Philosophical Perspectives, 6
Ethics, 1992

Previously Published Volumes
Volume 1, Metaphysics, 1987
Volume 2, Epistemology, 1988
Volume 3, Philosophy of Mind and Action Theory, 1989
Volume 4, Action Theory and Philosophy of Mind, 1990
Volume 5, Philosophy of Religion, 1991

Forthcoming Volumes
Volume 7, Philosophy of Language and Logic, Fall 1993
Additional Titles to be announced.

Philosophical Perspectives, 6
Ethics, 1992

Edited by
JAMES E. TOMBERLIN
California State University, Northridge

Ridgeview Publishing Company ● Atascadero, California

Paper Text: ISBN 0-924922-08-7
Cloth Text: ISBN 0-924922-58-3

The typesetting and illustrations were done by the CSUN Graphics Department (James W. Reese, Manager). The typesetter was Robert Olsen.

Published in the United States of America
by Ridgeview Publishing Company
P. O. Box 686
Atascadero, California 93423

Printed in the United States of America

This volume is dedicated to the memory of Hector-Neri Castañeda—
friend, teacher, and philosopher extraordinary.

Philosophical Perspectives, 6
Ethics, 1992

Contents

Philosophical Perspectives, 6
Ethics, 1992

PREFACE

Moral rights and rules, the nature of normativity, moral vs. nonmoral justification and explanation, consequentialism, deontology and naturalism, moral trust, abortion and free will—these are just some of the central issues addressed in twenty-three original essays included in the present volume devoted to ethics.

A new series of topical philosophy studies, *Philosophical Perspectives* aims to publish original essays by foremost thinkers in their fields, with each volume confined to a main area of philosophical research. The intention is to publish volumes annually.

Philosophical Perspectives could not have come to fruition without the precious encouragement it received from administrative officials at California State University, Northridge. I am particularly grateful to Dr. James W. Cleary, President of this institution, and Dr. Donald E. Bianchi, Acting Vice President for Academic Affairs, who provided essential financial support. I also thank Dr. Jorge Garcia, Dean, School of Humanities, and Dr. Daniel Sedey, Chair, Department of Philosophy, for their consistent efforts in advancing this project. Patricia D. Hackl, Administrative Program Specialist, School of Humanities, maintained logistical supervision and arranged for many valuable services. Irene Yarmak, Head Secretary of the department, and Pamela McClinton contributed ever so many hours of invaluable clerical assistance and support.

Finally, I am grateful to Michael Bratman, Geoff Sayre-McCord, and Holly Smith for generous and wise advice.

April 1992   **JAMES E. TOMBERLIN**

Philosophical Perspectives, 6, Ethics, 1992

A PUZZLE ABOUT THE
RATIONAL AUTHORITY OF MORALITY

David O. Brink
Massachusetts Institute of Technology

Commonsense morality recognizes various other-regarding duties to help, or forbear from harming, others. Most of us also regard moral obligations as important practical considerations that give agents reasons for action. But heeding these obligations may constrain the agent's pursuit of his own interest or aims. If we associate rationality with the agent's own point of view, we may wonder whether moral conduct and concern are always rationally justifiable. These thoughts reveal a tension in ordinary thinking about morality between living *right* and living *well*. That tension might be represented as a puzzle about the rational authority of morality that consists of a quartet of claims that can seem individually plausible but are mutually inconsistent.

I. Moral requirements—including other-regarding obligations—apply to agents independently of their aims or interests.
II. Moral requirements necessarily provide agents with reasons for action.
III. Reasons for action are dependent on the aims or interests of the agent who has them.
IV. There is no necessary connection between other-regarding action and any aim or interest of the agent.

Each element of the puzzle articulates a familiar and initially plausible idea.

(I) is a statement of the objectivity of ethics, familiar from Kant, according to which moral requirements are categorical norms; they apply to us independently of our antecedent desires and interests. The agent's own interests and inclinations are not, in the relevant way, among the conditions of application for moral requirements. This is clearest in the case of other-regarding moral requirements. I do not defeat an ascription of obligation to me to help another by pointing out that doing so will serve no goal or purpose that I have.

(II) captures the practical character of morality and moral deliberation. Agents typically engage in moral deliberation in order to decide what to do;

people give moral advice with the aim of guiding others' conduct; and most of us are quite sensitive to moral criticism. One explanation of these attitudes and expectations is that we think moral requirements give agents reasons for action. Such claims are sometimes defended as conceptual truths about morality. *Internalists* say that to be under a moral obligation to do something just is to have a reason to do it; they assume that norms of morality just are norms of rationality.[1]

(III) articulates the common assumption that a fact must affect the agent in some way to be of rational significance to her. Call this assumption about rationality *agent-relative*.[2] By contrast, rationality is *agent-neutral* just in case another's interests give an agent reasons for action directly, independently of any connection with her own interests or desires.[3] Agent-relative assumptions seem to underlie many formal and informal discussions of individual rationality in philosophy, economics, and politics. Moreover, an agent-relative theory provides a reliable link between reasons for action and motivation; we expect one who recognizes reasons for action to be motivated to act on them, and an agent seems more likely to be motivated by facts about his own interest or desires than by facts about the interest or desires of others. Also, when we explain an agent's behavior as an attempt to satisfy certain desires, given her beliefs, we are said to "rationalize" her behavior.[4] This suggests that genuinely rational behavior is that which would promote the agent's desires or at least those desires that she would have if she met certain epistemic conditions.

(IV) reflects a common assumption about the independence of different people's interests and attitudes that I will call the *independence assumption*. Of course, agents often do care about the welfare of others and desire to do the morally correct thing, and there will often be connections between an agent's own interests and those of others. But neither connection holds either universally or necessarily. My aims could be largely self-confined, and my own good can be specified in terms that make no essential reference to the good of others, say, in terms of my own pleasure or the satisfaction of my desires.

Despite their individual appeal, not all four claims can be true; we must reject at least one element of the puzzle if we are to avoid inconsistency. Indeed, we can make sense of a number of familiar positions at the foundations of ethics as tacit responses to this puzzle that reject one element of the puzzle in order to preserve others.

Moral relativism and *minimalist* moral theories, such as ethical egoism, reject the existence of categorical moral norms asserted in (I); they claim that moral requirements must further the agent's interests or desires in some way. *Externalists* reject the internalist assumption about the rationality of morality in (II). They distinguish between norms of rationality and norms of morality and recognize moral requirements such that failure to act on them is not necessarily irrational. *Kantians* and others reject the agent-relative assumptions about reasons for action in (III); they claim that the interests of other people can directly and necessarily provide an agent with reason for action. Finally, *metaphysical egoists* reject the independence assumption in (IV) and resolve the puzzle by arguing that, properly understood, people's interests are interdependent in ways such that acting on other-regarding moral requirements promotes the agent's own interests.

I'll sketch some of these solutions and their resources, limitations, and interrelations. My primary goal is not defend a particular solution to the puzzle, but to show that it provides a fruitful framework within which to address some foundational issues about ethics.

1. Relativist and Minimalist Solutions

Some writers begin with assumptions (II)-(IV) in place and conclude that we must reject the existence of categorical, other-regarding requirements.[5]

For example, in his article "Moral Relativism Defended" Gilbert Harman relies on Humean assumptions about the instrumental nature of rationality and internalist assumptions about the connection between moral obligation and reasons for action in order to defend a view that he calls moral relativism, according to which an agent's moral obligations must be relativized to her pro-attitudes.

> Formulating this as a logical thesis, I want to treat the moral "ought" as a four-place predicate (or "operator"), "Ought (A, D, C, M)," which relates an agent A, a type of act D, considerations C, and motivating attitudes M [1975: 10].

Harman claims, for instance, that Hitler is someone to whom obligations of fairness, decency, or respect for human life could not have applied because he (Hitler) lacked the relevant attitudes necessary for him to have had reasons to be fair, to be decent, or to respect human life (1975: 7-11).

Harman's argument has the following form.

1. Moral requirements generate reasons for action.
2. Reasons for action are desire-dependent.
3. Hence moral requirements are desire-dependent.

This is a version of relativism, because it relativizes moral obligations to people's variable aims. It is a version of minimalism, because it holds the content of one's obligations hostage to one's interests and aims and so seems unlikely to recognize the normal range of other-regarding duties that common-sense morality does.

Moreover, this view can be represented as an agent-relative ethical theory if it claims that promoting an agent's interests or desires is a sufficient as well as a necessary condition for moral obligation (1975: 11). An agent-relative ethical theory claims that an agent is obligated to do something just insofar as it would promote his own interests or desires.

Another view that can be represented either as an agent-relative ethical theory or as a skeptical view is Callicles' position in Plato's *Gorgias*. Callicles resolves the apparent conflict between the demands of justice and the agent's own interest by arguing that "real" or natural justice does not require the agent to help others or forbear from harming them, as conventional morality supposes (482de, 483ab, 488b-490a). The naturally just person satisfies her own unrestrained desires (488b). And, precisely because the revision in ordinary moral views that he makes is so drastic—his account of virtue is so minimalist—Callicles is usually thought of as a moral skeptic, even though he accepts the rational authority of real virtue.

Libertarian views might be motivated in a similar way. They recognize negative other-regarding obligations to forbear from harming others and interfering with their liberty but no positive obligations of mutual aid. Robert Nozick, for example, defends a moral theory incorporating libertarian side-constraints against utilitarianism by appeal to the *separateness of persons*. He writes

> Individually, we each sometimes choose to undergo some pain or sacrifice for a greater benefit or to avoid a greater harm... . Why not, *similarly*, hold that some persons have to bear some costs that benefit other persons more? But there is no *social entity* with a good that undergoes some sacrifice for its own good. ... To use a person in this way does not sufficiently respect and take account of the fact that he is a separate person, that his is the only life he has. *He* does not get some overbalancing good from his sacrifice, and no one is entitled to force this upon him... [1974: 32-3].

Nozick concludes that the separateness of persons grounds libertarian rights that protect individuals from other-regarding moral requirements that demand uncompensated sacrifices. His argument seems to have the following form.

1. It is unreasonable to demand uncompensated sacrifices.
2. Moral requirements must be reasonable.
3. There is no interpersonal compensation; benefits to another do not compensate me for my losses.
4. Hence moral requirements can include no other-regarding duties.

However, we might notice that libertarian minimalism is imperfectly supported by this argument. For, while she recognizes no positive duties of mutual aid that apply independently of the agent's own desires and choices, the libertarian does recognize negative duties to refrain from force and fraud that apply independently of the agent's own aims or interests. Even the libertarian thinks that negative duties of forbearance are other-regarding categorical norms.

Any agent-relative ethical theory that holds an agent's obligations hostage to the promotion of her immediate or unreflective interests or desires seems committed to a highly revisionary form of minimalism. Some agents are concerned about others. But such other-regarding attitudes are not universal. Moreover, benefiting others consumes time and resources that might have been spent in more self-confined ways. As long as people are psychologically malleable, we may ask why those who do not have other-regarding attitudes should *cultivate* them and those who happen to have them should *maintain* them. Unless there are answers to these questions agent-relative ethical theories will be quite minimal.

A sophisticated agent-relative ethical theory might try to avoid minimalism by arguing that it is in the long-term interest of agents to develop, maintain, and act on other-regarding attitudes. Such a theory would be a version of *ethical egoism*; it would claim that an agent is morally obligated to do something just insofar as that course of action would promote his own interest overall.[6] The ethical egoist's explanation of other-regarding moral requirements would exploit the idea that morality is concerned with the appropriate terms for personal and social interaction and cooperation and requires people to restrain their pursuit of their own aims and interests and accept a fair division of goods and resources. Each individual has an interest in the fruits of such interaction and cooperation. Though it might be desirable from a self-interested point of view to reap the benefits of others' forbearances and cooperation without incurring the burdens of one's own, the opportunities to do this are infrequent. Noncompliance is generally detectable, and others won't be forbearing and cooperative towards agents who are known to be noncompliant. So noncompliance secures short-term benefits that compliance does not, but compliance secures greater long-term benefits than noncompliance.

Because of the generally beneficial character of cooperative and restrained behavior, together with the cognitive and affective advantages of acting from fairly coarse-grained dispositions, people will have reason to develop and act on social sentiments and other-regarding attitudes. These attitudes will also receive external support. Because each has an interest in others' cooperation and restraint, communities will tend to reinforce compliant behavior and discourage noncompliant behavior. Community pressure, therefore, will also foster the development of fairly coarse-grained compliant dispositions. It's no accident, therefore, that people will have social sentiments and other-regarding attitudes, and these will give them agent-relative reason to act in other-regarding ways. And where they don't yet have these attitudes, they will nonetheless typically have agent-relative reasons to act in other-regarding ways (if only) as part of a process of developing such attitudes.

The strategic egoist reasons as follows.

1. It is in the agent's interest to receive the benefits of systems of cooperation and restraint.
2. The benefits of systems of cooperation and restraint are available only to those who maintain the appearance of cooperation and restraint towards strategic partners.
3. The least costly means of maintaining the appearance of cooperation and restraint is by being cooperative and restrained.
4. Hence it is in the agent's interest to be cooperative and restrained towards strategic partners.
5. Hence there are other-regarding duties that have agent-relative foundations.

In this way, the strategic ethical egoist tries to explain why one should both cultivate and maintain other-regarding attitudes by appeal to one's long-term interests. This form of ethical egoism attempts to justify other-regarding morality and avoid unacceptably minimalist conclusions while denying (I)'s claim that these moral requirements apply to agents independently of their interests and desires.[7]

But as long as ethical egoism recognizes the independence assumption, it must remain revisionary. In circumstances in which an agent would benefit from acting on selectively noncompliant dispositions, the ethical egoist cannot ascribe other-regarding moral obligations. First, (2) is not always true. In the case of public goods that are nonexcludable, the appearance of compliance is not necessary to receive the benefits of others' compliance, though fairness typically seems to require compliance. Moreover, if the stakes are sufficiently high in a particular case, and one's strategic partners have already complied, one may have no reason to maintain even the appearance of compliance. For the benefits of noncompliance in such a case can outweigh the costs of being excluded from future interaction. Second, (3) is sometimes false. Selective noncompliance may go undetected where it is difficult to monitor compliance and detect deception. But surely the moral obligation to comply does not cease just because successful deception is possible. Third, (4) doesn't support a sufficiently strong version of (5). Noncompliance towards those with whom one does not strategically interact will be in one's interest. So if the wealthy and talented have sufficient strength and resources so as to stand nothing to gain by participating with the weak and handicapped in a system of mutual cooperation and forbearance, then the strategic egoist can recognize no duties of mutual aid that the former have towards the latter. Finally, even if the strategic justification of other-regarding conduct were extensionally adequate, the independence assumption ensures that there are possible cases in which an agent has no strategic justification for compliant behavior, if only because the stakes are so high, her discriminatory capacities are so fine-grained, or she is such a successful deceiver. While our other-regarding obligations are presumably counterfactually stable, the strategic justification of other-regarding conduct is not.[8] These limitations in strategic ethical egoism are all limitations in the *scope of morality itself*, and not simply limitations in the rationality of other-regarding conduct and concern.[9]

One aspect of viewing minimalist moral theories as, perhaps tacit, solutions to this puzzle about the rational authority of morality is that it establishes a link between metaethical and normative issues and so undermines the common claim that metaethics and normative ethics are completely independent of each other. The link is simply that if one accepts certain metaethical claims—viz. internalism, agent-relative assumptions about reasons for action, and the independence assumption—then one is committed to a particular, indeed, extremely controversial kind of moral theory, viz. some form of minimalism. Conversely, if one is to avoid these normative views, one must reject at least one of three metaethical claims.

2. Externalist Solutions

Some accept the existence of categorical moral norms, agent-relative assumptions about rationality, and the independence assumption and so reject the internalist assumption about the rationality of morality in (II). This externalist solution denies that it is a condition of the application of a moral requirement that it provide the agent to whom it applies with a reason for action. While moral requirements apply to us independently of our antecedent desires and interests, they give us reasons for action conditional on their promoting our interests or desires.

We might motivate this externalist position by noting an ambiguity within Kantian rationalism.[10] Kant, of course, distinguishes between hypothetical and categorical imperatives (1785: 414). Hypothetical imperatives are conditional on whether the conduct enjoined promotes the agent's antecedent interests or desires, while categorical imperatives are not. Kant claims that moral requirements express categorical, rather than hypothetical, imperatives (1785: 416). But we might identify two distinguishable claims here corresponding to two distinct senses in which an imperative can be categorical. In one sense, imperatives are categorical just in case they *apply* to people independently of their aims or interests. Imperatives are categorical in this sense insofar as they generate *categorical norms*. (I) asserts that moral requirements—including other-regarding moral requirements—are categorical norms. Imperatives are categorical in another sense just in case they provide those to whom they apply with *reasons for action* independently of their desires, aims, or interests. Imperatives are categorical in this sense just in case they generate *categorical reasons*. Categorical reasons are agent-neutral reasons, and other-regarding moral requirements could provide categorical reasons only if there are agent-neutral reasons for action.

Once we distinguish these two Kantian theses we may not find them equally plausible. We might agree that moral requirements are categorical in the first sense—they are categorical norms—but deny that they are categorical in the second sense—they do not generate categorical reasons.

However, the internalist might argue that we cannot separate categorical norms and categorical reasons.

1. Moral requirements apply to people categorically (i.e. independently of their contingent desires and interests).
2. If a moral requirement (categorically) tells me to do x, then I have a (categorical) moral reason to do x.
3. If I have a (categorical) moral reason to do x, then I have a (categorical) reason to do x.
4. Hence moral requirements generate (categorical) reasons for action.
5. Hence it would be pro tanto irrational of me to fail to act on moral requirements (regardless of my interests or desires).

But the externalist can reply that the argument trades on an equivocation between different senses of 'reason'. In one sense (a) for there to be a reason for me to do something is simply for there to exist the relevant sort of behavioral standard or norm. In this sense, there are as many kinds of reasons as there are systems of norms; there are moral reasons, reasons of etiquette, reasons of state, etc. In this sense, the existence of categorical moral norms obviously does imply the existence of moral reasons and, hence, reasons. But when we call these reasons categorical reasons, we are just giving another name to what we had previously called categorical norms. The other sense of 'reason' (b) signifies more than the existence of a certain sort of behavioral norm; it indicates that there is a reason to behave in accordance with such a norm such that failure to behave in that way is ceteris paribus or pro tanto irrational. If there is reason, in this sense, to act on a norm, then practical reason endorses this norm. And it is this sense of reason and rationality that is at stake in the rational authority of morality and the debate about whether all reasons are agent-relative. Reasons, in this sense, do not follow from the mere existence of certain sorts of norms, as the case of etiquette seems to demonstrate. Norms of etiquette apply to my behavior independently of my interests or attitudes, but failure to observe them does not seem irrational unless this in some way undermines my interests or aims. So the externalist is justified in concluding that the argument trades on an equivocation between these two senses of reason: the argument for (4) is sound just in case it is understood as (4a), while (5) follows from (4) only if (4) is read as (4b).

In a similar way, the externalist may appeal to these two senses of 'reason' to dissolve the puzzle. On a univocal (b)-reading of 'reason', the externalist denies (II). On an (a)-reading of (II), (II) follows trivially from (I) and is not an independent premise. The externalist won't deny (IIa). But (III) clearly requires the (b)-reading of 'reason'. But, of course, the four claims do not form a genuine paradox if we read (II) as (IIa) and (III) as (IIIb).

We can better see this challenge to Kantian rationalism by considering Philippa Foot's useful analogy between morality and etiquette (Foot 1972). At some points it may be difficult to distinguish rules of etiquette and rules of morality; for instance, etiquette often enjoins the same sort of consideration and respect for others that morality does. Because we want to examine morality's relation to something agreed to be fairly unimportant, the focus on etiquette must be on those rules of etiquette that do not overlap with moral requirements, for instance, rules requiring that invitations addressed in the third person be answered in the third person. So we must compare morality and *mere* etiquette (those rules of etiquette that are not also moral rules).

Rules of (mere) etiquette, like moral requirements, are categorical norms. The moral duty to help others in distress, when you can do so at little cost to yourself, does not fail to apply to you—we do not withdraw our ascription of obligation to you—just because you are indifferent to your neighbor's suffering and in a hurry to read your mail, as would be the case if it was a hypothetical norm. In the same way, rules against replying to a third-person invitation in the first person don't fail to apply to you—we don't take back our ascriptions of duties of etiquette to you—just because you think etiquette is silly or you have a desire to annoy your host, as would be the case if rules of etiquette stated hypothetical norms.

But rules of etiquette seem to lack *rational authority*; they generate hypothetical, not categorical reasons. Rules of etiquette may state categorical norms, but failure to observe these norms does not seem irrational unless this in some way undermines the agent's interests or aims. Here too moral requirements may seem on a par with requirements of etiquette. If the independence assumption is correct, obligations of forbearance, mutual aid, and justice will sometimes further no aims or interests of the agent. Though we need not withdraw the ascription of obligation in such cases, perhaps we should allow that immoral conduct in such a case is not irrational. We can reproach such a person for immoral behavior, but not for irrationality.

But the analogy between morals and manners provides no explanation of the common belief that morality has a special authority. Now the externalist might conclude that the special authority of morality is just an illusion—an artifact of moral education and the internalization of moral norms (as Foot may seem to). But he might claim that morality and etiquette are imperfectly analogous. While alike in generating categorical norms whose rationality is hypothetical, not categorical, they need not be equally authoritative systems of norms. This is because of the *content* of the two types of norms. Different systems of norms make different sorts of requirements and have different *points* or *organizing principles*. The externalist might claim that the moral point of view has a more intimate and regular relationship to people's important interests and aims than the point of view of etiquette does.

The basic idea rests on familiar claims about what the moral point of view is (and what the point of view of etiquette is). One version appeals to claims about morality's other-regarding concerns with fairness, equality, and impartiality and the sort of strategic reasoning that we saw an ethical egoist might invoke. However, this sort of strategic reasoning figures here within a *rational* egoist attempt to defend the rationality of other-regarding moral considerations, not within an ethical egoist account of the content of morality. Rational egoism is the view that an action is *rational* just insofar as it would promote the agent's own interests, whereas ethical egoism is the view that an action is *morally obligatory* just insofar as it would promote the agent's own interests. The rational egoist, who is not an ethical egoist, allows that we can identify the content of moral requirements independently of the agent's own interest and then thinks that moral requirements can be shown to be rational just to the extent that they promote the agent's own interest. The rational egoist holds the rationality of conduct hostage to the agent's own interests and desires; but, unlike the ethical egoist, he does not hold the morality of conduct hostage in this way. Nonetheless, the same sort of strategic reasoning that the sophisticated ethical egoist employs can be invoked by the rational egoist. That reasoning purports to explain why agents have agent-relative reason to develop, maintain, and act on fairly coarse-grained other-regarding dispositions and attitudes. The rational egoist can employ these claims to provide a generally reliable contingent justification of the rational authority or other-regarding morality. We saw that there are actual or at least counterfactual limitations to the strategic justification of other-regarding conduct. But, unlike the ethical egoist, the rational egoist need not view these limitations as limitations in the scope of morality itself. They represent the limits of the rational authority of morality.

By contrast, I assume, the point of view of mere etiquette—whatever exactly it is—has no such intimate and regular relationship to people's important interests and aims. The rational authority of etiquette is not only contingent but weak and unreliable.

If so, the moral point of view is more centrally implicated in human interests and desires than is the point of view of etiquette. These constructive claims suggest how an externalist can try to show that morality has a special authority, not enjoyed by etiquette, while restricting herself to agent-relative reasons.

3. Agent-Neutral Solutions

Another solution to the puzzle is to give up the agent-relative assumptions about rationality in (III) in favor of agent-neutral claims. The trick, of course, is to make agent-neutral assumptions about reasons for action plausible. We have to explain how I can have reason to do something simply because it benefits someone even if it would further no interest or desire of mine.

We may find agent-neutral assumptions prima facie mysterious. Whereas the link between the agent's own interests and desires and his reasons for action seems intuitive, the link between the interests of others and his reasons for action may seem less clear or compelling. Moreover, agent-relative assumptions explain better why recognition of reasons for action should motivate the agent, whereas it seems possible to be unmoved by agent-neutral considerations. Further, agent-relative assumptions about rationality seem to be a natural extension of the "rationalizing" mode of explaining behavior, and this allows us to link normative and explanatory senses of 'reason for action'. By contrast, if an agent has not already formed desires for the welfare of other people, it's hard to see how the welfare of others could explain his behavior in any way. But then agent-neutral assumptions about rationality will not forge any link between normative and explanatory reasons for action.

Presumably, the friend of agent-neutrality believes that facts about another's welfare can and will be motivational when the agent understands *that* and *why* such facts provide reasons for action. If so, agent-neutrality can maintain a link between explanatory and normative reasons for action. Explanatory reasons consist of the agent's pro-attitudes, given her actual beliefs. Normative reasons represent an idealization of explanatory reasons. Genuinely rational behavior is behavior that would satisfy the aims the agent would have in an idealized epistemic state in which her various beliefs and desires were in wide reflective equilibrium (cf. Brink 1989: 63-6). If there are convincing arguments for agent-neutral reasons, then this will affect the agent's aims in reflective equilibrium. If so, there can be no a priori argument from the connection between rationality and motivation or between explanatory and normative reasons against the possibility of agent-neutral reasons.[11] We must consider particular arguments for agent-neutrality on a case by case basis. There are two main kinds of argument to consider: intuitive and theoretical.

Consider first an intuitive argument. Agent-relative theories of rationality assume that rational action must benefit the agent or further her aims. But surely, we might think, we have good reason to help others in distress or prevent harm to them if we can do so at little cost to ourselves, even if helping them won't benefit us or further our aims. Suppose that with a little effort I could warn you, before our jump, that your parachute is jammed or that I could easily step around your gouty toes. Surely, I have reason to warn you and avoid your toes even if doing so doesn't benefit me or further my aims.[12]

This claim has considerable force.[13] But the externalist who accepts agent-relative assumptions about rationality can accept it on one reading. She can agree that there is a moral reason for me to warn you about your jammed parachute and walk around your gouty toes, even if doing so does not benefit me or further my aims, and that I am immoral if I fail to do so. So she agrees that I have a reason to do these things in the sense that there is a categorical norm that enjoins such conduct. She denies only that there is a categorical reason for me to do these things. Assuming that I would receive no benefit from these actions, it would not be irrational of me to fail to warn you or avoid your gouty toes. What is intuitively clear is that it would be (grossly) immoral of me to let you jump or to tread on your gouty toes; it is not comparably clear that this would also be necessarily irrational.

Kant and neo-Kantians also offer theoretical arguments for recognizing agent-neutral reasons. One argument can be found in Thomas Nagel's *The Possibility of Altruism*. Nagel sees a parallel between intertemporal and interpersonal distribution of benefits and harms. He argues for agent-neutrality or altruism by analogy with prudence. Just as the interests of an agent's *future* self provide him with reasons for action *now*, so too, Nagel argues, *others'* interests provide *him* with reasons for action. Failure to recognize prudence involves temporal dissociation—failure to see the present as just one time among others—and failure to recognize altruism involves personal dissocia-tion—failure to recognize oneself as just one person among others. Both kinds of dissociation are mistakes. The parity of time and person within rationality, therefore, requires accepting agent-neutrality.

But the rational egoist will not be very impressed by this analogy with prudence. Rational egoism assumes that *sacrifice requires compensation*, that is, that an agent has reason to make a sacrifice, say to benefit another, if and only if the agent receives some sufficient benefit in return. Nagel himself accepts the "extremely strict position that there can be no interpersonal compensation for sacrifice" (1970: 142). But if sacrifice requires compensation, prudence and altruism must be importantly disanalogous. For, in the pruden-tial case, I am compensated for a sacrifice of my present interests in favor of my greater future interests; these future interests are mine. Because benefactor and beneficiary are the same, diachronic, intrapersonal compensa-tion is automatic. But interpersonal compensation is not automatic; benefactor and beneficiary are distinct. If the independence assumption is correct, the interests of other selves, however great, are not *ipso facto* interests of mine. Unless there is some connection between my interests and those of others (as, of course, there will in fact often be), I am not compensated when I sacrifice my interests (present or future) for those of others. But then justified concern for my own future does not itself establish justified concern for others.

A more promising strategy is to develop the Kantian attempt to link categorical norms and categorical reasons. Kant thinks that moral require-ments are categorical norms, because they apply to us insofar as we are rational beings and independently of our contingent interests and inclinations (1785: 408, 411, 425-7, 432, 442). If so, moral requirements apply to us in virtue of our rational features, and these are essential to our being agents who deliberate and possess reasons for action. If so, such requirements arguably provide agents with reasons for action independently of their contingent interests and inclinations. Any norms that apply to us in this way would generate categorical, agent-neutral reasons for action.

It remains to be seen whether there are any such moral requirements and whether they include familiar other-regarding duties. Kant thinks so. He understands the first formulation of the Categorical Imperative to require that one act on maxims that a rational being as such could will to be universal (1785: 421, 425-7). He thinks that the one thing that an agent would choose for its own sake insofar as she is rational, and independently of her contingent inclinations and interests, would be the realization of *rational agency*. If I choose rational agency solely insofar as I am a rational being, then I will choose to develop rational agency as such, and not the rational agency of this or that being, in particular, not just my rational agency. If so, then reason directs me to be concerned about other rational agents, as rational agents, for their own sakes. Kant concludes that insofar as we are rational beings we would will that all rational agents be treated as ends in themselves and never merely as means (1785: 429); this is his second main formulation of the Categorical Imperative.

The second formula imposes other-regarding duties. It prohibits treating anyone merely as a means. The negative requirement that no one be treated as a mere means requires that each be treated as an end, and this carries certain positive duties. For to treat other rational agents as ends requires treating them as agents whose deliberation and agency is valuable. This requires, ceteris paribus, not simply that we refrain from doing things that would harm the interests and agency of others but also that we do things to promote their rational agency. And this will involve a concern to promote or assist, where possible, others' opportunities for deliberation and agency, the effectiveness of their deliberations, and the execution of their choices and commitments (cf. 1785: 430).

This brief sketch of the Kantian strategy suggests a way of understanding the categorical application of other-regarding moral norms such that these norms generate categorical, agent-neutral reasons for action.

1. Moral requirements apply to people insofar as they are rational agents.
2. Hence moral requirements supply agents with reasons for action.
3. Insofar as an agent is rational, she will be concerned with rational agency.
4. Insofar as an agent is concerned with rational agency, she will treat rational agents as end in themselves.
5. Hence moral requirements include other-regarding duties to treat others as ends.

6. Hence agents have reason to act on other-regarding duties.

This is not the place to defend the details of this strategy, but it is a solution to the puzzle worth exploring further.[14]

4. Metaphysical Egoist Solutions

An agent-neutral solution would be unnecessary if the independence assumption were false. But that assumption looks very plausible as applied to the connection between other-regarding action and the agent's desires or pro-attitudes. We've already noted that other-regarding attitudes seem neither universal nor necessary. But there is a more abstract argument for denying that there is a necessary connection between any other-regarding action and any pro-attitude of the agent that appeals to the systematic plasticity of pro-attitudes. There are various connections between facts and people's pro-attitudes. Given some of my pro-attitudes, certain facts or their recognition may commit me to other pro-attitudes. If I want to hire a suitable person for the position, and you are the only suitable person available, then, if I realize this, I will want to hire you for the position. But this sort of connection is not a necessary connection between a fact or belief and a pro-attitude. For in response to the fact or belief, it is always possible to change the pro-attitude that had previously made the fact or belief relevant, rather than adopt the new desire that the fact or belief recommends. So in a context in which some background pro-attitudes are held fixed there are necessary connections between facts or beliefs and other pro-attitudes. But these connections are not necessary simpliciter, because systematic modification of one's pro-attitudes in light of the facts or one's beliefs is always possible. If so, this aspect of the independence assumption is secure.

But this does not rule out the possibility of necessary connections between other-regarding actions and the agent's interests, because we can construct non-conative conceptions of people's interests. If people's interests were interdependent in certain ways, this would undermine the independence assumption. We might call such a view *metaphysical egoism*. The metaphysical egoist claims that when the agent's own happiness or interest is correctly understood we will see that the good of others is, in the appropriate way, *part* of the agent's own good so that acting on other-regarding moral requirements is a way of promoting his own interests. If so, the rational egoist will be able to explain the rational authority of other-regarding moral requirements on agent-relative assumptions.

Metaphysical egoism is sometimes defended as part of absolute idealism, which claims that everything that there is exists as part of a single cosmic or divine consciousness. For then what we think of as distinct lives (distinct streams of consciousness) would stand to cosmic or divine intelligence as we now believe that the stages of a single life stand to the person whose life it is. There would be a super-personal entity that is both benefactor and beneficiary in the interpersonal case in much the same way that we take the person to be both benefactor and beneficiary in diachronic, intrapersonal sacrifice (contrary to Nozick's claim, quoted above). While this would make intradeity compensation automatic, it would not yet establish interpersonal compensation, because the *person* who is benefactor is not also beneficiary. And without interpersonal compensation, rational egoism will not recognize the rational authority of other-regarding demands. If absolute idealism is to establish interpersonal compensation, it must hold not only that there is a super-personal entity but also that persons are essentially parts of this super-personal entity such that their welfare is to be understood in terms of its. This, I gather, is roughly the view of idealists such as Hegel, Green, and Bradley.[15]

But, stated baldly, these metaphysical assumptions are likely to seem implausible. The general strategy, however, is also familiar from Greek philosophy. In the *Republic* Plato attempts to show that justice is in the agent's own interest, properly understood, because justice is part of having a well-ordered soul. In *Nicomachean Ethics* ix 4-12 Aristotle argues that friendship, which is the virtue appropriate to communities and includes the perfection of justice (1155a22-8, 1159b25-1160a8), is a virtue that promotes the agent's own happiness, because the virtuous friend is "another-self" (1168b2-6, 1170b6-9). If the friend is another-self, then benefiting her presumably benefits me. And if political communities are associations of friendship, then perhaps I can take this attitude towards others as well. If so, perhaps I can expect interpersonal compensation and so will have agent-relative reason to comply with other-regarding moral requirements.

One attempt to unpack these claims relies on familiar, though not uncontroversial, metaphysical claims. Indeed, I think that the basic strategy is Aristotelian.[16] Aristotle claims that we can justify concern for one's (best or complete) friends and family members (e.g. children and siblings) as cases of, or on the model of, *self*-love (1161b15-1162a5, 1166a10).

> The excellent person is related to his friend in the same way as he is related to himself, since a friend is another self; and therefore, just as his own being is choiceworthy for him, the friend's being is choiceworthy for him in the same or a similar way [1170b6-9].

One way to understand these claims is as a proposal to model the relationship between "other-selves" (e.g. intimates) on the relationship between a self and its temporal parts. I have reason to regard my intimates as other-selves, because they bear approximately the same relationship to me as future stages of myself bear to me, and this fact provides me with reason to care about them.

According to rational egoism, concern for my own future is rational; concern for my own future is concern for me, and I am compensated for sacrifices of my present self on behalf of my future self, because my future self is a part of me. But how must a future self be related to my present self in order for both to be parts of me? A common and plausible answer (which I shall employ but not defend) is *psychological continuity*.[17] On this view, a particular person consists of a series of psychologically continuous person stages. A series of person stages is psychologically continuous just in case contiguous members in this series are psychologically well *connected*. And a pair of person stages is psychologically connected just in case they are psychologically similar (in terms of such things as beliefs, desires, and intentions) and the psychological features of the later stage are causally dependent upon the earlier stage. On this view, self-love would seem to imply that I should be concerned about selves that are psychologically continuous with my present self.

But I can be psychologically continuous with other selves with whom I share a mental life and interact causally. Interpersonal, as well as intrapersonal, psychological continuity is possible. There will be psychological continuity between any people who share beliefs, values, and goals as the result of their causal interaction. This will be true to a significant extent in the case of intimates, such as spouses and friends. It will also be true to an interesting, though lesser, extent among members of the same community, because they have common goals and aims and because these shared goals have been produced at least in part by mutual discussion and interaction. Interpersonal psychological continuity can also be indirect, because it can hold between people who are not themselves connected but who are each connected to others in common. It can also be indirect when it is mediated by social institutions and practices (e.g. media and legal and political institutions) that otherwise isolated people both participate in. In these ways, interpersonal psychological continuity can extend quite broadly, even if the degree of continuity often weakens as it extends further.

To the extent that distinct individuals are psychologically continuous, each can and should view the other as another-self who extends her own interests in much the same way that her own future self extends her interests. If so, there can be automatic interpersonal compensation among other-selves just as there is automatic diachronic, intrapersonal compensation. One will have agent-relative reasons to promote the welfare of another proportional to the degree of psychological continuity one bears to her.

Degree of continuity will presumably affect the amount of other-regarding conduct and concern that can be justified in this way. Presumably, I have less agent-relative reason to benefit comparative strangers than my intimates, precisely because the former are less psychologically continuous with me than the latter. In this way, metaphysical egoism seems committed to a *discount rate of rational concern* proportional to the degree of psychological continuity the agent bears to others. But this need not be a threat to morality, because the extent of one's obligations to others is commonly thought to be a function not simply of the amount of benefit that one can confer but also of the nature of the relationship in which one stands to potential beneficiaries. Commonsense morality recognizes more stringent obligations towards those to whom one stands in special relationships (e.g. to family and friends and to partners in cooperative schemes) than towards others. Even impartial moral theories, such as utilitarianism or consequentialism, typically try to justify recognition of special obligations and the legitimacy of differential concern for those to whom the agent stands in special relationships.[18] The scale of stringency among our moral obligations to those to whom we stand in different relationships forms a *moral discount rate*. It remains to be seen whether the moral discount rate and the metaphysical egoist's discount rate of rational concern are isomorphic, but it is not a defect per se of its justification of other-regarding concern that it embodies a discount rate of concern, because there is a moral discount rate.

Because it is within one's power to affect the degree of psychological continuity one shares with others, there is a question whether one should cultivate or maintain other-selves. The metaphysical egoist can claim that having another-self *extends* my interests in important ways. A plausible conception of welfare can reasonably claim that it is in my interest to exercise those capacities that are central to the sort of being I am and that these capacities include, importantly, deliberative capacities (cf. EN i 7). Having another-self provides unique opportunities to exercise my deliberative capacities. My other-self brings me new information. I can learn and benefit from the experiences that my other-self has by adding them to my own. Moreover, deliberation includes practical deliberation. Practical deliberation is exercised in the reflective formation, assessment, and pursuit of projects and plans. By drawing on the experience of my other-self and engaging her in discussion, I improve my own practical deliberations, not just by reaching better informed decisions but also by forming my decisions in a reflective manner. I can also exercise new deliberative capacities by engaging in more complex projects requiring mutual cooperation. In these ways, my other-selves expand my deliberative powers, activities, and control.

These aspects of the way in which another-self extends one's interests constrain the degree of psychological similarity one has reason to seek in such a relationship. My activities will be more diverse and more complex if my other-self is no mere clone of me.[19] Clearly, I will diversify my experience more by interacting with someone who has somewhat different interests and experiences. My deliberations will be aided by input and criticism from new perspectives. And cooperation in complex projects will often be enhanced when participants have different strengths and talents. These considerations provide reason to participate in larger, more diverse groups as well small intimate associations. My experiences will be enlarged and my own practical deliberations will be enhanced by the input from people with different experiences, values, and perspectives; and larger groups with more diverse membership will typically make possible more complex forms of social cooperation and, hence, the exercise of new kinds of deliberative capacities.

Indeed, the arguments for cultivating another-self show that beneficial interaction with others is *itself* a way of extending one's interests. If so, one will have agent-relative reason to benefit others, as a way of establishing another-self, even towards those with whom one is not already continuous.

These are reasons to think that there are agent-relative reasons to cultivate and maintain other-selves, and because there is automatic compensation for sacrifice among other-selves, there is reason to think that other-regarding action can be a necessary part of an agent's good.

But we may wonder whether the egoist can justify the full range of moral demands, for morality seems to require not just that we perform the actions it demands of us but also that we fulfill its demands from the right sort of motives. Even if egoism can justify the moral demand that I benefit others, it may seem that it cannot account for the moral demand that I benefit others out of a *concern for their own sakes*. Because the metaphysical egoist justifies sacrifice on behalf of another by representing the other's good as part of the agent's own good, this seems to base the agent's other-regarding action not on concern for the other's own sake, but instead on self-love.

While the strategic egoist may find it difficult to defend other-regarding concern that is not, at bottom, instrumental, the metaphysical egoist can do better. The metaphysical egoist's argument for cultivating other-selves appeals to a deliberative conception of individual welfare and claims that the right sort of other-regarding relationships extend my interests by giving me opportunities to exercise more diverse and complex deliberative capacities. This argument justifies acquiring other-selves by appeal to its effects on one's capacities, but the capacities in question involve, among other things, one's relation to other people in cooperative and beneficial ways. So if I'm justified in entering such relationships because they exercise *these* sorts of capacities, my justification does not obviously reflect a purely instrumental attitude towards those with whom I'm entering such relationships.

Moreover, once my relationship with others is under way, psychological continuity begins to get established, and I can begin to see their welfare as part of my own. But if this is true, then my concern for them will not be purely instrumental. Recall the intrapersonal parallel. When I undergo a present sacrifice for a future benefit I do so because the interests of my future self are interests of mine; in this way, I make present sacrifices out of a concern for the sake of my future self. Of course, the on-balance rationality of the sacrifice depends upon its promoting my overall good. But, because the good of my future self is part of this overall good, concern for my overall good requires, as a constituent part, a concern for the good of my future self.

In this way, concern for my future self for its own sake seems compatible with and, indeed, essential to self-love.

Now the metaphysical egoist wants to model interpersonal continuity and concern on intrapersonal continuity and concern. Just as the agent's future self is a part of her, so too the interests of other-selves are part of her interests. And so just as egoism explains why the agent should be concerned about her future self for its own sake, insofar as it is continuous with her present self, so too it explains why she should be concerned about her other-selves for their own sakes, insofar as they are continuous with her.

My account of metaphysical egoism has appealed to both deliberative conceptions of welfare and psychological continuity accounts of personal identity. These may seem to be independent lines of argument. One could apparently justify cultivating and maintaining other-regarding relationships by appeal to deliberative conceptions of welfare without invoking the idea of another-self, and one could apparently appeal to interpersonal psychological continuity as a justification of other-regarding conduct even if one were, say, a hedonist. While these two lines of argument are somewhat independent, they are complementary and together strengthen metaphysical egoism. The deliberative conception of welfare plays a distinctive role in explaining why I should cultivate and maintain other-selves, while the parallel between interpersonal and intrapersonal psychological continuity provides a non-instrumental account of why I should be concerned about people to whom I am so related. Moreover, each line of argument arguably supports the other. We should expect to find interdependence between deliberative conceptions of welfare, deliberative conceptions of personhood, and psychological continuity accounts of personal identity in terms of reasoned control and modification of beliefs, desires, and intentions (psychological continuity, properly interpreted). Because personhood is itself a normative category and because psychological continuity is an account of what matters in personal identity, our views about these matters ought to affect our views about welfare or happiness. If what it is to be a person is to have certain deliberative capacities and what it is to be the same person over time is, roughly, for there to be reasoned continuity of intentional states, then we should expect one's exercise of deliberative capacities to be an important ingredient of one's welfare, in part because it will extend one's interests. And to the extent that deliberative activities seem to be principal ingredients in a good life, we should expect reasoned continuity of intentional states to be a principal ingredient in what matters in personal identity and deliberative capacities to be principal ingredients in personhood. In this way, the metaphysical egoist's dual appeal to deliberative conceptions of welfare and interpersonal psychological continuity promises to be a virtue.

The metaphysical egoist can provide agent-relative justification of other-regarding demands by showing how another's good can be part of the agent's own good. Whether an agent will always have an overriding reason to fulfill every other-regarding moral requirement is another matter, requiring further articulation of both the nature of morality's other-regarding demands and this neo-Aristotelian version of metaphysical egoism.

5. Solutions

I have tried to show how some familiar views about the foundations of ethics can profitably be seen as, perhaps tacit, solutions to the puzzle. This perspective may help us better assess these views.

For instance, when we view certain kinds of relativist and minimalist theories as solutions to the puzzle, we can both see their rationale and locate their implausibility. These theories are motivated by an attempt to preserve the other intuitively plausible elements of the puzzle. But rejecting the existence of categorical other-regarding duties (norms), while maintaining the independence assumption seems the least plausible response to the puzzle. It would be reasonable only if the sole alternative was to insist that moral requirements have no more rational authority than requirements of mere etiquette. But this is not so.

Suppose we accept not only (I) but also (III)'s claim that all reasons for action are agent-relative and (IV)'s independence assumption; this would require us to be externalists and reject (II). But this would not show that moral requirements had no more authority than the requirements of etiquette. For a rational egoist can employ certain forms of strategic reasoning to show how agents have generally reliable, albeit contingent, reasons to fulfill other-regarding requirements of forbearance, cooperation, and mutual-aid. And in those actual or merely possible circumstances in which acting on other-regarding moral requirements would not further the interests or aims of the agent, we can maintain the immorality of failure to act on those requirements even if we cannot maintain its irrationality. So, even if we had to accept (III) and (IV), it would still be more reasonable to reject (II) than (I).

What's objectionable is the combination of an agent-relative ethical theory *and* the independence assumption. An agent-relative moral theory that denied the independence assumption need not be unacceptably minimalist. Metaphysical egoism tries to establish that people's interests, correctly understood, are interdependent in ways that ensure that other-regarding conduct and concern necessarily promote the agent's own interests. I presented metaphysical egoism as a version of rational, rather than ethical, egoism—that is, as an account of rationality and the rational authority of other-regarding moral requirements, rather than as an account of the content of morality. But the resources of metaphysical egoism are available to the ethical egoist who insists that moral requirements must themselves be agent-relative. Insofar as metaphysical egoism can be articulated so as to justify other-regarding conduct and concern, an agent-relative moral theory incorporating metaphysical egoism can deny (I) while avoiding clearly unacceptable minimalist commitments. Indeed, we might conclude that the rejection of categorical other-regarding norms, asserted in (I), is plausible only if it is neither relativist nor minimalist; it will avoid relativism and minimalism only if it incorporates metaphysical egoism.

Of course, if we take (I) to be reasonably fixed, our views about the plausibility of any other element of the puzzle will vary inversely with our views about the plausibility of the other two. So, for instance, if we accept or hold reasonably fixed the claim that there are other-regarding requirements and the independence assumption, then we can see that the externalist denial of (II) and the agent-neutral denial of (III) will be inversely plausible. If, under these assumptions, we also think that all reasons for action are agent-relative, we must conclude that it is at least possible for there to be circumstances in which it would be immoral but not irrational for an agent to fail to fulfill her other-regarding moral requirements. We will, therefore, think (II) is false. And, similarly, if, under these assumptions, we also assume that moral requirements must supply reasons for action, we should think that not all reasons for action can be agent-relative. This will lead us to reject (III). If we reject (IV)'s independence assumption, then, whether we accept agent-relative or agent-neutral assumptions about rationality, we should accept (II)'s claim that moral requirements do supply reasons for action (though we needn't think, as the internalist does, that this is a conceptual truth about morality).

Moreover, we may *pool* resources. The friend of agent-relativity can combine the resources of both strategic and metaphysical egoists to provide a strong rational egoist defense of the rational authority of other-regarding moral demands. Even the friend of agent-neutrality may wish to enlist the aid of strategic and metaphysical egoists. For even if we reject (III)'s claim that all reasons for action are agent-relative and accept the existence of agent-neutral reasons, we are unlikely to think that all reasons for action are agent-neutral. There will still be agent-relative reasons for action. But this raises the possibility of conflict between agent-neutral reasons that support other-regarding moral requirements and agent-relative reasons that may not. If we are to vindicate the importance of moral requirements, agent-neutral reasons must not be systematically overridden by countervailing agent-relative reasons.

This suggests the need to distinguish stronger and weaker rationalist theses. A weak rationalist thesis claims that there is always some reason to fulfill moral requirements such that failure to do so is to that extent irrational. The strongest rationalist thesis would claim that for every agent there is always overriding reason to fulfill moral requirements such that failure to do so is on-balance irrational. And, of course, there are intermediate rationalist theses.

In fact, the strength of the rationalist thesis will affect our formulation of the puzzle. We might revise our formulation of the puzzle so that (II) reflects a strong rationalist thesis.

I. Moral requirements—including other-regarding obligations—apply to agents independently of their aims or interests.
II. Moral requirements necessarily provide agents with compelling or overriding reasons for action.
III. Reasons for action are dependent on the aims or interests of the agent who has them.
IV. There is no necessary connection between other-regarding action and any aim or interest of the agent.

A solution to the initial puzzle that establishes the existence of agent-neutral reasons to be moral may not solve the revised puzzle. The defense of agent-neutral reasons and the rejection of purely agent-relative assumptions about rationality, though significant claims, are not sufficient to vindicate the rationalist element of the revised puzzle. Unless agent-neutral reasons are necessarily superior reasons, the best solution would be to argue that agent-relative reasons, properly understood, support other-regarding moral requirements as well. So friends of agent-neutrality would do well to cultivate the resources of strategic and metaphysical egoists, even if they reject the rational egoist assumption that all reasons for action are agent-relative.

Further investigation of the puzzle would require more comprehensive investigations of (III) and (IV). Are there compelling arguments for agent-relativity? Can Kantian arguments for agent-neutrality be articulated plausibly? Are people's interests independent, as the neo-Aristotelian view claims? If so, do other-regarding moral requirements and other-regarding aspects of an agent's welfare dovetail appropriately? How strong is the authority of moral demands when the various resources for justifying other-regarding conduct are counted together? When we answer these questions, we will have the resources for a satisfying solution to the puzzle about the rational authority of morality.[20]

Notes

1. Because internalism assumes the norms of morality are norms of rationality, it implies, in effect, that (II) is an a priori constraint on moral theory and is not up for grabs. So understood, internalism is a *ground* for asserting (II). Internalism is sometimes understood as a claim about moral *motivation*, whereas the kind of internalism that supports (II) is a claim about the *rational authority* or morality. For a discussion of various forms of internalism, see Brink 1989: ch. 3. Internalism about moral motivation is relevant to a puzzle about moral motivation.

I. Moral judgments express beliefs.
II. Moral judgments imply motivation.
III. Motivation involves pro-attitudes.
IV. There is no necessary connection between any belief and any pro-attitude.

Noncognitivists (e.g. Stevenson and Hare) reject (I); externalists (e.g. Foot and I) deny (II); and new-wave theories of motivation (e.g. Nagel and McDowell) deny either (III) or (IV). Though I do not agree with their solutions, this second puzzle is usefully discussed by McNaughton 1988 and Smith 1989.

2. In some contexts it is important to distinguish the egoist claim that I have reason to do something insofar as it would promote my interests or advance my overall good and the instrumentalist claim that I have reason to do something insofar as it would satisfy my present desires. Among other differences, the latter has an important temporal restriction that the former does not. But both are agent-relative views, and my present purposes do not in general require that they be sharply distinguished. I will mark the distinction only where it seems relevant to my argument.

3. As I am understanding it, agent-neutrality says only that other people's interests can directly provide me with reasons for action, independently of any connection with my interests or aims; it says nothing about the scope or weight of various directly other-regarding reasons. So agent-neutral theories can be quite varied. For instance, Sidgwick's *rational benevolence* and Broad's *self-referential altruism* are both agent-neutral (cf. Broad 1953: 279-280).

4. Cf. Davidson 1963, 1974.

5. Cf. Hume 1739: III.i.1; Mackie 1977: ch. 1; Harman 1975, 1984.

6. My account of strategic egoism does not distinguish between *act* egoism and *motive* egoism. That's a topic for another occasion.

7. Cf. Epicurus *Kuriai Doxa* 31-38; Taylor 1987; Axelrod 1984; Gauthier 1986; and Frank 1988. Though each accepts a form of rational egoism incorporating such strategic reasoning, Epicurus and Gauthier are clearest about employing such reasoning as part of *ethical* egoism and its attempt to derive the content of morality from agent-relative rational choice.

There are various significant constraints on the models of social interaction in which cooperation and restraint are strategically rational. The model must be dynamic; actors must not discount future pay-offs too much; the environment must include a sufficiently large number of conditional compliers; and conditional compliers must be able to monitor reliably the compliance and noncompliance of others (this last condition tends to be more easily satisfied in small groups).

8. The Ring of Gyges exposes the counterfactual instability of strategic egoism; this is why Plato insists that justice be shown to be valuable for its intrinsic, and not simply extrinsic, consequences (*Rep* 359b-361d). However, *Republic* i-ii appears to be concerned with a rational egoist challenge to the rational authority of justice, not with ethical egoism. If so, it differs from the *Gorgias*, in which Callicles presents an ethical egoist challenge to conventional justice.

9. Indeed, Gauthier is quite candid about these limitations in his argument. His justification of other-regarding conduct among actors in strategic situations depends on the assumption that such actors are "psychologically translucent" (1986: 173-4), and he acknowledges that he cannot explain duties to those with whom one has no strategic interaction (1986: 16, 17).

10. My discussion here owes much to Foot 1972.

11. Any view, such as this, that treats rational action as action that would satisfy the aims the agent would have in an idealized epistemic state in which her beliefs

and desires are in reflective equilibrium might seem to be an agent-relative view about rationality. If so, it may seem that no arguments for agent-neutrality within reflective equilibrium could unseat agent-relative assumptions about rationality; the rationality of other-regarding conduct would still depend on facts about the agent's aims or desires (cf. Williams 1980). But this a priori defense of agent-relativity has two problems. First, *this* kind of agent-relativity is not a constituent element of the puzzle. If reflective equilibrium might be such that aims that are in reflective equilibrium must include direct concern for others, then there is no problem about the rational authority of morality on the kind of agent-relative assumptions characteristic of this reflective equilibrium account of rationality. If we understand the agent-relativity of (III) in this way, there is or need be no inconsistency in (I)-(IV). To put it another way, the kind of agent-neutrality sufficient to resolve the puzzle is not inconsistent with agent-relativity in this sense. Second, whether the reflective equilibrium account of rationality is agent-relative depends upon whether the arguments for agent-neutrality, if good, are good arguments because they're in reflective equilibrium or whether they're part of reflective equilibrium because they're good arguments. If the former, the rationality of other-regarding conduct is agent-relative; if the latter, it is agent-neutral. The friend of agent-neutrality presumably advances arguments for agent-neutrality the merits of which are intended to explain why agent-neutrality should figure in reflective equilibrium. As such, these arguments, if successful, would vindicate agent-neutrality.

12. The example involving gouty toes is Hume's (1751: ch. V, pt. ii), though his concern is with egoist theories of motivation, not rationality.

13. It will have even less force against agent-relative assumptions about rationality if we reject the independence assumption (cf. §4 below).

14. I explore this strategy more fully in Brink 1991.

15. Cf. Hegel 1821: §268, 1840: ch. 3; Green 1883: §§180-91, 199-203, 232-9, 286; and Bradley 1927: 69-81, 163, 166-92, 203-6, 219-25.

16. What follows is a condensed version of claims that I defend at greater length in Brink 1990; cf. Irwin 1988: ch. 18.

    This argument is also Platonic. Plato claims that (1) the virtuous person will have love for others (*Rep* 402d-403c, 412d), and (2) love (a) involves concern for the beloved's own sake, and (b) is, for the lover, the next best thing to immortality (*Symp* 206e-212c and *Phdrs* 243c-257b). (Cf. Irwin 1977: 241-3.) Plato's grounds for accepting (b) seem very similar to Aristotle's reasons for regarding one's friend as "another-self" (see below). (1)-(2) allow Plato to argue that the virtuous agent will be concerned about others for their own sakes and will necessarily benefit from benefiting them.

    Also, there is a reading of this project, which I won't pursue, that bears resemblance to the idealist strategy mentioned above.

17. Cf. Parfit 1984: part III; Shoemaker 1984. For some evidence that such a view appeals to Aristotle, see Irwin 1988: 241-255, 284-6, 345, 376-8.

18. Cf. Sidgwick 1907: 432-9; Railton 1984; and Brink 1986.

19. Psychological diversity is compatible with psychological continuity provided the diversity is the result of interaction in which the participants exchanged and discussed beliefs, goals, and values. For then differences result from a process in which there were common intentional states produced by causal interaction.

20. Work on this paper was done during a fellowship at the Center for Advanced Study in the Behavioral Sciences that was funded by an Old Dominion Fellowship from the Massachusetts Institute of Technology and by grants from the National

Endowment for the Humanities (#RA-20037-88) and the Andrew W. Mellon Foundation. I would like to thank these institutions for their support. I would also like to thank Randy Calvert, Stephen Darwall, Thomas Hurka, and David McNaughton for helpful discussion of some of these issues.

References

Aristotle. *Nicomachean Ethics* (EN), trs. T. Irwin. Indianapolis: Hackett, 1985.
Axelrod, R. 1984. *The Evolution of Cooperation*. New York: Basic Books.
Bradley, F.H. 1927. *Ethical Studies*, 2d. ed. Oxford: Clarendon Press.
Brink, D.O. 1991. "Categorical Imperatives and Kantian Rationalism." Unpublished.
Brink, D.O. 1990. "Rational Egoism, Self, and Others." In O. Flanagan and A. Rorty (eds), *Identity, Character, and Morality*. Cambridge, MA: MIT Press.
Brink, D.O. 1989. *Moral Realism and the Foundations of Ethics*. Cambridge: Cambridge University Press.
Brink, D.O. 1986. "Utilitarian Morality and the Personal Point of View," *The Journal of Philosophy*, 83, pp. 417-39.
Broad, C.D. 1953. "Self and Others." Reprinted in D. Cheney (ed), *Broad's Critical Essays in Moral Philosophy*. London: George Allen & Unwin, 1971.
Davidson, D. 1963. "Actions, Reasons, and Causes." Reprinted in D. Davidson, *Essays on Actions and Events*. New York: Oxford University Press, 1980.
Davidson, D. 1974. "Psychology as Philosophy." Reprinted in D. Davidson, *Essays on Actions and Events*. New York: Oxford University Press, 1980.
Epicurus. *Kuriai Doxa*. In Diogenes Laertius, *Lives of Eminent Philosophers*, vol. II, trs. R. Hicks (Cambridge, MA: Loeb Library, 1925).
Foot, P. 1972. "Morality as a System of Hypothetical Imperatives." Reprinted in P. Foot, *Virtues and Vices*. Los Angeles: University of California Press, 1978.
Frank, R. 1988. *Passions within Reason*. New York: Norton.
Gauthier, D. 1986. *Morals By Agreement*. Oxford: Clarendon Press.
Green, T.H. 1883. *Prolegomena to Ethics*. New York: Crowell, 1969.
Harman, G. 1984. "Is There a Single True Morality?" In D. Copp and M. Zimmerman (eds), *Morality, Reason, and Truth*. Totowa, NJ: Roman and Littlefield.
Harman, G. 1975. "Moral Relativism Defended," *The Philosophical Review*, 85, pp. 3-22.
Hegel, G.W.F. 1840. *Introduction to the Philosophy of History*, trs. L. Rauch. Indianapolis: Hackett, 1988.
Hegel, G.W.F. 1821. *The Philosophy of Right*, trs. T.M. Knox. Oxford: Clarendon Press, 1942.
Hume, D. 1751. *An Enquiry Concerning the Principles of Morals*. Indianapolis: Hackett, 1983.
Hume, D. 1739. *A Treatise of Human Nature*, ed. P. Nidditch. Oxford: Clarendon Press, 1978.
Irwin, T.H. 1988. *Aristotle's First Principles*. Oxford: Clarendon Press.
Irwin, T.H. 1977. *Plato's Moral Theory*. Oxford: Clarendon Press.
Kant, I. 1785. *Grounding for the Metaphysics of Morals*, trs. J. Ellington. Indianapolis: Hackett, 1981. (Prussian Academy pagination).
Mackie, J.L. 1977. *Ethics: Inventing Right and Wrong*. New York: Penguin.
McNaughton, D. 1988. *Moral Vision*. Oxford: Blackwell.
Nagel, T. 1970. *The Possibility of Altruism*. Princeton, NJ: Princeton University Press.
Nozick, R. 1974. *Anarchy, State, and Utopia*. New York: Basic Books.
Parfit, D. 1984. *Reasons and Persons*. Oxford: Clarendon Press.
Plato. *Republic* (Rep), trs. G. Grube. Indianapolis: Hackett, 1974.

Plato. *Gorgias*, trs. T. Irwin. Oxford: Clarendon Press, 1979.

Plato. *Symposium* (*Symp*), trs. M. Joyce. In *Collected Dialogues of Plato*, eds. E. Hamilton and H. Cairns. Princeton: Princeton University Press, 1963.

Plato. *Phaedrus* (*Phdrs*), trs. R. Hackforth. In *Collected Dialogues of Plato*, eds. E. Hamilton and H. Cairns. Princeton: Princeton University Press, 1963.

Railton, P. 1984. "Alienation, Consequentialism, and the Demands of Morality," *Philosophy & Public Affairs*, 13, pp. 134-71.

Shoemaker, S. 1984. "Personal Identity: A Materialist's Account." In S. Shoemaker and R. Swinburne, *Personal Identity*. Oxford: Blackwell.

Sidgwick, H. 1907. *The Methods of Ethics*, 7th ed. Indianapolis: Hackett, 1981.

Smith, M. 1989. *The Moral Problem*. Unpublished.

Taylor, M. 1987. *The Possibility of Cooperation*. Cambridge: Cambridge University Press.

Williams, B. 1980. "Internal and External Reasons." Reprinted in B. Williams, *Moral Luck*. Cambridge: Cambridge University Press, 1981.

Philosophical Perspectives, 6, Ethics, 1992

SOME QUESTIONS ABOUT THE JUSTIFICATION OF MORALITY[1]

Peter Railton
The University of Michigan, Ann Arbor

I

It is common enough to hear talk of moral justification, as for example when it is asked whether abortion is morally justified. It is less common to hear talk of the justification of morality. What might such a justification be—an answer to the question "Ought I to do what I ought to do?"? This has the look of a *question mal posée*.

But the question might be a sensible one, for there are multiple 'ought's.[2] That which I *morally* ought to do is at least conceptually distinct from that which I prudently ought to do, or ought to do as a citizen, or friend, or parent. So it would seem that various genuine questions can be asked about the justification of morality, though in order to be sure one is answering a genuine question when responding to a request for justification one must know what sort of 'ought' is at issue.[3] The very difficult first question that confronts any discussion of 'the justification of morality' is this: What *is* the purported standing of morality (as it is ordinarily seen), and so what (if anything) must be done to inquire into whether that standing is warranted? There may or may not be a coherent set of issues and concerns here.

For example, discussions of morality often emphasize its purported *practical* standing, though not always with a clear, agreed-upon idea of what this practical standing is. Moreover, among the important issues about the justification of morality are some that may resist ready assimilation to the practical. A central concern in this vicinity is what to *believe* about morality. To be sure, a sense of practical conflict is an excellent way of inducing concern about the epistemic standing of morality, and our moral beliefs are important to us in large measure because of their seeming practical implications. But belief should be, we think, responsive to theoretical as well as practical norms.

In this paper, I will seek to keep in tandem—in a way that, I hope, reflects our actual concerns—theoretical and practical issues about what there is (or isn't) to morality. An alternative way of proceeding would be to fix upon one notion of justification—I suppose the most important historically is called "rational justification"—and attempt to address more directly whether a justification of morality can be constructed. But I wonder whether this would not in the end amount to much the same thing, since I suspect that the expression 'rational justification' really covers a rather diverse, and ultimately not wholly practical, set of dimensions of justification. How could there fail to be interaction between thinking about what morality seems to ask of us practically and thinking about whether morality is the sort of thing that is, or could be, an object of knowledge?

Of course, it is common within the Kantian tradition of discussing the standing of morality to urge that we must not think of the justification of morality as a *metaphysical* task; and various interpretations of moral discourse and practice go a step further, holding that we should not treat our moral beliefs as genuinely cognitive at all. Perhaps so—but these are deliverances of pieces of theoretical inquiry. Now the theoretical may, for all that I will say here, ultimately be reducible to the practical (or, indeed, the other way around). What will occupy us here is simply the idea that the standing of morality involves interrelated questions of what we have theoretical reason to believe as well as what we have practical reason to do.

Just as questions about what justification would be typically express a diverse and not-wholly-articulated range of concerns, so do conceptions of what is to be justified vary. To more people than one would like to think, morality looms in the mind as a straight-laced and rather unsympathetic taskmaster, issuing prohibitions against various tempting activities and calling especially for rigid adherence to certain norms of sexual conduct and truth-telling. We can readily enough give an explanation of why morality strikes people in this way, but asking whether this motley of prohibitions is justified may not be the best way to reach the issues we find most philosophically perplexing about morality. If we are to be able to raise philosophically compelling issues about the justification of morality, we will need a more compelling conception of morality itself. Now any such conception seems bound to be either very thin or potentially controversial. There is much to be learned from raising questions about justification using as thin a conception of morality as we find recognizable, but I would like in this paper to pursue some thoughts about what one might learn by considering a more contentful, and therefore at least somewhat controversial, conception of morality. If, as I think, moral discourse does have content as well as form, then it is natural to wonder how—or whether—this content contributes to questions about justification.

II

Here is a familiar way in which genuine doubts about the justification of morality might arise. Consider (what I will call) a "modernist" attitude toward religion, which sees religious beliefs as projections of human aspirations, cultural norms, and social hierarchy. A theist might ask "Why did God create man in His own image?"; our modernist would ask instead "Why did men create God in their own image?", and leave to anthropologists, sociologists, and psychologists the task of explaining both the variety of religious doctrines and the underlying human tendency to treat such doctrines as representing an independent reality. The answers that social and psychological theory might provide could, for example, show that religious beliefs and practices served various useful functions in the societies or individual lives of those who promulgated or held them. However, answers of this kind would not ordinarily be understood to justify the *content* of religious belief. Likewise, social and psychological theory might be able to tell us why religious belief has been so irresistible for large numbers of people, but, *prima facie*, irresistibility is not tantamount to warrant.

In a similar way, a modernist asking herself what role *morality* should have in her life might wonder whether there really is anything to morality other than a social and psychological phenomenon requiring explanation. While people have deemed various behaviors to be morally right or wrong, and various sensibilities to be morally good or bad, this, too, might be seen as the reification of socially- and psychologically-grounded norms and aspirations as "objective" in some firmer sense. Indeed, this worry may involve more than a parallel to the religious case, for it has seemed to many theists and modernists alike that morality and religion stand or fall together—"If God is dead, then everything is permitted". If morality is to be objective, according to one variant of this view, an intelligently-ordered or divinely-governed universe must be presupposed.

Now sometimes when this sort of opinion is expressed the emphasis is on the policing and punishing functions of God—like an undeceivable and unmanipulable parent, God insures that we will pay a price for not minding. Yet it would be misleading to think this the whole story. For if it were sufficient to justify morality that there be a background system of sure and convincing punishment, then an earthly regime with a highly reliable repressive apparatus could do the job. If need be, some science-fictitious mind-reading devices and thought police could be added to fill the picture out. Such a regime would appear to have the power to make it prudent to go along with *whatever* social code it chose to enforce, but I suspect most of us would not think that this would show that code to be objectively correct (whatever this might mean), or to be justified *as a morality*. That is, most of us who pause to ask what to make of morality seek something other than a revelation that moral injunctions, though arbitrarily chosen to meet the needs of a dominant regime, are costly to break owing to the ruthless efficiency of the Space Gestapo. What God did, then, must have been more than policework.[4] While it is a quite deep question how the other, non-coercive features attributed to God *could* have given morality a foundation it otherwise would lack (as opposed simply to presupposing morality to be in order), nonetheless sheer coercive power—impressive as it certainly is in a practical way—seems insufficient to found an objective morality.

One way of thinking about what is lacking when an ideology is inculcated and enforced by an effectively repressive state is to notice that while a well-handled bludgeon can make belief in an arbitrary proposition prudent, it typically cannot serve as *evidence* for that belief. Perhaps, then, we should conclude that the justification of morality requires not just prudence in the practical sphere, but also *epistemic respectability* in the theoretical sphere, in this broad sense: moral beliefs must be shown not only to be advantageous, but also warranted.

But this will not suffice, either. Consider the view, which has not been entirely without advocates, that '*x* is wrong' just means "people in our society disapprove of *x*".[5] Social opinion is a real enough thing, and something about which we have (one may suppose) warranted beliefs. Moreover, it typically *is* prudent to avoid doing that of which people in one's society disapprove. For the sake of an example, let us suppose that this latter condition is very reliably met. Then we would have a view that affords a notion of wrongness that has both prudence and epistemic respectability on its side, but I suspect few would find this adequate for the sort of justification they had in mind. Indeed, this notion of wrongness would no doubt strike most modernists as a vindication of their suspicions: "If *that* is what morality consists in, then, as I always figured, morality is no more than an unholy alliance of social prejudice, highflown language, and the urge to punish deviants."

What is missing? In a phrase, the *peculiar normative standing* of ethics. Prudence and epistemology have their distinctive normative characters and their own sort of standing in relation to our thought and conduct, but it seems we cannot capture the purported normative status of morality simply by finding some notion that would combine prudence with epistemic respectability. How might we do better?

One answer with a long history is that one should look to the standing of *pure* practical reason, not mere prudence. To account for the peculiar normativity of ethics would be to show that morality gives people reasons for action not tied to particular individual interests, social settings, and so on, but categorical reasons, reasons for all (rational) agents as such.[6] This would give morality a special standing for all agents and secure independence from any particular repressive apparatus, even a divine one.[7] Let us for now set aside questions about the bare existence of categorical practical reasons, and ask instead whether, if they did exist, their special standing would suffice to capture the peculiar normative standing of morality.

Consider the following jury-rigged argument, with premises that might be borrowed from someone like Kant.[8] (I do not make any historical claims on its behalf.[9]) Suppose that the very exercise of practical reason requires that one believe that the world is benignly ordered in such a way that well-performed deliberation can be expected ultimately to yield good results for the agent, and perhaps for all humankind as well. (Or, alternatively, suppose that the exercise of practical reason requires that one believe in the objectivity of one's reasons, and that *this* belief is possible only on the supposition that the world is intelligently ordered.) Perhaps a divine, infinitely understanding mind could dispense with any such belief, but such a mind would also be beyond practical reason. (If an 'I ought' really becomes an 'I will' for a divine being, and if the future is as plain to it as the past is to us, then *deliberation* about the future might be no more a genuine possibility for it than deliberation about the past is for us. The incompatibility of a perfectly predictive 'I will' with a deliberative 'I ought' has been a favorite theme of incompatibilists.) It may therefore be the case that any being who is to be a deliberatively rational agent must *as such* believe in the existence of a benign world or a world-organizing benign intelligence. This would give a categorical reason (in our sense of the term: a reason stemming from agency alone) for such a belief. But would it make the belief epistemically respectable, or would the belief be a pure postulate, a mere article of faith?[10]

Imagine now running the same argument with the substitution of 'objective morality' for 'benignly ordered world'. Would that suffice for the justification of morality? Categorical practical reason, if it could be achieved, would add standing beyond merely prudential justification—specifically, it would remove any dependence on contingent ends—but it does not yet seem that this captures the essence of the normative standing we seek.

Perhaps we can say at least this much: categoricalness of practical reason would have to be combined with respectability of theoretical reason if belief in morality is to be justified. But rather than attempt to assess this possibility here,[11] I would like to shift more directly to questions of a theoretical nature, and only afterwards return to practical questions, once we have developed a somewhat different conception of the "inescapability" of morality.

III

How might one think about the normative standing of morality without appealing in the first instance to the idea of reasons that are compelling— even perhaps overriding—for all practically rational beings as such? It may be helpful to bear in mind just how philosophical this notion of a pure practical reason is, and how few of us can be said to have gained our original sense of what morality is, or requires of us, by grasping this conception. But—it might be countered—haven't we indeed at some level grasped it, for do we not in fact apply moral assessments non-hypothetically? Do we not, that is, apply the judgment that an act of cruelty is wrong even when committed by someone who does not happen to take an interest in moral conduct or the well-being of others?

Certainly our moral evaluations exhibit this feature. And perhaps a proper philosophical archaeology would unearth the idea of a categorical practical reason as the "real foundation" of our moral practice. But we might first consider a less dazzling claim: our notion of moral evaluation has a feature I will call *non-hypothetical scope*—we deem moral evaluations to be properly applied even to agents who, as a mater of fact, lack any significant intrinsic desire or extrinsic motive to give these evaluations (or the grounds upon which they rest) weight in their deliberation. This idea is sometimes put by calling moral evaluation "inescapable" or "unavoidable".

Some care is required here. First, the scope of our moral evaluations is restricted in various ways—a man who attacks an innocent person without provocation is subject to moral assessment, but not a baby who lashes out, or a crab which bites, or a fire that devours. One gets within the scope of moral assessment by being capable (and here we speak very loosely) of recognizing and conforming oneself to moral assessments, i.e., by being a moral agent. *Homo sapiens* who lack, temporarily or permanently, central properties of agency are not directly subject to certain kinds of moral evaluation (though morality need hardly be silent on their treatment as "moral patients", and morality may also deem it appropriate to employ the vocabulary of moral assessment with respect to such individuals instrumentally, for purposes of moral education). Second, many moral assessments have excusing conditions that depend upon the motivational or cognitive state of the agent. In the present discussion, we are especially interested in excuses relating to motivation. It is, for example, commonly said that, although rendering aid to those in dire need is morally good, nonetheless, agents are not ordinarily *obliged* to be beneficent when this calls for significant sacrifice on their part. Moreover, agents are often said to be entitled to distribute their charity according to special personal interests or ties. Those who render aid impartially, and at great cost to personal projects, act in a supererogatory, or more-than-obligatory, manner. The idea of inescapability therefore cannot be understood as the complete independence of substantive moral assessment from questions of the assessee's motivational character or state. Rather, at least in central cases, it is a matter of the *applicability* of moral standards even to those agents who do not find the standards themselves motivating. In the case of rendering aid, the moral standard might be something like: "Render aid when the effort involved is trivial in comparison to the good it could achieve, and when others are not evidently able to provide it". This standard applies to me, as an agent, whether or not I am already disposed to help. Should I fail to help in appropriate circumstances, I would be liable to moral criticism whether this concerned me or not.

Note that the standard might, but need not, be one of obligation—I may be *liable* to the criticism of acting morally badly, even if the criticism is not as severe as the criticism of violating an obligation. It would somewhat distort the object of our inquiry, I think, were we to take the notion of a moral requirement as our paradigm for the "inescapability" of moral evaluation, for we might thereby be led to see the particular features and stringency of obligation as essential to an explanation of "inescapability". The phenomenon is more generally present in moral evaluation.

My suggestion will be that we can account for this sort of "inescapability" without invoking the idea of a categorical imperative or a categorical reason. To help fix ideas, let us consider that there are various other classes of critical standards with non-hypothetical scope ("inescapability") in the relevant sense. We will consider three examples.

Aesthetics may be of special interest in this connection, since in aesthetics one is not initially tempted to think that the primary evaluative category is one of obligation rather than appraisal; rather, it seems to be oriented in the first instance more toward accomplishments than actions, and to be more a matter of greater or lesser value than of a trichotomy of the required, the permitted, and the impermissible. Like morality, aesthetics is a domain full of controversy, but not devoid of truisms. It is not, for example, anomalous to judge that a given choice of architectural detail is appropriate or inappropriate even when one (accurately) believes that the builder did not care about aesthetics and did not even have a non-aesthetic interest that would be served by a better choice of detail. A builder could not *rebut* a charge of inappropriate choice or "bad judgment" by claiming (sincerely) not to care—philistinism is an aesthetic criticism, not an exemption from it.[12]

Logic is much less controversial than aesthetics, and truisms abound. One such truism is meta-logical, and is so obvious that it attracts little notice: logical standards—often seen as centered on notions of what one *must do* or *is permitted to do*—have non-hypothetical scope in the sense that interests us here. That is, one's arguments cannot escape logical criticism by the fact of one's not caring: they are—and, by extension, one is—illogical whether one is concerned or not.

Now, at least on one familiar view, logic proper is not itself a set of norms of reasoning, but rather an account of relations among sentences or propositions, especially, relations of consistency and implication. These latter features are in turn explained by appeal to truth—inconsistent statements cannot simultaneously be true, non-valid inferences are not guaranteed to be truth-preserving.[13] Nonetheless, logic is used normatively by us as reasoners, since we hold that, non-hypothetically, one is liable to a decisive kind of epistemic criticism if one's beliefs are inconsistent or one's inferences fallacious. It could perhaps be claimed that this criticism depends in the end upon the fact that one always stands to benefit overall by avoiding contradictions and fallacies, but this strikes me as missing precisely the sense in which the criticism is *logical*. In any event, the claim that one always stands to benefit from eschewing illogical reasoning strikes me as much more controversial than the original claim about non-hypotheticalness. Moreover, aside from some homilies in introductory logic texts about the improved life prospects of those who learn to avoid affirming the consequent, it is striking how little attention philosophers (and others) have paid to the question whether one can demonstrate that logic always pays. Surely part of the answer is that it seems so obvious that illogical reasoning can lead one into trouble on various fronts. Yet with a little philosophical ingenuity one can construct possible cases in which what it would take to remove an inconsistent belief would be very costly to an individual, both practically, as an actor, and even theoretically, as a believer.[14]

The non-hypotheticalness of logical assessment does not appear to stem from some hard-to-establish fact about categorical reasons or guaranteed instrumental utility. One straightforward explanation suggests itself. The jurisdiction of logic, as applied to agents' beliefs and inferences, is not tied to questions about how well certain beliefs or inferences serve the agent's ends—even his necessary ends. In logical assessment our eye instead is fixed on matters of truth and truth-preservation in inference, however these might bear on the agent's concerns.

If we do not assume that rational agents always or necessarily have a compelling reason to overcome aesthetic shortcomings or logical defects, then what accounts for the normative force of such criticisms? One way of understanding this question is to put it thus: What accounts for the seriousness with which we (typically, at least) treat aesthetic or logical evaluation? Here is a very rough sketch for an answer. Logical standards play the role they (typically) do in public debate and private criticism because the truth and justifiability of what we believe (typically) matter to us, intrinsically as well as instrumentally, and because logic sheds light on what is necessarily true or false, or when an argument suffices for a conclusion, and so on. Aesthetic standards play the role they (typically) do because the beauty, harmony, proportion, and so on of what we create (typically) matter to us.

Now it would be a misrepresentation of this state of affairs to say that, therefore, logical or aesthetic standards are hypothetical. Logical and aesthetic criticism properly apply to my acts not only independently of whether I care, but independently of whether anyone cares.[15] As we have noted, logical standards have the standing for us that they do in part because they do not bend to our particular desires or ends, and are in that sense "external" to such considerations. Something similar can be said about aesthetic standards (despite their seeming dependency at some deep level upon the sorts of things that engage humans). The statement, "I don't know much about art, but I know what I like," is not, and does not purport to be, a piece of aesthetics.

One might be tempted to explain the non-hypothetical scope of logic and aesthetics in terms of the non-hypothetical content of the standards involved. But consider a third example of a standard with non-hypothetical scope, the theory of *instrumental rationality*. And consider this crude formulation: an act is rationally preferable for an agent if it would, prospectively, do a better job of advancing the agent's ends. This standard, though containing a reference to the particular agent's purposes, is not hypothetical in scope. An agent who fails to look beyond his immediate passions and ignores whether his acts can be seen as tending to advance or frustrate his own ends does not escape the brand "irrational", but earns it. Once again, one can ask why, unless there is some always or necessarily compelling reason to give one's ends weight in deliberation (and once one considers familiar quandaries involving now-for-then ends, the possible absence of such a general reason no longer seems altogether unintelligible), considerations of instrumental rationality (typically) have such significance for us. Once again, one can reply by noting that (typically) we take our own ends seriously, and following this standard (typically) helps us to realize them. Once again, that this concern might in some general or particular way be contingent does not show the standard itself to be hypothetical in scope.

What is it that *is* "hypothetical" about the standing of aesthetics, logic, or instrumental rationality? Let us say that their *evaluative impact* on us, as communities or individuals, does depend upon our desires or ends. After all, there are infinitely many standards for assessing beliefs or reasoning that possess the non-hypothetical scope of logic. Are the beliefs expressible in terms of first-order quantification theory? Do they occur in English? Do they exist before or after the Crimean war? And so on. To be told that one's beliefs do not meet—or only to a limited degree meet—any particular standard of this kind will not make much of an impression upon one unless one somehow cares about (or could be led to care about) this standard. Logical standards have, for us, significant evaluative impact—we feel keenly the criticism of inconsistency or fallacy, and devote a not insignificant amount of psychic energy to avoiding such criticisms. (To be sure, some of the strategies we follow in consequence lead us only into deeper error and self-deception.) But we can, it seems, imagine possible worlds in which illogic is the very thing to possess if one is to have a long and happy life, and we can imagine that happiness might be the only thing that, at bottom, could matter to us in its own right. (If psychological hedonism is false, it probably is contingently so.) Mere deliberation, one might claim, presupposes logic, but perhaps it really presupposes only *some* minimally coherent or practically effective set of dispositions to believe and infer. We need only imagine a world in which circumstances are so arranged that humans whose norms of belief-formation and inference depart from logic would encounter less frustration of the ends they actually possess than humans whose norms followed logic more faithfully.[16]

Nonetheless, I don't think that a sense of the contingency of our intrinsic or extrinsic concern for logic much affects the evaluative impact for us of logical standards. To learn that those who do not (and perhaps need not) care much about truth do not (and perhaps need not) care much about logic, either, does little to undermine my commitment to logic.[17] Partly this is because of the non-hypothetical scope and content of logic: to learn that there are or could be some who do not care about logic does not make me think there is nothing wrong with their beliefs or inferences when they violate logical norms (however much it might please them to do so). After all, it never was the distinguishing feature or peculiar point of logical criticism that those who fail to heed it will experience disappointment in life, even if, in fact, we have tended to assume that they will.

Now is it enough to capture the peculiar normative status of logic to appeal to its (essential) non-hypothetical scope and content and its (contingent but significant) evaluative impact for us? There remains at least one thing. Logic purports to have a necessary connection with truth, and that purport underlies the special significance of logic for us. But is the purport made good? That is, is logic *well-founded* in the broad, not-merely-technical sense that the notions of truth, necessity, consistency, validity, and so on, which it employs are not themselves bogus, and that the special connection it represents itself as having to truth is not specious? Suppose, as one sometimes hears in more melodramatic literary-critical circles, that what we call 'logic' is simply one set of socially-and historically-specific conventions for the regulation of belief or inference—the alleged special connection with truth, or perhaps even the notion of truth itself, being a piece of ideology, and logical criticism being just another form of social repression, used to extinguish or discourage creative views unfavorable to the status quo.[18] The fact that the standards are non-hypothetical no more secures a special connection between logic and truth than does the fact that the standard "Is the sentence in Hungarian?" is non-hypothetical secure a special connection between being in a Finno-Ugric language and truth.

Logical standards would not have the normative status they do for us if we did not believe they were well-founded. For logical standards to be justified in the normative status we do (at least, most of us) attribute to them, then, would require showing that they not only possess non-hypothetical scope and evaluative impact, but also are well-founded. For example, we often speak of logical criticism as *objective*. Whatever exactly that might mean, it seems clearly to involve us with the idea that the notion of truth in terms of which we explain the character of logic possesses itself something worth calling objectivity.

In similar ways, the normative status of non-hypothetical standards of aesthetics and instrumental rationality presupposes well-foundedness. If the very idea of aesthetic merit came to be seen as bogus, or if we could not find anything other than myth underlying our conceptions of personal continuity or agency, then we could be led to view the evaluative impact of aesthetics or instrumental rationality as ungrounded—even though, perhaps we found ourselves unable entirely to shake their psychological grip upon us.

IV

Let us now return to the status of morality. We are operating not with the notion of categorical reasons, but with the notions of non-hypothetical scope, evaluative impact, and well-foundedness. Do these categories help us to see what it might be for morality to be justified in the normative standing we attribute to it? Do they, for example, allow us to express the concerns we might have about this standing without raising concerns that we find, on reflection, at odds with (or inessential to) our conception of morality? We will take up the former question in this section, and the latter question in section V.

Our discussion of what had to be in place in order for logic to be vindicated in its standing depended upon a substantive claim about logic, namely, its purported connection to truth. This account of logic, though intended to be truistic, is nevertheless not utterly uncontroversial. Any attempt to give a similar, general characterization of ethics is bound to be yet more controversial. While I believe that a number of widely-held views about the nature of morality could profitably be used as the basis for the discussion that follows, it would quickly become unwieldy to attempt to keep several such accounts in play. I will, then, focus upon a particular characterization of ethics, saying only a bit about its plausibility and its relation to alternatives.

Consider the following standard for ethical evaluation: an act (or kind or act, or trait of character, or social institution) is better from a moral point of view, other things equal, to the extent that it can be expected to contribute to the well-being or to alleviation of the suffering of those it would affect. According to some moral theories, a standard of this ilk is the heart of morality. Classical utilitarian theories, for example, use this notion to account directly or indirectly for the whole of moral obligation. According to other moral theories, such a standard is one component of assessment among others, as for example in a Rossian deontology where beneficence figures as a *prima facie* duty. According to others still, such as classical Kantianism, that such a standard will be met by dutiful action is a necessary presupposition of the rationality of morality. Finally, contemporary rational social choice theories, including contractarian variants, typically make the efficiency of social arrangements at improving social welfare (perhaps with certain restrictions or once certain conditions have been met) count in their favor. It therefore is not utterly controversial to say that some such standard is part of what is at issue in moral assessment. Though it would be much more controversial to claim that this standard is the whole core of morality, we need not advance any such claim here. For there will be *something* to morality if this standard can be found to have appropriate standing.[19] Let us consider our three dimensions: scope, evaluative impact, and well-foundedness.

Scope. This standard can be seen, like the logical, aesthetic, and rational standards discussed above, to be non-hypothetical in evaluative scope. Suppose that I, rushing down the sidewalk like the others around me, hurry past a child who is wandering toward a busy street, noticing but doing nothing. To scoop her up, return her to her yard, and shut the gate would take an insignificant amount of time and effort on my part. Would a moral evaluation that I have acted badly be inapplicable simply because my plans for that afternoon did not include any rescues and because I just couldn't be bothered? Hardly. The standard of beneficence under consideration here has just this effect—nothing in its formulation necessarily limits its application to those beneficently motivated. To the extent that I am among those affected by my own actions, then effects on my own interests or well-being will enter into the content of beneficence, but this does not show a hypothetical scope of *application*—even if I happened not to care about my interests, beneficence would require that I take them into account. Whether act A, say, meets the standard will be settled, if at all, by the actual or prospective contributions of act A vs. available alternatives to the well-being of all affected. These contributions can exist and have whatever character they have even if I am oblivious or malevolent. As in the logical case, non-hypotheticalness can be grounded substantively rather than in a scheme of categorical reasons. The truth-preserving character of an inference is independent our interest in it, and so is the contribution of an action to the well- or ill-being of others.

Impact. To what extent does a standard of beneficence possess the features we have claimed to find in morality, the features we characteristically point to in explaining morality's special status? Certainly, moral evaluation is on its face non-hypothetical in character, but it would not suffice to vindicate the normative standing of morality simply to find a non-hypothetical standard with which to associate it. As in the logical case, there are altogether too many such standards. Indeed, the inverse of the standard of beneficence—a standard of malevolence which would favor an act in proportion as it increases suffering or decreases happiness—is equally non-hypothetical.

It therefore becomes important at this point to see that the standard of beneficence possesses certain other significant features commonly attributed to morality, many of which are also commonly associated with the notion of a categorical imperative. First, as we have already noted, the standard is *impartial*—it gives equal weight to the well-being of all potentially affected. Second, the standard is *universal* or *non- relativistic*. Etiquette has often been cited as a system of non-hypothetical norms,[20] but it does not appear to be part of etiquette to aspire to universality—the norms are non-hypothetical, but only within a local jurisdiction. It would manifest a misunderstanding of the normative status of etiquette to think that intersocial variability in codes of etiquette poses a challenge to the authority of our code comparable to the challenge that variability in moral code poses for the authority of morality—and this despite the many conventional elements that enter into the determination of which particular acts in which particular circumstances are morally right. For this reason, the 'must' of etiquette might be viewed as an unsatisfactory analogue to the 'must' of morality.[21] The standard of beneficence seems to accord their proper roles to both universality and variable convention: the principle itself is perfectly universal and non-relativistic, though it would approve looking to context and convention in order to determine how well-being might be realized. Third, the standard of beneficence is not only welfare-consulting, like the principle of malevolence, but it makes contribution to well-being *count in favor* of an action or institution. The principle of beneficence, thus, possesses a number of the features we are after in morality: impartiality, non-hypotheticalness, universality, and positive attention to the well-being of others as well as the agent.

Somewhat more impressionistically, the standard of beneficence can be seen to embody some of the things that have been very widely held to be part of what morality is about—and part of what gives morality its standing in our eyes. In their developed forms, theological and secular moral theories alike have often made an ideal of the sort of universal, impartial, generalized beneficence the standard embodies. Of course, not all codes of conduct we might in a descriptive sense call 'moral' have included this ideal. We can see beneficence as a compound of two elements: impartiality and an intrinsic positive concern for well-being.

It seems to me that when we reflect on codes that fail to assign fundamental significance—which is not to say exclusive significance—to these two elements and instead allocate the fundamental evaluative roles to such notions as filial loyalty, saving face, piety, honor, or caste, or, for that matter, to one's own well-being without regard to the well-being of others, we also find them lacking some distinctive features of a moral character. For example, a code in which acting to save face, or to avenge dishonor, or to show piety, cannot be subject to criticism despite its disastrous effects on the well-being of those concerned—either because the code will not consult well-being at all or because it insists upon partiality—would not support the kind of discourse about the justification of conduct that has become paradigmatic in our moral thought, whether contractarian or utilitarian or based upon natural law. Such a code, that is, would let questions of justification come to a halt well before the point at which many of the diverse moral theorists of recent centuries have thought moral justification to begin. Perhaps our current ways of talking about justification—and allied senses of the need for justification—merely reflect something that has gone badly astray in our ethical thought. But to the extent that this criticism itself takes the form of drawing our attention to forms or preconditions of well-being that are being overlooked or misunderstood, or of challenging a conception of impartiality by showing it to be in effect exclusionary, then this sort of criticism *is* recognizably moral; yet by the same token it falls beyond the point in thinking about justification that these honor- or face- or caste-based codes reach. On the other hand, to the extent that the criticism of the current justificatory norms shows no interest in well-being, or in supporting any possible challenges to partiality, then such criticism, though perhaps perfectly in order, and maybe even correct, it is not best understood as arising from distinctively moral concerns. And it is these concerns of which we are here trying to find some understanding, the better to raise the question: What would it take for morality to be in order?

Now a number of philosophers have found attractive the idea that the chief concern to which we should see morality as a response is a concern on the part of agents that they be able to see their actions as rationally justifiable. Early in this paper I forswore talk of rational justification as tending, it seemed, to bundle together too many considerations to be helpful in initially sorting out the questions that lie behind concerns about the standing of morality. But there nonetheless is something to be said for asking whether a standard of impartial beneficence can plausibly be seen as a candidate for a responding to concerns about rational justification on the part of agents.

Consider agents asking themselves how they might defend their actions to those affected in terms that the latter might reasonably accept.[22] Although it may be difficult to identify an uncontroversial sense of 'reasonably' that is sufficiently independent of substantive moral notions to be able to locate in this concern of agents a *grounding* for morality, that is a foundational issue which need not occupy us here. What is relevant to present purposes is that this concern on the part of agents seems clearly to capture something central to the impulse to morality, and that impartial beneficence affords a plausible way—though certainly not the only way—of addressing this concern. It seems, for example, reasonable enough (in some recognizable sense) for someone to ask that if I am to give a moral defense of my actions I not ignore how my actions might affect his well-being. And it seems reasonable enough (in our vague sense) to ask of him that he in turn see the well-being of others potentially affected by my actions in the same light. It would, on this view, be reasonable of him to ask me not to use my interests as a basis for ignoring his, but also reasonable of others to ask me that I not use his interests as a basis for ignoring theirs. Similarly, it would be unreasonable (in this sense) of anyone to ask me to use his interests as a basis for ignoring my own. Seen in this light, a standard of impartial beneficence is in some measure responsive to this fundamental justificatory concern.[23]

Relatedly, it has been a persistent thought in both commonsense and philosophical moralizing that morality at least purports to be *objective*. There does not appear to be an agreed-upon sense of 'objective' at work here. For some, talk of the objectivity of morality is merely a somewhat grand way of expressing the idea that moral assessment is non-hypothetical and universal. But most of us seem to have something more in mind. The difficulty lies in saying what this might be.

It seems unlikely that morality could sensibly be thought to be objective in the sense that (say) judgments about the external world are commonsensically (though perhaps mistakenly) thought to be objective, that is, independent of all facts about how that state of affairs is or would be seen from any perspective. Moral evaluation seems too tightly bound to questions of judgment and motivation. Indeed, even theological notions of the objectivity of morality typically make use of a divine subject—to ask "What matters from the point of view of the universe?" is to invoke a metaphor of *mattering* and *seeing*, concepts that require a subjectivity for their locus. It is unclear what would be left of this question without the metaphor.

This essential involvement of notions of judgment and motivation need not, perhaps, preclude morality from having whatever objectivity a theory of the attribution of psychological states might have. In whatever sense, then, that a theory of psychology can be objective in virtue of its "independence from arbitrary subjectivity" or "responsiveness to facts that hold independent of our conception of them", moral features could similarly hold true. Perhaps something like Thomas Nagel's view of "objective value" comes close to the mark.[24] If anything is "objectively bad" in itself, the argument runs, pain is. Pain's badness is intrinsic in the sense that when I experience pain, its undesirability depends entirely upon what the experience is like, owing nothing to the thought that it is *my* experience, and with no dependency upon further assumptions about my particular interests or ends, beliefs or inclinations. In general, our aversion to pain is not conditioned or ideological.[25] Yet surely this aversion or undesirability is a subjective phenomenon. It is, then, subjective in a nonarbitrary way, a way that can be seen as objective in virtue of owing its character to the nature of the thing—pain—itself, and not our theory or ideology of it. Recognizing this is part of an objective, non-ideological, non-arbitrary attitude toward the world, including the world of subjectivities. (This is certainly not yet to say, as Nagel recognizes, that one necessarily has a reason to care equally about, or assign equal deliberative weight to, the pain of others.) The standard of beneficence can express just this sort of objectivity in relation to pain—the pain of each is given the same standing, precisely in accord with what it is like wherever, so to speak, it occurs. To the extent that this picture of the intrinsic undesirability of pain makes sense, and to the extent that morality can be seen as resting upon the standard of beneficence, morality could be understood as *non-perspectival* in a way that captures something of our intuitive notion of the objectivity of morality: its evaluative stance does not depend upon the viewpoint of any particular agent or ideology, even as it is sensitive to the most deeply felt experiences of particular agents. Any given agent can fail to take an interest in the pains of another, yet this lack of interest will have no tendency to make the pains of another go away.

Of course, suggesting how a standard might address a concern about rational or objective justifiability leaves untouched the question of the status of that concern itself: What if it is not rationally mandatory to have such a concern? That is, what if the ideal of justifying one's conduct to those it affects, or of seeing one's deliberation as embodying a kind of "objective agency", or simply of acting in a beneficent manner, were something agents might lack while nonetheless being rational?

The first thing to say is that this notion of "rational optionality" should not be confused with hypothetical or non-universal scope. As we have noted, a standard need not be categorically rational in order to be non-hypothetical and universal.

The second thing to say is that we are drawn to asking moral questions about actions and institutions in part because we are drawn by the idea of a standard that is (in some sense) more validating than our own, personal perspective—less arbitrary, less partial, more objective, more defensible to others in terms responsive to all the interests at stake. A scheme for answering the questions I wish to raise about my conduct that made all answers hinge entirely upon my own likes or interests could not have the critical, or self-critical, role of morality, and so could not, *even for me*, afford to my judgments the backing, or standing, of morality.

The third thing to say takes a bit more breath. The idea that morality furnishes categorical reasons—reasons for all practically rational beings as such—has been intended, in part, to provide morality a stronger basis than inclination, to say that one *must* as a rational being give moral standards a role in deliberation. But of course nothing could take away the option of ignoring moral standards. One cannot use a theory of rationality to put deliberation in a vise. The only real question in this vicinity is: "What does one let oneself in for by exercising this option?"

If there were categorical reasons behind morality, one would let oneself in for the criticism that one is irrational if one assigned moral standards no weight in deliberation. Now what is the sting of this charge? Advocates of the categorical imperative are careful to distinguish rationality in their sense from mere instrumental rationality, but for that very reason someone could be irrational in their sense while living a well-organized, happy, productive life, a life devoted not only to self-interest, but to various projects, principles, and persons. Obedience to categorical reasons might by contrast be difficult and disruptive. If there is a penalty to being irrational in the noninstrumental sense, it is not the penalty of having a bad time or being unable to do what one wants or being cut off from all community of care or humanity. Rather, it is the penalty of being unable without deception to see oneself and one's actions in a certain way, of being unable without deception to defend oneself and one's actions in light of a certain standard, or to claim a kind of objectivity or autonomy in one's deliberative practice or agency. This will be a felt penalty only for someone for whom this way of seeing oneself has some evaluative impact, i.e., someone already inclined to take such a standard to heart. Categoricalness does not claim motivational force for all *Homo sapiens*, but rather *for anyone who is a (fully) practically rational agent*. If categorical reasons have evaluative impact for those of us who are *not* already practically rational, that is a contingent fact, perhaps reflecting an ideal we have come to cherish.

Something remarkably similar can be said within a noncategorical framework, though without the impressive invocation of Reason. The penalty for acting contrary to the standard of beneficence is not the penalty of having a bad time, but of being unable without deception to see oneself and one's actions in a certain way, of being unable without deception to defend oneself and one's actions to others in light of a norm that accords them an equal standing while resting upon the reality of their weal and woe—a reality that does not take on whatever color I wish to see in it. This is a penalty only to the extent that this way of seeing and justifying ourselves has evaluative impact for us. To the extent that we are moral agents and beneficence is part of being moral, this normative force is non-contingently part of us; to the extent that we are not, it may be an important ideal for us, but need not be. If it is objected that it should not be up to the agent whether he is liable to moral criticism, then we need only repeat that the non-hypotheticalness and universality of moral assessment are sufficient to achieve this sort of "inescapability", and that nothing—certainly not categorical reasons—could secure the "psychological inescapability" that moral criticism *must* have evaluative impact.

Well-foundedness. Yet non-hypotheticalness and *de facto* evaluative impact are not enough. As we saw in our earlier discussion of standards in logic, aesthetics, and rationality, it matters whether the standards are well-founded. How might the standard of beneficence fail to be well-founded?

For a start, there might be no such thing as well-being in the sense it presupposes. Of course, its presuppositions about well-being, while ambitious, are not detailed—appropriate variants of the standard might be formulable in terms of qualitative notions of pleasure and pain, or in terms of some more substantive notion of happiness, or in terms of preference-satisfaction, or in terms of the satisfaction of informed preference. But perhaps when formulated in certain terms the standard itself loses much of its evaluative impact. The idea of alleviating severe pain seems starkly compelling, but what is equally compelling in the idea of providing minor pleasures?—Yet couldn't beneficence permit us to balance lots of minor pleasures against a few severe pains? (Can compellingness be additive in this way?) The idea of satisfying just any preference, whatever it might be, may not strike us as compelling—would it help to qualify the preference as informed, or as (in some sense) non-optional?[26] To preserve the impact of the standard one may need a normatively compelling notion of well-being, and it is often claimed that no such notion could be epistemically respectable. This would tend to undermine claims about objectivity, and cast well-foundedness into doubt.

For my own part, I find many claims about the ineffability and incomparability of well-being, or the "subjective" or "arbitrary" nature of assessments of others' well-being, overstated.[27] It seems to me that there are lots of accessible facts about whether people are in pain or torment, or finding their lives rewarding. Moreover in many cases it is obvious whether a particular pain or pleasure, as experienced by a given individual at a given time, is greater or less than another pain or pleasure, experienced by that individual at a different time, or experienced by a different individual. And it seems to me not peculiar, but a common feature of our individual and collective life, to allow a great number of small costs or gains to offset a few of the larger sort—how else are we to handle risk, for example? A fair amount of vagueness or uncertainty will attend absolute and comparative judgments of well-being, and to that extent answers to the question "What is truly beneficent?" will themselves be vague or uncertain (as only seems right). But it seems to me quite unconvincing to say that we simply have no idea whether, on a given occasion, the pain of McAllister's wasp sting is greater or less than the pain of McMurtry's mosquito bite. It seems to me equally unconvincing to say that we typically have no idea whether the distress of McNeil at the loss of his job is worse than both together.

Such simple facts about pains, pleasures, and comparisons thereof, do not make up the whole subject matter of a theory of well-being, but they do constitute an important part of it, and enough to get a good deal of morality off the ground if the standard of beneficence is allowed a significant role. If, that is, we allow that, other things equal, people are better off experiencing less rather than more pain, this may give sufficient normative heft to the use of 'well-being' in our standard of beneficence to permit the argument to go forward. For there is *something* compelling to us—and compelling in an identifiably moral way—about the idea of alleviating anyone's pain, or making anyone's life more rewarding, other things equal. If pains and pleasures are genuine states about which we can have evidence, as it seems to me they are, then to that extent we have a notion of well-being that is epistemically respectable as well. Insofar as the standard of beneficence captures part of what we find compelling in morality in general (a question I have largely deferred), a non-hypothetical moral standard with evaluative impact can be well-founded.

We might for the sake of a contrast compare this basis for morality with divine bases. With the death of God, we have been told, everything became permitted—there were no divine commands, there was no set role for humankind in a cosmic order. But whether or not rumors of God's death are exaggerations, whether or not an intelligence has arranged the universe, people's lives continue to go well or ill. The question of how our lives go does not vanish, and remains of the utmost importance to those of us living them. Indeed, one can readily devise speculative anthropological explanations in which these individual and collective engagements on behalf of well-being—one's own and that of others one cares about—are part of a quasi-functional account of the emergence of religion. Without God the universal policeman is gone, but we have already seen that even a universal policeman could not by himself afford normativity of a distinctively moral kind. Without God, too, the capacity of humans to regulate themselves in greater or lesser accord with generalized beneficence remains a part of the universe, as do the needs to which beneficence answers and the widespread ideal it reflects.

The relation of theism to ethics can also be viewed from another perspective. Rather than seeing ethics as resting on religion, one might attempt to see religion as resting to a significant degree on ethics. That is, one might attempt to explain the sorts of gods to whom we have given life by seeing their characteristic features as reflections of the central concerns that give impulse to morality and to questions about the justification of morality. If God is the answer, then what was the question?

Clearly one central concern has been enforcement—how to insure that acting as morality requires is not imprudent? Yet, as we earlier observed, justifying morality as prudent is not justifying it as morality—conformity to any code could be made prudent by a suitable enforcer. What, then, are the questions apart from enforcement, the questions that God's existence might answer in such a way as to account for the non-prudential standing of morality? This is too large a question to undertake seriously to answer here, but perhaps something along the following lines is not altogether implausible.

The idea of a behavioral imperative is not hard to grasp once there is someone who issues and enforces it. In order for ethics as law to be other than arbitrary, however, we must know something about this law-giver—can he or she command respect as well as fear? A god who creates and chooses and judges must to that extent be a subjectivity, but not all subjectivities are alike. A parent also creates and chooses and judges, and commonsense holds that parents deserve respect, but some parents are more knowledgeable, committed, compassionate, and effective than others, and commonsensically they—and their choices and judgments—command the greatest respect. A divine subjectivity could command perfect respect if it perfectly embodied these features—its subjectivity would in some sense be wholly without arbitrariness, as objective as a subjectivity could me. Hence we come to an idea of morality as objectified subjectivity.

It is a remarkable fact about us that we have created such gods and then gone to such lengths to submit ourselves to them. As soon, it seems, as humankind settled down to the agricultural life and created a surplus, we began to pay some of it to larger-than-life gods: burying our dead with perfectly serviceable pots, worshipping with sacrifice and ceremony, and, eventually, supporting temples and priests to guide us in the ways of the gods. Our ancestors and our priests tied us to a larger, ordered, normative scheme, and as religion developed the order and norms became explicitly cosmic. Why did we bother to give life and sustenance to the means for judging ourselves against so grand a scheme? Even those social theorists who would see religion most instrumentally, as nothing more than a means of sanctifying the social inequalities that a surplus made possible, must explain why the "device" of religion proved so effective and so common, why it found and continues to find such resonance. The demand for a well-founded, objective, and normatively ideal code of behavior no doubt requires anthropological, sociological, psychological, perhaps even biological, explanation. Such an explanation would, among other things, throw into light the range, significance, and circumstances of the human needs to which a moral code answers.

It is a contingent fact that evolution was as it was, or that social circumstances were as they were. Gods, as necessary and eternal beings, perhaps should not owe their nature to such contingencies; gods should exist in their own right, and not be the ideal projections of human needs and aspirations. But morality need not similarly exist "in its own right" in order to be well-founded or "inescapable": if our non-hypothetical standards of moral requirement or value are seen as consequent from an idealization of conditions necessary for the well-being of actual humans, this would hardly seem to be undermining. Such a view of things need not lessen or imperil morality's evaluative impact for us, any more than it threatens the well-foundedness or "inescapability" or evaluative impact of logic that we might have been, or might yet become, beings who have little intrinsic interest in truth, in a world without a suprahuman grader who would mark us down for our logical failings.[28]

The demand for well-founded, non-hypothetical norms of behavior predates the onset of philosophical ethics and can survive the philosophical critique of religion. A modernist who views the gods of the past as a mystification of this justificatory impulse need not to see the impulse itself as a mystification—she can dispense with any middlemen between justificatory impulse and norms of behavior, and see that the core of the justificatory *basis* remains as it always was—the ill- or well-being of ourselves and our fellows, the manner in which the human condition depends upon our individual and collective behaviors, and our capacity to regulate our behavior in accord with general principles sensitive to effects on the human condition. Thus morality may be able to survive a certain kind of *Ideologiekritik*: we may be able to understand its origin and the interests it serves without losing our commitment to it.

V

The idea that morality is based upon a categorical imperative can be understood as part of a project for securing the "inescapability" of moral assessment, and to that extent securing the standing ordinarily attributed to morality. We have been considering an alternative way of going at least that far toward the justification of morality, a way that sees morality as essentially involving non-hypothetical standards which purport to be well-founded in concerns that would explain—and, on critical reflection, not undermine—morality's wide evaluative impact. Moral evaluation would be *formally* escapable were its scope hypothetical; it would be *substantively* escapable were its standards ill-founded (criticism based upon a mistake can be avoided by pointing out the mistake); and it would be *social- psychologically* escapable were it without widespread evaluative impact (there would be no "felt need" to be able to see oneself as morally justified, and no "social sanction"). It is important to distinguish the present approach from another, which bases morality upon hypothetical imperatives.[29]

First, not all moral standards need be imperatives. Indeed, the standard of beneficence we have been considering is not a standard of what one morally must do, but of what is morally better or worse.

Second, moral standards as understood here are non-hypothetical—their scope is not limited by a motivational condition. What is, in some sense, hypothetical is the extent of the influence of moral standards on our deliberation, that is, their evaluative impact. But whether moral standards apply to a given agent, and whether they are well-founded, do not depend upon the degree of interest the agent takes in them. In this respect, they are like the non-hypothetical standards of logic and aesthetics. Indeed, like these standards, morality owes part of its evaluative impact on us to this independence from the perspective and motivations of the particular agent.

For the sake of a contrast, let us briefly discuss a view that explicitly draws the implications of tying the evaluative scope as well as the evaluative impact of morality to the perspectives or purposes of particular agents.

In *The Nature of Morality*,[30] Gilbert Harman has in effect argued that if we combine three plausible doctrines about morality and motivation, the result will be moral relativism: (1) an internalist conception of moral obligation (according to which it is anomalous to apply an 'ought' judgment to an agent who lacks a reason to conform to it[31]); (2) an internalist conception of reasons for action (according to which an agent has a reason for acting only when she has a corresponding motive[32]); and (3) an empirical hypothesis that human motivation is contingent and variable, with no necessary, universal motives. Harman seeks to respect (1)-(3) by developing an account of morality according to which what a person ought to do depends upon the moral norms she accepts (and which therefore motivate her). Thus, perhaps, we cannot say "It was *wrong of Hitler* to have ordered the extermination of the Jews" or "Hitler *ought not* to have done it", because these latter expressions presuppose that Hitler had some motive not to pursue his Final Solution; but, given the extreme depravity of his character, he did not.[33] Of course, Harman's point is not that the actual Hitler had *no* motive not to carry out his design, for it might have advanced his project of the Thousand-Year Reich in various ways had he not ordered the extermination of the Jews. The point rather is that we can imagine a Hitler (or a Martian backed by legions of android troops) who in fact has no motive of any importance—even prudential—not to give such an order. Isn't it odd, Harman claims, to say of such a person that "He morally ought not to do X, even though he has no reason not to"? This oddness might be thought to arise merely from the enormity of Hitlerian schemes—'Hitler, you morally ought not to do it' is pale language for genocide. To Harman's ear, this sounds a bit too much like 'How naughty of you!'. But Harman believes this cannot be the whole explanation, for it would not be *as* odd to say, in a passive construction, "This morally ought not to be done". The locus of the additional oddness appears to be bringing the 'ought' to bear on the agent in an "internal" way, for how can we say "He morally ought not to do it" in the same breath as "but he has no reason not to"?[34]

But does the objectivity of morality require "internal" 'ought'-judgments of this kind? Or, put another way, if there exist species of moral assessment that do not presuppose such an "internal" bearing, then if they are non-hypothetical, universal, objective, and possess evaluative impact, then facts about variability in human motivation will not have the capacity to show them to be ill-founded.

Consider for the sake of an analogy a political leader whose demonic plans require that he not notice or correct a logical fallacy in his reasoning. We would not hesitate to brand him illogical in his reasoning, or to say that his inference is one that, logically, ought not to be made. Perhaps, however, we *would* find it strained to say "He ought not to make this inference" in the same breath as "but he has no reason not to". From this can we draw relativist conclusions about logic, or infer that the objectivity of logical standards of reasoning is compromised? Not if logic is well-founded. For if it is, then we can say "However this person views the matter and whatever his personal goals, still, he is running afoul of a necessary truth and his reasoning is logically defective."

When someone says "You ought not to do that", it sounds like a piece of advice, and a natural response is "Give me one good reason". If reasons are contingent and relative rather than categorical, then some possible persons will be able to carry off this reply with impunity. But such persons do not thereby escape logical or moral evaluation. After all, the basis of logical evaluation is not to be found in reasons but in reasoning, and bad reasoning is not made good by having compelling reasons for engaging in it. Similarly, the basis of morality is not to be found in the agent's reasons alone, but in the reasons or well-being of others he might affect, and bad actions are not made good when the agent has compelling reasons of his own for engaging in them. These are cases in which we want to say that the normative standing of logical and moral standards resides partly in their externality, in our incapacity to alter the standards' assessments by having devious plans, projects, or character. Once again, the externality is not that of a commanding deity, but rather that of truth, in the first case, or of the well-being of others, in the second. And neither truth nor the well-being of others depend for their reality upon my impressions or commitments.

Recall that our standard of moral assessment was put in terms of what is morally better rather than morally imperative. One advantage I hoped this would have would be to direct our minds to nonimperative ways of thinking of evaluative impact. But another advantage may be that it makes more evident what the objectivity of moral judgment might, at a minimum, come to. Enormity aside, I don't suppose anyone is tempted to say that there is anything odd about the phrase "It would have been morally better had Hitler not ordered the extermination of the Jews". Is this too much a judgment of Hitler's actions and not enough a judgment of Hitler? Then how about "Hitler was morally as bad as they come"? Is even this judgment too "external" to have the right normative character for moral evaluation—mustn't all moral evaluation look to *Hitler's* motives or reasons? No, not if this means giving his motives or reasons the power to regulate the scope of all moral evaluation, for no restriction capable of defining the full normative scope of *morality* could ever give motives or reasons such as Hitler's *that* power. The justification of morality is at the mercy of failures of well-foundedness, objectivity, and evaluative impact, but with these intact, it need fear nothing from Hitler.[35]

Notes

1. I am grateful to David Copp, William K. Frankena, and Alan Goldman for helpful discussion of some of the material contained in this paper.
2. Some philosophers deem it self-evident that moral 'ought's override all others, although this opinion seems less common than it once was. Even were it granted, questions of justification would not be forestalled; they simply would take the

form of questions about the existence of any such 'ought' as the moral 'ought'.
3. When in actual life questions about the status of moral considerations do arise, they often present themselves as involving more than one such 'ought', and it may be difficult or impossible to separate and identify the much-entangled considerations of (say) prudence, professionalism, law, friendship, and family. One may be as puzzled about whether or in what measure to take such considerations into account as one is about how morality stands with respect to them. So cleanly posed questions about the justification of morality may be hard to find in actual life.

Moreover, the questions that do arise may not always be best put in terms of an 'ought' at all. It will emerge in what follows that sometimes there is something to be gained by putting questions of justification not in terms of an imperative notion such as "ought", but rather in terms of such evaluative notions as "better".
4. It should not be overlooked that some religious conceptions do seem to allow that God's moral authority stems entirely from his power. Hobbes, in at least some passages, gives this impression. It is notable in this connection how little comfort the schoolmen seemed to find in Hobbes' philosophy.
5. A similar view is often expressed as a matter of the *function* of judgments of wrongness, rather than their *meaning* properly so called. (The tenability of this distinction might be denied, of course.) It will streamline our discussion to consider the position mentioned in the text.
6. I will for the most part drop the qualification '(rational)' hereinafter, partly out of deference to the view that "genuine agency" is, necessarily, rational. I will not attempt here a more precise characterization of "categorical practical reason" than "reason for all agents as such"—independent, that is, of any contingent feature of agents.
7. Actually, as we will see below, matters here can become more complicated than this conclusion suggests.
8. The argument is designed to create a tension between what might be categorical from the standpoint of practical reason, and what might be respectable from the standpoint of theoretical reason. But I admit to having only a dim understanding of how practical and theoretical reason are supposed to be related when, as in the case of actions that influence beliefs, they seem to apply to the same turf.
9. The obvious inspiration is Kant's *Religion Within the Limits of Reason Alone*, II.1.C.
10. I have tried to set up the argument so that we could not use our own practical rationality, as we experience it, as evidence for the belief.
11. For a discussion of difficulties one might have in finding the distinctive normative standing of morality even within a scheme of categorical reasons that is epistemically respectable, see P. Railton, "What the Non-Cognitivist Helps Us To See, the Naturalist Must Help Us To Explain", forthcoming in C. Wright and R. Haldane (eds.), *Realism and Reason* (Oxford: Oxford University Press, forthcoming).
12. One might, of course, claim not to care as a way of expressing aesthetic skepticism; and skepticism, if sustainable, *would* rebut the charge of "bad judgment". The point here is that there is simply no incoherence, or even oddness, in applying standards of taste to individuals who are so devoid of aesthetic sensitivity as not even to care.
13. One might explain validity in terms of consistency—an inference is valid if the falsity of the conclusion is inconsistent with the truth of its premises. So-called logical truths fall into place as valid "zero premise" arguments, or, alternatively, as statements whose negation is inconsistent. Of course, logicians are interested in various features of arguments beside validity, e.g., derivability.
14. Suppose that belief has as its essential object truth (that to believe that p is, necessarily, to believe p true). It still does not follow that removal of a given

inconsistency will effect net gain in truth for the believer.

15. This is not meant to be a deep fact about the constitution of aesthetic value or of the logical *must*; nor is it meant to be a powerful sociological hypothesis about the "purity" of the actual behavior of logicians or aestheticians. Rather, it is a surface fact about the dependencies "officially" recognized by existing evaluative practices—e.g., Does the practice of logical assessment license appeal to considerations of practical reason in the determination of logical status? As such, it is a part of the physiognomy of logical and aesthetic assessment, which must somehow be explained—or perhaps explained away—by any account of aesthetic value or the logical *must*.

16. Imagine a set of norms of belief or dispositions to believe which, thanks to favorable circumstances, have certain beneficial consequences in finite cases and lead to contradiction only in some practically unattained or unattainable infinite limit.

17. Mustn't agents at least *represent their inferential norms to themselves* as truth-preserving, given that believing must represent itself as believing-true? Even granting this, we have only a thesis about how agents must represent their inferential norms to themselves, not about the correctness of that representation.

18. Is such a claim even coherent? Demonstrating it not to be might be disallowed as presupposing logic. In any event, it strikes me that the evaluative impact of logic depends not so much on our confidence about the *incoherence* of such a claim as our confidence of its *falsity*.

19. To this it might be objected that some theories that have at least been called moral theories, such as moral egoism (understood *not* as the doctrine that things will be better overall if each pursues his own interest, but as an essentially token-reflexive doctrine), do not accept this standard even as one component of moral assessment. What I will say about the normativity of morality would not extend to such theories. This does not much trouble me, however, since it seems to me that such theories lack the distinctive normative character of more familiar moral theories.

20. See esp. P. Foot, "Morality as a System of Hypothetical Imperatives", reprinted in her collection *Virtues and Vices* (Berkeley: University of California Press, 1978).

21. Of course, it might be a part of (putatively universal) morality that one should show respect for others *in whatever form this is conventionally expressed in the local culture*, assuming that this form is not itself in violation of some other moral norms. But this is a moral norm, not a norm of etiquette proper. (Someone who thinks such a norm *is* part of etiquette has reason to think that the analogy between morality and etiquette is better for that.)

22. For discussion of such an idea, see T.M. Scanlon, "Contractualism and Utilitarianism", in A. Sen and B. Williams (eds.), *Utilitarianism and Beyond* (Cambridge: Cambridge University Press, 1982). Questions of this kind can be put by an individual concerned that his actions be defensible to others, or by a collectivity concerned that its terms of co-operation (and perhaps its "external relations") be defensible to all affected. On this latter point, see also J. Rawls, *A Theory of Justice* (Cambridge: Cambridge University Press, 1971), esp. sec. 3.

23. For a much more specific argument on a related theme, consider the hypothetical contractarian defense of utilitarianism in John C. Harsanyi, *Essays in Ethics, Social Behavior, and Scientific Explanation* (Dordrecht: D. Reidel, 1976). Of course, the rough argument in the text only shows one way in which it might be reasonable to defend one's actions to others; whether such a defense would be necessary or sufficient to answer fully questions about reasonableness is a much more difficult matter.

24. See his *View From Nowhere* (New York: Oxford, 1985), esp. pp. 156-162. (I do not claim here or elsewhere to be successful in capturing Nagel's sense, though I hope there is at least an affinity between the view discussed below and his.) It is striking that Nagel, whose work has elsewhere borne such a Kantian stamp, seeks in this work to explain the objectivity of morality via a value-theoretic concept. Such an approach seems especially congenial to a conception of morality that emphasizes beneficence as a kind of "objective agency" or "objectified subjectivity" (see below).

25. Of course, one might for instrumental purposes want to act in a painful way, all things considered. Here we speak only of intrinsic value.

26. Nagel objects that a preference-based account is simply incapable of capturing the objective character of the badness of pain that figured in the discussion of the objectivity of morality, above. Yet his explanation of the objective badness of pain seems to be that we have a particular sort of dislike of it, a dislike that is intense, immediate, and unrevisable:

> Without some positive reason to think there is nothing in itself good or bad about having an experience you intensely like or dislike, we can't seriously regard the common impression to the contrary as a collective illusion. Such things are at least good or bad *for us*, if anything is. ...The fact that physical pleasures and pains are experiences, and that our desires and aversions for them are immediate and unreflective, puts them in a special category. [*The View from Nowhere*, pp. 157-158.]

Perhaps what is at fault is not the idea of preference-satisfaction as an explanation of well-being, but rather the idea that optional, mediated preferences must be taken as fixed by a preference-satisfaction theory.

27. For an effort to suggest how a notion of well-being might simultaneously be (in some measure, at least) normatively compelling and epistemically respectable, see P. Railton, "Facts and Values", *Philosophical Topics* 14 (1986): 5-31.

28. For brief discussion of the intriguing idea that a commitment to truth is constitutive of belief, and thus necessary in the manner of a Kantian synthetic *a priori*, see Railton, "What the Non-Cognitivist Helps Us To See, the Naturalist Must Help Us To Explain".

29. See, for example, Foot, "Morality as a System of Hypothetical Imperatives". Foot writes in the preface to *Virtues and Vices* (pp. xii-xiv) that she no longer thinks the Kantian terminology of hypothetical imperatives best expresses her position.

30. (New York: Oxford University Press, 1977), see esp. section III.

31. This is a form of "existence internalism", in the sense distinguished by Stephen Darwall, *Impartial Reason* (Ithaca: Cornell University Press, 1983), pp. 54f. An alternative to (1) is a form of "judgment internalism" (again, see Darwall) according to which motivation is essentially linked not to being under a moral obligation, but to making a moral judgment. This alternative form of internalism has been an important source of support for non-cognitivism in this century. Harman's doctrine, by contrast, is cognitivist.

32. This again is a form of "existence internalism" (see previous note). In terms of Frankena's taxonomy, (1) and (2) yield an internalism about "exciting reasons" in ethics. See William K. Frankena, "Obligation and Motivation in Recent Ethics", reprinted in K.E. Goodpaster (ed.), *Perspectives on Morality: Essays of William K. Frankena* (Notre Dame: University of Notre Dame Press, 1976).

33. See *The Nature of Morality*, pp. 106-109. In the view as developed in this book, Harman distinguishes judgments of moral obligation (e.g., 'ought'-judgments) from

judgments of moral value (e.g., judgments of 'good' and 'evil'). Judgments of the latter sort are "external" in a way that judgments of the former sort are not. As a result, Harman observes that it may be possible to brand Hitler 'evil'.

34. Cf. Harman, *The Nature of Morality*, p. 107.

35. The boundaries of moral obligation might be something else. For an attempt to say something about the boundaries of obligation that would explain the appeal of internalism without conceding it the status of a conceptual truth, see Railton, "What the Non-Cognitivist Helps Us To See, the Naturalist Must Help Us To Explain".

Philosophical Perspectives, 6, Ethics, 1992

NORMATIVE EXPLANATIONS

Geoffrey Sayre-Mccord
UNC, Chapel Hill

Introduction

there is a great wind of moral force moving through the world and every man who opposes that wind will go down in disgrace

So wrote a widely respected historian, political scientist, and United States President—Thomas Woodrow Wilson.[1] Nowadays, Wilson's confidence in morality, his conviction that justice will out, that the righteous will rule, that morality can and does have an impact on what happens in the world, seems anachronistic, outrageously optimistic, and metaphysically peculiar. That it is anachronistic and outrageously optimistic, I don't deny. But I do hope to show that it is not nearly as metaphysically peculiar as many think. In particular, I hope to *make sense of the idea* that morality operates, if not as an over-powering wind, then at least as a gentle breeze in the course of history.

Less metaphorically, I want to explore the view that morality, and specifically moral rules, might help to explain social change.[2] I should emphasize, though, that my aim is to make sense of the idea, not to show that in fact morality actually does explain social change; I am after a plausibility argument, not an existence proof. Providing the first is hard enough.

Before moving directly to *moral* rules, and their potential role in explanations of social change, I will concentrate first on the more general issue of how rules (whether moral, legal, or social) figure in explanations. In what follows, I will be moving back and forth frequently between moral rules and other (metaphysically less presupposing) rules. Throughout, though, I shall be concentrating on normative rules—rules that forbid courses of action, impose obligations, or grant permissions—not on descriptive rules that serve simply to express empirical regularities. The contrast, I think, is intuitively clear, even if it doesn't lend itself to a rigorous definition: it is one thing to say that, in the U.S., there's a rule (in this case a law) forbidding speeds in excess of 65 mph; it is quite another to say that, as a rule, people in the United

State don't drive over 65 mph. Likewise, it is one thing to say that one ought to make rational choices; it is another to say that people do, as a rule, make such choices. And again, it is one thing to say that in baseball one is permitted by the rules of the game to steal second base; it is another to say that, as a rule, people do steal second base.[3] Mere regularities do not constitute normative rules, even though recognized and enforced normative rules may be expected to give rise to regularities. Whether normative rules that are unrecognized, or unenforced, or both, also give rise to regularities is less clear. That they do, or at least might, is something I argue for later in the paper.[4]

Normative rules are, it seems, ubiquitous; they apparently structure our interactions, inform our plans, define our options, and play a central role in our understanding of our own activities.[5] Yet the importance of normative rules, when it comes to explanation, as opposed to exhortation, remains dubious, at best.

Of course normative rules might explain why some action, for instance, counts as illegal, some utterance as ungrammatical, some proposal as rational, some institution as moral. Left lingering by this observation (right as it might be) is the suspicion that the facts explained by the relevant rules are just reflections of the rules. To say an act is illegal is, one worries, simply to say it violates a law; to say an utterance is ungrammatical is simply to say it violates a rule of grammar, and so on. Much more satisfying would be the discovery that the normative rules and corresponding normative facts they 'explain' themselves explain—*really* explain—some event, process, or situation, that is conceptually independent of the rules in question.[6] The nagging suspicion is that normative rules explain no such thing.

The doubts about the explanatory importance of normative rules come from many directions. Perhaps the most influential has its source in the conviction that there is a fundamental difference between fact and value, a conviction bolstered by the observation that what ought to be isn't always so, and that when it is so, it apparently isn't so *because* it ought to be. The inclination is to argue that only facts *as distinct from values* explain things that happen in the world. Notoriously, though, the distinction between facts and values is extremely difficult to articulate. Moreover, even those convinced of its existence are usually willing to count many normative social rules (such as those governing language, constituting legal systems, and defining games), even if not moral rules, as firmly on the side of facts.

Two Ways to Figure in Explanations of Social Change

If normative rules do figure in explanations it will be in either of two roles: as part of what is *being explained* or as part of what *does the explaining*. In the first case, when it comes to explaining rules, we would be interested in explaining the origin and stability of the rules in question and in explaining the various changes they might undergo. In the second case, when it comes to explaining by appeal to rules, we would be interested in using rules to help explain other rules, to explain particular actions, or to explain general trends and patterns. Either role, that of explainer or that of explained, will give normative rules a place in explanations.

Still, the two roles are not of equal significance. Normative rules only become interesting objects of explanation to the extent they are also themselves explainers—to the extent the rules being what they are makes some difference to what happens in the world. If rules never make such a difference, and so never help to explain what happens, we would have much less reason to bother explaining them. In fact, it is hard to imagine what grounds one might have for believing the rules exist if they have no impact.[7] Explained non-explainers seem just epiphenomena by another name with all the attendant problems. Nonetheless, before turning to how normative rules might explain, I would like first to mention briefly a couple of the ways they might be explained. I do this in part because some of our best explanations of rules themselves appeal to normative rules.

Normative rules fall fairly neatly into two groups. The majority owe their existence and their force to various social practices and conventions; the rules of chess, the requirements of etiquette, the standards of grammar, and the laws of the land (to take a few examples) all come into being, and lay a claim on us, only because of things people do or have done. Such rules wouldn't be, and wouldn't matter, save for the particular local practices of people. These rules are reasonably thought of as conventional. Other rules apparently transcend convention; the demands of morality, the rules of logic, and the standards of practical rationality, all appear not to depend (at least in any straight-forward way) on what people do or have done. The former are unmistakably human products, while the latter hover above, and seemingly free from the influence of, human practices and conventions. Whether this distinction between conventional and trans-conventional rules marks a real difference in kind, or just a difference in the degree to which the rules depend on more or less local practices and conventions, is both unclear and controversial. One might, and people do, argue that the apparently trans-conventional rules of morality, logic, and rationality, are, despite appearances, conventional rules that find their origin and force in very widely shared, and perhaps socially necessary, practices or conventions.[8]

Regardless, to the extent the normative rules in question are dependent for their existence and force on what people do or choose, or on practices and conventions, they lend themselves to psychological and social explanation. Among the most elegant of such explanations are those that, by making use of decision and game theory, explain the rules as products of rational behavior.

Some rules, for instance laws handed down from 'on-high' by a dictator, are plausibly explained as rational solutions to problems of parametric choice (that is, as rational solutions to problems where the agent chooses unilaterally from among what is viewed as a fixed set of options). Thus we might explain a Dictator's imposition of a curfew as his least-cost solution to the problem of containing insurgency; given his preferences, situation, and nearly unchecked power, passing laws that constrain the liberty of others might be (in some sense) the rational thing for him to do. On a less grand scale, the rules parents establish for their children are often designed as unilaterally imposed rational solutions to problems that would otherwise arise.

Other rules we might explain on the grounds that they are rational solutions, not to problems of parametric choice, but to problems of strategic choice (that is, as rational solutions to problems where the agents choose interactively among options that depend in part on the choices of others).[9] Plainly, social rules do frequently solve problems of strategic choice; they solve problems of coordination and problems of competition (usually with the help of enforcement mechanisms), and most often problems that mix elements of competition with the need for coordination. Moreover, that they solve such problems is plausibly taken to be the reason they exist. Traffic laws, to use a popular example, seem largely to have come about in order to coordinate behavior in a context where it doesn't much matter to people what exactly the laws are, just so long as there are some. Criminal laws serve primarily, although not exclusively, as a way of resolving predictable conflicts among the interests of people within a society. And anti-pollution laws have been introduced explicitly to militate against the tragedy of the commons, which is due to people exploiting unmercifully what is held in common and protected by no one.

Recognized, respected, and enforced social rules time and again shift expectations, circumstances, and motivations, so as to ensure that people won't act in ways that make all (or at least most) worse off. Without them social life would be impossible. Game theoretic explanations recommend themselves as well, though, for social rules of a less salutary cast. In South Africa, for instance, the laws of Apartheid were quite clearly the instruments of class interest, explainable in part as an immoral solution to a problem of collective choice faced by those in power.[10] In the same vein, a much more benign example can be found in casino gambling rules, which are calculated to give the 'house' a distinct advantage.

Still other rules may not themselves be consciously introduced solutions to choice problems, but instead by-products of social practices and conditions. Rules of etiquette, for instance, appear often to impose capricious constraints that are not themselves rational solutions to choice problems at all, despite their being predictable consequences of social conditions. Even in these cases, invisible foot explanations (that account for the rules as the unintended and detrimental consequences of rational behavior) and invisible hand explanations (that account for the rules as the unintended but beneficial consequences of rational behavior)[11] will sometimes be available. If they are available, such explanations will make use of decision and game theory to explain the behavior, practices, and social conditions, that produce the social rules as by-products.

Importantly, the fact that some rule would be a rational solution to a problem that would exist if there weren't such a rule, can't explain the rule's existence unless the relevant people acted *because* the rule offered a rational solution. Of course, the people needn't have acted because they *recognize* the rule offers such a solution; they may embrace and enforce a rule because the rule offers such a solution without knowing that is why they act as they do. Yet explanations that rely on decision and game theory will go through as *explanations*, and not simply as justifications or just-so stories, only if the people involved are suitably rational—only if their behavior is sensitive to what is rational under the circumstances. That people do live up to the demands of rationality, and act because of them, is a crucial presupposition of decision and game theoretic explanations.

Just exactly what the demands of rationality are, needless to say, is a matter of extensive debate even among those who take advantage of the formal apparatus of decision and game theory, along with the essentially maximizing conception of rationality that underlies it. Neoclassical economists, for instance, embrace an unabashedly narrow, even cynical, view that ties rationality to self-interest; while others hold that the preferences of rational agents may range over the welfare of others. And some hold that rationality is simply a matter of maximizing expected satisfaction of (brute) subjective preferences; others impose restrictions (usually having to do with reflection or information) on the subjective preferences that are to count; while still others replace subjective preferences in the account with objective interests.[12] Despite these differences, the common framework offered by decision and game theory provides a strikingly powerful explanatory tool.

Such explanations are often among the best we have of why many familiar rules and sets of rules have been imposed or adopted. Indeed, a powerful, though not always successful, strategy for figuring out why certain social rules have come into existence lies in discovering whose interests are served by the rules; where interests are served we are likely to find agents active. Clearly this works only as a heuristic strategy. It would be a mistake to claim that the mere fact that interests are served can itself explain the existence of rules; there must be some reason to think either that the people were aware of the benefits to come or that some feedback loop would have adjusted the rules had the interests not been served.[13] When the strategy fails, when the rules in question are not plausibly explained as rational solutions to choice problems, it will either be because the rules simply are not rational solutions or, if they are, be because their being rational solutions doesn't (under the circumstances) explain their coming into existence—say when the people don't recognize their interests, or when they haven't for some other reason lived up to the standards of rationality.

What is interesting, here, about decision and game theoretic explanations of conventional rules (whether of the rules directly or of the social practices that generate the rules as by-products) is not that they exhaust the sort of explanations we have for social rules—they certainly don't—but that they evidently explain social rules by appeal to the rationality of agents and thus to normative rules of rationality. Of course, the explanations will count as *normative* explanations only among those who accept the underlying theory of rationality as at least in the running as a normative theory of rationality. But this is a very large group. So let's turn from explaining rules to using rules to explain.

Explaining by Conventional Rules

To the extent we try to use normative rules to explain suitably independent events, processes, or situations, there are three ways the rules might enter into an explanation. In setting these ways out, I will concentrate first on conventional normative rules, only afterwards turning to the more problematic case of trans-conventional rules.

Most obviously, and least controversially, normative rules can figure in explanations as the *content* of agents' beliefs. People quite clearly often do things (say, drive under 65 mph or avoid splitting infinitives) because they believe doing so is required by certain rules (e.g. of law or grammar). Less often, perhaps, but no less clearly, people do things—out of perversity, indignation, or independence—because they believe doing so violates certain rules.[14]

It is tempting to stop here, saying that all the explanatory work done supposedly by rules is really done by appeal to beliefs, not rules. The beliefs do, of course, have rules as their content, but that hardly gives the rules themselves a robust role in explanations. After all, some people do things because they believe in Santa Claus, but we can explain their actions without sharing their conviction. Santa Claus himself, as opposed to beliefs about Santa Claus, figures nowhere in our explanations of things that happen in the world. In the same way, people may do things because they believe there are normative rules, but we might still be able to explain their actions without sharing their conviction. Normative rules themselves, as opposed to beliefs about such rules, might figure nowhere in our explanations of things that happen in the world. No doubter of the explanatory importance of rules need feel any discomfort allowing rules this role.

Nevertheless, the temptation to view the explanatory role of normative rules so narrowly should dissipate once attention is turned to explaining those beliefs that have rules as their content. For in many cases at least part of the explanation of why people believe the rules require them to act in certain ways is that the rules do. Part of the explanation will involve there actually being the rules about which the people in question have beliefs. Often enough, if the rules were different, people's beliefs, and their behavior, would have been different as well. For example, for several years, and until recently, the national speed limit in the United States was 55 mph. When the limit changed to 65 mph peoples' beliefs about the limit changed too, as did their driving habits. Were the limit to change again it is reasonable to think peoples' beliefs and behavior would change once more. In short, peoples' beliefs about the speed limit are explained (at least in part) by the speed limit itself, by the normative rule that forbids speeds in excess of 65 mph. Obviously, peoples' beliefs are not always sensitive to what the rules actually are; sometimes people believe rules require something of them when the rules don't. In these cases something other than the rule will have to explain their belief. Even so, rules will often explain the beliefs people have about rules and so they will explain indirectly the behavior caused by those beliefs. When they do, normative rules will figure in explanations not just as the content of beliefs but also as causes of belief and behavior. Presumably, when it comes to explaining our own beliefs about rules we are committed to thinking the rules being what we take them to be is part of why we hold the beliefs we do.

Normative rules can figure as well, though, in explanations where their effects on a person's behavior are unmediated by her beliefs about the rules. Sticking with the example of traffic laws, we might explain why a particular person is driving within the speed limit by noting that she is disposed to drive at roughly the same speed as those around her, and that those around her have slowed to 55 mph because they noticed what she did not—a new speed limit sign. Ignorant though she is of the new speed limit on that stretch of road, the fact that it is the limit helps to explain her behavior because it helps to explain the behavior of those around her (whose behavior in turn explains hers).

Switching from rule-following to rule-breaking behavior, it's clear as well that rules that are unrecognized, yet violated, by a person can contribute to an explanation of what happens (just as rules that are unrecognized but followed can contribute to explanations). We might, for example, explain someone being pulled to the side of the road by the police by appeal to the fact that he broke the speed limit and this explanation might go through even though the driver is ignorant of the law. His pulling to the side of the road will be explained partly by his having broken a rule about which he has no belief.

This particular explanation may initially seem plausible only to the extent we appeal to someone else's belief, for instance a police officer's belief that the speed limit was broken. But there are two points to keep in mind. First, the fact that the driver broke a normative rule—and the fact's explanatory relevance—is completely independent of the *driver's* recognizing that he was breaking the law. Second, the fact that the driver broke the speed limit might figure in the explanation *even if neither the officer nor the driver believe the speed limit was broken.*

Consider this case: imagine the officer has been ticketing people all day for speeding and has as a result become especially sensitive to those going faster than the limit allows. It is not that she thinks of them as speeders (she usually doesn't, unless and until she clocks them on the radar); it is just that she is disposed to notice them.[15] Suppose that, her awareness of speeders heightened, she notices our wayward driver and the fact that his car fits the description of a car recently stolen. Suppose too that because the officer thinks the car suspect, she takes chase without even thinking about whether the driver was speeding. In this case, the officer will have pulled the driver over because she believed he was driving a stolen car and not because she believed he was speeding (she didn't). Nonetheless, part of the explanation for why the driver was pulled over will be that he was speeding—had he not been, the officer wouldn't have taken notice of the car.

So rules might play any of the following three roles in explanations: (i) they might be the content of beliefs that in turn explain actions, (ii) they might themselves explain the beliefs (about rules) that explain actions, and (iii) they might explain actions, events, processes, or situations unmediated by beliefs about those rules. Unlike the first role, which leaves actual rules completely out of the explanatory picture, both the second and third roles have the rules themselves doing real explanatory work. The rules, and not merely peoples' beliefs about the rules, are accounting for events in the world.

It might seem as if the three roles are presented in successive order, from that allowing rules the least explanatory involvement to that allowing them the most. But there is no appreciable difference, in that respect, between the second and third roles. Once it is granted that rules can explain behavior when mediated by beliefs about rules, on the grounds that they explain the beliefs, it is no extra step at all to say they can explain things without the mediation of belief. *For the role a given rule will play in explaining a person's beliefs about that rule will of necessity be one itself unmediated by that person's belief about that rule.* While you can explain my belief concerning some law by appeal to that law, you can't explain my belief by appeal to the belief being explained. Still, it is important to recognize that rules (unmediated by belief) can explain things other than beliefs about those rules, not least of all because in this capacity rules frequently have their subtlest effects.

Although related, the second and third roles do differ—most significantly in that only when people have beliefs about what a rule requires can they *intentionally* obey or violate the rule. One can, of course, conform to or violate a rule without realizing it; but one can intentionally respect or flaunt a rule only if one is aware of the rule. Unrecognized rules, although they may sometimes help to explain what happens to people and what people do, cannot explain people consciously breaking these rules.

This difference suggests a stronger claim: explanations that give a rule the third role can account only for behavior that conforms to the rule, not behavior that violates it; while explanations that give rules the second role (that is, that invoke rules whose effects are mediated by beliefs about those rules) can explain behavior that violates the rule in question as well as behavior that conforms to the rule. One can of course break the speed limit, say, without having any beliefs about the speed limit, but it may look as if the fact that there is a rule setting the limit won't be relevant to explaining one's violation (even if it is relevant to the explanation of what happens once the rule has been broken). A rule that is neither recognized nor followed by a person may seem beside the point when it comes to explaining her breaking the rule.

But this stronger claim is simply too strong. It is easy to imagine cases where an unrecognized rule might explain its own violation, as when, for instance, a person wishing to stand-out from a crowd takes the necessary steps, only to discover (to her regret) that the crowd was simply obeying a strictly enforced rule. Here, the rule explains the crowd's behavior, and the crowd's behavior (along with the person's desire to stand-out) helps to explain her violation of the rule as well as her consequent woes.[16]

To press the point further, even a rule that is unrecognized by everyone (who fall under it) and followed by no one, might explain events in the world if, consistently, those who followed the rule (if ever there were any) would be, for instance, better off than those who violate it.[17] In such cases, at least part of the explanation of why the people are not better off is that they violate the rule.

More generally, but along the same lines, a rule will be part of a legitimate explanation if the actions the rule enjoins, or forbids, constitute causally significant categories; and it will be an especially informative explanation if the set of relevant actions are otherwise heterogeneous. Explanations of this sort are made most plausible, certainly, when there is some prospect of accounting for the causal feedback loop that renders reliable the effects of conforming to or violating the rule. However, even without a clear picture of how the feedback loop might work, if the effects are sufficiently reliable, and the pattern sufficiently evident, the rule will play a role in reasonable explanations.[18]

Explaining by Trans-conventional Rules

That conventional rules might explain what happens in the world is not, I take it, really all that controversial. In contrast, there are some apparently significant differences between conventional rules (of law, grammar, or games) and trans-conventional rules (of logic, rationality, or morality) that make much less palatable the suggestion that trans-conventional rules might explain.

The first difference has to do with what has become a standard test for explanatory import—the counterfactual test, which asks "what if the rules had been different?" and counts the rules as explanatorily important only if their being different would make a difference.[19] When we subject conventional rules to the counterfactual test, the test is conceptually unproblematic (since we can make sense of the rules being different than they in fact are). More impressively, it is quite clear that conventional rules can in principle pass the test; often, if the rules had been different, peoples' beliefs (and their resulting behavior) would have been different as well.

The second difference turns on the fact that both the metaphysical status and actual character of particular conventional rules is fairly unproblematic. People generally agree as to what the rules are and they share a sense of how to investigate and resolve differences of opinion when they arise.

On both counts, things get messy quickly when it comes to trans-conventional rules. First, in many cases it is hard even to make sense of the counterfactual test since it is hard to make sense of the trans-conventional rules being different than we take them to be. This is largely because the rules often don't seem to be contingent in a way that allows us to imagine easily and with any confidence what things would be like if they were in any significant way different. Suppose it were morally permissible for people in our situation to torture young children simply for amusement...what would people believe under the circumstances?[20] This seems similar to asking one to suppose that two plus two didn't equal four and then asking what people would believe under the circumstances. One is inclined to say these questions don't have answers because their suppositions are necessarily false, perhaps even inconceivable—a fact that makes it difficult, to say the least, to apply the counter-factual test.

Second, both the metaphysical status and the actual character of particular trans-conventional rules—especially those of morality, but also those of rationality—are very problematic. People frequently disagree as to what the rules are and also as to how one should investigate and resolve the differences of opinion that inevitably arise.

Despite these striking differences, sense can be made of trans-conventional normative rules (if there are any) contributing to our explanations of non-normative events, processes, and situations. To a great extent, the very real differences mentioned above, while they plague any attempt to defend one particular trans-conventional normative theory as over against another, leave largely untouched any particular conception's claim to explanatory import.

Recall that we already have on-hand a couple of plausible explanations that appeal to trans-conventional rules of rationality: the explanations of conventional rules mentioned early-on that made use of decision and game theory. There is room clearly to accept the decision and game theoretic explanations of conventional rules while at the same time rejecting as an inadequate normative theory the maximizing conception of rationality. Conversely, one might accept as right-headed the normative theory while doubting the success of the decision and game theoretic explanations. Yet for those who do accept both the normative view and the explanations (as many do), the decision and game theoretic explanations provide a nice example of normative explanations. The understandable controversy that will surround, say, the maximizing conception of rationality should warn devotees away from confident dogmatism; but to the extent they have reasonable (even if not conclusive) grounds for their view, there is no reason for them to refrain from using their normative theory in explanations. And, assuming the explanations are successful, there is no reason for them to refrain from seeing the normative theory they embrace as having explanatory credentials.

When it comes to trans-conventional normative rules, any attempt to develop a normative theory that will hold some promise of contributing to explanations will involve two steps. The first is to get some defensible account of what the relevant rules (of logic, rationality, or morality) are. This is the job of justificatory theory. Only if this first step is taken will the theory have any claim to normative force. Taking the first step usually involves defending one more or less controversial account among many. But it is a step people regularly take. The second step is to show that—on that preferred understanding of the normative rules—the fact that some inference, choice, or action, violates or accords with those rules (so understood) explains something outside the inner circle of the normative theory in question—i.e. explains why the inferences, choices, actions, were made or taken, or explains some other non-normative facts. Only if this second step is taken will the theory have any claim to explanatory force. Neither step is trivial. Yet, if the two steps can be taken successfully, one will be in a position both to justify one's account of the norms and to explain things that happen in the world by appeal to those norms.

It is worth noting that, as long as we are concentrating on trans-conventional rules, taking the second step involves making plausible the view that there is some nonconventional causal feedback loop that is responsive to the difference between what violates the rules and what accords with them. In the absence of some such nonconventional feedback loop the rules will have no role in explaining events independent of their recognition within convention. Significantly, though, when the explanation by rules is backed by a feedback mechanism, the problem involved in applying the counter-factual test to non-contingent rules doesn't arise; for the relevant counter-factual doesn't have to do with what would have happened *had the rule been different*, but with what would have happened *had the behavior being explained been different* in such a way as to make it conform with the rule rather than not (or vice versa).

Not only is it plausible to think defensible normative rules (even trans-conventional ones) might figure as the contents of peoples' beliefs; it is reasonable as well to suppose that, with a suitable conception in hand, one might have reason to think, first, that peoples' beliefs are sometimes respon-sive to the rules (as when the beliefs in question are one's own), and even, second, that peoples' prospects may vary, other things equal, according to whether they live up to the rules' demands or not. The maximizing conception of rationality is a clear case in point; for it flows naturally from that conception that those who fail to maximize expected utility will, on average, do worse than they otherwise would have. One doesn't have to look far, though, to discover plausible conceptions of morality that fit the bill as well.[21]

Two, in particular, are worth mentioning. One is a broadly utilitarian con-ception, the other broadly contractarian. Both—despite their deep and dramatic differences—hold the promise of giving morality not just a justifi-catory role but an explanatory role.

The utilitarian theory I have in mind begins with a conception of objective human good that is grounded in the satisfaction of informed preferences, and does not simply equate what is objectively good with what people happen to prefer. It then construes moral requirements as reflections of the demand that human good be maximized, without regard to whose good it is that is being advanced. On this view, actions, practices, and institutions, as well as particular moral claims, are seen as morally justified to the extent they contribute to the maximization of human good.

Within this view, so sketched, there is obviously a great deal of room for different specific views of morality, since a wide variety of accounts might be used to fill in more precisely the notion of objective human good. And there is room as well to embrace just the broader consequentialist outlines and, for instance, replace the appeal to objective human good with a purely subjectivist account that identifies human good with the satisfaction of human preferences whatever they happen to be (regardless of whether they are fully informed or reflectively held).[22]

The contractarian theory, in contrast, begins not with a conception of objective human good, but with a theory of rationality and, specifically, rational agreement. It then construes moral requirements as the products of rational agreement; the moral rules are those to which rational people would rationally agree, and with which they would then rationally comply, under appropriately specified conditions.

Within the contractarian view, too, there is a great deal of room for different specific views of morality, in this case because a wide variety of accounts might be used to fill in more precisely the notions of rationality and rational agreement. And there is room as well to embrace only the broadest contractarian outlines and, for instance, replace the appeal to appropriately specified, presumably hypothetical, conditions with simply the actual conditions real people happen to find themselves in.[23]

Despite the truly fundamental differences, both utilitarianism and contractarianism (of the sorts described[24]) maintain an over-all structure that makes the theories suitable candidates for use in explanations. For in each case, the demands of morality would be specified in a way that would make plausible the contention that there is a causal feedback mechanism that, by and large and in standard conditions, rewards compliance and penalizes non-compliance with (what each takes to be) the demands of morality.

Thus, for instance, on both the utilitarian and the contractarian accounts one might expect resentment, as well as dissatisfaction with the *status quo*, to grow roughly in proportion to injustice. Within societies (and also perhaps among societies) one could predict also that the social and political pressures would rise and fall in reaction to morally relevant changes in social institutions, consistently applying an impetus for moral improvement, if only with partial success. At the very least, unjustifiable institutions and practices likely suffer instability due to peoples' inability, on reflection, to endorse the norms to which they are subjected. Of course, because the social pressures will vary as well with factors other than the moral credentials of the institutions in place, the sanctions immorality suffers may be buffered, deflected, or simply neutralized. However, that forces will have no easily *predictable* effects in an exceedingly complex environment is no reason to deny their presence or their effect. And, to the extent morality is viewed in either a utilitarian or a contractarian way, there are even some grounds for thinking the effects of immorality are actually quite visible and predictable.

Needless to say, although the two approaches to moral theory each have the resources to make sense of how morality and immorality might be relevant to explaining both large scale and more local events and patterns of interaction, their differences will ensure that their various resources will be deployed in drastically different and fundamentally incompatible ways. They can't both be right about the nature of morality and so can't both be right about the ways and extent to which morality helps to explain social change. The important point for our purposes, though, is that either sort of moral theory—as long as it can be defended as a reasonable normative theory—will hook-up with our experiences, prospects, and fortunes, in such a way as to give morality itself, and not just beliefs about morality, a role in explaining what happens in the world. Either will give sense and substance to the notion that morality operates at least as a gentle breeze through the course of history.

Having spent all this time trying to defend the suggestion that morality might actually contribute to empirical explanations, a confession is in order. Much as I believe morality (at least on some plausible conceptions) does indeed have some explanatory force, I suspect as largely, perhaps even dangerously, misguided the view that moral theory's respectability depends on its having such force. The legitimacy of moral theory rests, I believe, not on its explanatory, but on its justificatory, force. But that is an argument for another time.[25]

Notes

1. Quoted in John Morton Blum's *Woodrow Wilson* (Boston: Little, Brown, & Co., 1956), p. 159.
2. Of course moral rules constitute neither the whole nor even the major part of morality. I concentrate on *rules* for two reasons. The first is that moral rules appear to be disembodied in a way that makes them especially problematic. Thinking that the rules of justice might explain social change is, initially at least, much less plausible than thinking, for instance, that someone's courageousness might explain why she does what she does. The second reason is occasion specific: the conference for which this paper was written revolved around the proposal that a logic of rules might contribute to explanations of social change. Two convictions guided the proposal: (i) that the social rules the logic could be used to represent themselves play a role in social change and (ii) that the rules of the logic could in turn help to explain why the social rules play the role they do. Both convictions presuppose that normative rules (whether normative social rules or normative rules of logic) can explain things that happen in the world.
3. Many (though not all) of the normative rules I have in mind contrast as well with the sort of 'ought' judgments that resolve neatly and easily into empirical 'if-then' claims. For instance, unlike "the gasoline ought to have an octane rating of at least 92," which might well be cashed-out as "if the gasoline has a rating of less than 92, then the engine won't run without pinging," claims like "You ought (as a matter of law) to drive under 65 mph" are less plausibly translated into 'if-then' substitutes that avoid mention of the rules in question. Others, though, for instance the requirements of practical rationality, seem at least to be candidates for such a reduction (e.g. if you don't do x, then your preferences will likely be more frustrated than they otherwise would be).
4. Even if, as I believe, there are some unrecognized and unenforced normative rules that apply to people and societies, it seems one could have no reason to ascribe a rule to a society *as a rule of that society* unless it was at least implicitly recognized and enforced. For a discussion of this point, see *Philosophy of Social Science*, David Braybrooke (Englewood Cliffs: Prentice-Hall, 1987), pp. 47-57.
5. See *The Reason of Rules*, Geoffrey Brennan and James Buchanan (Cambridge: Cambridge University Press, 1985).
6. It might be satisfying enough if normative rules could be shown to explain normative facts that are conceptually independent of the rules doing the explaining. Many, though, would hold that normative rules are doing real explanatory work only if they contribute to explanations of non-normative facts, for instance only if they helped to explain some of our perceptual experiences.

Behind this more stringent requirement is the conviction that an adequate epistemology must ground justification in sensation. See my "Moral Theory and Explanatory Impotence," *Midwest Studies* XII (Minneapolis: University of Minnesota Press, 1988), pp. 433-457, and Gilbert Harman's *Thought* (Princeton: Princeton University Press, 1973).

7. The underlying assumption here is that we have reason to believe only in those entities, properties, laws, and rules, that contribute to our best explanation of our experiences. See my "Moral Theory and Explanatory Impotence," *op. cit.*

8. I sketch a version of (what might be called) 'conventional moral realism' in "Coherence and Models for Moral Theorizing," *Pacific Philosophical Quarterly* 6 (1985), pp. 170-190.

9. See Jon Elster's *Ulysses and the Sirens* (Cambridge: Cambridge University Press, 1979) for a discussion of the difference between parametric and strategic choice.

10. I've concentrated in the examples on laws, but decision and game theoretic explanations seem to work too for many other normative rules, for example those governing membership in trade unions, and the authority of umpires in baseball, as well as less institutionally enshrined rules of social organization. David Lewis' *Convention* (Cambridge, MA: Harvard University Press, 1969) sets out elegantly the general structure of game theoretic explanations for social conventions (among which are all sorts of conventionally established normative rules). See also Russell Hardin's *Collective Action* (Baltimore: Johns Hopkins University Press, 1982).

11. Each person "intends only his own gain, and he is in this, as in many other cases, led by an invisible hand to promote an end which was no part of his intention. Nor is it always the worse for the society that it was no part of it. By pursuing his own interest he frequently promotes that of society more effectually than when he really intends to promote it." Adam Smith, *The Wealth of Nations*, (New York: P. F. Collier & Son, 1905), bk. 4, chapter 2, pp. 160-161.

12. See R. D. Luce and Howard Raiffa, *Games and Decisions*, (New York: John Wiley & Sons, 1957); Alan Hamlin, *Ethics, Economics and the State*, (New York: St. Martin's Press, 1986); David Gauthier, *Morals By Agreement*, (Oxford: Oxford University Press, 1986); Richard Brandt, *A Theory of the Good and the Right*, (Oxford: Oxford University Press, 1979); R. B. Perry, *General Theory of Value* (New York: Longmans, Green, and Co., 1926); Stephen Darwall, *Impartial Reason*, (Ithaca: Cornell University Press, 1983); and Peter Railton, "Moral Realism," *Philosophical Review* XCV (1986), pp. 163-207.

13. See Jon Elster's *Making Sense of Marx* (Cambridge: Cambridge University Press, 1985), and his *Ulysses and the Sirens, op. cit.*, and Richard Miller's *Fact and Method* (Princeton: Princeton University Press, 1987).

14. While these claims are, I take it, quite uncontroversial, they have (not surprisingly) been controverted, standardly on the grounds that talk of beliefs (not just beliefs about rules) is a relic of an outmoded conceptual framework ill-suited to explanation. In what follows, though, I will take for granted that at least sometimes beliefs may legitimately explain.

15. Such a disposition might, sometimes, reasonably be thought of as a (perhaps subconscious) belief, but not always. We may legitimately suppose, of the case at hand, that the disposition of the officer finds its expression unmediated by her cognitive states (even though she would not have acquired the disposition in the first place had she not had various beliefs).

16. Something like this apparently underlies the refrain: 'No wonder you got hurt, what you did was stupid!'; the idea being that, even if you didn't know that what you were doing was stupid, its having been so explains your pain.

17. This really is just a 'for instance'. The explanatory force of a rule doesn't depend on it having salutary effects when followed. As long as following a rule would have effects consistently different from those violating the rule has, the rule will be part of the explanation of why the effects are (or are not) in evidence. Yet the further away the effects are from being obviously valuable the less normative the rules in question will seem.

18. The importance of a patterned history, when it comes to explaining by appeal to rules *when the rules are not recognized by anyone involved*, does mean that in these situations the rules cannot provide a single-shot explanation of particular events—they can explain a single event only by relying on a pattern of events that the rule explains. See Alan Garfinkel's *Forms of Explanation*, (New Haven: Yale University Press, 1981); Richard Miller's *Fact and Method, op. cit.*; and for a slightly less lenient view, Jon Elster's *Ulysses and the Sirens, op. cit.*

19. This counterfactual test goes hand-in-hand with the counterfactual analysis of causation. See David Lewis' "Causation," *Journal of Philosophy* (1973), pp. 556-567; and his "Counterfactual Dependence and Time's Arrow," *Nous* (1979), pp. 455-476. See too my "Moral Theory and Explanatory Impotence," *op. cit.*, and Nicholas Sturgeon's "Moral Explanations," in *Morality, Reason and Truth*, edited by David Copp and David Zimmerman (Totowa: Rowman and Allanheld, 1985), pp. 49-78.

20. Notice that the relevant counterfactual does not ask us to suppose merely that people believe it morally permissible to torture for amusement, but instead to suppose such a belief true.

21. Although what follows is limited to a discussion of moral theories and their potential explanatory force, the problems faced by moral theory are exactly paralleled by problems faced by any attempt to defend the explanatory force of a normative system of logic or of practical rationality.

22. This sort of view goes back at least to Bentham's *Introduction to the Principles of Morals and Legislation* (New York: Hafner, 1948). For variations on this general theory, along with defense of its explanatory value, see Peter Railton's "Moral Realism," *op. cit.*; Richard Boyd's "How To Be A Moral Realist," in G. Sayre-McCord (ed.), *Essays on Moral Realism*, (Ithaca: Cornell University Press, 1988), pp. 181-228; David Brink's *Moral Realism and the Foundations of Ethics*, (Cambridge: Cambridge University Press, 1989); and Richard Brandt's *A Theory of the Good and the Right*, *op. cit.*

23. This sort of view has its own obvious roots, most clearly in Hobbes' *Leviathan*, (New York: Penguin Books, 1968). For variations on the general contractarian theme, see David Gauthier's *Morals By Agreement, op. cit.*, and his "Why Contractarianism?" in *Rational Choice and Moral Contractarianism*, edited by Peter Vallentyne (Cambridge: Cambridge University Press, 1990); James Buchanan's *Limits of Liberty*, (Chicago: The University of Chicago Press, 1975); and Gilbert Harman's "Justice and Moral Bargaining," *Social Philosophy and Policy* I (1983), pp. 114-131.

24. There is plenty of conceptual space within the paradigms of utilitarianism and contractarianism to allow for other versions that eschew the sort of contact with the world that these theories maintain. The non-natural moral ontology advanced by Moore and Ross, for example, leaves completely mysterious the impact morality is supposed to have on the world. Retreating to the claim that it does so by affecting our moral beliefs via (a special sort of) intuition hardly dissipates the mystery. See G. E. Moore's *Principia Ethica* (Cambridge: Cambridge University Press, 1903) and W. D. Ross' *The Right and the Good* (Oxford: Oxford University Press, 1930)

25. It is an argument I have begun in "Moral Theory and Explanatory Impotence,"

op. cit. This paper was written for, and delivered at, an interdisciplinary conference on "The Logic of Social Change" held at the Murphy Institute of Political Economy, Tulane University, in April 1988. I've since given versions of it at Vanderbilt University, Davidson College, the United States Air Force Academy, West Virginia University, the University of Kansas, and the University of St. Andrews, Scotland. Thanks are due to all seven audiences. They are due also to Christopher Morris, David Resnik, Michael Resnik, Walter Sinnott-Armstrong and, especially, to David Braybrooke, for detailed and perceptive comments on an earlier draft.

Philosophical Perspectives, 6, Ethics, 1992

WHOSE BODY IS IT, ANYWAY?

Holly M. Smith
University of Arizona

Opponents of abortion must typically[1] establish two separate claims: first, that the fetus has a significant right to life, and second, that the fetus has the right to utilize its mother's body for the support and nourishment of that life. One strategy sometimes used to bridge the gap between these two claims involves the general assertion that when an individual has a right to something, and another person can provide him with that thing at only moderate personal sacrifice, then the individual has a right to assistance from the second person. It is then asserted that pregnancy does not require too great a sacrifice on the part of the mother, so that she has an obligation to assist the fetus by allowing it to use her body for nourishment. But this strategy is a troubled one, since many reject the basic principle on which it relies. Cases such as Judith Thomson's famous violinist example have convinced many either that the principle itself is false, or else that pregnancy involves too great a sacrifice to fall under it.[2]

So opponents of abortion need some more effective way of arguing for the transition from the first claim to the second. One of the most common attempts to provide such an argument consists in showing that the pregnant woman has *given* the fetus that right by engaging in the act of sexual intercourse which created the fetus and made it dependent on her. But filling out this argument involves settling extremely complex issues about what counts as giving someone a right. How *voluntary* must the act of intercourse have been in order for it to count as the woman's giving the fetus the right to her body? Is it necessary (or sufficient) that the woman *knew* at the time of intercourse that she might become pregnant? Does the degree of *probability* of her becoming pregnant affect whether or not she gave the right to the fetus? If she took steps to *avoid* becoming pregnant can she claim she did not give the fetus a right? Can the woman make her gift of the right *conditional*, for example, can she specify that it becomes void if the pregnancy threatens her life or health? Answering all these questions is very difficult, and it is far from clear that the answers will support the right-to-life position on abortion.[3]

However, opponents of abortion have available still another strategy that evades all these issues, since it contends that the fetus's right to use its mother's body does not depend on her *giving* it that right, or indeed on any act or mental state of hers at all. This argument contends that the fetus has a right *by nature* to use the woman's body, in precisely the same way that the woman has a natural right to the use of her own body. What, after all, is the woman's claim to her own body? Primarily, it would appear, that she has been endowed with it by nature; but the fetus can make the same claim with respect to the woman's body that she herself can—the mother's body is part of the life support system with which the fetus, too, is endowed by nature. The fetus, on this view, has the same right to that body that the mother does—quite regardless of whether her act of intercourse was voluntary, knowing, or qualified by attempts to avoid pregnancy. And unlike the alleged right to assistance previously mentioned, this natural right of the fetus's would not depend on the degree of sacrifice the mother must undergo to satisfy it. Of course, the natural right of the fetus to the mother's body will conflict with the natural right of the mother to her own body in cases where the pregnancy is unwanted. But this conflict can be resolved by techniques that have been developed in other areas for handling conflicting rights; the territory here is familiar (if difficult) moral ground.

In this paper, I will elaborate and examine this argument that the fetus has a natural right to its mother's body. To my knowledge it has only been discussed in print by three philosophers, Mark Wicclair, Harry Silverstein, and Jim Stone[4], but a number of people find the argument to be a very natural expression of what seems wrong to them about abortion.

I.

I shall use the term "person" in a minimalist way to designate the possessor of at least one moral right. Of course, one of the major arguments concerning abortion is whether or not the fetus is a person in this sense. I personally find it difficult to agree that at least a very early fetus is a person in this sense. But for purposes of this argument we must assume the fetus is a person. Otherwise our question would be answered before we started, since a creature that lacks rights entirely could have no right to its mother's body.

What kind of entities are persons? Most of the debates on this subject have focused on the question of which creatures besides adult human beings are persons—whether fetuses, infants, higher animals, sophisticated computers, and so forth, qualify. But my concern in asking the question is different. Even with respect to adult human beings we can ask precisely what *part* or *aspect* of the adult is the right-bearer. Some would answer this question by saying that it is the *whole human body*, possessing the capacity to function in certain distinctive ways, that counts as the person and right-bearer. Others would say it is a *psychological entity*, typically associated with such a body, that is the right-bearer. It will streamline our discussion to adopt one or the other of these two views, although the issue of which one is correct cannot be resolved here. Probably the main questions can be formulated within either view, but since it appears they can be formulated more clearly if we assume the person is a psychological entity, I shall adopt this view. Note that this does *not* commit us to some form of non-materialism: one can hold that the entity in question consists (in the case of human beings) of psychological capacities that are identical with, or realized by, brain processes.

Of course a fetus, at least in its early stages, is not the kind of psychological entity typically envisioned when it is said that persons are psychological entities. Early fetuses, and probably late ones as well, do not have sufficiently complex mental lives. This is precisely what leads many, including myself, to deny that fetuses are persons. For purposes of our argument, then, we will have to assume that an entity can be a person despite absence of complex psychological characteristics. Since a *very* early fetus has no psychological characteristics, our remarks will only apply to fetuses at a later stage of development.

II.

The argument which we are examining contends that the fetus has a right by nature to use its mother's body, in precisely the same way that its mother has a natural right to the use of her own body. To assess this argument, we must first investigate the basis of the natural right to its own body possessed by the mother, or indeed any adult.

Many authors have assumed that individuals have a right, often characterized as a property right, to their own bodies. Most famously, John Locke states that "every Man has a *Property* in his own *Person*."[5] The content of this right often remains vague. However, most of us assume that the right to our bodies includes the right to use our bodies, to dispose them as we see fit (within certain limitations concerning the effects on other persons of our doing so), to exclude others from the use, disposition, harm or expropriation of our bodies unless with our consent, and the second-order right to transfer (by gift or perhaps sale) the right to certain parts of our bodies, their activities, or their products.[6] Some authors conceive of these rights as property rights, others deny they are property rights, while still others believe that they are a combination of personal and property rights.[7] It is commonly believed that the right to one's body is, in normal cases at least, stronger than one's right to other external objects or possessions, such as land or artifacts. This means that weightier claims are necessary to override someone's right to her body than are necessary to override her right to an ordinary possession. Thus, for example, many of us are willing that people be taxed in order to buy blood for the seriously ill, but we feel much less willing that anyone should be forced to give his own blood to the ill. Despite the commonly-felt centrality and strength of the right to one's body, few authors who acknowledge or rely on rights to one's body attempt to state the basis for these rights. Since the right to one's body is often seen as one of the most fundamental rights, the basis for this right is a deep issue in moral and political philosophy that deserves greater scrutiny that it standardly receives.[8]

There seem to be two generic possibilities concerning the source of a natural right to a body: either the right to a body is a *fundamental right*, arising directly from some natural or metaphysical fact, or it is a *derived right*, arising from some underlying more fundamental right. In this paper I will limit my discussion to five sub-possibilities: four versions of the claim that the right to a body arises from a metaphysical fact, and one version of the claim that the right to a body arises from a more fundamental right. In each case, I will argue that the claim under scrutiny cannot ground a natural right of the fetus to the use of its mother's body. Since I will not have exhausted all the possible groundings for a natural right to a body, clearly I will not have decisively disposed of the thesis that the fetus does have a natural right to its mother's body. However, this discussion at the minimum should alert those who are opposed to abortion that they will have to seek arguments elsewhere to support their position, and it may provide at least suggestive grounds for believing that this general strategy for arguing against the moral permissibility of abortion is unlikely to succeed.

III.

In everyday conversation, people often talk about some piece of a human body as "belonging" to them. Thus one hears people say "That's my foot you're standing on," and in philosophical contexts people often talk about an entire body as belonging to them. Thus Descartes states "...I possess a body with which I am very intimately conjoined."[9] Such talk tends to conflate two kinds of claim that we must keep distinct. On one hand, there is the *metaphysical* claim that a certain person (i.e., psychological entity) has a special metaphysical relationship, usually involving sensation and control, with a given body. On the other hand, there is the *moral* claim that a certain person has moral rights to the use and enjoyment of a given body. Clearly these two claims are conceptually distinct. One could be closely conjoined to a body without having special rights over it; Hobbes believed this was true in the state of nature.[10] Similarly one could have rights over a body without being closely conjoined to it. Or so it appears at first blush. However, it is plausible to think that the metaphysical claim forms the basis for the moral claim—that it is close conjunction that *grounds* the right to a body.

What constitutes "close conjunction" between a person and a body? The most natural proposal in this arena has been formulated by Sidney Shoemaker as a thesis about what it is for a person to be *embodied* in a certain body. According to Shoemaker, "volitional embodiment and sensory embodiment are together the primary criteria of, or constitutive factors in, embodiment simpliciter."[11] Shoemaker describes a person as "volitionally embodied in a certain body to the extent that volitions of that person produce in that body movements that conform to them or fulfill them, that is, movements that the person is trying to produce or which are constitutive of the actions he is trying to perform."[12] He describes a person as "sensorially embodied" in a certain body to the extent that the interactions of that body with its surroundings produce in the person sense experiences corresponding to, and constituting veridical perceptions of, aspects of those surroundings.[13] Most people would hold that this account of "sensorial embodiment" needs to be expanded to include the person's direct awareness of states of the body itself (by contrast with its surroundings): the body with which I am closely conjoined is, among other things, the body of whose states of cold, heat, pressure and pain I am directly aware.

This account is an attractive one. After all, your body *is* the one through whose eyes you see, whose injuries you feel, and whose movements you directly control. Moreover, the account handles certain hard cases in a satisfactory manner. For example it implies that split personality and split-brain cases are ones in which two (or more) persons are embodied in a single body, because each personality senses the world through that body, senses the states of that body, and is capable of directing that body's activities (although on a "time-sharing" basis).

Using this account of what it is to be embodied in a given physical body, one could then say that the metaphysical relationship of embodiment grounds a person's moral right to the body in which he or she is embodied. On this view, it is precisely *because* I sense through a certain body, am directly aware of its states, and control its movements, that I have a special moral right to control this body and determine what shall happen to it. As Cohen states, the factual truth that something is my arm provides a *prima facie* plausible basis for the claim that I alone am entitled to decide about the use of this arm and to benefit from its dexterity.[14]

It is obvious that this thesis does not provide any basis for the claim that a fetus has a natural moral right to its mother's body. The fetus does not detect its external surroundings through its mother's body in the same sense that she detects her external surroundings through that body. (For one thing, the mother's body *constitutes* part of the fetus's external surroundings.) The fetus does, of course, receive sensations of light, sound, and vibration through the interactions of the mother's body with the world external to the mother's body, and perhaps these give rise, in the fetus, to veridical perceptions of this external world. But this fact does not license us to say that the fetus is sensorially embodied in the mother's body, any more than the fact that a person enclosed in a flour sack receives sensations through its fabric licenses us to say that the person is sensorially embodied in the flour sack. The fetus is not directly aware of states of the mother's body in the same way that it is aware of states of its own body, or that she is aware of states of her body. And the fetus, even if it develops to the point of being able to initiate action rather than mere movement, does not act *with* the mother's body.

The most natural basis for the thesis that a person has a natural right to a given body—the metaphysical fact that the person is embodied in that body—cannot provide any support for the thesis that a fetus has a natural right to its mother's body. The mother alone is embodied in her body.

IV.

However, one could argue that embodiment in the sense just explained, although a sufficient condition for having a moral right to a body, is not a *necessary* condition. This view might receive motivation from the fact that there are certain physical objects that are not, properly speaking, natural parts of a given human body, and yet which may seem to come to have an analogous moral status to parts of the human body. For example, there are growing numbers of persons whose lives or health have been enhanced by organ transplants, or by artificial aids such as respirators, pacemakers, attachable insulin pumps, lens implants, kidney dialysis machines, and so forth. Consider Barney Clark and his implanted Jarvik-7 heart. Mr. Clark did not sense the world through his artificial heart; he was not directly aware of its states; and he could not directly control its movements in the same way that he could control the movements of his arms or legs. Nonetheless, if we ask ourselves what *moral rights* he had with respect to his artificial heart, we have some temptation—or at least I do—to say that his rights with respect to his artificial heart were no different (once it was plugged in and working) than my rights are to my natural heart.

The question of what rights individuals have to such artificial parts and aids is a difficult one.[15] However, reflection on this issue, in the context of reflection on the issue of fetal rights to the mother's body, might lead one to adopt what I shall call the "Extension Thesis": the thesis that the factual relationship between the fetus's body and its mother's body is such that the mother's body is not fully separate from the fetus's body, but rather forms an *extension* of it. On this view, during pregnancy the mother's body is *part* of the fetus's body. The view alleges that the boundaries we normally draw between the maternal and fetal bodies are misplaced: the fetus's body, instead of terminating at the periphery of the fetus's skin, actually extends through the mother's body and terminates with her skin. This claim certainly sounds bizarre. However, there is ample precedent for the claim that no true boundary exists between the maternal and fetal bodies, although historically this claim has more frequently taken the reverse form. For example, in Roman law and nineteenth century tort law in America, the fetus's body was conceived of as *belonging to the mother*—the fetus was considered a portion of the mother or her viscera.[16] And early advocates of the pro-choice position in the second half of the present century often assimilated the status of the fetus's body to that of the woman's appendix. The Extension Thesis simply reverses these claims.

It might be tempting to reject this view offhand on the ground that where there are two persons there must be two bodies. But this rejection would be too cavalier. We have already seen that there are other instances where it is plausible to recognize the existence of two persons but only one body— split-brain and split-personality cases. Where these personalities are sufficiently complete, one cannot deny them moral personhood. And this raises the specter (not merely theoretical in the case of split-personalities) of both persons holding rights to the single body, rights that may conflict. Recent legal cases in which a man has been accused of raping a woman with a split personality, only one of whose personalities consented to intercourse, are dramatic instances of this possibility.

It might also be tempting to reject the Extension Thesis on the ground that bodies (unlike artificial spare parts) can be decisively individuated by reference to their genetic material.[17] On such a view, two chunks of organic material count as parts of the same body if, and only if, they are genetically identical. Since the fetus and the mother are not genetically identical, of course it turns out that the mother's body cannot be an extension (and therefore part of) the fetus's. However, this criterion too runs afoul of counterexamples. It incorrectly implies that there is only one body, rather than two, in cases involving identical twins, or clones and their progenitors, or parthenogenetic offspring and their parents. It also incorrectly implies that there are two bodies, rather than one, in "chimera" cases in which innovative techniques have merged cells from three or more mouse embryos to produce a single mouse incorporating tissue masses having separate genetic materials.[18] Perhaps most puzzlingly, it implies that each of our bodies is not a single body, since all our cells include small but essential parts, the mitochondria, which replicate themselves independently and have different RNA and DNA from that of the cell nucleus itself.[19] Simple appeals to genetic differences are not going to provide a satisfactory assessment of the Extension Thesis.

A. (Mere) Organic Connection

What criterion could be used, then, to determine whether or not a given item counts as part of a given body? The most natural suggestion here, and the most promising one for a supporter of the Extension Thesis, is the claim that a chunk of living tissue counts as part of a given body if it is *organically connected* to that body.[20] This idea is expressed by Stephen Jay Gould when he states that "...physical separation is the essence of our vernacular definition of individuality,"[21] and it is certainly what first occurs to us when we ask why this finger or this toe counts as part of my body rather than someone else's—even when the finger or toe have suffered nerve damage, and I can neither feel them, or feel through them, or control their movements. Such a criterion implies that the Extension Thesis is true, since the fetal and maternal bodies are organically connected to each other in fairly elaborate ways, ways which permit the mother to provide the fetus with oxygen, nourishment, and waste disposal, and which allow chemical and hormonal signals to be sent from either side to the other, triggering an assortment of physiological responses.[22]

However, a closer look shows that organic connection does not provide a sufficient condition for bodily inclusion. The relevant examples are provided by the phenomenon of Siamese twinning. In some cases of Siamese twinning, it is quite plausible to regard the entity as one body with extra parts. For example, we would regard a creature with one head, two arms, and one trunk, but, say, four legs in this manner. But in other cases it is only plausible to regard the twins as having *two* bodies superficially joined. This can be seen in the original Siamese twins, Chang and Eng, who were physically complete human beings connected at the abdomen with a thin band of tissue, three and a quarter inches at its widest and one and five-eights inches at its thickest.[23] Precisely because Chang and Eng each had a full set of internal organs, limbs, etc., the mere fact of natural organic connection does not persuade us that there was only one body here rather than two (or persuade us that there were two bodies, each of which included the other as an extension). There is obviously a continuum of possible cases of Siamese twinning between the case I first described and that of Chang and Eng. We very likely do not know what to say about some of the cases that fall in the middle of this spectrum. But the existence of the Chang-Eng cases shows that *mere* organic connection is not sufficient to establish that the two connected parts are parts of one body.

B. Substantial Organic Connection

The proponent of the Extension Thesis might seek to circumvent this by enriching the organic-connection criterion to require, not *mere* organic connection, but *substantial* organic connection, where the required degree of connection is set so as to decide all the Siamese twinning cases the right way (perhaps with some undecided cases). But even if this could be done, it seems dubious that the resulting criterion would imply that the mother's body is an extension of the fetus's body. The fetal-maternal case seems to fall closer to the Chang-Eng end of the organic-connection spectrum than it does to the other end, or even in the middle. Both the mother and the fetus have a full set of organs and limbs, or at least (in the early stages of fetal development) the potential for a full set.[24] Granted, the connection between the fetus and mother is more substantial than the connection between Chang and Eng, since the mother's body performs some physiological functions for the fetus's body (although in later pregnancy the fetus's body is quite capable of performing these functions for itself). Nonetheless the connection is still pretty thin.[25] Appeals to organic connection, then, whether bare connection or enriched connection, do not seem to provide support for the Extension thesis.

C. Part of Natural Life-Sustaining Biological System

One last variant of this idea has been proposed by Mark Wicclair.[26] Wicclair suggests that a vital organ belongs to a person if that person was endowed with that organ by nature; or, as he sometimes puts it, if the organ is part of the biological system that naturally sustains the person's life. (Wicclair's discussion actually leaves it unclear whether he means the metaphysical or the moral sense of "belong." At this stage I shall interpret him as meaning the metaphysical sense.) This proposal has a number of virtues. For one thing, since it does not rely on *mere* organic connection, it avoids the unwanted implication that any crucial parts of Chang's body belongs to Eng, or vice versa. Moreover, it decides other cases in an intuitively acceptable manner. For example, we can imagine a Siamese twin case in which two body masses are readily discernable, but a single heart serves both bodies. On Wicclair's account, this heart belongs equally to both persons, and this conclusion seems apt.

However, there is a deep problem with Wicclair's approach. To see this, consider the case of parasites: for example tapeworms. A tapeworm makes its living by embedding its head in the intestinal wall of a large mammal, and then extracting nutrients from its blood. It appears that the mammal's intestine is part of the biological system that naturally sustains the tapeworm's life, and hence that Wicclair's account implies the mammal's intestine is part of the tapeworm's body. But clearly we not think that the mammal's intestine comprises part of the tapeworm's body. Unfortunately, Wicclair has no way to show this. For his argument to succeed, he would have to show (a) that the relevant sense of "biological system" excludes such systems as a parasite together with its hosts and vectors, and (b) that the features which exclude the parasite-host system do *not* rule out the fetus-mother system. Now clearly there *is* a distinction between the parasite-host system and the simpler kind of system that involves, say, the parasite alone. But if we asked what the difference is, the natural response is to say that the parasite-host system involves *two* bodies while the parasite simpliciter system involves only *one* body. This response of course is not available to Wicclair, since he is trying to use the notion of a biological system in order to explicate the notion of a single body. Wicclair might appeal to evolution at this point, and claim that the mammal's intestine counts as part of the mammal's system, but not as part of the tapeworm's system, because (crudely speaking) the intestine has evolved in order to support the mammal, but has not evolved in order to support the tapeworm. This would be correct in the case of tapeworms, and handle the case of fetuses in the way Wicclair wants, since the mother's organs *have* evolved precisely to support the fetus. But this criterion does not always draw the line in the right place. For example, many plants and animals have partners with which they live in mutualistic relationships. In many of these cases, organs of one or both partners have evolved in order to support the other partner. For instance, many flowers have evolved elaborate structures to attract and guide insects to their pollen. But we do not conclude that these floral structures are *part of* the insect's body; and similarly we cannot conclude that the mother's organs are part of the fetus's body.[27]

Wicclair does not directly address the question of what counts as the relevant kind of biological system, but he does argue that there is no analogy between a fetus and a parasite. He gives three reasons for this conclusion. (1) Parasites are normally "foreign" organisms which "invade" the body. Fetuses develop from eggs which are produced by natural processes within the woman's body. (2) Parasites commonly destroy vital organs within their hosts' bodies or deprive their hosts of essential nourishment. Hence, when a parasite invades a body, the latter is considered to be an abnormal, diseased condition. Pregnancy, on the other hand, is neither an abnormal condition nor a disease. (3) Parasites *always* require some host or other. For fetuses, on the other hand, occupying a host body is but one, relatively brief, stage in their natural development.[28]

Unfortunately, none of these alleged grounds for distinguishing between fetuses and parasites is accurate. With regard to the first reason, it is false that parasites are "foreign" organisms in any sense that excludes fetuses. A parasite and its host need not be of different species. For example, there is one species of anglerfish in which the male, who is considerably smaller than the female, attaches his mouth permanently to the female's flesh. Many of his internal organs then atrophy until finally he draws all his oxygen and nourishment from the female's bloodstream, which circulates freely throughout his body. His chief remaining independent function is to fertilize her eggs.[29] Clearly he counts as a parasite with respect to the female. Typically a parasite is "foreign" to its host in the sense that the two are distinct individuals in genetic and immunological terms. But the fetus is foreign to the mother's body in the same terms. Indeed the mother's body must erect elaborate defenses to protect itself from the fetus's foreignness. Some parasitologists recognize two categories of parasites; the heteroparasites, which are phylogenetically distinct from their hosts, and the homoparasites, which are closely related to their hosts. Fetuses are explicitly included among the homoparasites.[30] "Foreignness" does not provide a mark that can be used to exclude fetuses from the class of parasites.

With regard to Wicclair's second reason, it is a matter of controversy whether or not the term "parasite" should be restricted to those organisms that injure their hosts.[31] But even among the harmful parasites the injury in question is often so slight as to be unnoticeable to the host. On the other hand, under certain conditions human fetuses deprive their mothers of essential nutrients, and their existence not infrequently gives rise to processes that injure the mother's health or even result in maternal death. In other species this can be even more clear-cut. For example, in one variety of gall midge, the offspring develop live within the mother's body, eating her tissues from the inside until she dies and the offspring emerge to start the cycle all over again.[32] There is no interesting distinction between what these offspring do to their mothers and what many parasites do to their hosts. Finally, whether or not pregnancy is seen as an "abnormal, diseased condition" seems mostly to depend on fashions in medical and feminist thinking. Under any fashion, pregnancy can be unhealthy for the mother.

With regard to Wicclair's third reason, it is simply false that all parasites live their entire lives on their hosts. Many live only part of their lifespans on their host, and even must leave it in order to mature. Others, such as the tetanus bacillus, are facultative parasites: they can survive either on the body of a host, or by living freely in the soil.[33] The short-lived dependency of the fetus on its mother's body does not distinguish it from more standard parasites.

In short, then, none of Wicclair's reasons for distinguishing fetuses from parasites succeeds. In general it appears that there are good reasons to view fetuses precisely *as* a sort of parasite. Thus whatever reasons may be found for saying that the host's body does not constitute part of the parasite's natural biological system (in the relevant sense) will also imply that the mother's body is not part of the fetus's natural biological system (in the relevant sense). We must conclude that Wicclair's argument fails to show that the mother's body must be considered as part of the fetus's body.

We have now looked at three arguments for the Extension Thesis, the thesis that the mother's body must be considered as a part, or extension, of the fetus's body. Three criteria have been advanced for determining when something counts as part of a given body: the mere organic connection criterion, the substantial organic connection criterion, and Wicclair's sustaining-biological-system criterion. None of these criteria provided a foundation adequate to establish the Extension Thesis. We must conclude that no reason has been found to think that the mother's body belongs to the fetus in the metaphysical sense of "belonging," and hence no reason has been found to think that the fetus has a fundamental right to its mother's body arising directly from the natural or metaphysical relations between the fetus and its mother's body. Of course, it might be maintained that the fetus has a fundamental right to its mother's body arising from some different natural or metaphysical relation than any examined here. However, having reviewed the most salient proposals in this arena, I will now redirect our attention to the possibility that the fetus's right to its mother's body is not a fundamental right at all, but rather a derived right, arising indirectly from some more basic right.

V.

A derived right is one that derives from some more fundamental right. Thus it might be claimed that a creature has a derived right to food, because it has a fundamental right to life, and food is necessary for life. Unfortunately, although many of the rights important in political and moral discourse are clearly derived rights, very little is understood about the principles by which more concrete rights are legitimately derived from the abstract or generic rights that are generally held to be fundamental. We will have to proceed as best we can despite this lack in necessary theoretical apparatus.

The thesis to be examined asserts that the right to a body is not a fundamental right, but rather a derived right. There are various possibilities here, but perhaps the most natural position would be to hold that the right to a body is derived from the right to life, together with the proposition that control over a body is essential for continued life. Samuel Wheeler has proposed something like this view in maintaining that the fundamental right is the right to exist as an agent (which he connects with the right to exist simpliciter), and that the exclusive right to move and use our bodies derives from this right.[34]

A. Deriving Rights from the Right to Life

What is the content of the right to life, and how can we derive other rights from it? I shall take it that the right to life is the right to continued existence as a psychological being. Such a right has traditionally been thought to have two components: the right not to have one's life terminated by others without one's consent, and the right to maintain one's life without interference from others. From these two sub-rights we could derive bodily rights by the following pair of arguments. The first argument invokes the following general principle:

P₁. If a person P has a right that someone else S do x, then P has a derivative right that S do anything y that is a necessary and sufficient condition for S's doing x.

For example, if Peterson has a right that Smith return a borrowed book, and the only way to return the book is to mail it, then Peterson has a derivative right that Smith mail the book. We have just seen that P has a fundamental right that S not terminate P's existence as a psychological entity. But P's existence as a psychological entity is closely bound up with what happens to the body with which he is closely conjoined. Hence P has a derivative right that S not interfere with P's body in ways that would result in the termination of P's existence. The exact content of this right is specified by the actions that are necessary and sufficient conditions for any S's not terminating P's existence.

The second argument starts from a slightly different general principle:

P₂. If a person P has the right to do x himself, then P has a derivative right to do anything y that is a necessary and sufficient condition for P's doing x.

For example, if Peterson has a right to sell his land, then Peterson has a derivative right to sign the documents necessary and sufficient for selling his land. We have just seen that P has a fundamental right to maintain his existence without interference. But under most circumstances, it is a necessary and sufficient condition that P move his body in various ways in order to maintain his existence. Hence by the second principle, P has a derivative right to move and use his body in various ways without interference by others. The exact content of this right is specified by the movements that are necessary and sufficient to maintain his existence.

Taken together, principles P₁ and P₂ establish important components of the right to one's body as it was earlier characterized: they give each of us a right that others not interfere with one's body in ways that would terminate one's existence, and a right to move and use one's body in ways that are necessary and sufficient to maintain one's existence. In particular, these principles give a pregnant woman these rights with respect to her body. But they also give the fetus these rights with respect to its mother's body, since the fetus depends on the mother's body for its life just as it depends on its own body. Thus the fetus has a derivative right that no one (including the mother herself) interfere with its mother's body in ways that would terminate the fetus's existence, and it also has a right to use its mother's body (for example, for nourishment) in ways that are necessary and sufficient for the maintenance of its own existence. Of course the rights of the mother and those of the fetus may conflict with each other, for example in cases where pregnancy would be lethal to the mother. But this kind of conflict must be settled in whatever way such conflicts are normally settled: the important point is that the fetus's right will be just as strong as the mother's right in such cases.

Before proceeding, it is important to note two caveats regarding this derivation of bodily rights from the right to life. First, this derivation is not sufficient to establish bodily rights of the full scope that we normally assume such rights have. For example, the derived rights will not prohibit interferences with one's body that would not affect one's existence—even though such interferences would result in pain, injury, destruction of bodily parts, frustration of will, and so forth. By the same token, the derivation is insufficient to secure any right to use one's body to obtain any good less important than life itself—no right to use one's body to obtain comfort, good health, affectionate relations with others, better tasting food, and so forth. Indeed, these derived rights would license no complaint at all against a powerful but benign oppressor who assumed complete control of one's body and used it entirely for his own purposes—so long as those purposes were compatible with one's continued existence. What this shows is that the right to one's body that we believe ourselves to have cannot be derived completely from our right to life, but must be derived from other fundamental rights as well, such as the right to be free from pain, to experience pleasure, to have rewarding interpersonal relationships, and so on. Whether or not deriving a right to one's body from a larger range of fundamental rights would secure the requisite scope for that right is a matter that cannot be pursued here.[35]

The second caveat concerns the two principles used for deriving a right to one's body from the right to life. Both these principles are suspect. Neither accommodates the fact that what is necessary and sufficient for fulfillment of a fundamental right may already have moral claims on it that preclude derivation of a right to its use. For example, in one case described above, Peterson is described as having a right that Smith return a borrowed book, and therefore a right that Smith mail the book by way of returning it. But suppose the only stamp available for mailing the book belongs to Brown, who doesn't consent to Smith's using it to return Peterson's book. Does Peterson have a right nonetheless that Smith use Brown's stamp, because doing so is necessary and sufficient for Smith's returning the book? Clearly not, yet Principle P_1 implies that he does. We could deal with this problem by denying that (in these circumstances) Peterson has a right that Smith return the book; or by qualifying Principle P_1 to accommodate such cases. Or perhaps we need some rather different principle for deriving rights. This is too large a problem to be settled in the context of this paper. Rather than attempting to do so, since *something* like principles P_1 and P_2 must be true, I will make use of these principles as stated, and attempt to frame cases in such a way as to avoid this kind of problem.

B. Problems with Deriving Bodily Rights from the Right to Life

We have now formulated a way of deriving bodily rights from the right to life, and seen how it implies that the fetus has a right to use its mother's body as necessary to sustain its life, and a right not to have its mother's body interfered with in ways that would be detrimental to the fetus's continued existence. The existence of such rights, clearly, would be very helpful to opponents of abortion.

However, I will now argue that deriving the right to one's body from one's right to life does not provide an acceptable ground for the right to one's body, and hence must be rejected. If we reject it, we have not found any acceptable foundation for the right to a body that supports the thesis that the fetus has a natural right to its mother's body.

The first difficulty with the strategy of deriving one's bodily right from one's right to life arises because the strategy implies (contrary to our earlier assumption) that one's right to one's own body has no different status from one's right to certain external objects.

To see the problem, consider a case in which you are dangling by one hand over a vat of boiling oil. Since falling into the vat would cause your death, you have a (bodily) right that no one cut off your hand and send you to destruction below. But now suppose you are dangling from a rope over the vat of boiling oil. (We can assume that you own this rope, or that no one owns it.) In this case you have a right that no one cut the rope in two and send you to your death below. On the account of rights we are examining, your right with respect to your hand in the first case is precisely analogous to your right with respect to the rope in the second case. The two rights derive from the same source, and so are of equal strength and importance. But this violates our assumption that the right to one's body is importantly different from, and stronger than, the right to other objects.

It is difficult to know how decisive an objection is raised by this case. On the one hand, it is true that we believe one has a stronger right to one's body than one has to other, external objects. On the other hand, we certainly feel that it would be *very* wrong for anyone to cut the rope. But if we analyze this reaction, it seems plain to me that what underlies the reaction is not the feeling that the wrongness in cutting the rope derives from your property rights to the rope. Rather what makes cutting the rope wrong is the fact that it would be very wrong for anyone to kill you, and cutting the rope in these circumstances is killing you. It would be just as wrong to cut the rope if someone else besides you owned it, and even consented to its being cut. These feelings contrast with our feelings in the case where your hand is cut: here, too, it is wrong to cut your hand because doing so would be killing you. But it is *also* wrong because your hand belongs to you, and that means you have a right that it not be interfered with without your consent. We do not feel this additional wrong is present in the case where the rope is cut.[36]

The rope case should at least raise suspicion that deriving bodily rights from the right to life may result in judgments that fail to accord with our normal moral views. That suspicion can be strengthened by considering the following case. Suppose you are starving, and there are apples hanging from a branch in front of you. You have a right to move your hand to secure the apples, since if you do not, you will die, whereas if you do, you will live. Now suppose you can't reach the apples by yourself, but could knock them within your grasp by swinging the arm of a taller person at them. The taller person has no particular need to use his arm at the moment. Then, on the account of rights we are examining, you have a derivative right to swing the arm of the taller person to secure the apples. Your right to his arm is precisely parallel to your right to your own arm in a case in which you need only reach out to grasp the apples. This violates our normal assumption that bodily rights are *exclusive* rights, or that each person has primary rights to his or her own body that supersede those of other persons. If bodily rights are derived from each person's right to life, then no one has a greater right to his own body than he does to anyone else's body that might prove useful for sustaining his life; and he has no prior right to his own body if his body proves useful for sustaining another's life. Each person's body will have numerous claims on it during its history, none of them weaker or less important than the claim of the person whose body it is. All this violates our ordinary assumption that bodily rights are normally exclusive. And of course it is precisely this feature that makes it possible to derive a fetal right to the use of its mother's body.[37]

These cases show that the attempt to derive one's right to one's body from one's right to life results in rights that run afoul of two of our central assumptions about the nature of a right to one's body—the assumption that this right is importantly different from, and stronger than, one's right to other objects, and the assumption that one's right to one's body is normally an exclusive right. But there is a third, and perhaps more damaging, consequence of deriving bodily rights from the right to life. Such rights do not have the correct normative import. To see this we need to develop a slightly longer story. The first thing to note is that the two components of the right to life that were mentioned originally, the right not to have one's existence terminated, and the right to maintain one's existence, can easily come into conflict with each other. To take a standard example, to maintain my life I might need to extract your heart and transplant it to my body. But of course doing so would kill you, so there is a conflict between my right to maintain my life and your right not to have your life terminated. Such conflicts must be resolved by some sort of priority rule. It is sometimes suggested that the relevant priority rule in such cases is one that gives priority to the right to the individual whose body is needed, since that individual has not only a right to life but also an additional right to control his or her body. Clearly such a priority rule is unavailable to the theorist who believes rights to the body are simply derived from rights to life, since on this view bodily rights are not importantly distinct from rights to life, and each individual in the case just described has the same right to the bodily part that is necessary and sufficient for the continued life of each of them. Thus in the context of our discussion, the only available priority rules for resolving such conflicts (in cases where other moral considerations do not bear on the problem) are the rule that (A) the right not to be terminated always outweighs the right to maintain oneself, and (B) the right to maintain oneself always outweighs the right not to be terminated. To see which, if either, of these two rules is acceptable, let us consider two further cases.

In the first case, you are hiking along a precipitous trail when a severe earthquake hits the area. The tremor throws your body over the precipice, where luckily it lodges in the branches of a tree growing below the trail. You are wedged into the branches in such a way that you cannot extricate yourself. Meanwhile, another hiker, a complete stranger to you who was hiking in the same area at the time of the earthquake, has similarly been thrown off the precipice. Luckily for her, her jacket became hooked over your foot as she hurtled past, and she is now dangling there. If she falls, she will be killed on the rocks below. Unfortunately, her weight is such a strain on your body that if she continues to hang from your foot, your backbone will snap and you will be killed before help arrives. However, even if you die, your corpse will remain wedged in the tree, and the other hiker will remained hooked over your foot and eventually be rescued. On the other hand, you could kick her off before the strain on your back proves too great. In other words, it's a straight conflict between your right to life and hers. You have a right to maintain your life by kicking her off, and she has a right not to be killed by your kicking her off.

Now consider a second case. The initial scenario is the same: you and a stranger are both hiking in a remote area when an earthquake flings the two of you over a precipice. In this case, each of you is caught in a branch of a single tree below the trail. Neither of you can move from her position. Eventually help will arrive. However, the tree is not strong enough to bear the weight of both of you, and even now is starting to split down the middle. If it splits, your side of the tree will rip away and plunge you to your death in the abyss below. The remainder of the tree will remain rooted to the cliff wall, and the other hiker will survive. On the other hand, her entanglement in the tree is fairly insecure (unlike yours). If you kick and thrash, you will knock her off into the abyss, at which point the splitting process will halt and you will survive. In other words, it's a straight conflict between your right to life and hers. You have a right to maintain your life by kicking her off, and she has a right not to be killed by your kicking her off.

How are these conflicts to be resolved? Within the context of the theory we are examining, we saw that there are only two possibilities: either one person's right not to be terminated always outweighs the other person's right to maintain her existence, or else one person's right to maintain herself always outweighs the other person's right not to be terminated. Whichever of these rules is correct, both cases must be handled the same way. Either you have a right in both cases to maintain your life by kicking the other hiker into the abyss below, or else she has the right in both cases not to have her life terminated by being kicked off, and you must die. But does this agree with our intuitions about what is right and wrong in these cases?

It must be admitted from the start that it is hard to have clear intuitions about these cases. They are extreme and bizarre examples of the sort about which it is always difficult to marshal firm convictions. The problem is compounded by the fact that any beliefs about what it is right or wrong to do are easily overwhelmed by our knowledge of what we personally would be likely to do anyway in order to save our lives, regardless of whether it is right or wrong. Despite all this I have intuitions about these cases, and my feeling is that they are *not* morally equivalent. I think you have the right to kick the other hiker off your foot in the first case, but do not have the right to shake her out of the tree in the second case. Or to put it more accurately, I am more *inclined* to believe you have the right in the foot-hanging case than I am inclined to believe you do in the splitting-tree case. Perhaps a better way to tease out this intuition from those who do not immediately share it has been suggested by John Deigh.[38] Suppose someone proposed, in the splitting-tree case, that the two hikers use some sort of lottery to settle which of them would get to use the tree to save herself. They might, for example, flip a coin. This would seem to be a cold-blooded but reasonable and appropriate method for settling a horrible dilemma. Indeed judges have proposed exactly this sort of solution in analogous real life cases.[39] But suppose someone suggested that a lottery be used to resolve the foot-hanging case: heads you get to kick the other hiker off your foot, killing her but saving yourself; tails she gets to continue hanging from your foot, killing you but saving herself. Using a lottery to settle *this* conflict seems far less reasonable and appropriate.

I think the reason we have different intuitions about the two cases can be understood as follows. You and the other hiker are in symmetrical moral positions in the splitting-tree case, but you are not in symmetrical positions in the foot-hanging case. In the splitting-tree case, you and the other hiker each depend on a third object, the tree, to save your lives, and your relations to that object are the same: neither of you has any special or prior claim to it. But in the foot-hanging case, the third object on which both your lives depend is *your body*, and your respective relations to that object are not the same. *You* have a special, morally prior claim on it. If anyone gets to use your body to save her life, it should be you, not some stranger who adventitiously comes to need it. For this reason, it is permissible for you to dislodge the other person when her using your body will result in your death. But since you have no special claim on the tree, it is not permissible for you to dislodge the other person when her using the tree will result in your death. And for this reason you need not accede to the use of a lottery in deciding who gets to use your body to save herself: you *already* have a claim on that body. But it is suitable to use the lottery in deciding who gets to use the tree, since neither of you has a claim on the tree.[40]

If this is correct, it completely undermines the theory under examination. That theory asserts that a person's right to his body is derived from his right to life, and hence that his right to his body cannot be distinguished from his right to any other vitally important object. For this reason the theory cannot distinguish your right to your body from your right to the tree, and so entails that our two cases must be handled alike: either you have the right in both cases to kick the other hiker off, or you have the right in neither case to kick the other hiker off. But this disagrees with my intuitions, and I presume those of other people, that the two cases should be handled differently, and in particular with the feeling that the reason for this difference is that you have a different kind of claim on your body than your claim on the tree, and that your claim on your body is prior to the other hiker's claim on your body. It follows that the right to one's body cannot derive solely from one's right to life. Indeed, the right to one's body, rather than deriving from the right to life, must be independent from the latter, since the right to one's body helps specify what one may do to save one's own life, and sets limits on how much others may do to your body in order to save their lives.

We have found, then, three serious defects in the theory that one's right to one's own body derives from one's right to life: the strength of the derived bodily right fails to exceed that of one's right to other objects or possessions; one's right to one's body fails to be an exclusive right in the normal case; and the derived right fails to yield the correct normative judgments in cases where rights conflict. I conclude the theory is mistaken. Since it is mistaken, it cannot be used to provide a foundation for a natural fetal right to the use of its mother's body. Opponents of abortion can find no help in this quarter.

Still, it might be claimed that even though the theory itself is incorrect as an account of the nature and genesis of bodily rights, nonetheless it relies on two general principles for deriving rights that may be of assistance. As yet no direct suspicion has been cast on the utility of these general principles, and they can be used to derive a fetal right to the mother's body—a right, since it is merely derived, that may have a different status or strength from the mother's own right, but a right nonetheless.

But such a derived right appears to be of little help to opponents of abortion, since it is evidently secondary to the mother's own fundamental right. And we cannot be sure as yet that there is such a derived fetal right, since it remains to be shown whether one can derive a right in this fashion to something on which there is already a prior claim. This is precisely the problem in the kind of case where one person needs the stamp belonging to another in order to receive a book to which he has a right, and where we said that the implications of the principles seemed incorrect. It is just such debates that opponents of abortion hoped to avoid by showing that the fetus and the mother have parallel and equal natural rights to the mother's body.

Of course it is possible that the right to one's body can be derived from some different fundamental right or rights, and that this derivation would support the anti-abortion case. But I am not optimistic that any such derivations will succeed; most of the obvious candidates for the relevant fundamental right, such as the right to be free from pain, can be shown to succumb to the same problems that vitiate the attempt to derive bodily rights from the right to life.[41] Barring future arguments to the contrary, our conclusion must be that the strategy of deriving bodily rights from more fundamental rights fails, and so can afford no support to those who wish to show that the fetus has a derived right to its mother's body equal in stature to her own right.

VI.

In this paper I have examined the thesis that a fetus has a natural right to its mother's body, a right commensurate with the mother's own right, and in no way dependent on her choices or mental states at the time of conception. We have looked at several different ways of spelling out this idea: the thesis that the fetus has a right to the mother's body because the fetus is embodied in the mother's body, the thesis that the fetus has this right because the mother's body is organically connected to the fetus's body, the thesis that the fetus has this right because the mother's body has a substantial organic connection to the fetus's body, the thesis that the fetus has this right because the mother's body is part of a biological system that naturally sustains the fetus's life, and finally the thesis that the fetus has a derived right to its mother's body because it has a right to life and use of its mother's body is necessary and sufficient for maintaining that life. None of these theses has proved convincing. If the fetus has an equal, natural right to its mother's body, that fact still remains to be shown.[42]

Notes

1. Some opponents of abortion base their view on reasons with quite a different structure, e.g., obedience to a purported direct Divine injunction against abortion.
2. Judith Jarvis Thomson, "A Defense of Abortion," *Philosophy and Public Affairs*,

I (Fall 1971), pp. 47-66. The argument in this article has come under significant attack since its publication. See, for example, Ann Davis, "Abortion and Self-Defence," *Philosophy and Public Affairs*, 13 (Summer 1984), pp. 175-207.

3. See Thomson, *ibid.*; Donald Regan, "Rewriting Roe v. Wade," *Michigan Law Review* 77 (August 1979), 1569-1646; and Holly M. Smith, "Intercourse and Moral Responsibility for the Fetus," in William Bondeson, H. Tristram Engelhardt, Stuart Spicker, and Daniel Winship, eds., *Abortion and the Status of the Fetus* (Hingham, Mass.: D. Reidel Publishing Co., 1983).

4. Mark Wicclair, "The Abortion Controversy and the Claim that This Body is Mine," *Social Theory and Practice*, Vol. 7 (Fall 1981), pp. 337-346; Jim Stone, "Abortion and the Control of Human Bodies," *The Journal of Value Inquiry*, Vol. 17 (1983), pp. 77-85; and Harry Silverstein, "On a Woman's 'Responsibility' for the Fetus," *Social Theory and Practice*, Vol. 13 (Spring 1987), pp. 103-119.

5. John Locke, *Second Treatise of Government*, Section 27.

6. Some theorists would place severe restrictions on these rights, for example by denying that one has the right to destroy one's body, or permanently to alienate it to the control of another person (as in slavery).

7. See, for example, Lori B. Andrews, "My Body, My Property," *Hastings Center Report*, Vol. 16 (October 1986), pp. 28-38, and Stephen Munzer, *A Theory of Property* (Cambridge: Cambridge University Press, 1990), Chapters 1-3.

8. For a valuable discussion of the role this right plays in contemporary political philosophy, see G. A. Cohen, "Self-Ownership, World-Ownership, and Equality," in Frank S. Lucash, ed., *Justice and Equality Here and Now* (Ithaca: Cornell University Press, 1986), pp. 108-135. As Cohen points out, certain influential political theorists, including John Rawls and Ronald Dworkin, deny that there is any exclusive natural right to one's own body. Cohen, *ibid.*, p. 113, 114-115. For a discussion of the centrality of bodily rights (without any attempt to explain their foundation), see Judith Jarvis Thomson, *The Realm of Rights* (Cambridge, Massachusetts: Harvard University Press, 1990), Chapter 8.

9. Rene Descartes, "Meditation VI," from "Meditations on First Philosophy."

10. Hobbes believed there was no exclusive right to one's own body in the state of nature: "every man has a right to every thing; even to one anothers body." Thomas Hobbes, *Leviathan*, ed. W.G. Pogson Smith (Oxford: Clarendon Press, 1909), ch. 14, p. 99.

11. Sydney Shoemaker, "Embodiment and Behavior," in Amelie Rorty, ed., *The Identities of Persons* (Berkeley: University of California Press, 1976), p. 112. See also Arthur Danto, *Analytical Philosophy of Action* (Cambridge at the University Press, 1973), pp. 141-142; Descartes, *op. cit.*; and Daniel Dennett, "Where Am I?" in *Brainstorms* (Bradford Books, 1978), pp. 310-323. Samuel Wheeler III argues against sensation and agent-type control as providing the moral foundation for bodily rights in "Natural Property Rights as Body Rights," *Nous* XIV (May 1980), pp. 175-176.

12. Shoemaker, *ibid.*

13. Shoemaker, *ibid.*

14. Cohen, *op. cit.*, p. 112.

15. One issue: is one's right to items that merely enhance one's functioning (eyeglasses, hearing aids) different from one's right to items that are critical to essential functions (implantable insulin pumps, pacemakers, etc.)?

16. John T. Noonan, "How to Argue About Abortion," in Tom Beauchamp and Leroy Walters, eds., *Contemporary Issues in Bioethics* (Encino, California: Dickenson Publishing Co., Inc., 1978), p. 216.

17. See Stephen Jay Gould, "Living with Connections," in *Natural History Magazine*, Vol. 91 (November 1982), p. 22, for a similar suggestion.
18. Karl Illmensee and Leroy C. Stephens, "Teratomas and Chimeras," in *Scientific American* 240 (April 1979), pp. 120-132.
19. Lewis Thomas, *The Lives of a Cell* (New York: The Viking Press, 1974), p. 4, 70-74; and Leslie A. Grivell, "Mitochondrial DNA," *Scientific American* 248 (March 1983), pp. 78-89.
20. Note that this suggestion provides no help in the case of non-organic artificial body parts. Samuel Wheeler III argues that any kind of attachment is unnecessary for moral rights to a bodily part. See Wheeler, *op. cit.*, pp. 176-178.
21. Gould, *op. cit.*, p. 22.
22. Note that on this criterion, the fetus's body is just as much an extension of the mother's body as her body is of the fetus's. Her rights to its body would be equivalent to its rights to hers.
23. Gould, *op. cit.*, p. 20.
24. Note the somewhat bizarre implications of the "substantial organic connection" thesis for abortion policy: as the fetus acquires more and more fully developed organs as the pregnancy continues, its organic connection with its mother decreases, so that the claim her body is part of the fetus's body decreases, and the fetus's moral claim to the use of her body decreases (and, presumably, abortion becomes *more* acceptable) in late pregnancy. Normally we suppose late abortions are *less* acceptable.
25. As Robert Cummins has pointed out to me, the more plausible it is to view the fetus as a person (as it develops in later pregnancy), the *less* plausible it is to view the mother's body as an extension of the fetus's body, since the latter body becomes more and more complete and self-sufficient. On the other hand, the more plausible it is to view the mother's body as an extension of the fetus (in early pregnancy), the less plausible it is to view the fetus as a person. So even a decision that the mother's body does count as an extension of the fetus's body, say in early pregnancy, would tend to be associated with a concurrent denial that the fetus is a person with any rights.
26. Wicclair, *op. cit.*, p. 341. A similar idea has been proposed independently by Jim Stone, *op. cit.*, pp. 82-83, and by Harry Silverstein, *op. cit.*, p. 115. However, both these authors propose direct moral theses concerning the fetus's rights to use of its mother's body, on grounds that such use is part of the natural and normal course of human development, without any intermediate thesis that the mother's body is (factually) a part of the fetus's body. Hence I shall not directly discuss their theses here.
27. It might be claimed that the case of flowers and insects is not apt, since the floral structures have evolved to benefit the insects but ultimately to serve the flower itself through dispersion of its pollen. But better cases of unqualified altruism could be adduced to make the same point. For example, when the antelope flashes its white tail to warn other herd members of danger, we do not conclude that the tail belongs to the other herd members.
28. Wicclair, *op. cit.*, p. 345, note 2.
29. Stephen Jay Gould, *Hen's Teeth and Horse's Toes* (New York: W.W. Norton and Company, 1983), Chapter 1. Gould himself denies the male is a parasite (although most accounts refer to it as such), since he holds that parasites must injure their hosts.
30. J.F.A. Sprent, *Parasitism* (London: Bailliere Tindall and Cox, 1963), pp. vii.
31. See P.C.C. Garnham, *Progress in Parasitology* (The University of London, The

Athlone Press, 1981), p. 91; and R. Alan Wilson, *An Introduction to Parasitology* (New York: St. Martin's Press, 1967), Preface.

32. Stephen Jay Gould, *Ever Since Darwin* (New York: W.W. Norton and Company, 1977), pp. 91-92.

33. Sprent, *op. cit.*, p. 31.

34. Samuel Wheeler III, *op. cit.*, pp. 187-189.

35. The artificiality of deriving a right to one's body from the other rights mentioned in the text suggests to me that the derivation may be proceeding in the wrong direction: perhaps our right to our bodies is fundamental, while our rights to be free from pain, experience pleasure, and so forth, derive from that right.

36. Unfortunately there are disanalogies between the rope case and the hand case that prevent them from providing fully decisive arguments here. Your life depends on the rope only on this rare occasion, so you have no continuing right to the rope, whereas (arguably) your life depends on your hand on many occasions, so your right to your hand continues (albeit intermittently). Cutting the rope only results in your death, so your right to the rope only derives from your right to life; whereas cutting your hand results in significant (if brief) pain, so your right not to have the hand cut also results from your right not to be in pain.

37. Note that on this view, the fetus's right to its mother's body will fade at the time of viability (since it no longer needs to use its mother's body in order to maintain its own life). Thus "abortion" in late term would be morally permissible even though earlier abortion might not be. This consequence might depend on the availability of artificial support systems for use in providing the fetus with whatever it needs to survive. This is another example of a case in which pinning the moral status of abortion on the fetus's natural right to its mother's body gives us a moral result very different from the one many people assume is correct.

38. In conversation.

39. In *Regina v. Dudley and Stephens*.

40. Part of Judith Jarvis Thomson's discussion in "Killing, Letting Die, and the Trolley Problem" is relevant to this point. See Chapter 6 in Judith Jarvis Thomson, *Rights, Restitution, and Risk*, ed. William Parent (Cambridge, Massachusetts: Harvard University Press, 1986).

41. One prominent suggestion must be dealt with differently. Some theorists have wanted to view the right to freedom of action as the basis for all other rights, or at least the right to one's body. But this suggestion is of little help. To see why, notice that one can distinguish three different types of actions: mental actions, basic actions, and non-basic actions. The right to perform mental actions (such as making decisions or choices), provides no support for rights to one's body. One has the right to desire, and even decide to do, many things, without having the right to carry out those desires or decisions. On the other hand, the right to perform non-basic actions (such as the right to open a door) might be thought to entail the right to control any objects, such as one's body, involved in the doing of those actions. But this would place one's right to one's body on the same footing as one's right to external objects involved in the action, such as the door itself. Hence this would not form a derivation for the sort of right to one's body we want. Finally, the right to perform basic actions just *is* one aspect of the right to one's body, so we cannot say that the bodily right is *derived from* the right to perform basic actions. For discussion by theorists who have suggested the right to free action as the basis for other rights, see Wheeler, *ibid.*; H.L.A. Hart, "Are There Any Natural Rights?" in David Lyons, ed., *Rights* (Belmont, Ca.: Wadsworth Publishing Co., 1979), pp 14-25; and Jan Narveson, *The Libertarian Idea*

(Philadelphia: Temple University Press, 1988).

42. I am grateful to Marcia Baron, Stephen R. Munzer, and Harry Silverstein for helpful comments on earlier versions of this paper.

Philosophical Perspectives, 6, Ethics, 1992

NONMORAL EXPLANATIONS

Nicholas L. Sturgeon
Cornell University

Moral explanations of nonmoral facts, including moral explanations of our holding the moral views we do, often look plausible. But so do nonmoral explanations of the very same facts. My aim here is to pursue farther than I have elsewhere the question of what difference this makes.[1]

I

Nonmoral explanations sometimes strike us as undermining moral ones. For example, the thesis that moral condemnation of homosexuality is just due to the condemner's unacknowledged fears about his or her own sexual identity seems to undermine any suggestion that the judgment is due to there being anything really wrong with homosexuality—a point perhaps implicitly acknowledged by friends of the latter explanation in their uniform rejection of the former. So one question is whether nonmoral explanations always undermine moral explanations in this way. The answer, I believe, is no. Consider another explanation easily read as an undermining one. David Donald has maintained, in a study of the militant abolitionism that emerged suddenly in the United States of the 1830's, that "it was the reaction of a class whose leadership had been discarded." The abolitionist leaders came primarily from a former New England professional elite displaced by such social changes as industrialization, and their "abolitionism should be considered the anguished protest of an aggrieved class against a world they never made." So, on this account, the evil of slavery played no role in explaining why they thought it an evil.[2] But if this explanation undermines a moral one, it does not do so simply in virtue of being nonmoral. For contrast it with another possible explanation, equally nonmoral, of someone's coming to think slavery a great evil. This time, let us suppose, our abolitionist notices, as she had not before, that slaves are fully as human as she, subject to the same hopes, affections and vulnerabilities; that slavery is a source of immense and avoidable misery to them; that slavery prevents them from realizing capacities for self-development and self-respect that they in fact have; that it encourages in the (male) master class tendencies towards cruelty, arrogance and massive self-deception, dispositions not then easily confined to relations with slaves; and that this last is only one among many reasons that slavery is incompatible with democracy, even democracy among those not enslaved.[3] This second explanation is hardly an undermining one. Indeed, if it were in question whether a particular abolitionist's opposition to slavery was actually due to the evil of that institution, it would be as natural to take a nonmoral explanation of this latter sort to support an affirmative answer as it would to take a nonmoral explanation in Donald's style to support a negative one. Nonmoral explanations do not always compete with moral ones, and as often *corroborate* as *undermine* them.[4] The point can be seen, in fact, even in my initial example. If one's judgment that homosexuality is wrong is due just to fears about one's own sexual identity, then it isn't due to anything really wrong with homosexuality; but, plausibly, it *is* then due to a moral flaw in oneself, that of letting one's judgments be influenced by such feelings. Our nonmoral explanation undermines one moral explanation, the one that would explain the judgment by its approximate truth; but it does not conflict with, and even appears to support, a different moral explanation of why the judgment is made.

Nonmoral explanations also often stand in another important relation to moral ones which they do not undermine and may or may not support. For lack of a better term I shall say that these explanations *amplify* the moral ones. There are cases in which we are at least provisionally more confident of the truth of a moral explanation than we are of any precise view about which nonmoral facts the explanatory moral fact supervenes on or consists in; and we appeal to nonmoral explanations of the same explanandum to help settle this question. This can happen when it is central to our idea of a moral quality—as it is, I believe, to our idea of the virtues, individual and social—that it play a certain causal role. If we expect social justice to be a condition that will stabilize a society in normal circumstances, and without undue reliance on deceit or coercion, then we can test competing conceptions of justice by investigating the (nonmoral) question of which conditions will have this effect, and amplify our provisional moral explanation accordingly.[5] It can also happen when we trust someone's moral judgment, assuming that the explanation of his thinking some act wrong is probably that it *is* wrong. Investigation of his standards—that is, of the nonmoral determinants of his judgment—may then shape or reshape our own. This may sound like a situation in which no philosopher of a skeptical temper would ever find herself. In fact, it appears to be the situation of anyone whose arguments in normative ethics appeal at any point to the moral judgments, at any level of generality, that we do or would make under favorable and (as we think) nondistorting conditions—that is, of just about everyone who debates normative ethics. For the relevance of this appeal looks to depend on the assumption that it is under these conditions that our judgments stand the best chance of being explained by their approximate truth, thus making an investigation into their nonmoral grounds a reasonable guide to moral theory.[6]

Interesting complications are possible. We may start out looking for an amplifying explanation and find instead only an undermining one, one that undercuts our initial moral explanation. And there can be disagreement about whether this has happened. I can illustrate with one of Gilbert Harman's arguments for his relativism about "inner judgments" (Harman 1975, 12-13; 1977, pp. 110-11; 1980, p. 114). According to this thesis certain moral judgments ascribe to agents reasons they have in virtue of practical conventions they accept, conventions that typically result from implicit bargaining. On behalf of this thesis, Harman argues that it provides the only reasonable explanation of our common view that duties not to harm are more stringent than duties to aid, a view that would otherwise seem "irrational and unmotivated" (Harman 1977, p. 111). The explanation is that (1) our moral judgments are sensitive to the actual practical conventions to which agents subscribe; and (2) that it is predictable that such conventions place a higher priority on not harming than on bringing aid. This is predictable because the conventions are a compromise among people who vary greatly in power and wealth. The strong and wealthy have much to lose and little to gain from a strong principle requiring mutual aid; but the poor and weak, who would benefit greatly from such a principle, might refuse to agree even to refraining from harm, which benefits all, unless there were some commitment to aid. The result is the mixed convention we have and the moral judgments that reflect it.

I can see no way of making sense of Harman's argument as an argument *for his relativism* unless he is presenting it as what I have called an amplifying explanation, the use of a nonmoral explanation to fill in a moral one. He begins, on this understanding, with the assumption that our common moral judgments about aid and harm are well-founded, caused by the very facts that make them true; he then proposes his nonmoral explanation for these judgments, that they are responsive to a practical convention that has the structure it does because it has emerged in the way he describes; and he concludes that the existence of conventions that agents accept is all that makes such judgments true—that is, that his relativism is correct.[7] My own view of his accomplishment, however, is quite different. I do not know whether he is right that his is the only reasonable explanation for our common view. But if it is, then that view looks to me to be in serious trouble.[8] If our according greater moral weight to duties not to harm than to duties to aid is really nothing but the influence on us of a convention that reflects the much stronger bargaining position of the rich and powerful, an advantage they have for no morally relevant reason, then our belief appears to me no more to be shaped by moral facts than are the beliefs of Donald's abolitionists. In short, Harman's explanation looks to me like an undermining explanation rather than an amplifying one.

This example naturally raises the question of how we decide when nonmoral explanations conflict with, or support or amplify moral ones. The answer, I believe, is that abstractly the procedure is no different from that used in answering similar questions about chemical and biological explanations, or about psychological and sociological ones. Conflict between explanations is virtually never a matter of outright contradiction. We locate such conflict, rather, when against a background of theoretical assumptions we accept about the fields in question we find it hard or impossible to see how both explanations could be true. (And we see one explanation as supporting another, similarly, when on these same assumptions the truth of the one makes the other more likely.) All that is special about the moral case is that some of these background assumptions will have to be about morality. Donald's explanation appears to us to conflict with one ascribing moral insight to the abolitionists because, on our moral views, we can see no way in which the cause cited, the displacement of a certain New England elite, was either a part or a symptom of the evil of slavery; whereas we can easily see this about the nonmoral features cited in the contrasting, more flattering explanation that I mentioned. If two people differ in their assumptions about morality, therefore, they may differ also about the relation of nonmoral to moral explanations. That appears to have happened to Harman and me. I see a conflict between explanations where he sees none, because we bring to the assessment different pictures of what moral facts could be like.

This conclusion will disappoint anyone who hoped to find in our judgments about the relation of nonmoral to moral explanations an entirely independent, unassailable foundation for moral theory. There is no such foundation, here or anywhere else. Even so, our intuitions about such questions often do provide an important purchase in argument, that may contribute to resolving disputes. As an example, someone who has read Mackie 1977 may find himself initially convinced that real moral facts would have to be very special, guaranteed to influence the will of any rational being who is aware of them. If he also thinks (as Mackie does, and I do) that no natural facts could be like this, he will be committed to the conclusion that any fully naturalistic, nonmoral explanation of a moral belief must be an undermining one: it will display a moral belief as caused entirely by facts of a sort that could not possibly constitute moral facts. He may find this conclusion less plausible when he looks at its applications, however. He may for example agree that my second imagined nonmoral explanation of moral opposition to slavery seems to support rather than undermine the view that the opposition was due to slavery's really being an evil. And this agreement may continue—I find it often does—even if we add that slavery had, in addition to the natural features cited, no magic ones such as Mackie describes. If so, then someone initially persuaded by Mackie's view may be convinced to adopt a less extravagant general conception of what moral facts would have to be like. In this way confident views about the relation of particular nonmoral to moral explanations may help shape our general theories, even if those theories also shape them in return.

(Since Mackie's thesis is a metaethical one, this example illustrates another point worth noting. Reasoning in metaethics, as much as in normative ethics, typically involves moving dialectically in this way between plausible general theses and plausible views about cases, seeking a reflective equilibrium. Those philosophers who are confident that this procedure can yield nothing objective in normative ethics should ask themselves, therefore, whether they are prepared to draw the same conclusion about metaethics. They should especially wonder, perhaps, whether they are prepared to apply this conclusion to their own thesis, itself metaethical.)

II

Not all nonmoral explanations appear to undermine moral ones, then. But some do, and that leaves open one further troubling possibility, to which I shall turn for the remainder of my discussion. For the doubts that some philosophers have about moral explanations would not be allayed, I suspect, by the observation that many nonmoral explanations, viewed locally, appear to support or amplify moral ones. Their concern is more global and foundational. They appeal to some plausible, comprehensive naturalistic explanation, not just of this or that moral judgment but of our moral thought as a whole; and this most basic explanation they see as an undermining one. There are suggestions of such a view in Marx, Nietzsche, Freud and, if not Darwin, then in some Darwinists. Local nonmoral explanations appear to corroborate or amplify moral ones, on this view, only because they are incomplete; as they are filled in they will be seen to conflict with moral explanations, whose plausibility will then vanish.

Doctrines of this sort appear to support skepticism not just about moral explanations but about all our moral views. When we become convinced, about a particular moral view, that the only possible explanation of it would undermine any that explained it by appealing to its truth, we seem to be required to reject not just the undermined explanation but also the view itself—for we cannot see ourselves in any instance as holding it because it is true. Many of us think, for example, that the only plausible explanations available for anyone's thinking homosexuality immoral are undermining ones of this sort (even if more complex than the stereotype mentioned above), and see this as undermining the view itself, not just moral explanations of it. Or, again, if Harman is right that his is the only plausible explanation of our views about aiding and not harming, and if I am right that his is an undermining explanation, then the consequence appears to be (as I indicated) that the view itself is discredited along with any moral explanations of it. So any convincing story that undermined *all* moral explanations would appear to have achieved a triumph for moral skepticism. We might find for psychological reasons that we could not abandon moral thought entirely as we might a particular judgment, but it would be hard to see this inability as a vindication against the undermining challenge.

There are too many proposals of this latter sort for me to canvass all of them. I shall focus on a suggestion that has been advanced by a number of writers over the last decade, that plausible Darwinian explanations of our moral faculties undermine moral explanations of their exercise and so cut against moral realism. The suggestions have been diverse and often hard to pin down.[9] Sometimes they appear to mean only that Darwinism supports metaphysical naturalism (as I agree) and that naturalism in turn leaves no room for objective moral properties. I believe that this latter assumption has been dealt with adequately elsewhere.[10] But often the appeal is to more specific hypotheses about the origins of moral thought, motivation and language, some of which merit attention. I shall consider one of the clearest and most carefully worked out, by Allan Gibbard. Gibbard takes his story to yield "a kind of noncognitivism" (Gibbard 1982, p. 43), a view according to which (a) moral discourse serves merely to express sentiments rather than moral beliefs, and (b) moral thoughts represent no real uniform sort of fact. Since I believe that there are (as I shall explain) objections to (a) that are largely tangential to Gibbard's argument for (b), I shall focus more on his argument for (b), his irrealism. I do not deny that we *could* have evolved, genetically or socially, to use moral language as noncognitivists or irrealists claim, but I shall deny that Gibbard's story supports the conclusion that this has in fact happened. Such difficult issues in metaethics as the choice between realism and irrealism, in my view, depend on details that a general Darwinian outlook leaves quite undetermined.

Some will doubt that noncognitivism in any form is a proper target for my discussion. For Simon Blackburn has recently maintained that "projectivism" (as he calls noncognitivism) can straightforwardly accommodate moral explanations, and can even attribute causal efficacy to moral properties (Blackburn 1991a, 11-13). If this were so, then it would seem that accepting Gibbard's evolutionary story about the origin of our moral faculties should in no way preclude our accepting moral explanations for the same development or for moral judgments we now make; and his story would thus undermine neither moral explanations nor the views themselves. This is not Gibbard's understanding, however. He sees his project as competing with any attempt to explain our moral judgments as detecting moral facts (Gibbard

1990, p. 107). Nor, in fact, can it be Blackburn's understanding. For he, too, argues for noncognitivism, and against moral realism, by claiming that from a suitably naturalistic perspective, one that relies on all we know of ourselves and our place in nature, no plausible explanation of our moral thought (or of anything else) will postulate moral facts or properties.[11] Accommodating moral explanations means, for him, finding a principled way for a noncognitivist to mimic accepting them without actually doing so. I have argued elsewhere that neither Blackburn nor any other noncognitivist has succeeded in this project; but success would not in any case bring noncognitivism any closer to accepting moral explanations.[12]

Gibbard emphasizes that his story about the origins of our sense of justice is "highly speculative" (Gibbard 1982, p. 39) and I agree: I am undoubtedly more suspicious than he of evolutionary stories in this genre. But a story like his *could* be true, and I would not have it thought that the case for moral explanations depends on denying it. So, for the sake of discussion, I shall not challenge its main outlines. I assume that Gibbard's claim is modest in another respect as well. When he describes a recent elaboration of his views as illustrating "how biology could settle whether there are normative facts," I take him to be allowing not only that the biology (which here means: surmises about selection pressures on the psychology of our distant ancestors) is speculative, but also that the moral irrealism follows from the rest of the story, not deductively, but rather with the kind of plausibility characteristic of scientific inference.[13] On this understanding, it will be no objection just to point out that his story leaves it *conceivable* that realism is true. I shall claim much more. What I shall argue is that noncognitivism is implausible for independent reasons, and so is best put aside; that, for the evolutionary environment he is considering, Gibbard's story is *more* plausibly read as a realist than as an irrealist one; that it is *as* easily elaborated to support moral realism as irrealism, when extended to apply to contemporary thought and discourse; and that the evidence for deciding among any of these options will not come from evolutionary biology.

III

Gibbard's story centers on what he calls *bargaining situations*, which surely confronted our ancestors as often as they do us. These are situations in which it helps everyone get what they want for there to be some scheme of cooperation rather than none, but in which there remains a conflict of interest over which cooperative scheme to adopt. On the plausible assumption that in the evolutionary past getting what you wanted would normally also promote your biological fitness, there would have been a selective advantage for psychological capacities and dispositions enabling people to do as well as possible for themselves in these situations. What capacities and dispositions might these have been? Gibbard knows that there are numerous possibilities, but introduces his favored proposal by noting a difficulty with one of the more obvious ones. What is obvious is that this would have been a good time for the evolution of intelligence and conscious self-interest. Smart, self-interested bargainers could then solve these problems using the kind of "high rationality" explored by Thomas Schelling (Schelling 1960): "because of past experience, it is common knowledge that everyone expects a certain outcome, and so everyone insists on that outcome because he expects to benefit by doing so and expects to lose by insisting on more" (1982, p. 36).

The problem with this solution, unsupplemented, according to Gibbard, is that

> purely self-interested bargaining often breaks down: there is too much advantage to be gained from altering expectations in one's favor, and once expectations are confused, it may happen that each party insists on more than he can get. (1982, p. 36)

So he proposes an alternative that involves what he calls "attaching a moral sentiment" to an outcome. What is crucial is mutual knowledge of certain behavioral dispositions.

> Instead of everyone's wanting as much as he can get in a bargaining situation, suppose there is some outcome such that everyone cares very much about getting his share under that outcome, but cares very little, not at all, or even negatively about getting more. Suppose also that each person prefers carrying out his threat to settling for less than his share under that outcome. If these facts are known, the situation will be very stable: there will be no advantage to altering expectations.

"Sentiments" come into the story as emotional dispositions supporting these behavioral ones: "a disposition to be resentful or angry if one gets less than one's share under that outcome, and to be satisfied if that outcome does obtain" (1982, p. 37). Finally, there is a facilitating role for language, with some word used to express this constellation of behavioral and emotional dispositions. The words involved, Gibbard suggests, are "just" and "fair." "To regard something 'as fair,' then, simply is to attach this moral sentiment to it." More precisely, since none of these distant ancestors spoke English, his suggestion is that although there are various possibilities—a theological term might have served—"the words 'just' and 'fair' do the job in our language," and so to that extent translate whatever term served in this evolutionary scenario (1982, p. 38).

This is the heart of Gibbard's proposal. But the story is still indeterminate in a crucial respect, as we can see by considering two more precise versions. For reasons that will become clear, *neither* of these versions can be Gibbard's; but we can learn something important from seeing why, and from seeing how each approximates to his final account.

Story One. There is a property of possible bargaining outcomes that humans are able to detect. What evolved is a tendency to favor, in the manner described, outcomes with that property and to reject others. Humans, being language-users, had a term (which we might translate as "just" or "fair") for this property, and the ability to identify the property linguistically was no doubt essential to the evolution of the tendency to care deeply about it.

Story Two. Humans evolved a tendency to favor, in the manner described, some bargaining outcomes and reject others: not, however, the same outcomes or kinds of outcomes, for some favored one sort of outcome, some another. Being language-users, they naturally had a term (which we might translate as "just" or "fair") for expressing this special sort of favorable attitude, and possession of this term no doubt facilitated the evolution of the attitude itself.

These are both accounts of why humans should have come to care about justice—that is, about what they think of as, and call, just. But they differ strikingly in several respects.

1. The first story is a cognitivist and, potentially, a moral realist one, according to which it is crucial to humans' coming to favor the property they call justice that they be able to detect it and have a term referring to it. (The story is only potentially realist because nothing in it *guarantees* that, when we find out more about the property in question, the story will not strike us as undermining rather than amplifying the suggestion that our ancestors sometimes called bargaining outcomes just because they really were. I have explained how this could happen. On the other hand, there is nothing at all in the story to *preclude* our finding it compatible with, or corroborative of, this moral explanation, either.[14] In a discussion of whether an evolutionary view of human origins supports moral irrealism, the latter of these points seems the salient one: it explains, among other things, why this story *cannot* be the one Gibbard ultimately intends. So I shall, with this much warning, call this story a realist one.) The second story, by contrast, is an explicitly noncognitivist and irrealist one, according to which attributions of justice express attitudes rather than moral beliefs and ascribe no single property to anything. It insures that everyone "cares about justice" only by requiring that the caring form *part* of any state of mind recognizable as the thought that some bargaining outcome is just.[15]

2. The second story is more vulnerable than the first to doubts about whether we would happily translate as "just" or "fair" a term used as the story describes.[16] A general doubt applies equally to both stories, but could largely be met, I shall assume, by supplementing both in an obvious way. For we might be reluctant to accept these translations for terms applied to bargaining outcomes in the ways described, if their application was in no way guided by what we think of as standards of justice or fairness. So assume in both cases that it is so guided.[17] There remains a more specific doubt that

applies to the second story but not the first. I can press it most forcefully by first noting a point easily accommodated, that we apply our term "just" in related ways not only to outcomes and procedures but to institutions and persons. Just institutions are, perhaps, those that embody just procedures and secure just outcomes, and just persons those with the right dispositions to support just procedures, outcomes and institutions. These formulas are too simple, but it is enough that something like them be true. For the problem for the second story is that the justice of persons and of institutions are often appealed to in explanations of their flourishing.[18] The justice of a society, as I noted above, is supposed to stabilize it; and people are alleged to prosper precisely because of their justice. Of course, there is also a tradition that attacks this latter claim as a pious fiction. But the most prominent opposing view also treats justice as explanatory. That justice always pays, and that justice sometimes costs, are both views that cast justice as a property with causal efficacy.

We would not regard as satisfactory, I think, any translation that precluded these claims or debates. As I have remarked, however, noncognitivism must reject all such moral explanations on their straightforward readings, and no one has displayed a satisfactory alternative way for the view to accommodate them. Insofar as the second story is a noncognitivist one, then, I conclude that it would involve a term or family of terms applied expressively to outcomes, procedures, institutions and persons, but never used to frame explanations. I believe that we would not regard any term limited in this way as translating ours.

There is another way to see this point. Recall that Gibbard allows that "a term with theological meaning might do the job" accomplished by the term he proposes to translate as "just" or "fair" (1982, p. 38). So suppose that our ancestors evolved as in Gibbard's story, but came to say of the relevant outcomes not that they were just but that they were favored by the gods. If these gods were then thought to act on this preference, or indeed to do anything at all, then a noncognitivist account of this assertion would be implausible; reference to the gods is here thought to be explanatory, and this assertion about bargaining outcomes is linked to the explanatory network. (Noncognitivist analyses of theological discourse have of course been proposed. But one of their costs has always been that they have to say of much that looks explanatory that it is not—not even *intended* as explanatory, whatever other functions it may fulfill as well.) But ascriptions of justice and injustice fit into an explanatory network, too, and that makes noncognitivist analyses of them implausible as well.

Of course, as a glance at this theological analogy illustrates, this argument for moral cognitivism is not yet an argument for moral realism. I favor a cognitivist stance toward much theological discourse, but I do not believe in any more gods than Gibbard does. So I entirely grant that from the fact that some talk is intended as explanatory it does not follow that the entities or properties it postulates actually exist, or that it fully succeeds in any function but a noncognitive one. But it does follow, I believe, that an irrealist account of such an area must be an error theory, according to which users of the discourse are mistaken about what they are doing and about the world. And an important implication of my argument in this paper is that error theories about morality are harder to defend, from a naturalistic standpoint, than are error theories about theology. Moral explanations often appear supported or amplified, rather than undermined, even by very full naturalistic, nonmoral explanations. Of course, whether they are nevertheless globally undermined by some plausible, and fundamental, naturalistic explanation is the very question I am discussing, and I cannot fully settle it here; but I am arguing that no evolutionary explanation like Gibbard's will have this effect.

The upshot, then, is that if we are to recognize any terms as translatable by our terms "just" and "fair", they or closely connected terms must be put to explanatory use; but in that case the story of their use, even if it is irrealist, must be cognitivist. This applies to my second story but also to any other, including the more elaborate version that serves, for reasons I am about to explain, as Gibbard's final account. So, although Gibbard calls his account noncognitivist, I shall take the live, interesting issue to be, not whether it supports noncognitivism, but whether there is anything in it to favor irrealism over moral realism.

3. A third difference between the two stories is that, of the two, only the first, the realist version, describes a *solution* to the problem of instability that Gibbard thinks evolution might have set out to solve by giving us a sense of justice. The second story, in fact, not only describes no solution, it describes what is surely an exacerbation of the original difficulty. We were to imagine smart, self-interested bargainers who too often upset established expectations by miscalculating and holding out for too much; but now we picture bargainers whose preferences for competing outcomes are driven not just by self-interest but by anger and moral indignation at those who disagree. We have replaced competing egoists with competing fanatics, and that is no recipe for peace.

Gibbard knows this. "If different people attach their moral sentiments to different outcomes...bargaining can break down in ways much more intractable than in rationally self-interested bargaining" (1982, p. 38). That is why neither of these two stories can be his. The first is ruled out because it is realist, the second because, though irrealist, it provides no solution to the evolutionary problem. To get moral irrealism out of evolution, therefore, he needs a more elaborate version of the second story, which he provides by suggesting a more complex role for moral language. His suggestion is, he admits, schematic (1982, p. 39), and we shall see that it requires interpretation. The requirement is for "a mechanism for adjusting the objects of moral sentiments to make them compatible. That mechanism could be provided by language and the workings of small group consensus which language makes possible" (1982, p. 38). People may start out with conflicting views about justice, and so with emotional and behavioral dispositions attached to incompatible outcomes. But if they had also evolved a tendency to discuss issues of justice with others, and to adjust their views in discussion in the direction of consensus, then this whole package of psychological dispositions would have provided a solution to the evolutionary problem after all.

This is, I believe, a fair statement of Gibbard's considered proposal. But it still leaves some questions we need to settle. The main problem is that it is still not clear how the proposal will serve his philosophical purposes. For either these discussions normally produce agreement about what is just or they do not. If not, then we still have no solution to the evolutionary problem. But if they do, then we are entitled to wonder why Gibbard's story is not just an elaborate version of realism: that is, why it has not now become a version of my first story rather than just my second. If the problem is not apparent, consider that the most common and persuasive argument against moral realism is an argument from disagreement. Many disagreements about justice and other moral issues are, it is claimed, too deep to be rationally resolvable; irrealism would explain why. But Gibbard's story requires that, in the evolutionary environment he is considering, disputes about the justice of bargaining procedures and outcomes have been not just resolvable but regularly *resolved*. So it doesn't sound like a story that would support irrealism. If people who have come to care about justice are also able to resolve disputes about it, why doesn't this mean that they are, in those discussions, referring to a real property that they care about, and about which their views are often correct?

Gibbard does not address this question as I have framed it. This may be partly because he overlooks the possibility that achieving consensus in debate might be a way, in this case even an especially appropriate way, of detecting a property.[19] It can be. Consensus among experts is often an indicator of at least approximate truth on many topics, and if moral expertise is as widely shared (on ordinary cases, and barring special distorting factors) as many think, then on these issues a broad consensus should count for something. Justice seems a special case even among moral properties, moreover. Notice the sort of property, if there were such a property, that it would be. On any plausible account it will involve balancing the competing interests of different parties; and the parties will be ones who (1) know that respect for justice is a shared motive of some importance, but who (2) are also strongly concerned about their individual interests. A familiar consequence is that they will all (3) have a standing motive for seeing the requirements of justice as favoring their own case more than they actually do. If there really were such a property, therefore, and if human beings were to evolve, either genetically or socially, a strategy for countering these predictable biases and determining where it really lies, it is hard to see how they could do much better than to aim at consensus in a debate in which all the competing interests are represented.[20] That is another reason why Gibbard's story, according to which natural selection has got us to do just that, looks like one a realist might tell. We still need to know how it is supposed to support irrealism.

The answer appears to be that Gibbard is relying on an assumption about what would solve his evolutionary problem that he barely states, and that looks implausible once it is made explicit. He notes quite correctly that what is essential to preventing destructive conflict in bargaining situations is just that for (almost) every such situation there be a resolution, based on some agreed standard or other. What he assumes is that this solution could obtain, stably and over time, without there being any single set of standards, however abstract, on which the members of a population (usually) agree, however implicitly, and which they bring to bear to resolve individual cases. That is why he emphasizes the usefulness of language in achieving "*small group* consensus" (1982, p. 38, emphasis added), and says that although his story "predicts a strong concern for justice and substantial small group consensus on what is just," it nevertheless "offers no reason for expecting that the same standards will direct the sense of justice in all people" (1982, p. 39). There is no single property being detected and referred to in people's discussions of justice, as they regularly resolve disputes about it, because the resolutions are merely piecemeal.

This story is logically possible. But I believe that it is not very plausible, for a couple of reasons that depend on things we know about human psychology. One is that any individual will be party to different disputes, and human psychology does not seem flexible enough for A to have a strong emotional attachment to ranking, say, effort over output in her dispute with B, but output over effort in her dispute with C, unless she can see both rankings as the application of some reasonable but more abstract principle to differing circumstances.[21] The other depends on another interesting feature of our sense of justice, one for which Gibbard admits that his basic story provides no explanation, though various emendations might serve (1982, p. 39). This is that we are often deeply concerned about injustice among third parties, including strangers. So it will not guarantee peace simply for A and B to resolve their dispute by mutually agreed standards, if C regards their standards as unfair to one of them and is prepared to intervene.[22] These are features of our current psychology; it is conceivable that they were different in the past. But unless they were, it seems to me quite unlikely that our moral emotions could have evolved as Gibbard suggests, for their advantage in stabilizing bargaining, except in a population that was at the same time coming to have (mostly) shared standards of justice. So the story still sounds realist, in its most plausible version. It explains why people would come to care about a complex social property they call justice, at the same time that they are learning to identify it through discussion and debate.

IV

Must anyone who accepts Gibbard's story be a moral realist, then? No. It is not hard to extend his story to support irrealism, by taking advantage of a familiar point: that Darwinian solutions do not foresee future environments, and that the human social environment, since the advent of agriculture, has changed far too rapidly for natural selection to keep pace. It might be, for example, that human beings evolved standards tolerably sufficient for picking out a single outcome in the sorts of bargaining situations that confront hunter-gatherers, but that these same standards proved woefully inadequate in more complex societies. Different cultures and individuals, on this story, have developed supplementary but conflicting standards, so hopelessly diverse that their talk of justice fastens on no one property. Attempts to reach consensus often fail, so the evolutionary solution Gibbard describes has broken down.[23] It could be, as Gibbard seems inclined to maintain, that through these differences there remains a constant, intrinsic emotional attachment to whatever one *regards* as just; or it might be allowed, I think more plausibly, that among the conceptions of justice are some (think of Marx, or Thrasymachus, or just of what Glaucon and Adeimantus offer as "what people consider the nature and origin of justice" to be (*Republic*, 358b)) that would undermine most people's commitment to it for its own sake, while leaving room for some to have an instrumental concern for it. Either way, thought and talk of justice would have no determinate reference, nothing to divide truth from falsehood in any of the pervasive and interesting disagreements about it. So the indicated metaethic would be irrealist.

It is just as easy, however, to tell a more optimistic story. Gibbard's evolutionary solution has broken down: the pervasiveness of unresolved disputes about justice establishes that. But perhaps we are nevertheless left with the resources for resolving most of them. The varying conceptions of justice that have arisen may have been sufficiently shaped by the commonalities of human life to make this much true: (1) that under the pressure of rational argument and with adequate nonmoral information, these varying conceptions would mostly agree in their application to actual cases, however much they continued to disagree about mere thought-experiments, and (2) what makes this so is that, in the actual world, the different features to which these conceptions attach importance stand in relations of mutual causal support.[24] (Thus, to illustrate, the idea would be that the sort of equal liberty that proponents, after sufficient argument, would agree is worth valuing, and the sort of equality in other respects that others would likewise defend, prove each in fact sustainable only with a good measure of the other. And so with other goods.) We may add that this conception of justice would probably strengthen rather than undermine most people's intrinsic attachment to it. If all this were so, then the best account of moral thought and talk would be what I and many others regard as a realist one.

As an account of our current situation I incline to the second, realist story. Many readers will strongly disagree. The only point about the disagreement that I mean to establish here, however, is that Gibbard's account of the evolution of our moral sentiments—itself speculative, but accepted here for the sake of discussion—does *nothing whatever* to favor the first, irrealist extension of his story over the second, realist one. Evidence in this argument will have to come from the sources from which it has always been drawn: from our experience of what moral argument can accomplish, and of how human social systems work. Gibbard's story seems neutral between the two possibilities. If we were pressed to find *some* asymmetry in its relation to the two extended stories, however, so as to let it suggest a working hypothesis, then we might note that it is the second story rather than the first that preserves the realism implicit (I have argued) in Gibbard's own, for the environment that it deals with.

As I explained, I have selected Gibbard's story for this detailed examination because it is by far the clearest and most carefully worked out of the accounts that begin with an evolutionary story about our moral sentiments and conclude with an irrealist view of moral thought and discourse. If it shows no clear path along which evolutionary considerations should steer us from the former toward the latter, we may reasonably doubt that there is any to be found. Although I have not argued the point, I should record that I find Gibbard's story typical in a broader respect as well. When historical and contemporary evidence leaves room for serious debate about aspects of human psychology (including ones that would underlie possible cognitive relations to moral facts), evolutionary speculation is unlikely to contribute much, if anything, to resolving the issues. To the question whether biology matters to ethics, my reply is that *psychology* matters a great deal to both metaethics and normative ethics: not because ethical positions can be deduced from psychological ones, but because in the sort of dialectical argument characteristic of both metaethics and normative ethics, psychological premises significantly restrict the conclusions we can find plausible. Biology will matter in turn if it helps us learn about psychology.[25] Although our basic psychological makeup is an evolved one, however, what we know of our evolutionary history is so sketchy, and evolutionary theory is so flexible, that together they provide almost no basis for settling debates among what we already knew were the reasonable options about how humans have turned out.[26] The more promising disciplines on these issues are history, anthropology, sociology and, of course, psychology itself.

My conclusion comes in two parts, then, one confident, the other more tentative. What I am sure of is that, viewed locally, nonmoral explanations do not always appear to undermine moral ones. They often corroborate them instead; and their role in amplifying moral explanations is central to much philosophical argument in moral theory. About whether there nevertheless remains some basic and convincing naturalistic explanation that will undermine moral explanations globally, I am more tentative because I have not surveyed all the candidates. But I take my discussion of Gibbard to have shown that nothing we know of our evolutionary history supplies such an explanation, or makes moral irrealism any more plausible than the moral realism I am prepared to defend.

Notes

1. I have touched on this issue in Sturgeon 1985, 1986, 1991.
2. Donald 1956, pp. 31, 36. A careful reading suggests that Donald does not see his explanation as undermining entirely one that imputes moral insight: he says that his aim is to explain why a longstanding evil was only then *recognized* (p. 22). And it is important to notice that it is actually rather difficult to construct *completely* undermining explanations, that are at all plausible, for moral judgments that seem obviously correct (Sturgeon 1985, p. 76, n. 23). Even if the abolitionists attacked slavery only (unconsciously) to have a pretext for expressing anger about something else, for example, there is the question why they found this a plausible pretext. Perhaps only because they sensed that some of their audience would, but then why was that so? So long as our explanation leaves open the possibility that the evil of slavery accounts in some measure for any of these things, it is not completely undermining. Still, without being certain of the truth of the matter, I shall assume that with imagination one could construct, under Donald's inspiration, a story that would make the actual wrongness of slavery entirely irrelevant to the explanation of these abolitionists' thinking it wrong.
3. A list compiled from accounts opponents of slavery themselves gave of factors moving them. For a recent study attributing considerable truth to these allegations, including the last two (which were politically very important), see Freehling 1990.
4. For complementary suggestions see Miller 1985, 526-29. I have benefitted from Miller's discussion of the topic of this paragraph, on which I touched only tangentially in Sturgeon 1985.
5. See Sturgeon 1991, 27-30. John Rawls argues (Rawls 1971, Sec. 76) that, given certain psychological assumptions, a society just by his standards would be significantly more stable than one just by utilitarian standards. (This is not merely a claim about the effects of the society's being *thought* just, for that factor is held constant in the comparison.) He does not offer this as one of the "main grounds" favoring his view, but does regard it as helping to rebut possible doubts.
6. See Sturgeon 1986. Of course, this is not the description that all philosophers give of their method. R. M. Hare, for example, denies any "probative" force to ordinary moral judgments, no matter how carefully filtered (Hare 1981). There is some irony, therefore, in the fact that Hare's argument for utilitarianism from first principles (about the meanings of some moral and psychological expressions) appears to have convinced almost no one, whereas his (and, to be fair, others') resourceful deployment of a "two-level" strategy, to show how utilitarianism can accommodate many ordinary judgments apparently unfavorable to it, has contributed importantly to keeping that view among those taken seriously.

7. Two caveats. (1) First, Harman's view is that a "full-fledged" inner judgment not only states a proposition capable of truth or falsity but also expresses the speaker's endorsement of the agent's reasons. This latter feature he appears in fact to treat as no more than a kind of cancelable implicature, since the same words can be used just to state the proposition if one indicates appropriately that the endorsement is absent (Harman 1975, 8-11). If it is supposed to be more integral to the judgment than that, however, then the assumption I attribute to him must be, more precisely, that our common moral judgment, *insofar* as it is capable of truth, is caused by whatever facts make it true; and his relativistic conclusion is that what makes such judgments true, *insofar* as they are capable of truth, is just the agent's acceptance of the relevant convention. (2) Harman of course does not *say* that his argument rests on initial acceptance of a moral explanation for our moral belief; but I claim that there is no way of getting from his explicit premise—his nonmoral explanation of our belief—to his relativism, without relying on this additional assumption. Whether I am right matters to another disagreement between Harman and me. He has argued in criticism of my views that a philosophical naturalist will rely on moral explanations only *after* establishing a naturalistic reduction for moral judgments (Harman 1986, 63-66). I have argued in reply that there is no way to establish any naturalistic reduction without accepting some moral explanations to start with (Sturgeon 1986). If the reading I suggest here is correct, then Harman's practice fits my view rather than his. For his relativism *is* his favored reduction for "inner judgments"; but his argument for the reduction rests partly on the assumption that the explanation of our thinking duties not to harm more stringent, is that they are.

8. As others have alleged on different grounds: see, for example, Glover 1977, pp. 92-112.

9. See, for example, Murphy 1982 and Ruse 1986. Neither of these writers even mentions the sort of ethical naturalism that I and a number of others have defended, according to which moral terms refer to natural properties that matter to us because of their role in human life; so neither explains how evolution would undermine this thesis. Simon Blackburn does address this view by implication in Blackburn 1988, arguing that philosophical naturalism "demands" his projectivist, noncognitivist view of ethics partly because "only if values are intrinsically motivating, is a natural story of their [evolutionary] emergence possible" (p. 363). But Blackburn defends this claim with only one example, concerning the evolution of cooperation: "Evolutionary success may attend the animal that helps those that have helped it, but it would not attend an allegedly possible animal that thinks it ought to help but does not." It is easy to think of examples that appear to cut in the opposite direction. The ability to tell, of unfamiliar people, whether they have a morally decent attitude toward strangers, can be a matter of life and death. And if morality is even in part (as Blackburn's example suggests) a system of cooperation for mutual advantage, it is not hard to say why knowledge of what it requires would be useful even if not intrinsically motivating: Glaucon and Adeimantus provide part of the explanation in *Republic* II, Hobbes and Hume the rest. On all these issues Allan Gibbard's metaethical conclusions are similar to these authors', but his argument is more patient and detailed.

10. See Sturgeon 1985, Brink 1989, Boyd 1988, Railton 1986, among others; also my comments, above, on Mackie.

11. "The projectivist holds that our nature as moralists is well explained by regarding us as reacting to a reality which contains nothing in the way of values, duties,

rights and so forth;..." "Moral 'states of affairs,' above all, play no role in causing or explaining our attitudes, their consequences, their importance to us." (Blackburn 1981, pp. 164-65, 185-86) Compare Blackburn 1984, pp. 256-57, and Blackburn 1988, p. 370.

12. Sturgeon 1991, 27-33. In response, Blackburn has objected that he does not "deny outright" that there are moral properties or that events occur because objects possess these properties: these are things he denies when he *starts out*, but nevertheless *ends up* allowing himself to say (Blackburn 1991b, 41-42). Presumably, however, he does not end up *contradicting* what he says at the outset, for that would be to withdraw his opposition to realism. So I take the claims affirmed at the end to mean something different from the ones denied at the beginning—an interpretation confirmed by his ever-more-elaborate searches for something acceptable to a noncognitivist that these affirmations *could* mean. That leaves the initial denials standing, outright and robust.

Will noncognitivism's rejection of moral explanations for our moral views undermine the views themselves, as I have suggested? I believe so, but this thesis, too, will be sharply contested by Blackburn and others, and the issue is too complex to pursue here. (Gibbard discusses it in Gibbard 1990, pp. 153-250.) My argument here is just that the moral explanations are not undermined.

13. Gibbard 1990, p. 107. In Gibbard 1982, Gibbard considers only judgments of justice or fairness (mostly interchangeably, as I shall; but see his n. 5). His view there would be consistent with a different treatment of other moral judgments. But in Gibbard 1990 the argument is generalized. The conclusion is also more complex. Though judgments of justice are not specifically mentioned, he would now presumably treat them as expressing norms one accepts about emotions directed towards actions or outcomes, rather than the emotions themselves, for example. Despite the greater scope and subtlety of the more recent discussion, I believe that the most general points I make about the earlier discussion will also apply to it. Consideration of its positive proposals and rich detail will have to await another occasion.

14. I here assume the conclusion of the arguments cited in note 10, that the property is not precluded from being moral merely by its being natural.

15. Strictly, the second story does not have to be noncognitivist. As stated, it leaves the possibility that attributions of justice are belief-stating but ambiguous, in that different speakers use them to attribute different properties, perhaps without realizing that this is so. This option is usually held by noncognitivists to conflict with intuitions about univocality. I think that some of these intuitions are challengeable and that this relativist view deserves a serious hearing, but I follow Gibbard in ignoring it here.

16. Gibbard does not claim that the term would have to be a good translation of "just" or "fair"; he thinks his example of a theological term would not (1982, p. 38). But he appears to think that any term that *merely* served this function, without importing additional meaning, would translate ours; I deny this. He also clearly thinks that *some* term that played the role described could be translated by ours; but my second doubt, especially, is about whether *any* term that functioned as the second story describes could be a translation of ours.

17. This assumption ought not to appear to noncognitivists and other irrealists to rule out the second story: for since they regard our current standards as insufficient to settle disputes about justice, they should allow that they might also have been insufficient in our ancestors' environment. On the other hand, this assumption goes some way to support the reading of the first story as a genuinely realist

one, though without, I concede, guaranteeing this interpretation.

The most obvious omission in Gibbard's schematic story is any explicit reference to fair *procedures* rather than outcomes. For we judge, and care about, the fairness of procedures not only when we view them as determining that of outcomes but when we do not (that is, in cases of what Rawls (1971, pp. 84-86) calls perfect and imperfect procedural justice, as well as pure procedural justice). I doubt that we would recognize a notion of justice that attached no importance to procedures; Gibbard might allow this if, as I suspect, he is using "outcome" broadly.

18. So is the justice of outcomes, like any other moral property, thought to explain something: why, under proper conditions, people think them just. I find it fatal to noncognitivism to fail to accommodate explanations of this sort, moreover, for they are, I have argued, central to our reasoning about ethics. But many noncognitivists, I discover, remain convinced that these explanations are peripheral to moral thinking, that it can somehow be reconstrued so as not to rely on them. Hence my emphasis here on other explanations that are obviously not peripheral.

19. Our sense of justice might be responding to a single real property, he allows, were we genetically programmed to possess "moral sentiments which are rigidly directed so as to be compatible: say, toward leaving possessors in possession and the like"; but he objects that this solution "might well be too inflexible to cope with the variety of bargaining situations hunter-gatherers faced" (1982, p. 38). He then presents his own suggestion, that we are programmed to work towards consensus, as an *alternative* to the view that we are responding to a property. The natural first response to his objection, however, is surely that the evolutionary solution would be more flexible if the property to which our sentiments were directed were more abstract; and all the reasonable candidates are, plausibly, properties well detected by debate aiming at consensus.

20. They might also seek the opinion of a disinterested but appropriately informed third party, of course—as they often do.

21. In more recent presentations of his view Gibbard has emphasized that a susceptibility to being pressured towards normative consistency is central to the psychology whose emergence he postulates (1990, pp. 74-75). But more than consistency is at stake in the example, for there is no inconsistency in thinking merely that justice requires one ranking in the one case, a reverse ranking in the other. We seem to care here—as in other intellectual endeavors, any cognitivist will point out—not just about consistency but about explanatory generality, about *why* the different rankings are appropriate.

22. We seem most easily to identify with victims who themselves feel aggrieved; but real life is also full of cases in which we regard people as oppressed despite their having accepted the standards of their oppressors.

23. The adaptive value of a sense of justice as an evolutionarily stable strategy depends, Gibbard says, on this: that "either all will regard the same outcome as fair and settle on it, or language will enable all to reach a consensus on which outcome is fair" (1982, p. 38). But recorded history is full of disputes for which neither disjunct obtains, and in the contemporary world they are commonplace, with moral emotions nevertheless engaged on all sides. Whether this makes a sense of justice now maladaptive would depend on what one is comparing it to; what seems clear is that it could hardly emerge, by the mechanism Gibbard proposes, under contemporary circumstances.

24. For a similar account of moral properties and of many other natural properties, and a naturalistic semantics to fit, see Boyd 1988.

25. Of course it matters in other long-recognized respects, too. Humans are vulnerable to harm from one another; they need food and shelter to survive; that infants take so long to mature requires societies to make some provision for raising them; and more. But crucial to all of the recent philosophical suggestions about the relevance of evolutionary biology to ethics, as to most human sociobiology, are attempts to predict features of human psychology from evolutionary scenarios.

26. Someone asking whether biology matters to ethics might have in mind not evolutionary history but current neurophysiology (though they usually do not). I have no doubt that increasing knowledge of neurophysiology may throw light on some psychological questions related to ethics.

On the relation of evolutionary biology to psychology I draw on many conversations with Richard Boyd, with whom I have for a dozen years jointly taught a course on Darwin, Social Darwinism and Human Sociobiology. We hope to publish a more systematic discussion, which would provide needed qualifications and, of course, argument.

References

Blackburn, S.: 1981, "Reply: Rule-Following and Moral Realism," in Steven Holtzman and Christopher Leich, eds., *Wittgenstein: To Follow a Rule*, London, Routledge and Kegan Paul, pp. 163-187.

Blackburn, S.: 1984, *Spreading the Word*, Oxford, Clarendon Press.

Blackburn, S.: 1988, "How to be an Ethical Antirealist," in Peter A. French, Theodore E. Uehling and Howard K. Wettstein, eds., *Midwest Studies in Philosophy*, Vol. XII, Minneapolis, University of Minnesota Press, pp. 361-76.

Blackburn, S.: 1991a, "Just Causes," *Philosophical Studies* 61, 3-17.

Blackburn, S.: 1991b, "Reply to Sturgeon," *Philosophical Studies* 61, 39-42.

Boyd, R. N.: 1988, "How to be a Moral Realist," in Geoffrey Sayre-McCord, ed., *Essays on Moral Realism*, Ithaca, Cornell University Press, pp. 181-228.

Brink, D. O.: 1989, *Moral Realism and the Foundations of Ethics*, Cambridge, Cambridge University Press.

Donald, D.: 1956, "Toward a Reconsideration of Abolitionists," in *Lincoln Reconsidered*, New York, Viking Books, pp. 19-36.

Freehling, W.: 1990, *The Road to Disunion*, Vol. I, New York, Oxford University Press.

Gibbard, A.: 1982, "Human Evolution and the Sense of Justice," in Peter A. French, Theodore E. Uehling and Howard K. Wettstein, eds., *Midwest Studies in Philosophy*, Vol. VII, Minneapolis, University of Minnesota Press, pp. 31-46.

Gibbard, A.: 1990, *Wise Choices, Apt Feelings*, Cambridge, Harvard University Press.

Glover, J.: 1977, *Causing Death and Saving Lives*, Harmondsworth, Penguin Books.

Hare, R. M.: 1981, *Moral Thinking*, Oxford, Clarendon Press.

Harman, G.: 1975, "Moral Relativism Defended," *The Philosophical Review* 84, 3-22.

Harman, G.: 1977, *The Nature of Morality*, New York, Oxford University Press.

Harman, G.: 1980, "Relativistic Ethics: Morality as Politics," in Peter A. French, Theodore E. Uehling and Howard K. Wettstein, eds., *Midwest Studies in Philosophy*, Vol. III, Minneapolis, University of Minnesota Press, pp. 109-121.

Harman, G.: 1986, "Moral Explanations of Natural Facts—Can Moral Claims Be Tested Against Reality?" *The Southern Journal of Philosophy* 24, Supplement, 57-68.

Mackie, J. L.: 1977, *Ethics: Inventing Right and Wrong*, Harmondsworth, Penguin Books.

Miller, R. W.: 1985, "Ways of Moral Learning," *The Philosophical Review* 94, 507-56.

Murphy, J. G.: 1982, *Evolution, Morality and the Meaning of Life*, Totowa, N. J., Rowman and Allenheld.

Plato: 380BCE, 1974, *Plato's Republic*, tr. G. M. A. Grube, Indianapolis, Hackett Publishing Company.

Railton, P.: 1986, "Moral Realism," *The Philosophical Review* 95, 163-232.

Rawls, J.: 1971, *A Theory of Justice*, Cambridge, Harvard University Press.

Ruse, M.: 1986, *Taking Darwin Seriously*, Oxford, Basil Blackwell.

Schelling, T.: 1960, *The Strategy of Conflict*, Cambridge, Harvard University Press.

Sturgeon, N.: 1985, "Moral Explanations," in David Copp and David Zimmerman, eds., *Morality, Reason and Truth*, Totowa, N.J., Rowman and Allenheld, pp. 49-78.

Sturgeon, N.: 1986, "Harman on Moral Explanations of Natural Facts," *The Southern Journal of Philosophy* 24, Supplement, 69-78.

Sturgeon, N.: 1991, "Contents and Causes: A Reply to Blackburn," *Philosophical Studies* 61, 19-37.

Philosophical Perspectives, 6, Ethics, 1992

ANCIENT ETHICS AND MODERN MORALITY

Julia Annas
University of Arizona

It is no news to moral philosophers that it is extremely hard to define morality, at least convincingly. Those of us who do ancient philosophy face a further problem. When we study Plato's *Republic*, Aristotle's *Ethics*, the Stoics and Epicureans, it's not at all obvious that these famous figures in moral philosophy are talking about morality at all. They all take it for granted, for a start, that the main focus of their enquiry is the agent's happiness; and this doesn't sound much like morality. We explain at this point, of course, that they are not talking about happiness as we understand that, but about *eudaimonia*, and that *eudaimonia* is the satisfactory, well-lived life. But a little reflection shows that this doesn't help, or at least that it doesn't help as much as one might have hoped; it still doesn't sound much like morality. And this initial feeling of unease is only reinforced when we find other differences, such as that in ancient ethics the good of others enters in as part of one's own good, justice is a virtue of character rather than being introduced *via* the rights of others, and so on.

We study the ancient theories, then, but sometimes with some doubt as to what they are theories of. We tend in fact to talk of ancient *ethics*, not ancient morality, and we do the same for modern theories containing elements that are prominent in the ancient ones: thus we talk of virtue ethics, not virtue morality. There is a fairly widespread attitude that ancient theories of virtue and the good life are concerned not with what we take to be morality, but with something different, an alternative which can be labelled ethics.[1]

Recently the issue has been sharpened by Bernard Williams.[2] The ancients did indeed, Williams claims, lack our notion of morality—and were better off without it, since it is confused and in many ways objectionable. However, one need not be hostile to morality to think that ancient ethics is an alternative to modern morality, rather than part of the same endeavor. We might have taken a wrong turning, but there again we might have made progress.[3] There are, moreover, a variety of possible viewpoints as to how central to our own outlook morality is. We might find ancient ethics useful to us in our own attempts to produce moral theory; but equally we might find it attractive but irrelevant, perhaps not really available at all in the modern age.

Whatever we do with the contrast, it is widely taken that there *is* such a contrast; ancient ethics is another country, and they do things differently there—and think differently about them. I am not convinced that this contrast, as it is commonly conceived, exists. Of course there are important differences, but they do not compel us to deny that ancient ethics is also ancient morality.

Because of the difficulty of demarcating the notion of morality, we are, I think, guaranteed to make no progress if we try first to define morality and then see how it measures up against what we find in the ancient theories. A more tractable project is to examine prominent features of morality which, it is alleged, we do *not* find when we examine the ancient theories. The result will fall short of a complete account, but it does at least constitute progress in showing whether or not ancient ethics and modern morality can be taken to be, as wholes, so distinct as to be alternatives.

Moral and non-moral reasons

The most prominent feature of modern moral theories that we fail to find in the ancient ones is the thought that moral and non-moral reasons are different in kind. Moral reasons have a special, compelling force, for when properly appreciated they have a special status in our deliberations: they override or silence all non-moral considerations. Of course, stated thus blankly the difference between moral and non-moral reasons can seem quite mysterious; it is more plausible if it is taken to be a formal one. Moral reasons will then be taken to acquire their force from the fact that they recommend themselves to our reason by being, for example, universalizable without contradiction.

Ancient Greek lacks words or concepts corresponding at all closely to those of the moral and non-moral. Further, no ethical theory suggests that practical reasons come in two kinds, which, just as a ground-floor fact, have basically different kinds of force. Rather, all the ancient theories claim that the good person is marked by possession of *phronēsis*, practical wisdom or practical intelligence, which is an undivided excellence in reasoning over one's life as a whole. Aristotle in chapter 5 of book VI of the *Nicomachean Ethics* says that it is characteristic of someone with this excellence 'to be good at deliberating about what is good and expedient for himself, not in particular matters...but about the kinds of thing that conduce to living well in general'. He instances Pericles and other successful politicians, not the most obvious kind of moral exemplar to the modern mind.

Since ancient theories don't distinguish moral reasons as a special kind of reason, *a fortiori* they don't distinguish them as a special kind of reason by their form. We can even go further: ancient theories show no particular interest in the form of ethical reasoning as such. There is a modern pre-occupation with 'the correct form of moral reasoning'; commonly it is assumed that there is such a thing, the only question being, what it is (rule-following, calculating consequences, etc.). But in ancient theories there is no kind of reasoning, employing which ensures ethical correctness.[4]

Given all this, it may be tempting to conclude, with Williams, that '[Greek ethical thought] basically lacks the concept of *morality* altogether, in the sense of a class of reasons or demands which are vitally different from other kinds of reason or demand'.[5] But this would be premature.

If we ask what the point is of distinguishing moral from non-moral reasons, we find something that has a striking likeness. For the point is to show that moral reasons have a special place in our deliberations. Suppose I consider an action in terms of how much it would cost, how long it would take, and so on. Then I find out that it is dishonest. This is not just another consideration to be taken into account and weighed against the others. If I understand what dishonesty is, this reason just stops the deliberating; for this kind of reason does not outweigh, but overrides or silences the other kinds.[6] Of course I may do it anyway; to understand what morality requires is one thing, to do it another. The point is rather that to consider this fact, of dishonesty, as though it were merely another reason like the others, possibly to be out-weighed by profitmaking, is to misconceive what dishonesty is. Moral reasons are special just because of this role they have in our deliberations: they silence or override other kinds of reason just because of the kind of reason that they are.[7]

But now we don't find a difference with ancient virtue ethics. For all ancient theories think exactly the same way about the fact that the action is dishonest: this is a consideration which is not just weighed up against the profit and time expended, but which sweeps them aside; and to think otherwise is to misconstrue what dishonesty is.

The Stoics make this point in the clearest and most uncompromising way. Only virtue, they say, is good; other things that we desire should be called not good but 'indifferent'. This does not mean that we have no more reason to go for them than not; it simply marks the difference between virtue and everything else. Some things, like health and wealth, are natural advantages, and it is rational for us to seek them; these are 'preferred indifferents', illness and poverty being 'dispreferred' since nothing is bad but vice. Along with this goes a whole set of new vocabulary; thus only virtue is 'chosen', while health, wealth, etc. are 'selected'. The point of all this is to stress the special role of virtue in our reasoning; if we have to use different words for virtue and for other things which we conventionally call good, then there is an initial barrier to our thoughtlessly treating them as considerations all of which are on a par.

'We judge health to be worthy of a kind of value, but we do not judge it a good, and we do not think there to be any value so great as to be preferred to virtue...Compare the way the light of a lamp is obscured and overpowered by the light of the sun, and the way a drop of honey is lost in the extent of the Aegean sea; compare adding a penny to the riches of Croesus and taking one step on the journey from here to India—if the final good is what the Stoics say it is, it is necessary for all the value of bodily things to be obscured and overwhelmed, indeed to be destroyed, by the brilliance and the extent of virtue.'[8]

The analogies suggest two points. On the one hand, virtue is not straightforwardly incommensurable with other things, in the sense of not being on the same scale at all. A penny has the same kind of value (monetary) as Croesus' riches; one step does get you *some* of the way to India. On the other hand, there is a difference so marked that seriously to compare these items shows a lack of understanding of what they are. Someone who seriously congratulated herself on the progress she had made towards getting to India after taking one step would be showing lack of understanding of what one step is and what the journey to India is; someone who seriously counted a penny as the first step towards a billion-dollar fortune likewise. Similarly, while we can at the intuitive level talk of virtue, health and so on as considerations all of which have value in an agent's life, seriously to compare the value of money as against that of honesty, say, shows a misconstrual of what money is and of what honesty is.

This is less familiar to us than the distinction between moral and non-moral reasons, both because the ancients do not pose the issue in terms of different kinds of reason and because they do pose it in terms of the ways we can and cannot compare virtue and other kinds of thing. (In particular, we find in the ancient sources less stress on overridingness in cases of conflict, doubtless because of the fact that in ancient discussions less stress is put on conflict and disagreement.)[9] Nonetheless, we could easily reformulate the ancient point as a point about the kinds of reason that the virtues give rise to. And even without reformulation the distinctions seem congruent, for their point is the same: they are emphasizing a feature of our practical deliberation, the fact that one kind of consideration, if rightly understood, cannot simply be weighed up against the other kinds, but knocks them out of the running. Of course the reasons that modern theories give as to *why* dishonesty is to be avoided will be different from the ancient reasons; modern theories may point to alleged formal features of reasons deriving from honesty, whereas ancient theories will point us towards analysis of the nature of the virtue of honesty. But there is agreement on the main point: dishonesty is not just another reason to be factored in, it is a consideration which stops the others in their tracks and sends us back to square one.

Admittedly the Stoics are the only school who insist so uncompromisingly on the difference between the value of virtue and the value of any other kind of thing. Aristotle does not insist that virtue is marked off from other kinds of thing that we seek in this way, and later his followers, the Peripatetics, defined their position against that of the Stoics by saying that virtue and other kinds of natural advantage are all good, ridiculing the Stoics for saying that things that we all rationally seek are not good. Aristotle is thus not in as strong a position as the Stoics are to mark off the special deliberative role of virtue. Nonetheless, Aristotle insists in different ways that virtue has special kinds of benefit which other goods do not. The virtuous person will take pleasure in being virtuous, even if it leads to disadvantages, or even to wounds and death; thus he is not losing anything by his virtuous activity that can be balanced against the value of virtue. Thus virtue has a special place in relation to the other goods.[10]

Aristotle also describes virtuous action in ways which bring it close to other modern characterizations of what is done for a moral reason. The virtuous person does the virtuous action for its own sake,[11] and because it is *kalon*, 'fine' or 'noble'.[12] The *kalon* is the aim of virtue.[13] Alexander of Aphrodisias, the later commentator on Aristotle, puts the point more precisely: 'Virtue does everything for the sake of the *kalon quā kalon*, for virtue is such as to do things that are *kala* in the field of action.'[14] The virtuous action is done for its own sake, without ulterior motive, as is commonly taken to be true of an action done for a moral reason. And it is done with the *kalon* as its aim, rather than benefit or pleasure, which are the other characteristic human aims.[15] Aristotle does not, in the *Ethics*, further analyze the *kalon*. It is distinguished not only from what is pleasant and beneficial but also from what is necessary,[16] but we learn little more about it; Aristotle assumes that it motivates the virtuous person, and that this is something that we can recognize. It can be analyzed in different ways, which we cannot examine here,[17] but what matters for the present issue is that Aristotle clearly recognizes that the virtuous person does the virtuous act for its own sake, and that this is a distinctive kind of motivation.

Again we seem to have agreement with the demands of modern morality rather than disagreement, since moral reasons are commonly taken to have just these features: to act for a moral reason is to do the action for its own sake and not for any further motive, and it also involves a distinct kind of motivation. Thus in different ways Aristotle and the Stoics seem to agree with modern theories of morality. Aristotle's position is the weaker (hence it is no surprise that it is his theory which is most often invoked in contrasts with modern morality).[18]

The Stoics have the sharpest and most satisfactory position about virtue, though other schools have a weaker view along similar lines; but in both cases there seems no reason to deny that the role of virtue in our deliberations is essentially that which modern theories take morality to have. Only Epicurus does not mark off the deliberative role of virtue in even the weaker way; but just this point forms a standard ancient *criticism* of him.[19] And if this kind of force in our deliberations is taken to be characteristic, or even definitive of morality, the ancient theories seem to be telling us something about morality.

Moral responsibility

In modern moral philosophy it is a cliché that 'ought implies can', that moral appraisal implies moral responsibility, where this in turn implies that the agent was in some way free not to do what is in question. Ancient ethics, it is often claimed, is by contrast less concerned about this; ethical appraisal is sometimes handed out in cases where the agent was not in this way free not so to act. Sometimes this is put as a point about 'moral luck': the agent can be morally held to account for actions which it was not in her power to avoid doing. If one accepts this claim, one will indeed tend to think that ancient ethics is not modern morality, since it is central to all going modern theories that if one was not free not to do the action one cannot be morally held to account for it.

This point is often buttressed by pointing out that the Greek word *aretē* (and the same goes for the Latin *virtus*) does not mean 'virtue'; it means 'excellence', and can apply to what makes a house or a horse an excellent house or horse. From this point it is often inferred that even for humans the *aretai* are not the virtues. (Some modern translations reflect this belief.)[20] Virtues are states where we are concerned with particularly moral appraisal, and judge that the person can be praised or blamed and hence is morally responsible for what he did. But if the *aretai* are just the human excellences, there will be no division of kind between being brave or just and excellences like being healthy or handsome, no way of marking off an area of peculiarly moral appraisal where it is assumed that the agent is morally responsible.

This charge against ancient ethics is a venerable one, and can be found in Hume's fourth appendix to his *Enquiry Concerning the Principles of Morals*. Hume claims there that even in English we do not make a marked distinction between what are usually called the moral virtues and other kinds of non-moral excellence, a claim rebutted by Sidgwick.[21] More to our present point, Hume claims that 'the ancient moralists, the best models, made no material distinction among the different species of mental endowments and defects, but treated all alike under the appellation of virtues and vices', and, 'In general, we may observe, that the distinction of voluntary or involuntary was little regarded by the ancients in their moral reasonings.' It was, he claims, only with the incursion of religion, specifically Christianity, into moral philosophy that philosophers began to be obsessed by the question of voluntariness.

Hume's analysis, and its accompanying diagnosis, have been often repeated, so it is worth pointing out that what Hume says is quite false. Aristotle devotes a prominent part of book III of the *Nicomachean Ethics* to discussing the conditions for voluntariness, precisely because this is needed in an enquiry into virtue, since 'praise and blame are bestowed on what is voluntary, pardon and sometimes pity on what is involuntary'.[22] Further, what is true of Aristotle remains true for all the ancient schools: virtue requires voluntariness, the free exercise of choice to act one way rather than another. Nothing could be less true than the claim that the ancients were uninterested in the difference between this kind of state and a state like health or beauty.

What of the point about *aretē*, however? It is true that *aretē* means 'excellence', not 'virtue'. But it is quite compatible with this that the excellences of a human life should be the virtues, indeed what we might call the moral virtues. And this is in fact what we find. We might, of course, disagree that this is the form an excellent human life should take. But the human *aretai*, from Plato onwards, are routinely taken to be courage, 'temperance' (moderation and self-control), practical intelligence and justice, with the other virtues as subdivisions of these.[23] And if we look more closely at courage, justice and so on, we cannot doubt that they are not regarded as being on a par with natural endowments, nor are they simply regarded as some among a lot of desirable dispositions. They are dispositions *to do the ethically right thing*, and as such involve the agent's choice, and presuppose that this is voluntary.

By the time of the Stoics we find it explicitly recognized, and enshrined in technical terminology, that the virtues are special kinds of excellence or *aretē*, precisely because they involve choice and are, as they say, 'reasoned', based on accepting certain principles:

'As for *aretē*, it is in one sense generally anything's reaching completion. So it is with a statue. And there is the unreasoned kind, like health, and the reasoned kind, like intelligence. Hecaton says...that the *aretai* that involve knowledge and are reasoned are those whose constitution is formed from principles,[24] like intelligence and justice; unreasoned are those that are observed to be co-extensive with those constituted from principles, such as health and strength.'[25]

Indeed, the use of *aretē* or *virtus* for the moral virtues of a person came to be seen as the standard or primary use, and the application to statues and horses as secondary, as we can see from later passages, where *virtutes voluntariae* are said to be *virtutes* in the proper sense of the word,[26] and where it is claimed that *aretē* is actually ambiguous because it can be used both of the virtues of a person, which are developed by accepting moral principles, and of aptitudes and natural excellences.[27]

No understanding is gained, then, by translating *aretē* as 'excellence', or by pointing to *aretē* as applied to statues and healthy bodies. Indeed, understanding is lost. For the *aretai* that concern ethics are courage, justice, etc.; and these are precisely different from the statue and health uses in that they do presuppose a freely choosing and developing agent.

It is certainly true that in some ancient texts we find reflected a belief in 'moral luck'—in tragedy, for example. But it is striking that we do not find it in ancient moral *theory*. The main reason for this seems to be that ancient moral theory is centrally concerned with the virtues, and the virtues are, as we have seen, reasoned states presupposing freedom of choice. Ancient moral theory in fact is committed to being *critical* of the acceptance of 'moral luck' in other areas of ancient intellectual life, and in very similar ways to those in which modern moral theories are committed to being critical of such an acceptance in areas of modern intellectual life. Thus it would be a mistake to think that deontological and consequentialist theories are committed to rejecting moral luck, while virtue ethics is not; it finds precisely the same problem that they do. It is sometimes claimed[28] that it is a profound mistake to reject the notion of 'moral luck'. If this is so, it is a mistake on the part of ethical theory generally, as opposed to pre-reflective ethical beliefs. It is not a mistake of modern as opposed to ancient ethical theory.[29]

Scope

Reflection on Aristotle's list of virtues has often suggested to modern readers (especially those who read no ancient ethics but Aristotle's) that there is a fundamental difference of scope between modern morality and the ancient ethics of virtue. Aristotle's virtues range over areas of life that we would not at all naturally take to be the domain of morality. Thus Aristotle opposes the virtue of 'temperance' or self-control in bodily pleasures such as those of eating, drinking and sex not just to self-indulgence, in his terms the 'excess', but also to the 'defect', *anaisthēsia*, the disposition not to enjoy food, drink and sex as much as much as one should. (This disposition, he remarks, is rarely encountered.) He also sketches large-scale social virtues, such as that of paying for public works in a tasteful and appropriate manner. If we are to take him to be talking about virtue in a sense which is recognizably moral, then we seem forced to absurd conclusions such as that not enjoying food is a moral vice, or that tasteful expenditure is a moral virtue. And similar conclusions follow for many of Aristotle's virtues.

This criticism can be partially deflected, whatever else we say about it, by the point that Aristotle's list of virtues is rather unusual. His successors revert to Plato's habit of regarding virtue as consisting of the four 'cardinal' virtues, subdivided. So Aristotle is at least not typical. Further, his theory of virtue as a mean, which directs many of his distinctions, was likewise unusual, and it, not a view about virtue in general, is responsible for some of his odder views, such as the status of *anaisthēsia*. But even taking this into account the fact remains that Aristotle talks of virtues covering areas of life which we would not be inclined to bring under morality.

There are other responses, however, than the usual one of claiming that Aristotle's virtues are not concerned with morality. For it might be that Aristotle is prepared to moralize more of everyday life than we are. Perhaps he thinks that indifference to food and sex is not (always) a blank physical given, but an insensitivity which involves or flows from a moral insensitivity. And perhaps tastefulness in public expenditure, and the large-scale public virtues generally, are matters of moral concern, either in their results or in their origin or both. The plausibility of this thesis about Aristotle obviously depends on a detailed account of all Aristotle's virtues, which cannot be done here; but the general strategy is clear enough.

Is this an absurd position? All the ancient ethical schools accepted the assumption that ethics is not a distinct compartment in one's life. Taste, style, and social behavior generally are not neutral matters, indifferent between the good and the bad: because of the centrality of character, ethical differences will affect all aspects of your life. Most ethical theories do not follow Aristotle by structuring actual virtues for all aspects of social life. Aristotle is unusual, and arguably over-ambitious, in trying to work out these matters in detail as part of a theory of virtue. But the other schools do not disagree with Aristotle's point that the possession or otherwise of the virtues makes a great difference to how one spends money, enjoys food, makes jokes and so on. Your ethical stage of development is relevant in your life as a whole, in every aspect of your interactions with others.

Does this contrast with morality? Only if morality is compartmentalized in our lives, if our stage of moral development has little or nothing to do with the way we live the rest of our lives. And while some hold that this can be the case, it is not obviously true. In fact quite compelling arguments can be put forward to show that it is not true—arguments effectively articulated by Bradley. As he puts it,

> It is...an error to suppose that in what is called human life there remains any region which has not been moralized... . The character shows itself in every trifling detail of life; we can not go in to amuse ourselves while we leave it outside the door with our dog; it is ourself, and our moral self, being not mere temper or inborn disposition, but the outcome of a series of acts of will.[30]

We may reject this; and Bradley is not typical of modern moral theory here, which in general ignores the problem. But it certainly ought not to be taken for granted that morality can be restricted to part of one's life only. And if we take this point we may find it a matter of detail whether, with Aristotle, we take it that areas of social life demarcate distinct virtues, or, with the other schools, that the virtues, more narrowly defined, affect one's conduct in all areas of social life.[31]

Actions and agents

Williams characterizes morality as a system of thought making *obligation* primary, indeed the only form of moral requirement.[32] He points out that if we try to reduce all aspects of the moral life to the holding of obligations, we shall find the account drastically impoverished. While this is certainly true, one might well doubt whether modern moral theories really are characterized quite as strongly as Williams suggests by the primacy of obligation. Consequentialists, for example, think that what matters is maximizing good consequences of some kind; even if they think that this is what one ought to do, they are often not happy with the idea of starting from such notions as obligation and duty.

A weaker position captures what has widely been felt to be an important difference, one summed up by calling modern morality *act-centred*. The thought is this: morality is primarily a matter of how one ought to act, what one ought to do. Morality starts from what are called our intuitions, the judgements we pre-reflectively make about what we ought to do. It examines the ways we come to make those judgements and the kinds of grounds that we consider relevant. The task of moral theory is to clarify to ourselves, and make more rigorous, our ways of coming to decide what we ought to do. Some forms of moral theory aim to produce a decision procedure—a mechanical way of finding out what to do, which is to be so constructed as to come to the right results. But even theories which fall short of this tend to take as their primary aim that of improving our ability to decide what to do.

By contrast, ancient ethics does not see this as its aim; relatedly, it does not spend time on tasks which are important to modern theories, such as studying hard cases. Ancient theories have been labelled *agent-centred*; they take their primary aim to be that of delineating the good person and of helping us to understand what constitutes the good life. Assuming that we all seek the good life, they examine what it consists in; and they ask what it is about certain of our dispositions that makes them virtues, and how possessing these helps one to achieve the best life.

Broadly stated in this way, the contrast is obviously right. But it needs some refinement. Modern theories don't just seek decision procedures; especially if they have revisionary views as to what the right thing to do is, they have to examine the relation between doing the right thing and being the kind of person who will do the right thing. And ancient theories don't just discuss virtue and the good life; they also discuss what is the right thing to do. They can hardly avoid this, since a virtue is a disposition to do the right thing. In fact a little reflection shows that no sensible theory could be act- or agent-centred in the sense of *just* considering acts or agents; all theories have to consider both.

The contrast, then, must lie in the relative importance that ancient and modern theories give to acts and agents. And it at first seems that we still have a striking contrast. For modern theories tend to take questions about what one should do to be the primary ones, in that it is only when these are in hand that one can consider the question of what kind of person to be. The good person, to put it crudely, is the person who is so disposed as to do the right thing; but we find out what the right thing to do is independently, without appeal to what the good person is. Thus, since virtue notions will not help us to discover or clarify what the right thing to do is, they will be secondary in moral theory. By contrast, ancient theories are seen as taking virtue notions to be primary, and questions of right action to be secondary. The important point for ancient ethics will be to establish what the virtuous person is like; the right thing to do will just be what the virtuous person would do, and thus will be a secondary issue.

It is widely accepted that there is something like this contrast between ancient and modern theories. Indeed, it is often made the basis for criticisms of ancient theories, on the grounds that they have nothing to say about right conduct that is not trivial.[33] For if one is faced by a difficult decision, and is told that the right thing to do is what the virtuous person would do, one does not feel much helped.

However, the more one looks at this alleged contrast, the shakier it seems to be. Few modern theories are so crude as to work out a decision procedure for action and then simply define the good or ideal agent as the person who applies that procedure. For if an account of right action is to be an account of how people act rightly, some account of how people are and ought to be has to be fed into it; it is pointless to develop it in a void. What use could a theory be as a *moral* theory if nobody could internalize it and act on it?[34] And on the other side, ancient theories do not develop an account of what the virtuous person is in the void, adding that right action is just what this person would produce. Rather, the virtuous person is the person with developed dispositions to do the right thing. We have to have some idea of what the right thing to do is in order so much as to get going a notion of a *virtue*, as opposed to some other kind of disposition. In fact it is obvious on reflection that any ethical theory has to say something by way of criticism and clarification of our intuitive views on both rightness of action and goodness of people.

In the end there does remain a difference. For modern theories often demand that particular answers to hard cases be built into the theory itself, in such a way that all one needs is to feed in a fairly simple description of a particular problem for the theory to produce an answer to it. Ancient theories, on the other hand, are more impressed by the complexity and difficulty of particular situations. The completely virtuous person will be able to come to particular decisions which do justice to all features of a particular situation, because he has internalized the ethical theory; but the decisions are not themselves part of the theory.

(It should be added, however, that this is the ideal; you and I, not being completely virtuous, are best advised to follow the best available rules or principles, rather than relying on the capacity we have developed to make particular judgements. So for unideal people the gap between ancient and modern closes somewhat.)

Sometimes modern morality is characterized by its emphasis on rules, as a guide to right acting, and ancient ethics is held up as a more humane alternative, more interested in developing good dispositions, since it is interested in people. Rule-following is often supposed to be of interest only if one is concerned only or primarily about acts. But moral rules clearly have a place in both kinds of theory. Moral rules are a guide to acting rightly; but just for that reason they are the way to develop a virtuous disposition. Aristotle says little about rules, being more interested in the following of virtuous models, and so rules are often under-stressed in modern discussions of ancient ethics. But the Stoics make a fairly large place for rule-following within the development of virtue. It is true that in an ethics of virtue rule-following will not be, on its own, enough to make one virtuous. But then few modern theories would hold that rule-following on its own is enough to make one act rightly either.

Myself and others

Ancient ethical theory begins by specifying what, really, when I understand it, is my 'final end' or 'final good'. It is taken for granted that each of us does have a final good—an overall good which we seek to bring about in all we do. It is also assumed that this is happiness, though this point is regarded as trivial and settling nothing; real debate centres on how one's final good is to be informatively specified. Epicurus claims that it is pleasure; Aristotle and the Stoics disagree as to whether it requires only the development of virtue, or some material advantages as well. Thus ethical enquiry takes place within a framework in which the fundamental ethical question which faces me is, how I shall achieve my own final good.

This is, to put it mildly, not the fundamental ethical question in modern theories. The fact that these tend to characterize morality in terms of concern for others, whereas ancient ethics begins from concern with oneself, shows that there is certainly a contrast here. And if one takes a basic and non-derivative concern for others to be definitive of morality, one will, as is often done, take the contrast to show that ancient ethics is not morality, or at best is grossly defective as morality. But again the supposed contrast is a slippery one.

It is still sometimes claimed that, because ancient ethical theory works to answer the question, what constitutes my final good, that it is egoistic; in pursuing my own final good I am pursuing my own self-interest. This claim is mistaken. For what ancient theory demands that I develop, in pursuing my final good, are the *virtues*, and these include justice, courage and the like. Some of them have a direct connection with the good of others, for example justice. All of them involve at least having a disposition to do the right thing, where this is established independently of the agent's own interests. An ethics of virtue is at most formally self-centred, since its framework is that of the agent's own final end; its content can be fully as other-regarding as that of other ethical theories.

Nonetheless, the idea persists that ancient ethics, since its framework is that of the agent's final end, is at bottom egoistic. This has, I think, two main sources, one confused, the other not, but in the end mistaken. The confusion comes from the thought that if the good of others is introduced into the agent's own final good, it cannot really be the good of *others*, but must in some way be reduced to what matters *to the agent*. But why must this be the case? Perhaps the thought is that the good of others must matter to me *because* it is the good of others, not because it is part of my own good. But no ancient theorist would dispute this. The good of others does not matter to me because it is part of my own good; it matters to me because it is the good of others. This is quite compatible with its being part of my overall final good. The second thought does not undermine the first.

A more creditable objection goes as follows: If ethics begins from the question, what my final good is, then this can indeed include *philia* or friendship, caring for particular other people for their own sake. It can even include justice understood as a concern for fair dealing. But it cannot extend to impartiality, the thought that I matter, from the moral point of view, merely as one among others, and should give my interests no more weight than those of anybody else. And impartiality is required by (many, at least) modern moral theories.[35]

This is an interesting claim, but false. Not all ancient theories demand that I think of myself as merely one person among others from the ethical point of view, but Stoicism does. The Stoics think that a rational person will naturally be led to extend her rational concern to all other people (rational people at least) until she is impartial between her own interests and those of 'the remotest Mysian', that is, someone living in a far-off country of whom she has no personal knowledge at all, and to whom she has no personal links.[36] They draw conclusions from this which were attacked by ancient critics in much the way that Williams has attacked Kantian theories. In a shipwreck, for example, where there is one plank and each of two people wanting to be saved, the Stoic view is that the person who ought to have the plank is the morally worthier. If both are equally morally worthy, they will use a fair random procedure. An ancient critic attacks this on the ground that in such a case each person would in fact save himself; to claim that he ought to be impartial between his own interests and those of others, and settle the matter by appeal only to considerations of ethical worth, appeals to motivations that people don't in fact have.[37] The Stoics, that is, do exactly what is supposed not to be possible: they take ethics to be an examination of what constitutes the agent's good, and claim that ethical development leads the agent eventually to do two things. One is to see morality as not just one of her concerns, but as a concern that can override all her other concerns. The other is to see morality as a perspective from which one is impartial between one's own concerns and interests and those of other people concerned. We may find it strange that eudaimonism can accommodate these thoughts, but it is part of the data of ancient ethics that it can.

It is true that not all ancient theories think that this kind of impartiality between one's own interests and those of anyone else *is* demanded by ethical considerations. Aristotle's account of justice, for example, does not make the demand of impartiality between oneself and all others that the Stoic account does. Theories that derive from Aristotle do not make this a requirement of morality generally or even of justice in particular; they start from the agent's concern for the good of particular other people and tend to stop when a group of people is reached with whom the agent has a feeling of community, such as the citizens of one's city-state. The important point here is that while impartiality between one's own interests and those of any other rational human was not taken for granted as a requirement of morality or even of justice in ancient theories, the idea was familiar and a matter of debate. A eudaimonistic form of ethics does not prevent the agent from reaching this impartial viewpoint.

So we cannot deny that ancient theories are moral theories on the grounds that they do not recognize that morality requires impartiality; some of them do, and it is a topic of argument. And since in recent years there has been debate as to whether modern theories are right to require impartiality of this kind, any division of principle seems to evaporate.

Conclusion

My account has been sketchy and partial. But I hope that I have at least isolated, and tried to meet, a common line of thought. There are indeed large differences between ancient and modern ethical thought, and it is easy to be over-impressed by them, and to conclude that, since our notion of what morality is must answer to our own type of theory, we have to regard the ancient theories not as moral theories, but something different. I have tried to focus on the main reasons for thinking this, and the reasons for rejecting them.

My project may seem to have been an irenic one; I have been trying to reconcile positions that are often taken to be hopelessly diverse. I have done so by way of minimizing differences: what appear to be competing positions turn out not to be in competition, since they are doing the same thing in different ways. But this does not leave everything where it was before. For it undermines two attitudes to ancient ethical theories, and to modern theories that hark back to ancient texts. One is the hostile attitude that the ancient theories are simply outdated: they are inadequate to cope with the problems that modern moral theories have to deal with.[38] I hope I have shown that this attitude rests on some mistakes about ancient ethical theories. But there is another attitude, equally harmful, I think, of romantic nostalgia: the feeling that it would be nicer if we could shed the problem-area that we have and go back to a very different set of problems, that ethics would be a kinder, gentler place if we could forget about hard cases and talk about friendship and the good life instead. Like much nostalgia, this is misplaced.

Both of these attitudes neutralize the ancient theories as answers to our problems: whether passé or inspiring, these theories are seen as out of our reach, not applicable to the moral problems we now have. But if what I have suggested is right, ancient ethics is not so easily disposed of. The possibility remains open that one of the competing ancient theories might have just as much chance as the modern competitors of being, not just interesting, or edifying, but a true theory, of morality.[39]

Notes

1. I take it that in everyday language 'ethics' and 'morality' are used interchangeably. There seems at any rate to be no single principled difference between them. The use of 'ethics' to label an alternative distinct from morality is the product of certain assumptions made when discussing ethical theory, and I have used it in conformity with those assumptions. I do not know of any general argument to establish the difference; hence my opponent in this paper is not one single argued position, but a set of assumptions which are widespread in discussions of ancient philosophy, though possibly no one would explicitly subscribe to all the assumptions I criticize here.
2. In the chapter 'Philosophy' in M. I. Finley, *The Legacy of Greece*, Oxford, Oxford University Press, 1981; also in *Ethics and the Limits of Philosophy*, London, Fontana/Collins, 1985. My criticisms of Williams are not aimed at his own position in the book, but merely at his historical claims about ancient ethics.
3. Bernard Williams in his Sather Lectures labels as 'progressivist' the idea that we have outgrown ancient ethics, that we now have more mature responses to the problems in question.
4. Rather, what is important in Greek ethical theory is the difference between the beginner and the ethically developed person. This is commonly seen on the model of a beginner in a craft, who is dependent on following rules and models, and the expert, who has internalized the principles of the craft and need not follow rules and models so rigidly. (Whether, however, this amounts to a difference in

the form of ethical reasoning between beginner and expert is a difficult matter, and may well differ between the different schools.)

5. 'Philosophy' p. 251.
6. For the silencing metaphor see J. McDowell, 'The Role of *Eudaimonia* in Aristotle's Ethics', in A. Rorty (ed), *Essays on Aristotle's Ethics*, Berkeley/Los Angeles/London, University of California Press 1980, 359-376.
7. To avert misunderstanding: this is what I take the intuitive notion of a moral reason to be. I am not providing a theoretical defence of it against theories which would try to weaken or erase the difference.
8. *Fin* III 44-5.
9. For the Stoics, virtue is the *technē* or skill which is exercised in putting non-moral advantages (the 'indifferents') to use. This conception of the relation of moral to non-moral value is strikingly different from a conception which assumes from the start that they are likely to come into conflict, as John Cooper has emphasized to me. Nonetheless it is compatible with considerations of virtue having what I have called the special deliberative role.
10. It is necessary for happiness, since without it the other goods cannot be appreciated at their true worth, but not sufficient, since external goods are needed also. See my article, 'Aristotle on Virtue and Happiness', *University of Dayton Review* Winter 1988-9, 7-22, and the relevant parts of my book (n. 39), where I argue that this position is inherently unstable.
11. E.g. 1105 a 31-2.
12. E.g. 1116 a 11.
13. 1115 b 11-3. For a more detailed account of the occurrences of these phrases, see the excellent article by T. Irwin, 'Aristotle's Conception of Morality', in *Proceedings of the Boston Area Ancient Philosophy Colloquium* vol 1 (1985), 115-143. See also 'The *Kalon* in the Aristotelian Ethics' by J. Owens, in *Studies in Aristotle*, ed. D. O'Meara, Catholic University of America Press, 1981.
14. *de An* II 154.30-32.
15. 1104 b 30-1105 a 1.
16. See Irwin, op. cit., pp. 125-126.
17. Compare Owens, who understands it as 'the intrinsic obligatory character of moral goodness' with Irwin, who explicates it, via passages from the *Rhetoric*, as essentially connected with the good of others.
18. The stronger Stoic position implies something like the Aristotelian, but not the other way around. The question, whether Aristotle really recognizes the nature of moral reasons, thus depends on how strong you take the contrast between moral and other reasons to be. I have assumed that intuitively we suppose the stronger view, but have not here defended this assumption.
19. See *Fin* II 44 ff. Epicurus is often interpreted as giving virtue only instrumental value as a means to producing pleasure. I have argued that Epicurus is driven by various constraints into allowing virtue intrinsic value (see my 'Epicurus on Pleasure and Happiness', *Philosophical Topics* XV (1987), 5-21, and the relevant parts of my book (n. 39).
20. For example, the revised Oxford translation (ed. J. Barnes, Princeton 1984), which replaces 'virtue' by 'excellence' throughout. This produces the odd result that people interested to see what Aristotle has contributed to 'virtue ethics' find in this translation that he has nothing to say about virtue. J. O. Urmson, *Aristotle's Ethics*, Blackwells 1988, pp. 26 ff, explicitly defends the translation 'excellence' rather than 'virtue' on the grounds that Aristotle is not making 'hopelessly wrong' claims about moral virtue, but is concerned with acting effortlessly and with enjoyment, as a result of one's character.

21. *The Methods of Ethics* III ii.
22. Hume, we should note, says that 'We need only peruse the titles of chapters in Aristotle's Ethics to be convinced' that Aristotle's virtues are not restricted to what is voluntary; there is little sign that Hume perused the actual chapters. Indeed, while Hume is clearly at home with ancient literature, history and oratory, his grip on ancient philosophy is surprisingly weak.
23. Aristotle is the exception; his list of virtues includes these, but is wider and messier. Concentration on Aristotle's ethics has tended to obscure the extent to which these four are in the ancient world quite standard. Even later versions of Aristotelian ethics conform more to the standard pattern.
24. The word is *theorēmata*. This is used by the Stoics for mathematical theorems, but also for the principles which give structure to any craft or skill (cf. the passages in von Arnim, *Stoicorum Veterum Fragmenta* III 214, where *logos...kata ta theorēmata* is distinguished from mere habituation; also III 278, 295.) Virtue for the Stoics is a skill, so its 'theorems' are the principles which structure a virtue, the rules or principles which you have to accept to be dispositionally brave, just and so on. (There is no implication that the agent's moral reasoning has a deductive or mathematical structure.)
25. Diogenes Laertius, VII 90. Cf. also the parallel passage in Arius Didymus; account of Stoic ethics in Stobaeus, *Eclogae* II, 62.15-63.5 .
26. *Fin* V 36-38, in a description of Antiochus' ethical theory.
27. Alexander of Aphrodisias, *de An* II 155 24-8.
28. Influentially by Martha Nussbaum, in *The Fragility of Goodness*, Cambridge University Press 1986.
29. And of course I have not in the least shown whether it is a mistake or not.
30. *Ethical Studies* 2nd ed, Oxford University Press 1962, Essay VI, pp. 217-218.
31. The latter is certainly more plausible, as we can see from the difficulties we tend to find with Aristotle's more 'social' virtues. We can presume that the later schools shared these difficulties, and that this explains why they took the alternative course.
32. *Ethics and the Limits of Philosophy* ch. 10.
33. See R. Louden, 'On Some Vices of Virtue Ethics', *American Philosophical Quarterly* 1984 (reprinted in R. Kruschwitz and R. Roberts, *The Virtues*, N.Y. Wadsworth 1987) for a trenchant statement of this.
34. Some modern versions of consequentialism do not recognize this constraint, distinguishing the role of a moral theory as motivating and as justifying. I do not think that this move is as successful as often thought, but cannot argue that here.
35. This issue is discussed more fully in the relevant part of my book (n. 39), and also in 'The Good Life and the Good Lives of Others', forthcoming in *Social Philosophy and Policy*.
36. Plato has Socrates use 'the remotest Mysian' as a proverbial expression for someone far off and unknown to us, at *Theaetetus* 209b. The Anonymous Commentator on the *Theaetetus*, probably first century B.C., of whose work we possess a substantial papyrus fragment, uses it as an example in an ethical context (cols. 5-6) when discussing the Stoic theory.
37. The Anonymous Commentator (see last note). The shipwreck example is in fact fragmentary in the Commentary, though the author's view is clear enough from the substantial objections which do remain, and from the parallel passage in Cicero's *de Officiis* III 89-90.
38. This attitude is often accompanied by the romantic thought that modern moral philosophy faces problems that are unprecedented, and that our ways of dealing with them owe little or nothing to past traditions.

39. This paper has been read at the University of Arizona, Columbia University, the University of Oklahoma, Brown University, Johns Hopkins University, Brigham Young University and the political thought seminar at Princeton University. I have benefitted from comments on each occasion, and apologize to the numerous people whose questions and problems have greatly helped me to clarify the issues, but whose individual contributions I can no longer accurately distinguish. I am grateful for written comments from Michael Slote and Jonathan Kandell. The need for reflecting on these issues arises from a book I am writing on the intellectual structure of Greek ethical theory, *The Morality of Happiness* (Oxford University Press, forthcoming).

Philosophical Perspectives, 6, Ethics, 1992

TRUSTING PEOPLE[1]

Annette C. Baier
University of Pittsburgh

My title is deliberately ambiguous. Some of us, in some contexts are trusting people, while others in the same contexts are suspicious people. That is one sense of my title. The other sense of my title and part of my topic concerns trusting *people*, as distinct from trusting human institutions and the roles we and our ancestors have designed for them, for a succession of persons to fill—trusting presidents and vice presidents, trusting fathers and clergymen. For it may well be that some roles tend to pressure a not-so-trustworthy person into being more trustworthy, or tempt the formerly trustworthy person into treachery or corruption. My assumption will be that we would, other things equal, prefer to be able both to trust individual persons and rely on the institutions that structure their conduct, so prefer to be able to regard it a good thing if people are trusting people. But of course we cannot afford to encourage our children or one another to be more trusting until we have reasonable assurance that those whom we are encouraging them to trust by and large will not let them down. We cannot simply label trustingness a virtue, any more than we can simply call loyalty and trustworthiness virtues. Those who are worthy of the trust of their co-workers in say the drug business, or are loyal gang members, are not necessarily the better for their trustworthiness, and those who put their trust in those who perpetuate exploitation or domination are not to be admired for their willingness to trust. Still despite these clear cases of deplorable forms of trusting and meeting trust, I think that an adaptation of Royce's[2] claim about loyalty can be made out for the pair trust and trustworthiness, namely that the bad forms tend to be temporary since self-undermining, while the forms that are self-strengthening, and that tend to produce meta-trust, trust in trust-involving relationships and forms of cooperation, are the ones that we have good reason to welcome, from a moral point of view. Not loyalty to loyalty, but trust in sustained trust, trust in it in full knowledge of its risks as well as its benefits, and trustworthiness to sustain trust, these may well be the supreme virtues for ones like us, in our condition.

Diego Gambetta, in his concluding essay to the collection of essays on trust which he edited,[3] raises the question of whether we can trust trust, or whether our well documented experience of betrayals would not rather suggest that we should be suspicious of it, and minimize the contexts in which we expect it of others or offer it to others. He quotes Elster and Moene, "We may hope that trust will come about as a by-product of a good economic system...one would be putting the cart before the horse were one to bank on trust, solidarity and altruism as the precondition of reform."[4] Elster and Moene allow that "some amount of trust must be present in any complex economic system".[5] Even the most competition-encouraging systems do rely on some trust in contracts, the most controlled economies on some trust in those administering the controls. But whatever may be the case for economic systems, what are we to say about moral networks? Can we trust trust, at least outside our business deals? Gambetta's answer to this question is a fairly pessimistic affirmative. After noting how distrust tends to spread and to disable, he writes "Trust, even if *always* misplaced, can never do worse than that, and the expectation that it might do at least marginally better is therefore plausible." His guarded conclusion that "it may be rational to trust trust, and distrust distrust"[6] really endorses the rationality not so much of trusting trust, as of relying on it, since if our choice is between doing very badly by encouraging distrust and doing marginally better by encouraging trust, then it is dubious that choosing the latter option really counts as *trusting* trust, by Gambetta's own definition. Trust, he writes (here drawing on the analyses given by the others who contributed to the volume) "is a particular level of subjective probability with which an agent assesses that another agent or group of agents will perform a particular action, both *before* he can monitor such action (or independently of his capacity ever to be able to monitor it) *and* in a context in which it affects *his own* action...[a probability] high enough for us to consider engaging in some form of cooperation with him."[7] But Gambetta's own estimate of the disastrous costs of mistrust is based on a fairly careful monitoring of its record, for example in the Mafia, and of the better record of trust-involving social structures. His is a dubious case of meta-trust, precisely because his knowledge-based case for the "rationality" of encouraging trust is so strong. "The condition of ignorance or uncertainty about other people's behavior that is central to the notion of trust"[8] is not met in his version of meta-trust. We might, fairly implausibly, suppose that Gambetta's considerable knowledge of the comparative record of trust-relying and mistrust-relying social strategies might be merely historical, and without projective predictive value. The excessively risk-averse will, I suppose, find the philosophical "problem of induction" a *practical* problem, so that any attempt to learn from experience will involve risk-taking, but it still will not yet amount to trusting, if that is risk-taking reliance on others' hoped for behavior. In any case Gambetta does not appear to be suspicious of all reliance on probability estimates, and in particular on past monitorings of people's performance as a guide to their future behavior, so this way of importing some ignorance into his guarded preference for trust over distrust, enough for it to count as trust in trust, is purely hypothetical.

Is there then any such phenomenon as trust in trust? That depends on our definition of trust. For the individual, as distinct from the social scientist and the would-be reformer of human habits, there surely are frequently cases where our previous experience of where trust has more or less worked, and where it invited disaster, give us very little basis for any probability estimate about the other's reliability in the case before us. A Peruvian artist selling his paintings at a fair in a U.S. city was recently faced with strangers and possible clients, a couple who would buy a certain large painting only if the artist could arrange its transport to their home. The artist, unable to close his stall right then, and unwilling to miss or postpone the sale, proposed that one of the couple watch his stall while he transported the painting, guided by the other buyer. Perhaps he had done this on previous occasions, without mishap, but there must have been a first occasion when twenty or thirty paintings were left in the custody of a stranger, just because she had shown herself willing to purchase one such painting. Social scientists may know the frequency with which con-men in this country lure merchants away by promising to complete a sale elsewhere, while leaving their accomplices minding the store, but the foreign artist was innocent of such statistics. He just trusted the couple who wanted to buy, and such fairly ordinary trust, shown by an adult in a novel situation, might well be seen to involve meta-trust, a snap judgment that on this occasion trust is more sensible than losing a sale through suspiciousness. If trust is taken to be always trust in people,[9] then this meta-trust is best construed as trust in one's own judgment concerning the others' trustworthiness. Then there will be trust in trust, and it may be displayed quite often by ordinary people. It may be harder for social scientists to find room for it. The more one knows about people (oneself included), the less one has occasion strictly to trust them, or to trust trusting them. An omniscient and otherwise omnipotent God will of necessity lack one ability that his human and animal creatures have—to give or withhold trust. The traditional religious commandment has been that we should trust God, not that we should live up to any divine trust in us. It is an important fact about trust that it cannot be given except by those who have only limited knowledge, and usually even less control, over those to whom it is given.

It was not trust in trust which I tentatively promoted to supreme virtue for ones like us, with finite mutual knowledge and mutual control, but trust in sustained trust, along with trustworthiness to sustain trust. And the temporal stretch is important. Gambetta defined trust as willingness to cooperate with another *before* monitoring her performance, perhaps even without any capacity ever to monitor it. I have put a similar point by saying[10] that it is willingness to give discretionary powers, to postpone checking and account-ing. But except in rare cases there will eventually be some contrived or fairly automatic accounting, and with it some discovery of how well or badly the trusted person performed. One-shot brief trustings do occur, but, except when fatal, usually they will be followed by retrospective "monitoring" of their outcomes by the trusters. It is the cases where we repeat a previously ventured type of trusting, or sustain an old trust, that present the most interesting dimensions of trust, and those most important for our lives together. (What we *see* as a repetition of a familiar form of trusting, or see as a mere con-tinuation of an old trust, will of course affect our willingness to give trust.) Because sustained trust is experienced trust, is a willingness to postpone any further accounting because past accounts have been satisfactory, its conditions are both some relevant knowledge and some relevant ignorance about the trusted. Should any form of meta-trust be put forward as candidate for the position of moral centrality that Royce believed "loyalty to loyalty" to have, it had better not be one of the blinder variants of trust or of meta-trust.

But I am not really concerned to elevate any virtue to supremacy. Even if we could effect some sort of unification of the virtues by relating them all to due trust and due trustworthiness (and some often-neglected virtues from gentle ones like tact, discretion, patience, and the avoidance of bitterness, to feistier ones such as resilience, alertness to the oppression of those who are too oppressed to protest on their own behalf, and inventiveness in the redesign of roles, do come to the fore once we look at trust relationships), we will still need a whole host of virtues, more or less democratically ruling in our souls, balancing each other's likely excesses. The theoretical exercise of seeing how we could illuminatingly map the interrelationships of the virtues is of course one that appeals to philosophers, but it is not part of my present aim to show that due trust and due trustworthiness can lord it over other virtues. My aim here is less imperial, more modest—to imitate Hume, it is to bring the topic of trust and distrust a little more into philosophical fashion (its fashion in films, novels, and short stories is already established and it is catching on in applied ethics) to increase our understanding of our own selective trust in selective trust, to increase our self consciousness of our own capacities for creating the conditions for sensible trusting.

Parents of small children these days surely face a very difficult problem—on the one hand they want to surround the child with an atmosphere of mutual trust, to help the growing child to trust them, trust herself, and trust their will to help not hinder her in her attempts to explore, enjoy, and also to control, the world around her, to learn to walk, talk, and generally participate in human activities. On the other hand the child has to be put on guard against dangers, not just deterred from too adventurous experiments with the non-human environment, but also from unselective trust in older persons, since some do not wish her well. How to strike the right balance in the child between undue trust in others and in her own ability to do things safely with others, on the one hand, and undue timidity, fear and suspicion, on the other, seems a task that would require the wisdom of a Solomon or a Queen of Sheba. But somehow many parents bring it off. We do seem to have some innate capacities, not merely for trusting and meeting trust, but also for trustworthy transmission of discriminating trusting, despite our inability to analyze, let alone to reduce to any kind of rule, the dispositions that we manage to encourage. Of course not all do manage to pass on their own more or less functional mix of trust and vigilance, and not all have it to pass on. Still, praise be, some have it, and do pass it on.

After a lecture on trust that I gave recently, where I had retold John Updike's story "Trust Me," in which a child is forgiving of his father's failure to catch him when he jumps trustingly into a swimming pool, in response to his father's assurance that he will catch him,[11] a friend told me the following bit of family legend. His father had reported his childhood experience (trauma?) of having been encouraged by his father to climb up onto a fairly high and slippery place, under which the father stood with outstretched arms, as if to catch the child, or at least to break his likely fall. The child duly climbed, and duly fell. His father stepped aside, simply watching while his child fell and injured himself, and then helped him up, and tended his wounds. The hurt and bewildered child of course demanded of his father "Why did you do that?" and got the reply "So that, from now on, you will know that *no one* is to be trusted." Having heard this grim tale, I marveled a bit that my friend trusted me with it—indeed that he and his father had anything but extreme suspicion of apparent friendship. For those whose willingness to trust has been so dramatically punished will have to make very special efforts if they are to transmit anything but watchful suspicion to their own followers. Still, the wish to do better for the next generation than the previous generation did for us is a force not to be underestimated, even if the wish is only occasionally father to the successful deed.

And how would we recognize success in this transmission of attitudes? What mixture of caution and enterprise, trust and wariness, does the benevolent godmother wish the child's parents to somehow encourage in the child, either by providing models to be imitated, or at worst by providing object lessons of what to avoid? Can anything except unhelpful platitudes be said about the mixture that we reasonably welcome in young people, or in one another? Do we welcome different degrees and kinds of trust and mistrust at different ages? Is it healthier for the four year old than for the fourteen year old to trust the stranger who is offering some sort of treat? Is it any better or worse for the forty year old, or for that matter for the eighty year old?

We do seem to expect that with increase of age there will come increased acceptance of the truth of the maxim that there is no free lunch, so that the question "what does this person count on from me?" will reliably arise for, say, the fourteen year old who is invited to accept favors from strangers. But for the four year old it is usually just false that there is no free lunch—her lunch does not normally come with strings attached, so there is no very good reason why she should be suspicious of what seem to be free gifts. And even for forty and sixty year olds, there can be free gifts, which it would be graceless to refuse because of our suspicion that Hume may be right, that even "the more generous and noble intercourse of friendship" involves some expectation of return service, of some "recompense"(*Treatise*, 521). A. S. Byatt puts it nicely in her story "Art Work" (*New Yorker*, May 20, 1991), a story about an artist, his wife Debbie, and their cleaning woman, Mrs. Brown. "Mrs. Brown has always had an awkward habit of presuming to give the family gifts..." (A description follows of the "awful" and "flamboyant" sweaters she has knitted for the children.) "... The real sufferer is Debbie whose imagination is torn all ways. She knows from her own childhood exactly how it is to wear clothes one doesn't like, isn't comfortable and invisible in, is embarrassed by. She also believes very strongly that there is more true kindness and courtesy in accepting gifts gratefully and enthusiastically than in offering them. And, more selfishly, she simply cannot do without Mrs. Brown, she needs Mrs. Brown,..." (p. 42). Receipt of gifts can alter a relationship, create expectations of some return, and the exchange of gifts can cement relationships more than we sometimes welcome.

As Hume noted, we come to like those whom we have benefitted (or whom we think we have benefitted), and as Kant noted, for some people, himself clearly included, graceful acceptance of gifts, and so of indebtedness, does not come easily. Kant in his lectures on ethics said "A friend who bears my losses becomes my benefactor and puts me in his debt. I feel shy in his presence and cannot look him boldly in the face. The true relationship is canceled and friendship ceases." (Infield edition, p. 205.) Gratitude is for Kant a duty, and against the grain of the autonomy-loving man. In *The Metaphysics of Virtue*, sec. 32, he writes that "a person can never, by any recompense, acquit himself of a benefit received, because the recipient can never wrest from the giver the priority of merit, namely to have been first in benevolence". But true benevolence, for Kant, will not risk humiliating its beneficiary, it will disguise itself, and the virtuous benefactor will "express himself as being obligated or honored by the other's acceptance (of the benefit)" (sec. 31). This Kantian game of debt-avoidance and fake debt-acknowledgment by proud mutually respectful persons is clearly an adolescent or an adult game—children are innocent of its ploys and counterploys. They do not naturally fear those bearing gifts, nor are they hesitant to appear to be making gifts. Belief in the possibility of making and taking free gifts is one of the blessings of childhood, and so it seems a terrible condemnation of our society that this innocent blessing has to be withdrawn or circumscribed. It is one thing to encourage reciprocity and the expectation of the expectation of reciprocity, quite another to warn against all bearers of gifts.

It is not in all cultural settings that young children have to be instructed to beware of strangers offering sweets. There are varying climates of trust. Indeed the move from one, my native New Zealand, that was fairly kind to innocent trusters, and where houses were regularly left unlocked, to more menacing social climates, in Great Britain (where I was warned against gypsies and where unlocked doors were certainly discouraged), in the United States (where one must give only store-wrapped candy to children coming to the door at Halloween, since unwrapped or home wrapped sweets might be poisoned), in Austrian towns (where not just doors but front gates are often kept locked and even not-so-young women are warned that unaccompanied women in the city streets or cafes at night may be taken as "fair game" for men on the prowl) was what first led me to think about trust, and the historical and cultural factors affecting its presence and types. A city like Vienna, as long as its memories of its Nazi period and its occupation by foreign armies are still vivid, will be understandably uncertain of the safety of its streets at night. (On my arrival there by train shortly before the allied occupation ended, in 1955, a concerned gentleman who had shared a train compartment with my woman friend and me insisted on taking us to some religious society for the protection of women, who had an office at the station, and who duly found us "safe" lodging in a nunnery. Even on my return ten years later to a much more relaxed city, going to evening concerts alone was still regarded as risky for a woman.) To some extent it is an accident of military history, and of whether one was victor or vanquished, what climate of trust a city or a nation enjoys. But it is also a matter of the culture that continues through and between wars, and the sort of upbringing it gives to its young. A friend of mine who attended a parochial Catholic school for girls in the United States recently told me how puzzled she was by the religion classes she had to attend at school, until she was informed by more clued-up school mates that what this mysterious stuff amounted to was simply slightly coded instructions on how to remain a virgin. Sex education is all very well, but one hopes that it need not come in the guise of theology, nor come in a way that gives a girl to understand that the world she is part of divides into wise and cautious virgins on the one hand, and, on the other, predatory males along with their "fallen" victims, along with two dubious fringe groups—those who have chosen to marry rather than burn, and those who have been called to be priests, administering the moral rules for others, and making interesting rules for themselves.[12]

Religious traditions are places where we find it preached that trust in God, and in religious superiors who claim to speak on God's behalf, are virtues. It is not so surprising that philosophers have tended to shy clear of talking much about trust, given its guilt by association with such suspect monkish virtues as obedience. The current mini-revival of philosophical interest in trust in applied ethics, brings some dangers of a return to that unholy alliance of moral commands to "trust and obey". Wherever the roles of an institution have given some people authority to give orders to other people, as in the church, in hospitals, in the military, and in most political systems, there will be a tendency to construe trust in a more powerful person as involving willingness to obey orders, rather than to take instruction or counsel, to take advice, to be patient and defer satisfying one's reasonable desire to understand what is going on, to learn some valuable discipline, or to conform to authoritative laws which others have made. Even in the military, where a case can be made for the need for some to give commands and for others to obey them, we now encourage moral checks by the commanded on the content of some of the orders. By and large, *trust is a virtue only when it is not trust in authoritative commanders*. Where such positions of command are deemed unavoidable, then vigilance and non-paralyzing distrust will displace judicious trust as the functional virtues of that sort of highly asymmetrical cooperative scheme. Even when we agree that we need them, we should maintain some continuing distrust of those institutions that create commanders, since if we have learned anything from our individual and collective lessons in regrettable trusting, it surely is that power corrupts. Trustworthy institutions will be those that distribute power in such a way that this corruption is less likely. So, for example, in a medical context, we should not expect physicians who are dictators within their realm to exhibit trustworthy behavior, any more than we should expect it of any other would-be almighty ones, or their favored spokesmen, in religious or in non-religious organizations. *Trustworthy people*, we could say, *are to be expected only to the extent that the roles we have given them to play are trustworthy roles*. Of course there will be occasional saints who do not succumb to the temptations a badly-designed role puts in their way, and some especially vicious people who function badly even in the best-designed of social roles. The most we can hope for is that both the places we encourage or allow people to occupy, and the procedures we have that select who does occupy a given role, will both control the damage done by the very vicious, and, while placing no reliance on the likelihood of saints, give any who turn up the chance to show their special gifts not in resisting temptation, but in wonders of a more positive kind.

Granted the need for trustworthy institutions and institutional roles, it will still be rightly said that relationships of trust are not always between role-players, or structured by institutions and the power that they distribute. Do we not sometimes just trust a *person*, as a person, rather than as priest, as military commander, as chief surgeon, as customer, or whatever? Yes we surely do, and sometimes we trust animals, put ourselves in their power. In extreme cases, another person looks us in the eye and says "follow me," and we drop everything and do so. But it may on the whole be better to give such instant devotion to friendly cats than to those with pretensions to be kings. It is a pretty remarkable fact about us that we do form quick judgments about the trustworthiness of strangers, on the basis of some combination of eye contact, tone of voice, and other cues given by bodily expression, and perhaps, who knows, by our unconscious sense of smell, judgments that serve to launch us into personal relations of trust on matters great and small. I stagger under the load of heavy suitcases in a foreign airport and a stranger says "Let me help you with those." I glance at him, and do, although I have no assurance that he is not a thief in bourgeois clothing. I offer my assistance in an airport to a stranger, a man trying to carry both his suitcase and a one year old child, expecting that he will be glad to have me take his case, since I am walking unladen in the same direction. He glances at me and says "Thank you. Could you take her?" I marvel that the child is willing to cling to a stranger, and wonder as I carry her if she should be so willing. And so I ponder trust, wise and foolish trust, and ponder the mysterious bases of our trustings and distrustings.

This may be the appropriate point to apologize, if that is what I am now doing, for the excessively anecdotal nature of my remarks about trust. I do have some distrust of abstract theorizing in moral philosophy,[13] so I am in general more tolerant than are many of my colleagues of other approaches, of case studies (from fictional or real cases), of "natural histories" such as those of Hume or Rousseau, of perusal of autobiographies and biographies, of consultation with anthropologists, sociologists, historians. But on this topic in particular it would seem that a bit of self revelation is only proper—to borrow all my examples of rash or wise trusting from other people's lives would be to misrepresent the basis for whatever considered views I have about trust. I do not take my own case to be atypical, or at least not atypical for women,[14] but of course I may have been luckier or unluckier than most in some sorts of trustings and distrustings, so that some bias may be present in my approach. We have to trust others to discern such bias, since we are very bad at doing it for ourselves, so a little bit of relevant life history along with our more general reflections on trust seems only right and proper. I know, however, that I will not convince many of my fellow moral philosophers on this matter.[15] The impersonal style has become a pretty sacred tradition in moral philosophy, and examples of departure from it, such as Rousseau's *Confessions* (or St. Augustine's) are not altogether encouraging examples. Selective anecdote is very far from purportedly full confessional flow, but certainly has its own dangers, including those of bias. But it seems to me time to experiment a bit with styles of moral philosophy, especially for those of us who like Hume hope that moral philosophy can be accurate without being "abstruse," and might even "reconcile truth with novelty".

We do all make snap judgments about people, as a basis for our decisions to put or not to put ourselves in their hands on some matter, and even "profound inquiry" and the most "abstract speculations" into our moral capacities will have to accommodate not just the fact that we do this, but that bad judgment here is the exception not the rule.[16] Is it that the really bad judges on this matter do not survive to get into our epistemological records? Unfortunately infants depend more on their parents' willingness to encourage trust and a developing judgment of whom to trust than they do on their own initial capacities. Those who die in infancy do not often die from their own bad judgment. Any who are burdened from the start with distrust of those who offer food or care will be severely handicapped, and trustworthiness towards them will call for special skills and virtues, but it will not be judgment that such special caretakers will be trying at first to impart, as much as pre-judgment attitudes, the very capacity to trust. Unless we have that, there will be no scope for judgments about whom to trust, nor for judgments about what matters to trust to a particular person.

Some innate or soon acquired willingness to show some trust in those who stand in a parental capacity to the child is the primitive basis of other more judgment-mediated trustings. But this does not give us exactly a case of trusting persons *qua* persons, as distinct from trusting those in a given role. For parenthood is a social role, even if we want to call it also a natural role. Even our most spontaneous trustings may be trustings (or distrustings) of those in a given role, where the role filler cannot be entirely separated from the role filled. For we do engage fairly instinctively in natural "rituals," such as hugging, exchanging smiles, taking and shaking hands, and these can be seen to define simple roles, with some primitive role differentiation. *Those for whom trustworthiness or treachery are possibilities, we might say, are ones who can have eye contact with one another, or answer each others calls.* Calling and answering are primitive cooperative practices,involving a role for caller that is distinct from that of answerer. Infants delight in learning variations of these responsive activities, and playing games involving them. They may risk little by a smile in return for a smile, but more perhaps by taking another's offered hand. The handshake is learned in almost all societies as the symbol of some mutual trusting, and it grows out of more asymmetrical trustings of small hands into larger ones, offered to support or to guide.

The supporting hand can turn into the abducting or the abusive hand, and the guiding hand can lead into traps and dangers. The trusting one always puts herself in the trusted's power, and by her trusting increases the power of the one who is trusted. In the case of the very young, the trusted older person whose hand is taken will be one who already has more power than she does, more physical strength and more knowledge of how to get what is wanted. By cooperative trusting behavior the truster renounces some of her own small power to control matters, and as long as the more powerful trusted one wants what she wants, this voluntary renunciation of control will advance her goals, will get her where she wants to be, and often will help her to increase her own strength and ability. When matters work out well, her voluntary giving up of power will be an investment whose returns will be ultimate increase for her. But if things go badly, she will be harmed not helped by her trusting. Risk is of the very essence of trust.[17]

When the trust is mutual, the risks are on both sides, and most trust is to some degree mutual. Even the youngest child has some power to hurt and harm—when I take the stranger's little girl into my arms in the airport, I *might* be rewarded by having my ear bitten or my hair pulled. Normally we do not even think of such possibilities, and nor do we expect the very small child to think of the bad possibilities of being in the stronger arms of another. Should one actually review all the possible bad outcomes of some avoidable dealing with another before embarking on it, the calculated risk which one then took, if one went ahead, would scarcely warrant the label "trust". Trusting is taking not-so-calculated risks,[18] which is not the same as ill-judged ones. Part of what it is to trust is not to have too many thoughts about possible betrayals, since they would turn the trust into mistrust.[19] There can be mistrustful reliance on another, reliance accompanied by predictions that the relied-upon will prove unreliable. The alternative to trusting another is not always avoidance of being in their power—that is sometimes unavoidable, and sometimes when it is avoidable it is nevertheless chosen, but mistrustfully, and with some misgivings. It takes a fairly generous person not to respond to such mistrust with mistrust of her own. Francis Bacon wrote that "base natures, if they find themselves once suspected, will never be true"[20] and not-so-base natures, who remain true, may still develop mistrust of their own. There can be mistrustful fidelity. Mistrust can bring out the worst in the mistrusted, as trust can bring out the best. Albert Hirschman has pointed out that trust, like other of our moral resources, increases with use, decays with disuse.[21] Both trust and mistrust tend to be self-fulfilling, and tend to be contagious.[22]

The handshake, that sacred sealer of deals, is a nice example of a gesture that combines trust and caution. It is the remnant of a mutually disempowering gesture, a mutual putting out of full action of the strong manipulative right hand. The mutuality of its disempowering effect protects each party, so that little is risked by the gesture itself. Yet there is still a sense in which one must trust the partner to a handshake—not merely trust him to honor whatever deal the handshake seals, but trust him to be what he purports to be, a partner in a reciprocal and non-harmful gestural exchange. Even when the handshake seals no bargain, but is merely a greeting, it does make some pretenses, and these like all pretenses can be false. The pretense is of equality, reciprocity, good will. Should the hand I shake have a concealed spiked mitt in its palm, I will be a victim. Should the hand have an open wound, and the shaker have some deadly disease communicated by body fluids, I may become the victim of an ill-judged handshake. Normally we do not think at all of such possibilities—as John Locke said, we live on trust. Sometimes we are surprised in less unpleasant, but nevertheless disturbing ways. I recall my first introduction in Austria, when I trustingly held out my hand to shake that of the man to whom I was being introduced, and was astounded to find it lightly taken and raised to the man's lips. Why should this have upset me? Is this not a charming old world gesture? It is a gesture intended not merely for use between gentlemen and ladies who spend time on the care of their hands (as distinct from women with hands rough and earthy from gardening, or inky from writing) but also between those unequal in perceived power to take the initiative. The man is active, the woman passive. Her hand is taken and subjected to a kiss. There is a mutual vulnerability of a sort—the man does risk a dirty or germy hand at his lips. But the symbol is quite other than that of the handshake, a symbol of fake devotion to a more delicate and more passive person. To submit to this custom is, for a woman, indeed to submit. For one reared in more egalitarian cultural climates, in New Zealand where handshakes or mutual nose rubbings are the rule (and bowings and curtseyings are hastily improvised for the occasional royal visit), Austrian polite greetings came at first as a genteel shock, a matter for wonder and later for amusement. ("Handküsse an die Frau Gemahlin," as bit of telephone pleasantry, surely cries out for ridicule.)

Our everyday gestures do put us into short-lived roles vis-a-vis one another, ones that involve some mutual trusting, and that may be symbolic of the longer lasting roles that we fill or are expected to fill. I have dwelt on variations of the greeting and of hand-takings, because they are simple cases putting ourselves in the power of others, and they show both how natural it is for us to do this (the embrace is common to all cultures, the handshake between equals to very many) and how cultural variation can come in to shift the power relations, to vary the degree of reciprocity. Earlier I claimed that trustworthy people are to be expected only to the extent that the roles we give them to play are trustworthy roles. I modified this claim by allowing that spontaneous trust, cued by some hard to analyze feature of the trusted person's face, stance, voice and general aura certainly happens, as does spontaneous distrust, and is minimally role-affected, but our lasting relationships with others are rarely based only on such instant recognitions. We may, on the basis of eye contact, or other sorts of instant attraction, be willing to have more intimate contact with another for a night or so, but few of us would take marriage vows just because we had looked into another's eyes and liked what we saw. (Liked the version of ourselves we saw there?) Some do marry and marry happily, on the basis of very selective pre-marriage mutual knowledge of one another, so we do seem able to make fairly sound judgments of trustworthiness on the basis of fairly restricted data, and that is clearly a vital human cognitive skill. But we also make bad errors here, and how disastrous their consequences are will often depend on just how the lasting roles that we enter are structured. The design of the roles of husband and wife has changed, is still changing, and pretty obviously such changes both pressure the spouse into certain sorts of trustworthiness, while perhaps also creating temptations for other sorts of infidelity, and limit the severity of the harm that comes from disappointed trust. That people married when divorce was not yet a possibility is a fact to marvel at—it shows either their amazing confidence in their powers of mutual assessment for trustworthiness, or the compelling force of those drives that, in traditional societies, were channeled into matrimony—the need for a sexual mate, and the wish to have children socially recognized as ones own.[23] If it was better to marry for life than to burn, the fires had to be very fierce indeed.

Women, when faced not merely like men with a no-exit form of marriage, but also with the loss of their property rights at marriage and with the obligation to obey their husbands, took extraordinary risks, and often bad risks, by choosing to marry. But of course their options were limited. Choosing to be an unmarried governess or a housekeeper was also choosing to be in the power of some master, and so for all its horrors, Victorian marriage may well have seemed, to women who had any choice, to be the safer bet. The changes in the design of marital roles in the last hundred years in our society have radically altered the climate of trust and distrust between marriage-inclined men and women, and show us just how "manners makyth men". Novels such as those of Ivy Compton Burnett, describing terrible family tyrants and the protective ploys and counterploys of those forced to live under one roof in intimacy and mutual distrust, document for us not so much the nastiness of our own nature, as the horror that was the Victorian family. The raw material, male and female, is doubtless much as it always was, but husbands are less likely to be ruthless bullies, wives and daughters less likely to be wily schemers, sons less likely to be plotting takeovers from their fathers, once we have the changes we now have in the rights of wives, in women's opportunity to have careers outside the home, as well as in young men's freedom to move away from paternal control, and to have ambitions finer than becoming patriarchs in their turn. Whatever the problems facing us now, real problems that are the results of greater sexual freedom and the breakdown of a patriarchal tyranny, and problems that create their own climate of insecurity and distrust, they are a great advance on those faced by people living in the straitjacket of the sort of family described for us by Compton Burnett, or in the plays of Ibsen. The specter of deadly venereal disease haunting human sexual intimacy, in and out of marriage, is no new phenomenon. When the marriages it entered were "till death do us part," there was no protection. When a double standard operated, making divorce easier for husbands than for wives to initiate, women were at special risk, risk over and above that which childbirth then involved. Tragic as our present sexual scene may be (given the AIDS epidemic), what woman in today's society would choose to change places with her 1890s counterpart?

Changes in marital and other family roles (for example in children's rights) affect the expectations it is reasonable for us to have of one another, affect what we can trust each other with, and for. Other changes in institutional design are equally effective controllers of our climate of trust. Universities who have appointed an ombudsperson, to whom complaints can be made without alerting complained-of superiors into punitive reaction, thereby alter all the other roles in their hierarchy. Chairpersons and deans become more trustworthy by the sheer background presence of well designed procedures for complaint. This is not because these officers will fear exposure of any abuses of power they may be tempted to, it is because they will be less likely to feel the temptation. Just as the procedures for judicial appeal affect the powers and role of judges in lower courts, so the creation of the job of ombudsperson alters the powers and role of other university officers, and so alters the opportunities and temptations they have for abuse of their power. These are pretty obvious ways by which we can mold people to make them more trustworthy, and so be able to afford to encourage people to be more trusting.

Niklas Luhmann[24] distinguishes between our "familiarity" with and "confidence" in our customs and institutions and our "trust" in one another, as we encounter each other in the society that is structured by our customs and institutions. He pairs confidence with danger, trust with risk. Both involve our willingness to act in ways that we cannot be sure will not lead to disappointment or disaster. If we are confident, we ignore the danger, which is quite different from saying that we are ignorant of its existence. If we have confidence in, say, our court procedures, then if we are accused of a crime of which we are innocent, we will expect acquittal, even though we know of cases where the system failed. Risk is unlike danger, Luhmann thinks, in that we *take* risks, whereas we can have no choice but to face dangers. To trust is to venture, to assess and accept risks, to distrust is to be averse to, and to avoid, such risk-taking. I have not drawn a sharp distinction between danger and risk, or between our confidence or lack of confidence in our institutions and our trust or distrust of those who fill roles in them, and whose lives are lived in the structure they impose. This is because I think that there is a continuum between our most and our least "chosen" vulnerabilities to others, so that Luhmann's "danger" and "risk" will merge. Nor do I think that all our trusting and risk taking is towards individuals, in or out of institutional roles—we take risks when we redesign roles, we place our trust, in Luhmann's sense of the term, in procedures as well as in people. Luhmann emphasizes the interdependence of confidence in our social systems and trust, understood as risk-taking by individuals. When there is unhappiness with and lack of confidence in structures that we take ourselves to be powerless to change, we have no choice but to keep on living within them, but if we are also so risk-averse that most of us will not invest, say, in government bonds or in industries vital to that system, then the system may change. "Thus lack of confidence and the need for trust may form a vicious circle. A system— economic, legal, or political—requires trust as an input condition. Without trust it cannot stimulate supportive activities in situations of uncertainty or risk. At the same time the structural and operational properties of such a system may erode confidence and thereby undermine one of the essential conditions of trust."[25] By parity of reasoning, where the societal and institutional conditions of trust are met, there will be willingness to take risks to support the structure, and also to venture to try to improve it. Since I have refused to separate the human role-filler very sharply from the variety of natural and humanly designed roles that she finds herself filling, sometimes by necessity and sometimes by choice, I have not drawn Luhmann's distinction between confidence in structures, despite their structural flaws and dangers, and willingness to give trust. For those we give our trust to, or withhold it from, are themselves molded by these structures, and the position from which we trust or distrust will be one of natural or social power or powerlessness. We begin as natural beggars, trusting that our begging hands will get bread not a stone, and having no natural inclination to bite the hand that feeds us. From the start we engage in some more or less equal exchanges (of smiles) and venture into some mutual trustings, slowly progressing to less restricted equalities and more equal reciprocities. And we learn soon enough whom and what to distrust—those brandishing whips, guns, or other means of attempting to get others in their power, those attempting to hold a monopoly of power, to prevent rather than to assist the less powerful from advancing towards equality, and so towards the optimal conditions for mutual trust.[26]

Notes

1. A version of this paper forms the Bugbee Lecture, given at the University of Montana, Missoula, October 9, 1991.
2. Josiah Royce, "The Philosophy of Loyalty," especially Lecture III, "Loyalty to Loyalty," in *The Basic Writings of Josiah Royce*, ed. John J. McDermott (Chicago: University of Chicago Press, 1969), vol. II, pp. 855-1014.
3. *Trust: Making and Breaking Cooperative Relations* (Basil Blackwell, 1988).
4. J. Elster and K. Moene, eds., *Alternatives to Capitalism* (New York: Cambridge University Press, 1988), introduction.
5. Here they agree with most analysts of economic transactions. Kenneth Arrow, in "Gifts and Exchanges," *Philosophy and Public Affairs* 4 (Summer, 1972) p. 357, writes "virtually every commercial transaction has within itself an element of trust, certainly any transaction conducted over a period of time."
6. Gambetta, op.cit., p. 234.
7. Gambetta, op.cit., p. 217.
8. Gambetta, op.cit., p. 218.
9. In "Trust and Antitrust" (*Ethics* (96), January, 1986, pp. 231-260. Reprinted in

Feminism and Political Theory, ed. Cass Sunstein, University of Chicago Press, 1990), I defined it as accepted vulnerability to another person's power over something one cares about, in the confidence that such power will not be used to harm what is entrusted.

10. In my Tanner Lectures on Trust, forthcoming in *Tanner Lectures on Human Values*, vol. 13, (Salt Lake City: University of Utah Press).

11. John Updike, *Trust Me*, Short Stories, Fawcett Crest, New York.

12. My protestant upbringing gave me, as a child, such a distrust and terror of "priests in their gowns making their rounds" that when I was about ten, and sent by the headmaster of my school to take some message to the nearby parochial Catholic school, it took real courage for me to control my fears enough to walk into that school and hand over the note. I remember it as my first test of courage. So ashamed of this attitude was I later, as a young woman, that I eagerly welcomed an opportunity I was offered to become acquainted with a young priest, with shared literary interests. The acquaintance ended fairly abruptly when he proposed that my current accommodation problem, in a city where rents were high and apartments scarce, be solved by his providing me with a comfortable place, since his responsibilities gave him some control over housing owned by the church, in return for his having rights of visit and sexual favors. When I inquired how such a proposal sat with his religious and moral conscience, he cheerfully assured me that he would not dream of making such a proposal to one of his own flock, but lapsed protestant women were a different matter. So my initial irrational distrust of priests in their gowns was replaced by a more rational distrust.

13. I discuss this in "Trust and Distrust of Moral Philosophers," forthcoming in the proceedings of a conference on applied ethics held at the University of British Columbia, Vancouver, June 1990.

14. After my anecdotal Tanner Lectures on trust (given at Princeton in March 1991, forthcoming in *Tanner Lectures on Human Values*, op.cit.), several women members of the audience, mostly younger women, expressed appreciation of my willingness to break the traditional reticence on these matters of personal experience.

15. A respected older mentor, after an anecdotal talk of mine about trust, said "This may all be great fun, but is it real professional work?"

16. Diego Gambetta, "Can We Trust Trust?" in Gambetta, op.cit., p. 217, note 6, cites Woody Allen's insight, in *Hannah and Her Sisters* that "Why the Holocaust?" is the wrong question—what we should ask is rather why it does not happen more often.

17. See Niklas Luhmann, "Familiarity, Confidence, Trust: Problems and Alternatives" in Gambetta, op.cit., pp. 84-107.

18. Luhmann, op.cit., p. 97, distinguishes trust from confidence, requiring some sort of risk assessment to be present in the case of trust.

19. I discuss this, in the case of trust in intimates, in "Trusting Ex-Intimates," *Person to Person*, ed. H. Lafollette & G. Graham, Philadelphia (Temple University Press) 1989, pp. 269-281.

20. Francis Bacon, *Remains* (London: Robert Chiswell, 1679), p. 70.

21. Albert Hirschman, "Against Parsimony: Three easy ways of complicating some categories of economic discourse," *American Economic Review Proceedings* 74 (1984) pp. 88-96.

22. See Thomas Schelling, *Micromotives and Macrobehaviour* (New York: Norton, 1978) for a study of such self fulfilling beliefs about how others will behave.

23. Distinguished opponents of divorce, such as David Hume, in his essay "Of

Polygamy and Divorces," rest much of their case on the duty of parents to put the good of their children before their own preferences, but the empirical assumption that young children are more harmed by the break-up of their parents' marriage than by sustained mutual hostility in marriage seems very dubious. Significantly, after making his case for no-exit marriages, Hume kept clear of matrimony.

24. Luhmann, op.cit.
25. Luhmann, op.cit., p. 103.
26. I develop this claim that distrust is properly directed at those who try to prevent their inferiors from advancing, trust at those who assist them, in my Tanner Lectures, op.cit.

Philosophical Perspectives, 6, Ethics, 1992

INTERNALISM AND AGENCY

Stephen L. Darwall
University of Michigan

As interest has refocused in recent years on fundamental questions of meta-ethics, a group of loosely-related ideas collectively referred to as *internalism* have come in for increasing attention and controversy. A good example would be recent debates about moral realism where question of the relation between ethics (or ethical judgment) and the will has come to loom large.[1] Unfortunately, however, the range of positions labelled internalist in ethical writing is bewilderingly large, and only infrequently are important distinctions kept clear.[2] Sometimes writers have in mind the view that sincere *assent* to a moral (or, more generally, an ethical) judgment concerning what one should do is necessarily connected to motivation (actual or dispositional).[3] This necessity may be conceptual, or perhaps metaphysical, the thought being that it is not merely a contingent matter that people have motives to do what they think or sincerely say they should. I call internalism of this variety *judgment internalism* and distinguish it from another set of theses that concern, not what it is to accept an ethical judgment, but what it is for such a judgment to be true.[4] According to *existence internalism*, someone morally (or ethically) ought to do something only if, necessarily, she (*the agent*) has (actually or dispositionally) motives to do so. Again, this necessity might be conceptual or metaphysical, the thought being that it is not merely a contingent matter that agents have motives to act as they ought.

Already, several comments are necessary. It may be wondered, for example, what the point is of adding 'ethical' to 'moral' in these two formulations. Falk is generally read as having originally introduced 'internalism' to refer to a view about the moral 'ought', viz., that, necessarily, an agent morally ought to do something, say *A*, only if she has a motive to *A*.[5] Falk did not distinguish between this claim and the thesis that, necessarily, an agent morally ought to *A* only if there exists *reason* or justification for her to do so. Indeed, the view he had in mind was that a moral 'ought' claim is true only if its grounds are themselves reasons to act, *both* justificationally and (at least potentially) motivationally.[6] These claims came to the same thing for him because, evidently, he believed that the existence of (justifying) practical reasons also necessarily depends upon motivation.[7] This is controversial, however. Someone might think that there being reasons to act—indeed, an agent's having such reasons—has no necessary connection to motivation. (Justifying) reasons *for* someone *to* do something can be distinguished from an agent's actual (motivating) reasons for acting, and it can be held that whether there are good or justifying reasons for an agent to do something is completely independent of her motives, actual or hypothetical.[8]

Falk's suppressed premise was an internalism about practical reasons, but it was no less a meta-*ethical* thesis for that.[9] Whether there are reasons to act is a normative and thus, in the broad sense, an ethical matter.[10] It concerns what the agent rationally *ought* to do. Moreover, the rational 'ought' is almost never treated by philosophers as simply one 'ought' among others, on all fours with 'ought''s *internal to*, e.g., etiquette, baseball, or bridge. It is regarded, if only implicitly, as *unqualifiedly normative*—not just an ought-according-to-the-norms-of-rationality, as there might be oughts-according-to-the-norms-of-etiquette, or -baseball, or -bridge. What a person rationally ought to do is whatever he ought to do *simpliciter—sans phrase*, as it were.[11] It is, with some redundancy, what he ethically ought to do.

Consider in this light the position of those who assert existence internalism of practical reasons, but deny it of morality, and conclude from this that morality has no warranted claim to unqualified normativity. Such a line of thought can impugn the unqualified normativity of the moral 'ought' only if the rational 'ought' has it.

A different picture would be that morality lacks unqualified normativity, but then, so does everything. There are 'ought''s of morality, rationality, etiquette, bridge, baseball, and whatever other systems of norms one cares to imagine, but none of these bear on some further issue—what a person should do *simpliciter*; there is no such further issue. This, however, amounts to a form of ethical skepticism. Insofar as it is practical, ethics' fundamental question is what a person should do. Unqualified normativity would appear to be its subject.[12]

Judgment and existence internalisms are always asserted, I believe, of what their proponents *take* to be unqualifiedly normative. Judgment internalists about morality, for example, see their view as recommended by the fact that the (unqualified) normativity of moral judgment cannot be adequately understood except by way of connection to judge's-motivation. And existence internalists about morality reason that the (unqualified) normativity of the moral 'ought' requires agent's-motivation as a necessary condition of its truth.[13] Judgment or existence internalism about morality will seem plausible, I submit, only if one thinks that morality *is* unqualifiedly normative.[14] Thus, internalists about practical reasons who are externalists about morality also deny that moral 'ought''s have unqualified normativity. In the end, internalism is offered as a thesis about unqualified normativity and normative judgment.

Sometimes the view that morality is unqualifiedly normative is simply taken to *be* a form of internalism.[15] This makes reasons to act internal to morality, but the internalisms we shall be concerned with are views that hold the normative, or normative judgment, to be necessarily related to what is internal *to us*.

Or again, 'internalism' sometimes refers to a view about motivation—for example, to the view that belief by itself is motivationally inert and that all motivation derives from desire.[16] The issues to which ethical internalism is addressed, however, can be treated somewhat independently of these matters of philosophical psychology. If, for example, ethical judgment is necessarily connected to motivation, the latter might be carried by a desire, or by a distinctive conative state—such as Gibbard's "acceptance of a norm"—, or, perhaps, by a peculiar variety of motivating belief.[17] *Ethical* internalism is addressed to the nature of ethics and ethical judgment, and even if issues of philosophical psychology cannot be postponed indefinitely, the initial focus is different.

Existence internalism, a preliminary distinction

Existence internalism is a metaphysical claim. It is the nature of unqualified normativity, it holds, to be necessarily related to motivation. But this general characterization admits of two very different kinds of view. On one, the ethical is such that motivation is necessarily an effect of engaging it epistemically. On the other, motivation is a constituent of ethical facts themselves. The most familiar versions of the former are rational intuitionisms such as Plato's which hold that it is of the nature of the Good that it cannot be fully grasped with indifference. Richard Price held a similar view about moral obligation: "When we are conscious that an action...*ought* to be done, it is not conceivable that we can remain *uninfluenced*, or want a *motive* to action."[18] These may seem to be versions of judgment internalism, but they are not. They say, not that ethical belief or sincere assertion necessarily motivates, but that actual consciousness of or cognitive contact with the ethical does.[19] But Price also stresses that motivation has nothing to do with what ethical facts themselves are. Motive is "the *effect* of obligation perceived, rather than *obligation itself*."[20] This, however, is precisely what views of the second kind assert. Seeking an understanding of the unqualifiedly normative—of what it is for an act to be something an agent ought to do—they look to motivation. They hold that, ultimately, normative force must be understood as a kind of motivational force.

Thus, although both these varieties of existence internalism assert that, necessarily, an agent ought to do something only if, necessarily she would have under certain circumstances a motive to do so, only the latter is a *constitutive internalism*. Only on the latter sort of view does the agent's (dispositional) motivation have anything to do with what makes it the case that he ought to act. Only constitutive internalism, we might say, situates normativity itself *within* agency.

This difference reflects two different ways of looking at practical reason. For rational intuitionists such as Plato and Price, there is no fundamental difference between practical and theoretical reason. Reason is the faculty of cognition, and ethical facts are no less available to it than, say, mathematical ones. The difference consists in the objects of cognition. Unlike other objects of knowledge, the ethical is such that, necessarily, to know it is to be moved. For constitutive internalists, on the other hand, practical reason is not simply theoretical reason applied to the discovery of ethical truths. Rather, as I shall argue, constitutive internalists view practical reason as realized in the practical reasoning that *agents* do. And facts concerning what agents *ought* to do are constituted by motives they can acquire through practical reasoning. The formula "reason can be practical" is thus ambiguous as between two quite different ideas.

Some kind of non-constitutive existence internalism appears to be the crucial premise in J. L. Mackie's well-known argument that ethical properties are too "queer" to exist.[21] If anything really were "objectively valuable," as he puts it, it would have to have an unqualified normativity that would necessarily motivate when grasped. "An objective good would be sought by anyone who was acquainted with it, not because of any contingent fact that this person, or every person, is so constituted that he desires this end, but just because the end has to-be-pursuedness somehow built into it."[22] But it is mysterious how there could be such a property, precisely because it seems to require a bridge between knowledge, or its object, and *action*. Constitutive internalisms also hold that ethical knowledge necessarily motivates, at least when it is gained by an agent for herself within the deliberative process of practical reasoning and judgment.[23] But that is because, for such views, practical knowledge is *of motives* deriving from the agent's practical reasoning. For non-constitutive internalisms, however, there is no such connection between the *object* of ethical knowledge and agent's-motive. And practical reason, on such views, can refer only to the fact that when the general faculty through which we cognize truth grasps ethical truth, motivation necessarily results. How this connection might be effected nonetheless remains a mystery. There is no necessary connection in general between knowledge and motive, and non-constitutive existence internalists have traditionally eschewed any account of the object of ethical knowledge in particular that would relate it to agent's-motive.

Recently, however, another form of non-constitutive existence internalism has been proposed that promises to relate ethics to motivation in a new way.[24] Inspired partly by the concerns just registered, but also by a resistance to non-cognitivism *and* to constitutive internalism, John McDowell and David Wiggins have articulated a meta-ethical position, which because it aims to model our understanding of ethical properties on that of secondary qualities such as color, we might call *sensibility theory*.[25] Simplifying significantly, sensibility theorists claim (a) that we have distinctively ethical sensibilities, which have affective and motivational aspects; (b) that these sensibilities cannot be understood projectively, but only in terms of ethical properties they implicitly attribute; and (c) that, nonetheless, ethical properties can themselves adequately be understood only by relation to a relevant sensibility, including its motivational aspects.

As an analogy, consider the sense of humor. A person lacking in a sense of humor does not perceive the humor in a situation and simply fail to be amused; sensing humor apparently includes its distinctive affect. But neither can we well understand what it is to *be* humorous independently of amusement and a sense of humor. Sentiment and property seem to require each other in something like the same way color and color sense interdepend.

Sensibility meta-ethical theories make similar claims about the relation between ethical sensibility and ethical properties. Someone lacking moral sense, they claim, will not perceive that a certain situation, say the avoidable suffering of a child, calls for action, but simply fail to be moved. Sensibility theory is thus an existence internalism, but unlike rational intuitionism, it holds motivation not to be an effect of ethical cognition, so much as a component or condition. And contrary to constitutive internalism, sensibility theorists argue that what is cognized is a *sui generis* space of reasons that apply to an agent irrespectively of her motives—not something constituted in any way out of her practical reasoning. An agent suffering no defect of practical rationality might fail to perceive an obligation she was genuinely under simply through lacking the power to be appropriately moved.

Sensibility theories may thus be thought of as non-constitutive existence internalisms that seek to explain an otherwise puzzling connection between moral cognition and motivation by the mutual dependence of moral property and sensibility. It is not clear, however, that this can suffice for an adequate account of unqualified normativity. Even if it is part of moral sensibility that, as McDowell argues, some properties it enables one to discern have the effect, when recognized, of silencing or outweighing other sorts of reasons in practical deliberation, we might imagine this also to be true of other matched sets of sensibility and property. What about the sense of the sacred, for example, or even the diabolical? Just as, according to sensibility theorists, only properly motivated agents can perceive the right, and then do so as authoritative and silencing other considerations, it may be no less true that only the devout can discern the sacred, and that they discern it as properly regulating conduct. And similarly, perhaps, for the diabolical. So long as the justificatory force of the moral can only be grounded within a moral sensibility that can in principle conflict with other "practical" senses, there seems nothing to give its reasons any weight except, as it were, *within* that sensibility, and certainly nothing to give them greater weight than those tied to any other. But if this is so then sensibility theory is apparently an inadequate account of unqualified normativity.[26]

Judgment internalism

Judgment and constitutive internalists share the belief that the unqualified normativity which is the hallmark of ethics is best explained by the idea that ethics is an inescapably *practical* subject. Consider Moore's famous open question argument against any attempt to reduce (what he regarded) the fundamental ethical property, intrinsic goodness, to any complex of naturalistic or metaphysical properties. We can always intelligibly ask of any such complex, Moore argued, whether that complex is itself good. The open question argument has had remarkable staying power, despite the fact that Moore's formulation has been known to rest on widely rejected assumptions in the philosophies of language and mind.[27] Why is this? Recall that intrinsic goodness for Moore (in *Principia*) has unqualified normativity built into it.[28] Moore alternately formulated an option's being intrinsically good as its "ought[ing] to exist for its own sake," and this entails that anyone who can realize it *ought*, other things equal, to do so. We can therefore put the thought behind the open question argument in this way: for any complex of naturalistic or metaphysical properties, it seems we can intelligibly ask of an arbitrary agent in a position to realize this complex, whether she *ought* to, other things being equal. But what explains why this question should prove so difficult to close? Judgment and constitutive internalists believe the explanation has to do with the necessary connection between unqualified normativity (or normative judgment) and motive.

This is clearest with judgment internalism. Moore explained the open question by the hypothesis that goodness is a *nonnatural* property, but exactly what he meant by this was not entirely clear.[29] Later Moore remarked that the contrast he had in mind could be put by saying that

> an intrinsic property is 'natural' if, in ascribing it to a natural object you are *to some extent* "describing" that object...and that hence an intrinsic property, e.g. the sense of 'good' with which we are concerned, is not 'natural' if, in ascribing it to a natural object you are not... describing that object *to any extent at all*.[30]

This may provide some confirmation of Stevenson's diagnosis that the seeds of non-cognitivism were already implicit in Moore's thinking. A nonnatural, intrinsic property, Moore is here saying, is one the attribution of which involves no description at all. Stevenson concluded that Moore's idea of a "nonnatural quality...must be taken as an invisible shadow cast by confusion and emotive meaning."[31] Similarly, Hare argued that the open question can be explained by the hypothesis that the judgment that something is good, unlike any descriptive judgment, necessarily expresses the speaker's *commendation*. Were 'good' to mean some complex of descriptive properties, *C*, it would "become impossible to commend [something] *for being C*."[32] Judging that it was good would add nothing to the judgment that it was C.

The cleanest way to be a judgment internalist is to be a *motive non-cognitivist*—to hold, that is, that the reason why ethical judgments are necessarily connected to judge's-motivation is that they *express* such motives, and that this exhausts their distinctively ethical content. Not all forms of non-cognitivism are judgment internalisms. For example, if Hume is read (anachronistically) as a non-cognitivist, rather than, say, a kind of naturalist or, perhaps, an error theorist, it is at least doubtful that he is best read as a motive non-cognitivist or, on these grounds, as a judgment internalist.[33] Humean moral judgments express *sentiments* directed towards contemplated motives or character traits, and these sentiments are only doubtfully motives themselves. Any form of non-cognitivism can "explain" the open question, of course, by the familiar fact that what is non-cognitive—whether sentiment, motive, or itch—cannot follow from anything, but if what is to be explained is the irreducibility of practical 'ought' judgments, then the appropriate non-cognitive candidate would seem to be a motive. Hare's view is that 'ought' judgments express a universal prescription, a preference for anyone doing a kind of thing in a kind of circumstance.[34] And Gibbard holds that judgments about what is reasonable or sensible express the acceptance of a norm permitting it, and that the latter state of mind includes a tendency to be governed by the norm oneself in like situations.[35] I say this is the cleanest way to be a judgment internalist since, for a motive non-cognitivist, the state of mind expressed by a judgment of unqualified normativity is exhausted by its motivational powers. Since it is not also a belief, the question cannot even arise, how can a belief of this sort motivate?

We have, then, three fundamentally distinct kinds of view, all of which have been called "internalism": judgment internalism and two sorts of existence internalism, constitutive and non-constitutive. What lies behind judgment internalism—at least in its purest form—is a view about, to paraphrase Stevenson, the "non-cognitive content of ethical terms." The reason why sincere assent to ethical judgments is necessarily connected to judge's-motivation is that expression of such motivation is all that ethical judgment *is*. What such judgments express is non-cognitive, a motivating attitude: a preference, perhaps, or the acceptance of a norm.[36]

Non-cognitivists do not offer this, of course, as an account of normativity (as distinct from normative judgment), since for them there really is no such thing. But unlike error theorists, who agree with this latter thesis, motive non-cognitivists believe that ethical judgments express no belief which can be confounded by this philosophical discovery. And if there need be no such thing as unqualified normativity to make sense of normative judgment, no question arises concerning what it might consist in, and no philosophical incentive to think that 'ought''s have anything essential to do with agent's-motive. To be sure, a motive non-cognitivist might hold the *ethical* position that agents ought only to do what they can be motivated to do under certain conditions, but his meta-ethics provide no particular ground for this view.

Constitutive internalism and philosophical naturalism

Constitutive internalists maintain, on the other hand, that there is something deserving to be called unqualified normativity, and seek to understand it as having a realization in the *practical realm*, from an *agent's* point of view, in motives generated through practical reasoning. Consider, for example, how the laws of nature function on Hobbes's view. On the one hand, Hobbes refers to these as "*dictates* of reason" and defines them as "precept[s] or general rule[s], found out by reason, by which a man is *forbidden* to do that which is destructive of his life, or taketh away the means of preserving the same; and to omit that, by which he thinketh it may be best preserved."[37] On the other, he says that the laws of nature are "but conclusions, or theorems concerning what conduceth to the conservation and defence of themselves."[38] And while he writes that "we ought to judge those actions only wrong, which are repugnant to right Reason," what he means by right reason is not some faculty of rational intuition, but simply a correct "reckoning" of consequences.[39]

But how is it possible for reason to *dictate* anything if the only thing it can tell us is what is likely to happen if we act in one way rather than another? What turns the latter, *theoretical* conclusion into an 'ought to do'? Hobbes never faces this question directly, but we can see how he must be thinking. Any of us, Hobbes believes, "by natural necessity...intend[s] the procurement of those things which are necessary to his own preservation."[40] Self-preservation is an inescapable human end. Thus reckoning concerning what is necessary to achieve self-preservation has an inescapable *practical* relevance for us. *As agents*, unavoidably viewing the world *sub specie* the end of self-preservation, our conclusions regarding how our lives are "best preserved," give rise to dictates, to 'ought to do''s. Of course, could we give up this end, the most we could conclude would be that we ought either to do what is necessary for self-preservation or renounce it as end, but the latter, Hobbes believes, is not an option that is open to us.

According to this line of thinking, theoretical reasoning becomes practical when placed in the service of ends—from the agent's point of view. Viewed from an observer's perspective, the thought that keeping covenants is, for anyone, the strategy necessary to achieve self-preservation is simply an observation about how things lie in nature. But if self-preservation is the end at which we unavoidably aim, it becomes, from our point of view as agents, a sufficient ground for the thought that keeping covenants is the strategy one *ought* to pursue. For Hobbes, this strategy's being unqualifiedly normative for human beings just *is* its being the case that human agents have a rationally conclusive *motive* for pursuing it.

Here, then, is a way of maintaining a view about the distinctive normativity of ethics within a comprehensively naturalist metaphysics and a broadly empiricist epistemology. There is no *sui generis* normative metaphysical order; nor have we a cognitive faculty that might access it if there were. Viewed from the observer's perspective, ethical truths do not differ fundamentally from those regarding any other natural connections in the world. They have a distinctive subject—the relations between human action and consequence— but they nonetheless concern the same natural order as does natural philosophy. Viewed, however, from the agent's point of view, ethical truths have an inescapable motivational force, since they concern the necessary means to an unavoidable end. And this is what their distinctive normativity consists in. Its being the case that a person *ought* to keep covenants, as this is the necessary means to an inescapable end, consists in his therefore having, as agent, an unavoidably conclusive motive for so doing. Ethics' distinctive normativity consists in practical relevance from the agent's point of view.

Although Hobbes pioneered this way of viewing normativity in general, and that of morality in particular, his near contemporary Richard Cumberland was more methodologically explicit.[41] Cumberland quite straightforwardly announces his belief that "the whole of moral philosophy, and of the laws of nature, is ultimately resolved into natural observations known by the experience of all men, or into conclusions of true natural philosophy."[42] How then is morality's normativity to be understood? For Cumberland, as for his contemporaries more generally, this was the same as asking how morality can *obligate* agents, how it can *bind*.[43] This latter idea, however, is "some-what obscure from metaphors; for the mind of man is not properly tied with bonds." "There is nothing," he continues, "which can superinduce a necessity of doing or forbearing any thing, upon a human mind deliberating upon a thing future, except thoughts or propositions promising good or evil to ourselves or others, consequent upon what we are about to do."[44] Since any rational agent "necessarily seeks his own greatest happiness," propositions concerning what is necessary for that have an inescapable practical relevance, and this is their normative force.

There is, Cumberland believes, a single law of nature: "the greatest benevolence of every rational agent towards all, forms the happiest state of every, and of all the benevolent, as far as is in their power."[45] So stated, this is a finding of natural philosophy. To appreciate its normative force, we must view it from the perspective of an agent "deliberating upon a thing future." From this standpoint, it has an unavoidable practical relevance, as it concerns the necessary means to a necessary end, and this is its normative force. Cumberland holds that the law of nature is a "practical proposition" which can be expressed variously as a proposition of natural philosophy concerning the connection between acts and consequences, as an imperative ("Let that action, which is in thy power, and which will most effectually, of all those which you can'st exert, promote the common good in the present circumstances be exerted"), or "in the form of a gerund; 'Such an action ought to be done.'" "In my opinion," he concludes, "these several forms of speech...mean the same thing."[46]

It is important to realize that even in its purest, instrumentalist form, the sort of view we are considering requires a distinction between actual motivation of actual agents, on an occasion, and motives they would have if their practical reasoning were in order. Both Hobbes and Cumberland take it that practical reasoning transfers motivation from end to necessary means, but it is surely conceptually possible for a being to have an end, believe that the only means to it is an action at hand, and not be motivated appropriately. Cumberland, indeed, recognizes this is a real possibility. "Upon discovering the law of nature," he writes, "all men are obliged, whether it be of so great weight with them, as perfectly to incline their minds to what it persuades" or not. They are obliged because belief in this proposition "would certainly prevail; unless the ignorance, turbulent affections, or rashness of men, like the fault in the balance, opposed their efficacy."[47] The law of nature is normative, therefore, because it would motivate an agent whose practical reasoning was not faulty. And correct *practical* reasoning involves, not just having correct beliefs about practice, but also deliberating about these, bringing them to bear on choice, in the right way. For an instrumentalist, this requires that motivation transfer from end to means. A failure to do so is a failure of practical reasoning.[48]

At this point, the sort of view we are now considering faces a dilemma. A purely instrumentalist version confronts the problem that our actual, uncriticized ends seem to provide an inadequate basis for normativity since we can surely also ask what ends we should have. The connection the instrumentalist proposes between means and ends seems uncontroversially defensible, at least, on grounds of something like practical coherence.[49] But that it is incoherent to maintain an end while refusing the only available means can provide no more reason to take the means than to renounce the end. On the other hand, any attempt to strengthen instrumental rationality to provide a more adequate basis for normativity, through specifying rational ends, seems to bring an accompanying increase in controversy, if not implausibility. Why, for example, must a rational agent aim at his own happiness?

An increasingly popular strategy has been to enhance instrumental reasoning with an account of the rational criticism of ends that looks primarily to an uncontroversial ideal of theoretical rationality. An agent's end may be based on ignorance in the straightforward sense that, were she to know more about it, she would renounce it. When the pursuit of an end is rooted in error, then, as Brandt (among others) has argued, it is plausible to suppose that this undermines the justification for taking necessary means.[50] Normativity cannot derive simply from the relation between means and end; it is also necessary that the agent would be motivated to adopt (or retain) the end were she to be perfectly informed about it and its place in the natural order. The first step in this strategy, then, is to hold that a necessary condition of its being the case that an agent ought to do something is that she would be motivated to do so were she *epistemically* perfect and instrumentally rational.[51] This will not be sufficient, however, since mere knowledge may fail to enter into deliberation or practical reasoning at all. As in Cumberland's example, "turbulent affections, or rashness" may impede judicious consideration of what one knows.[52] Correct theory must be brought properly to bear on practice in the agent's deliberative reasoning.

Of course, the constitutive internalist's standard for correct practical reasoning cannot be set externally, by whether the agent is motivated to do what she (independently) ought. The independent variable must be some procedure of practical reasoning whose correct exercise can be specified internally and not by its approximation to some external, independently specifiable result.[53] Thus, for Brandt, whether an action is rational depends on whether there is a stable truth concerning what the agent would be dominantly motivated to do were she knowledgeable about her situation *and* vividly to represent and think about what she knows.[54]

We may think of this as the appropriate outcome of a certain kind of philosophical naturalism. Concerned to place normativity in the natural order, the philosophical naturalist can hold that normativity consists in the *practical* consequences of accurately representing *that very order*. Thus, not only does normativity become a natural fact; it becomes the natural fact concerning whatever stable effect an agent's accurately representing the natural order itself has on her motives. So conceived, normative force is motivational force, not from just any motives, but from those arising from the contemplation of experience and correct natural theory. This situates normativity within an agency maximally improved by the experience and knowledge of nature.

Constitutive internalism and autonomy

Historically, philosophical naturalism was a major force leading to the original constitutive internalisms of the early modern period, as it continues to be today. But it is not the only line of thought leading to constitutive internalism whose influence dates from that period. A second begins by thinking about the capacity to be subject to norms, with the thought that only agents of a certain kind *can* be normatively bound. It then seeks to understand what normativity is by relating it to this capacity. Locke, for example, identifies himself in the *Essay* with "those who cannot conceive, how any thing can be capable of a Law, that is not a free Agent."[55] And, beginning in the second edition, he provides an account of the distinctive capacity for self-determination "intellectual beings" have owing to their ability to step back from present desires and critically examine alternatives. Moreover, while he never renounces his usual theological voluntarism, Locke includes along with his new theory of autonomy an argument that agents can only be obligated by motives created by self-determining practical thinking, and at points suggests that obligation just consists in this.[56]

We are most familiar, of course, with the shape this line of thought takes in Kant—viz., that practical laws are realized in the self-legislation of a free rational agent—but in some form or other it runs deep in the thinking of many philosophers. Among the early modern British moralists, for example, it can be found in Cudworth, Shaftesbury, and Butler (as well as Locke).[57] And in addition to Kant and post-Kantian idealists, it often appears in recent philosophers influenced by Kant, such as Thomas Nagel.[58] One way into this way of thinking is to begin with Kant's discussion of his claim that we unavoidably regard ourselves as free to do what we ought.[59] Sometimes the doctrine that 'ought' implies 'can' is understood to mean that a person must be able to do what he ought in the sense that, were circumstances to be such that he wanted so to act, he would—nothing is stopping choice from eventuating in action. What is most interesting about Kant's discussion, however, is that he explicitly distinguishes between the sense in which we might say that someone could have refrained from doing something, meaning that he would have if, say, a policeman had been at his elbow, and the sense with which he is concerned. Kant's claim is that when, for example, one is asked by a tyrant to betray an honorable man, and thinks one ought not, one is committed thereby to the thought that one *can* not do so *for the very reasons one thinks one ought not.* By Kant's lights, this is not a theoretical conjecture that might falsified, say, by a proof of determinism. It is an irreducibly *practical* thought, one we cannot avoid *as agents* deliberating about what to do, or in judgments of others (or ourselves) that involve an imaginative projection into their deliberative standpoints.[60]

The *deliberative* thought that, for certain reasons, one ought to choose an alternative requires the thought that one can choose that alternative for those very reasons. Nor is this latter thought confined to actual deliberation. Imputations of responsibility, either to ourselves or others, also require it, albeit by way of imaginative projection. To impute responsibility is to regard someone as a person—to relate to her as someone who can determine herself by reasons.[61] When we reproach ourselves for not having acted as we ought, and thereby impute responsibility, we must suppose we could have so acted for the reasons we (now think) we ought—that these could have been *our* reasons for acting. We project ourselves into our earlier deliberative standpoint from which we take such action to be (have been) a practical alternative. Likewise, when we blame, and impute responsibility to, another, we commit ourselves to a deliberative judgment we think he should have made and could have acted on from his (agent's) viewpoint.[62] We judge there were reasons *for him to act*, and, in so thinking, think he could have acted for those reasons.[63] In this way, reproach and blame differ from mere sanction or retaliation. Reproach does not just aim to *give* the agent a reason to do what we think he ought; it expresses the judgment that there *existed* sufficient reason, reason on which the agent could have acted. We can hardly blame others for doing what we think they had good and sufficient reason to do.

Suppose, then, that thinking a person is genuinely bound by a norm, and appropriately held responsible for following it, commits us to thinking she has the capacity to determine herself to conform to it. We will then require a philosophical understanding of normativity that can explain this connection. We will need an explanation of what normativity is such that a person is normatively bound to do A only if she can autonomously choose to do A. Constitutive internalists who take these concerns seriously give various versions of the following answer: being obligated consists in having a dominant motive resulting from the proper exercise of the capacity for autonomy. They proffer an account of autonomous practical thinking, and hold obligation to consist in motives resulting from the correct exercise of that. Thus Locke, holding that the only rational end is the agent's greatest happiness, and that autonomy involves the exercise of a free agent's power to step back from the press of present desire and, by imaginatively considering the objects of desire "on all sides," make a genuinely practical judgment of available future happiness with appropriate motivational force, maintains that this motive is an obligation to happiness.[64] And what makes morality, the law of nature, obligatory for Locke, is that God has divinely sanctioned it with eternal punishment and reward, and given human agents sufficient evidence of this that they can determine themselves to act morally.

For Kant, of course, this is a description of heteronomy. No material end, whether the agent's happiness or the happiness of all, can serve as an autonomous agent's governing motive. A Kantian autonomous agent governs her conduct by a conception of unqualified normativity, by a conception of law. Autonomy is *normative self-regulation* or self-*government*. This involves two, somewhat distinguishable elements in Kant's thought. First, an autonomous agent can act on a *rule* or "maxim" he gives to himself. And second, an autonomous agent can act on a conception of *law* (of unqualified norms that apply to any agent capable of normative self-regulation) by virtue of a distinctive second-order capacity for self-regulation (a capacity to regulate her self-regulation by maxims). "Nothing is left," ultimately to ground autonomous action than the idea of "the bare conformity of actions to universal law as such, this alone must serve the will as its principle." And the only way an autonomous agent can discipline rule-guided conduct by this idea is, Kant argues, to do so by the Categorical Imperative. An agent fully governs herself by a conception of law only if she subjects her will to the form of law—only if, he argues, she constrains her maxim-guided conduct by those she could will *as law*. "That is to say," he concludes, "I ought never to act except in such a way *that I can also will that my maxim should become a universal law...*".[65]

Locke's agent determines himself by judgments about his greatest happiness or good, but is unable to question whether this is an (or the only) end at which he *ought* to aim. Nor, indeed, does he aim at his own happiness because he thinks he ought to do so.[66] The idea of the normative plays no deliberative role. For Kant, however, autonomy is realized only by an agent for whom the idea of the normative (a conception of law) fundamentally governs practical deliberation. And it can do so only if an agent can act on rules and descipline her doing so by the Categorical Imperative.[67] If, for a given situation, she finds only one of a set of contenders she can will universally, she acts on it. She wills her acting on the maxim as an instance of willing that all do. And her being obligated to do so consists in the fact that she has a conclusive motive for doing so as a result of the practical thinking that realizes autonomy.[68] Thus are practical laws "laws of freedom." Unqualified normativity is the practical force for the agent of guiding herself by a conception of the unqualifiedly normative.

There are, then, two quite different lines of thought leading to constitutive internalism. For the philosophical naturalist, concerned to place normativity within the natural order, there is nothing plausible for normative force to be other than motivational force, perhaps when the agent's deliberative thinking is maximally improved by natural knowledge. This gives the naturalist a way of holding that while there is a sense in which, as Cumberland put it, "the whole of moral philosophy,...[can] ultimately [be] resolved into...conclusions of true natural philosophy," moral philosophy is not the very same subject as natural philosophy. What is distinctive about ethics, unqualified normativity, is the practical force some natural propositions have for us as agents.

For the line of thought we have just been considering, however, the attraction of constitutive internalism is primarily that it provides a philosophical understanding of the connection between being appropriately held subject to a norm and the capacity for normative self-determination. Only persons, it seems, can be subject to norms. But if to regard someone as a person subject to a norm is to think her able to determine herself by that very norm, then we need some understanding of what it is to be subject to a norm that assures this connection. But if normativity just is the force of motives resulting from self-determining practical reasoning, this connection is assured.

We have, then, two traditionally distinct philosophical rationales for constitutive internalism.[69] The thought that normativity can only adequately be grasped from within the agent's standpoint is, however, common to both— both situate normativity within agency. In this they contrast with the purest form of judgment internalism, motive non-cognitivism, which takes normativity to be a projection of the motives of the ethical judge, and with non-constitutive existence internalism, which locates it independently either of agency or judgment, in a distinct metaphysical order.

Notes

1. See, e.g., David Brink, *Moral Realism and the Foundations of Ethics* (Cambridge: Cambridge University Press, 1989), pp. 37-80.
2. Brink is a notable exception.
3. For a recent example see James Dreier, "Internalism and Speaker Relativism," *Ethics* 101 (1990): 6-26. Robert Audi calls this position "motivational internalism" in "Internalism and Externalism in Moral Epistemology," *Logos* 10 (1989): 13-37; see esp. p. 22. Mostly, however, he is concerned with internalist and externalist theses regarding moral knowledge, by analogy with a familiar contrast in epistemology.
4. I make this distinction in *Impartial Reason* (Ithaca: Cornell University Press, 1983), p. 54. See Brink, p. 40 for a similar distinction between what he calls "appraiser internalism" and "agent internalism."
5. Putting it this way is a little misleading, since Falk's point was that one conception we have of morality is a wide one in which we take the moral 'ought' to dictate whatever, on balance, there is reason to do. See "'Ought' and Motivation," *Proceedings of the Aristotelian Society* 48 (1947-8): 111-138; reprinted in Falk, *Ought, Reasons, and Morality* (Ithaca: Cornell University Press, 1986), pp. 21-41. Further references will be to the latter. For convenience, I will sometimes omit the qualifiers "necessarily" and "actually or dispositionally."
   The other classic article on internalism and externalism is William K. Frankena's "Obligation and Motivation in Recent Moral Philosophy," in A. I. Melden, ed., *Essays in Moral Philosophy* (Seattle: University of Washington Press, 1958), pp. 40-81.
6. Falk writes that Prichard is an externalist because "he holds that the man who while granting a duty doubts he has also a motive has a real axe to grind: there is no convincing him that he has a motive except by considerations additional

to those which already convince him that he has the duty." (27)

7. As he argues in "Action-Guiding Reasons," in *Ought, Reasons, and Morality*, pp. 82-98.

8. See Kurt Baier, *The Moral Point of View* (Ithaca: Cornell University Press, 1958), pp. 148-156, for the distinction between *justifying* and *motivating* reasons. Baier is an example of a philosopher who holds that justifying reasons are independent of motivation. For Baier's critique of an internalism about reasons, see "The Social Source of Reason," *Proceedings of the American Philosophical Association* 51 (1978): 707-733.

The remark has sometimes been made (including by the present author), that the distinction between justifying and motivating reasons derives from Hutcheson's distinction between "justifying" and "exciting" reasons. This is misleading since Hutcheson meant by the former a ground for moral approval (of character, motive, or motivated action), and he also held that such grounds cannot be reasons to act. Thus they are not justifying reasons in the present sense. See Francis Hutcheson, *Illustrations on the Moral Sense*, ed. Bernard Peach (Cambridge: Belknap Press of Harvard University Press, 1971), p. 121.

9. Note the emphasis on "-ethical" rather than "meta". We need presuppose no sharp line between meta- and normative ethics.

10. On this point, see Sidgwick's chapter "Ethical Judgments," in *The Methods of Ethics*, 7th ed. (London: MacMillan, 1967), pp. 23-38.

11. Some of the resonances of this latter phrase are misleading, since the intended contrast is orthogonal to one between a *prima facie* (or *pro tanto*) 'ought' and one "all things considered."

12. It is notable, in this connection, that G. E. Moore, whose ethics are fundamentally axiological, nonetheless understands intrinsic goodness to be essentially unqualifiedly normative. He regards 'what ought to exist for their own sakes' as a synonym for 'what is good intrinsically' or 'absolutely'. (*Principia Ethica* (Cambridge: Cambridge University Press, 1966), p. viii) It is essential to Moorean intrinsic goodness that, other things equal, everyone ought to do what they can to realize it. On this point see William K. Frankena, "Obligation and Value in the Ethics of G. E. Moore," in P. A. Schilpp, ed., *The Philosophy of G. E. Moore*, 3rd ed. (La Salle, Ill.: Open Court, 1968), pp. 99-110. See also Moore's reply, pp. 560-581, 592-606.

13. This is evident, for example, in Harman's argument that moral relativism follows from a certain form of existence internalism about morality. Unless this latter premise were true, he in effect argues, morality would not be unqualifiedly normative. See Gilbert Harman, "Moral Relativism Defended," *The Philosophical Review* 85 (1975): 3-22; and "Metaphysical Realism and Moral Relativism: Reflections on Hilary Putnam's *Reason, Truth, and History*," *The Journal of Philosophy* 79 (1982): 568-575.

14. Hare may seem to be a counterexample since he is a judgment internalist about morality, but holds, nonetheless, that whether it is rational to be moral may best be approached by Brandt's method of determining what course of conduct the agent would prefer under cognitive psychotherapy. On such a view there will be no necessary connection between judging what a person morally ought to do and judging what it would be rational for him to do. But by Hare's lights the latter is a descriptive rather than a normative question. In fact, not only does Hare hold moral judgment to be of the unqualifiedly normative, he holds it to be of the *overridingly* unqualifiedly normative. R. M. Hare, *Moral Thinking* (Oxford: Clarendon Press, 1981), pp. 20-24, 214-216.

15. E.g., by Brink, *Moral Realism*, p. 39.

16. See, e.g., Alfred Mele, "Motivational Internalism: The Forms and Limits of Practical Reasoning," *Philosophia* 19 (1989): 417-436.

17. Allan Gibbard, *Wise Choices, Apt Feelings* (Cambridge: Harvard University Press, 1990), pp. 55-82. For the last alternative, see, e.g., David McNaughton, *Moral Vision* (Oxford: Blackwell, 1988).

18. Richard Price, *A Review of the Principal Questions in Morals*, ed. D. D. Raphael (Oxford: Clarendon Press, 1974), p. 186. This passage is reprinted in D. D. Raphael, ed., *British Moralists* (Oxford: Clarendon Press, 1969), v. ii, p. 194.

19. Note that this is also different from thinking that being in the right motivational state is necessary for epistemic access.

20. Price, *A Review*, p. 114; Raphael, *British Moralists*, v. ii, p. 167.

21. J. L. Mackie, *Ethics: Inventing Right and Wrong* (Harmondsworth: Penguin, 1978), pp. 38-42.

22. *Ibid.*, p. 40.

23. Such deliberation may be only imaginative, of course.

24. By, independently, John McDowell and David Wiggins. For McDowell, see, e.g., "Are Moral Requirements Hypothetical Imperatives," *Proceedings of the Aristotelian Society*, supp. vol. 52 (1978): 13-29; "Virtue and Reason," *Monist* 62 (1979): 331-350; "Values and Secondary Qualities," in *Morality and Objectivity*, ed. Ted Honderich (London: Routledge and Kegan Paul, 1985); and "Truth and Projection in Ethics," Lindley Lecture (University of Kansas, 1987). For Wiggins, see, e.g., "Truth, Invention, and the Meaning of Life," "Truth as Predicated of Moral Judgments," and "A Sensible Subjectivism?," reprinted in Wiggins, *Needs, Values, and Truth: Essays in the Philosophy of Value* (Oxford: Basil Blackwell, 1987).

25. For a discussion of sensibility theories, see Stephen Darwall, Allan Gibbard, and Peter Railton, "Towards Fin de Siècle Ethics," *The Philosophical Review*, forthcoming, on which the discussion in the text draws.

26. For further discussion of these and related points, see *Ibid.*

27. William K. Frankena, "The Naturalistic Fallacy," *Mind* 48 (1939): 464-477; Gilbert Harman, *The Nature of Morality* (New York: Oxford University Press, 1977), pp. 19-20; David Brink, *Moral Realism*, pp. 151-154, 162-163.

28. See note 12 above.

29. Including perhaps, it is fair to say, to Moore himself. See Moore's "Reply to My Critics," in *The Philosophy of G. E. Moore*, pp. 581-592.

    For an extremely illuminating discussion of 'nonnaturalness' and the open question argument within the context of G. E. Moore's early thought, see Darryl Wright, *Refuting Idealism: G. E. Moore's Metaethics in Historical Context* (Ph.D. diss., University of Michigan, 1991).

30. *The Philosophy of G. E. Moore*, p. 591. See also note 24 above.

31. Charles Stevenson, *Ethics and Language* (New Haven: Yale University Press, 1944), p. 109.

32. R. M. Hare, *The Language of Morals* (London: Oxford University Press, 1964), p. 85.

33. For Hume as naturalist, see, e.g., Barry Stroud, *Hume*, (London: Routledge & Kegan Paul, 1977), pp. 171-218; for Hume as error theorist, see J. L. Mackie, *Hume's Moral Theory*, (London: Routledge & Kegan Paul, 1989); for doubts about Hume's judgment internalism, see Charlotte Brown, "Is Hume an Internalist?," *The Journal of the History of Philosophy* 66 (1988): 69-87.

34. On the latter point, see Hare, *Moral Thinking*, p. 91.

35. *Wise Choices, Apt Feelings*, pp. 68-82. Note that, unlike Hare's view, this does not imply any preference for others being governed by the norm.

For Gibbard, moral judgments (in the narrow sense) do *not* directly express judge's motive; rather they express acceptance of norms for having certain *reactions* (viz., feelings of guilt and resentment). Note also that the open question argument takes a distinctive form in Gibbard's hands. For him, the core phenomenon is that genuine disagreement about what it is rational to do apparently survives complete agreement about factual matters. For example, those who think it rational to take one box in Newcomb's Problem, and those who disagree and think both boxes should be taken, can agree completely about the features of the situation and the respective properties of Bayesian and causal decision theory. The best way to understand the issue between them is, Gibbard argues, noncognitively, viz., that these different judgments express conflicting non-cognitive states of mind: the acceptance of conflicting norms. On this point see *Wise Choices, Apt Feelings*, pp. 9-22, 36-54.

36. Obviously, on the latter view, we must be able to understand what it is to accept a norm non-cognitively.

37. Thomas Hobbes, *Leviathan*, chs. xv and xiv, respectively.

38. *Ibid.*, ch. xv.

39. *De Cive*, ch. ii; *Leviathan*, ch. v.

40. *De Cive*, ch. iii.

41. Richard Cumberland (1631-1718) was known as one of the three great modern writers on natural law, the other two being Grotius and Pufendorf. His *De Legibus Naturae disquisitio philosophica* (1672) was published in an English translation by J. Maxwell as *A Treatise of the Law of Nature* in 1727. Selections from this work can be found in J. B. Schneewind, ed., *Moral Philosophy from Montaigne to Kant* (Cambridge: Cambridge University Press, 1990), v. i, pp. 138-155; and in D. D. Raphael, ed., *British Moralists* (Oxford: Clarendon Press, 1969), v. i, pp. 79-102.

   Although Cumberland may be considered a follower of Hobbes in some significant methodological respects, a major purpose of his *Treatise* was to criticize Hobbes.

42. *A Treatise of the Law of Nature*, trans. J. Maxwell (London: 1727), facsimile edition, (New York: Garland Publishing, Inc., 1978), p. 41.

43. I sketch this phenomenon in "Motive and Obligation in the British Moralists," in Ellen F. Paul, *et al*, eds., *Foundations of Moral and Political Philosophy* (Oxford: Basil Blackwell, 1989), pp. 133-150. (Also published as v. 7, no. 1 of *Social Philosophy & Policy*.)

44. *Treatise*, p. 233. Note that Cumberland says that propositions concerning good consequences for others can also "superinduce a necessity of doing of forbearing." Cumberland's position is actually a good deal more complex than I am presenting it here.

45. *Treatise*, p. 41.

46. *Treatise*, p. 180. The "fitness, which is expressed by a gerund, wants explanation, which is to be fetched, either from the necessary connexion of the means with the end, or from the obligation of a law." And ultimately, Cumberland resolves the latter itself into the "necessary connexion of the means with the end."

47. *Ibid.*, p. 234.

48. On this point, see Christine Korsgaard, "Skepticism About Practical Reason," *The Journal of Philosophy* 83 (1986): 5-25.

49. For a discussion of this point, see *Impartial Reason*, pp. 43-50, 62-77.

50. Richard Brandt, *A Theory of the Good and the Right* (Oxford: Clarendon Press, 1979).

51. I am indebted to Connie Rosati here.

52. This is the theme of W. D. Falk's "On Learning about Reasons," in *Ought, Reasons, and Morality*, pp. 67-81.
53. Compare Rawls's distinction between pure procedural and perfect (or imperfect) procedural justice. In the former case, as in a fair gaming wheel, there is no independent specification of a just outcome to which a just procedure approximates. The independent variable is the idea of a just procedure, and a just outcome is whatever eventuates. In the latter case, as when one person divides and the other chooses, the independent variable is the notion of a just outcome and a just procedure is what best approximates that. See *A Theory of Justice* (Cambridge: Belknap Press of Harvard University Press, 1971), pp. 85f.
54. Richard Brandt, *A Theory of the Good and the Right*, pp. 110-129. Peter Railton provides a similar, but interestingly different account of a person's good in "Moral Realism," *The Philosophical Review* 95 (1986): 163-207. The major wrinkle in Railton's account involves the idea of an epistemically-improved second-order desire. Roughly, X is part of A's good [and hence something at which A ought to aim, other things equal], if a fully knowledgeable, experienced, and imaginative A (call her A*) would want A, given A's actual situation, to want X.
55. John Locke, *An Essay Concerning Human Nature*, Peter H. Nidditch, ed. (Oxford: Clarendon Press, 1985), p. 76.
56. *Essay*, pp. 263-264, 266-267, 271; for the latter point see, especially, pp. 266-267.
57. For a short discussion of Shaftesbury on this topic see Darwall, "Motive and Obligation in the British Moralists." For Butler, see Darwall, "Conscience as Self-Authorizing in Butler's Ethics," in Christopher Cunliffe, ed., *Joseph Butler's Moral and Religious Thought* (Oxford: Clarendon Press, forthcoming). Cudworth's version of this view can be found in his manuscripts on free will, held in the British Library. One of these has been published: John Allen, ed., *A Treatise of Freewill* (London: John W. Parker, 1838). An excerpt appears in D. D. Raphael, ed., *British Moralists* (Oxford: Clarendon Press, 1969), v. i, pp. 120-134.
58. Especially in Nagel, *The View from Nowhere* (New York: Oxford University Press, 1986), pp. 110-137. I discuss this aspect of Nagel's views in "How Nowhere Can You Get (and Do Ethics)?," *Ethics* 98 (1987): 137-157. The view I sketch in *Impartial Reason* can also be understood as a version of this line of thought, as I try to make clearer in "Impartial Reason," in *Contemporary Ethics*, James Sterba, ed. (Englewood Cliffs, N. J.: Prentice-Hall, 1989).
59. Immanuel Kant, *Critique of Practical Reason*, Lewis White Beck, trans. (Indianapolis: Bobbs-Merrill Co., Inc., 1956, p. 30.
60. Thus, Kant writes of the agent deliberating about refusing the betrayal: "Whether he would or not he perhaps will not venture to say; but that it would be possible for him he would certainly admit without hesitation." For an excellent discussion of Kant's ideas here, stressing their practical character, see Christine Korsgaard's "Morality as Freedom," in Y. Yovel, *Kant's Practical Philosophy Reconsidered* (Dordrecht: Kluwer Academic Publishers, 1989), pp. 23-48.
61. Thus Locke's famous passage: "*Person*...is a forensic term appropriating actions and their merit; and so belongs only to intelligent agents capable of a law...," *Essay*, p. 346.
62. As Nagel puts it, the "defendant" in a judgment of responsibility is an agent, and in imputing responsibility we implicitly "enter into the defendant's point of view as an agent" and "evaluat[e] his action from within it." *The View from Nowhere*, p. 120, 121.
63. It is, of course, consistent with this (indeed, it is required) that we take diminished capacity to act for reasons to diminish responsibility.

64. *Essay*, pp. 266-267.
65. Immanuel Kant, *The Groundwork of the Metaphysics of Morals*, H. J. Paton, trans. (New York: Harper Torchbooks, 1964), Ak. p. 402.
66. For an argument that such naturalisms as Brandt's and Railton's concerning an agent's good are incapable of adequately capturing normativity, because they do not connect up with autonomy in the right way, and that the normativity of ethics highlighted by Moore's open question argument is best understood in relation to autonomy, see Connie Rosati, "Agency and the Open Question Argument," unpublished manuscript, and *Self-Invention and the Good* (Ph.D. dissertation, University of Michigan, 1989).
67. For further discussion of the connection between autonomy and the search for unqualified normativity, see Darwall, "Autonomist Internalism and the Justification of Morals," *Nous* 24 (1990): 257-267.
68. Various qualifications are necessary here. Kant generally reserves 'autonomy' for "the property the will has of being a law to itself (independently of every property belonging to the objects of volition)." (Ak. p. 440) It is clear, however, both that Kant takes our capacity to determine ourselves by a conception of law as essential to what makes us subject to law, and that he thinks this is a capacity we can succeed or fail in exercising properly. In the text I am using 'autonomy' to refer to the result of the successful exercise of this capacity.

Second, he generally reserves 'obligation' and 'ought' for a constraint the objective law imposes on a "will which is not necessarily determined by this law in virtue of its subjective constitution." (Ak. p. 413)
69. It may, of course, be possible to combine them. I argue that David Gauthier can be understood as having done this to some extent. See my "Rational Agent, Rational Act," *Philosophical Topics* 14 (1986): 33-57; and "Kantian Practical Reason Defended," *Ethics* 96 (1985): 89-99. Both rationales are also at work in Locke's thought.

Philosophical Perspectives, 6, Ethics, 1992

THE SOCIAL IMPORTANCE
OF MORAL RIGHTS

Joel Feinberg
University of Arizona

Many philosophers who are skeptical about moral rights are less concerned to deny that moral rights exist than to doubt the value or importance they would have if they did (or if they do) exist. Some of these are "skeptical" in a stronger sense, not merely doubting or even denying that moral rights have positive value, but claiming that they actually have negative value on balance. These distinctions thus yield four categories of moral-rights skeptics: (1) those who deny that moral rights exist at all, but also deny that such rights would have positive value on balance if they did exist, (2) those who deny that moral rights exist at all, and also claim that that is a good thing because such rights would have disvalue on balance if they did exist, (3) those who concede that moral rights do exist but deny that they have the positive value that is often claimed for them, and (4) those who concede that moral rights do exists but regret that this is so, since they believe that the consequences of such rights on balance are more harmful than beneficial, hence of negative value.

The fourth of these positions may seem paradoxical in its very formulation, for if a *moral* right, by definition, is one whose existence is not derived from any political enactment, and not subject to alteration by human volition, one which is discovered rather than invented or created, then to say that such a right exists and has disvalue seems to be to say that "true morality" (as opposed to any particular conventional morality) is inherently askew, and there is nothing whatever we can do about it, and *that* does have the sound of a paradox. I think the paradox can be avoided, however, if we interpret the fourth position as saying that the evil sometimes produced by appeals to moral rights is not a flaw in those rights themselves but in the way people tend to understand and exercise them. If the supporting argument for the fourth position, for example, is that possession of rights encourages a kind of self-righteous defense of selfishness, we might point out that this unhappily widespread phenomenon can better be ascribed to a deficiency in care for others and sensitivity to their needs and feelings than to the possession of a valuable moral instrument (a right) that is, alas, subject to abuse, and dependent for its intended good effects on supplementary virtues that are not easily acquired.

Skepticism about moral rights is easy to come to by another route. Imagine a couple cowering in their bed awaiting an early morning peremptory knock of the Gestapo, as heavy booted footsteps are heard outside their door. A legal right to due process would do them some good, but only if that right's correlative duty were reliably enforced. The legal right without enforcement would give them no protection. What good would it do them in that case to have a moral right? Such a possession would give them control over the moral duties of their persecutors but what good would that moral power do them without physical power to back it up? With a moral right they would have the "satisfaction" of knowing that they were being wronged and not just suffering through their own fault or through the capricious occurrence of some natural accident. This would give them the opportunity to feel righteous and morally superior while they are whipped and clubbed. A moral right in these circumstances is like a "moral victory" (so-called) in a game that is hopelessly lost. Every honest supporter of moral rights, it seems to me, must concede this point to the skeptic. Even if moral rights are valuable commodities in general, they are not sufficient to reward their possessors to some degree in all circumstances. One can say in their behalf only that the world is better off generally for having them, that they do in many cases confer subtle benefits, but at most they are necessary not sufficient for one's overall good, and in no case are they guaranteed protections.

1.

Philosophical writers who doubt the value of moral rights, even as so qualified, can be divided, as we have noted, into two groups: those who charge rights with having an actual *disvalue*, and those who reject the claims of positive value that their defenders make for them. In the former group are some (but not all) feminists, some (but not all) Critical Legal Studies theorists, and communitarians both of the left, following Karl Marx, and of the right, following among others, Edmund Burke. Common to all these writers is the view that rights function to separate people rather than draw them closer together in tighter communities, that rights are both an expression and a reinforcement of individual selfishness, and a threat to social solidarity. Jeremy Waldron, after carefully interpreting Bentham, Burke, and Marx, writes that "the great recurring theme in all three of these attacks is that the rights of man embody as the be-all and end-all of politics a demand for the immediate and unqualified gratification of purely selfish individual desires...For all of them, human life, to be bearable, involved a substantial commitment to living together in community that is belied by the abstract egoism of a theory of human rights."[1]

Assuredly, rights claims are demands for things the claimant desires; if a person doesn't want something, then why make claim to it? It hardly follows, however, that the only desires any person ever has, and thus the only desires whose satisfaction he ever lays claim to as a matter of right, are "purely selfish" ones. In fact the desires protected by the most fundamental moral rights, the human and civil rights mentioned in the leading manifestos, are precisely those most plausibly designated as natural, understandable, and *unselfish*. It is morally absurd to accuse the pre-teenage girl in an African village of a purely selfish desire not to have her sex organ mutilated as a precondition of eventual marriage (female circumcision), or to charge the Indian widow with a purely selfish desire not to be burned alive on her husband's funeral pyre, (suttee), or to level similar charges against the suffering terminal patient for insisting that he be released from his painful losing struggle, the Bahai worshipper in Iran for attempting to practice his religion, or the Gestapo victims for claiming a moral right to due process, or second parties for judging with all of them that they do indeed have such rights. Do such judgments, which can be made in the first, second, or third person, singular or plural, really serve primarily to make people selfishly unconcerned about one another? The very opposite would seem to be closer to the truth in these examples.

Perhaps some moral rights, property and contract rights in particular, are instruments of and contributors to a kind of righteously callous self-centeredness. Among the more prominent uses of such rights, after all, is their employment as counters in acquisitive commercial strategies, and we are all familiar with the sort of person who, although affluent himself, thinks that taxation for the support of the needy is a kind of theft—a violation of his sacred property rights. People to whom the words "mine" and "thine" come readily to the lips, and are frequently uttered with emphasis and passion, are hardly social paragons, contributing to the sense of community among the rest of us. But we must remember that those of us who would rather own some things in common, and in some contexts cooperate rather than compete, and to whom the words "we," "us" and "ours" come more readily to the lips than "mine" and "thine," will nevertheless treasure *our* rights and the possessions held in common that *we* have. A sense of community does not render rights obsolete; it just assigns some of them collectively to groups who then can assert them collectively against outsiders or against individual members who would harm the collective good. The group has a right not to have its facilities damaged or its treasury pillaged by anyone, and this right contributes to its general cohesiveness. It can hardly be the case, therefore, that all rights by their very nature serve to separate people.

Moreover, moral rights often resemble those legal rights that blend claims against others with what are called "powers." A power is a capacity under the rules to create, alter, or extinguish legal or moral relations (sometimes called "positions") both of oneself and of others. So, for example, my claim-right against you corresponds to your duty to me, but in addition I have the power of altering, suspending, or extinguishing your duty by choosing, for example, to waive my right and thus release you from your duty. In short, rights give us *control* over other parties' duties to us and (sometimes) over their duties to third parties. How we exercise this control is morally up to us, which is to say that we are morally at liberty to release or not release the other party from his duty as we see fit. There is no reason why we can't exercise our power wisely, compassionately, or cooperatively if we choose. We don't have to demand our pound of flesh just because we have a right to it. So again we can see that rights, even if morally necessary, are by no means morally sufficient. Virtues of good judgment, sympathy, and considerateness are necessary also, if the rights are to be used constructively. These excellences of character are an essential part of morality too. But there is nothing in the very nature of a moral right that militates against the acquisition and cultivation of these gentler social virtues.

The main point in response to those who condemn moral rights as selfish and divisive, however, must rest on a specimen list of acknowledged moral rights of which the moral right to due process is perhaps prototypical. The German citizens made subject to Gestapo arrests, detention, torture, and death were up against the whole massive force of the totalitarian state, and condemned by a transformed community moral code and the explicit content of the state's enacted laws. The following entry appeared in Marie Vassilichev's *Berlin Diaries*: "On 26 August 1942 the dummy-reichstag had voted a law conferring on Hitler discretionary powers in the administration of justice. The preamble to the law read: 'At present in Germany there are no more rights but only duties...' A few days later, in his weekly 'Das Reich,' Goebbels made clear what lay ahead: 'the bourgeois era with its false and misleading notion of humaneness is over'..."[2] It was evidently Goebbels' ideological conviction that a system which includes citizens' rights against the state is *morally inferior* to a system in which a united citizenry eagerly accept duties assigned by the state but never consider making any claims of their own against the state, or of supporting the claims made by any other person against the state. How admirable, chorused Nazi philosophers, what self-denying devotion to duty, how pure and uncorrupt! To those of us who react with repugnance and horror to this conception of social morality, it seems plain that when a community becomes highly cohesive and tightly organized, where togetherness prevails and dissent is muted, that is *precisely when there is the greatest need for moral rights*, their acknowledgement, and where possible their enforcement.

What does it mean after all for a person or her conduct to be selfish? A selfish person is not simply one who is devoted to the pursuit of her own ends. If that were true, then we could all be called selfish. In contrast, a genuinely selfish person is one who cares *unduly* or *supremely* for herself, whose conduct manifests an *excessive* concern for her own welfare, and who pursues her own comfort or advantage, in *blamable disregard of or at the expense of others*. It is grotesque to apply this word to victims of the Nazis or to the victims of the Argentine terror in the 1980s whose final desires and hopes were directed only to their own bare survival. Charging those who with trepidation and alarm point to what they call human rights violations against themselves or others with being selfish, socially dangerous persons, and citing their pliant conforming fellow citizens as moral exemplars, selflessly devoted to community values, is a transparent moral perversion. It is good that we have heard the last of it from the evil Nazis. Now it would be welcome if we could stop hearing similar perversities from respectable well-intentioned intellectuals.

2.

I turn now to the second group of those who doubt the importance that moral rights have or would have if there were any. These are philosophers who deny the case that others have made for the value of moral rights without going quite so far as to assert their actual disvalue. The proposition these philosophers deny is one I have defended, which we can call "the moral impoverishment thesis." I borrow this term from Richard Wasserstrom, who as a Justice Department attorney was a leader in the movement to implement the Civil Rights Acts of the 1960's in the southern states. Wasserstrom found that there were some older blacks who had adapted so well to their assigned role under the old system as second class citizens that they were wary of the equal status conferred on them by their newly declared constitutional rights. Writing in 1964 he states that "To observe what happens to any person who is required to adopt habits of obsequiousness, [and] deferential behavior in order to minimize the likelihood of physical abuse, arbitrary treatment, or economic destitution is to see graphically how important human rights are and what their denial can mean."[3] If this is what tends to happen to people when they have no legal rights and lack a belief or even a conception of their own moral rights, what would the consequences on human character be generally of a normative system which assigned no rights to anyone even though it did impose duties on people of a more privileged class to treat their inferiors decently? Wasserstrom replies that "Such a system would be a morally impoverished one. It would prevent persons from asserting those kinds of claims...which a system of rights makes possible."[4]

In my 1970 article "The Nature and Value of Rights,"[5] I tried to provide further content and support to Wasserstrom's moral impoverishment thesis. A good part of the argument is empirical; people who must live as slaves tend to become servile simply as a survival mechanism. The situation of rightless dependence on more powerful persons naturally breeds a servile character, imprinted with fear and characterized by obsequious flattery, flaunted obedience, submissive cringing, fawning and meanness. The servile person is also likely to have a clever manipulative side; he turns his false humility off when he is with his own kind and will bully the less powerful. As C. S. Lewis put it, he is "alternately fawning and insolent."[6]

People who are confident of their own rights are less likely to develop servile characters. They are not forced to secure their needs by begging "favors" from masters who have no relational duties to them, on the one hand, or by stealing and cheating, or resorting to plain force on the other. To say they have moral rights is to say that morally they are in a position to *claim* what they want as their due, what they have coming, and what the other party is under a moral obligation *to them* (not merely regarding them) to provide. A claim is different from a mere demand like that of a gunman for your money or your life, and it is different from begging, imploring, or beseeching, for to claim is to invoke the authority of governing rules or principles by producing reasons certified by those principles as relevantly applicable and binding. The claimant has control over the claimee's duty which he activates by making the claim, but which he has the power to alter or even suspend as he wishes, just as he has the physical power to turn on or off a light by pushing a switch one way or the other. The right-holder has more dignity than a mere beggar who is not in a position to make claim to what he wants, or a highwayman who, in abandoning the moral posture altogether, forfeits, in large part, any claim he might have had to moral respect.

I concluded that to respect a person is tantamount to respecting her rights, that is to thinking of her as a prospective maker of weighty moral claims. If a person is thought to have no rights, not even the basic moral rights, she is by the same token thought to be unworthy of respect, and if she thinks of herself that way she can only cringe and beg, or cheat and steal, and will lack the virtue of self-respect, not to mention respect for others. No wonder that a whole human population without rights, lacking even the concept of a right, would be "morally impoverished."

A great many critics registered their disagreement with this analysis. Most of them countered that a community which acknowledged moral duties of fairness and benevolence could dispense with rights. William Nelson, following Jan Narveson,[7] asks "Why does Feinberg think that people who do not regard themselves as possessors of rights but [do] regard others as having obligations and duties towards [regarding] them, will be unable to demand that those others perform their duties and discharge their obligations? Why should they not be able to stand up, look...[the] other in the eye and complain just as loudly as anyone else when someone behaves toward them in a way which he was obligated not to behave?"[8]

Nelson anticipates my reply when on a later page he writes that "...when Feinberg suggests that in morals someone who lacks rights is prevented from claiming or complaining he surely does not mean that he opens his mouth but no sound comes out...". Exactly so. If A has a duty to treat his slave B decently, but B being a mere slave, has no right that A do his duty (or any other right against A for that matter), and A proceeds to violate his own duty by treating B cruelly, then B will be "able to demand" that A do his duty in the sense that if he opens his mouth to utter words of complaint, the intended sounds *will* come out, or if he merely speaks to remind his master, with the utmost tact, of his duties, (say) under a code of *noblesse oblige*, those sounds *will* come out. If he chooses incredibly to look his master in the eye and "complain loudly" that the master is neglecting his own duty, even those sounds will come out. But it isn't a question of B's physical abilities, his being able to utter certain sounds; it is a question not of what he *can* do, but of what he *may* do under the accepted rules that govern his conduct and A's, and under those rules any claim he may make will be infirm; he will have no legal or moral *power* to affect his master's duties or his own; he will be *able* to complain but not *entitled* to complain; he will in a sense "have a complaint" but he will not have a genuine moral *grievance*; since he had no rights against A, he could not be *wronged* by A's conduct but only hurt or harmed by it. If he tries to voice a grievance anyway, he is vulnerable—morally vulnerable—to A's cogent reply: "What business is it of yours whether or not *I* perform *my* noble duties? The rules that govern our relations do not make me answerable to you." That reply does not exactly express respect for B, and under the rules, B is not worthy of respect since he has no rights. So adding to B's moral repertoire a moral claim-right correlative with A's moral duty to him, does make a moral difference.

3.

A strategic digression. Philosophers have given thorough attention to moral rights to act, omit, possess, or be something or other, but they have neglected the widespread use of rights-idioms applied to states of mind like belief, feeling, attitude and emotion. That surprising omission may be the consequence of taking legal models as the sole guides to the interpretation of rights-talk, for legal models like that of Hohfeld simply do not fit "the right to be certain," "the right to believe in the absence of evidence," "the right to feel proud," or (to come back to our primary concerns) "the right to feel aggrieved" or "morally indignant." The concept of a right in these contexts is to serve as a *warrant of appropriateness*. This kind of usage is sufficiently widespread to be standard and fixed, and cannot be dismissed as merely idiosyncratic, voguish, or slang. It is especially interesting in that it does not even superficially appear to rest on legal analogies. So the analysis of such terms will have to rely upon such words as "fitting," "suitable," and "appropriate," drawn from the nonlegal-like part of our moral vocabularies. Moreover, as we have seen, the account we have sketched of what it is to have a standard moral right to do, omit, possess, or be *X*, includes as one of *its* elements, a right in certain circumstances to feel indignant or aggrieved, which in turn, will have to be analyzed in terms drawn from the nonlegal-like sector of morality—from terms like "fitting," "seemly," and "appropriate."

Two examples might be helpful here. The first is the old jazz lyric, "I've got a right to sing the blues." The second is the common situation in which one person gives expression to her fatigue at the end of a busy day, and the other replies reassuringly, "You've got a right to be tired." What does it mean to say "I've got a right to sing the blues"? It means that I am depressed, but more than that, I am *understandably* depressed, *naturally* depressed, depressed for *just cause* and *good reason*. I am not clinically depressed, or depressed for insufficient reason, or from illusory and neurotic causes. Objectively depressing things have happened to me. Even if I am not in fact depressed, I have an objective and natural warrant for depression. (My children have died; my wife has left me; I've lost my job.) It is only appropriate that I be depressed. I've got a *right* to sing the blues.

Much the same analysis applies to "You've got a right to feel tired." You have put in a long hard day, and fatigue is the natural consequence of that. It is not the weariness of ennui you feel; not a bodily expression of torpor or lassitude, but honest, well earned tiredness. ("Earned" in that usage is deviate or ironic. Benefits are the sorts of things that are earned. Here perhaps what are earned are "bragging rights": "What a lot of labor I expended today.") In any event, fatigue in this case is nothing mysterious, unnatural, inexplicable (in a normal way) or neurotic. And certainly the concept of *irrational* doesn't apply at all. Don't worry; your fatigue is *appropriate*. Its explanation gives warrant of that appropriateness. You've got a *right* to be tired.

Returning to the jazz lyric title, how would we analyze it if we understood it on a Hohfeldian legal model? Perhaps the jazz title refers to a *claim-right*, in which case it asserts that I am at liberty to be depressed if I choose to be (which sounds a little paradoxical already) *and* I am in a position to make claim to your noninterference, a claim which grounds your duty not to interfere. That is, you and all others have a duty to leave me alone in my depression. The analysis of what is meant, however, seems to undermine its truth, because it is not plausible to say that you violate my right by trying subtly to cheer me up and hurry my mending when my depression is understandable. Second, suppose the affirmed right is a mere *bilateral liberty*, and what the lyric says, therefore, is: I have no duty not to feel depressed just as I have no duty to be depressed. I can be either as I wish, or as I feel about it. Maybe there are "duties of reason," in this instance "a duty, if I am to be rational, to be depressed" (or, as the case may be, undepressed). But rationality does not appear to be the critical element here. The statement in the lyric title is not about what I am required or not required to do if I am to be rational, so much as about whether my feelings, which are not subject to my firm control in any event, are in a larger sense, *appropriate* in the circumstances. The third possibility is that the lyric claims a Hohfeldian *power*, in which case if the lyric speaks truly, it is possible for me to create a duty in you not to "interfere" with my feeling, or perhaps better, that you not make adverse critical judgments, voiced or not, about my feeling, for example about its "irrationality" or "inappropriateness." Notice also that on this interpretation I also have the moral power to alter, weaken, or cancel your duty altogether, so that you become free after all to judge me adversely, (as having irrational or inappropriate emotions). This is surely nonsense. Finally, the statement in the song title might claim an *immunity*, in which case I, the speaker, say to you that in respect to my blue mood, you have *no power* to alter my liberties, claim-rights, powers or other immunities by anything you can do. This is more plausible, though a bit artificial.

Perhaps in the right to be tired example, the most fitting Hohfeldian gloss would be in terms of immunity. Your long labor gives you rightful immunity from certain kinds of criticism. It cannot be said of you that you are a weakling, or a lazy goof-off, or that you are feigning exhaustion to get out of doing the dishes. If you have a right to be tired, then none of these adverse judgments can be true or at least properly made. But this isn't exactly like a Hofeldian immunity. What is the correlative disability? What moral powers do others lack as a consequence of your immunity? There is no reference here to powers others do not have to *change your moral position or relations.* The "power" whose absence is affirmed is only the "power" (ability) to assert adverse critical judgments of a certain class and assert them properly or truly. But that is a big departure from a Hohfeldian power and a very weak analogy to it. The other Hohfeldian elements do even worse. Is your right to be tired a *liberty*? If so it means that you have no duty not to be tired, as well as no duty to be tired.[9] As if you had any choice in the matter! Is your right to be tired a claim-right? If so, I and others have a duty subject to your power—a duty to do what? To not interfere with your fatigue? To give or to withhold a cup of coffee? To offer a bed for the night? None of this coheres very well with what we understand by "a right to be tired," which, unlike typical moral and legal rights, does not affect the moral positions of others at all.

It does appear then that "appropriateness-rights" (as we can call them) are a quite distinct species of right, irreducible to rights in any of the Hohfeldian categories that classify ordinary moral and legal rights so well. What makes them relevant to the present discussion is the possibility, developed in section 4 below, that an appropriateness-right lies at the heart of our tacit criteria for determining whether a wrongdoer's misbehavior has violated another party's rights (in the more familiar legal-like sense). If the second party now has a right to feel aggrieved or indignant, in our estimation, (or if another party has a "right" to have those feelings vicariously in his behalf), that is a sign that we believe that the misbehavior of the wrongdoer was more than just wrongful; rather we believe, on the basis of this test, that it specifically *wronged* the other party, who now can be considered its *victim* in the sense that requires not only harmed interests but violated rights.

In one way at least we can welcome the requirement that an appropriateness-right be involved in this way, for it obviates the danger of falling into an infinite regress of rights. It is often said that if one party's right is violated by a second party, then the first party is "entitled to complain." If this moral entitlement itself is understood as a moral right, how do we know when *it* is violated? The answer might seem to be that we apply the same test that we used in the case of the original right. If a party's *right* to complain has been violated then (we can be tempted to say) he has a new right to complain about the violation of his other right to complain, which in turn, had as its target the violation of the original right. In this way, it is possible to generate an infinite regress whose effect on our original analysis would be less than benign. But if the "right to complain" is a right in the quite different sense of "appropriate fit" between a wrongful action and a responsive feeling or attitude, the regress can be avoided. No sense can be given to *violating* a right to complain if that right consists merely in the appropriateness of an aggrieved response to another party's wrongdoing.

The philosopher who has made the most of the idea of being entitled to complain is Daniel Lyons,[10] some of whose insights are well worth borrowing. When we wish to distinguish between the party (*B*) who has a legal right violated by another's (*A*'s) behavior and the party (*C*) whose injury is only incidental—or to put the distinction in an equivalent way, between the party *to whom A* had a duty (*B*), and the party merely *regarding whom A* had that duty (*C*)—then we sometimes give "operational point" to the distinction by asking "who has the right to sue, to enjoin, or to prosecute." The moral parallel to these legal operations, Lyons suggests, is some "special right to complain and feel aggrieved." Lyons is quite convincing in this contention, though I think he fails to appreciate how special this "special right" is, being not a moral analogue to a legal right, but a right in a totally different sense, consisting simply of the relation of appropriateness. Lyons' examples well illustrate this point.

> Consider this exchange: "You have no right to complain about welfare-cheats [said to a person who claims that his own *rights* have been violated by the cheaters]; you're on a pension yourself; you pay no taxes." "Nevertheless, since every welfare cheat discourages

the community from giving legitimate pensioners their full due, my rights are involved—I do have a right to complain." Or this [example]: "Mother, *you* have no right to be angry with Jim because he called off our wedding; I'm the one who was jilted." "Yes, but I spent a thousand dollars on the preparations."[11]

There are many examples, of course, as Lyons himself points out, of people feeling personally aggrieved and indignant, even when they are not entitled to those feelings: "For instance, the temperance people Mill mentions in *On Liberty* took other people's simple drunkenness as an offense directly against themselves. They undoubtedly felt this special indignation, but Mill would deny that they were entitled to it."[12] The disagreement between Mill and his opponents in the temperance movement was a substantive one, not merely a theoretical quarrel about the analysis of the concept of a right. Each side understood that aggrieved feelings are part of the test of whether a person genuinely believes that a right has been violated, but they disagreed in the case that divided them about whether such feelings were appropriate, a matter to be settled, if at all, by extensive moral argument.

The word "complain" which Lyons, following common usage, employs so frequently, could trap the unwary into the very regress from which appropriateness-rights were meant to protect them. Complaining appears to be a kind of linguistic *doing*, so that one can do that thing in response to a violation of his right, unless prevented from doing so, in which case one can try to complain (act) in response to *that* constraint, and if further restrained, complain again, etc. *ad infinitum*. But Lyons is not unwary. He distinguishes complaining from protesting, interpreting the former as one kind of species of the latter, so that he can define complaining as "protesting, accompanied by a certain special kind or degree of aggrieved indignation." The "special kind" of feeling is the important thing, the complaining is merely giving it voice. One can have an appropriateness-right to the feeling, while either having or lacking the legal-like moral right to its expression at a given time or place, or in a given manner.

Despite the importance of the idea of an appropriateness-right there are some clear limits to its utility. It will be of little or no assistance in settling the question of whether a given wrongful action violated a right of some particular person or whether a duty had been owed *to* that person in the first place by the wrongdoer. After all, the feelings of grievance may themselves be inappropriate, in which case one has no "right" to them, and the reasons that settle the question of the appropriateness of the grievance feelings will be precisely those that will settle the substantive moral questions. *B* was a right-holder wronged by *A*'s conduct if and only if his feelings of grievance were warranted. Of that we can be sure. But the only way to show that the grievance was warranted is to show that *B* was a right-holder against *A*, and that *A* violated his right, a question more amenable to standard moral argument. So the point about appropriateness-rights offers no quick short-cut to a resolution of substantive disagreement, but only a circular trip around the problem.

Secondly, we should not look for more precision than is possible in the application of the grievance-feeling test even to the problem it is better suited to solve: that of determining whether a given person *believes* that he (or another) has had his rights violated. As an emotion, a sense of grievance (or indignation) is subject to different degrees of intensity, just as the moral grievance itself is subject to different degrees of seriousness, or moral gravity. But the emotional intensity is no reliable gauge for determining the degree of moral gravity, being itself the product of many factors in addition to moral judgment—irascibility, vulnerability, emotional volatility, bias, self-preference, and so on. If elements of that sort play too large a role in the production of grievance-feelings, those feelings may be, at least to some degree, mere animal anger or hatred self-deceptively masquerading as moral indignation. We would be better advised to rest with the cautious position that some minimal threshold of grievance-feeling must be met if we are to ascribe to the aggrieved party any belief at all that his rights have been violated. It does not follow from this that the moral importance of the right believed to be violated is directly proportional to the intensity of the aggrieved party's anger.

Closely related to this point is the fact that our feelings of indignation are targeted at the *persons* we believe to have wronged us, not simply at their actions, so that the intensity of the feeling will vary more with such factors as our perception of the other party's motivation and intention, than with our appraisal of the importance of the right violated. Many of us will have little or no anger at all, raw or moralized, at the person who violates our rights inadvertently through clumsiness or absent-mindedness. "You should have watched what you were doing" may be the strongest moral denunciation we can muster, and even then we may prefer to say "Forget it pal; it could have happened to anyone. Just pay for the repair job (or medical bill) and we can forget all about it." But if that is followed by an expressed unwillingness to pay compensation, indignation is sure to flower, and it will extend back to the original negligence (initially forgiven) as well as to the subsequent refusal to compensate. Then there will be no doubt that the victim believes he has been wronged.

There is one final set of complications in the idea of an appropriateness-right. Radical moralists and philosophers sometimes argue that some feelings or attitudes toward others are, in their very nature, *never* appropriate. It is understandable and natural perhaps (a philosopher might argue) that one experience envy at the good fortune (especially the undeserved good fortune) of another person, but envy is so corrosive of character, so unseemly in a person of moral dignity, that it is always inappropriate. So also, Nietzsche in a wonderfully subtle way has argued that pity is always inappropriate,[13] and

Clarence Darrow has reached a similar judgment about vindictive anger.[14] I would not be surprised to learn that some radical moralist or other has in the same sweeping fashion denied the appropriateness of a sense of grievance and moral indignation at the mistreatment of one person (oneself or a third party) by another. If a sense of grievance is one of the conditions that must be satisfied if we are correctly to attribute to a person the belief that his or another's *rights* have been violated, and our hypothetical moralist denies that we ever have an appropriateness-right to such a feeling, it follows that the moralist denies that anyone ever has his rights violated, not because all who could violate those rights are too honorable to do so, but because there are no rights to be violated in the first place. That conclusion is so startlingly unwelcome that we might even take it to be the *reductio ad absurdum* of the premises from which it follows, in which case having what one believes to be a complaint, being morally indignant, having a sense of grievance against another for what he did to oneself, or a vicarious grievance for what he did to a third party—none of this is necessary, after all, for one to believe that one has had a right violated.

The best way to cope with this difficulty, I suspect, is to separate, somewhat more sharply than I have done, the emotional or affective element in the feeling that one has a grievance from the basic moral conviction that one has been wronged and is entitled to protest in a self-confident and righteous manner. Moral indignation is moralized anger, that is the anger that is a natural response to injury accompanied by the disposition to respond in a similar way to any similar wrong—"out of principle." But one could press one's rights or affirm the rights of others righteously, indeed "indignantly," with only a trace of genuine emotion. One could "feel" that one has a complaint without feeling angry at all, and one could voice a grievance in a matter-of-fact business-like way, with hardly a trace of emotion in one's consciousness, as when one confidently claims the compensation believed to be one's due from a merely negligent wrongdoer against whom one has no animus. When such an "innocent" tortfeasor absentmindedly delays his payment of compensation, one may smile inwardly at the person's eccentricity, but voice one's grievance against him firmly nonetheless. The grievance is simply the claim that the other has wronged one, normally but not necessarily accompanied by "appropriate" anger. The belief that one has a complaint, that it would be morally appropriate, if one chooses, to *make* that complaint, is so essential to the belief that one's right was violated, that it almost defines that belief. And that remains true even if one's grievance ("complaint") is unaccompanied by a trace of the anger or resentment that some sensitive moralists would judge unseemly. Explaining rights infractions in terms of "having a complaint" and its near synonyms makes a very small theoretical advance, but as I hope to show below, locates a factor (obvious though it might be) of crucial psychological significance for the right-holder.

4.

The moral impoverishment thesis, apart from explaining how some rights are valuable, has a further advantage of a practical kind: it provides us with a test for distinguishing cases where one party has a right against another from cases in which he merely stands to gain from the performance of the other's duty or from the other's supererogatory act of beneficence toward him. Let us consider two kinds of cases in which that distinction is unclear and controversial. In both of these examples, it is agreed that A ought to have helped B, that it would have been a good thing and indeed the morally right thing for A to have done, and maybe even A's duty to have done, but the question then arises after A's failure to do it: did his failure to assist B violate B's rights? The first example is the problem of third party beneficiaries of promises made to second parties. In one clear and uncontroversial example, a life insurance company (Alpha) promises Baker that if Baker pays the agreed upon premium, then upon his death an enriched sum will be paid to Charley, his designated beneficiary. Charley may not even know of the existence of this agreement. Still when Baker dies, Alpha is under an obligation to Charley to pay him the agreed sum, and Charley has a correlative right against Alpha that puts him in a position validly to claim that amount from Alpha, even though Alpha's original promise was not made to Charley, the beneficiary, but to Baker, the policy holder and promisee. If Alpha, the company, refuses to pay Charley, the third-party beneficiary, then clearly it will be violating Charley's right, for the money is owed to Charley even though the promise was made to Baker.

In contrast, suppose Alpha promises Baker to do something which, as it turns out, will incidentally benefit some total stranger, Carlos, and Carlos learns of the deal and eagerly looks forward to, even acts in reliance upon, his expected lucky windfall. Alpha then breaks his promise to Baker, thus incidentally ruining Carlos's hope of profit. In that case, clearly Carlos, the would-be third party beneficiary of Alpha's promise to Baker, has not had his own rights violated since he did not have a personal right in the first place that Alpha keep his promise to Baker.

I am not interested now in deriving the grounds for the distinction between the two kinds of cases, although that seems an easy enough thing to do in these clear instances. Instead, I wish to propose what I call "a phenomenological test" for determining whether or not a person who believes that a benefit to one party was wrongfully withheld by another party is committed by his other judgments and moral responses to the further judgment that the unhelped party suffered a violation of his *rights*. It isn't sufficient to generate that belief in a person to point out that he *already* believes that the one party was *wrong* not to behave in a way that would have been helpful, that he *ought* to have so behaved, indeed even that he had a *duty* to behave in that way. We can believe all that and still deny that the unhelped party had a right violated by the wrongdoer. How does one tell, if one is confused about the concept of a right, whether one holds the further belief that a *right* was violated? I suggest, combining the analysis adumbrated in my earlier articles with the interpretation suggested in the preceding section, that one does in fact hold that further moral belief if and only if one also believes the following:

(1) Charley[15] could have appropriately *claimed* in advance the assistance from Alpha as his own due (by saying upon the fulfillment of the agreed conditions "You owe me as my due..."). Therefore, Charley can appropriately press his claim with greater moral dignity than by mere begging or bullying, imploring or intimidating.

(2) Charley can voice a grievance against Alpha afterward (if the promise is broken) by saying to him appropriately "You wronged me by violating your agreement with Baker."

(3) At any time during the life of the agreement Charley can release Alpha from his duty if Charley pleases, that is he has the legal or moral power to control Alpha's duties in that way.

(4) It is for Charley's sake that Alpha has its duty to act in the agreed upon way and not merely for some extraneous reason unrelated to Charley.

(5) Whether or not Baker does his duty is Charley's "business," his proper moral concern.

If you believe that all five of these statements are true of a given transaction, then and only then do you believe that the third party beneficiary in that transaction had a right to the benefit in question. These five statements do not provide a full and useful criterion for deciding whether Charley had a right; indeed they presuppose that substantive moral questions have all been settled. Instead they constitute a test of whether an outside judge is already committed by his other judgments and moral responses to that belief. And the interesting thing about this test for our present purposes is that several of the elements in it, particularly being in a position to make claims and afterward to voice grievances, are the grounds of the greater dignity and self-respect that are associated with the role of right-holder.

The other example is that of the notorious bad samaritan. Unlike the more celebrated good Samaritan of the New Testament, the bad samaritan lets an injured person, a stranger to him, lie where he fell on the street after being beaten and robbed, even though getting assistance for the battered victim would have cost him little more than minor inconvenience. Most, but not all, commentators on this matter agree that morality imposes a duty on the "samaritan" even though the injured party is a stranger, to assist him if he can, but there is great disagreement over whether the battered stranger has a *right* against the samaritan to his help. If you agree with the duty judgment but are not sure whether you hold the further right-judgment or not, I suggest that something like the five part test proposed above will tell you whether you have that belief or not. If this test is inconclusive, if follows that you have no definite belief at all on the matter, and should apply the appropriate substantive criteria, whatever they are, to the facts to help you make up your mind. But if the test tells decisively one way or the other, it follows that you already have a belief on the question, entailed by your other moral beliefs, and you were confused about that only because of uncertainty about the meaning of the expression—"a right."

I have argued elsewhere that the test shows that most of us, whatever we may say, do in fact believe that the crime victim had a right to the stranger's help. Suppose, first of all, that you were a friend or relative of the battered victim, yourself lying there with no life-threatening injuries of your own but with a serious disablement, say two broken legs. You ask the samaritan's assistance for your unconscious friend whose very life is endangered. When the stranger hesitates, you are surely in a position, morally speaking, to make claim to his assistance for your friend. "You can't just leave him there to die!" you might say. Clearly you are not in such a position, morally speaking, that you can only beg or implore the stranger for help; rather you and the friend you represent are in moral control over the other's duties, a role that confers much greater dignity on you than a belief that your friend's life had no value worthy of commanding even a stranger's respect.

Secondly, we can ask after the fact whether the stranger's failure to offer help is any business of the one neglected, whether it would be appropriate for him and his loved ones to feel, not just animal anger, but moral indignation against the nonfeasant stranger, and whether they are in a position to voice a genuine moral grievance against the stranger for his neglect of his acknowledged duty. When we agree that passing strangers *ought* to offer assistance in cases like this, indeed that they must offer assistance, I submit that most of us also think that moral indignation on behalf of the recipient of the duty would be fitting if the stranger failed to do his duty. The alternative is just to give the stranger low moral grades, adding that his flaws are no business of the person he declined to aid, nothing that person is entitled to complain about. There are examples, to be sure, where this sort of response *is* fitting. If some person, Abel, is pompous, vain, silly, dull-witted, or unimaginative, what is that to Baker, who is a mere stranger, a passive observer? Baker can make these adverse judgments about Abel and avoid his company, but can he claim as a personal grievance about Abel that Abel has these failings? Clearly not, and that is a sign that he has *no right* that Abel be a better person in those respects. That is Abel's business and not his. But the parents (say) of the battered victim in the samaritan case will feel understandably and plausibly aggrieved, and we can share that indignation vicariously with them. We would not acknowledge that their child's right was infringed if we thought of the bad samaritan's neglected duty as something like a duty of *noblesse oblige* (i.e. a duty with no correlative right in the beneficiary). But clearly we cannot think of it that way; the persistent sense of personal grievance will not permit it.[16]

5.

Armed with this analysis, we can now return to a charge against moral rights that we considered earlier, that they are in their very nature a threat to worthwhile community. The simplest models of worthwhile community are marriages, families, friendships, and simple partnerships. Confining his attention to marriages and families, Robert Young writes that

> It is frequently where there has been a breakdown in the caring or loving relationships that hold between people that appeals to rights are made. When loving relations break down and the caring for another's interest which is morally proper goes by the board, people fall back on the auxiliary apparatus of rights. This is often understandable, but is not morally desirable since it does nothing to mend the ruptured relations.[17]

I have three quick replies to this. I can concede the subordinate role of reciprocal rights claims in loving relationships. But having a right does not require one to raise hell every time one perceives an infraction on the part of another. It only "puts one in a position" morally speaking to make claims or complaints. One can exercise those liberties and powers as one sees fit, and a loving party will see fit to speak softly and gently, to forgive quickly, and so on.

Secondly, loving relationships do break down, alas, and probably more often than not, and when this happens rights possession is not merely valuable; it is indispensable if one is to protect one's interests and preserve one's self-respect. Moreover, there is a real moral value in respecting the other person as a genuine maker of moral claims, even—Kant might say "especially"—in the absence of affection. But most important, thirdly, rights are more than a "fall-back auxiliary apparatus," for they are as necessary to love as affection itself is, even during the period when affection flourishes. Part of what is involved in caring for a person is a concern that she have those things that she just happens to have a right to anyway—consideration for special sensibilities and handicaps, fairness in the distribution of burdens and labors, freedom from arbitrary hurts and embarrassments, and so on. The rest of what is involved in caring is a concern that the loved one have more than that minimum she could claim as a matter of right—unexpected delights, unique tenderness, gifts, favors, symbolic gestures. Love may, in this way, demand more than respect for rights, but it cannot survive with less.[18]

Young quotes with approval a passage from Simone Weil meant to show

how poorly rights serve a genuine community of reciprocally caring individuals. The very notion of a right, Weil claims, "has a commercial flavor, essentially evocative of legal claims and arguments. Rights are always asserted in a tone of contention; and when this tone is adopted it must rely upon force in the background or it will be laughed at."[19] A twofold reply can be made to these bold assertions. In the first place, it seems false that rights are always asserted in a tone of contention.[20] Rights, in fact, can be asserted coolly, automatically, with dignity and calm, or with embarrassment, regret, or even apology. Indeed they can be asserted without uttering words at all, as when a person makes claim to his coat by presenting his coat check token to the coat room attendant.[21]

An especially interesting example comes from a recent syndicated newspaper column by Zeke Wigglesworth, defending the quality of food service on international air flights by citing the many difficulties the airlines must surmount in order to serve hot meals at all. After an enumeration of these difficulties, he adds another one—"Then there is always some clod who tries to go to the washroom while the meals are being served, creating a traffic jam and demanding loudly that the stews [stewards or stewardesses] get the trolley out of the way."[22] I have on occasion played the role of the "clod" myself, and it is very embarrassing. The clod either forgets to stop in the restroom before boarding the plane or is so rushed he has no opportunity. By the time he feels the call of nature, it is too late; the luncheon trolley already fills the aisle and there is no room to squeeze by.

Fortunately, there is a well understood moral convention governing situations of this kind. The clod has the right of way, given that his natural need can be presumed to be more pressing, and the stewardesses must back their cart out of the way, thus delaying the service. (This suggests a new interpretation of "natural rights.") Both the stewardesses and the clod understand that he has the right to proceed and they have the duty, under the convention, to get out of his way. But the clod need not assert his right by "demanding loudly" that the trolley be removed. Right-possession is not a license for vulgarity. He can assert his right without speaking at all, except for an embarrassed mumbled "sorry" as he passes the stewardesses. His right-assertion in that case would consist in his signalling his intention clearly, and his confident goal-directed strides toward the barrier, with the demeanor of a person who knows the rules and proceeds without hesitation, and with as much dignity as he can muster. Claiming in these circumstances is simply exercising a legal-like, conventional moral "power," as if one were thereby pushing a button that creates—or "lights up"—the other parties' duties. This *can* be done apologetically, regretfully yet firmly.

6.

Weil's other point, in the passage quoted by Young, is about the impotence of rights claims, even when "asserted in a tone of contention," if they are made in the face of superior physical force and thus are incapable of being enforced. In replying to it, I return full circle to the topic with which this paper begins. If Salman Rushdie had been captured by the Iranians and presented to the Ayatollah, he could on that occasion have contentiously asserted his right of free expression, and righteously demanded to be released. The Ayatollah was not known to laugh easily, but Weil refers in her quote to the laugh of derision not the laugh of amusement, and Rushdie's situation would not have been very dignified if he had been dragged off by burly guards to be imprisoned. The truth is that rights may be necessary for respect and dignity but, except perhaps in the case of genuine heroes, they may not be sufficient. It also helps to have the rights recognized by the other party or even backed up by some physical or military force.

Moral rights, then, do not help much, or not at all, in the face of machine guns manned by the lackeys of powerful immoralists or other unimpressed antagonists, even from the point of view of moral dignity. But before one dismisses moral rights for that reason, consider the alternatives. The dissident couple seized in their home by the Gestapo have at least three options. They can affirm their moral rights calmly and firmly, thus triggering derision and cruelty, or they can abandon moral language to make idly heroic demands, as if *they* had the monopoly of force in the situation, or they might prostrate themselves and beg for mercy. Surely, the hopeless assertion of right is not any *less* consistent with dignity than its alternatives, although all three are hopelessly doomed. My analysis of rights as claims, in any case, implies only that the right-holder by virtue of his right is in a *moral position* to make claims against others, not necessarily that he is in a physical or political position to make claims without having his face kicked in. For this so-called "moral advantage" to be a genuine advantage it is necessary that those to whom rights-claims are made have some capacity of moral recognition and at least some minimal moral responsiveness. It is no wonder that Ghandi maintained his impressive moral dignity even in the teeth of superior force from his enemies in British India. The Nazis would have allowed him no moral dignity at all.

It is interesting that one of the most impressive of the proposed techniques for retaining dignity in the face of tyrannical power does not employ the concept of a moral right at all. The Stoic moralist Epictetus makes no claim that he or anyone else has moral rights of any kind. The only thing of value to him is his unsoiled excellence of character, or "virtue." Virtue, in turn, consists in doing one's duty, or rather in trying one's best to do one's duty, since actually succeeding in doing one's duty is sometimes beyond one's power. One's subjective duty, however, which is to try one's best to do one's objective duty, is *always* within one's power. The next step is to value, and consequently to desire, nothing but one's own moral excellence, and since *that* virtue is always possible to achieve, one can never be harmed or disappointed. Thus, he says in his chapter of the *Discourses* entitled "Of the Right Treatment of Tyrants":

> When the tyrant says to anyone,
>   "I will chain your leg,"
> he who chiefly values his leg cries out for pity; he who chiefly values his own moral purpose says
>   "If you imagine it for your interest, chain it."
>   "What! Do you not care?"
>   "No, I do not care."
>   "I will show you that I am master."
>   "You? How should *you*? Zeus has set me free. What! Do you think he would suffer his own son to be enslaved? You are master of my carcass; take it."
>   "So that when you come into my presence you pay no attention to me?"
>   "No, I pay attention only to myself; or if you will have me recognize you also, I will do it, but only as if you were a pot."[23]

Epictetus is a writer with no conception of himself as a right-holder or maker of moral claims against others. What matters to him, and all that matters to him, is his duty, and since no one and no thing can ever prevent him from doing that duty, the virtue that consists in fidelity to duty is always within his grasp. No tyrant can deprive him of *that* by preventing him, for example, from dying bravely rather than cravenly or theatrically.

Without question, there *is* a kind of dignity in the Stoic slave's defiance of the tyrant, though if he soon becomes a bloody corpse, his dignity does not last long. And the dignity is surely different, qualitatively different, from that of the righteous resister who thinks of himself as dying in defense of his rights or the rights of other parties rather than in discharge of his duty. The Stoic resists in a spirit of genuine indifference to whether he succeeds or fails. The important thing is that *he* do *his* duty, not that any other fancied good is achieved thereby. There is something disturbingly make-believe about his mental disposition. His duty is to play well the part assigned to him, while aware all along that it is only a "part," only an occasion for virtue, nothing more. There can be a pretended compassion but never real compassion, for that would imply that there can be something other than one's own virtue that is worth genuinely caring about. If a closely related person—a spouse, a child, or a friend—suffers severe pain, says Epictetus, "do not disdain to accommodate yourself to him, and if need be, to groan with him. Take heed, however, not to groan inwardly too."[24]

Moral duty conceived in the Stoic fashion, unlike moral rights, purports to be a comprehensive and self-sufficiently valuable thing. Rights are important only when backed by power, whereas Epictetan duty is important even without power, even without genuine goals of any other kind, without success in one's projects, without victory in one's conflicts, without compassion, without love. It is not likely that Simone Weil, a woman of genuine warmth and courage, would prefer the exclusively duty-devoted Stoic conception to that of the human rights partisans. To respect rights after all is to respect all the aims and goals and interests that rights defend. To give one's total devotion to playing well one's part in a play in a spirit of indifference to real life outcomes, on the other hand, is to detach one's behavior from anything else worth caring about, in a spirit of unbecoming moral egotism. Weil disdains rights in part because, unbacked by power, they cause tyrants to laugh derisively. The best answer to the problem of the immoral tyrant is not to crawl into a self-insulating shell of selfish "virtue," giving up all desires and cares but one all-consuming concern for one's own invulnerable goodness, but rather to leash real power to one's moral rights.

Moral powers, so-called, without back-up physical power will be impotent against physical force unrestrained by moral responsiveness. But before leaving this depressing topic, we should look at the idea of a "moral power" a little more closely. Moral and legal powers are not just alternative techniques—like nuclear power, hydroelectric power, psychological power, persuasive power, and political power—for producing the same kinds of effect within the physical world. Rather they provide ways of producing their own distinctive types of effect within their own distinctive realm—effects on people's moral positions, their duties, liberties, claims, immunities, liabilities, and further moral powers—and these distinctive effects are produced, not by some other kind of natural power, on a par with electric power or military power, but by rule-defined offices and statuses, offers, acceptances, transfers, acts of consent, and so on. Between two parties who are in some way potential competitors, yet have not rejected the whole moral game in favor of physical force, rights-claims, more than any of their alternatives, dispose the parties toward reasonableness. Carl Wellman makes this point well: "Claiming is an appeal to...the grounds of one's rights, and thus an appeal to reasons rather than to mere force."[25] In the case of moral rights of the sort listed at the start of this paper, appeal is not made literally to titles, chits, receipts, warranties, and so on—these are *legal* or legal-like reasons—but to moral reasons, in Wellman's words, "statements that imply some moral conclusion."[26]

It is an important source of the value of moral rights then that—speaking very generally—they dispose people with opposed interests to be reasonable rather than arrogant and truculent. The more widely spread the respect for the general practice of rights-claiming, the less likely (or at least the less quickly) people are to resort to physical force. That is part of the full case for the importance of rights. That case is not undermined by the truism that general reasonableness will not impress the unreasonable.

There is a lamentable tendency among social philosophers to conclude that if something is not "*the* good" then it cannot even be *a* good; that if something is not self-sufficiently good, as Epictetan "virtue" claims to be, then it cannot be in its own right intrinsically good; that if something is not all by itself sufficient for human well-being, then it cannot be a necessary element of, or even an important contributor to, that well-being. To cite a familiar example, *liberty* without minimal health or wealth or opportunity does its possessor no good, as is commonly and correctly observed. Therefore (the argument goes) political liberty, conceived "negatively" as an absence of state coercion, is a counterfeit good and an unworthy goal. That these inferences are *non-sequiturs* is too obvious a point to dwell upon. Similarly, we can concede to Robert Young and Simone Weil that rights to autonomy and privacy, to free expression, to freedom from physical assault and from verbal incivility, to due process, to equal treatment, to free association, to free religious practice, and so on, will not compensate one for the lack of affection and loving care, or the absence of physical safety, but that shows only that moral rights are not enough for a good life, not that they are unnecessary or undesirable. (Actually what it shows is that a lot of other things are necessary too.) And the insufficiency of rights possession as a defense against ruthless totalitarian oppression is a feature that rights share with every good thing, including affection and loving care. (Perhaps the Stoics' total and exclusive devotion to duty-based "virtue" is an exception, but it comes—as Madame Weil, I suspect, would be the first to acknowledge—at unacceptable cost to one's humanity.) In the end, every form of goodness can be said to presuppose the protection of political and ultimately physical power. But that is not even the slightest reason for devaluing rights.

Notes

1. Jeremy Waldron, *Nonsense Upon Stilts, Bentham, Burke, and Marx on the Rights of Man* (London and New York: Methuen, 1987), p. 44.
2. Marie Vassilichev, *Berlin Diaries* (New York: Knopf, 1987), p. 78. I am indebted to Professor Ruth Marcus for this reference.
3. Richard Wasserstrom, "Rights, Human Rights, and Racial Discrimination," *Journal of Philosophy*, Vol. 61, (1964), p. 636. For an illustration of the sort of thing Wasserstrom may have meant, consider this World War I example from "Billie Dyer," by William Maxwell, in *The New Yorker* (May 15, 1989), p. 44:

   Camp Funston, in Kansas. It was the headquarters of the 92nd Division, which was made up exclusively of Negro troops—the Army was not integrated until thirty one years later by executive order of Harry Truman.

   At Camp Funston, a bulletin was read to all the soldiers of the 92nd Division: "The Division Commander has repeatedly urged that all colored members of his commands, and especially the officers and noncommissioned officers, should refrain from going where their presence will be resented. In spite of this injunction, one of the Sergeants of the Medical Department has recently...entered a theatre, as he undoubtedly had a legal right to do, and precipitated trouble by making it possible to allege race discrimination in the seat he was given...Don't go where your presence is not desired."

Is it possible for a white reader to imagine what it would be like for a black soldier to read this bulletin and *not* seethe with moral indignation? Is it possible that a black soldier could accept the claim that his rights end where the desires of others for his nonpresence, no matter how arbitrary or ill-founded, begin? To imagine such a person is to appreciate what Wasserstrom means by 'moral impoverishment.'

4. Wasserstrom, *loc. cit.*
5. Joel Feinberg, "The Nature and Value of Rights," *Journal of Value Inquiry*, Vol. 4 (1970).
6. C. S. Lewis, *Studies in Words* (Cambridge: Cambridge University Press, 1961), p. 14.
7. Jan Narveson, *Journal of Value Inquiry*, Vol. 4 (1970).
8. William Nelson, "On the Alleged Importance of Moral Rights," *Ratio* (1976), p. 150.
9. There may be a related use, however. You are a soldier on guard duty, whose duty is to be wide awake and alert. But you have "a right to be fatigued," and fatigue makes alertness impossible, etc. That it was not inappropriate for you to be fatigued in the circumstances gives you an excuse for the inefficient performance of your duties.
10. Daniel Lyons, "Entitled to Complain," *Analysis*, April, 1966, pp. 119-22.
11. *Ibid*, p. 120.
12. *Loc. cit.*
13. Friedrich Nietzsche, *The Will to Power*, trans. Walter Kaufmann and R.J. Hollingdale (New York: Vintage Books, 1968), sects. 365-68, Book IV, *et passim*.
14. Clarence Darrow, *Resist Not Evil* (Montclair, N.J.: Patterson Smith, 1973). First published in 1902.
15. Of course "Carlos" or any other proper name would serve as well as "Charley."
16. The preceding five sentences are taken from my "The Moral and Legal Responsibility of the Bad Samaritan," *Criminal Justice Ethics*, Vol. 3, No. 1 (1984), p. 64.
17. Robert Young, "Dispensing with Moral Rights," *Political Theory*, Vol. 6 (1978), p. 68. See also an astute recent article by Jeremy Waldron of which I was unaware when I wrote this paper. See his "When Justice Replaces Affection: The Need for Rights" in the *Harvard Journal of Law & Public Policy*, Vol. 11, No. 3 (1988). In this paper Waldron works out a kind of compromise between Kant and Hegel on the role of rights in marriage. Hegel's view is similar to that of Robert Young quoted in the text. Waldron paraphrases it thus: "To stand on one's rights is to distance oneself from those to whom the claim is made; it is to announce, so to speak, an opening of hostilities; and it is to acknowledge that other warmer bonds of kinship, affection and intimacy can no longer hold. To do this in a context where adversarial hostility is inappropriate is a serious moral failing. As Hegel put it in an Addition to *The Philosophy of Right*: 'To have no interest except in one's formal right may be pure obstinacy, often a fitting accompaniment of a cold heart and restricted sympathies. It is uncultured people who insist most on their rights, while noble minds look on other aspects of the thing'." (Waldron, p. 628.)
18. One way to define "love" that does justice to its honorific associations is as a relation between persons characterized by mutual affection *and* moral respect, among other things. For a striking and persuasive example of how affection

without respect falls short of love see Henrik Ibsen's play, *A Doll's House*. The benighted husband, Torvald Helmer, has genuine affection, of a sort, toward his young wife Nora. He predictably beams when he beholds her pretty face. He is even "proud of her," as a parent might be of a child, or an owner of an art object. He is constantly petting her, as one might pet a cat or dog. Indeed, his favorite forms of address are the names of "cute" little animals. ("Is that my little lark twittering out there?," "Is my little squirrel bustling about?") Its bland conventionality aside, Helmer's affection may well be genuine. After all, we can be genuinely affectionate with animals (another class of playthings) too. But Helmer lacks all respect for his little pet, not only in the sense of esteem, but also in the sense of recognition of the other as a potential maker of moral claims against one, and against others too. When she does finally make a claim against him, it is as if a mechanical doll had suddenly spoken. He just cannot take her seriously as a claimant, being unable even to conceive of her in that role.

This interpretation, I think, goes one step beyond that of Waldron, who writes, "To go back to the marriage example, I will suggest that there is a need for an array of formal and legalistic rights and duties, *not to constitute the affective bond* [as Kant almost seems to say] but to provide each person with secure knowledge of what she can count on in the unhappy event that there turns out to be no other basis for her dealings with her erstwhile partner in the relationship." (Waldron, *op. cit.*, p. 629). I would treat respect as closely tied to the idea of moral rights, and those rights as valuable not only for fallback security, but, as the object of moral respect, an essential constituent—not of "the affective bond" necessarily, (if that means simply "affection")—but of the full bond of love. (Other elements are no doubt necessary too, like simple liking, for example.)

19. Simone Weil, *The Need for Roots* (London, 1952), p. 18. The words quoted here are apparently a paraphrase of Weil's own words, quoted by Young (*op. cit.*, p. 68) from their author, Mierlys Owens, in "The Notion of Human Rights: A Reconsideration," *American Philosophical Quarterly*, Vol. 6 (1969), p. 244.

20. Even Carl Wellman appears (perhaps through inadvertent overstatement) to make this mistake. He writes, for example: "Claiming is striking a blow in a struggle to prevail over one's opposition"—Carl Wellman, *op.cit.* p. 209.

21. Having held this view for over twenty years, though perhaps having given it insufficient emphasis, I was quite astonished to read in Jeremy Waldron's *Nonsense Upon Stilts* (*op.cit.*, p. 196) that my theory is that "self-respect and human dignity really depend upon being in a position to make strident, querulous, adversarial claims *against* other people...that my fulfillment, my freedom and self-realization depend on my muscular and self-assertive capacity to place limits on yours."

22. Zeke Wigglesworth, Knight-Ridder Newspapers, April 16, 1989.

23. Epictetus, *Discourses*, Book I, Chap. 19, "Of the Right Treatment of Tyrants."

24. Epictetus, *The Enchiridion*, XVI.

25. Carl Wellman, *A Theory of Rights* (Totowa, NJ: Rowman & Allanheld, 1985), p. 210.

26. *Ibid.*, p. 170.

Philosophical Perspectives, 6, Ethics, 1992

MORAL CONCEPTS: SUBSTANCE AND SENTIMENT

Allan Gibbard
University of Michigan

Decent people heed morality: They don't kill or steal, or hit people to see them wince. They help others in need. We learn all this young—though even then we know that life isn't as plain as the maxims. Morality, though, is only part of life, and within its constraints, the moral person has a range of choice. He can decide what he wants in life and how best to pursue it.

Moral philosophers widely accept this picture. They see morality as part of the best life, but not all of it by far. Morality may be specially authoritative, overriding in the sphere where it does issue commands—but still, the sphere is limited. This narrow view of morality is not universal: some understand morality as taking in all of how to live.[1] But many reject such moral totalitarianism, some with vehemence.

To explain these widespread views, we have to say what morality is. What delineates moral precepts from other fine precepts for living? We can ask this as a question of substance: What is the nature of morality, and how does morality, narrowly taken, differ from the rest of living well? Analytic philosophers, though, would think there is a prior difficulty to solve: What does this question mean? What is a person saying if he calls one consideration moral and another not?

In my book *Wise Choices, Apt Feelings*,[2] I make a proposal for how to delineate morality. This paper is a partial defense of one part of my proposal. It confines itself to one set of moral concepts: moral right and wrong. Its aim is to develop one chief competitor to my own account of these concepts, and then say why to prefer mine.

My criteria must be multiple: First, I want my proposal to fit pretty well our clear judgments of how our terms apply, and what ranges of statements employing those terms we can imagine people accepting. I want also, though, to develop concepts that are coherent, and I am looking for concepts that might be well worth keeping. These goals may compete, but my aim will be to reconcile them. I am exploring whether ordinary thought suggests important, coherent ways of thinking about life and human relations, and if so, how we might regiment its suggestions.

We live now in a post-analytic period, we philosophers in the analytic tradition. We are united not by our tenets or procedures, but by our history and the way it has left us suspicious of claims of meaning. Like our predecessors, though, we need meaning in some form. We too can find ourselves talking at cross-purposes if we don't ask ourselves what to mean by our terms. We may not be able to see our problem as one of straight analysis; there may be no clear fact of what a term means. Morality as we know it, after all, has a wide range of features. When we think of evaluations with some of these features but not all, then although sometimes we will have a clear sense of how our words apply, sometimes we will be puzzled. The constraints on a satisfactory account of meaning will then be slack, but it may still be useful to ask how best to satisfy those constraints.

I. My Proposal

A morality confined to right and wrong is narrower than morality on ordinary conceptions. We assess people as morally admirable or morally praiseworthy. Other evaluations too might count as moral: judgments of shamefulness (though not, say, of shameful birth), and judgments couched in thick terms: that one is a swine, say, or disrespectful, or lazy. Here, though, I focus on right and wrong. These lie at the core of what we normally count as morality, and if we can deal with them, we may be able to apply the same pattern to other concepts. (Thick concepts, however, may need quite a different kind of treatment, and so I set them aside for other studies.) I speak in this paper as if morality were entirely a matter of moral right and wrong. You should read all talk of "morality" in this paper as talk of morality *insofar as it concerns moral right and wrong.*

I want to explain moral right and wrong in terms of moral sentiments: guilt or remorse on the one hand, and impartial resentment or anger on the other. Wrongness, I propose, is a question of blame—of the kinds of acts that are blameworthy or blameless. (The connection of wrongness to blame is complex, but in the book I try to draw it.[3]) A blameworthy action is one that warrants blame: self-blame on the part of the agent as feelings of guilt, and blame from others as impartial resentment or anger. My proposal, then, is to start with the moral sentiments of guilt and impartial resentment, and proceed from there to the narrowly moral concepts of right and wrong.

One reason to develop these concepts is to interpret wholesale criticisms of morality, such as Nietzsche's and Williams'.[4] Can these writers be criticizing morality as such, or are they criticizing one conception of morality in favor of another? Perhaps they are criticizing the place we give in our lives to moral right and wrong. Another reason is to understand the question

"Why be moral?" For this question to make sense, morality cannot be characterized simply as the study of what we have reason to do. To ask why do something, after all, is to ask for reasons. At stake may be the place of moral right and wrong in good reasons for action.

This is not right and wrong of just any kind. There are right and wrong answers on tests, and perhaps we could even speak of right and wrong choices for the man pursuing riches with a contract murder business. As morality concerns right and wrong actions, it concerns *morally* right and wrong actions. We then have to say what it means to call an action right or wrong morally— the topic of this paper. Now moral theorists often regiment the term 'right' to mean not wrong, or morally permissible. The regimentation probably won't fit all significant connotations of the term, but here I accept it. My aim, then, is to understand moral permissibility and impermissibility.

The root idea of my proposal is this: When we assess actions as morally wrong or not, we tie our assessments to blame. Acts can be undesirable or defective in other ways too, but 'wrong' in its moral sense gets its force from the way it invokes standards of blame. Can anyone think that certain kinds of acts are morally wrong, but that no one could ever be blamed for doing them? If he said he did, we would want to hear more.

What, then, is blame? It would be hard to explain it apart from the feelings expressed in blaming someone: feelings of indignation, we might say. Indignation we can see as a species of anger or resentment, along with a sense that the feeling is justified, even from an impartial standpoint. Justification is required: I might resent you for something you have done, but if I think these feelings unwarranted, I do not sincerely blame you. Then too, if I think resentment warranted, then even if I cannot summon it up, I do think you to blame. Blame goes with thinking resentment warranted. A person is *to blame* for doing something, we can say, if and only if resentment against him for doing it would be warranted. Resentment is a narrowly moral sentiment, and so blameworthiness is a matter of warrant for narrowly moral sentiments of blame.

Self-blame, though, is not self-resentment. I kick myself when I have blundered and let myself down, but my typical response to my moral transgressions is different. Feelings of self-blame are not indignant and punitive, but agonized and conciliatory. They are feelings not of resentment, but more of acceding to the resentment of others. We call these feelings of guilt or remorse.

When I think myself to blame for an act, in short, I think two things: that resentment is warranted on the part of others, and that feelings of guilt are warranted on my own part. This, I propose, gives us the concept of blameworthiness.[5] That leaves moral wrongness. To act wrongly is not always to act blamably: one sometimes acts wrongly but excusably. How to derive moral wrongness from blameworthiness is a difficult problem. I try it in my book, and I'm not sure whether or not I succeed.[6] When we think an act morally wrong, in some sense we rule it out. We can also rule out actions, say, as stupid or ill-advised, or as wounding to our prestige. One way to ask what 'morally wrong' means is to ask this: When one adopts a set of standards for ruling out actions, what makes these standards ones of moral wrongness? My rough answer is that the standards are sanctioned by blame. Standards of moral wrongness, we can try saying, are standards identified by this characteristic: if an agent violates them because of inadequate motivation to abide by them, guilt is warranted on his part, and resentment on the part of others.[7] My account of the concept of moral wrongness is thus related to emotivism: Like emotivists, I think that criticisms of actions as morally wrong have a special emotional flavor. The way to explain what constitutes moral thinking, they and I maintain, is to show its tie to specific moral sentiments. I differ from the emotivists, though, on what this tie is: Moral convictions, I hold, do not consist precisely in emotions. They consist in judgments of warrant for emotions: judgments of whether and when certain moral emotions are warranted.

This analysis gives central place to a notion of warrant, and of warrant as applied to feelings. Many people reject the claim that feelings can be warranted or not. I think this is more in the abstract than in particular cases: If your next door neighbor is angry with you for not raking his leaves, won't you find his anger unwarranted? And suppose he is angry with you for sleeping too late in the morning. Won't you again find his anger unwarranted, even if you yourself are cursing at having slept so late? Further stories might lead you to answer no to these questions, to be sure, but if this is all there is to it, then isn't he being a self-righteous sponger and busybody? In any case, I try in the book to reconcile us to the idea of warrant for feelings: I exclaim how much of social life consists in sorting out how to feel, in working toward common standards of warrant for feelings. I develop a proposal for what 'rational' or 'warranted' means—as applied not only to feelings, but to actions and to beliefs. *To call a feeling warranted, I say, is to express one's acceptance of norms that permit the feeling.*[8] Nothing in this paper, though, will depend on this part of the theory—so long as we accept that feelings like guilt and anger can somehow be assessed as warranted or not. The two parts of my proposal are separable, and this paper concerns the first: that wrongness should be explained in terms of warrant for guilt and impartial resentment. For purposes here I leave it open how warrant for feelings is best explained.

This means I am leaving aside questions of metaethical cognitivism and non-cognitivism. My theory of what 'warranted' means is non-cognitivistic, but this is the half of my theory I am setting aside for now. You can, if you wish, be a non-naturalist about warrant, and claim that warrant is a simple, non-natural property. This was the position of A.C. Ewing.[9] Or you can adopt an ideal observer or qualified attitude theory: warranted feelings are the ones a person will have when he is informed and vividly aware of everything pertinent.[10] Both these accounts treat warrant as a property in the strict sense, and so if you combine either with my definition of 'morally wrong' you will have a cognitivistic theory of moral terms like 'wrong'. You will be treating moral wrongness as a property.

Some people challenge guilt: they think it is never warranted. In proposing that moral wrongness boils down to warrant for guilt, I do not mean to reject this challenge. Rather, I am offering terms for framing the challenge. The person who thinks that guilt is never warranted thinks that nothing anyone does is, strictly speaking, morally wrong. Actions may be lamentable in other ways, but not in this way. This is how I interpret his challenge.

II. Cluster Constraints

Why characterize wrongness in terms of blame? Wouldn't it be better to characterize wrong acts substantively, in terms of the sorts of things that make acts wrong? Not just any kind of act, after all, can count as wrong. Suppose a high Pythagorean priestess claimed it is wrong to count beans, and that this is simply a moral axiom. We would find her claim unintelligible. Aren't we forced, then, to define moral wrongness by the characteristics in virtue of which acts are wrong?

In the remainder of this paper, I follow this thought as far as I can take it. I ask how we could use it to develop an alternative account of what the term 'wrong' means, in its moral sense. I then assess the two proposals against each other: mine and the alternative. In this section and the next, I put the alternative in as strong a form as I can find.

Concede (at least for now) that not just any sort of action could be called wrong for no further reason—not with linguistic propriety, that is. Moral concepts are substantively constrained. To work toward a definition of 'wrong', we can first ask what these constraints might be.

Perhaps they constrain morality to questions of benefit and harm. A consideration bears on moral right and wrong only if it boils down, in the end, to good or ill for someone.[11] Now our question, recall, is one of meaning, and so for our purposes, this must not only be true, it must be true as a matter of meaning. It must hold true not only of considerations that really are morally valid, but of anything a person could regard as a valid moral consideration—so long as he makes no mistake of language or logic. Meanings, after all, are shared by people with correct moral views and people with mistaken ones. What shared meanings put these people in disagreement on a common subject matter? I might well agree to a substantive claim that all valid moral considerations boil down to benefits and harms. In question here, though, is a claim of meaning: that anyone who says otherwise is botching language. Could a person meaningfully and coherently think an action wrong, and not think its wrongness somehow a matter of benefit and harm?

We seem to find many examples of this. People widely think certain sexual practices wrong. Sometimes they have stories that tie the wrongness to harm, but sometimes they do not. A person who does not may, to be sure, think that such a story could be given—though he himself can't give it. He then stands prepared to withdraw his claim of wrongness if no tie to harm can be sustained. But he might not: he might think the wrongness a matter, say, of dignity. Or he might just think we can recognize the wrongness, that the upright person knows moral right from wrong.

Must we take such views seriously? Even if for me they are not live options, I want to be able to talk with people for whom they are. There seems to be disagreement between them and me, and I want to be able to explain it as disagreement. Is it disagreement over moral wrongness, or disagreement of some other normative kind? Wrongness is what seems to be at issue, and moral wrongness at that. It is hard to see how else to name the disagreement.

In any case, I think I can say what is at issue. Some people think that certain kinds of sexual conduct warrant blame—guilt on one's own part, and resentment on the part of impartial, engaged observers. They think that such conduct warrants blame independently of whatever harms it does. I do not, and so here, at least, is a dispute we can interpret.

Still, aren't some views so incredible that we should be happy not to shape our language to accommodate them? Some people do think that certain sexual practices warrant blame, independently of whatever harm they do. We for whom such views are not live options, though, might want to identify some narrower range of inquiry—a range we find genuinely problematic. We might pigeonhole only views in this range as views about "moral wrongness". Practical disputes about benefits and harms permeate our lives, and it seems useful to have some label for this topic. 'Moral wrongness' might be the best.

Such a stipulation, though, threatens to exclude far too many views from our discussion. Even if we put sexual taboos beyond the pale, many are our friends who think, for example, that human dignity matters in itself. Many think respect for humanity is basic. Do we want by linguistic fiat to rule these views out? (And if indignity, say, might make for moral wrongness in some realms, why stipulate that it can't count with sex?)[12] We could, to be sure, recognize the disagreement, but deny that it has to do with moral right and wrong. Something else is at issue, we might say. Some people think that acts that manifest disrespect for human dignity warrant blame, independently of any harm they do. Others don't. This is a dispute, but because it is not a dispute grounded in considerations of benefit and harm, we might call the dispute non-moral. We might—but again, it is hard to see the point. Isn't the dispute just the kind we would regard as deeply moral? Isn't the topic the bases of morality, the kinds of grounds that go, ultimately, to make acts morally right or wrong?

I have belabored a point that may seem plain, because we need to see where it leads us. Moral concepts have substantive constraints built in, I am conceding. These constraints, though, must be broader than a restriction to benefits and harms as the bases of moral claims. Dignity and respect count too, and so perhaps do some other considerations. Some are still ruled out, to be sure: whether the act is one of hand-clasping, say, or of counting beans— unless some further story is in the offing. The upshot is this: Moral wrongness is a cluster concept. The concept, it turns out, is best identified by citing a whole cluster of kinds of considerations the concept admits.

Alternatively, we might cling to the view that by its very meaning, moral wrongness is a matter of benefit and harm, and still admit dignity and the like by giving a broad reading to benefit and harm. We then count disrespect and assaults on dignity as harms, even to someone who welcomes them and whose pleasure in life is not lessened by them. But then—unless we can say what unites the things we now count as benefits or harms—these notions too have become loose clusters. Moral wrong is then still a cluster concept. Its meaning is still characterized by the loose group of considerations one could think, with linguistic propriety, bear on moral wrongness.

This outcome should stir misgivings, if nothing more can be said. What is it about the group that gives wrongness its special importance? Is the classification of some views as moral and others as not any more significant than the fact, say, that the French word *'sauce'* applies to gravy, salad dressing, and Hollandaise sauce, whereas Americans have no such term?

III. The Alternative

Waive for now all objections to clusters. The meaning of 'morally wrong', let us agree, is to be explained by citing a set of considerations the concept admits. Linguistic rules allow just the members of this set to bear on whether an act is morally wrong. How is all this supposed to work?

Benefits and harms belong in the set, but not all statements grounded in benefit and harm are moral statements. One can cite benefits and harms explanatorily, to explain Mme Dufarge's hatred, say. And a person can deny that certain considerations of benefit and harm have moral import. The Hopi studied by Brandt did not see anything wrong with a game that hurt chickens—though they agreed the game caused the chickens a lot of pain.[13] Once we have listed the considerations in the set, then—the considerations that can count as moral—we still need to say how the constraints work. I can think of two possible schemes. One, though, is a non-starter: naturalism in Moore's sense. The term 'wrong', a naturalist thinks, has a purely natural meaning, derivable from substantive constraints on its application. To maintain this, however, we would have to think the constraints are strong enough to determine, all by themselves, a moral term's full meaning. That there are such constraints does not entail that the constraints are this tight.[14] One person may think that indignity goes toward making an act morally wrong, even when no one minds. Another may deny this. Neither need be confused about language. Theirs is a dispute of moral substance. Are these merely cases of ordinary vagueness? If they were, either party could accede to the other's vocabulary without change in moral views—and there would be nothing left to discuss. These disputes are really, though, over the ways dignity matters in conduct, over how to treat considerations of dignity in settling what to do. They should not be assimilated to a dispute, say, over whether a love seat is a couch.

What besides Moorean naturalism, then, might account for the substantive constraints that seem built into the concepts of moral right and wrong? Though constraints of substance do somehow enter into moral meanings, we now must say, they do not by themselves give the entire meanings of moral terms. Something is missing, and so we need to identify it. What might it be? Many philosophers would say it is the "normativity" or the "action-guiding character" of moral terms. Let us try to follow this up. Could we get the meaning of 'wrong', then, by somehow combining action-guidingness with constraints on the kinds of considerations that get to count as moral?

My own view is that action-guidingness is indeed built into the meaning of 'wrong'—along perhaps with constraints on the application of the term— but that this is not enough. The action-guidingness, on my view, must be of an indirect kind: it must proceed through warrant for blame. It must go by way of the narrowly moral sentiments of resentment and guilt. A more direct view, though, must seem a prime alternative to my own. Will action-guidingness plus substantive constraints give us, all by themselves, the meaning of 'morally wrong'? We should develop this possibility into the strongest form we can, and see how it fares.

Let me try this—recognizing that someone may find a sturdier version. First, action-guidingness: Start with the idea of a *valid practical considera-tion*—or in one sense of the term, a *reason* for acting one way rather than another. When I use the term 'reason', I need to warn against a pitfall. We sometimes speak of "a person's reasons" for doing something, without endorsing those reasons as cogent: the Little Moron's reason for jumping off the Empire State Building was to make a big hit on Broadway. In another sense, we could tell the moron "That's no reason to jump!"—and it is this latter sense I want to give to the term 'reason'. A reason to act one way or another is something that reasonably bears on what to do. It bears on what it makes most sense to do, on what one has most reason to do. The totality of one's reasons to do one thing or another somehow combine to endorse an alternative as the best thing to do, or to endorse some range of alternatives as equally well supported.[15] A person who claims something to be a reason, in this sense, is taking a normative stand. He is endorsing the reason as good or cogent or valid. What this claim amounts to will be disputed: I have my own view, but in this paper, I am keeping neutral on this question.[16] Suppose, then, we understand what 'reason' in this sense means. Suppose we understand what it means to say that the reasons combine, in such-and-such a way, to make a course of action the one an agent has most reason all told to take. I assume that however this talk of reasons is best explained, the normativity or action-guidingness of moral concepts is somehow a matter of reasons in this sense.

We can now formulate a claim about the meaning of 'morally wrong'—a claim that builds the meaning out of action-guidingness plus linguistic constraints of substance. Start with a fairly empty framework principle: That an act is *morally wrong* means that it is ruled out on valid moral grounds. We then have to explain the phrase 'valid moral grounds'. What constitute such grounds will be a matter both of rules of language and of normative substance. Start with the idea of a *possible consideration*: something that is a candidate for being a valid reason to do something or not—something a person might take to be a valid reason, without linguistic or conceptual error. For a possible consideration to constitute a *valid moral ground*, it must satisfy two requirements: that it be valid, and that it be moral as opposed to non-moral. Whether it counts as a possible *moral* consideration is a linguistic or conceptual matter: the concepts of moral right and wrong invoke a set of possible considerations that are linguistically eligible to be accepted as moral considerations. Whether a possible consideration is a *reason*—a *valid ground*—is in contrast a substantive issue. Conceptual analysis does not settle which possible considerations are genuine reasons.[17] Suppose, for instance, fighting a duel would make me admired by my rivals. This is a possible consideration in favor of fighting the duel. We may deny that this in itself is any reason to fight the duel, but at least it is a candidate reason: someone might think it a reason and have full command of language. Whether he would be mistaken is a substantive normative question; it will not be settled linguistically; one could take either side of the issue without misusing the term 'reason'. If, though, this is a reason—a valid consideration, that is to say—then language settles that the reason is not a moral one. If the fact that fighting the dual would impress my enemies constitutes a reason for fighting it, and does so on no further ground, the reason is non-moral.

An act is morally wrong, the proposal now goes, if it is ruled out on valid moral grounds. Valid moral grounds are grounds that are valid—they constitute genuine reasons in favor of courses of action or against them—and they are moral as opposed to non-moral. Whether the grounds are valid is a matter of normative substance. Whether, if so, they are moral or non-moral is settled by the meaning of the term 'moral'. The proposal is that this gives the meaning of 'wrong' in its moral sense.

More needs to be said. In the first place, do moral grounds have to be valid as ultimate grounds? Must they constitute good reasons for no further reason? Or may they be grounds that make for good reasons derivatively? Suppose, for example, my theory of good reasons for action is hedonistic egoism: I think that all good reasons to act one way rather than another are ultimately a matter of prospective pleasures and displeasures for the agent. I also think that honesty is the hedonically best policy: it always gives an agent the best long-run prospects for pleasure. When I rule out an act as dishonest, do I think it morally wrong? Here is a quandary: By conceptual rules, honesty, if a consideration, counts as a moral consideration. One's own prospects for pleasure, if what makes them a consideration is that they are one's own, counts as a non-moral consideration. So if honesty is a consideration only because one's own pleasure is, are considerations of honesty moral considerations? Are acts to be ruled out as dishonest morally wrong, if the rationale is at base egoistic?

It may be best to allow that they are. Many people have thought, after all, that the justification of common sense morality is one of enlightened long-run self-interest. Sidgwick may have dealt such views a definitive refutation—questions of afterlife aside [18]—but we should avoid, if we can, saying that none of these thinkers really ever thought anything morally wrong. This quandary, then, may turn out not to be serious.

IV. A Dilemma

Here is a second quandary for the construction of this position. This quandary, I argue later, tells against the alternative I have been developing, and in favor of my own analysis.

Moral reasons, we have said, may not be all the reasons that bear on a decision. That is to say, rules of language do not settle whether all reasons for action—in the sense of good or cogent reasons—are moral reasons. A person could think that not all are without misusing language. What if he does, then: what if he thinks that some reasons to act one way rather than another are moral reasons and some are non-moral? By definition, he thinks an act morally wrong if he thinks it ruled out for moral reasons—on valid moral grounds. But what does this mean? I can think of two possible interpretations. The first is that the moral reasons by themselves, taken all in all, tell against the act. This leaves it open whether all things considered, there is most reason to perform the act nevertheless. A person might coherently think this and violate no rule of language—though such a possibility might be ruled out on substantive grounds, by an account of the proper role of moral considerations in practical reason. That linguistic rules alone leave the question open may be as it should: We puzzle why be moral. Perhaps the question amounts to asking whether, sometimes, we have most reason to do things that are morally wrong. If we never do, that ought to be a deep fact about the rational power of moral considerations, not a tautology.

Alternatively, we might say that by the very meaning of the term, an act is morally wrong only if, on moral grounds, one has most reason to rule it out. For an act to be morally wrong, the moral considerations must not only speak against it, all told; they must carry the day. This requirement, we might want to maintain, is a rule of moral language. To say that breaking this promise is morally wrong is not only to say the moral considerations, taken together, come out against it. It is to say too that the good reasons as a whole—moral and non-moral together—come out against it. If that is what we mean, it is analytic that a morally wrong act cannot be the one a person has most reason, all told, to perform. The question "Why be moral?" is senseless.

Now to be sure, we might be convinced that valid moral reasons, taken as a whole, always carry the day whenever they pronounce. Where morality commands, practical reason obeys. In that case, these two theories of meaning will always yield like findings of whether an act is morally wrong or not. When the moral reasons, all told, speak against an act, then in the first sense it follows by definition that the act is wrong. In the second sense, it follows that the act is wrong not from this alone, but from this plus a deep finding: the finding that moral considerations always trump when they come into play. The moral considerations alone speak all told against the act; therefore by the deep finding, the totality of good reasons speak all told against the act. It then follows from these two premises that the act is wrong in the second, stronger sense. A person who thinks that moral reasons always trump can use 'wrong' in either of these two senses indifferently; he thinks they always coincide in their application.

We are looking, though, for a meaning that might be shared even by people who disagree on whether moral considerations always carry the day with practical reason. Those who think it does not may sometimes think, and without linguistic mistake, that an act is morally wrong in the first, weak sense but not in the second, strong sense. The moral reasons tell against the act, but the moral and non-moral reasons combined tell on balance in its favor.

Now for the dilemma: It stems from an asymmetrical way we ordinarily treat personal burdens and opportunities. Suppose an act would lose you an opportunity for great enjoyment. This does not count as a moral consideration when the other considerations are non-moral. An opportunity comes up, say, for a long weekend skiing trip with friends. You would enjoy the trip greatly, but if you stay home and work, that will help you get the promotion you want. This choice we count as non-moral. On the other hand, enjoyment might defeat a moral obligation—especially if the obligation is slight. Last week, let us say, you didn't have money when the paper girl came to collect. You promised to have it this Friday. She isn't desperate for the money, but you promised because you fully expected to be home on Friday. Now the skiing expedition has come up, and if you go you won't be there to pay her. The decision is moral, but the conclusion may be to break your undertaking to pay her Friday. You can, after all, pay her with apologies next week, and it won't much bother her. All told, it will not be wrong to do so—or so you may conclude. Here the only straightforwardly moral consideration is your slight obligation to pay this week rather then next. The moral considerations thus speak all told for staying home, since that is the only way to pay the girl as you promised. In the weak sense, then, it is morally wrong to go skiing in this circumstance—though you have most reason all told to do so. This seems a mistaken assessment of the case, given ordinary views. In the strong sense, it is not wrong to put off paying her, and this seems the right thing to say.

We have a dilemma, then. We seem forced by this case to the strong version of the proposal. But the strong version too is problematic. It rules out, as a matter of proper language, all possibility that an act could ever be morally wrong and still be the thing one has most reason all told to do. This seems wrong: the possibility or impossibility of such a case seems a question of moral substance.

In developing this alternative to my own view, then, I encounter a dilemma. The alternative comes in two versions, and neither allows us a distinction we may want to make. When personal considerations enter into moral calculations, one version allows them to defeat the claim that an act would be morally wrong. The other allows them to prevail over moral conclusions in valid practical reasoning. Neither version, though, allows that each of these things might sometimes happen, the one in some cases and the other in others.

V. Comparative Assessments

I myself think that moral reasons apply to actions indirectly: moral judgments concern not reasons for actions directly, but reasons for moral sentiments about actions. The sentiments are ones of guilt and resentment, and it is the flavor of these sentiments that makes certain judgments moral as opposed to non-moral. We now have two competing strategies on the table for picking out a class of normative judgments as moral. The alternative developed in the last two sections, we can say, is *direct* and *substance-constrained*: moral reasons are directly reasons for or against actions, but rules of language make for substantive constraints on what grounds can count as "moral". The proposal in my book—the one I favor—is *sentiment- routed* and hence *indirect*: moral reasons are to be explained in terms of reasons not for actions directly, but for moral sentiments about actions. And the proposal includes no stipulation of substance constraints.

How do these two kinds of proposals fare against each other? The initial presumption must be for a direct account. Doesn't moral thinking have its primary home in practice? Aren't moral questions primarily questions of what to do—and not of what to feel about the things we might do? Sometimes, to be sure, we decide on the basis of what we would hate ourselves for in the morning, but that's unusually roundabout. Normally we think more directly about what to do, and only move to an indirect view when we fear our direct view is getting clouded.

A second advantage of the direct view may lie in its substance-constraints. It builds in substantive constraints on the kinds of considerations that count as moral. This, we might think, fits a sense we have that not just anything counts as a possible moral view: that if our priestess claims to think that only counting beans is morally wrong, we would find her claim baffling.

This second advantage, I claim, is spurious. In the first place, if we do need to build in substantive constraints like these, we can add them to either a direct or an indirect account. With substance-constraints added, the indirect, sentiment-routed account will go something like this: First, valid *moral* grounds for ruling out an action (as opposed to non-moral grounds) are the ones that satisfy these two conditions: (i) Their violation (through insufficient motivation, by a normal person) is reason for guilt on the part of the agent, and resentment on the part of impartial, engaged observers. (ii) They are members of the following set: ..... The dots are then filled in with the kinds of grounds that our language would allow us to regard as moral. Having defined valid moral grounds, we again define an act as *morally wrong* if it is ruled out on valid moral grounds. A sentiment-routed view, then, can be specified to include whatever substantive constraints we need.

It is not at all clear, though, that we need a list of substantive constraints—or even that we can build one in if we want and still get the right verdicts. Anyone who thinks substantive constraints are needed will think too that the correct ones rule out silly, spurious reasons, like that the act is one of counting beans. Our rules of language tell us, he will say, that barring some further story, this could not genuinely be thought grounds for thinking an act wrong. But suppose our priestess really did think guilt warranted when one counts beans, and anger on the part of others. Suppose she found this self-evident, a starting point for moral reasoning and not a conclusion from deeper premises. Wouldn't we say that she thinks bean-counting wrong? Her view would be bizarre, but would her mistake be one of meaning? Wouldn't it rather lie in her bizarre view of the kinds of things that warrant guilt and resentment? If we think this, then our linguistic judgments for this case fit an indirect, sentiment-routed account, with no substantive constraints added.

They clash with any account of meaning that builds in plausible substantive constraints on the kinds of grounds a person could think moral.

Still, what if she claimed to think that counting beans is the *only* kind of action that warrants guilt or resentment? Wouldn't her claim be quite unintelligible? Whatever bad feelings she manifests toward counting beans, what identifies these feelings as moral ones? What identifies them as guilt and resentment? Now I agree that guilt and resentment are identified partly by their typical subject matter, the things they are typically about. Still, the objection is not yet on target: What we need to rule out is not that she might *feel* guilt and resentment only over bean-counting. It is that she might think bean-counting the only thing that *warrants* guilt and resentment. Perhaps she does resent it when people kick her, and she would feel guilty if she went around kicking others—but she thinks these feelings of hers unwarranted. We identify her feelings as guilt and resentment partly by what they are typically over, but can't we still attribute to her a bizarre view of what warrants these feelings?

The answer might be no. When we get to the point of attributing to her such a bizarre view of the warrant for guilt and resentment, haven't we lost our grip on the concepts involved? Haven't we lost our grip on the concepts of warranted guilt and resentment? I'm not sure: When we declare her views unintelligible, perhaps we just mean that we can't imagine how anyone could really hold them. We can't think ourselves, even fantastically, into a frame of mind of finding such a view plausible. This is different from saying that there is nothing we would even count as thinking so—nothing we would recognize as her meaning what she says when she says these bizarre things. Even once we agree that interpretation requires agreement on most truisms, we can still interpret our subject as dissenting from some minority of truisms. Could her dissent encompass all truisms about the kinds of things that warrant resentment or guilt?

Let me concede that they could not. There is nothing we would interpret as the belief that, as a matter of first principles, guilt and resentment are warranted for counting beans and for nothing else. Does this mean we need substantive constraints as an add-on to our account? Must we add substantive constraints to a sentiment-routed account of what 'morally wrong' means? Not at all: the upshot is that such added constraints are superfluous. Substantive constraints, we have concluded, are already built into the concept of warrant for guilt and resentment.

This conclusion was derived from a concession I thought I might not need to make: that nothing would count as the conviction that bean-counting alone is what warrants guilt and resentment. Accept the concession or not, then; in either case no substantive constraints need to be *added* to a sentiment-routed account. Either they are not needed at all, or they are built in already for free.

The simplicity argument is therefore a wash. A sentiment-routed account is no less simple than a direct account. It has the drawback of being indirect, but the virtue that if any substantive constraints survive scrutiny, they are built in automatically. A direct account has the advantage of being direct, but the disadvantage of needing added substantive constraints.

We found earlier, moreover, that the added substantive constraints yield bad conclusions in some cases: where the priestess has some isolated quirk in her moral views, like the thought that bean-counting too warrants guilt and resentment. This goes not only for indirect accounts, but for direct ones. Either way, the constraints entail an implausible conclusion: that she can't be counted as having, along with fairly normal moral views, the bizarre view that for no further reason, bean-counting is morally wrong. This seemed mistaken: once she bizarrely thinks that bean-counting warrants guilt and resentment, we would think that she bizarrely regards bean-counting as a subject for moralizing. She thinks it morally wrong.

In short, then: A direct account needs added substantive constraints whereas a sentiment-routed account does not. The added substantive constraints will misfire for some cases. A direct account, then, cannot be made to work.

At the outset I had another complaint about add-on substantive constraints. An account with a list of them has an unexplained, arbitrary element: the list itself. Now we see that a sentiment-routed account gives a rationale for the list. It explains the phenomenon that led us to construct the list in the first place: our sense that there are things we can't really imagine a person regarding as moral reasons. These, we can now say, are considerations such that we cannot really imagine what it would be like to find it plausible that they warrant guilt and resentment.

A final technical virtue of sentiment-routed accounts: They get us out of the dilemma of last section. A direct account, I complained, does not have the resources to distinguish two ways moral grounds can interact with personal considerations. You fail to pay the paper girl when you promised, because the chance to go skiing with friends has suddenly come up. If you have most reason to go off and delay paying her, there seem to be two things we might say: that failing to pay her is morally permissible, or that it is morally wrong but nevertheless the thing you have most reason to do. We might conclude, in the end, that this is a distinction without a difference, but the sentiment-routed account allows us to avoid this conclusion.

The distinction is this, on my sentiment-routed account. Personal considerations might play either of two roles in thinking what to do and how to feel about it. They might swing the balance not only in favor of skiing, but against feeling guilty about it, and against others' resenting you for it. In that case, going off to ski is morally permissible. Or the personal considerations might swing the balance in favor of skiing, but not against blaming you for it—not against your feeling guilty about it, or against others' resenting you for not staying home to pay the girl. This may seem a wild view to have of this particular situation, but anyone who had it, I am proposing, would think this: that going off skiing was morally wrong, but it was nevertheless the thing you had most reason to do.

Moreover, in other cases of similar structure, this second kind of view will not seem wild—though it may be gravely mistaken: By poisoning your brother, suppose, you can gain a grand inheritance; otherwise you are condemned to spend your life as a junior army officer in the far colonies, a life you will find miserable. Clearly enough, it is morally wrong to murder your brother. Is it so clear, though, that you don't still have most reason to do so, all things considered? I hope you don't, but must I be linguistically confused to wonder whether you might—even if I am firm in thinking such poisonings morally wrong?

VI. Mill's Thesis

My arguments so far have run along this general line: There are distinctions we seem to make in our moral thinking that a sentiment-routed view captures, but that a direct view must dismiss as confused. Our linguistic intuitions deliver verdicts that a direct account will contradict. Still, we can ask whether the distinctions are ones we really need, and whether the intuitive verdicts are ones we need to maintain. Is there real value to adopting a sentiment-routed account?

Such accounts stem from John Stuart Mill,[19] and Mill, I claim, offers one quite strong reason to adopt a sentiment-routed account: it lets us formulate his claims for liberty (1859). If we want to accept these claims, or even weaken them, a direct account will not do. It will not even give us the words to formulate his views—or at least I do not see how it can. Let me explain.

Mill delineates a personal or self-regarding sphere of action; these are the acts that have no direct good or ill effects on others.[20] An act in this personal sphere, Mill tells us, is not to be condemned as morally wrong, even if it is gravely misguided. Direct ill effects on oneself do not make a course of action morally wrong, and neither do indirect ill effects on others.[21] If, say, a movie actress turns to drink, we can think badly of her. We can urge her to pull herself together, to think about what is most important to her in life and whether chronic drinking will permit her to get it. We can entreat her not to jeopardize a brilliant career. We can even appeal to the difference she makes to the lives of millions when she is in top form. We cannot, though, condemn her drinking as morally wrong—unless it leads her to violate assignable duties, say by driving when drunk.[22] On a sentiment-routed account, these distinctions are easy to formulate. Whether or not we agree with Mill, can say what he is claiming. Acts that directly harm others, he thinks, warrant guilt and resentment. Dissoluteness—even when it has serious indirect effects on others—does not. It may warrant concern, pity, or even dislike and contempt on the part of others, but not indignation or resentment.[23] Mill might have added that it warrants soul-searching, dismay, and shame on one's own part, but not the special sanctions of conscience that acts directly harmful to others can warrant.[24] Mill's thesis, of course, has been controversial. Most people reject it for extreme cases, such as drug-abuse. Still, he does seem to be making an important claim: If an act harms other people indirectly but not directly, then however important it is for a person to avoid it, the act is not on that account morally wrong. So claims Mill—and though most people will reject his particular way of drawing the line, they will think there is still a line to be drawn. Some matters are a person's own business. These include matters that are bound to have significant indirect effects on others.

How might a direct account interpret such claims? If benefits and harms to others count as moral considerations, then on a direct account, Mill's view is incoherent. The actress on the verge of a dissolute breakdown might think of the enjoyment and insight she can bring into the lives of millions, and see this as ample reason to take hold of herself and reform. Friends might urge this consideration on her, and Mill would applaud. These benefits, he could say, give her sufficient reason to rule out, say, laying in a stock of booze for the night. Still, though, Mill must insist, buying the bottles would not be morally wrong. Now on this direct account, these two claims do not jibe. Mill must think that her stocking up is morally wrong. For an act to be morally wrong, after all, is for it to be ruled out on valid moral grounds. On a direct account, valid moral grounds are (i) reasons—genuine ones, good or cogent as opposed to bad—and (ii) classified as moral, as opposed to non-moral, by linguistic rules. Mill thinks her reasons for ruling out the trip to the liquor store are genuine, cogent reasons. They are reasons of benefit to others, and so—as we are now supposing—they count as moral rather than non-moral. Mill must think, then, that for her to stock up would be morally wrong.

We can avoid this outcome by changing our claims about language, thereby moving to an alternative direct account. Rules of language, we might say, dictate that indirect harms and benefits shall not count as moral grounds. However good reasons for action they may be, they are non-moral. Mill's claims are now coherent—but too coherent: Now we cannot dissent without a mistake of moral language. Now it would be linguistically incoherent to think her morally wrong to stock up for the night on Grand Marnier. Yet this seems to be something that anti-Millian friends might very well think: that someone of her talents has a moral duty to pull herself together, to bring to millions the enjoyment and insight her talents permit. These friends will then think it morally wrong for her to stock up, knowing that then she will be soused the next day and unable to act. But their grounds for thinking this wrong are now declared non-moral, by rules of language. Therefore they cannot think her stocking up to be ruled out on moral grounds—and so on this second direct account, they cannot really coherently think it wrong for her to stock up on the booze.

On one direct account, then, Mill's views are linguistically incoherent. On an alternative direct account, the views of his opponents are linguistically incoherent. No adjustment of the list of linguistically eligible moral grounds will make both views coherent at once. Both views, though, do seem linguistically coherent: there seems to be a genuine, substantive dispute between Mill and his opponents, and not just a dispute over words. Indeed it is a dispute of great importance. A sentiment-routed account interprets the dispute: It is a dispute over warrant for guilt and resentment. A direct account must dismiss one side or another as confused over language. A language that robs us of all vocabulary to conduct this dispute has taken something of value.

To be sure, we could make the term 'morally wrong' mean whatever we want, and then paraphrase Mill's thesis using other language. But then we lose a simple and plausible formulation of Mill's thesis, and one that Mill himself pretty much adopts: that although for this actress, going off the wagon would be tragically ill advised, it would not be morally wrong.

VII. Looser Accounts

I have been assuming in this paper that narrowest morality deals with moral wrongness and moral permissibility. I have thus been asking what we can best take the term 'morally wrong' to mean, not how far beyond moral right and wrong we can best conceive of morality as extending. And chiefly I have been developing and examining just one kind of alternative: the kind I have called a direct, substance-constrained account. This account has three features: (i) A neutral, framework principle: An act is *morally wrong* if and only if it is ruled out for reasons that are cogent as opposed to spurious, and moral as opposed to non-moral. (ii) The directness thesis: Moral reasons are directly reasons for or against acting in certain ways. (My own indirect alternative is that, directly, they are reasons for moral sentiments that favor or oppose acting in certain ways.) (iii) Substance-constraint: What counts as a moral ground (as opposed to non-moral) is stipulated by linguistic rules. This is the most plausible view of the meaning of 'morally wrong' that I have been able to construct along these lines. It is inadequate, I have been arguing: On linguistic grounds it rules out various distinctions we are prone to make, whereas disputes over these distinctions seem to raise questions of genuine normative substance.

Still, my own reading of morality is constricted—avowedly so. I am framing issues of prime significance not as questions within morality, but as questions of whether to moralize at all, and if so how widely. Others will want to treat these same issues as questions of what the broad content of our morality ought to be. On my treatment, a vast range of evaluative standards count as non-moral: the normative systems of exotic cultures, perhaps, and radical transformations we might advocate for our own normative life. These standards may well be worth serious consideration, to be sure, as alternatives to morality as we know it. I count them, though, not as alternative moralities, but as alternatives to morality.

We might want to use the word 'moral' in a far more inclusive way. To this I am not opposed; I only insist that if we do, our usage must be fairly loose. In any sharply different alternative to our own familiar ways of normative thinking, we can label as "morality" whatever subsystem plays a role roughly analogous to morality as we know it. This may not allow for great precision: it may be hard to individuate normative subsystems, or to say which candidate yields the best parallel to familiar morality. But looseness can often be no grave defect.

Along these lines we might develop an alternative, looser meaning for the term 'morally wrong'. The *morality within* a normative system, we are saying, is whatever sub-system bears the best analogy to morality as it figures in our old, familiar ways of thinking. A normative system, we can now say, *treats* an act *as morally wrong* if the morality within the system forbids the act. An act *is morally wrong*, then, if the normative system that validly applies to the agent treats it as morally wrong. (What moral system validly applies is a question of normative substance—a question of high generality which we might fiercely dispute.)

If we take this line, we can still regard my own proposal as one for regimenting and elucidating the content of familiar moral views. An adherent of familiar views, so regimented, will think that an act is wrong in this new, loose sense if and only it is wrong in my constricted sense. For he thinks that familiar ways of normative thinking validly apply to everyone, and he accepts my description of how morality operates within these familiar ways of thinking. The best valid analog to familiar morality, he thinks, is familiar morality itself. The proof he must treat them as equivalent now runs as follows: We have stipulated that (a) an act is morally wrong in the *loose* sense iff (b) it is ruled out by the morality within the normative system that validly applies to the agent. This holds, he thinks, iff (c) the act is ruled out by familiar morality. This holds, he accepts, iff (d) by the standards of familiar morality, the act warrants guilt and resentment.[25] Since he accepts familiar morality, he thinks this holds iff (e) the act really does warrant guilt and resentment. That is to say, (f) the act is wrong in my constricted sense. This completes the proof that an adherent of familiar moral views, if he conceives of them as I propose, must think that an act is wrong in this loose sense if and only if it is wrong in the sense I advocate.

Things come out quite differently with someone who rejects familiar moral thinking—for someone who rejects according warrant for guilt and resentment its traditional place in our thought. As I describe matters, he will think that nothing is ever wrong in a moral sense. Acts can be bad in other ways, even terrible, but moral right and wrong are not what matters. In the looser sense, in contrast, he will think lots of things morally wrong, and think moral wrongness important—though he rejects tying it to warrant for guilt and resentment.

Which set of meanings shall we choose? Both may be worth having. We should know how to take Nietzsche at his word when he rails against morality, and we should have a meaning for 'morally wrong' that makes clear sense of distinctions we tend to draw in our moral thinking. We may also, though, want to have words for talking in loose ways about standards roughly analogous to morality as we know it. Then we can call Nietzsche a radical moralist.[26]

Notes

1. Sidgwick, 1907, esp. Bk. I, Ch. iii, sec. 1.
2. Gibbard, 1990. Hereafter referred to as *Wise Choices*.
3. *Wise Choices*, 44-5, 47-8.
4. Nietzsche (1887) and Williams (1985, esp. Ch. 10).
5. Nietzsche (1887) and Williams (1985) both attack morality under something like this conception. Nietzsche attacks *ressentiment* (Essay I) and bad conscience (Essay 2). Williams writes "Blame is the characteristic reaction of the morality system. The remorse or self-reproach or guilt...is the characteristic first-personal reaction within the system, and if an agent never felt such sentiments, he would not belong to the morality system or be a full moral agent in its terms" (177). Some philosophers argue that guilt and resentment cannot be appealed to to explain the meaning of 'wrong', because the concepts of these emotions themselves depend on the concept of a moral transgression. I speak to this objection in *Wise Choices*, Ch. 7. Wiggins (1987, Essay 5) and McDowell (1988, 7-10) think that wrongness and moral sentiments are benignly to be explained in terms of each other; I leave this view for other studies.
6. *Wise Choices*, pp. 44-5, 47-8.
7. This account is close to Brandt's characterization of a "social moral system" (1979, 165-70). He lists its characteristics as (i) intrinsic motivation, (ii) guilt-feelings and disapproval, (iii) believed importance, (iv) admiration or esteem, (v) special terminology, and (vi) believed justification. I am leaving aside admiration and esteem (iv). As for believed importance (iii), I take it a code couldn't have the other features Brandt lists without its adherents believing that it deals with important matters—though I allow for minor moral issues too. My picture has guilt feelings and disapproval (resentment, ii) with believed justification (warrant, vi). I treat judgments of warrant as intrinsically motivating (i) and tied to special terminology involved in normative discussion (v).
8. Or more precisely, it is to express one's acceptance of a whole system of norms that permit the feeling on balance. Or more precisely, see Chapter 5 of *Wise Choices*, where I treat the logic of normative judgments on a norm-expressivistic

theory.

9. Ewing (1939, 14) thinks 'ought' has two senses; in one of these, his ought seems roughly my warrant.

10. Brandt's "quasi-naturalistic definition" schema for moral terms (1959, 265-6) in effect includes a definition of warrant for attitudes: an attitude is *warranted* (my term) if it "satisfies all the conditions that would be set, as a general policy, for the endorsement of attitudes...by anyone who was intelligent and factually informed and had thought through the problems of the possible different general policies for the endorsement of such attitudes." He argues that those conditions are those of the "qualified attitude method: that the attitude not be partial, uninformed, a consequence of an abnormal state of mind, or incompatible with having a consistent and general system of principles" (249-50). Similar conditions are offered by Rawls (1951) and Firth (1952).

11. Philippa Foot may at one time have had a view like this; see Foot (1978), xii and 96-109, the latter a reprinting of "Moral Arguments" (1958).

12. I don't mean that dignity is unproblematic as a basis for morality. It may deserve the treatment Frankena gives respect (1986): Perhaps we can't appeal to considerations of human dignity to ground morality, because we can't settle what constitutes human dignity, in the appropriate sense, until we have settled what the demands of morality are. See also my *Wise Choices*, 264-9.

13. Brandt, 1959, 102-3.

14. Recent "moral realists" generally do not disagree with what I am saying here. They often say they are asking not about meaning in the sense I am discussing, in which sameness of meaning is synonymy. See, for instance, Sturgeon (1985, 26) and Sayre-McCord (1988, 7), who writes, "For the most part, realism is a matter of metaphysics, not semantics." Rather, they are offering an account of the properties to which moral terms refer, as 'wet' refers to the property of being covered in H_2O. We are then owed an account of how a word like 'wet' could have gained this reference—even before anyone knew of molecular structure. This account would fill the role of more traditional theories of meaning and synonymy. Boyd offers such an account; he speaks of "homeostatic property-cluster definitions" (1988, 196-9). I do not attempt here to assess that account. Others offer definitions as reforms, and so are not asking about current meanings. See Brandt (1979, Ch. 1) and Railton (1986, 204).

15. Reasons for or against an action may weigh against each other, but this is not the only way that reasons that tell against each other can interact. See, for instance, Raz (1975) on "exclusionary reasons".

16. See *Wise Choices*, 163: To call a possible consideration *C* a *reason* to do *X* is to express one's acceptance of norms that say to treat *C* as weighing in favor of doing *X*. Brandt (1979), if he adopted my vocabulary, might say that a *reason* for action is a possible consideration *C* that satisfies this condition: *C* would motivate the agent if he had undergone cognitive psychotherapy—that is, had repeated representation of all relevant, scientifically available information, in an ideally vivid way, at appropriate times (11, 113).

17. This corresponds somewhat to Frankena's characterization of a narrow, "material and social" concept of morality (1966)—though with some differences. Frankena asks when the action guide of a group (or person) is to be called a moral one. The group must take the guide as prescriptive and universal; this fits my proposal that to think a directive moral, one must think that it constitutes a reason. In addition, the guide appraises actions "simply because of the effect they have on the feelings, interests, ideals, etc. of *other* persons or centers of sentient experience,

actual or hypothetical (or perhaps simply because of their effects on humanity, whether in his own person *or* in that of another)" (126). In effect, then, he identifies a range of grounds that can count as moral. He requires a moral action guide, though, only to *include* such considerations (128-9). I am supposing that the total action guide a person accepts might be partially moral and partially non-moral, so that we need to know how to distinguish its moral and its non-moral components.

18. 1907, Bk. II, Ch. v.
19. *Utilitarianism* (1863), Ch. V, para. 14 (or on the scheme I shall use with Mill, V.14).
20. *On Liberty* (1859).
21. He discusses indirect effects in 1859, IV.8, 10-11, where he speaks of "merely contingent" or "constructive injury". These, he says, do not make an act self-regarding.
22. What I say about this example sticks pretty close to Mill's own words. On "assignable duties", see IV.10. "The moral coercion of public opinion", he says (I.9), is to be confined to acts that harm others; when acts merely harm oneself, others may remonstrate, reason, persuade, or entreat. Injuries to others and the like are "fit objects of moral reprobation" and "immoral"; the dispositions that lead to these acts are "moral vices", whereas self-regarding faults are "not properly immoralities" (IV.6).
23. This contrast is explicit in IV.7; he speaks of being "an object of pity, perhaps of dislike, but not of anger or resentment." On dissoluteness, see IV.10-11.
24. I have found no discussion of attitudes toward oneself in *On Liberty* (1859), but in *Utilitarianism* (1863, V.14) he says "We do not call anything wrong, unless we mean to imply that a person ought to be punished in some way or other for doing it; if not by law, by the opinion of his fellow-creatures; if not by opinion, by the reproaches of his own conscience". I am reading this reference to conscience into the doctrines of *On Liberty*.
25. Again, this abbreviates a more complex statement. See *Wise Choices*, 47-8.
26. Work on this paper was supported by a Fellowship from the John Simon Guggenheim Memorial Foundation. Peter Railton discussed an earlier draft with me and was very helpful.

References

Boyd, Richard N. (1988). "How to be a Moral Realist". Geoffrey Sayre-McCord (ed.), *Essays on Moral Realism* (Ithaca: Cornell University Press), 181-228.

Brandt, Richard B. (1959). *Ethical Theory* (Englewood Cliffs, NJ: Prentice-Hall).

Brandt, Richard B. (1979). *A Theory of the Good and the Right* (Oxford: Clarendon Press).

Ewing, A.C. (1939). "A Suggested Non-Naturalistic Analysis of Good". *Mind* 48: 1-22.

Firth, Roderick (1952). "Ethical Absolutism and the Ideal Observer". *Philosophy and Phenomenological Research* 12: 317-45.

Foot, Philippa (1978). *Virtues and Vices* (Berkeley: University of California Press).

Frankena, William (1966). "The Concept of Morality". *Journal of Philosophy* 63: 688-96. Page references to reprinting in Kenneth Goodpaster, ed., *Perspectives on Morality: Essays of William K. Frankena* (Notre Dame, IN: University of Notre Dame Press).

Frankena, William (1986). "The Ethics of Respect for Persons". *Philosophical Topics* 14: 149-167.

McDowell, John (1988). "Projection and Truth in Ethics" (Lawrence, KA: Department of Philosophy, University of Kansas).

Mill, John Stuart (1859). *On Liberty*. (Many editions; cited by chapter and paragraph numbers).

Mill, John Stuart (1863). *Utilitarianism*. (Many editions; cited by chapter and paragraph numbers).

Nietzsche, Friedrich (1887). *Zur Genealogie der Moral*. Trans. Walter Kaufmann and R.J. Hollingdale, *On the Genealogy of Morals* (New York: Vintage Books, 1967).

Railton, Peter (1986). "Moral Realism". *Philosophical Review* 95: 163-207.

Rawls, John (1951). "Outline of a Decision Procedure for Ethics". *Philosophical Review* 60: 177-97.

Raz, Joseph (1975). "Reasons for Action, Decisions and Norms". *Mind* 84: 481-99.

Sayre-McCord, Geoffrey (1988). *Moral Realism* (Ithaca: Cornell University Press).

Sturgeon, Nicholas (1985). "Gibbard on Moral Judgment and Norms". *Ethics* 96: 22-33.

Wiggins, David (1987). *Needs, Values, Truth: Essays in the Philosophy of Value* (Oxford: Basil Blackwell).

Williams, Bernard (1985). *Ethics and the Limits of Philosophy* (Cambridge, MA: Harvard University Press).

Philosophical Perspectives, 6, Ethics, 1992

THE STRUCTURE OF NORMATIVE ETHICS

Shelly Kagan
University of Illinois at Chicago

If you open a typical textbook on normative ethics, it will have a discussion of what it thinks of as rival theories: there might be a chapter each on, say, utilitarianism, contractarianism, and virtue theory. The assumption seems to be that these three are alternative attempts to answer the same basic questions.

This seems to me exactly incorrect. At least as they are ordinarily understood, these three are addressing three different concerns in normative ethics, and in principle—although almost never in practice—they are completely compatible. Failure to see this, I believe, is due to our failure to have an adequate "map" of the structure of normative ethics. We lack an adequate account of what the various theories in normative ethics are trying to accomplish.

It is not that there is nothing at all like a received view concerning the nature of normative ethics: roughly, normative ethics involves the attempt to state and defend the basic principles of morality. It is concerned with determining which actions are right, which wrong, what is permitted and what forbidden. Similarly, it might be said to treat the basic moral rights, duties, virtues, and so on.

So far as it goes, there is nothing wrong with this account. But it does not go very far. It is like a map of a country which only displays its border. Such a map can serve to distinguish one country from another—as our account can help to set off normative ethics from metaethics—but it gives no significant detail about the internal features of the country. What we lack—what the received view does not give us—is a sense of the major regions of normative ethics and how they are related to one another. Lacking an adequate guide to the structure of normative ethics we can fail to recognize what we are doing when we compare and evaluate the specific normative theories that have been offered.

In this essay, then, I want to try to lay out the basic outlines of a more adequate map. My goal is not to argue for a particular theory in normative ethics, but rather to try to give a perspicuous way of sorting out some of the most important theories and disputes. If I am successful, the account I offer should not strike you as a description of a new, exotic land or alien terrain. For although we may lack an adequate *map* of normative ethics, as moral philosophers we are not, of course, unfamiliar with the various internal doings of normative ethics itself. So the map should have a familiar feel to it, at least in the sense that we should recognize it as a plausible account of what we have been doing in normative ethics—one that does not distort too much of the field, and is not hopelessly idiosyncratic in its concerns.

As a first step, it seems to me useful to distinguish between two sorts of activities that go on in normative ethics. One thing we try to do is to articulate the various factors that are relevant to determining the moral status of an act. I'll say more about these factors later, but to fix the basic idea quickly, here is an example. Suppose that in order to save the life of someone drowning, I must row out to her in a boat. The fact that the act of rowing out and pulling her in would have a good result—saving a life!—is one morally relevant factor in determining the rightness or wrongness of the act. In saying this, I do not mean to be making the epistemological claim that we *appeal* to the presence of such a factor in *deciding* whether the act is right or not, although in fact I think that this is often the case. Rather I mean to be making the ontological claim, that the interplay of the various morally relevant factors is what makes it *be* the case that the given act is right or wrong. It seems quite plausible to think that goodness of outcome is one morally relevant factor in this sense.

It certainly need not be the only factor. Suppose that the only boat at hand is not mine, so I must steal it, if I am to rescue the drowning person. This might plausibly be thought to be a second morally relevant factor—that is, the fact that I must violate someone's rights, in particular, property rights. Whether, morally speaking, I should still take the boat or not depends on which of these two factors outweighs the other. And there might be other factors as well. The person drowning might be my wife, and so it might be thought that this gives me a special obligation, stronger than the general obligation to save a mere stranger. And so on.

Real life cases might get fairly complex. From a moral point of view, the complexity lies in the fact that several distinct morally relevant factors come into play. Whether a given act is forbidden, or required, and so on, is a function of these various factors. We might think of them, loosely, as right-making or wrong-making factors, although we should not assume in the absence of a worked out theory that an adequate classification will be that simple.

The task of articulation of the normatively relevant factors is an astonishingly complex one. There is considerable debate over which purported factors are of genuine relevance. Even when there is some agreement that a particular factor belongs on the list, there remains the difficult and contentious task of demarcating its precise content and contours. And beyond this, there is the further task of determining how the various factors interact, and what outweighs what in cases of conflict.

Much of what takes place in contemporary moral philosophy is an attempt to work out answers to these questions. It is theory building at the level of normative factors. Many articles in normative ethics are primarily concerned with the precise specification of some part or parts of one or more normatively relevant factors, or with determining the outcome of the complex interactions of the given factors.

Such investigation of the normatively relevant factors is one of two major activities in normative ethics. The second activity is this. We offer rival theories of what I call the *foundations* of normative ethics. Roughly, we propose and evaluate alternative "devices" or "mechanisms" that purport to generate and thus explain the favored list of normatively relevant factors. Once again I will say more about this below, but to get a few examples on the table will be helpful: Contractarian theories claim that the correct list of moral rules, or morally relevant factors, consists of those that would be chosen by a group of rational bargainers, with various motivational and informational constraints. Contractarianism is thus a foundational theory, in my sense. (Strictly, it is of course a family of theories, but that won't concern us for the moment.) An adequate contractarian theory would provide an explanation and justification for the specific normative factors generated by the theory.

Another foundational theory (or family of theories) is rule consequentialism, which claims that the correct rules or factors are those that would lead to the greatest amount of good, that is, the best results overall. Yet another theory is the ideal observer theory, which claims that the correct list is that which would be endorsed by a suitably characterized observer, for example, one with full information, and impartial benevolent concern for all parties.

In calling theories of this sort "foundational" I do not mean to be claiming that beliefs about such theories are more certain than intuitions about the normative factors, nor do I mean to suggest that these theories provide some sort of bedrock and do not stand in need of further justification. Claims of these sorts are common in theories of epistemology or justification that often go under the label "foundationalism". I have no sympathy for them in ethics, or elsewhere. I simply mean to be claiming that those who offer foundational theories in my sense typically take their favored foundational theory to offer an explanation and justification of their favored list of normative factors.

In principle, a foundational theory—at least if worked out—will yield a list of normatively relevant factors. If the foundational theory itself has any independent plausibility, then the fact that it yields the specific factors that it does provides something of a justification for the claim that those factors are indeed the genuinely relevant factors. But of course the very fact that the foundational theory yields plausible factors also provides support in turn for the plausibility of the foundational theory. So the support can go in both directions. That is one of the reasons that I think that the various epistemological foundationalist views should be rejected.

My aim here, however, is not to discuss the metaethical questions of moral epistemology, but simply to distinguish the distinct sense in which I think of theories such as contractarianism or rule consequentialism as foundational: a contractarian thinks that the rules selected by the specified bargaining process are the morally relevant rules, and he presumably thinks that it is the very fact that they would be so selected that explains or is the ground of their being the correct or genuinely relevant rules. Similarly, a rule consequentialist thinks that it is the optimal rules that are the genuinely relevant rules, and she thinks that what makes them so is the very fact that they are indeed the optimal ones in terms of their results. And so on for the other foundational theories. Each foundational theory not only yields a favored set of normative factors, it purports to explain and justify the relevance of those factors.

By providing a mechanism which generates or selects some candidate normative factors and not others, a foundational theory strives to settle the debate over which factors have genuine moral relevance, and which are spurious, or of merely derivative significance. Ideally, an adequate foundational theory would go further. It would help to settle disputes over the precise content and contours of the favored list of factors. And it would illuminate how the various factors interact in determining the moral status of an act, explaining which factors outweigh the others in cases of conflict, and why. It would in effect provide and vindicate the tradeoff schedule in complex cases involving conflicting factors.

Of course in practice foundational theories are virtually never worked out in this kind of detail. Often in fact there is little more than a hand or two waved in the direction of showing that the given foundational theory will indeed yield anything like the list of normative factors that we are independently inclined to accept. But in principle, at any rate, one of the advantages of having an adequate foundational theory is that it would provide us with guidance in our articulation of the normatively relevant factors.

As a first approximation, then, normative ethics has these two different kinds of components. There are alternative theories about the morally relevant factors. And there are alternative theories about the foundations of normative ethics.

One of the things that is of interest is the extent to which these two activities can be—and are—conducted largely independently of one another. People frequently attempt to fine-tune our understanding of the normatively relevant factors without appealing to any particular foundational theory. (They may appeal, instead, to intuitions about various hypothetical examples.) And at least in part, people often evaluate alternative foundational theories by considering what independent rationales, if any, can be provided for the various theories.

This is not to say that people never attempt to settle questions about factors by considering the implications of some favored foundational theory. And I certainly do not mean to deny that people frequently evaluate foundational theories by considering their implications at the level of factors. But for all that, the two activities have a surprising degree of independence.

The relative independence surfaces in a second way. Two people might agree about the list of normative factors, and yet disagree about the correct foundational theory. After all, it might be the case that two distinct foundational theories would generate the same list of factors. Or, at any rate, two people who agreed about the relevant list might still disagree over which foundational theory would in fact generate that list. Similarly, two people might agree that a given foundational theory is the correct one, while still disagreeing over which factors are generated by that theory.

This distinction between discussion of normative factors and discussion of foundational theories seems to me one of the most important divisions in normative ethics. But I said that thinking of normative ethics in terms of these two activities is only a first approximation. For it seems to me helpful to distinguish as well a third activity, involving debate over what I will call *evaluative focal points*. However, I want to postpone a discussion of these focal points for the time being, since what I have in mind is best brought out in the context of a more careful look at the foundational theories. And before turning to that, I first want to say something about the basic types of normative factors.

As I see it, the intuitively plausible normative factors fall under four main heads. (Perhaps it would be more accurate to say that I think that they can be usefully grouped in this way; other classificatory schemes are certainly possible.) The four major types of factors are as follows: (1) overall goodness of results; (2) general constraints; (3) special obligations; and (4) options. Although I do not intend to go into great detail about any one of these groups, I want to say enough—if only by way of offering some examples—to give a sense of what I have in mind for each.

As I have already indicated, it seems quite plausible to suggest that one morally relevant factor in determining the moral status of an act is the outcome of that act—that is, whether the act leads to good results overall, or better results than those of the alternative acts available to the agent. But this factor is itself a function of more than one subfactor. (Incidentally, I think it is mostly a matter of convenience, in any given case, whether we speak of "groups" of factors or, alternatively, of various "subfactors" coming together to determine some larger "single" factor.)

To begin with, most would agree that the overall goodness of an outcome will turn, at least in part, on the levels of well-being of the various individuals who are part of the given outcome. So one thing needed by normative ethics is an adequate theory of individual well-being. Clearly, however, since typical cases involve more than one individual, there will also have to be some principle governing the aggregation of facts about the welfare of the various relevant individuals into overall evaluations of outcomes with regard to welfare. Here we need to settle whether what matters is the total amount of well-being, or the average level, or something captured by a still more complex formula.

But matters obviously do not stop there, for it is often suggested that the *distribution* of well-being is itself a relevant factor in determining the overall goodness of an outcome. Egalitarians will claim that it matters directly whether the welfare is distributed equally, and will presumably sometimes be willing to settle for a smaller total amount of well-being in exchange for a more egalitarian distribution. And this will be rejected by those—the welfarists— who think that distribution has no intrinsic importance (although of course it is often instrumental to an increase in welfare). Furthermore, even if we agree that distribution matters, there is still room for disagreement over the correct distributive principle: for example, should our concern truly be with equality per se, or should we instead have a special concern for the worst off? And even among strict egalitarians there will still be the need to establish the precise tradeoff schedule between welfare and equality.

Still other good-making factors might be *impersonal* in the sense of not being functions of well-being or its distribution at all. Perhaps the existence of beauty, or of knowledge, might directly contribute to the overall goodness of a state of affairs (that is, above and beyond any contribution it might make to increasing welfare). And other more exotic candidates have been entertained as well.

There are of course many other factors that might plausibly be claimed to have direct weight in determining the overall goodness of an outcome, such as desert, fairness, or entitlement. But since all I am trying to do is to give a sense of what sorts of factors fall under each of the four major headings, I hope that the examples I have already discussed will suffice.

In trying to articulate a theory of the overall good we face the same three tasks here as elsewhere. First, there is disagreement over which of the proposed factors have genuine weight: for example, does distribution genuinely matter directly in determining the goodness of an outcome, or are we simply misled into thinking so by the fact that distribution typically affects the amount of well-being? Second, there is disagreement over the precise specification of the relevant factors: for example, assuming that distribution does have genuine weight, should our concern be with equality or with, say, maximin (which gives lexical priority to the worst off)? Third, there is disagreement over the tradeoffs between distinct factors: for example, assuming that gains in equality can sometimes outweigh gains in total well-being, exactly how much of the former outweighs how much of the latter?

As I have suggested, theory construction and evaluation in this area— as with the other major groups of factors, and the theories of their interplay— can be conducted with a surprising degree of autonomy. Considerable debate over the nature of good outcomes takes place without recourse to particular foundational theories. At the same time, I find it implausible to think that the debate can be concluded autonomously. Appeal to an adequate foundational theory may well be necessary to answer questions about the precise content or weight of various proposed factors; and at any rate it seems inevitable if we are to have a satisfying explanation of why the normatively relevant factors are indeed morally relevant in the first place.

Now most of us believe that although the value of the outcome of an act is indeed one relevant factor in determining the moral status of that act, it is not by any means the only relevant factor. Intuitively, certain acts seem to be forbidden even if the results of performing those acts would be good overall. This brings us to the next group of factors, that of general constraints.

By constraints, I have in mind the types of features that have recently been discussed under such headings as side-constraints, deontological restrictions, and agent-relative prohibitions. Most of us believe, for example, that there is a prohibition against harming people. The fact that my act will harm someone is generally taken to be a morally relevant factor, a factor that generates moral reason not to perform the act. This factor is typically thought to be so powerful that it virtually always outweighs other relevant factors, in particular the possibility of promoting good consequences. I cannot kill an innocent person, say, even if this is the only way to save two other innocent people from being killed. When we say that there is a prohibition against harming, we are expressing the belief that this factor generally outweighs any opposing factors.

It is worth noting that one can give weight to a constraint against harming without viewing that weight as absolute. One might hold that if *enough* is at stake—for example, the avoidance of nuclear war—then promotion of the overall good will indeed outweigh the constraint against harming. In short, constraints can have finite thresholds. And in principle, these thresholds might be fairly modest; the prohibition against killing might be overridable, say, even in order to save as few as five lives. But in fact it seems likely that anyone who hopes to capture our intuitive beliefs on these matters will hold the thresholds to be extremely high. Some—the absolutists—would argue that the threshold is infinitely high, so that harming the innocent is never permitted. But one can be more moderate on this score without abandoning the view that this constraint is indeed a genuinely relevant factor, and outweighs other factors in many or most cases.

As always, the precise specification of the constraint against harming is a controversial matter. For example, exactly what type of act is forbidden by the constraint in question? Is it the *doing* of harm that is especially morally offensive (as opposed to merely allowing harm)? Or is it rather the *intending* of harm as a means (as opposed to merely foreseeing harm as a side-effect)?

Another familiar debate concerns exactly which setbacks constitute harms: Should mental discomfort or offense be included along with bodily injury? What about invasions of privacy? Or appropriation of one's property? To a certain extent some of this debate is merely terminological. Nothing prevents us from listing distinct constraints for different types of setbacks. But much of the debate can be understood as involving the substantive issue of which setbacks are genuinely protected by a constraint at all, and for those that are protected, whether the grounds of that protection are of fundamentally the same sort.

This last question reemerges when we consider plausible constraints that are typically not subsumed under the rubric of a constraint against harm. We might well want to include a constraint against lying, or a constraint against paternalistic interference with another's autonomy. To my mind, at least, there are interesting questions about whether or not these are best understood as simply being particular forms of harm after all. And if they are best understood in this way, then the question arises whether there are indeed any general constraints other than various versions of the constraint against harming.

In contrast to such general constraints, special obligations involve the particular duties and responsibilities that we have by virtue of our own individual circumstances and history. The most familiar and relatively uncontroversial examples of such special obligations involve moral requirements generated by acts freely undertaken in the past: promises generate special obligations to keep those promises, and so one factor relevant in determining the moral status of an act is the fact that the act is the keeping (or breaking) of a promise. Similarly, the principle of fair play may generate special obligations to do my fair share in sustaining a joint practice from which I have knowingly and willingly benefited in the past. And I may have special obligations toward my infant daughter, generated in part by the fact that I am directly responsible for her existence.

But mention of this particular family obligation brings to mind the thought that not all role-related obligations can be traced to previous free acts of the agent. Even within the family it might be argued that one has special obligations toward one's parents, although the relation to one's parents is not one freely undertaken. Similarly, it might be argued that one's determinate social role generates a host of specific obligations, even though one may not be completely free with regard to one's social role. (Political obligations might sometimes work like this.) Now it can of course be argued that many of these involuntarily generated special obligations are best explained as instances of the obligation of gratitude; but since the obligation of gratitude itself can have this involuntarily entered character, the basic point remains. Against all this, there is of course considerable contemporary scepticism about whether there are any genuine special obligations not grounded in free acts of the agent.

There is one other obligation that I think merits our attention. Many of us feel that there is a fairly strong obligation to rescue particular individuals when we find ourselves facing the immediate opportunity to do so. The fact that we do not consider ourselves under a similarly strong obligation to aid unnamed persons who are, say, starving at the other end of the globe, provides some evidence that we are indeed describing what we take to be a special obligation, rather than merely an instance of the general ("weak") obligation to promote better consequences overall (for example, by saving lives). Even more evidence emerges when we consider that the opportunity to directly rescue a known individual is often taken to generate an obligation which must be met even if more good could be done elsewhere by diverting the resources necessary for the rescue.

It is perhaps worth observing that the obligation to rescue appears to be a special obligation that is not grounded in voluntary acts of the agent. Of course general constraints have had this "involuntary" character all along, so friends of the thesis that all special obligations must be "voluntary" might suggest that the obligation to rescue should actually be classified as a general constraint.

Now I am not in fact convinced that there is any deep distinction to be found between the category of general constraints and that of special obligations. For some purposes it might be more illuminating to collapse the two into one. Even a constraint against lying, or against harming, for example, will only yield a specific determinate obligation with regard to the performance of a specific act in the right kinds of circumstances; so the distinction between "general" constraints and "special" obligations may only be one of degree, rather than marking a sharp break. Or perhaps we should simply move directly to marking the voluntary/involuntary distinction, or some other distinction (such as that between negative and positive obligations). But these are questions I will not attempt to pursue here.

The last major type of factor is that of options, or what have elsewhere been called agent-relative permissions, or agent-centered prerogatives. Most people believe that even if an act would have good results (one morally relevant factor) and even if the act would not involve the violation of any general constraints or special obligations (two other types of morally relevant factors) the act might nonetheless *not* be morally required. For agents have the option of pursuing their own personal projects and interests, even if greater good overall could be done in some other way. Many morally praiseworthy acts are above and beyond the call of duty—meritorious, but not required.

What exactly is the factor at work here? The matter is not uncontroversial, but I think the most likely account is that the relevant factor is an appeal to the cost to the agent that can be involved in sacrificing the pursuit of her projects for the sake of the overall good. If the cost to the agent is significant, this is one more normatively relevant factor in determining the moral status of the act: an act might be optional (permitted but not required) if it would involve a significant sacrifice on the part of the agent, even though an act with similar results might well be required if the cost to the agent would be slight.

Here too the need remains for considerable further discussion. We need to specify which other factors can be outweighed by an appeal to cost, and to what extent. The size and nature of the options that we have will be a function of this tradeoff schedule. Most of us believe, for example, that although we have options to allow harm, we do not have similar options to do harm: I can devote my income to my family, rather than to famine relief, but I cannot *kill* to provide a comparable income for my family. Thus cost appears to outweigh the possibility of attaining good results, but is itself outweighed by general constraints. Even the option to allow harm, however, is not unlimited: when enough is at stake, the appeal to cost to the agent may indeed be outweighed by a consideration of results.

These, then, are the four basic types of factors that come into play in determining the moral status of an act: results, constraints, special obligations, and options.

It may be worth explaining, parenthetically, why the concept of rights has not appeared in my discussion of the basic types of normative factors. The main reason is simply that I think that talk of rights frequently lacks sufficiently determinate content to be helpful in analysis. A related reason is that talk of rights is often meant to bring in more than one of the types of factors that I have been distinguishing. When we say that someone has such and such a right, often we mean to be drawing attention to what I have called constraints or special obligations. But sometimes we mean—in addition, or instead—to be drawing attention to the existence of an option. A right may involve one of these elements without the other, and so it seems to me clearer to lay out the possible elements directly.

The picture of the normative factors that I have sketched is not, I trust, an unfamiliar one. Whether an act is required or not turns on such matters as what the results of the act would be, whether it involves keeping or breaking any general constraints or special obligations, and what the cost to the agent would come to. As I have explained, one of the major activities of normative ethics involves the specification of the various factors and subfactors, debates over which of these have genuine weight, and attempts to determine which genuine factors take precedence in cases of conflict.

Some of these debates are legitimately seen as in-house debates over details. This might be true, for example, for disagreements over the correct version of maximin, or disagreement over the precise location of a finite threshold for a constraint against doing harm. In other cases the disagreement will be far more radical. The most familiar example of a large-scale debate is that between consequentialists and deontologists.

Consequentialists hold that the only normative factor that has any genuine weight in its own right is that of the overall goodness of the results. (This still leaves room for debate among consequentialists over the nature of the good. If welfare is taken to be the only good-making feature of outcomes, then the resulting normative view is utilitarianism.) Other factors may have derivative significance, insofar as attending to them rather than directly to consequences can often contribute to making the results better or worse; but no other factor has any direct significance. At this level of normative factors, then, a *deontologist* should be understood to be anyone who believes in the direct significance of further factors, in particular general constraints or special obligations.

What this means is that rule utilitarianism is *not* from this point of view a utilitarian or even a consequentialist theory! Rule utilitarianism (and, more broadly, rule consequentialism) is, rather, a *foundational* theory which attempts to explain why other normative factors than the goodness of results have direct normative relevance in determining the status of an act. Thus at the level of the normative factors themselves, rule utilitarianism does not support a utilitarian theory, but rather a deontological one.

Similarly, although contractarianism—another foundational theory—is typically thought to underwrite a deontological normative view, at a sufficiently general level of description this cannot be assumed. Some versions of contractarianism end up supporting utilitarianism at the level of the normative factors.

This debate over who is a deontologist and who a utilitarian or consequentialist takes a rather different cast if we turn to the foundational theories. For consequentialism reappears as a family of foundational theories as well. At the level of normative factors, as I have just explained, consequentialism is the theory that goodness of results is the only directly relevant factor in determining the status of an act. But as a foundational theory, consequentialism is the view that whatever the genuinely relevant normative factors may be, the *ground* of their relevance ultimately lies in their connection to the promotion of the overall good. As a foundational theory, that is, consequentialism holds that an explanation of the significance of the normative factors must ultimately be in terms of an appeal to the good.

Classical consequentialists at the normative level often justified their views by appealing to consequentialism at the foundational level. For some, the conception of the good has been metaphysical or platonic; for others it has taken a more naturalistic form. But it is important to recognize that one can be a consequentialist at the factoral level without favoring consequentialism at the foundational level. As I have just noted, one might prefer instead to ground one's factoral consequentialism in a foundational contractarianism, or for that matter in an ideal observer theory, or some other alternative.

And it is equally important to recognize that one can be a consequentialist at the foundational level without believing that this supports consequentialism at the factoral level. Rule utilitarians (or, more broadly, rule consequentialists) should be understood in just this way. They ground the moral relevance of the various normative factors in terms of the good—saying that those factors that would (if acted on) lead to best results have direct weight—but they do so in a manner that generates a nonconsequentialist theory at the factoral level. So there is a sense in which rule utilitarians deserve to be called utilitarians after all—namely, at the foundational level. But this is compatible with insisting that there is another sense in which they should be called deontologists—namely, at the level of normative factors.

This prompts the question of whether there is any useful notion of being a deontologist at the foundational level. The thought that initially suggests itself is that foundational deontologists are those who think that an adequate foundational theory will select normative factors not simply with an eye to the promotion of the good, but rather (in addition, or instead) on the basis of features that are somehow more "intrinsic". But I am not sure how to spell out the second half of this suggestion. After all, many would take contractarianism to be a deontological theory at the foundational level, but I am hard pressed to think of any interesting sense in which contractarian approaches turn on especially "intrinsic" properties—whether of acts, or of the normative factors. So I am inclined to think that deontology at the foundational level should be understood simply in terms of the negative, first half of the suggestion. That is, deontological foundational theories are those that select the normative factors on the basis of something other than, or more than, the promotion of the good.

We would come close to this by saying that foundational deontologists are those that offer a foundationally nonconsequentialist theory. But this would be too wide a definition. For consequentialists appeal, in particular, to the promotion of the *overall* good, and we presumably also want to exclude as nondeontological foundational theories—such as egoism— that appeal instead solely to promotion of one's *personal* good, or self-interest. So we may prefer the following. Call a foundational theory *teleological* if it appeals solely to promotion of the good, however this is construed—whether personal good, or overall good. We can then say that deontological foundational theories are those that are nonteleological.

I will not attempt to give a more fine-grained system of classification for the foundational theories than this. Unlike the four major divisions of the normative factors, I do not know of any typology for the foundational theories that is comparably useful. At any rate, the task of producing an illuminating classificatory scheme for the foundational level will be made more difficult by the fact that foundational theories can combine with one another, mixing their elements.

Consider, for example, universalization theories, which claim that the correct normative factors are those that can be appropriately universalized, that is, those for which it is possible to have a world in which everyone acts on the proposed factors without something "going wrong". Now in pure versions of such theories, the thing that can "go wrong", and that universalization tests for, is this: for illegitimate factors, the concept of such a world of universal compliance entails a logical or practical contradiction. But some advocates of universalization theories think that it is insufficient to rule out only those factors that when universalized generate a contradiction. They suggest, instead, that a proposed factor should also be ruled out if its universalization would yield unacceptable results.

Here too, of course, there is room for disagreement as to the type of results that are relevant: some ask whether universalization would lead to bad results overall; others whether it would lead to bad results in terms of the agent's personal good; and so on. For our purposes, however, the point to note is this. However "bad results" is understood, a theory of this latter sort seems to combine the idea of universalization with teleological elements. It is a hybrid—combining elements from two "pure" theories to form a new theory. (Is this new type of theory a deontological one? It depends on whether assessing results from the standpoint of universalization in this way means that justification is no longer simply a matter of the promotion of the good. I think that people's intuitions will differ on this.)

This possibility—of combining elements from more than one foundational theory to form a distinct foundational theory—should not be confused with pluralism at the foundational level. And pluralism at the foundational level should in turn be distinguished from pluralism at the factoral level.

This last point is by now a familiar one. A pluralist at the factoral level believes that more than one normative factor has weight in its own right. Factoral consequentialists deny this; but most others accept it. As we have already seen, however, one can be a pluralist in this sense and still believe that there is a single foundational theory that justifies and explains the relevance of this plurality of normative factors. Rule consequentialists and contractarians, for example, typically hold this view.

But a pluralist at the factoral level need not believe that there actually is a single foundational theory that generates all of the relevant normative factors. (Indeed, scepticism on this score sometimes leads people to deny that there exists any foundation at all for the normative factors.) For there is another possibility: one could be a pluralist at the foundational level as well—

holding that certain of the factors are grounded in a particular foundational device, while other factors are grounded in some second device, and still other factors are grounded in yet another device. On such a view pluralism at the factoral level would not be underwritten by monism at the foundational level; the justificatory picture would be more like a patchwork or a quilt.

There is of course a sense in which any given version of foundational pluralism will itself be one more foundational theory—one compounded out of the original foundational devices. Nonetheless it seems to me useful to distinguish between this case—where combination is largely a matter of mere conjunction—and other cases (like that of the hybrid of teleology and universalization) where the elements being combined are "synthesized" so as to form a foundational theory that intuitively possesses some internal unity.

If we do have a case of pluralism at the foundational level, the pluralism may well be ultimate and irreducible. But I think that even here it need not be. On some views, at least, there may be—at a "deeper" foundational level still—some single foundational theory that grounds and explains the legitimacy of the plurality of more "superficial" foundational theories.

Indeed, this possibility that a given foundational theory might be under-written or supported by a distinct foundational theory seems to me to arise even in cases where there is only a single foundational theory at work on any given level. Thus, rather than directly generating the various normative factors, the machinery of a given foundational theory might generate—and thus support—one of the other foundational theories. Presumably, this process could be repeated. For example, egoism might generate contractarianism, which might in turn generate rule consequentialism before, finally, generating the relevant normative factors. There are in fact theorists that have held such multi-leveled foundational views, and it can be illuminating to see them in this light.

Rather than pursue such exotic possibilities any further, however, I want to return to an earlier point. As we have seen, consequentialism at the foundational level can support deontology at the factoral level, if the foundational theory takes the form of rule consequentialism. We thus need to distinguish at the foundational level between rule consequentialism and act consequentialism (a distinction familiar, of course, from the debate between act and rule utilitarians). Act consequentialists think that the given act should be evaluated directly in terms of *its* consequences; thus it emerges at the factoral level that the *only* factor with genuine weight is that of goodness of results. Rule consequentialists in contrast think a given act should be evaluated in terms of its conformity to the optimal set of rules (where the rules are themselves evaluated in terms of their results) rather than directly in terms of its consequences; this is what generates the possibility that other factors may have genuine weight at the factoral level beyond goodness of results.

The distinction between act and rule consequentialism might be put this way: both share the foundationally consequentialist thought that moral justification must ultimately be in terms of promotion of the good; both use impact on the promotion of the good as the method for evaluating their particular favored objects, whether acts or rules. But the two approaches differ as to what kinds of objects provide the *primary* evaluative focal point. Rule consequentialists select *rules* as their primary evaluative focal point; they then evaluate acts in a secondary or derivative way, in terms of the directly evaluated rules. In contrast, act consequentialists select *acts* as their primary evaluative focal point, evaluating them directly. (This last claim is potentially slightly misleading, but will do for the moment.)

Although it has not been widely appreciated, this debate concerning the proper primary evaluative focal point is not at all limited to foundational consequentialists. It seems to me, in fact, that for all, or almost all, of the major types of foundational theories there are distinct versions of that foundational theory which differ in terms of their choice of primary evaluative focal point.

Consider, for example, the ideal observer theory. The basic idea of such a theory is that moral justification is ultimately in terms of the choices or preferences of a suitably ideal observer. An act version of this approach would hold that a given act is morally right provided that the ideal observer would approve of or favor this act. The foundational machinery of the theory—the device of the ideal observer—is here being applied directly to the evaluation of acts. (Incidentally, it might still turn out, of course, that the ideal observer is sensitive to a number of features of acts, and so nothing here yet rules out the possibility that at the level of normative factors there will be several factors with genuine weight. Until the details of the theory are filled in, there is simply no way to tell.)

The rule version of this approach does not apply the device of the ideal observer directly to the evaluation of acts, but rather to the evaluation of rules. It holds that a given act is morally right provided that the act conforms to the various rules favored by the ideal observer. (Once more, it may be worth noting that until the theory is filled in, we simply cannot tell what would emerge at the level of normatively relevant factors; in particular nothing yet indicates whether a rule ideal observer theory would give genuine weight to more than one normative factor.)

Here is another example of a foundational theory where we face the same choice between act and rule as our primary evaluative focal point: egoism, or the self-interest theory, which holds that moral justification must ultimately be in terms of the promotion of the agent's self-interest, or personal good. Ethical egoism is almost always understood as having acts as the primary evaluative focal point. So construed—that is, as act egoism—it holds that an act is morally right provided that the given act best promotes the agent's self-interest. As has been widely observed, this is actually a rather unpromising suggestion for the foundations of normative ethics; at the level of normative factors, no factor will emerge as having genuine weight except for the agent's own well-being. What has been largely (although not completely) overlooked, however, is the possibility of *rule* egoism, which holds that an act is morally right provided that it conforms to the rules, conformity with which on the part of the agent would best promote the agent's self-interest. This is actually a much more promising suggestion, for it seems at least possible that the optimal set of rules from this point of view will give genuine weight to many of the normative factors that we intuitively think of as having moral force.

Unlike egoism, where it is generally assumed that the primary evaluative focal point will be acts, when it comes to contractarianism people have generally assumed that the primary evaluative focal point will be rules. Standard versions of the theory hold that an act is right provided that it conforms to the rules that would be selected by the suitably specified bargainers. The contractarian machinery is used for the direct evaluation of rules; acts are only evaluated indirectly. But nothing rules out the possibility of an act contractarian approach, which would use the contractarian machinery to evaluate acts directly. Such a theory would hold that a given individual act is right provided that the hypothetical bargainers could agree to it.

Acts and rules do not exhaust the list of plausible primary evaluative focal points. Motives belong on the list as well. Thus we have motive consequentialism, which asks which set of motives would lead to the best results overall, and then derivatively evaluates acts in terms of whether a person with the ideal set of motives would perform them. We might similarly consider the merits of motive contractarianism, motive egoism, and so on for the various other foundational theories.

Other possible primary evaluative focal points include institutions, norms, character traits, and intentions. For each of these, I think, we can construct a variant of any given foundational approach. Abstractly described, the general idea is this: the machinery of the given foundational theory is used to directly evaluate instances of the favored type of evaluative focal point, and these direct evaluations are used to provide derivative evaluations of instances of the other types of focal point.

This choice of primary evaluative focal point can have an influence—potentially, a rather significant one—on what exactly is generated at the level of the normative factors. For the same basic type of foundational device may well support different lists of normative factors, or different weights for those factors, depending upon the particular evaluative focal point chosen. For example, as we have noted, act consequentialism supports the view that the only normative factor with direct weight is the overall goodness of results, whereas rule consequentialism appears to support the conclusion that other normative factors have independent significance as well.

The choice of evaluative focal point will also influence the precise *form* that the favored normative factors will take. Roughly speaking, on the rule version of a given foundational theory, the normative factors that are selected will emerge—naturally enough—in the form of rules or principles that are to be conformed to. On the motive version, the normative factors will take the form of various motives that are to be had and acted upon. On the act version, the normative factors will appear as positive and negative "values"— features of acts that are to be displayed (or not displayed) in one's actions. And so on, for the various other focal points.

It will be noted that I have been writing as though a fully specified theory at the foundational level must always choose one particular focal point and elevate it to the special status of *primary* evaluative focal point, evaluating the other focal points only indirectly, in terms of the primary one. But this is not in fact the only option. One could have a theory that refrained from selecting any of the focal points as primary, evaluating all of them, instead, directly.

Given this possibility, we need to distinguish between *act* theories—strictly so called—which directly evaluate only acts (and evaluate the other focal points only indirectly), and what might be called *direct* theories, which directly evaluate not only acts but also the other focal points as well. (I think, incidentally, that what many people have in mind by the position that is generally referred to as "act consequentialism" is actually direct consequentialism. Of course, not being aware of the distinction, most people have not had either theory determinately in mind.) The differences between these two types of theories can be rather subtle, and I won't explore them here. But it should, I think, be borne in mind that the choice of focal point includes this possibility of taking a direct approach to all of the focal points, and not only the possibility of selecting one particular focal point for primacy.

Now from one point of view, of course, the specification of the evaluative focal point is simply one way among many in which any given basic type of foundational theory needs to be elaborated if it is to assume a more determinate form. After all, even if we know that we are dealing with act contractarianism, say, we still ultimately need to specify the motivation of the bargainers as well as what kinds of information they possess. Similarly, even if we know that we are dealing with a universalization theory, we still need to specify whether it is logical contradiction that we are testing for, or practical contradiction, or some particular form of "bad result". But for the most part, the particular details that need to be filled in vary from one basic type of foundational theory to the next.

In contrast, as I have been trying to bring out, the choice of focal point is one that each foundational theory faces. For this reason it seems to me helpful to think of the chosen focal point as one of two basic components— the other is the given type of foundational mechanism or device—that together determine the fundamental character of the theory at the foundational level. (Of course, for all that, it remains natural to think of foundational theories that differ only in terms of their choice of evaluative focal points as variants of the same basic type of theory. Accordingly, in those contexts where a contrast is being drawn between the choice of foundational device and the choice of focal point, I will continue to use the expression "foundational theory" to refer to the basic foundational device itself.)

If the choice of evaluative focal point is indeed duplicated by each of the foundational theories, then it seems plausible to think that the focal points may deserve study in their own right. This is not to suggest that discussion should or could take place in complete isolation from discussion of the foundational theories, but only that a certain degree of autonomous investigation might be illuminating, just as it has proven to be in the case of the normative factors or in the case of the foundational theories.

For the most part, however, discussion of the various evaluative focal points has taken place only within the context of examining one or another foundational theory. What I am suggesting is that we would do well to bring the evaluative focal points into the philosophical light, and investigate them directly.

One obvious way in which there is some benefit to be had from thinking of the focal points in this way is that it suggests possible normative theories that might otherwise be overlooked. The example of rule egoism illustrates this point.

Secondly, at least some of the arguments that have been offered for running a given foundational theory in terms of one or another evaluative focal point seem to stand on their own, and thus may carry over to the choice of focal point for other foundational theories. Alternatively, investigation might reveal what it is about a given focal point that makes it a plausible choice for one particular foundational theory, but implausible for another.

Here is an example. There has been considerable debate over whether or not rule utilitarianism provides a genuine alternative to act utilitarianism. The thought is that since the rules are to be evaluated in terms of the goodness of results when the rules are acted on, the best rule will simply turn out to be act utilitarianism, which (after all) already directs agents to bring about the best results! If rule utilitarianism does indeed "collapse" into act utilitarianism, then this prompts the question whether for *all* foundational approaches, the given rule version similarly collapses into the corresponding act version. Direct investigation of the properties of rules and of acts at work in this argument should help clarify for which foundational theories, if any, this objection is sound.

Another possibility is this: it might turn out that the arguments for some particular evaluative focal point are sufficiently powerful and general that they succeed in establishing the superiority of that focal point—independently of being committed to any particular foundational theory. This parallels a phenomenon we have observed previously, in which claims at a given level of normative ethics can apparently be made while maintaining neutrality concerning the other levels. The contractarian, for example, holds that the correct *foundational* theory is the contractarian one; in itself this claim is neutral on the question of the correct account at the level of normative factors. And utilitarianism, I have suggested, should typically be taken as a claim at the level of the normative factors, a claim that is in itself neutral about the correct foundational approach. Similarly, then, one might argue that a given focal point is the uniquely correct primary evaluative focal point, while at the same time maintaining neutrality concerning the correct foundational approach or the genuine normative factors.

Virtue theory, I suggest, is best understood in this way. Particular virtue theorists, of course, may well be committed to a host of claims concerning the foundational or factoral levels. But what virtue theories have in common, as a class, is the claim that it is virtues, rather than acts or rules, that should be our primary evaluative focal point. Virtue theorists thus provide the single most important exception to my earlier observation that the study of focal points has received little direct attention. The nature of a virtue, at any rate, has received considerable attention. And much of that discussion has been concerned at the same time with arguing for the relative superiority of virtues over the other potential primary evaluative focal points.

I have now, I hope, made good on my promise to explain why I believe that it is a mistake to think that utilitarianism, contractarianism, and virtue theory are all rival attempts to do the same thing. Let me quickly review the outlines of my answer.

It is helpful to think of normative ethics as having two major levels—foundational and factoral. But investigation at the foundational level can itself be further subdivided into discussion of foundational devices and of focal points. Foundational devices are combined with, or directed toward, a choice of evaluative focal point and thereby generate the favored list of normatively relevant factors. In principle, a complete theory of normative ethics will include all three components, and will show the interconnections between these elements.

But there is something to be learned from incomplete theories as well, and a theory might confine itself to claims involving only one of these three areas. On at least one plausible construal, utilitarianism is a theory about the normative factors, contractarianism is a theory about the foundational device, and virtue theory is a claim about the evaluative focal points. Far from being incompatible or rival views, one could in fact endorse all three!

This is not to deny that once spelled out, choices in one area may constrain one's choices in another area. Perhaps there is no plausible way to fill in the details of the contractarian approach, for example, and still hope to generate goodness of results as the only genuinely relevant normative factor. But many claims in normative ethics are initially offered at a fairly high level of generality, and tensions and incompatibilities may only surface after considerable investigation. At any rate, the point remains that we might be prepared to make a claim concerning one of these areas, without yet knowing for sure where we stand with regard to the others.

Obviously enough, the picture I have been drawing of the structure of normative ethics is incomplete in many ways. It will be apparent, for example, that I have made no attempt at all to be complete in my listing of potential evaluative focal points. Indeed, in my own mind, at least, the list is at present rather open ended, and unstructured. As I have noted, there has been little systematic discussion of the focal points, and I am not at all sure how best to organize the candidates or even what all the most plausible candidates are.

In contrast, the examination of foundational theories is at least more well trod terrain, and I have somewhat greater confidence here that I have a handle on the most important proposals that have been made. Unfortunately, I have not had the space to discuss or even to introduce all of them.

Even for those foundational theories that I have discussed, I have said little or nothing about the various rationales that might be offered on their behalf. Of course, as I have noted, one kind of support that a foundational theory can have is the very fact that it succeeds in generating the various normative factors that we are independently inclined to accept. But foundational theories can be attractive in their own right, and it is always worth asking of a given approach why an approach of that *kind* should seem plausible.

As often as not, if we do start to explain why a given kind of foundational approach seems attractive, we will soon find ourselves appealing to alternative conceptions of the very nature of morality—its point, and its place in the world of persons, reasons, and things. In short, we will find ourselves appealing to alternative metaethical views. But this is just as it should be. For normative ethics is not, in the final analysis, independent of metaethics. Each leads inevitably to the other.

Philosophical Perspectives, 6, Ethics, 1992

MORALITY AND PARTIALITY

Susan Wolf
Johns Hopkins University

The great moral theories that have dominated moral philosophy for at least the last forty years have taken impartiality to be a core defining feature of morality. That is, they have identified morality with the idea of acting from a position that acknowledges and appreciates the fact that all persons (or even, on some views, all sentient beings) are in an important sense equal, and that, correspondingly, all are equally entitled to fundamental conditions of well-being and respect. Recently, however, many have called attention to the fact that relationships of friendship and love seem to call for the very opposite of an impartial perspective. Since such relationships unquestionably rank among the greatest goods of life, a conception of morality that is in tension with their maintenance and promotion is unacceptable.

Thus a debate has arisen between, as we may call them, the impartialists and the partialists. In defense of their position, the impartialists note that someone's being your friend or relative does not make her more morally deserving than anyone else, and they point to the grave moral dangers of moving that acknowledgment from the center of moral thought. Rather than allow our personal affections to compromise our commitments to justice and equality, they argue, we must shape our ideals of friendship and love to fit the demands of impartial morality. The partialists reply that this denigrates the value of special relationships to friends and loved ones, at best according them the status of acceptable extracurricular activities and at worst regarding them as a consequence of human nature to be warily tolerated.

For my own part, I am quite sympathetic to the partialists' concerns. But I think that they locate the problem in the wrong theoretical place. The problem is not that impartiality is too closely or centrally identified with morality, but that morality as a whole is being expected to do too much. I shall, then, defend a conception of morality that, in the context of the debate sketched above, might be labelled a moderate impartialism. But at least as important as its location within the impartialist-partialist debate is its self-conscious acknowledgement of the limitations of that debate, and indeed of the limitations of morality itself in settling some of the most important questions of our lives.

Types of Impartialism

The position that impartiality is a central and defining feature of a moral perspective is open to many interpretations. The most extreme, if also the most obvious interpretation directly identifies the moral point of view with the impartial point of view. According to Extreme Impartialism, a person is morally required to take each person's well-being, or alternatively each person's rights, as seriously as every other, to work equally hard to secure them, or to care equally much about them, or to grant them equal value in her practical deliberations. A person acts immorally, on such a view, if she fails either to do or to try to do what is best from a perspective that takes each person's interests, rights, or welfare as of equal importance to every other. Such an extreme form of impartialism seems to me patently absurd. For it is absurd to suggest that morality requires one to care, or to act as if one cares, no more about one's own child than about a stranger's, or that it is immoral to go to the movies with a friend whenever more good could be done by working at a soup kitchen. Only slightly less absurd, though much more popular, is a view that permits partisan emotions and behavior, as long as in fact they promote nonpartisan goals. For the acceptability of coaching one's daughter's soccer team, or taking one's friend to dinner on her birthday does not rest on the fortuitous coincidence that this action, or even the way of life that gives rise to it, is the one that will maximize human welfare or equal respect all around.

The grip that such views have on moral theory, despite their apparent absurdity, comes, I think, from the fact that they seem able to claim for themselves a special kind of objectivity. For it is an objective truth that my daughter is no more deserving than anyone else just for being mine. If one's aim in acting (or in forming one's values) is first and foremost to *reflect* objective truth, then, the extreme impartialist perspective seems better than any alternative.[1]

But it is neither rationally nor morally required that this *be* one's first and foremost aim. If Italian food is objectively no better than Thai food, this surely does not impose a requirement that I consume equal quantities of each. If Botticelli is objectively no better a painter than Tintoretto, this does not oblige me to spend equal time looking at their paintings. Similarly, it would seem, in the absence of further argument, the fact that my daughter is no better than some stranger does not require me to care about them equally or to act in a way that equally promotes their welfare. Unless one thinks that we are put on this earth for the sole purpose of serving it or its subjects, the idea that morality, much less rationality, requires us solely or dominantly to do so seems totally unjustified. We are, after all, subjects as well as objects, with interests of our own.

The idea that impartiality is part of the core of morality admits of more moderate interpretations than this, however. If we refer to the claim that all persons are equally deserving of well-being and respect as the Impartialist Insight, then we may characterize impartialism generally as the position that a moral person is one who recognizes and appreciates the Impartialist Insight and integrates it into her life. Understanding impartialism this way allows us to see the variety of views that may fairly be called impartialist. For integrating the Impartialist Insight into one's life need not mean letting it absolutely take over. There are both formal and substantive ways of shaping one's life so as to reflect people's basic moral equality which fall far short of identifying morality with living, as it were, from the impartial point of view. The familiar idea that morality requires one to act only in ways that one thinks any reasonable person would accept is one formal and more moderate interpretation of impartialism. The notion that one must hold oneself to whatever standards one expects of others is another. The first counts as impartialism because it treats all persons as equally deserving of a say in setting the moral standards. The second counts as impartialism because, although one sets the standards oneself, one sets them in such a way as expressly to avoid granting oneself (or one's friends) special privilege. These forms are more moderate because the standards thus set are apt unconditionally to allow a good deal of partiality in one's psychology and behavior. One would not expect or demand a stranger to take one's own interests as seriously as the interests of her loved ones, nor would a stranger expect or demand this of oneself.

What would, or what ought strangers (or enemies) expect of each other in the way of concern and respect? A defect of the formal characterizations of morality above is that they do not say. But the spirit of impartialism obviously urges something more than indifference to others. Rather than try to derive this something more from the formal requirements mentioned above, we may directly and explicitly add a more substantive, though still indeterminate requirement to the interpretation of moderate impartialism. What I have in mind is simply the idea that reflection on the fact that everyone is equally morally deserving should in itself move one some way in the direction of universal benevolence. Thus, for example, people (like us) who live, with their friends and their children, in relative luxury, must, if they are moral, realize that others, no less deserving, are starving, homeless, abused. The substantive element of moderate impartialism insists that appreciating and integrating this fact into one's life must have some practical effect—on one's politics, on one's activities, on one's choice of how to spend one's money.

I shall defend Moderate Impartialism, understood as a conception of morality that endorses all three of the less extreme interpretations of impartialism mentioned above. A moral person, on this view, does act only in ways that she believes any reasonable person would allow. She does hold herself to the same standards that she expects of others. And she is moved to practical effect by the thought that others—all others—are as deserving of the fundamental conditions of well-being and respect as are she and her circle of friends and loved ones.

Moderate Impartialism and the Status of Friendship and Love

Since this view gives impartiality a much more limited role in morality than Extreme Impartialism, some may regard Moderate Impartialism as itself a conciliatory view. After all, few, if any, critics of impartialism meant to deny that impartiality had any role in morals at all. The issue dividing the parties of the debate is about the size, or centrality, or ubiquity of that role. Extreme Impartialism makes impartiality loom very large in moral thought. Moderate Impartialism gives it a distinctly less intrusive position. Still, I mean to understand this position in a way that gives impartiality not just a place, or even a very important place in moral thinking, but also a special, and especially absolute place. Moderate Impartialism, as I understand it, is still a form of impartialism because, insofar as impartiality does generate any requirements of us, these requirements are morally absolute. They cannot be traded off or balanced by other considerations. Indeed, this is the point of endorsing the formal characterizations of morality mentioned above. This endorsement implies that anyone who acts in a way that reasonable others would not allow, or anyone who violates standards that she would expect others to uphold acts immorally. Anyone who knows that her action cannot be justified to others but who chooses to act despite this, thereby defies morality—and does so whether she is motivated by self-interest or by friendship or love.

Moderate Impartialism, like Extreme Impartialism, then, conceives of morality as fundamentally and absolutely connected to the Impartialist Insight that all persons have a kind of moral equality. Let us now see what implications this has for the moral status of friendship and love and for the moral evaluation of acts that are performed in their contexts. To see how far such a conception of morality goes in the direction of positively accommodating and valuing such relationships, at least four points should be made.

First, and most obviously, Moderate Impartialism allows the existence of deep friendships and love without apology. Consequently, many, if not all, of the preferences for loved ones most of us express in our daily lives will turn out to be unequivocally permissible. Since Moderate Impartialism never asks a person to value every human or sentient being as much as every other, there is no problem about coaching *one's own* daughter's soccer team or taking *one's own* friend out to dinner, or loving *one's own* spouse more than the equally deserving but much less interesting man across the street.

Second, preferential actions on behalf of loved ones are sometimes not just permitted but positively required by (moderately) impartial morality. Thus, the common sense view that there are special obligations of friendship seems supported rather than contradicted by morality thus conceived. For relationships of friendship, and love, not to mention family ties, tend to give rise to special expectations in their participants and frequently put individuals in positions that make them uniquely capable of benefitting and protecting another. Even from a purely disinterested perspective, one can see how such expectations and circumstances may be thought to generate special duties. Thus, there will be many occasions on which a Moderate Impartialist will be able to say that acting on behalf of one's friend or loved one is not merely morally permissible, but morally good.

Third, a defender of Moderate Impartialism should acknowledge that even if impartiality plays a distinctive, unconditional role in moral thought, it is not always salient in moral evaluation. Morality is not just about treating people equally or fairly, but about treating them well. And in many, perhaps most, contexts where moral deliberation or evaluation is called for, issues about partiality and impartiality do not arise. Kindness and cruelty, sensitivity and thoughtlessness, honesty, deception, respect and manipulation can be noted and appropriately encouraged or condemned without any reference to the issue of partiality. Though impartiality is related to morality in a fundamental and unconditional way, it is not always useful to dwell on this or place it in the forefront of moral judgment.

Related to this is the fourth and final point that from a moderately impartialist moral point of view, there is abundant reason to encourage friendships and love and to be dedicated to structuring society so that such relationships can flourish. Of course, morality sets limits on what one can do in the context of a friendship or love relationship, but, for the most part, these relationships advance moral goals rather than threaten them. For in addition to being an immeasurable and profound source of human happiness—a moral goal if ever there was one—such relationships provide by far the most natural and effective setting for the development of moral sentiments and virtues. Sympathy for a friend teaches and encourages one to have sympathy also for a stranger. Thinking about the feelings and interests of a loved one helps develop the habit of thinking about others more generally.

In light of all the positive things a moderately impartial moralist can say about partial relationships—in light of the wide room within morality in which friendships and love can develop and flourish and the sincere praise and encouragement that a moralist can offer to the participants of these relationships—is there anything left for a partialist to complain about?

At least some partialists think that there is. For even if the kind of impartial morality sketched above acknowledges a value to friendships and love, they think it is the wrong kind of value; even if impartial morality endorses these special relationships, they think it endorses them for the wrong reasons.

The Partialist Complaint

To begin with, the partialists will point out, the primary impartialist attitude to friendship and love is that within limits, it is perfectly permissible. But what a weak and paltry thing that is to say about one of the most gratifying and meaningful forms of human activity! To put it in the class of the permissible is to rank it with such acceptable activities as stamp-collecting and golf. Surely, relationships with friends and family have a different and deeper kind of value. It is not just alright but positively good that a person goes hiking with a friend, that she help a neighbor start his car, that she bring her children presents, bake them cookies, teach them songs. More generally, it is not just alright but positively good that such relationships form part of a person's life.

The remarks made earlier make the impartialists' response to this easily predictable. The fact that friendships are like stamp-collecting in both being permissible carries no implication that these activities are comparable in kind or amount of value. Of course, it is positively morally good that one helps a neighbor, or brings joy to one's children. Helping people is always morally good, and one's children are hardly an exception. Besides, as has already been noted, one has special responsibilities to those in whom one has encouraged special expectations, and an obligation to take extraordinary measures for those whom one is in a unique or nearly unique position to help. For these reasons, the impartialist, like the partialist, will not only praise the person who does help her friends, but, on some occasions, morally criticize the person who fails to do so (even if she fulfills all her duties to treat them and others decently). And, at a more general level, the impartialist has plenty to say to support the partialist's point that friendships are immeasurably more valuable than stamps. For one thing, they provide much more pleasure, and, lest pleasure seem too shallow a benefit, they provide further satisfactions, including a sense of purpose and meaningfulness. Moreover, they provide these benefits, not just to the agent who loves, but to the beloved as well. Thus, friendship and love are unusually efficient in being able to spread and intensify positive experience in ways solitary activities and interests cannot match. And finally, as we have already noted, people who are involved in warm special relationships are more likely to be or to become generally sympathetic and generous than are people without such relationships. For all these reasons, impartialists may be said to agree with the partialist statement that friendships and love are of positive moral value.

But this perfectly illustrates the partialist complaint—that although the impartialist values these relationships, she values them in the wrong way, for the wrong reasons.

Thus, the impartialists say that you ought to make special efforts for your friends—but not because they are your friends and you love them. Rather it is because you have encouraged special expectations on their part, or because you are in a unique position to help. This explanation of obligations of friendship likens such obligations to contractual or professional duties, or to the duty to respond to emergency situations that chance happens to throw in one's path. This seems a cold and detached way to respond to a friend, hardly representative of the kind of psychology the partialists want to praise. And though the impartialists support friendship and love more generally, they support these relationships as means to another end—to the production of pleasure or meaningfulness, to the development of a more generalized altruism. The partialists want to insist that friendship and love are valuable *in themselves*, independently of their contribution to these other goals. Even if, as sometimes happens, a friendship leads to more sorrow than joy, and even if it makes no contribution to the more generalized moral virtues of those involved, the relationship enhances rather than detracts from the participants' lives.

The partialists seem to me right to note the coldness of impartial morality's support of special relationships and the actions they urge on us; they seem to me right in pointing out that on this conception of morality, love and friendship are not moral ends in themselves. What does not seem right is the further thought that these facts count against an impartialist conception of morality. This issue depends on how complete and perfect a guide to life morality can be expected to be.

Tensions between Impartiality and Personal Ties: Reasonable Disagreement

It is time to look at the practical concerns to which these issues abstractly refer, to take note of the problems in ordinary life that the tension between impartial morality and discriminating love create. I shall focus on the most discussed controversy—namely, that concerning how much one *may* do for friends and loved ones. Within this realm, two different sorts of issues arise.

First there is an issue about how much of one's time, money, and effort one may direct towards the benefit of those one specially cares about in light of the greater and more pressing needs of people not part of one's circle. May one buy one's child a Nintendo game even though other children don't even have coats to keep them warm? What about private school? Summer camp? Psychotherapy? One's multimillion dollar estate? Moderate Impartialism as such offers no determinate answer to these questions. Rather, it recognizes an imperfect duty to give some attention to others, independent of any special ties to you. How much and what kind of attention, and what one gives up in order to meet this demand, will vary with one's resources and the other morally significant claims upon one. Presumably, partialists will want to recognize such an imperfect duty themselves. They are rarely so callous as to suggest we have no obligation to care about strangers. In this area of moral life, then, the abstract debate about partiality and impartiality might engender no substantive disagreement. Still, the tone of impartialism might lead one to assume that the impartialists want to draw the line of permissible expenditures for loved ones somewhat closer than their opponents.

More interesting, theoretically, are issues concerning apparently perfect duties. When, if ever, may one break the rules (or bend them) for a friend or relative? May one lend a friend one's apartment, knowing she wants it for an adulterous affair? Is one allowed to commit perjury for a friend, or hide her from the police? May one vote for a friend's tenure, knowing that one would have voted against it if there had been no special relationship? May one let a friend sneak through the turnstile as one collects tickets for a Bruce Springsteen concert? Traditionally, impartialisms of the more moderate type have been interpreted as answering no to all these questions, presumably on the grounds that if an impartial perspective demands the laying down of a rule, it demands that the rule be obeyed absolutely. But Moderate Impartialism as I have sketched it contains no such theoretical commitment. Moderate Impartialism requires that one ask what standards any reasonable person would set for everyone to follow. What would you demand of others, it urges you to ask, and what may others reasonably demand of you? Taking myself as an example of a reasonable person, I can only report that I would not take it amiss if a ticket-taker let a friend slip into a Springsteen concert, even bearing in mind that some people who camped out in front of a ticket booth all one cold, rainy night, had to be turned away. As I see it, these are matters where luck acceptably—even sometimes, delightfully—plays its part. Some people are unlucky in being just ten places too far back in line; a few are fortunate enough to have a friend at the turnstile. And I can imagine a morally virtuous individual deciding to take advantage of her position to give a friend—who is seriously into Springsteen—the peak experience of seeing this concert which she would otherwise be unable to afford.

But, of course, when it comes to taking special advantage, one must draw the line. It is one thing to let one friend into one concert without a ticket, another to let thirty friends in every week. Or to get one's friend's daughter into medical school, even though her record is not as good as other applicants', or to drop criminal charges against one's ex-roommate for old times' sake. The point is that Moderate Impartialism *as such* is as indeterminate about these matters as about those mentioned earlier. It is, in both instances, a matter of where to draw the line.[2]

Though one cannot literally derive substantive disagreements about specific practical issues from the theoretical debate about impartialism, however, one can expect such concrete disagreements to accompany the more abstract one. By imagining and explaining the trains of thought some possible concrete disagreements might provoke, we can gain insight into some implicit assumptions operating in the background of both parties of the partialist/impartialist debate.

Consider the case of the woman who is moved to vote for a friend's promotion to a tenured position, conscious that in the absence of the friendship she may have been inclined to vote against him. We may assume that the impartialist would judge that morality requires her, at the very least, to withdraw herself from the vote. The partialist, on the other hand, thinks this shows insufficient appreciation of the pull of loyalty and mutual commitment, and so accuses her opponent of taking the impartial point of view too seriously. Who is right?

In dealing with this controversy, the natural tendency is to try to defend one's initial position by deepening one's characterization of it and drawing out the negative implications one suspects to develop from the opposing view. One can imagine the debate getting ugly, with the impartialist painting the partialist (at least, the one that we imagine actually does vote for her friend) as totally unscrupulous and the partialist painting the impartialist as smugly self-righteous and cold.

In fact, however, I would guess that nine times out of ten this tendency leads us astray. The right thing to do for both parties of the debate is, essentially, to accommodate the other. To be sure, the impartialist's *first* reaction to the case is to think that in tenure cases one must put friendship to one side. (For the record, this is my first reaction.) But after listening to the partialist, and perhaps to added details that are plausibly claimed to be relevant, it may be more appropriate simply to accept that this is a case where reasonable people disagree. Moreover, this concession should be enough to satisfy the partialist, unless she thinks that it is positively immoral for someone to refuse to compromise her professional standards for her friend.

Earlier I said that whether one is a partialist or an impartialist, the question of what and how much one can do on behalf of a friend or loved one must be a question of where to draw the line. Acknowledging the possibility of reasonable moral disagreement, however, suggests a modification of that claim. For, strictly speaking, it seems, one need not draw a line. One may instead shade an area, encompassing a range of behavior patterns of varying degrees of moral tone.

In contexts where nonmoral values are at issue, we are ordinarily quite ready to acknowledge that our preferences, even our judgments of what is best, may legitimately differ from others. We may have different tastes--within reason—in music, movies, and men, without any of us being irrational or obtuse. There is no reason—though no doubt there is an explanation—why we shouldn't be similarly tolerant about some moral issues. Disputes about the limits of permissible partiality seem to me to be connected with just such an issue.

Accepting the existence of reasonable disagreement in this area does, however, complicate the version of Moderate Impartialism that I have proposed. Specifically, it creates difficulties in interpreting the condition of morality that requires one to act in accordance with standards that all reasonable others would accept. This condition appears to require that our behavior conform to the *strictest* standards of impartiality that fall within the reasonable range, for to do anything less would fail to be in accord with what *all* reasonable others would accept. At the same time, the acknowledgment that some reasonable people have more lenient views about the degree to which impartial concerns should prevail ought to incline those who are initially drawn to strictness to loosen up on what they think morality universally requires.

Ideally, conscientious and imaginative reflection on the range of reasonable moral views in this area will lead in the long run to more consensus as well as more tolerance. Those who tend initially to set more lenient standards will pull themselves up to conform to the standards of others they respect, and those who tend toward strictness will take a less moralistic and condemnatory attitude towards those they come to see as falling within the reasonable, if less demanding, range. That there should still remain borderline cases in which it is unclear what counts as reasonable and correspondingly what counts as morally required does not, I think, constitute a significant objection to this view.

Tensions Between Impersonal and Personal Ties: Radical Choice

As I have suggested, many cases in which a tension between love and impartiality is a source of moral controversy can be explained and accounted for by recognizing a range of reasonable disagreement about what standards people should expect and require of each other. But there are some cases which cannot comfortably be interpreted in this way. What I have in mind are cases where there is no controversy about what reasonable people—and so, what impartial morality—may require, but where the pull of love and loyalty urge the agent to consider flouting those requirements nonetheless. What is such a person to do, and how are we to judge her? Impartial morality unequivocally instructs her to refrain, and issues a negative judgment on her if she does not (how negative, of course, depends on how serious her sin). But with sufficient imagination, one may paint such an agent in sympathetic colors—not only as one who deserves our sympathy but as one with whom we may be *in* sympathy. This may suggest that impartial morality is somehow wrong.

Consider the case of a woman whose son has committed a crime and who must decide whether to hide him from the police. He will suffer gravely should he be caught, but unless he is caught, another innocent man will be wrongly convicted for the crime and imprisoned. I shall take it as needing no argument that impartial morality forbids protecting one's son at the expense of another innocent man's suffering. Impartial morality forbids it—but we are talking about a woman and her son.

For many people, this case is unproblematic. The woman should turn in her son, and that's that. This view is perfectly compatible with feeling great sympathy for her, and even for excusing her, partially or wholly, if she cannot bring herself to do what she ought to do. But there are others who regard the dilemma in a different light, and whose view of the woman who protects her son is more positive than the one just depicted. To these others there is something positively reasonable (and not just understandable) about the woman who, having recognized that impartial morality instructs her to turn her son in, wonders whether to act according to impartial morality or not. After all, if the meaning of one's life and one's very identity is bound up with someone as deeply as a mother's life is characteristically tied to her son's, why should the dictates of impartial morality be regarded as decisive? One can imagine a woman recognizing the dictates of impartial morality, and accepting without protest the judgment of others that she ought to turn in her son. She might believe that they have a right to disapprove, even to punish her for protecting her son, but nonetheless find that these considerations pale in significance beside thoughts of her child's welfare. "Do to me what you like," she may say, "Judge me as you will. I will go to hell if I have to, but my son is more important to me than my moral salvation." One may regard such a woman not just with sympathy, but with a kind of admiration and respect, perhaps as much admiration and respect as one regards the woman who, after equally tortured deliberations, makes the opposite choice.

The thought that there is nothing wrong with the woman who protects her son, or that, at any rate, nothing wrong with deciding in *some* contexts to act on behalf of a loved one despite the recognition that others fairly disapprove is perhaps the strongest motivating thought behind partialist morality. For if one thinks it is reasonable for a person to act a certain way, one is inclined to think that it must be moral, too. And so, one may think, it must be moral occasionally to choose to act one way despite the fact that even a moderately impartialist perspective forbids it. From this one concludes that even a moderately impartialist perspective is only a conditional, if typical, feature of morality, and that the bonds of love and friendship can reasonably compete with the demands of impartiality for moral priority.

As I have hinted throughout the paper, I believe that this line of reasoning is mistaken. Rather than interpret the woman's dilemma as one in which different sorts of moral concerns compete, I prefer to characterize it as a conflict *between* morality and the demands of love. It is morality itself, and not just an aspect or facet of it, that stands on one side of the dilemma. The problem the mother faces is not the problem of weighing different moral concerns against each other; it is rather the problem of whether to attend ultimately to moral concerns at all. In this sense, it is a problem of radical choice.

Conflicts Between Love and Morality

Conceiving of the woman's problem in this way reveals a commitment to conceiving of morality as impartial morality, to regarding judgments of moral permissibility as completely and unconditionally bounded by impartialist constraints. Yet, because I have not assumed that rationality and reasonableness are completely and unconditionally bound by moral constraints, my evaluation of the mother's possible responses significantly coincide with the partialists' evaluation in this case. For, while I agree with other *im*partialists that it would be immoral for the woman to hide her son from the police, it seems to me that a willingness, in such special circumstances as these, to consider acting immorally, and even to act immorally, is compatible with the possession of a character worthy of respect and admiration.

At this point, the reader might well feel exasperated, wondering whose side I am really on, or even whether, in my effort to appreciate both sides of the debate, I manage to maintain a consistent position at all. For evidently I want to have it both ways: to claim, on the one hand, that the woman is morally required to turn in her son, and, on the other, that she may be reasonable, even admirable, if she refuses to turn him in. Since I understand morality as defined, at least in part, by what it is reasonable for people to demand of one another, this may appear self-contradictory. But it is not *quite* contradictory to believe both that it is reasonable to morally demand that the mother turn her son in and that it is reasonable for the mother to refuse to meet the demand. This would be contradictory if one understood, as part of the *meaning* of a moral demand that it be a demand that, all things considered, any reasonable, decent person should meet. But I believe there are strong reasons for understanding the meaning of "moral" differently, and thus for allowing that on rare occasions, a reasonable and decent person may find herself considering, and even deciding to defy morality.

Specifically, there are strong reasons for using "moral" to refer to whatever is dictated by an impartial perspective. For the impartial perspective, or, more precisely, the constraints on action that this perspective would urge have a uniquely important and distinctive role in our thought and in our lives. They are, first of all, constraints which, as members of the human community, we have a deep and abiding interest that people follow. But they are not just constraints that we *want* people to accept—they are constraints that we are justified in insisting that they accept. For these constraints offer a way of integrating into our lives an appreciation of an unassailable truth—the truth that you or I are ultimately no more deserving of having our interests satisfied or our point of view respected than any other human being. This is a truth, moreover, which, without some help, people are apt to neglect or ignore.

To return to the mother's dilemma, it seems completely legitimate for us, as voices, if you will, of a reasonable humanity, to forbid—insofar as it is in our power—that she protect her son. For no matter how much she understandably values her son's welfare, someone else's son's welfare is also at stake, and he is innocent. Given the history of our language, to say to her, or to ourselves, that turning her son in is the action that follows from the impartial perspective is hardly sufficient to express the urgency, the seriousness, or, what is perhaps most to the point, the finality of the judgment that is appropriate here. For these reasons, we want to use the words: morality requires it.

At the same time, once we have realized that a moral requirement just is a judgment about what kind of behavior is tolerable from an impartial perspective, it would be unrealistic and even perhaps undesirable to expect people to be committed to morality unconditionally. Even if, as one hopes, moral values reach to the very core of a person's identity, they are not, nor do we want them to be, the only values or attributes that comprise that core. So there is the possibility of conflict, and of reasonable, decent people, resolving the conflict in favor or against morality.

Moderate, as opposed to Extreme, Impartialism recognizes limits to the degree to which one can expect people to integrate and practically express the fact that all humans are equally deserving. People have their own lives to live, after all, they are not just servants to humanity. Moderate Impartialism sets moral standards with this limitation in mind. One who accepts this perspective, however, must also recognize the possibility that even these moderate standards may call for wrenching sacrifices, and that a person's commitment to upholding these standards, and to remaining, as it were, in good standing with reasonable humanity, might not hold its own against some other legitimately deep feature of that person's life. Recognizing this does not call for the conclusion that the standards were set unreasonably high after all: the mother who protects her son does act wrongly, and deserves whatever guilt and punishment flow from that judgment. At the same time, if she turns him in, she will irreparably alter a relationship that has, perhaps, been the most fulfilling thing in her life. She will suffer a huge loss either way.

To describe the woman's conflict as one *between* morality and the bonds of love seems to me to capture or preserve the split, almost schizophrenic reaction I think we ought to have to her dilemma. It allows a part of us to disapprove of the option of protecting her son, while allowing another part of us to withhold judgment. Though one wants as far as possible to avoid being torn, split, dis-integrated, the more unified alternatives in this case seem to me less reasonable. And, anyway, what would be accomplished, what message would be sent, and to whom by a more unified conclusion? It seems gratuitously vindictive to insist that a moral judgment against the woman who protects her son is the last, or the only, word on her. Yet it seems disturbingly smug, as well as morally lax, to say that, on the contrary her act was morally all right. In any event, *she* had reached a point where the issue of moral approval had ceased to be decisive.

Conclusion: Morality's Job

Earlier I suggested that the debate between partialists and impartialists, insofar as it was not built upon confusion, betrayed what I take to be unreasonable expectations for morality, on the parts of both sides. It is unreasonable, first, to expect morality to have determinate answers to every question, to expect morality always to be able to draw a line on which everyone can agree. It is also unreasonable to expect that once morality has drawn a line, one's practical deliberations must be over. It is sometimes hard to say whether an action is morally justified. It may also be hard to say, on occasion, whether, or at least how much, it matters.

Still, it is to be expected that occasions of this latter sort will be rare. In ordinary circumstances, a well-meaning person will have integrated the minimal constraints of (impartial) morality in such a way that the question of whether to violate them will simply not arise for her. One does not even consider robbing or cheating or hurting innocent people even to confer some very great benefit on one's child. And, if all goes well, one's children do not consider such options either, thus allowing most of us to avoid such dilemmas as the unfortunate woman in our example faces.

In light of all the concessions to the importance and value of personal relationships that I have urged, both within and without the framework of impartialist morality itself, it is hard to imagine a substantive reason for rejecting an impartialist conception of morality. However, one source of dissatisfaction for the partialist may remain. Specifically, my support of an impartialist conception of morality has relied heavily on the way such a conception generates moral *requirements* and *constraints*. Throughout this discussion, I have concentrated on questions about what is morally permissible, what forbidden. Someone initially sympathetic to a partialist conception of morality might object to this. In particular, she might point out that the tendency to focus on questions of permissibility and prohibition is itself symptomatic of the coldness and distance inherent in impartialist morality. This, she might note, is part of what generated the partialist critique in the first place.

To think in terms of what one may do, what one must do (what one has to do), is to express and reinforce a sense of dichotomy between oneself and those represented by morality. It reflects or engenders a sense of isolation from others, even in the attempt to secure a certain kind of minimal attention to others. It may be that for those who are afflicted with this sense of isolation, an impartialist conception of morality offers the best advice available for how to cope with the inescapable social world. But, the defender of partialist morality will go on, it would be better to avoid the sense of isolation in the first place. By loosening the connection between impartialist thinking and moral thinking, by according love and commitment to specifiable others to have fundamental intrinsic moral worth, we can offer a happier, more harmonious vision of the moral life and encourage people, not to grudgingly overcome their selfish instincts in favor of what they perceive to be their duty, but rather to replace these instincts, or perhaps expand their conception of their selves so as to embrace and identify with a larger social community. Thus, we can avoid the need to think in terms of duty altogether.

This objection contains considerable truth. In particular, it is true that by focusing on questions of obligation and duty, of permissibility and prohibition, we focus on the persons or on the situations in which a person's interests are *in tension* with the interests of society at large. To ask what one may do, and what one has to do, is to express a reluctance to help or to respect the wills of others. When the voice of morality comes down in answer to these questions, it is like the voice of an umpire settling a controversy between opponents.

To be sure, we do not for the most part want people to think about their neighbors, much less their children, in these terms. But is it the job, or the place of morality to see to it that they do not?

There are so many reasons to love your children and even to help out your neighbors. Some reasons are grounded in natural sympathy; others are grounded in self-interest. And in the case of *my* children, there is their objective—albeit nonmoral—superiority to all other living creatures. There is no need for morality to tell you to love your children and have friends. Moreover, it seems inappropriate for morality to condemn those who, whether for psychological or geographical reasons, are unable to have friends or children to love.

At the same time, we must acknowledge the existence of people who have no love, or even sympathy, for others, and the existence of the much larger group who love some others but who care not a jot for the rest. Further, we must acknowledge that all of us are sometimes faced with conflicts between our own interests and the interests of strangers, between the interests of loved ones and the interests of strangers, even between our own interests and the interests of those we deeply love. We need some way of dealing with these people and these conflicts, some way of thinking about them that will set a minimum standard of tolerable behavior. It is a tough job, but somebody has to do it. Specifically, morality has to do it. And for this job, an impartialist conception of morality works best.[3]

Notes

1. Even so, this perspective has problems of its own. For acknowledging that my daughter is no more deserving than anyone else leaves open the question of whether anyone is deserving of anything at all.
2. Among contemporary moral theories, the one defended in Bernard Gert's *Morality: A Defense of the Moral Rules* is especially good in appreciating this.

3. In thinking about these issues and in correcting some of the errors of previous drafts, I have greatly benefitted from discussions with Evelyn Barker, Lawrence Blum, Don Garrett, Shelly Kagan, and audiences at Connecticut College, Northwestern University, Temple University, and the University of Utah.

Philosophical Perspectives, 6, Ethics, 1992

THE "POSSIBILITY" OF A CATEGORICAL IMPERATIVE: KANT'S *GROUNDWORK*, PART III

David Copp
University of California, Davis

In part III of the *Groundwork for the Metaphysics of Morals*, Kant attempted to solve a problem that he took to be an especially serious one for his moral philosophy. He described it as the problem of showing "the possibility of a categorical imperative".[1] At the end of part II of the *Groundwork*, he said that he needed to show this possibility in order to show that morality is "something real, and not a chimerical idea without any truth"—"that morality is not a mere phantom of the brain" (Ak 445).[2] The importance of this problem to Kant's argument in the *Groundwork* can scarcely be denied.[3]

The "possibility problem" must be faced by any non-skeptical moral philosophy, as I will explain. My goal in this paper is to show how Kant saw the problem, to show how it arose in the context of his moral philosophy, and to explain his attempt to solve it. I shall explore Kant's argument in *Groundwork* III, and the intuitions that underlie it. I shall also examine two recent reconstructions of the argument, by Henry Allison and Thomas Hill, Jr. My overall goal is to locate a problem for moral theory in the work of Kant, but to discourage the idea that it can be solved by means of a Kantian strategy. I will argue that there are major hurdles in the way of a Kantian solution.

1. The Possibility Problem

We are able to formulate any number of putative moral standards. For example, we can formulate a standard or a rule against money-lending. Of course, most people in capitalist societies would deny that money-lending is actually wrong. But they can admit the existence of a rule that purports to prohibit money-lending, while denying that any actual prohibition corresponds to the rule. The issue whether money-lending is wrong therefore does not turn on the mere existence of a rule (or family of rules) to the effect that interest is not to be charged when money is lent; it turns on the *status* of this rule.[4] The issue is whether the rule has the status of delineating an actual moral prohibition.

A standard does not delineate an actual moral prohibition or requirement, or a class of actual moral goods or bads, unless it has a relevant authoritative standing, status, validity, credibility, or justification. I will usually simplify by speaking only of requirements, and I will speak of the "justification" of corresponding standards. A non-skeptical moral philosophy therefore must specify a condition, which I have elsewhere called the justification criterion or *J* criterion, and argue that all and only the standards that meet the condition correspond to actual moral requirements.[5] Moreover, I would argue that a moral proposition is true only if a corresponding moral standard has an appropriate justification.[6] For example, if it is true that money-lending is morally wrong, then a moral prohibition against it has an appropriate authoritative status or justification. Accordingly, in order fully to explain the truth-conditions of moral propositions, and to show that there are in fact moral truths, a theory would have to specify and defend a *J* condition, and it would also have to show that certain standards meet the condition.

In short, it is incumbent on a non-skeptical moral philosophy to explain the status which is possessed by standards that delineate actual moral requirements, and to show that some standards actually have this status. This is the possibility problem in contemporary dress, and it is essentially the problem confronted by Kant. It is a problem with three components: to specify the *J* condition for moral standards, to defend the proposition that all and only the standards that meet the condition correspond to actual moral requirements, and to show that certain standards meet the condition.

A Kantian "imperative" is an *authoritative* or *justified* standard, one that delineates an actual requirement or prohibition. An imperative is expressed by a sentence to the effect that someone "is to do" something or other; that someone is "required to", or "must", or "ought to" do something. The quoted words express a kind of "necessitation" that Kant thinks must be explained. The difficulty he sees is both to explain how to conceive of "the necessitation of the will expressed by an imperative in setting a task" (Ak 417) and to show that there is such necessitation. It is not, of course, that an agent's performing the action in question is necessary in the way that it is a necessary truth that seven plus two equals nine. The sense in which it is "necessary" is elusive and must be explained.

As is well known, Kant distinguishes between hypothetical and categorical imperatives (Ak 414), and he argues that moral imperatives are categorical. He says,

> the question of how the imperative of morality is possible is undoubtedly the only one requiring a solution. For it is not at all hypothetical; and hence the objective necessity which it presents cannot be based on any presupposition, as was the case with the hypothetical imperatives. (Ak 419)

Since my topic is the possibility of a categorical imperative, I shall not pause to discuss the possibility of hypothetical imperatives in any detail. Yet Kant does offer an explanation of their possibility.[7]

Hypothetical imperatives postulate actions as required given a presupposed goal, purpose, end, or desire of the agent. They are of the form: An agent P ought to perform action A assuming that, or given that, P has purpose E. A rule of this form is not an imperative unless P's doing A is necessary to P's achieving E. An example is the rule that one ought to change the oil regularly in one's car, assuming that one wants the car to continue running well. If this is in fact an imperative, then changing the oil is in fact necessary if a car is to run properly. And in this case, the proposition that I ought to change the oil in my car will be true if I do have the purpose that my car run well. More generally, the proposition will be true only if there is *some* hypothetical imperative specifying a purpose relative to which one is to change the oil in one's car and if I have that purpose.[8]

Clearly the requirement to do A that is postulated by a hypothetical imperative is contingent on the agent's having a purpose appropriately related to A. And, as Kant says, "the precept can always be ignored once the purpose is abandoned" (Ak 420). For instance, it may be true that I ought to change the oil in my car, but if so, the requirement that I do this is conditional on the presupposition that I have purposes the achieving of which require me to change the oil. If my purposes were to change, it might no longer be true that I ought to change the oil. Hence, as Thomas Hill, Jr., remarks, the requirement postulated by a hypothetical imperative, to do A given that one has purpose E, can be conformed to either by doing A or by giving up the purpose E.[9] As Hill points out, this ensures that there is no conflict between conformity to the requirements of morality and conformity to the hypothetical requirements of one's ends. For a person can give up her ends, if required to do so by morality, and in doing so she need not be violating any hypothetical requirement.[10]

Kant asks how hypothetical imperatives are possible. The issue is "how it is possible" that a person be *required* to do something A on the basis that she has a purpose E. What does it mean to say a person is required to do this, and on what basis is she required? Kant says no special discussion of this is needed.[11] For,

> Whoever wills the end, wills (so far as reason has decisive influence on his actions) also the means that are indispensably necessary to his [ends] and that lie in his power. This proposition, as far as willing is concerned, is analytic. (Ak 417)

Let me call the proposition Kant says is analytic the "base principle" for hypothetical imperatives. Kant's idea is I think expressed by the following "base property" and "base equivalence" for hypothetical imperatives.

(1) The rule that one is to do A in circumstances C if one has purpose E is a (valid) hypothetical imperative just in case the rule has the following property: if a person had the purpose E and realized both that doing A in C is in his power and is necessary for him to achieve E, then he would intend to do A in C if reason had "decisive influence" on his intentions.

(2) If P's doing A in C is in P's power and is necessary for P to achieve E, then P is *required* to do A in C, given that P has the end E, just in the sense that, and in virtue of the fact that, given that P has purpose E, if P realized that doing A in C was in his power and was necessary to his achieving E, P would intend to do A in C if reason had "decisive influence" on his intentions.

Notice that the requirement that P do A is contingent on P's actually having the end E, and on A's actually being within P's power and actually being necessary for P to achieve E. But the proposition that P is required to do A is *explained* in terms of what P *would* intend, presumably in a circumstance in which P *believed* the action A to be both within his power and necessary for him to achieve E. It is controversial whether the base principle is analytic. But since Kant thinks that it is, he takes it to follow that standards of the appropriate form actually are imperatives, and actually do delineate requirements.

Categorical imperatives delineate requirements that are not conditional on any presupposed ends of the agent (Ak 415). Hence, their possibility must be explained in a different way. Kant's account is captured, at least in part, by the following "base property" and "base equivalence" for categorical imperatives (Ak 449):

(1) The rule that one is to do A in circumstances C is a (valid) categorical imperative just in case the rule has the following property: any person *would* (intend to) do A in C if he were fully rational and "affected" only by "purely rational incentives".

(2) If there is a categorical imperative that one is to do A in C, then P is required to do A in C just in the sense that, and in virtue of the fact that, any fully rational person would (intend to) do A in C if he were "affected" only by "purely rational incentives".

Kant is again attempting to explain the idea an agent is required to do something in terms of the intentions the agent *would* have, given the counter-factual hypothesis that reason has "decisive influence" on his willing. But here there is the additional counter-factual hypothesis that the agent is affected only by "purely rational incentives".

The ends that ground hypothetical imperatives are not restricted to ends that Kant would regard as "purely rational incentives" (Ak 449). For example, the desire that one's car continue to run is obviously not a fully rational incentive in Kant's sense—i.e. it is not a desire that any fully rational agent would have just in virtue of being rational (Ak 415-416). Hence, the imperative to change the oil in one's car, assuming one wants his car to continue to run, does not have the base property of categorical imperatives. To be sure, any agent with an appropriate desire would intend to change his car's oil regularly, provided he understood the need for doing so, and provided he were *otherwise* unaffected by incentives that are not purely rational, and provided reason *otherwise* had decisive influence on his willing. But categorical imperatives meet the more stringent condition that *any* fully rational person would intend to comply with them if she were affected *only* by purely rational incentives. (In the interest of brevity, I will in general delete the qualification about purely rational incentives).[12]

I said above that any non-skeptical moral theory must specify a *J* condition for moral standards. I can now say that, in Kant's theory, this condition has two parts. First, a standard must have a specific "purport" or content, in order to qualify as a moral standard. And second, standards with this purport delineate actual moral requirements just in case they have the base property for categorical imperatives.[13]

In the first two sections of the *Groundwork*, Kant claims to derive the *purport* of the Categorical Imperative from the ordinary and "universally accepted concept of morality" (Ak 445), together with the concept of a rational being (Ak 426). He thinks that the ordinary concept of morality implies that the moral law would be binding on every rational being as such (Ak 412, 440). His argument in these sections would establish the formulation of the Categorical Imperative, the "supreme principle of morality" (Ak 392), on the assumption that such an imperative is possible. Consider then one of Kant's formulations: "Act only according to that maxim whereby you can at the same time will that it should become a universal law" (Ak 421). Even if this is implicit in the concept of morality, the issue still remains whether it is a genuine requirement. A skeptic can agree with Kant that any moral imperative would be a categorical imperative, and even that the Categorical Imperative would be the supreme principle of morality if there were such a thing. Yet, prior to the argument of *Groundwork* III, the skeptic can reject the possibility of any such imperative, claiming that no one is in fact bound in any way except by his purposes.

Kant himself points this out, of course. He claims to have shown that "if duty is a concept which is to have significance and real legislative authority for our actions, then such duty can be expressed only in categorical imperatives", but he concedes at the end of *Groundwork* II that he has not yet shown "that there actually is an imperative of this kind, that there is a practical law which of itself commands absolutely and without any incentives" (Ak 425, also 431). He claims to have shown that anyone who "holds morality to be something real" must admit "the principle of autonomy" (Ak 445). He claims that this "can quite well be shown by mere analysis of the concepts of morality". But he concedes that one cannot show in this way that this principle "is an imperative, i.e., that the will of every rational being is necessarily bound [by it]" (Ak 440).

As I said, the possibility problem has three parts. First is to specify a J condition. For Kant, standards that correspond to actual moral requirements have both the required purport and the relevant base property. Second is to show that exactly the standards that meet the condition delineate actual moral requirements. Kant needs to show that all and only the standards that have both the required purport and the base property would actually delineate moral requirements. Kant unfortunately devotes no attention to defending the base property. Third is to show that some standards meet the J condition. Kant needs to argue that the standards that have the specified purport also have the base property and therefore, according to the theory, specify actual moral requirements. The argument of *Groundwork* III is devoted primarily to the third of these issues. It is meant to show that the Categorical Imperative has the base property and that it is therefore binding on every rational agent (Ak 446-448).

2. From Reason to Freedom to Morality

Kant's argument can be divided into two stages: In the first, Kant argues that every rational agent must be assumed to have free will, and in the second, he argues that every agent with free will is subject to the moral law. The second stage argument is actually given at the beginning of *Groundwork* III, but it will be easier to postpone discussing it until after I discuss the argument from rationality to freedom.

The argument turns on the idea that the concept of a rational agent is the concept of an agent with the ability to bring about his own actions by means of decisions that he makes for his own reasons. That is, first, a rational agent would have the capacity to reach a decision just as a result of reasoning, where the course of his reasoning is a result of his own thought, and where his reasoning brings about his decision. And, second, he would have the capacity to act on the basis of his decision, where the action he performs is caused by his decision. It follows that the conception of a rational agent is the conception of an agent with a kind of freedom. For if we imagine that a person's "actions" or "decisions" are fully determined by factors that have nothing to do with any reasons that the person has, then the person does not qualify as a *rational agent*. Even if the person is rational, in the sense that he has reasons for his "actions" and "decisions", if these reasons are *causally* irrelevant to his actions, then his rationality is irrelevant to his agency, and he is not a rational *agent*. Hence, if one thinks of anyone as a rational agent, then one must think of him as having the capacity to reason "freely" and to act "freely" on the basis of decisions based in such reasoning.

But are there any rational agents? Does anyone have this kind of freedom? Kant seems to say that a being "cannot act otherwise than under the idea of its own freedom" (Ak 448, note). The idea here appears to be that one cannot *act* unless one conceives of oneself as free. But why not? I think Kant's intuition must be that one who conceives of himself as an *agent* cannot avoid conceiving of himself as *rational*, and conceiving of himself as rational, he thereby conceives of himself as having the above kind of freedom.

A person of any degree of conceptual maturity and normal physical capacities can hardly avoid conceiving of himself as an *agent*. For this is just to conceive of oneself as capable of acting, as not being entirely passive. But an action is not merely a movement of the body. It is at least a movement of the body brought about by the agent for certain reasons. Hence, one who conceives of himself as an agent thereby conceives of himself as rational, in that he has the capacity to act for reasons. But this capacity involves the kind of freedom in question. For to conceive of oneself as having the capacity to act for reasons requires conceiving that one's actions and decisions are not fully determined by factors that have nothing to do with one's reasons. If this is correct, then anyone who conceives of himself as an agent must conceive of himself as "free".

One might worry that it is not sufficient for Kant to show that we must *conceive* of ourselves as rational agents, for if we are not *in fact* rational, then the argument does not show we are in fact free, even if it shows we must conceive of ourselves as free. Yet Kant claims it is enough to show that in acting we must conceive of ourselves as free, for this means that, "from a practical point of view", every rational agent is free (Ak 448-9). And if, as the second stage of the argument is supposed to show, the conception of a free agent is the conception of an agent subject to the moral law, then if we must think of ourselves as free, we must regard ourselves as subject to the moral law (Ak 448, note). If a person who views herself as an agent must see herself as rational, she is committed to regarding herself as bound by the moral law.

The second and more difficult stage of the argument is meant to show that "if freedom of the will is presupposed, morality...follows by merely analyzing the concept of freedom" (Ak 447). We begin by developing the concept of an agent with "negative freedom" (Ak 446): She would have the power to bring about her actions and choices "independent of any determination by alien causes", so that her actions would not be causally determined by anything other than the decisions that emerge from her reasoning. But an agent's power to bring about her actions is the power to *cause* her actions. And, Kant insists, causation is a relation between cause and effect that can be expressed in a law. Hence, the relation between the reasoning and actions of a free agent can be expressed in a law (Ak 446).

But this relation is not expressed in a law of "natural necessity". Laws of this kind, the causal laws of the natural world, express causal relations between natural events every one of which is the effect of some other natural event in a way that is covered by natural law (Ak 446, 453; *Critique*, Ak 95). But a free agent is able to bring about an action just as a result of a reasoned decision, without either her decision or her action being causally determined by anything else. It follows that neither her decision nor her reasoning is itself the effect of any other event in a way that is covered by natural law. It follows in turn that her decision and her reasoning are not related to the actions they bring about by any natural causal law. Her decision making is "contra-naturalistically free", as I shall say.

Yet, Kant holds, since the decision of a free agent causes her action, the relation between them can be expressed by *some* law. Moreover, this could not be a law whose content is fixed independently of and prior to the decision and the reasoning of the agent. For such a law would specify what the effect would be of any given process of reasoning or decision-making, and the effect would not then be due solely to her reasoning. Her freedom would be limited. Hence, the content of the law in question must be dependent in some way on her reasoning and decision. Kant infers that this law must be a law of the will itself, a "special kind" of law (Ak 446). "[T]he will is in every action a law to itself" (Ak 447). And since autonomy simply is "the property the will has of being a law to itself", freedom of the will entails autonomy of the will (Ak 447). That is, a free agent has the capacity to bring about actions in a way that is expressed by a law of the will itself, the content of which is dependent in some way on the nature of her reasons and decision. I will refer to an agent who is free in this sense as "morally free".[14] Kant would say she has "positive freedom" (Ak 446).

If the "maxim" on which a person acts captures the intentions or reasons with which she does what she does, then a law of the will would have to correspond to, or be dependent in some relevant sense on the maxim on which the agent acts.[15] At the same time the law would enter into the explanation of the agent's action by explaining why she performed it. It would be a general principle or universal proposition corresponding to her maxim.[16] But not every such proposition is a law. We have concluded that a free agent acts only on maxims that correspond to laws that are dependent on her reasoning, and Kant's account of the Categorical Imperative supplies an account of maxims that correspond to laws in such a way. For it says that a person is to act on a maxim only if, without contradiction, she could will it to "become a universal law". Kant concludes, then, that a free or autonomous agent is one whose maxim "corresponds" to a law in the sense that the universal proposition which corresponds to her maxim, and which could be cited in explaining her action, is one which the agent could will to become a law, without contradiction. Thus a morally free agent acts only on maxims that the agent could at the time of acting will to become universal laws. And, according to Kant's analysis of the concept of morality, "the principle of morality" just is the principle of "acting according to no other maxim than that which can at the same time" be willed "that it should become a universal law" (Ak 421, 447); "this is precisely the formula of the categorical imperative... . Thus, a free will and a will subject to moral laws are one and the same" (Ak 447).

Given the first stage of the argument, we can now conclude that a rational agent would be a free agent, and, given the second stage, that a free agent would act only on maxims that correspond to laws, in the sense that they pass the Categorical Imperative test. Hence, a rational agent, or at least one whose rationality is not "hindered" by the influence of "incentives that are not purely rational", would be moral.[17]

Our failures to act morally are due to the fact that we are "affected by sensibility, i.e., by incentives of a kind other than the purely rational". But an agent who is affected by such "hindrances" is nevertheless *required* to comply with the moral law in the sense that she *would* comply if she *were* rational without hindrances. And Kant argues that every rational agent would act morally—would comply with the Categorical Imperative—if reason controlled her behavior without hindrances (Ak 449). Hence, the Categorical Imperative has the base property and it therefore delineates an actual moral requirement.

3. Two Worlds, Two Standpoints

I have not yet taken into account Kant's idea that there are "two worlds". He says categorical imperatives are possible

> because the idea of freedom makes me a member of an intelligible world. Now if I were a member of only that world, all my actions *would* always accord with autonomy of the will. But since I intuit myself at the same time as a member of the world of sense, my actions *ought* so to accord. (Ak 454)

What does Kant mean by a "world"? He says, "The concept of an intelligible world is...only a point of view which reason sees itself compelled to take...in order to think of itself as practical" (Ak 458). So we can take the distinction to be between two points of view, or "standpoints" (Ak 455). But what role does the distinction play in Kant's argument?

Kant introduces the distinction in an attempt to avoid "a sort of circle" (Ak 450). He says,

> we assume that we are free so that we may think of ourselves as subject to moral laws... . And we then think of ourselves as subject to these laws because we have attributed to ourselves freedom of the will. Freedom and

> self-legislation of the will are both autonomy and are hence reciprocal concepts. Since they are reciprocal, one of them cannot be used to explain the other or to supply its ground... . (Ak 450)

It is not entirely clear what is going on here, but I think Kant invoked the distinction between the "two worlds" in an attempt to deal with the following problem.

Kant's conception of the will as "a kind of causality" (Ak 447), together with his view of natural events as existing in a nexus covered by causal law, leads to a dilemma. As we have seen, the stage one argument turns on the claim that anyone who conceives of herself as an agent must conceive of herself as "free". She must have the view that her reasoning and decisions are contra-naturalistically free. However, if her actions and their effects are natural events, they are subject to natural law. Suppose, for example, that my decision to throw a baseball results in my throwing the ball, and my throwing the ball causes a window to break. Now Kant holds that if my decision was contra-naturalistically free, then it was not caused by other events in accord with "natural law". It follows that its relation to its effects also is not covered by natural law. Hence, if my decision to throw was contra-naturalistically free, then, according to Kant, it follows that the relation between my decision and my throwing cannot be expressed by a "natural law". But our actions have effects, and the relation between an action and its effects must be explained by natural law. On Kant's view, since my throwing caused the window to break, it follows that my throwing was the effect of natural causes. It cannot then have been the effect of my decision to throw unless that decision caused my throwing and was itself brought about in accord with natural law. Hence, given that my throwing caused the window to break, there is the following dilemma: If my decision caused my throwing, it was not contra-naturalistically free; and if it was contra-naturalistically free, then it did not cause my throwing. More generally, if decisions are causes of natural events, they are not contra-naturalistically free. If they are contra-naturalistically free, they are not causes of natural events. Kant apparently must hold that a causally effective and free act of will is incapable of altering the natural world.[18]

Kant introduced the distinction between "appearances" and "things in themselves" in an effort to deal with this problem (Ak 451). The appearances constitute the "world of sense", and Kant acknowledges that insofar as a person views himself as part of the world of sense, he views his actions and decisions as subject to laws of nature (Ak 452). From this standpoint, he does not view himself as contra-naturalistically free. Yet Kant claims that there is another available standpoint, for a person can regard himself as rational and morally free. This then is Kant's reply to the dilemma: From one standpoint, our reasoning and decisions are or can be viewed as events that are causally effective in the natural world, but not as contra-naturalistically free.

But from the other standpoint, they are or can be viewed as a product of our reason, and when viewed in this way, they are viewed as contra-naturalistically free but not as causally effective (Ak 450, 453). Moreover, since it is our reason which distinguishes between appearances and things in themselves, and which perceives limits to its own activity, a person must regard his rational nature as what he is "in himself", and not merely as yet another appearance (Ak 452). In viewing myself as rational, I must view my rationality as my real nature, as I am in myself, and not as mere appearance. I must therefore view my reasoning and decision-making as contra-naturalistically free, for the laws of nature pertain to appearances, not to things as they are in themselves.

The intuition here is perhaps that since it is our reason that theorizes about our nature and our place in the world, and since we know this, we cannot view our reasoning as mere appearance. We must view our reasoning as taking place in reality; we must view our reasoning as a kind of fulcrum that we can use to assess the veridicality of the way things appear to us.[19] Moreover, while we are reasoning and deciding, we cannot view our thinking as determined causally by preceding events together with natural law. We must view our reasoning as contra-naturalistically free, for we have to think that the process of reasoning will determine its own result. But then, by the stage two argument, we must view ourselves as free in the sense that we would act only on maxims that would pass the Categorical Imperative test. This, however, is the way we must view matters while we are deliberating and reasoning. We can also view our reasoning and actions as part of the natural world, and this view enables us to explain both how morally improper behavior is possible and how our reasoning can cause our actions.

Unfortunately, on Kant's view, it remains that it is not possible for a decision, such as my decision to throw the baseball, to be both causally effective and contra-naturalistically free. Given Kant's assumptions, the propositions that the will is contra-naturalistically free and that the will is causally effective in the natural world appear to be inconsistent. Perhaps some would argue that these propositions are somehow rendered consistent by Kant's theory of two standpoints. But there is no point of view from which one can consistently affirm that, say, my decision to throw the ball is both causally effective and contra-naturalistically free. In order to solve the difficulty, it seems that we would have to introduce a third standpoint, a "philosophical" one, from which we could say that the will has "two aspects" that are not mutually incompatible, a causally effective aspect that is not free and a free aspect that is not causally effective. But this stratagem is not Kant's. His view is that the causally effective will is a mere appearance, which does not seem real from the other standpoint. Hence, I believe, Kant's introduction of the two standpoints does not permit him to escape the dilemma.

4. Why the Argument Fails

I see four additional problems with Kant's argument. First, the stage one argument does not succeed in attaching contra-naturalistic freedom to rationality. Second, because of this, the overall argument is invalid. Third, the argument is vitiated by an equivocation in the notion of law. And finally, Kant has offered no defense of his proposed base property of categorical imperatives.

First, Kant has not shown that an agent who views himself as rational must view himself as contra-naturalistically free. I agree that if a person regards himself as a rational or deliberative agent, he thinks of himself as acting for reasons. This means he regards himself as bringing about actions by means of his reasons. Moreover, he regards his decisions as the result of his own reasoning or deliberation. He regards himself as able to determine what he will take to be a sufficient reason to act in a given way. Perhaps all of this is included in the self-conception of someone who views himself as a rational agent. Beyond this, however, Kant seems to think that a person who views himself as rational cannot think that his decisions are causally determined by events distinct from his own deliberation, nor that the course of his deliberation is determined by events or processes other than his own reasoning, and still consistently think that he is a rational agent.

These additional claims are false. Many people accept the theory that actions are caused by events in ways that can be explained by ordinary empirical science, and that the events we conceptualize as instances of reasoning are in fact simply biological events in our brains which are causally determined by other such events. There does not seem to be anything incoherent in this theory, and Kant himself accepts it as one point of view we can correctly take of ourselves (Ak 450).

Perhaps, however, at the moment of action and choice, an agent who conceives of himself as rational must view himself differently, from the other standpoint, as willing freely (Ak 450). Yet I do not see that a person who views herself as rational must take this point of view. There is no inconsistency in deliberating while at the same time having in mind a naturalistic and deterministic theory of human reasoning. Nothing seems to prevent a person from being in the grip of the conviction that the upshot of his deliberation is determined by antecedent causes other than his own reasoning, and nothing seems to force him to lose this conviction while he deliberates about what to do. After all, if he has to decide what to do, he has no option but to consider what to do, even if he thinks that the course of his reasoning is already determined. To be sure, there is a limit to how much information we can have in the forefront of our minds at any one time, and the belief in a deterministic theory of reasoning is hardly relevant to most of our decisions, so we might not typically be thinking of it when we deliberate. If we were thinking of it, we might become despondent. Yet these psychological points hardly show that while we are deliberating we *must* conceive of our deliberation and acting as outside of a deterministic causal nexus. So it seems possible to conceive of oneself as a rational and deliberative agent even while regarding one's deliberation as causally determined. Viewing oneself as rational seems compatible with the theory of oneself as an organism with a natural history existing in a network of causally related events and processes.

Let us turn now to my second objection, which concerns the relation between the two stages of the argument. The upshot so far is that if the stage one argument can show that an agent who regards himself as rational must conceive of himself as free, the relevant sense of freedom is compatible with causal determinism. Yet the stage two argument requires an incompatibilist conception of freedom whereby "acts of will", such as decisions, are not causally determined by any other events according to natural law. Otherwise, there would not be room for Kant to argue that causally effective acts of will must be related to their effects in accord with laws of the will itself (Ak 446). As we saw, the stage two argument requires that a rational agent be contra-naturalistically free. Therefore, there seems to be a gap between the stage one and stage two arguments: The first stage shows at best that a rational agent conceives of himself as free in a sense compatible with determinism under natural law. The second stage requires contra-naturalistic freedom, which implies that decision making is not a natural process covered by natural law.

My third objection is that there is an equivocation in the notion of law. Kant needs ultimately to show that any free will is bound by the moral law. The argument is supposed to work by showing that the occurrence of actions or any other events that are caused by the decisions of a free will requires that the will be bound by the moral law, for these causal relations are not covered by natural law. At best, however, the argument shows that if the decisions of a free will cause any other events, then there are laws which are not ordinary causal laws, but which cover or describe the causal relations between the decisions and these other events. *Moral* laws *governing* the relations among states of the will, or between states of the will and actions, are or would be laws of a different sort, for they would express how states of the will *ought* to be related to one another and to actions, not how they are in fact causally related. Kant's premise was that the existence of causal relations implies that there are laws that cover or describe those relations as relations that have to be as they are by causal "necessity". It does not follow that there are laws that describe how those relations ought to be by moral "necessity". Kant's argument depends on an assimilation of causal necessity, by which a causally effective free will would be related to its effects, with the moral necessities or requirements that he hopes to show a free will is bound to respect.

There are additional puzzles about causation and laws. First, when a rational and deliberative agent acts *immorally*, her maxim, to do *A* if *B*, does not correspond to a law in the relevant sense. For Kant would say that she could not will without contradiction that it become a law that everyone do *A* if *B*. So if Kant is going to allow that a rational agent can freely choose to act immorally, then he cannot rely on there being a law corresponding to the agent's maxim, in the sense that the maxim passes the Categorical Imperative test, in every case of freely chosen action. Moreover, even if on a given occasion an agent *could* will without contradiction that the universal proposition corresponding to her maxim should become a law, it does not follow that that proposition is an explanatory or causal law. This does not follow even if the proposition states the principle on which she acts, so that her accepting it can help us explain her choice. But if it *were* a causal law that everyone does *A* if *B*, then, one would think, given that *B* is the case, her doing *A* would be causally determined, in accord with this law.

The upshot is not what Kant desires. It is his own thesis that causation is a relation covered by laws according to which the cause "entails" its effect (Ak 446). It follows from this thesis that if a will can bring about changes in the natural world or it itself, then states of the will entail their effects in ways that can be expressed in causal laws. Kant argues that these are not natural laws, that they are laws of "a special kind" (Ak 446). But Kant speaks of relations of causal necessitation between states of the will as "no better than the freedom of a turnspit" (*Critique*, Ak 97). So it appears he must give up either the idea that a free will can be causally efficacious, or the idea that causation is a relation by which a cause "necessitates" its effect. The main thing, however, is that there is no reason here to think that a causally efficacious contra-naturalistically free will would be bound by *moral* law.

Finally is the problem of the base property. Kant's argument depends on the idea that a moral standard delineates an actual moral requirement just in case any person would comply with it if he were fully rational and affected only by purely rational incentives. It is unfortunate that Kant does not offer any explicit defense of this idea. But the text suggests an argument based on the idea that, as a person is "in herself", she is a contra-naturalistically free and fully rational self who belongs to the "intelligible world". Hence, if *any* fully rational person would comply with a given moral standard, then I can conclude that *I* would comply with it, or that my "real self" would comply with it. It does not follow, however, that I am *required* to comply with it. The fact that my "real self" would comply does not entail that *I* am required to comply, *as I am in fact*.

Moreover, Kant does not have a satisfactory argument to show that my real self is *fully* rational and affected *only* by purely rational incentives. He seems to argue that since it is our reason that distinguishes between appearances and things as they are in themselves, a person must regard his rational nature as what he is in himself (Ak 452). But the most that follows is that a person must regard his reason as part of his nature. It does not follow that I must regard the incentives I have that are not purely rational as not actually possessed by my "true self".

The key point is that Kant is able to show neither that possession of the base property is sufficient, nor that it is necessary, for a moral standard to delineate an actual moral requirement. For all that Kant has shown, it could be that there is some other property, one quite different from Kant's base property, the possession of which by a moral standard would mean that the standard delineates an actual requirement.

In summary, then, the first stage of Kant's argument gives us no reason to believe that rational deliberative agents are contra-naturalistically free, or must regard themselves as such. And the second stage does not show that a rational agent who was contra-naturalistically free would be bound by the moral law. It seems, then, that a person can regard herself as rational and as free in the sense that her deliberation can itself lead to action, but she need not regard herself as having contra-naturalistic freedom, and she need not regard herself as bound by moral law.

5. Two Reconstructions of the Argument

It is widely recognized that there are enormous problems with the argument, but many philosophers have been convinced nevertheless that Kant was correct to think that morality is an expression of freedom and rationality. In this section, I shall briefly explore two perceptive reconstructions of the argument, each of which attempts to put it on a more secure footing by strengthening its premises.

Henry Allison's reconstruction depends on two key assumptions.[20] First, an agent who views herself as rational views her choices as justified. And second, the rational agents in question are, or at least view themselves as, "transcendentally" free; in my terminology, they view themselves as both contra-naturalistically and morally free.[21] I take this to mean that the agents in question are not only contra-naturalistically free, but they have the capacity to act and adopt maxims on the basis of reasons, and to do so in accord with a law of the will itself (Ak 447). In effect, this second assumption gives to Kant the conclusion, which he reaches in the second stage of the argument, that a contra-naturalistically free agent would bring about her decisions and actions by means of a "special kind" of law (Ak 446). A stronger assumption would give away too much.

A maxim can always be formulated that expresses the intentions or reasons with which an agent acts when she acts intentionally, and a rational agent acts on maxims.[22] It will help to work with an example. Suppose that I threw the baseball intending to break my neighbor's window because I wanted revenge for his having interfered with my vandalizing a car. I acted on the maxim to revenge myself for an annoyance by causing trivial damage to the person who annoyed me. Given Allison's first assumption, if an agent views herself as rational, she must think that she has reasons that justify her *adopting* her maxim, as well as having reasons that justify her *acting* on it. But if she views herself as contra-naturalistically and morally free, she must think that she could have selected and acted on a maxim that would have frustrated her desires and her nature. The implication of this for the example, Allison would say, is that I cannot view my justification for adopting my maxim as resting in the mere presence of my desire for revenge, nor even in the idea that it is human nature to seek revenge, for viewing myself as free means viewing myself as free to choose in a way that frustrates my desires and nature. Allison therefore concludes that any sufficient justification possessed by a rational and free agent for "selection of a maxim can never be located in an impulse, instinct, or anything 'natural'", such as her empirical nature or any of her desires or purposes.[23]

An "unconditional practical law" would be a law that is "valid" for all rational agents independently of any ends or desires they may have. An imperative expressing the requirement to comply with such a law would be a categorical imperative.[24] Allison now claims that one is justified in adopting a maxim only if it conforms to an unconditional practical law. For an agent is justified in adopting a maxim only if the maxim is permissible. And since the maxims at issue are "the desire- or interest-based maxims of transcendentally free rational agents", such as my maxim to seek revenge, their permissibility "cannot be construed as a function of desires or interests, even the most fundamental ones." Their permissibility must be a function of conformity to a "rule or set of rules governing the pursuit of any end at all, including desire- or interest-based ends." Given this, Allison concludes, "it is apparent" that this rule or set of rules must "apply to all transcendentally free rational agents...regardless of what desires or interests they may happen to have." Hence, this rule or these rules must be unconditional practical laws.[25]

There are fatal problems with this argument. We may agree that an agent who views herself as rational must view her actions as justified and must also view her adoption of the maxim on which she acts as justified. And if she views herself as contra-naturalistically and morally free, she must hold that she could have done what she did even if she had had different desires and purposes. But it does not follow that her justification for adopting her maxim cannot "be located in" her empirical nature or in any of her desires or purposes. To see this, consider my example. Suppose I claim it is not contrary to reason for me to adopt the maxim about revenge, because adopting and acting on it enables me to regain self-respect in a situation where someone is annoying me.[26] That is, I claim that my desire for self-respect justifies my adopting the maxim to seek revenge. In this sense, I say, the maxim's "permissibility" is "a function of" my desire for self-respect.

Now, if Allison's argument is correct, I cannot in this situation consistently view myself as rational and morally free. Yet I do view myself as acting for the reasons given by my maxim, and as adopting the maxim for the reason that doing so will contribute to my self-respect. Since I view myself as free, I hold that I could have chosen to frustrate my desire for self-respect, but since I view myself as rational, I hold that I *would* have chosen to frustrate my desire only if I had had sufficient reason to do so. Perhaps it will be said that I am following a higher-order maxim to pursue self-respect (and nothing incompatible with self-respect). But I claim that my choice to adopt this higher-order maxim was justified by my desire for self-respect, and further that my choice to adopt it was in conformity with that very maxim. Allison would claim that the permissibility of my maxims must be a function of their conformity to a set of rules governing the pursuit of any end at all. I reply that this adds nothing. For my higher-order maxim about self-respect is a rule governing the pursuit of any end at all, including the end of self-respect. Allison would claim that this rule must "apply" to all rational and morally free agents "regardless of what desires or interests they may happen to have." But I can deny this, if it means that any such agent would be acting contrary to reason if he failed to comply with my rule about self-respect. Nothing in the argument shows that in this imaginary situation I must view the pursuit of self-respect as required by reason. I simply view it as permitted by reason. In short, Allison has not shown that if I am morally free, I will aim to act only on maxims that conform to a rule that any agent must comply with at the price of irrationality.

Allison would claim that if my choices are "ultimately governed by" something that is a "fundamental drive or natural impulse", such as a desire for self-respect, I am not "transcendentally" free. For my choices are "limited to the determination of the best means for the attainment of some end implanted by nature."[27] Yet suppose that I am seeking self-respect as a "final end", not as a means to anything else, and suppose this is my reason for adopting the higher-order maxim about self-respect. I may be unable in principle to give any deeper reason than one that cites my desire for self-respect. The fact that I am normatively "governed" by the desire for self-respect in this way does not mean that I am causally "governed" by it in a sense that would undermine my moral freedom, or my *capacity* to choose any maxim in accord with a law of the will itself. My moral freedom can perhaps be understood as a capacity to govern myself normatively. But the fact that I have chosen to govern myself *by a desire* does not mean I have not *chosen* to govern myself.[28]

Allison's argument would at best leave us a long way from any moral requirements. Perhaps it is true that a free agent cannot provide a final or ultimate justification for adopting and acting on a maxim by citing any of his desires or objectives, and perhaps it is also true that as a rational agent he must ultimately justify every choice. Then it may be that the criterion of justification for his maxims would have to be a principle that would be valid for every agent regardless of his desires. There remains a gap, however, between "conformity to practical law" in this sense, and conformity to "the moral law as Kant defines it." Allison attempts to bridge the gap with the following argument. He says, "for a transcendentally free agent, conformity to a practical law must provide the reason to adopt a maxim", and "an inclination or interest is never in itself a sufficient reason for a transcendentally free agent." He continues, "to say that conformity to universal law must be the reason for adopting a maxim is just to say that its mere legislative form must provide the reason...; and this is precisely what the categorical imperative requires."[29]

Consider, however, the rule to adopt a maxim only if (or if and only if) adopting it can be justified relative to one's desires. Nothing in Allison's line of reasoning entails that this could not be the "practical law", conformity to which provides the justification for a transcendentally free agent to adopt a maxim. Allison does claim that an interest is never sufficient reason for a free agent to adopt a maxim, but I have just argued, using the example of self-respect, that he has not established this key claim. Moreover, an agent who regulated his maxims by assuring their conformity to the above rule would not view a desire as providing a sufficient justification, for he would view conformity to the rule as an important part of any justification of his adopting a maxim. In short, Allison's argument does not show that the "mere legislative form" of a maxim must be the reason for adopting it.

Thomas Hill Jr.'s reconstruction of the argument turns on distinguishing causal explanations from explanations in terms of reasons. He says that the actions of a rational agent are properly to be explained by reference to the "principles, laws, or reasons on which the person acted", not by reference to empirical causal laws.[30] When a rational agent performs an action for certain reasons, she is committed to an underlying principle according to which reasons of this sort justify actions of this sort, and she is committed to regarding the principle as rationally acceptable. If she is also free, then her "acceptance of such principles cannot be causally determined".[31] Now, a hypothetical imperative would be a principle "indicating a means" to satisfy a desire, and Kant regards our desires as alien to reason.[32] Hence, if an agent were committed only to principles that are hypothetical imperatives, then all of her reasons would be fixed by her desires, and given that she is rational, her reasons would fix her choices; this means she would not be free, for it means her desires would fix her choices. That is, as Hill says, a free agent can have "sufficient determinate reasons to act" independently of her desires.[33] So a rational and free agent must be committed to some principles that are not hypothetical imperatives.

Moreover, a rational agent must see herself as free when deliberating and acting, for she must see her decision and her principles as not fixed by her desires and her beliefs about how to satisfy them. Given the above argument, this means a rational agent must accept that she is committed to some principles that are not hypothetical imperatives.[34] Hill suggests that a rational agent must accept this "undeniable formal principle": "Act in such a way that you conform to laws, or rational principles of conduct, you...accept independently of desire".[35]

I am not persuaded by this argument. Even if we grant that a rational agent must see her decisions as not causally fixed by her desires and her beliefs about how to satisfy them, it does not follow that she cannot hold that the *rationality* of her decisions is a function of her desires and her beliefs about how to satisfy them. Perhaps, too, a rational agent must view the fact that she accepts certain principles of rational choice as something that is not causally determined by her desires. But it does not follow that a rational agent could not accept as her sole guiding principle an injunction, say, to maximize the satisfaction of her desires. For if it is possible to decide freely to accept a principle of rationality, it seems possible to decide freely to accept this one. To be sure, if a fully rational agent accepts this principle and complies with it, she will do what she believes will maximize the satisfaction of her desires. Her actions and decisions will be predictable on the basis of her desires and beliefs. Yet it does not follow that her actions and decisions are causally determined by her desires, for her acceptance of the criterion may not itself have been causally determined by her desires.

Most important is that the argument does not show that a rational agent is committed to any moral principle. As Hill himself asserts, Kant's argument requires an "illegitimate" transition from the above "formal principle" to a dubious "substantive supreme moral principle".[36]

Allison and Hill have suggested ways of deepening and extending our understanding of Kant's argument. Yet, as Hill acknowledges, the most their reconstructions accomplish is to show that Kant's argument is "more coherent and plausible than it may at first appear".[37] We are left with the conclusion that Kant's attempt to show the possibility of a categorical imperative is unsuccessful.

6. Kant's Legacy

Kant's fundamental thesis is that morality is binding on all rational agents and that compliance with morality is a requirement of reason. This thesis is intended as part of the explanation of the possibility of a categorical imperative. The sense in which one is *required* to comply with morality is that one *would* do so if one were fully rational. This thesis is not entirely intuitive, of course, for there is a temptation to think that immoral behavior might be rational in certain circumstances. Therefore, it would be implausible simply to claim it is *analytic* that immorality is irrational, and this claim would beg the question against the skeptic about the rationality of compliance with morality.

A Kantian strategy does not aim to *prove* that immorality is irrational but rather to show the conceptual penalty for denying it. Allison says that Kant has shown "the price of moral skepticism" to be "the rejection of transcendental freedom".[38] Kant describes his own argument in similar terms. He admits that he has not proven that we are actually free, yet he claims to have shown that "we must presuppose [freedom] if we want to think of a being as rational and as endowed with consciousness of its causality as regards its actions". His idea is that there is a price to be paid for denying that morality is binding on all rational agents; *viz.*, the inability to conceive of ourselves as rational agents in a sense which would imply that we are capable of performing actions for reasons that are fully our own, or of which we are the "author" (Ak 448). If I am correct, however, Kant failed to show that we must pay this price. A successful Kantian strategy would have to show that the price of skepticism about the existence and rationality of moral requirements is too steep for any sensible theoretician to pay. Of course, I cannot prove the impossibility of a successful Kantian argument, but I am not aware of one that is successful.[39]

Any non-skeptical moral philosophy faces the problem of explaining the nature of the authority which is possessed by actual moral requirements, as distinguished from merely putative ones. Kant's failure to explain the possibility of a categorical imperative was his failure to solve this fundamental problem. Yet I believe we must solve it in one way or another if we wish to develop an adequate non-skeptical moral philosophy.[40]

Notes

1. The phrase, "the possibility of a categorical imperative" appears in Section III of the *Groundwork*, on p. 447 of the Prussian Academy edition (Ak 447, also see Ak 417-19). All references in this paper to the *Groundwork* are to Immanuel Kant, *Grounding for the Metaphysics of Morals*, translated by James W. Ellington (Indianapolis, Indiana: Hackett, 1981; original publication, 1785). I use the page numbers of the standard Prussian Academy edition, which is in *Kants gesammelte Schriften* (Berlin: Konigliche Preussische Akademie der Wissenschaften, 1911), volume IV. Page numbers from this edition appear as marginal numbers in the Ellington translation. I will place them in parentheses in the text. Unless otherwise noted, page references in the form, Ak nnn, found in parentheses in the text, are to the *Groundwork*.

2. At the end of Section II, Kant speaks of the need to show how "a synthetic practical a priori proposition is possible" (Ak 444). Earlier in the *Groundwork*, he spoke about showing that duty is not "a vain delusion and a chimerical concept" (Ak

402), and that morality is not "a mere phantom of human imagination" (Ak 407).

3. However, Kant does seem to see his project differently in the *Critique of Practical Reason*. He views his argument there as *based* in the assumption that "pure practical laws" have "reality", and as offering no "deduction" or "justification" of them (*Critique*, Ak 46). In fact, he says in the *Critique* that the moral law itself *needs* "no justifying grounds" (Ak 47). My goal in this paper is to understand Kant's argument in the *Groundwork*. All references in this paper to the *Critique* are to Immanuel Kant, *Critique of Practical Reason*, translated by Lewis White Beck (Indianapolis, Indiana: Library of Liberal Arts, Bobbs-Merrill Company, 1956; original publication 1788). Page numbers given represent the pagination, provided in the Beck translation, of the standard Prussian Academy edition, *Kants gesammelte Schriften* (Berlin: Konigliche Preussische Akademie der Wissenschaften, 1911), volume V.

4. To be sure, a dispute about usury might be partly concerned with the precise terms of the prohibition. I am assuming that there is agreement as to which rule is at issue and disagreement only about the status of the rule. It is worth mentioning that the terms of such a rule could be as specific as one likes. John McDowell has argued against the idea that "an adult moral outlook" is "codifiable" in rules, in "Virtue and Reason", *Monist*, 62 (1979), pp. 331-350, at p. 336. But his arguments seem directed against the idea that a moral outlook must be codifiable in "universal principles" that contain within themselves all the information needed to apply them without error. See pp. 337-342. Nothing in what I shall say turns on the idea that the standards at issue are of this nature. For example, one standard is a rule to the effect that money is not to be lent for interest in circumstances like *this*, where one could not understand the rule without having an appreciation of the details of the specific situation picked out by the demonstrative pronoun.

5. See my "Moral Skepticism", *Philosophical Studies*, 62 (1991), pp. 203-233, at p. 216.

6. See my "Normativity and the Very Idea of Moral Epistemology", *Southern Journal of Philosophy*, Volume 29, 1990 Spindel Conference Supplement (1990), pp. 189-210.

7. Thomas E. Hill, Jr. has an excellent discussion of this in his "The Hypothetical Imperative", *Philosophical Review*, 82 (1973), pp. 429-50. My account differs from Hill's in some minor respects.

8. Hypothetical imperatives are conditional, but they need not be expressed by conditional sentences. The context can make it clear that the agent is assumed to have some purpose that is appropriately related to the action in question. For example, the imperative that one ought to change the oil regularly in one's car, assuming that one wants the car to continue running well, could be expressed in most contexts by the sentence, "One ought to change the oil regularly in one's car."

9. Hill, "The Hypothetical Imperative", p. 436.

10. Thomas E. Hill, Jr., "Kant's Theory of Practical Reason", *The Monist*, 72 (1989), pp. 363-383, at p. 368.

11. His remark is actually that no special discussion is required to explain how an "imperative of skill" is possible. Imperatives of skill are hypothetical imperatives in which the relevant purpose is well enough defined that it can be strictly true that a required action is necessary if the purpose is to be achieved (Ak 415-417). Kant contrasts them with "imperatives of prudence", which recommend actions as means to one's happiness. But since the concept of happiness is "indeterminate", in Kant's view, no (or few) actions can be said to be definitely necessary for happiness, and so "imperatives of prudence, strictly speaking, cannot command

at all, i.e., present actions objectively as practically necessary" (Ak 418). Yet, he says, "if the means to happiness could with certainty be assigned", the same story could be told about imperatives of prudence as can be told about imperatives of skill (Ak 419).

12. According to my account, if there is a desire D that is a fully rational incentive, and if doing A in C is necessary to satisfying D, then the rule to do A in C qualifies as a categorical imperative. For example, Kant says that "rational nature" is necessarily an end for every fully rational agent (Ak 428-9). This presumably means that the desire to treat "rational nature" as an end is "fully rational". Actions that are necessary to treating rationality as an end are required, and a rule that requires such an action is a categorical imperative. Unfortunately, the rule to do A in C if one has D might seem to qualify as a hypothetical imperative, according to the base property I specified, even if D is a fully rational incentive. I am not sure that this is a problem, but I could add to the base property the qualification that a rule is a hypothetical imperative only if the assumed end E is not a "fully rational incentive". Mark Timmons helped me here.

13. Kant distinguishes between "purport" and "possibility" at Ak 420.

14. Henry E. Allison speaks of "transcendental freedom" in this connection. I use the term "moral freedom" partly because it sometimes seems to me that Allison builds more into his account of transcendental freedom than I want to build into the condition that I call moral freedom. See Henry E. Allison, *Kant's Theory of Freedom* (Cambridge: Cambridge University Press, 1990), pp. 202, 204, 207-10.

15. Kant introduces the notion of a maxim in the *Groundwork* as a "subjective principle of volition" (Ak 400). Henry Allison suggests that a maxim is "roughly equivalent to an intention" so that if an agent intends to do A if B, he has a maxim "To do A if B", and vice versa. See Henry E. Allison, "Morality and Freedom: Kant's Reciprocity Thesis", *Philosophical Review*, 95 (1986), pp. 393-425, at pp. 402-403.

16. If her maxim is "To do A if B", then the corresponding universal proposition is "Everyone does A if B".

17. In the *Critique*, Kant argues in reverse, from morality to freedom, and so he holds a kind of equivalence between freedom of the will and a will subject to morality. He claims, in the *Critique*, that "the moral principle itself serves as a principle of the deduction of...the faculty of freedom" (*Critique*, Ak 47). Hence, if one assumes freedom of the rational will, as in the *Groundwork*, then Kant thinks it can be shown that the will is bound by the moral law, and if one assumes that the rational will is bound by the moral law, as in the *Critique*, then he thinks it can be shown that the will is free. This is Kant's "reciprocity thesis" (*Groundwork*, Ak 450). There is an excellent discussion of this thesis in Allison, "Morality and Freedom: Kant's Reciprocity Thesis".

18. This is not a contradiction. Perhaps a decision can be causally effective in some other realm or way than by altering the natural world. (1) Perhaps a free act of will can be conceived to alter the *will*. But if a free will is able only to affect its own states, then the duties of a free will may be limited to duties regarding its own states. We may be led to a morality of states of the will. This reasoning may explain why the Kantian Categorical Imperative, at least in the universal law formulation, is a principle that governs states of the will; it states a condition to be met by any maxim one acts on. (2) Kant tries to explain, in the *Critique*, how a free will could be effective in causing events in the natural world. His position seems to be that my free will can be conceived as causing at once the entire empirical sequence of my actions and the character of my life and person, so that even if my throwing the baseball was causally determined by past events, I still could have refrained in the sense that I could have brought about a different

empirical life by an originating and free act of will (*Critique*, Ak 97-98). This is a fantasy we should be happy to reject.

19. Onora O'Neill suggests that the second analogy in the first *Critique* has shown that agency is "the presupposition of causal judgment". If we conceive of ourselves as "confronting a natural world that is causally determined, and so resists our control", we cannot "think of ourselves merely as members of the sensible world." I claim, however, that it does not follow that we must think of ourselves as morally free, nor even as contra-naturalistically free. See O'Neill, *Constructions of Reason: Explorations of Kant's Practical Philosophy* (Cambridge: Cambridge University Press, 1989), p. 63.

20. Henry E. Allison, "Morality and Freedom: Kant's Reciprocity Thesis". See also Henry E. Allison, *Kant's Theory of Freedom*. The argument of "Morality and Freedom" appears in Chapter 11 of the book. In the following, I will use the abbreviated titles "Morality and Freedom" and *Kant's Theory*.

21. Allison, "Morality and Freedom", p. 413; *Kant's Theory*, pp. 207-8.

22. Allison, "Morality and Freedom", pp. 400-404; *Kant's Theory*, Chapter 5 and Chapter 11, p. 204.

23. Allison, "Morality and Freedom", p. 414; *Kant's Theory*, pp. 207-8. Strictly speaking, Allison is entitled to conclude at best that an agent who *views* herself as rational and free must *think* that she has sufficient justification for her actions and that her justification does not rest in any of her desires or purposes. However, Kant says that agents that must view themselves *as* free *are* free, "from a practical point of view" (Ak 448). For the important thing is whether an agent views herself as subject to morality, and so it will be enough if an agent who views herself as free must view herself as subject to morality. We can therefore carry on the argument as if the agents we were discussing are rational and free, even though, strictly speaking, we should speak only of their viewing themselves as rational and free. If a rational and free agent would be subject to morality, then an agent who views herself as such is committed to viewing herself as subject to morality.

24. Allison, "Morality and Freedom", p. 399; *Kant's Theory*, p. 203.

25. Allison, "Morality and Freedom", pp. 416-17; *Kant's Theory*, pp. 208-210.

26. There are less perverse examples. For instance, I might adopt the maxim of speaking my mind forthrightly, and claim that my adopting the maxim is justified by my desire for self-respect. The argument would go through, *mutatis mutandis*. I use the example of seeking revenge partly because we would not ordinarily think that self-respect is a good reason for seeking *revenge*, especially not revenge for someone's having interfered with one's vandalizing a car. I think Allison's argument ought to be able to show that this is not a good reason.

27. Allison, *Kant's Theory*, p. 207.

28. Allison cites Ak 440 in this connection and adds some details to the argument in his "On a Presumed Gap in the Derivation of the Categorical Imperative", forthcoming in *Philosophical Topics*. But I believe that the additional detail does not help the argument. Remember that Kant needs to *show* that a will that is a law to itself would be autonomous in that it would comply with the categorical imperative. He cannot make this a matter of definition without opening gaps in other places in the argument of *Groundwork* III.

29. Allison, *Kant's Theory*, pp. 212-13.

30. Thomas E. Hill, Jr., "Kant's Argument for the Rationality of Moral Conduct", *Pacific Philosophical Quarterly*, 66 (1985), pp. 3-23, at pp. 8-9.

31. Hill, *ibid*, p. 12.

32. Hill, *ibid*, pp. 11, 10.

33. Hill, *ibid*, p. 15.
34. Hill, *ibid*, p. 17.
35. Hill, *ibid*, p. 19.
36. Hill, *ibid*, pp. 19-20.
37. Hill, *ibid*, p. 18.
38. Allison, "Morality and Freedom", p. 423; see *Kant's Theory*, p. 213.
39. There are contemporary Kantian arguments, among which I would include the arguments of Thomas Nagel, in *The Possibility of Altruism* (Oxford: Oxford University Press, 1970), and Alan Gewirth, in *Reason and Morality* (Chicago: University of Chicago Press, 1978). Discussion of these arguments is beyond the scope of this paper.
40. I am indebted to Henry E. Allison, Thomas E. Hill Jr., Richard Kraut, Andrews Reath, and Mark Timmons for helpful comments and suggestions about earlier versions of this work. I am grateful to the following institutions for their support: the Social Sciences and Humanities Research Council of Canada, for a Research Grant and Research Time Stipend (410-82-0640), which I held during 1983 and 1984 when I began work on this paper; the Campus Research Board of the University of Illinois at Chicago, for granting me a Short Research Leave during 1985; Simon Fraser University for allowing me to take leaves of absence; and finally, the Research Triangle Foundation and the National Humanities Center, North Carolina, for granting me a fellowship during 1988-89 that enabled me to complete the major part of my work on this paper.

Philosophical Perspectives, 6, Ethics, 1992

A KANTIAN PERSPECTIVE ON MORAL RULES

Thomas E. Hill, Jr.
University of North Carolina, Chapel Hill

Both Kantian and utilitarian theories are in need of further development, and in fact even their strongest advocates now tend to see the theories more as projects in progress than as finished products with every detail engraved in stone. My main concern in this paper is to develop some ideas within the Kantian tradition, without worrying about whether the views presented are orthodox or radically revisionary. More specifically, I sketch some features of a Kantian perspective for reflection on moral rules, contrast this with some other views, and briefly call attention to some problems and strategies for addressing them.

My discussion is meant to be suggestive rather than argumentative, for too many details need to be filled in before one can draw more than tentative conclusions about these matters. Such abstract and incomplete reflections are no substitute, of course, for more narrowly focused attention to theoretical and practical issues. But sometimes it is useful to step back from more detailed issues to ask what large projects in moral philosophy seem most worth developing. Since, as most proponents agree, current versions of both Kantian and rule-utilitarian theories need to be further refined, revised, and supplemented, one cannot decide between these approaches by first seeing exactly what they prescribe for particular cases and then comparing these outcomes with intuitive judgments. In this situation, other sorts of comparison become more important. We should consider, for example, *the sort of moral reflection* each theory recommends, independently of how (or whether) the theories may in the end lead to different judgments about specific cases. My concern here will be with a Kantian normative theory considered at this more abstract level. One should not suppose, however, that at this level moral judgment is unnecessary and we can evaluate competing theories by purely theoretical criteria, such as simplicity, comprehensiveness, and formal elegance. We have relevant moral convictions not only about what it is right to do but also about how we should decide what is right to do.

What are called "ethical theories" are sets of ideas designed for various purposes, arising in different contexts, often addressing distinct problems. The perspective to be sketched here is not a comprehensive moral theory; nor is it an answer to the "metaethical" issues that have recently returned to center stage in moral philosophy. Rather, what I call "the Kantian perspective" is meant to be considered as a way of framing and guiding the moral reflection of conscientious agents when they are deliberating about certain practical questions. The usual candidates for this role are other "normative ethical theories", as often presented in ethics text-books: for example, act-utilitarianism, rule-utilitarianism, Rossian pluralism, Rawlsian contractualism (as sometimes adapted for ethics), and Kant's "universal law" and "ends in themselves" formulas of the Categorical Imperative. With many variations and a few alternatives, these normative theories are often offered as candidates for acceptance to students presumed to be conscientious and morally sensitive about many familiar local matters but not yet reflective and articulate about how to assess unfamiliar and troublesome cases. The context of discussion, typically, is not a metaphysical debate about the reality of moral properties, a chaplain's sermon to cynical or sociopathic criminals, or the project of a Cartesian moral philosopher who, doubting all his previous moral opinions, now seeks to build an entire moral system from sparse but indubitable premises. Theories are considered not as self-evident truths or even theorems to be proved but as possible frameworks to use in shaping one's moral reflections, and they are offered not as having morally neutral credentials but as ideas themselves subject to moral evaluation.

My remarks here presuppose a similar context. More specifically, I want to consider how certain aspects of Kant's ethics, or some reasonable adaptation of them, might serve us if we were sincerely trying as reasonable, conscientious persons, to resolve some practical questions about how to conceive, specify, and apply certain moral rules and principles.[1] For these purposes an ethical theory is no use to us unless it can guide our decisions or help to structure our dialogue; and, even if choice-guiding, the theory will carry no authority for us unless it coheres with our basic outlook as reasonable, conscientious moral agents.

One further caveat. Though discussion here will focus on moral rules, we should acknowledge that rules are not applicable to all aspects of moral living. Even in situations that fall under moral rules, it is not always necessary, best, or even appropriate for an agent to be thinking primarily of rules. Also though rules have a place in moral reflection, they generate problems that must be faced. For example, any system of rules raises worries about conflicts, gaps, alternative interpretations, and hard cases. Too often familiar moral generalizations ignore relevant differences among particular cases or are defended from a perspective alien to our outlook in daily life.

Assuming, then, the context of discussion as I have described it, my aim and plan is as follows. The main object is to sketch the elements and outlines of a way of thinking about moral rules that is drawn from one of Kant's less influential formulations of the Categorical Imperative, namely, the principle that one ought always to conform to the laws of a possible kingdom of ends. As liberally reconstructed here, this principle combines central ideas from Kant's other formulas. The principle calls for a way of thinking analogous in structure to John Rawls's theory of justice, but the differences are important. Like rule-utilitarianism, the Kantian principle distinguishes moral reflection about rules from moral judgment on particular cases, and both theories require us to think about what would happen if various rules were generally adopted. But despite these similarities, the Kantian perspective on rules is fundamentally different from rule-utilitarian perspectives.

More specifically, in the *first* section I indicate how the elements, or construction materials, of the kingdom of ends are drawn from Kant's more familiar ideas of a good will and the previous formulas of the categorical imperative. No simple formula, I think, can meet the unreasonable demand for a precise and morally adequate decision procedure; and, as is well known, there are special difficulties in trying to use Kant's famous formulas of universal law and ends in themselves as comprehensive and decisive tests to determine in particular cases what one ought to do. Nonetheless, as Kant suggests, these formulas, along with the ideas of a good will and the formula of autonomy, provide the basic ideas from which a further idealized model of moral legislation can be built, and it may be that the ideas stand better together than they do alone.

Then, in the *second* section, I outline an ideal of moral legislation that results when these preliminary ideas are put together in a certain conception of the kingdom of ends. The ideal, both in Kant's work and as briefly sketched here, is obviously underdefined in important ways and needs to be refined and supplemented if it is to be of any practical use. But even in its somewhat indeterminate form the kingdom of ends, construed as an perspective for moral legislation, contrasts significantly with Rawls's idea of the original position, rule-utilitarianism, and Kant's other formulas of the Categorical Imperative.

In the final section I discuss briefly some problems raised when we try to use the idealized Kantian perspective as a heuristic for thinking about real world issues.

I. Elements of the Kantian Legislative Perspective

The Kantian idea to be considered here is a reconstruction and modification of Kant's idea of a "Reich der Zwecke", or "kingdom of ends."[2] It has obvious affinities with ideas of John Rawls and others, but my focus will be on its roots in Kant's ethics. Kant presents the ideal of a "kingdom of ends" as in some way a combination of the ideas expressed in other formulations of the Categorical Imperative. It expresses a "complete determination" of maxims, he says, in a way that helps to bring the abstract universal law formula "nearer to intuition" and so better able to "secure acceptance."[3] In the *Groundwork* Kant does not give examples to illustrate the application of his kingdom of ends principle, and he even suggests that for guiding moral judgment the "universal law" formula is better.[4] In Kant's later ethical writings the principle is largely passed over in favor of the more famous first two formulas. Thus in a scrupulously balanced interpretative account of Kant's ethics, the kingdom of ends principle would not play the central role that it will have in this discussion. Nevertheless, the idea is worth considering in its own right. Moreover, as Kant suggests, it brings together many of his other ideas, and these stand better united than they do alone.

In this section I want to review some basic features of a moral attitude that would, I think, be endorsed not only by Kant but also by most contemporary philosophers who count their theories as Kantian. Kant himself goes beyond these minimal points in various ways, but my aim here is to draw from these ideas, not to give an exact representation of Kant's position. The idea is to draw out some central elements of a moral attitude from Kant's discussion of a good will, the idea of duty, and three formulas of the Categorical Imperative (universal law, humanity as an end in itself, and autonomy). These are the building blocks for a reconstruction of the idea that we "legislate" moral rules in a kingdom of ends.

(A) Like other forms of the Categorical Imperative, the kingdom of ends principle is supposed to express basic commitments of reasonable conscientious persons, that is, ourselves so far as we have "good wills." One of these commitments is implicit in Kant's initial idea that a good will is *good unconditionally* and *above all else*.[5] We begin with a thought experiment. Among the many things we find worth seeking and preserving, which do we count as good in all possible contexts, that is, as things that we cannot, on deep reflection, justify (to ourselves and others) sacrificing for anything else? Many things, such as money, fame, and power, we would find it reasonable to sacrifice under some imaginable circumstances. If the legendary Satan offered you continual "happiness" in return for your basic commitment to live as a reasonable moral person, even then, Kant thought, you could not really justify the choice to yourself, though you might in fact be tempted to accept the bargain. Reasonable moral agents, in Kant's view, are deeply committed to trying to live as they should, not just "as a rule" but always. Though of course not wanting to sacrifice other goods, they acknowledge that they should forego any desired goods if the price were to be abandoning or violating their commitment to do what, in their best judgment, they find morally obligatory.

This leaves open, of course, the content of what each will judge to be morally required. It is misguided, or at least premature, to object that acknowledging the supreme value of a good will might require one to sacrifice even one's family for the impartial good of all; for the Kantian idea as construed here is formal and modest. That is, it says, "Do what you must to maintain your good will", which is to follow your best judgment as to what, all considered, is morally and rationally required in the situation. If, as is likely, you judge the sacrifice of your family to be morally wrong, then you are committed to avoiding it, no matter what public or "impartial" goods may thereby be lost.

The commitment to the overriding value of a good will, for Kantians, is not matter of pursuing any general end of the kinds philosophers have typically urged, such as personal happiness, self-realization, or the general welfare. Nor is it a commitment to the rules of external authorities, such as God, state, or community. Abstractly, it is a will to "conform to universal law as such."[6] One conceives of something as a "universal law", in Kant's sense, if one sees it as a principle of conduct for everyone that is "practically necessary", a principle the violation of which one could not justify to oneself or others. In sum, as reasonable conscientious agents we are deeply committed to conforming to *whatever general principles* our reflections as such agents prescribe. The presumption at this point is that there will be principles of this sort; but that has yet to be seen.

(B) Kant reaches a similar point from a different angle by analyzing the idea of duty.[7] To acknowledge that one has moral duties, as any conscientious person does, is to accept that there is at least one general principle of conduct that is a "categorical imperative", that is, a rational moral requirement for everyone not based or conditional on its serving one's contingent personal ends (and not merely saying "take the means to your ends"). The only principle that could, strictly, fit this description, Kant says, is (once again) "Conform to universal law as such."[8] Thus, again, what we know of all reasonable, conscientious agents is that they are deeply and overridingly committed to constraining and guiding their conduct by whatever principles for everyone they find, in appropriate reflection, supported by compelling reasons. The sort of reasoning in which we are to find the content of moral principles cannot be exclusively self-interested or instrumental reasoning, for that would yield not duties but only prudential and conditional requirements. These conceptual points are, of course, no proof that there are moral duties; they are only preliminary clues as to how to look for them.

(C) Kant's first effort to give more content to the abstract idea of "conforming to universal law" was to simply identify this requirement with his famous first formula of the Categorical Imperative and then to give examples to illustrate how that formula could guide moral judgment. Kant makes the crucial move twice,[9] but critics find it baffling and even sympathetic interpreters can see a gap in the argument. If we assume for now my loose and informal reconstruction of Kant's thought up to the crucial step, the problem is this. Even though it is a commitment of conscientious agents, "conform to universal law" is only a very minimal requirement, telling one very little about how to go about moral deliberation. Kant and his followers, however, find quite substantive procedures for moral judgment in the universal law formula: one ought never to act except in such a way that one can also will that one's maxim should become a universal law.[10] Interpretations of this vary, but on any account one must identify a maxim for proposed actions, try to "conceive" that very maxim *as* a universal law in some sense, and (if successful) determine whether one "can will" that universal law along with one's initial maxim. There are many ways of construing these several steps; but, whatever the way, if it yields substantive guidance in particular cases without borrowing from independent moral principles, it seems clearly to have gone beyond the minimal requirement "conform to universal law", understood in the thin sense that makes the latter initially plausible.

Whether or not the universal law formula really follows from "conform to universal law" in the initial sense, its content is meant to express something fundamental about a moral attitude. However one construes the details, it is supposed to be concerned with willingness to reciprocate, to avoid being a free-rider, and to checking one's personal policies by reflecting about what would be reasonable from a broader perspective. This much seems rather uncontroversial as a partial characterization of the attitude of a conscientious person. The problems begin, however, when one tries to work out the details behind the hope (which Kant encouraged) that this simple formula, by itself, could serve as a direct test for determining right and wrong in particular cases. A massive literature has developed over many years as Kant's sympathizers have constructed ingenious devices to make the formula work as an action guide and Kant's critics have invented new counter-examples to undermine their attempts.[11]

It is not to my purpose to review or take sides in this debate, but it is worth noting one persistent problem and one constructive suggestion that have emerged from the controversy. The problem stems from the notorious difficulty of specifying the maxim of an action. The difficulty is not that we cannot easily or certainly tell what maxim a person has acted on in the past; for in Kant's theory the primary task is deliberating about prospective conduct and, surprisingly, assessment of the moral worth of past acts is of little importance for that task.[12] The problem is that it difficult to find any way of characterizing the proper description of the maxim to be tested without relying upon one's antecedent sense of how the test should come out. But if that is so, we do not really have any sort of litmus test of the rightness or wrongness of particular acts; for our independent judgments regarding the latter are guiding our selection of inputs for the alleged test. The formula might still be acceptable as a framework within which to conceptualize the results of one's moral judgments, but not by itself as a guide to such judgments.

Admittedly some conditions on the description of maxims are implicit in Kant's theory, both in what he says about them and in the role they are supposed to play. For example, it is clear that my maxim cannot include features of a prospective act that I am not aware of in deliberation. For example, if Mary has no idea that her accepting a job will result in John's losing his, then her maxim could not include reference to that fact. Also most details that are not salient for an agent seem not to belong in an honest statement of the agent's maxim. For example, if I am thinking of repeating a rumor, then it is unlikely to be relevant that the victim is 49 years old, dark-haired, left-handed, and English-speaking. It is tempting to say that factors unimportant to the agent should be excluded from the description of that agent's maxim, but this would raise problems. Suppose, for example, that I know that my repeating a rumor will severely damage another person, but I am indifferent to this fact. Testing a maxim that makes no reference to the damage seems likely to give a morally wrong result; and, quite apart from this, it seems bizarre to suppose that I could assess my proposed act morally without reference to the pertinent fact that I would be knowingly harming another person.

Much has been, and more can be, said about what is relevant in constructing the maxim, but it seems that ultimately conditions of relevance must be guided by independent moral judgment. In fact one finds again and again that both sides in debates about Kant's formula tend to pick the maxim description that yields the results they want, relying on their prior sense of the morally appropriate conclusion in the case. For them, at least, the formula is not working as a test.

Struggling with another problem in applying the universal law formula leads to a more constructive suggestion. The problem is raised by the familiar example of a fanatic, who is willing to accept everyone's living by maxims that most of us find morally repugnant. A fanatical Nazi, for example, might be willing to accept everyone's persecuting those who have, or whose immediate ancestors have, certain physical characteristics.[13] That is, we are to imagine that he would accept this even if he knew that he himself were to fit the description. (Imagine that if someone were to convince him, with real or forged papers, that he falls into the hated class, he would accept persecution and even ask to be destroyed.) Now there are various ways to approach the case, but one suggestion is this. What counts is not what the fanatic personally, with all his prejudices and idiosyncrasies, would be willing to accept for all to do. The relevant question is, "what can he *rationally* will (or will *as a rational agent*)?" This seems to call for reflection from a broader perspective, where "reasons" are not exclusively person-relative. In effect, maxims that one *can will qua rational* can be construed as simply those that one can personally adopt without conflict with whatever "universal laws" one is committed to as a reasonable, conscientious agent.

The suggestion makes the universal law formula more similar to the abstract requirement from which it was supposed to follow, namely, "conform to universal law as such." Moreover, as will be evident, construing the formula this way points towards the sort of reflection that characterizes legislators in the kingdom of ends.[14] By requiring agents to assess their "maxims", the formula at least expresses the idea that moral deliberation requires one to evaluate not only the expected consequences of one's act but also, under other descriptions, what one sees oneself as doing, one's aims, and underlying policies and reasons. The formula represents the conscientious person as one who evaluates his or her own acts and policies, not merely in terms of their effectiveness towards desired goals, but as implicitly taking a stand on what others may reasonably do. But this is not to suggest, of course, that the universal law formula can function by itself as a moral litmus test, for no results emerge until we add some other basic ideas to supplement the formula and we do some substantive thinking as reasonable, conscientious agents with relevant empirical information.

(D) Further elements of a Kantian conception of a basic moral attitude are suggested by the idea of humanity as an end in itself.[15] Familiar in general but controversial in detail, this expresses the thought that human beings have dignity, not mere price. Independently of talents, accomplishments, and social status, each person is to be regarded as having a special worth that conscientious agents must always take into account. This value is not derived from one's being useful or pleasing to others, and it takes precedence over values that are contingent in those ways. More controversially, dignity is not value that can be quantified but is "without equivalent."[16] One cannot, for example, justify disregarding or violating the dignity of a few persons with the thought that thereby one would promote more dignity in many other persons. One acknowledges the dignity of other rational agents by constraining one's pursuit of one's own ends, restricting oneself solely to means-ends activity that those affected by one's action could, in appropriate reflection, agree with. The ground of dignity, on Kant's view, is a person's rational and moral capacities, but to respect a person's dignity one must take into account appropriately the whole person. We must pay attention to the reasonable claims and conscientious opinions of others and give special weight to what preserves, promotes, and honors each person's capacity to live as a reasonable conscientious agent. Since they are *human* beings, the only rational persons we must deal with have a full array of natural human needs as well as personal loves and individual projects. One cannot treat them with dignity without giving due regard to their quite reasonable concern for these matters as well.

These ideas about human dignity add some substance to a Kantian conception of a basic moral attitude, but they do not encourage one to treat Kant's formula of humanity as an end in itself as a self-contained, definitive moral guide to be used on a case by case basis. The formula expresses in a general way an important conception of a moral attitude, but this does not translate immediately into simple action principles. The basic attitude leaves many unresolved questions for further dialogue and reflection. Any resolution, it seems, will require further moral judgment, and universal agreement is not guaranteed. While it is clear that one must not trade or sacrifice the dignity of anyone for "more dignity" for others, this leaves it distressingly open how to decide notorious hard cases where it seems one cannot fully respect the dignity of all. What exactly one must do (and avoid) to respect dignity remains a matter of judgment, as does the question how much and in what ways one must promote other's ends. Others must be *able to agree* with one's choice of ends and means, as I said, "in appropriate reflection;" but what sort of reflection is appropriate needs to be further specified.

(E) Kant's formula of autonomy provides further material for characterizing a Kantian conception of a basic moral attitude.[17] The formula tells us that conscientious agents view every rational agent as, in a sense, legislating moral laws. The most general moral principles that characterize a basic moral attitude express, not divine, natural, or conventional requirements, but rather our "wills" as conscientious reasonable agents, what we find upon deep reflection to be pervasive and overriding commitments.[18] Less general moral rules, regarding lies, promises, mutual aid, and so on, are to be seen ideally as joint products of all moral agents deliberating with due regard to both necessary and contingent values of each person. As in theological conceptions of morality, moral rules are legislated by (or expressive of) the will of an authority; but, as in Rousseau's ideal political society, the authority is not external but a "general will" that includes, crucially, each person's own acknowledged commitments.

We are supposed to think of moral agents as having *autonomy* of the will and so as legislating, in some sense, independently of inclinations and contingent desires. This invokes a quasi-theological idea of the law maker as standing, God-like, outside the world, devoid of both personal feelings and natural human preferences, and then declaring what is rational for human beings in utter disregard for their natural needs and individual concerns. Scholars disagree about whether Kant was in fact captivated by this sort of picture, but one can draw out some main points about the role of autonomy in moral judgment without invoking any metaphysical images of a quasi-noumenal world.[19]

At a minimum, when we deliberate morally we cannot count the fact that we are inclined to do something, or even that it will promote our happiness, as in itself a sufficient reason for choice. Similarly, one cannot determine what is reasonable to choose by relying uncritically on authorities, precedents, social demands, ties of friendship, or claims about natural human tendencies. All of these may figure in one's reasoning at some stage, but one should not assume prior to critical reflection that they give decisive reasons for choosing. The autonomy of moral agents, however, means more than these negative points.[20] More positively, agents with autonomy acknowledge reasons of another kind that may conflict with and override their personal desires. They presuppose that they can recognize, and in appropriate reflection would accept, such reasons as justifying. Though they feel "bound" by them, they do not regard the obligation as externally imposed because they deeply identify themselves as persons committed to acknowledging the force of such considerations.

Further, the ideal of deliberating with autonomy would mean trying, so far as one's can, to identify one's preferences, hopes, and fears so that one can consider reflectively whether or not they are good reasons to act. Empirical states, as Kant acknowledged, must figure in the psychological explanation of what we do; but this does not mean that all judgment is blind or that every desire is a prima facie good reason for action. The ideal of autonomy prescribes trying to assess relevant facts and arguments squarely and nonevasively, taking into account ways in which judgments can be skewed by our impulsivity, wishful thinking, and preference for what is close and familiar. Since, if honest, we realize how poorly we approximate the ideal by ourselves, it should encourage us to submit our opinions and values to the challenge of others with divergent viewpoints.

The formula of autonomy, like the previous ones, raises many questions and obviously cannot function as a self-standing moral decision procedure. It proposes a way of conceiving of moral deliberation and its conclusions, but it is not an abstract rule-generator that can replace factual inquiries, hard thinking, and moral dialogue. Moral deliberation, so conceived, cannot ultimately rest with appeals to authority, the untested voice of individual conscience, or even universal (if uncritical) moral conviction. A sober, nonevasive, and comprehensive awareness of the relevant empirical realities of the world in which one lives is what any rational person seeks as the ideal *background* for particular judgments, but values and moral imperatives cannot simply be *inferred* from such facts.

The ideal of moral agents as jointly legislating moral laws, I suggested, urges us to curb our moral self-complacency by consulting others, listening to divergent views, and submitting our own convictions to criticism. But, unfortunately, we see ample evidence that, even among reasonable conscientious people, real moral discussion often fails to produce the convergence of judgment that Kant expected among ideally rational legislators with autonomy. This is one reason, among others, that the principle that we should regard each person as a rational autonomous legislator of moral laws cannot serve by itself as a determinate decision guide. The idea behind the principle, however, can still help to frame morally appropriate attitudes. In practice, we should not only deliberate appropriately but also seek dialogue with other reasonable moral agents, especially those whose lives we will most affect. When disagreements persist, we must often judge and decide how to act anyway; for to suspend judgment and remain passive is itself to take a moral stand. Then, having taken into account the reasoning of others and admitting our fallibility, as conscientious persons we must still act on our own best judgment. In this nonideal (but typical) situation, we can perhaps still partially express the ideal of acknowledging others as moral legislators by restricting our conduct to what we ourselves can sincerely endorse *as justifiable to other moral deliberators*, even though we lack assurance of their agreement.[21]

II. The Kingdom of Ends as a Legislative Perspective

The Kantian themes of the last section can be combined in a conception of an ideal point of view for deliberation about moral rules. The conception is admittedly abstract, incomplete, and problematic. It has obvious structural similarities with Rawls's theory of justice, and this is no accident[22] though the dissimilarities are also important. The key points can be summarized briefly, for my purpose here is only to show how the legislative ideal is a natural extension of the ideas sketched in the last section and to distinguish it from some views with which it might be confused.

The main idea is that one must always conform to the moral laws that would be legislated by oneself and others in a kingdom of ends. This principle itself is supposed to be a basic moral requirement that indicates how to think about more specific moral rules, for example, about deception, promises, mutual aid, imposing risks, killing and letting die. Since the legislators in the kingdom of ends are meant to represent abstractly basic features of a reasonable attitude regarding moral rules, the idea is that one *should* accept the norms that *would* be adopted by legislators in the kingdom. The judgments of the ideal legislators are expected to converge because they are conceived as having the same basic moral attitudes and as being uninfluenced by the many factors that commonly distort ordinary moral judgment. Assuming this ideal convergence of judgment, reasonable conscientious persons could see the resulting moral rules as, in a sense, self-imposed, that is, not merely demands from others but as reasonable applications of their own deep commitments.

The defining elements of the legislative perspective are drawn from the ideas sketched in the last section.[23] The members are *rational* in a robust sense, implying more than instrumental rationality. They will not make rules unless they judge that there is good reason to do so, and they are concerned with reasons that anyone falling under the rules could acknowledge. They have *autonomy* of the will, and as rational and autonomous legislators they will *universal laws*. They recognize one another as *ends in themselves*, with dignity above price. Accordingly, they place a high value on preserving, developing, exercising, and respecting the rational and moral capacities of persons, and they unconditionally attribute a worth to persons that cannot be quantified and is not subject to trade-offs. Acknowledging that each valued member has personal ends of his or her own, they give weight to whatever enhances members' abilities and opportunities to pursue those ends successfully within the bounds of the moral rules they adopt.

In addition to these stipulations, Kant describes the legislators in his kingdom of ends as "abstracting from personal differences."[24] This condition reflects that idea that the appropriate attitude for deliberating about moral rules requires a kind of impartiality, a willingness to set aside irrelevant differences between oneself and others for whom the rules are intended. Any useful interpretation of the ideal, however, would need to specify this morally appropriate sense of impartiality. There are familiar problems with interpreting it as a "veil of ignorance" as extensive as that which characterizes Rawls's "original position", and even more serious problems with treating it as abstraction from everything empirical, leaving members to reflect about only what is essential to rational agency.

Requiring decisions to be made in ignorance of certain facts is a useful thought experiment or psychological device that can help decision makers to discount irrelevant personal preferences and minimize other distorting influences on judgment. It serves this function, for example, both in Rawls's theory and in the practice of sequestering juries. But in many common contexts the "impartiality" that is called for is not selective blindness to facts but rather being guided effectively by given standards, without being distracted by irrelevancies, when one has to judge or decide about cases understood in full detail. If one can make oneself judge by specified standards rather than by irrelevant concerns, then the better one understands the situation in question the wiser one's decision should be.

This suggests a way of interpreting "abstracting from personal differences" that may be more useful, at least if the conception of a kingdom of ends is to serve for any practical action-guiding purpose. The idea would be not to exclude empirical information about the context for which legislators are to make rules but only to insist that their decisions about rules be guided so far as possible by specified moral procedures, values, and criteria of relevance instead of by special preferences and attachments they have as individuals that are morally irrelevant to the matter at hand. To be realistic, however, we cannot expect that all standards of moral relevance are already implicit in the abstract model, and so we must rely to some extent on our independent judgments about what is morally relevant in the context at hand. But a Kantian perspective is clearly incompatible with at least these two extreme ideas about moral relevance: *first*, the idea that a rule's being especially beneficial to a particular individual (e.g. oneself) rather than to others is a relevant reason in itself for a legislator to favor the rule, and, *second*, that all that counts is maximizing the satisfaction of preferences, no matter whose preferences or how they are to be satisfied.

For the kingdom of ends to be of practical use, many details would need to be supplied and some troublesome questions addressed. But already we can note some contrasts between the Kantian legislative ideal as sketched here and some more frequently discussed approaches to moral deliberation.

First, consider the contrast between the kingdom of ends principle and the universal law formulation of the Categorical Imperative. Many of the problems with using the latter as a moral guide stem from the fact that, on the usual readings, it requires us to settle on a particular description that we can identify as *the maxim* of a proposed action. The kingdom of ends formula, like rule-utilitarianism, asks us instead to work out a system of moral rules, which can then serve as a standard as we review our proposed action considered in detail, under many descriptions, without having to select a privileged description as expressing "the maxim." Furthermore, the universal law formula tells us to test particular acts by considering them in a possible world different from ours in one way (and whatever else that entails), namely, that everyone adopts our proposed maxim. But the kingdom of ends principle asks us to assess acts by considering them in a more radically and system-atically changed world, that is, the world as we think it would be under an ideal system of moral rules. In shifting to the second perspective, we can acknowledge that different sets of interrelated rules shape forms of life in such a way that particular rules and acts typically cannot be assessed in isolation from their normative context. The universal law formula asks us to consider what *particular maxims* we *can will* as universal law, and the kingdom of ends principle invites us directly to consider what *general rules* we *would will* as universal laws. And the sense of "willing as universal law" is not quite the same.

Second, the formula of humanity as an end in itself is also commonly taken to be a specific action guide that one can apply case by case without raising questions about the network of rules and social relations within which the initial problem arises. This approach leads too easily to conflicts of duty and simplistic moral judgments. What is needed to respect the dignity of one person often seems contrary to the dignity of another. To avoid moral paralysis it is necessary to try to adjudicate such problems at a higher level of deliberation, reflecting on what general rules and policies best reflect the dignity of all. Though some problems may unresolvable, by incorporating the value of human dignity into the broader legislative perspective of the kingdom of ends we introduce constructive ways of thinking about the troublesome cases.[25] Rather than trying to determine in isolation whether Mary is now treating John as an end, we can try to work out what general moral rules would we reasonably urge for adoption if we had, constraining and shaping our other concerns, an overriding commitment to human dignity. Hard cases would still need to be addressed, but rather than considering them individually we would think about what broad policies are relevant and how, if at all, we can specify legitimate exceptions.

Third, the main idea here is obviously similar to Rawls's abstract model for reflecting on the principles of justice, but one should not overlook important dissimilarities. For example, Rawls' original position was designed for the specific purpose of resolving controversies about the principles of justice governing the basic structure of society, and the defining features of that deliberative position were selected for their suitability for this particular aim.[26] Another difference is that, though the original position is supposed to "represent" some basic moral values, its members do not presuppose or make any moral judgments. They do not, for example, rely on their sense of what is morally relevant, and they select principles from prudent self-interest rather than judgment as to what is just. The Kantian legislators are not mutually disinterested. They are overridingly committed to human dignity, which implies not only that they are constrained in their choice of means but also that they value to some extent the personal ends of each. Further, the Kantian legislators are not exclusively focused on the distribution of the "primary goods" that Rawls considers most crucial when the focus is the justice of the basic economic and political institutions. The goods inherent in the idea of dignity, or humanity as an end in itself, are overriding for Kantian legislators; and, in addition to considering these, anyone trying to use the ideal as a heuristic guide would presumably have to rely on their best judgments regarding other human needs and values as well as more contextual factors.

Fourth, the Kantian legislative perspective needs also to be distinguished from rule-utilitarianism.[27] Both propose ways of thinking about what moral rules there should be and how they should be specified. But from the rule-utilitarian perspective the aim of deliberators is exclusively to find the set of rules that, if generally adopted by the appropriate community, would maximize utility. Utility can be defined, of course, in different ways, for example, as happiness, satisfaction of actual preferences, or fulfillment of a purified set of informed and considered preferences. But the point is always to find the rules that produce the most utility, without prior constraint regarding its distribution or the means of achieving it. Kantian legislators, by contrast, are trying to find rules they can reasonably endorse and justify to one another under the severe constraint of their overriding commitment to the dignity of each person.

By hypothesis, Kantian legislators respect each other as persons with ends of their own and they are not indifferent to what enhances the ability of individuals to realize their ends. But the legislators should not be conceived as having the unlimited project and authority to determine, over all matters, which ends are to be promoted and how. Although their jurisdiction is wide-ranging and their sovereignty is complete within its scope, their legislative agenda is limited. The commitments presupposed in taking up the Kantian legislative perspective, as suggested earlier, are to ideas such as the priority of conscientious judgment, acceptance of constraints on self-interest, some form of reciprocity, respect for human dignity, autonomy as an ideal of deliberation, recognition of the autonomy of others, and abstracting from morally irrelevant concerns when deliberating about rules. These commitments are substantial, but they do not, even in theory, propose for legislators an overarching goal of maximizing some given value. Importantly, they do not imply that the law makers have unlimited authority, or any rational basis, to make whatever rules they prefer or think best as they try, God-like, to empathize completely with the wishes of everyone. In taking up the Kantian legislative position one does not magically become so empathetic, nor does one commit oneself to obeying the rules of those who do. One does not, as it were, agree to join others in placing all one's preferences into an anonymous pool so that impartial rule-makers, more empathetic and less morally constrained than we, can decide what rules will satisfy the most preferences in the pool. Though they must be prepared to accept the constraints of the rules that, as Kantian legislators, they make, they are not committed to legislate from a point of view that places all their life-plans on the agenda for decision by legislators concerned only to maximize global happiness, preference satisfaction, or even realization of ends.

III. Problems of Bringing the Kingdom Down to Earth

Comparisons of the kingdom of ends principle with rule-utilitarianism and Rawls on justice lead naturally to conjectures about how the Kantian perspective might look if developed more fully as a theoretical model that philosophers might use in trying to derive and justify a set of moral rules. But, as I said initially, my concern here has been with a more modest inquiry, namely, to see how the Kantian principle might serve as a heuristic guide for reasonable conscientious agents who are trying to resolve some practical questions, especially concerning how to conceive, specify, and interpret moral rules. Kant presented his idea of a kingdom of ends, not as a guide to moral judgment, but as a part of a highly abstract discussion of the most basic issues in moral theory. The problem, then, is to see whether the abstract ideal can have a practical use. To deal adequately with this problem would be a large project, and here, in my final remarks, I will only mention some of the obstacles it faces and hint at strategies for meeting them.

First, since the kingdom, as construed here, is a perspective for deliberating about rules, its use requires us to make judgments about what sorts of issues are appropriately placed under moral rules. When we think there is, or ought to be, a moral rule regarding some conduct, we are presumably considering standards that are meant to be publicly acknowledged, represented in moral education, appealed to in moral criticism, as well as used as action-guides by individual agents. As rule-utilitarians have noted, there are costs as well as advantages in having conduct governed by moral rules. And advocating rules tends to make less sense the less likely one is to find agreement, within the relevant group, on how to handle the issue in question. With regard to many moral decisions, reasonable people can get along well enough without public agreement on rules, by relying instead on the individual judgments of people who internalize some basic moral attitudes. But on other matters, for example, recurrent questions of life and death, it seems essential to work towards a widely accepted common framework for decisions. Also we must keep in mind that there are rules of many kinds, defined and enforced in different ways. All this may seem obvious, but the practical point is that Kantian legislators, like rule-utilitarians, must face prior questions about what issues call for treatment by rules and then about what types of rules are appropriate. Kant makes suggestions about these matters in his *Metaphysics of Morals*,[28] but that is only a beginning.

Second, the kingdom of ends ideal, like any rule-generating procedure, must face the possibility that, in practice, it will produce moral dilemmas, gaps, and disagreements. Given the central role of dignity, one naturally suspects that reflection from the Kantian perspective will result in commitment to rules absolutely forbidding each of two types of conduct, even though we may face situations where to avoid one is to do the other. Given how limited and imprecisely specified the commitments of Kantian legislators are, it seems obvious that some questions about moral rules will not be determinately resolvable. And finally, given the above together with inevitable human ignorance, fallibility of judgment, and impurity of heart, even the most sincere and conscientious deliberators are likely to disagree about some significant issues.

How, for practical purposes, should those sympathetic to the Kantian perspective take these problems? First, as Alan Donagan has noted, strict moral dilemmas are conceptually impossible in a Kantian moral theory, as presumably they are in any rationalist ethics.[29] That is, treating duties as absolute practical commands, the theory cannot concede that persons have all-considered duties that they strictly cannot meet. Thus, if it seems a duty forbids A and forbids B but we cannot avoid doing one or the other, then we must go back and rethink the issue, including if necessary the reasoning that led us initially to think that refraining from A and refraining from B were strict duties in all circumstances.

For practical Kantians, then, *apparent* dilemmas pose tasks for further moral thinking rather than a reason to abandon the framework or simply to marvel at the tragic absurdity of life. A similar attitude seems advisable about both moral gaps and disagreements. The heuristic ideal, perhaps, is definitive resolution and rational agreement on every significant issue, but the practical imperative is only to seek it and to be honest in admitting that we rarely have it. Rule-utilitarianism, we might note, usually contains stipulations that make it less likely *in theory* to generate dilemmas, gaps, and disagreements, but theoretical neatness, of course, is no guarantee of actual agreement on determinate solutions in practice.

Third, the kingdom of ends principle, unless qualified, is in danger of encouraging *utopian* thinking. That is, unless we are wary, it may lead us to draw unreasonable inferences about how we should act in our very imperfect world from our thought experiments about ideal agents in a more perfect world. If, for example, we imagine that in the kingdom of ends all citizens conscientiously obey the laws, then we will ignore the problems stemming from the fact that there is no such strict compliance in our world. Questions regarding punishment and incentives will not even arise. There is a further problem even if Kantian legislators can agree which rules are best for situations where partial compliance is all that they can expect. Our actual moral community may be deeply committed to a quite different set of rules that are not ideal but yet not bad; and in this situation, though recommending reform may be admirable, simply to follow blindly the more perfect rules, ignoring the actual forms of social life, may be morally inappropriate, and even disastrous. A rule-utilitarian theory that advocated following the "ideal code" for a community would, of course, face a similar problem.

A practical Kantian strategy for thinking about such problems would have to concede at once that there is no unqualified imperative to follow those rules that we would legislate under the unrealistic assumptions that these rules will in fact constitute the moral code of our community and that everyone will automatically follow the rules. Perhaps thinking what such rules would be is useful, but it must be followed by reflecting on the differences between that world and ours. We could try to decide on rules with the basic attitudes of Kantian legislators but under the more realistic assumption of partial compliance, that is, assuming that most, but not all, can be convinced to obey the rules. This might suggest constructive criticisms and reforms of actual practices. But, as long as even these more realistic reform rules diverge from the actual moral code of one's community, it is a matter for further moral judgment whether, in any given case, one should follow the reform rules we would endorse or instead adjust to the demands of the actual situation. Kantian deliberative attitudes may help here, but it is unlikely that for such decisions further rules will be of any use.

Fourth, a final problem that should be mentioned is the currently influential objection that any two-level theory that calls for impartial thinking, like rule-utilitarianism and our Kantian perspective, alienates the living agent from what allegedly gives authority to moral rules.[30] On these theories, it is charged, "we" are expected to live by prescriptions that "they" would make, when "they" and "we" have importantly different moral outlooks. This is an important line of objection, though hard to make clear. It asks each of us to consider seriously whether the higher order perspective recommended for determining moral rules is really one that, in honest and deep reflection, we can acknowledge as authoritative for us. Perhaps the answer is not the same for all, and, if so, it is hard to imagine the proof that it should be. I suspect, however, that the Kantian perspective on rules is in important respects more likely to meet the concern than is rule-utilitarianism.

In other words, my conjecture is that when duly qualified and adapted for practical use, the Kantian principle in significant ways comes closer than rule-utilitarianism does to reflecting a deep and widely shared moral sense of *how* we should try to conceive, specify, and apply moral rules. Many of the standards of the Kantian perspective seem to be already implicit in the questions we raise in a practical context. Other constraints built into the Kantian perspective reflect a common moral conviction that certain values, such as basic human dignity and autonomy, are morally prior to any moral imperative to satisfy more preferences.

Also despite its current reputation to the contrary, the Kantian perspective, I suspect, more nearly expresses what readers of this volume normally take for granted and would be reluctant to abandon, namely, that we are not required to place every aspect of our personal lives and relationships with others on an agenda to be authoritatively reviewed, endorsed, or possibly squelched by impartial legislators whose primary attitude is to maximize utility. If my conjecture is right about what most of "us" think, then even if it happens that rule-utilitarian legislators would make just the rules that we would, their attitude towards rules may be so foreign to ours that the fact that they would legislate a rule carries no evident moral authority with us. Seeing rules as prescribed from an alien perspective would not help us to see why *we* count them important, that is, why it makes sense for us as conscientious agents to accept that we must constrain *ourselves* by them.

Notes

1. Throughout this paper I will repeatedly use the expression "reasonable and conscientious" to convey an ordinary, indefinite idea of sensible, well-intentioned people trying to decide well and act as they morally ought. This is the audience, at least in their best moments, that Kant thought he was addressing. The word "rational" has acquired too many technical associations among philosophers to serve the same purpose. Also I should note that, though I mostly write of "rules" rather than "rules and principles" in this paper, the longer phrase might serve as well or better. I mean to facilitate eventual comparison about publicly affirmed general moral norms with rule-utilitarian thinking about the same, and for this

purpose the term "rule" is apt. However, in Kant's philosophy the sort of norms in question are the intermediate "principles" in *The Metaphysics of Morals*, not the Categorical Imperative itself, not specific local norms, and not merely personal "principles" of individuals.

2. My discussion of the Kantian perspective here is draws from and continues my discussions in the following essays: "The Kingdom of Ends", "Making Exceptions Without Abandoning the Principle: or How a Kantian Might Think About Terrorism", and "Kantian Constructivism in Ethics", in *Dignity and Practical Reason in Kant's Moral Theory* (Ithaca: Cornell University Press, 1992).

3. See Immanuel Kant, *Groundwork of the Metaphysic of Morals* (hereafter abbreviated simply as G), trans. H.J. Paton (New York: Harper & Row, Publishers, 1964), pp. 100-107 [433-440], especially p. 104 [437]. Numbers in brackets refer to the Prussian Academy edition.

4. G 104 [437].

5. See G 61-64 [393-396].

6. See G 70 [402].

7. See G 82-88 [414-421].

8. G 88 [420].

9. G 70 [402] and 88 [420-21].

10. See G 70 [402], 88 [421], 104 [436]. Most commentators, reasonably, distinguish the strict uninterpreted (or not yet "typified") version of the formula from the interpreted versions that are applicable to cases. Thus, for example, "Act only on that maxim through which you can at the same time will that it should become a universal law", G 88 [421], expresses the former, whereas "Act as if the maxim of your action were to become a universal law of nature," G 89 [421], expresses the latter. See Kant's *Critique of Practical Reason*, trans. Lewis White Beck (New York: The Liberal Arts Press, 1956), pp. 70-74 [68-73]. See also H.J. Paton, *The Categorical Imperative*, (London: Hutchison & Co., 1958) pp. 133-164, especially, 157-164.

11. See, example, Nelson T. Potter and Mark Timmons, *Morality and Universality: Essays on Ethical Universalizability* (Dordrechdt: Reidel, 1985), M.G. Singer, *Generalization in Ethics* (New York: Atheneum, 1971), Onora (O'Neill) Nell, *Acting on Principle* (New York: Columbia University Press, 1975) and *Constructions of Reason* (Cambridge: Cambridge University Press, 1989), and Christine Korsgaard, "Kant's Formula of Universal Law," *Pacific Philosophical Quarterly* 66, 1985, pp. 24-47.

12. This is a theme I develop in "Kant's Anti-Moralistic Strain" in *Dignity and Practical Reason in Kant's Moral Theory* (Ithaca: Cornell University Press, 1992).

13. The example is from R.M. Hare, *Freedom and Reason* (Oxford: Oxford University Press, 1963), pp. 158-185.

14. There remains a significant difference, however, between the reconstructed universal law formula and the kingdom of ends principle to be discussed. The difference is that, even as modified, the universal law formula still requires one to identify a maxim for the proposed action and try to figure out what this very maxim would be "*as* a universal law," where this can be understood in various ways, for example, a law of permission ("everyone may..."), or a psychological law ("everyone does..."), or a teleological law ("our natural end is to..."). The kingdom of ends principle, by contrast, allows one to assess one's proposed act, under any description, by the standards of the prescriptive "laws" for everyone that one would endorse in morally appropriate reasonable reflection.

15. See G 95-98 [427-430].

16. G 102-103 [434-36]. My way of understanding these ideas is more fully developed in chapters 1 and 9 of *Dignity and Practical Reason in Kant's Moral Theory*.
17. See G 98-100 [431-433]. There is further discussion of autonomy in chapters 5, 6, and 7 of *Dignity and Practical Reason in Kant's Moral Theory* and in Henry Allison's *Kant's Theory of Freedom* (Cambridge: Cambridge University Press, 1990), especially Part II.
18. Admittedly Kant held that we should view moral duties as if they were commands of God and he implies that, along with all rational beings, God legislates moral laws in the kingdom of ends (though without being "subject" to them). But Kant never maintains that divine command is the source of the authority of moral laws.
19. I say "quasi-noumenal" rather than "noumenal" because Kant repeatedly insists that the latter term marks not only what is beyond empirical knowledge but also what cannot be pictured.
20. See G 114-115 [446-447] and the references in note 16.
21. The metaphor must shift to accommodate deep disagreements. Rather than guiding ourselves by laws that we can see ourselves legislating together with all others by unanimous agreement, we must at least guide ourselves by "bills" or proposed legislation that, in good conscience, we can stand up to defend before other legislators as worthy of their concurrence.
22. This is not accidental, of course, because Rawls draws from Kant and I draw from Rawls.
23. See note 1. Also I should add that my way of understanding how members "make universal laws" (analogous to political legislation rather than "universalizing one's maxims"), while supported in Kant's texts, is not the only, or perhaps even the most straightforward, reading of all the relevant passages.
24. G 100-101 [433].
25. I attempt to show how this might work in chapter 10 of *Dignity and Practical Reason in Kant's Moral Philosophy*.
26. See John Rawls, *A Theory of Justice* (Cambridge: Harvard University Press, 1971).
27. There are many versions, but one classic is Richard Brandt's "Toward a Credible Form of Utilitarianism" in Hector-Neri Castaneda and George Nakhnikian, *Morality and the Language of Conduct* (Detroit: Wayne State University Press, 1965). See also Richard Brandt, *A Theory of the Good and the Right* (Oxford: The Clarendon Press, 1979), and R.M Hare, *Moral Thinking* (Oxford: Clarendon Press, 1981).
28. This is available in translation in two volumes. John Ladd, *The Metaphysical Elements of Justice* (Indianapolis: Bobbs-Merrill, 1974) and Mary J. Gregor, *The Doctrine of Virtue* (Philadelphia: University of Pennsylvania Press, 1971).
29. Donagan argued this in an unpublished paper presented at the University of Minnesota in the spring of 1991, just shortly before his death.
30. See Michael Stocker, "The Schizophrenia of Modern Moral Theories", *Journal of Philosophy* 73 (1976), pp. 453-466, and Bernard Williams, "Persons, Character, and Morality", in *The Identity of Persons*, edited by Amelie Oksenberg Rorty, (Berkeley: The University of California Press, 1976), pp. 197-29.

Philosophical Perspectives, 6, Ethics, 1992

CREATING THE KINGDOM OF ENDS: RECIPROCITY AND RESPONSIBILITY IN PERSONAL RELATIONS[1]

Christine M. Korsgaard
Harvard University

> As the virtuous man is to himself, he is to his friend also, for his friend is another self.
>
> Aristotle[2]

When we hold a person responsible, we regard her as answerable for her actions, reactions, and attitudes. We use the concept of responsibility in two contexts, the legal and the personal. We use it in the legal context when we must determine whether to punish someone for a crime or make him liable for another's losses. We use it in the context of everyday personal interaction, when we are pressed to decide what attitude we will take toward another, or toward some action or reaction of another. It is frequently assumed that these two uses are the same or at least continuous. Because I have doubts about this, and some worries about the appropriateness of using the notion in the legal context, I want to lay that use aside.[3] In this paper, my focus will be on our practice of holding people responsible in the context of personal relations.

I begin by offering an account of personal relations, derived from Kant and Aristotle, along with an explanation of why they require us to hold one another responsible. I then distinguish two views about what holding someone responsible involves. Specifically, I argue that to hold someone responsible is to adopt an attitude towards him rather to have a belief about him or about the conditions under which he acts. This view gives rise to a problem: if holding someone responsible is something that we *do*, why and how do we decide to do it? In the rest of the paper, I argue that Kant's theory of personal and moral relations provides some answers to this question.

I. Personal Relations, Reciprocity, and Responsibility

In the British Empiricist tradition, the concept of responsibility has been closely associated with the ideas of praise and blame, and these in turn have played a central role in its moral philosophy. In the theories of Hutcheson, Hume, and Smith, the approval and disapproval of others is the fundamental moral phenomenon, from which all our moral ideas spring.[4] There is something obviously unattractive about taking the assessment of others as the starting point in moral philosophy. One of the appealing things about Kant's ethics, by contrast, is that in it moral thought is seen as arising from the perspective of the agent who is deciding what to do. Responsibility is in the first instance something taken rather than something assigned. And this fact about the structure of his view is complemented by a fact about its content. Kant is not very interested in praise and blame and seldom mentions them. And when he does discuss issues of moral assessment, much of what he says favors a taking a generous attitude. His metaphysical view that we cannot know even our own most fundamental maxims (G 407/19) combines with a set of moral injunctions—to respect others, avoid scandal, and "never to deny the wrongdoer all moral worth" (MMV 462-464/127-129)—to give philosophical foundations to the Biblical injunction "Judge not."[5]

But in a broader sense it is not possible for us to avoid holding one another responsible.[6] For holding one another responsible is the distinctive element in the relation of adult human beings. To hold someone responsible is to regard her as a *person*—that is to say, as a free and equal person, capable of acting both rationally and morally. It is therefore to regard her as someone with whom you can enter the kind of relation that is possible only among free and equal rational people: a relation of reciprocity. When you hold someone responsible, you are prepared to exchange lawless individual activity for reciprocity in some or all of its forms. You are prepared to accept promises, offer confidences, exchange vows, cooperate on a project, enter a social contract, have a conversation, make love, be friends, or get married. You are willing to deal with her on the basis of the expectation that each of you will act from a certain view of the other: that you each have your reasons which are to be respected, and your ends which are to be valued. Abandoning the state of nature and so relinquishing force and guile, you are ready to share, to trust, and generally speaking to risk your happiness or success on the hope that she will turn out to be human.

I borrow the idea that personal relations are characterized by reciprocity from both Kant and Aristotle, two of the very few philosophers in our tradition who have written about this topic. And it will be important to my argument that I hold along with them that the territory of personal relations is continuous with moral territory. That is to say, I accept their view that the forms of friendship, at their best at least, are forms of the basic moral relation among human beings—particular forms of that relation which have been rendered perfect of their kind. Aristotle holds that the most perfect human relation is the friendship of virtue, in which two people of good character share their lives and activities, and in particular, share those virtuous activities that make their lives worth living. (NE IX.9 1169b28ff./1089-1090) And Kant holds that the ideal of friendship is that of "the union of two persons through equal mutual love and respect," a relation in which the two basic attitudes we owe to one other as moral beings are realized in spontaneous natural sentiment (MMV 469/135). Characteristically, Aristotle holds that achieving such a relationship is a virtue, and Kant, that striving to achieve it is a duty. For friendship, Aristotle tells us, it is "not only necessary but noble" (NE VIII.2 1155a29-31/1059); and Kant echoes the thought: "friendship...is no ordinary duty but rather an honorable one proposed by reason." (MMV 469/135)

Both define this perfect relation, as well as the less perfect variants of it, in terms of reciprocity, and both cite reciprocity as the reason why friendship is found above all among people who are good. For Aristotle, friendship is characterized by acknowledged reciprocal good will, in which each person loves the other for his own (the other's) sake. (NE VIII.2 1155b28-1156a5/ 1059-1060) This requires trust in the other's goodness, for as Aristotle says "it is among good men that trust and the feeling that 'he would never wrong me' and all the other things that are demanded in true friendship are found." (NE VIII.3 1157a22-24/1062) Kant characterizes friendship in the *Lectures on Ethics* as "the maximum reciprocity of love" (LE 202). There he argues that friends exchange their private projects of pursuing their own happiness, each undertaking to care for the other's happiness instead of his own. "I, from generosity, look after his happiness and he similarly looks after mine; I do not throw away my happiness, but surrender it to his keeping, and he in turn surrenders into my hands" (LE 203). This requires the maximum reciprocity of love because "if I am to love him as I love myself I must be sure that he will love me as he loves himself, in which case he restores to me that with which I part and I come back to myself again" (LE 202). The later account in *The Metaphysics of Morals* adds another element. Friendship in its perfection involves what Kant calls "the most intimate union of love with respect." (MMV 469/135) While love moves you to pursue the ends of another, respect reminds you that she must determine what those ends are; while love moves you to care for the happiness of another, respect demands that you care for her character too. Kant means here the *feelings* of love and respect, for he is defining the friendship of sentiment, but this does not sever the tie to morality. Love and respect are the primary duties of virtue we owe to others. Although only the outward practices can be required of us, Kant makes it clear in many passages that he believes that in the state of realized virtue these feelings will be present. In one place he even defines love and respect as the feelings which accompany the exercise of our duties towards others (MMV 448/112; see also R 23-24n /19n). Feelings of sympathy, gratitude, and delight in the happiness of others are not directly incumbent upon us, but they are the natural result of making the ends of others our own, as duty demands. The feeling of respect, a still higher achievement, is the natural result of keeping the humanity of others and so their capacity for good will always before our eyes. So this kind of friendship really is in Kant's eyes the friendship of *virtue*, the moral relation in a perfected form.

"When men are friends they have no need of justice," says Aristotle, and there are two ways to understand what he means. (NE VIII.1 1155a25-26/1059) The wrong way is to suppose that he is referring to an idea like Hume's of the "circumstances of justice": justice is only useful and so is only required when moderate scarcity holds among people who are only moderately benevolent.[7] Friends, because they are endlessly benevolent to each other, are not in the circumstances of justice and have no use for it. Now this clearly cannot be Aristotle's meaning, for he thinks that "the truest form of justice is thought to be a friendly quality" (NE VIII.1 1155a27-28/1059) and that "friendship and justice...seem to be concerned with the same objects and exhibited between the same persons" (NE VIII.9 1159b25-27/1068). Justice is, at its best, a kind of civic friendship. And indeed, friendship, like justice, is not primarily a matter of doing things *for* one another, but of doing things together. "Those in the prime of life it stimulates to noble actions—'two going together'—for with friends men are more able both to think and to act." (NE VIII.1 1155a14-16/1058) Aristotle sums up his account with these words:

> And whatever existence means for each class of men, whatever it is for whose sake they value life, in *that* they wish to occupy themselves with their friends; and so some drink together, others dice together, others join in athletic exercises and hunting, and in the study of philosophy, each class spending their days together in whatever they love most in life; for since they wish to live with their friends, they do and share in those things which give them the sense of living together. (NE IX.11 1172a2-9/1093)

Justice isn't necessary between friends because the reciprocity (NE V.5-6) and unanimity (NE VIII.1; NE IX.6) characteristic of justice are already present. And this is because they want above all to act together. Kant would again agree. Kant thinks that justice is reciprocal coercion under a general will, made necessary by geographical and economic association (MMJ 232/36-37; 256/64-65). When we share a territory we may have a dispute about rights. But I may enforce my rights against you only on the understanding that you may enforce your rights against me, and in this way we make a social contract and constitute ourselves a state. (MMJ 315-316/80-81) Friendship is a free and uninstitutionalized form of justice, where the association is created by love rather than geographical necessity, and regulated by mutual respect rather than reciprocal coercion.

But it is not merely the narrow relation of political justice, but rather the moral relation generally, that friendship mirrors. For to join with others as citizens in the Kingdom of Ends is to extend to our inner attitudes and personal choices the kind of reciprocity that characterizes our outer actions in the political state. This is seen best in the way Kant uses the Formula of Humanity to explain our duties to others.[8] In the positive sense, to treat another as an end in itself is to make her ends your own: "For the ends of any subject who is an end in himself must as far as possible be my ends also, if that conception of an end in itself is to have its full effect in me." (G 430/37) In the negative sense, to treat another as an end in itself is to respect her autonomy—to leave her actions, decisions, and ends to her own choice. But this respect gets its most positive and characteristic expression at precisely the moments when we must act together. Then another's right to choose becomes the "limiting condition" of my own. (G 431/37) If my end requires your act for its achievement, then I must let you make it your end too. Both what I choose and the way I choose it must reflect this constraint. You must be free to choose whether you will contribute to the success of my project or not. Kant says anyone engaged in a transaction with me must be able to agree with my way of acting towards him and to share in the end of my action. (G 430/37) If I force you to contribute to an end you have had no opportunity to decide for or against, or if I trick you into contributing into one end under the guise of soliciting your help with another, then I have used you as a mere means. Kant illustrates this with the example of the lying promise. If I ask you to lend me money, knowing I shall not be able to pay you back, I trick you into contributing to an end you have had no opportunity to choose. I make you think that the end produced by our transaction is my temporary use of your money, when in fact it is my permanent possession of it. Neither my way of acting nor the end produced by it are things that you are in a position to accept or reject, and this renders them morally wrong. Thus I must make your ends and reasons mine, and I must choose mine in such a way that they can be yours. But this just is reciprocity. Generalized to the Kingdom of Ends, my own ends must be the possible objects of universal legislation, subject to the vote of all. And this is how I realize my autonomy. Paradoxically if you like, my ends and actions are most truly my own when they are chosen under the restrictions of a possible reciprocal relation—a kind of friendship—with everyone.

I do not say this to join forces with those who believe that there could be no room in aa Kantian life for personal as opposed to moral relations.[9] Nor, certainly, do I mean to suggest that being friends is just a matter of being good. My point is only that moral and personal relations are not different in kind. The difference between them is the difference between the degree of reciprocity that is *required* of us as one human being relating to another, and the degree of reciprocity that we are capable of when our relations are at their best. Anyone must tell the truth when the circumstances call for it, but between friends there is a presumption of intimacy, frankness, and confidence. Anyone must help another in need or emergency, but friends promote each other's projects as routinely as they do their own. Anyone must refrain from leading others into temptation; but friends help each other to

be good. The difference is the difference between the absolute moral requirements we must meet if human relations are to be decent at all, and the further
reaches of positive virtue, where our relations with one another become
morally worthy. Friendships are human moral achievements that are lovely
in themselves and testify to the virtue of those who sustain them. To become
friends is to create a neighborhood where the Kingdom of Ends is real.[10]

Kant's faith in the moral force of reciprocity shows up best when he believes
that the basic moral relation is at risk. In both the *Lectures on Ethics* and
the *Metaphysics of Morals* Kant gives inarticulate voice to the view that there
is something morally troublesome, even potentially degrading, about sexual
relations. It is important to understand that what bothers him is *not* the idea
that one is using another person as a means to one's own pleasure. That would
be an incorrect view of sexual relations, and in any case any difficulty about
it, would, by Kant's own theory, be alleviated by the other's simple act of
free consent. What bothers Kant is rather that sexual desire takes a *person*
for its object.[11] He says: "They themselves, and not their work and services,
are its Objects of enjoyment." (LE 162) And he continues:

> Man can, of course, use another human being as an instrument for his
> service; he can use his hands, his feet, and even all his powers; he can use
> him for his own purposes with the other's consent. But there is no way in
> which a human being can be made an Object of indulgence for another
> except through sexual impulse...it is an appetite for another human being.
> (LE 163)

Regarding someone as a sexual object is not like regarding him as an
instrument or a tool, but more like regarding him as an aesthetic object. But
in this case the attitude is not just appreciation but desire. (MMV 426/87)[12]
Viewed through the eyes of sexual desire another person is seen as something
wantable, desirable, and, therefore, inevitably, possessable.[13] To yield to *that*
desire, to the extent it is really *that* desire you yield to, is to allow yourself
to be possessed. The problem is how you can do that in a way that is consistent
with respect for your own humanity.[14] And the solution rests in reciprocity:

> If, then, one yields one's person, body and soul, for good and ill in every
> respect, so that the other has complete rights over it, and if the other does
> not similarly yield himself in return and does not extend in return the same
> rights and privileges, the arrangement is one-sided. But if I yield myself
> completely to another and obtain the person of the other in return, I win
> myself back; I have given myself up as the property of another, but in turn I
> take that other as my property, and so win myself back again in winning
> the person whose property I have become. In this way the two persons
> become a unity of will. (LE 167)

The language of self-surrender and retrieval here is strikingly similar to that
Kant uses elsewhere for both friendship and justice. In making the social
contract, Kant says, we do not sacrifice part of our freedom for a particular
purpose, but rather sacrifice all of our lawless freedom in order to regain

our freedom again, undiminished, under law. (MMJ 316/80-81) In the case of friendship Kant says I surrender my happiness completely into the hands of my friend, but that in loving me as he loves himself "he restores to me that with which I part and I come back to myself again" (LE 202).[15] This perfect reciprocity is the only condition under which the sexual relation is morally legitimate; and Kant thinks this condition is only possible in marriage, where the reciprocity of surrender has been pledged. Extramarital sex is forbidden only because the woman, as Kant supposes, does not then have the same rights over the man that he has over her. Of course marriage as it has usually existed has hardly been a solution to *this* problem. The equality necessary for reciprocity is far more likely to be distanced even further by marriage, which has usually given the husband rights over his wife *additional* to those that accrue from the superior social position he has held as a man. Kant admits as much in the *Metaphysical Elements of Justice*, asserting that an unequal marriage is not a marriage in his sense at all. Thus marriage as it has been practiced in most societies·has not sanctified but rather degraded sexual relations. (MMJ 278-279)[16] But perhaps the most startling ramification of Kant's view emerges in what he says about incest. As strong as our natural aversion to it may be, and however risky and therefore *conditionally* wrong it is from a reproductive point of view, incest is only morally wrong in itself, *unconditionally*, in one case: the case of parent and child. And this is because, according to Kant, the equality of respect required for reciprocity cannot and should not be achieved in that relation. (LE 168)

Which brings me back to my topic. The relations of reciprocity are relations that obtain between free and equal persons. As such, they call for mutual responsibility for two important reasons. In order to make the ends and reasons of another your own, you must regard her as a source of value, someone whose choices confer worth upon their objects, and who has the right to decide on her own actions. In order to entrust your own ends and reasons to another's care, you must suppose that she regards you that way, and is prepared to act accordingly. People who enter into relations of reciprocity must be prepared to share their ends and reasons; to hold them jointly; and to act together. Reciprocity is the sharing of reasons, and you will enter into it only with someone you expect to deal with reasons in a rational way. In this sense, reciprocity requires that you hold the other responsible.

It is certainly a concomitant of holding someone responsible that you are prepared for blame, resentment, and the other reactive attitudes.[17] If my friend fails me in a serious way and I do not blame her, shrugging it off as I would the misdemeanors of a child or a pet, then I was not holding her responsible after all, and probably I was holding myself back. But it is a mistake to make these reactions central. Blame is important, not as a tool of training or the enforcement of social norms, but as an expression of the tenacity of disappointed respect. At its best, it declares to its object a greater faith than she has in herself. Yet still it is not central. The willingness to take a chance on some form of reciprocity is the essence of holding someone responsible.

I mean in these words both to acknowledge the affinity of my position with P.F. Strawson's in "Freedom and Resentment" and to notice one point of difference. Strawson also emphasizes the employment of the concept of responsibility in everyday personal relations. But he tends to focus more on the effect of attributions of responsibility on our sentiments than their effect on our practices. His topic, as he describes it, is "the non-detached attitudes and reactions of people directly involved in transactions with each other;...the attitudes and reactions of offended parties and beneficiaries; of such things as gratitude, resentment, forgiveness, love, and hurt feelings."[18] I want to focus less upon the exchange of benefits and harms, and the feelings that result from that exchange, and more upon the willingness to act in concert. But my point is similar to his. In everyday personal interaction, we cannot get on without the concept of responsibility. And therefore we cannot rest with the view that agents take responsibility for their own actions but can refrain from judging others. For a Kantian, this means it is necessary to say more than Kant himself did about what, on his view, is involved in determining when and whether to hold people responsible.

II. Theoretical and Practical Conceptions of Responsibility

Attributions of responsibility may be understood in either of two ways, which I will call theoretical and practical. Construed theoretically, responsibility is a characteristic of persons. Construed practically, holding one another responsible is something that we do, the more or less deliberate adoption of an attitude. In what follows I will distinguish these two ways of understanding attributions of responsibility, and show that according to Kant we must understand attributions of responsibility in a practical way. I believe that this view of responsibility is implicit in our actual practices, and therefore that, on this point at least, Kant's account can make us more transparent to ourselves.

Responsibility is construed theoretically by those who think that it is a fact about a person that she is responsible for a particular action, or that there is some fact about her condition either at the time of action or during the events which led up to it which fully determines whether it is correct to hold her responsible. It is a fact, say, that she could have done otherwise, or that she could have avoided the condition which made it impossible for her to do otherwise. Similar although somewhat more complicated claims would be made about the person's reactions and attitudes: facts about the person settle the question whether she is accountable for them. Deciding whether to hold someone responsible is a matter of assessing the facts; it is a matter of arriving at a belief about her. It seems probable that we arrive at this model by a certain route: we think about legal responsibility first, and we suppose that in that case we *must* find facts which can settle the matter, and then we imagine that personal responsibility is an extension of this.

Responsibility is construed practically by those who think that holding someone responsible is adopting an attitude towards her, or, much better, placing yourself in a relationship with her. While of course facts about the agent and about her condition at the time of the action *guide* your decision whether to hold her responsible, they do not fully *determine* it. It is important to see that the facts still do provide guidance, for a practical conception need not be envisioned as completely voluntaristic. On either a theoretical or a practical conception, we will, when deciding whether to hold someone responsible, say such things as "he is very nervous about the interview he has tomorrow" or "he's been hurt so often that now he can never trust a woman." But in a practical conception these considerations appear in the role of practical reasons for not holding the person responsible rather than as evidence that he could not have helped what he did. When responsibility is viewed this way, we need not suppose that there is a *fixed degree* of nervousness or past heartbreak beyond which someone is *in fact* no longer responsible for the way he acts and reacts; deciding whether to hold him responsible is therefore not a matter of determining whether this fixed degree has been reached. A resulting feature of the practical conception which I take to be one of its virtues is that it distances the question whether to hold someone responsible from the question whether he acted voluntarily. I do not believe there is a stable relationship between the voluntariness of an action or attitude and the appropriateness of holding someone responsible for it. If a bad action is found to have been involuntary in some straightforward way, we will withdraw blame; we may also do this if the person is under severe emotional stress. But there is neither need nor reason to reduce the second kind of excusing condition to the first and say that people under severe emotional stress *cannot* control themselves. We do not need to understand a form of debilitation as a form of impossibility in order to make allowances for it; we need only to know what it is like. Conversely, we may well blame people for involuntary attitudes or expressions, because we blame people for lack of control itself. If you cannot repress a victorious grin on learning that your rival has met with a gruesome accident, you ought to be blamed, precisely on that account. The impulse to reduce all excusing conditions to claims about the voluntary comes from the theoretical conception of responsibility, which demands an answer to the question whether one could have done otherwise or not. On the practical conception excuses need not completely determine our decisions about whether to hold people responsible. If the decision to attribute responsibility is practical, it may be reasonable to make it partly on the basis of other kinds of considerations: in particular, which reciprocal relations you already stand in or plan to stand in or hope to stand in to the person in question.

Construing responsibility practically opens up possibilities that would not make sense if responsibility were a fact about the person. It is because we both accept and avail ourselves of these possibilities that I claim that we implicitly understand attributions of responsibility practically in everyday life. For instance, it may be perfectly reasonable for me to hold someone responsible for an attitude or an action, while at the same time acknowledging that it is just as reasonable for someone else not to hold the same person responsible for the very same attitude or action. Perhaps it is reasonable for *you* to forgive or overlook our friend's distrustful behavior on the grounds that he has suffered so much heartbreak, but not for me, *not* because I fail to appreciate how hurt he has been, but because I am the woman whose loving conduct is always met with distrust.[19] Again, if deciding whether to hold someone responsible is something that we do, it is something that we may in turn be held responsible for. Holding someone responsible can be insensitive or merciless; failing to hold someone responsible can be disrespectful or patronizing. Moral requirements will apply to our attributions of responsibility, just as Kant believes they do.

Consider, for instance, the appropriate reaction to a case where one is disappointed in friendship. Kant thinks the perfect friendship I described earlier, characterized by *feelings* of equal mutual love and respect, is impossible to achieve. But he does think we can achieve what he calls "moral friendship." (MMV 471-473/138-140) The form of reciprocity central to this relation is the frank conversation, the sharing of sentiments, of which Kant believes we all stand in need. Like other reciprocal relations it calls for good character on the part of the participants, because it is hedged with dangers— ranging from the crude risk that you will tell your secrets to an unreliable person who will publish them, to the more subtle risk that your confidences will be met with disrespectful attitudes.[20] I do not want to share my ambitions with someone who is inwardly amused by my vanity, nor whisper my temptations to someone who will place a harsh construction on them. One who consents to receive my confidences is committed to avoiding the vices of mockery and calumny, serious failures of respect in the Kantian catalogue (MMV 466-467/131-133). And I will blame her if she fails in these ways, without regard to the available evidence of her character or of the circumstances in which it was formed. Her circumstances must have been very bad indeed, or her failures very frequent, before I may decide it was simply *my* error to trust her. For in deciding this I write her off as a person, and I do this at my own moral peril.

I suppose that most of us have at one time or another had the experience of being tempted to "write somebody off." The extent to which we do this is a matter of degree, and hopefully we do not go so far as to give up treating the person with the most basic forms of moral decency. But we may avoid interaction, as far as possible; we may choose to execute our projects in the company of others; where interaction is necessary, we may come to treat the person as an obstacle to be worked around. In an extreme case we may cease to have reactive attitudes altogether, or at least we may scold ourselves, as for irrational feelings, when we have them. "You know that she always ends up infuriating you. Why don't you just stay out of her way?" Taking such attitudes towards others seems disrespectful, but it can certainly sometimes be tempting all the same. How do we decide what to do in such a case? On a theoretical construal of responsibility, we simply ask whether the person is in fact responsible for the offensive behavior, and treat her accordingly. On a practical construal, we must discover moral and practical reasons that will guide us to the right attitude. Kant's theory of moral and personal relations, I believe, can show us where these reasons are to be found.

III. Kant's Two Standpoints

I will approach these issues in a roundabout way, however. I begin by discussing the way Kant reconciles free will and determinism, and by showing how his reconciliation gives rise to some apparent problems about holding people responsible. Kant's theory of moral and personal relations show us how he might have resolved one of these issues, and how we might resolve the other.

Kant's solution to the problem of freedom and determinism is clear enough in outline, however much philosophers may disagree about what it means. We must view ourselves from two standpoints, from which we appear as members of two different "worlds." (G 452/53-54) Complete causal determinism holds in the phenomenal or sensible world, the world of things as they appear to us; but we cannot know that it holds in the noumenal world, the world of things as they are in themselves. Indeed, since we must suppose that there are some undetermined first causes, or free agencies, which generate the appearances, we must suppose that things which exist in the noumenal world are free.[21] Insofar as we regard ourselves as "intelligences," the spontaneity of reason induces us to attribute a noumenal existence to ourselves. (G 452/53; C2 42-43/43-44) Insofar as we consider ourselves to be intelligent *agents*, then, we must regard ourselves as free: indeed, completely and transcendentally so. Yet at the same time we must view our actions, like all phenomena, as fully determined.[22]

Despite Kant's strictures against trying to envision what occurs on the boundary between the two worlds, it is natural to want a picture that reconciles these two views of ourselves. At one point in the *Critique of Practical Reason*, Kant supplies the beginning of such a picture. He proposes that we should think of ourselves, and also that we do think of ourselves, as if we created our own characters. Although a person may know that his actions are determined in the phenomenal world, Kant says:

> ...the same subject...is conscious also of his existence as a thing-in-itself...determinable only by laws which he gives to himself through reason. In this existence nothing is antecedent to the determination of his will; every action, and...even the entire history of his existence as a sensuous being, is seen...only as a consequence...of his causality as a noumenon. From this point of view, a rational being can rightly say of any unlawful action which he has done that he could have left it undone, even if as an appearance it...was inescapably necessary. For this action and everything in the past which determined it belong to a single phenomenon of his character, which he himself creates... . (C2 97-98/101)

Kant then applies this picture to our attributions of responsibility:

> From this point of view...judgments may be justified which...seem at first glance to conflict with equity. There are cases in which men...have shown from childhood such depravity...that they are held to be born villains and incapable of any improvement of character; yet they are judged by their acts, they are reproached as guilty of their crimes; and, indeed, they themselves find these reproaches as well grounded as if they...were just as responsible as any other men. This could not happen if we did not suppose that whatever arises from man's choice...has a free causality as its ground...the vicious quality of the will...is...the consequence of...freely assumed evil and unchangeable principles. (C2 99-100/103)

Here one's life is regarded as the phenomenal representation or expression of a single choice, the choice of one's character or fundamental principle. This choice must be understood as occurring outside of time, in the noumenal world. The choice is the one described in the first book of *Religion Within the Limits of Reason Alone*: the choice of how incentives are to be ordered in one's most fundamental maxim, the choice between morality and self-love. (R 36/31) As Kant sees it, human beings are subject to certain incentives—impulses which present themselves to us as candidates, so to speak, to be reasons for action. Among these are our desires and inclinations, as well as respect for the moral law. Kant believes that we are not free to ignore such incentives altogether. Instead, our freedom consists in our ability to rank the incentives, to choose whether our self-love shall be governed by morality or morality shall be subordinated to self-love. This fundamental choice then governs our choice of lower-order maxims. The fundamental choice is an act—in the *Religion* Kant calls it an intelligible act—and it is ultimately this intelligible act that is imputable to us, and makes our phenomenal actions imputable to us. (R 31-32/26-27)

When first exposed to Kant's view, one may be tempted to try to picture how and where the choice of one's character enters the processes which ultimately issue in action. Suppose, with violent oversimplification, that it is a law of nature that children raised in certain conditions of poverty and insecurity tend to become somewhat selfish as adults, and suppose that such a childhood has had this effect on Marilyn. Are we to say to her: "Your childhood insecurity gave you an incentive to be selfish, but it is still your own fault if you elevate that incentive into a reason?" Then we are thinking that Marilyn's freedom inserts itself in between the causes in her background and their ultimate effect.[23] Or are we supposed to think that, in her noumenal existence, Marilyn *wills to be* a selfish person? Or, to get even fancier, should we think that in her noumenal existence Marilyn wills the law of nature that deprived children become selfish adults? Obviously, if we try to picture *how* Marilyn's freedom is related to the forces that determine her, we must imagine it either inserting itself somewhere into the historical process, or standing behind the laws of nature from which this historical process necessarily follows. And both of these pictures seem crazy.[24]

And of course they are crazy. Kant's response to this problem is to maintain that the question should not be asked. To ask how freedom and determinism are related is to inquire into the relation between the noumenal and phenomenal worlds, a relation about which it is in principle impossible to know anything. But our understanding of what this response amounts to will depend on how we understand the distinction between the noumenal and phenomenal worlds, and the related distinction between the two standpoints from which Kant says we may view ourselves and our actions.

This is a large issue which I cannot treat here in a satisfactory way; I shall simply declare my allegiance. On a familiar but as I think misguided interpretation, the distinction between the two worlds is an ontological one; as if behind the beings of this world were another set of beings, which have an active and controlling relation to the beings of this world, but which are inaccessible to us because of the limits of experience. According to this view, we occupy both worlds, and viewing ourselves from the two standpoints we discover two different sets of laws which describe and explain our conduct in the two different worlds. We act on the moral law in the noumenal world, the law of self-love in the phenomenal world. This view gives rise to familiar paradoxes about how evil actions are even possible, and how we could ever be held responsible for them if they were.[25]

On what I take to be the correct interpretation, the distinction is not between two kinds of beings, but between the beings of this world insofar as they are authentically active and the same beings insofar as we are passively receptive to them. The "gap" in our knowledge exists not because of the *limits* of experience but because of its essential *nature*: to experience something is (in part) to be passively receptive to it, and therefore we cannot have experiences of activity as such.[26] As thinkers and choosers we must regard ourselves as active beings, even though we cannot *experience* ourselves as active beings, and so we place ourselves among the noumena, necessarily, whenever we think and act. According to this interpretation, the laws of the phenomenal world are laws that describe and explain our behavior. But the laws of the noumenal world are laws which are *addressed to us* as active beings; their business is not to describe and explain at all, but to govern what we do.[27] Reason has two employments, theoretical and practical. We view ourselves as phenomena when we take on the theoretical task of describing and explaining our behavior; we view ourselves as noumena when our practical task is one of deciding what to do.[28] The two standpoints cannot be mixed because these two enterprises—explanation and decision— are mutually exclusive.[29]

These two ways of understanding the noumenal/phenomenal distinction yield very different interpretations of Kant's strictures against trying to picture the relation between the noumenal and phenomenal worlds. On the ontological view, the question how the two worlds are related is one which, frustratingly, cannot be answered. On the active/passive view, it is one which cannot coherently be *asked*. There is no question that is answered by my descriptions of how Marilyn's freedom interacts with the causal forces that determine her. For freedom is a concept with a practical employment, used in the choice and justification of action, not in explanation or prediction; while causality is a concept of theory, used to explain and predict actions but not to justify them.[30] There is no standpoint from which we are doing both of these things at once, and so there is no place from which to ask a question that includes both concepts in its answer.

So, if I am myself Marilyn, and I am trying to decide whether to do something selfish, reflections on the disadvantages of my background are irrelevant. I must act under the idea of freedom, and so I must act on what I regard as reasons. Being underprivileged may sometimes be a cause of selfish behavior, but it is not a reason that can be offered in support of it by a person engaged in it. So although *we* do not necessarily say of Marilyn: "her background gave her some tough incentives to deal with, but still it is up to her whether she treats them as reasons," that is what she must say to herself. I say that we do not *necessarily* say this, because, as I am about to argue, whether we say it depends on whether we have decided to enter into reciprocal relations with her and so to hold her responsible. But in that case, it is better regarded as something we say not *about* but *to* her. The second-person grammatical form, so rarely privileged in philosophy, is exactly right here, for if anyone besides Marilyn has the right to make this judgment, it is her friends, those with whom she interacts. On the other hand, if I am not Marilyn's friend but a social scientist who is trying to understand and explain her behavior, then my business is not to try to justify her conduct, and for my purposes the causal explanation which makes her selfish actions seem inevitable is the right one to pursue.

The two worlds, or the two views of the world we get from the two standpoints, may seem strangely incongruent, but it is important to see that there is no contradiction. The incongruity simply follows from the fact that we stand in two very different relations to our actions: we must try to understand them, but we must also decide which ones to do.

IV. Practical Grounds for Holding People Responsible

But we cannot just leave the matter there. For there are contexts in which we have to mix considerations derived from the two standpoints, and make a moral assessment of someone's action, on the basis of a theoretical explanation of what she did. This occurs when we are making judgments about responsibility: when we must decide whether, for instance, someone is to be exonerated, excused, forgiven, blamed, or not held responsible for a bad action at all.

There are really two problems here. First, given that we can view people and their actions either way, or from either standpoint, what reason do we have for settling on the practical point of view, and holding people responsible, at all?[31] Second, even if we can discover such a reason, won't Kant's view be intransigent? For if we do regard people as free agents, fellow citizens in the Kingdom of Ends, then it seems as if we must treat them as transcendentally free and so as completely responsible for each and every action, no matter what sorts of pressures they may be under. Yet the obvious fact is that we live in neighborhoods which are at different distances from the Kingdom of Ends, and it seems merciless to give this obvious fact no weight. But it also seems as if the only option Kant provides is to switch to the theoretical standpoint and regard candidates for forgiveness as if they were no more responsible for their actions than small children and animals. The very idea of an action's being excusable or forgivable or understandable seem to bring together explanatory and justificatory thoughts. The doctrine of the two standpoints seems to keep such thoughts resolutely apart.

In response to the first problem, why we hold people responsible at all, it is important initially to separate two issues. One is the issue of holding yourself responsible for your own actions in the context of deliberative choice, and the other is the issue of holding other people and your self at other times responsible. On Kant's view, we first encounter the idea of freedom when we are deciding what to do. We encounter it in the necessity of acting under the idea of freedom, and in the commands of the moral law.[32] At the moment of decision, you must regard yourself as the author of your action, and so you inevitably hold yourself responsible for what you do. It is only when you think about the actions of other people, and when you think about your own actions at other times, that you can view them from either standpoint. You can take up the position of the social scientist, and regard actions as psycho-social phenomena that need to be explained. Or you can put yourself in the other person's shoes as a decision-maker, and think about what it is like to *choose* or to *do* an action of that kind.

Now it seems clear that you cannot restrict the concepts of freedom and responsibility to yourself in the context of deliberative choice. If you did, you would think that the only free agent in the world is me-right-now. But the moral law, which according to Kant presents itself to you in exactly these moments, commands that you treat everyone as an end in himself (C2 29-30/29). Unless you hold others responsible for the ends that they choose and the actions that they do, you cannot regard them as moral and rational agents, and so you will not treat them as ends in themselves. Indeed, unless you regard others and your future self as moral agents, there will be no content to your duties at all, for all duties (according to Kant) are owed either to other persons or to the enduring self (MMJ 241/47; MMV 442-444/105-107). The moral law, announcing itself as the law of your will, would be without content or application. Your relations to other people, and to your self at other times, would be, at best, like your relations to small children and the other animals. But there is more at stake here than just whether you have any duties, for you cannot enter into *any* reciprocal relations with people whom you do not hold responsible. Nor can you do this if you do not take responsibility for your own actions at other times, since relationships after all are enduring things.

This is why our reaction to Derek Parfit's nineteenth-century Russian nobleman is that he's wrong, and in particular, that he wrongs his wife. The story goes like this. Parfit's Russian nobleman is now, in his youth, a socialist, and plans to distribute large portions of his inheritance, when he comes into it, to the poor. But he also anticipates that his attitudes will become more conservative as he grows older, and so that he may not think this is the right thing to do, when the inheritance is actually his own. So he asks his wife to hold him to the promise he makes *now*, to distribute the land, even if he tells her *then* that he has changed his mind.[33] Parfit makes it clear that the case is not like that of Ulysses binding himself to the mast to resist the Sirens' song. The young nobleman does not anticipate that he is going to become irrational, that his judgment will be clouded, or that he will be out of control. He merely believes that he is going to think differently than he does now. This case illustrates my point well. The young nobleman's attitude towards his own future attitudes is essentially a *predictive* and theoretical one, and, because it is so, he abdicates the kind of responsibility that is necessary for reciprocity: the kind of responsibility that enables people to act in concert. His way of making himself do the right thing is not to take responsibility for doing so, but to give the responsibility to his wife. This may be one way to form the "united will" that Kant says is necessary in marriage, but it is not the right way. The Russian nobleman leaves his wife alone in the standpoint of practical reason, where people who are married must stand together. Her decision is not, as Parfit says, which of these two men, older and younger, is her real husband, the man she loves, the man she has married. Nor, for that matter, would *that* be just a question about how she feels about them or what she thinks of them. She cannot be married to the older man, later, unless she holds him responsible, and takes him at his word. She cannot be married to the younger one, now, because he has already abandoned her. And further than that: to the extent that it is important to this woman's sense of her own identity, morally and personally, that she is his wife, he leaves her without anything clear to be, and so without anything clear to do. You cannot act in concert with one who does not act in concert with himself. Where our relations are constitutive of our ongoing identities, those with whom we have them must have ongoing identities too.[34]

So if you only apply the concepts of freedom and responsibility to yourself at the moments of deliberative choice, you do not have any sort of recognizable moral life at all. No Kingdom of Ends on earth can be sought or realized if responsibility is restricted to its original home in the first person deliberator's perspective.

But notice that all of the reasons I have just given are moral and practical ones. I have been suggesting that holding people responsible is something that we do for moral reasons. The reason we must view another as a fellow rational person rather than as a psycho-social phenomenon is not that he is *in fact* one of these things rather than the other. In fact, he is both. That another is responsible is what Kant calls a postulate of practical reason: a belief or attitude that can be formulated theoretically, but is practical and moral in its basis. (C2 132-134/137-139) We hold others responsible in the same way that, according to Kant, we "will that there be a God", because it is a condition of our obedience to the commands of the moral law. (C2 143/149) Or, when a more personal relation is at stake, because it is the condition of our submission to the imperatives of love.

No doubt this way of putting it makes it all sound more deliberate and voluntary than it really is. We do not, of course, simply decide whether to hold other people responsible in general; reciprocal relations and the attitudes that characterize them are, as Strawson argues, too deeply imbedded in the framework of human life to "come up for review", and reactive attitudes, or at least the feelings that accompany them, cannot always be helped.[35] But as Strawson himself observes we do make these decisions in particular cases, and even more frequently we make decisions about whether to identify with our reactive feelings or not. If I have decided not to hold someone responsible, I may view my rage at him as mere inevitable emotion, like the rage provoked in everyone except saints by recalcitrant home appliances and fractious infants. Still, it might be better to put my point a different way. The idea is not that we deliberately decide to hold people responsible in general, but that our commitment to this view of others and our commitment to the moral life issue together from the standpoint of practical reason. Holding others responsible is an inevitable concomitant of holding ourselves so, both in particular personal relations and in more general moral ones. To share our ends and reasons is to share the standpoint from which those ends and reasons are generated. The citizens of the Kingdom of Ends make their decisions in congress; the noumenal world is, above all, a place that we occupy *together*.

V. Mitigating Moral Judgment

Now while this explains why we hold others responsible, and why our doing so has and must have a practical basis, it does not solve the problem of what now appears to be Kant's intransigence. The moral command that we hold others responsible seems as absolute as it would be if we had theoretical knowledge that they were indeed transcendentally free. Kant does not separate the grounds for holding people responsible in general, from the grounds for holding them responsible for particular actions. And so it seems as if holding someone responsible in general amounts to holding her responsible for everything she does. The flexibility with which I credited the practical account of attributions of responsibility does not seem to follow readily from Kant's view.

Some of the things Kant says, however, suggest that there is room for such flexibility. I will discuss two kinds of considerations, mentioned by Kant, which may be used to guide our decisions whether to hold people responsible for particular actions and reactions, and in particular, to mitigate the intransigence that seems required by the commitment to treating others as persons.

The first consideration springs from what I call Kant's practical compatibilism. Although Kant endorses both free will and determinism, he is not a theoretical compatibilist. Kant does not believe that these two things can be reconciled from a single point of view, as his contempt for Leibniz's *automaton spirituale*, which he says has "the freedom of a turnspit," shows. (C2 97/100-101) And yet this does not stop him from adjuring politicians that "a good constitution is not to be expected from morality, but conversely, a good moral condition of a people is to be expected only under a good constitution." (PP 366/112-113) Nor does it stop him from detailing a theory of moral education designed to awaken our sense of our own autonomy.[36] To the extent, or in the sense, that Kant believes that virtue can be taught, or made to flower by a good constitution, he must believe that it can be caused.[37]

Readers of Kant may want to deny this, for in the *Groundwork*, Kant says that insofar as we are members of the world of sense, our actions "must be viewed as determined by other appearances, namely, desires and inclinations." (G 453/54) But this remark is actually somewhat misleading. Insofar as we view our actions as phenomena we must view them as causally determined, but not necessarily as determined by mere desires and inclinations. We can still view them as determined by moral thoughts and moral aspirations; only from this point of view, those must themselves be viewed as determined in us. For instance, I might explain someone's doing the right thing by saying that she did it because she values humanity as an end in itself, and I might in turn explain that fact by showing how she received a moral education. And, for that matter, I might explain how that kind of education is possible by appealing to a psychological or even psychoanalytic theory, such as Freud's, of how human beings develop a conscience or superego. A deterministic account can be a deterministic account of moral motivation itself—it does not have to bypass morality and pretend we do everything for the sake of happiness. The element of truth in what Kant says is that a deterministic account necessarily leaves out what is distinctively good about moral motivation. From a merely theoretical and explanatory point of view moral interest is on a footing with inclination. We may imagine the cynic saying: "it doesn't really matter how she came to treat humanity as an end in itself. It is what she likes to do, so she is still pursuing her own happiness." When moral motivation is viewed theoretically, it can be distinguished from inclination only by its content. It's special *source*, in the agent's autonomy, does not show up.

Kant's practical compatibilism suggests that it may be reasonable, when we are deciding whether and when to hold people responsible, to take into account such things as upbringing and education. Depending on the particular circumstances, the fact that someone has had a good moral education may provide a special reason either for forgiveness or for blame, and our decisions about whether to hold him responsible may be governed accordingly. Or it may by itself, quite apart from prediction, provide a special reason for holding someone responsible. When the community has done all it can to make someone good, then there may be no further outlet for respect for humanity, than to blame him if he goes wrong.[38]

Another kind of consideration comes from Kant's iterated demand, in the *Metaphysical Principles of Virtue*, for generosity of interpretation. As I mentioned at the beginning of my discussion, Kant believes that we cannot know people's most fundamental or intelligible characters. But he censures contempt, calumny, and mockery as much for their disrespectful and ungenerous nature as for their lack of a theoretical basis. (MMV 462-468/ 127-133) He says, for instance, "One should cast the veil of philanthropy over the faults of others, not merely by softening but also by silencing our judgments." (MMV 466/132) Our theoretical estimate of another person's character may be set aside in favor of our respect for the humanity within him. The reproach of vice, according to Kant,

> ...must never burst out in complete contempt or deny the wrongdoer all moral worth, because on that hypothesis he could never be improved either—and this latter is incompatible with the idea of man, who as such (as a moral being) can never lose all predisposition to good. (MMV 463-464/129)

Kant compares this to the duty, when someone makes an error, not just to deem him stupid but to try to determine how the mistaken view could have seemed reasonable to him. We are to do this in part in order to "preserve the mistaken individual's respect for his own understanding." (MMV 463/129) But regarding a person as stupid or making her errors seem reasonable are not our only options in these cases. Sometimes we can best preserve someone's self-respect, as well as our own respect for her, not by making her errors seem reasonable, but by laughing them off as the result of transitory emotion or exhaustion. The same is surely true in the moral realm. Respect for someone's humanity is not always best expressed by holding him responsible for each and every action. It may be better to admit that even the best of us can just slip. Indeed Kant's own doctrine of moral progress, in *Religion Within the Limits of Reason Alone*, has this implication. The phenomenal expression of a noumenally good will is not perfect action in all cases, but progress towards the better. (R 47-48/43) If an anomalous action intrudes into a course of steady progress in virtue, we might find it in our hearts simply to dismiss it as atavistic or transient, or sometimes without any explanation at all. We simply say "He isn't himself."

VI. Conclusion

On the whole, Kant's view is that we must always hold ourselves responsible, and that we should as far as possible always hold other people responsible. But this is not because people's noumenal freedom is known to us as a theoretical fact. It is because of the respect which the moral law commands us to accord to the humanity in every person. We hold one another responsible because this is essential to our interactions with each other as *persons*; because in this way we together populate a moral world. We may disagree with Kant about some of the details of how respect for humanity is best expressed, but his theory captures the essential idea that attributions of responsibility have a practical basis. To view people theoretically, as objects of knowledge, is to view them as part of the world that is imposed upon us through the senses, and, to that extent, as alien. But insofar as we are noumena, or active beings, we join with others in those intersubjective standpoints which we can occupy together, either as thinkers or as agents. When we enter into relations of reciprocity, and hold one another responsible, we enter together into the standpoint of practical reason, and create a Kingdom of Ends on earth.

Notes

1. I have many people to thank for help with this paper. Ken Simons provided extensive and helpful comments which prompted me to make a number of

revisions. Sidney Axinn, Charlotte Brown, Dan Brudney, and Jay Schleusener read and commented on various versions. I presented the paper to several philosophy departments and found all of the discussions helpful; special thanks are owed to audiences at UCLA, the University of Vermont, and the University of Michigan. A short version of the paper, entitled "Holding People Responsible," was presented at the VIIth International Kant Congress and is forthcoming in the proceedings of that meeting.

2. *Nicomachean Ethics* IX.9 1170b 6-7, with parentheses removed. From the translation by W.D. Ross in *The Basic Works of Aristotle*, ed. Richard McKeon (New York: Random House, 1941), p. 1090. Henceforth cited parenthetically in the text as NE followed by the Bekker page, column, and line references and then the page number from the translation.

3. My reasons for these doubts will become apparent in the course of the paper, although I will not discuss them in the text. If the argument of this paper is correct, the decision whether to hold someone responsible is governed by a variety of considerations, rather than determined wholly by facts about the person. One might think that the legal use of the concept of responsibility requires that the issue of whether a person is responsible be determinable by such facts. Did he understand what he was doing? Does he know right from wrong? If so my view might cause difficulties for it, unless the legal use is not as continuous with the moral use as some believe. However, it is important to notice that my doubts concern the *particular* uses to which the concept of responsibility is sometimes put in our legal system. In a general and philosophical way, the justification of the penal system may rest on our will, as social contractors, to hold one another responsible. But *this* legal use of the concept of responsibility admits of the moral and practical foundation I describe in this paper, and indeed probably requires it. We have no general reason to believe that our fellow citizens are for the most part rational and moral people, who only occasionally go haywire or fall into sin. If I am right, we do have a general reason to hold them responsible: it is *because* they are our partners in the social contract.

4. This is clear from the structure of their theories. But for some more specific statements, see for example the opening paragraph of Francis Hutcheson's *Inquiry Concerning Moral Good and Evil* (in D.D. Raphael, *British Moralists*, (Hackett, 1991) Volume I, p. 261); Hume's statement of the central question of his moral philosophy on p. 456 of *The Treatise of Human Nature* (ed. L. A. Selby Bigge and P. H. Nidditch. Oxford: Clarendon Press, 1978). The complaint applies less straightforwardly to Smith, whose theory in general is more sensitive to the perspective of the agent than those of his predecessors. But see, for instance, the opening lines of I.i.5 of *The Theory of Moral Sentiments* (Indianapolis: Liberty Classics, 1982), p. 23.

5. Matthew 7:1. Where I have cited or referred to Kant's works in this paper I have inserted the reference into the text. As is standard, in each case except the *Critique of Pure Reason* and the *Lectures on Ethics*, the first page number refers to the Prussian Academy Edition of Kant's works *(Kants gesammelte Schriften. Preussische Akademie der Wissenschaften*: Berlin, 1900-1942), and the second to that of the translation used. The following abbreviations are used:

G   *Grounding for the Metaphysics of Morals.* (1785) Prussian Academy Edition Volume IV; James Ellington's translation in *Immanuel Kant: Ethical Philosophy*. Indianapolis: Hackett, 1983. Although I have used Ellington's translation, I refer to the *Grundlegung* as the *Groundwork*.

C1   *Critique of Pure Reason.* (1st ed.1781, 2nd ed.1787) Page numbers of the A and B editions are followed by those of the translation by Norman Kemp Smith. New York: Macmillan, St. Martin's Press, 1965.

C2   *Critique of Practical Reason*. (1788) Prussian Academy Volume V; Lewis White Beck's translation. Indianapolis: Bobbs-Merrill Library of Liberal Arts, 1956.

LE   *Lectures on Ethics*. (1775-1780) edited by Paul Menzer from the notes of Theodor Friedrich Brauer, using the notes of Gottlieb Kutzner and Chr. Mrongovius; translated by Louis Infield. London: Methuen & Co., Ltd., 1930; rpt: New York, Harper Torchbooks, 1963; current rpt: Indianapolis, Hackett Press.

MMV *The Metaphysical Principles of Virtue*. (1797) Prussian Academy Volume VI; James Ellington's translation in *Immanuel Kant: Ethical Philosophy*. Indianapolis: Hackett, 1983.

MMJ *The Metaphysical Elements of Justice*. (1797) Prussian Academy Volume VI; John Ladd's partial translation. Indianapolis: Bobbs-Merrill Library of Liberal Arts, 1965.

PP   *Perpetual Peace*. (1795) Prussian Academy Volume VIII, translation by Lewis White Beck in *On History*, edited by Lewis White Beck. Indianapolis: Bobbs-Merrill Library of Liberal Arts, 1963.

R   *Religion Within the Limits of Reason Alone*. (1793) Prussian Academy Volume VI; translation by Theodore M. Greene and Hoyt H. Hudson. La Salle, Illinois: Open Court, 1934. rpt. New York, Harper Torchbooks, 1960.

6. We have two somewhat different uses of the term "responsible." When we say someone is responsible for an action or attitude, we imply that she is a candidate for praise or blame. But when we say someone is a responsible person, we imply that she is reliable, resourceful, trustworthy, and self-controlled. The notion I want is a combination of these but more like the second: we think of the person as someone who should be regarded as reliable and trustworthy and so forth, and *therefore* as a candidate for praise and blame.

7. See David Hume, *An Enquiry Concerning Human Understanding* (in *Enquiries Concerning Human Understanding and Concerning the Principles of Morals by David Hume*. ed. L.A. Selby-Bigge, 3rd. ed. with text revised and notes by P.H. Nidditch. Oxford: Clarendon Press, 1975): pp. 183-192. I borrow the term "circumstances of justice" from John Rawls in *A Theory of Justice*. (Cambridge: Harvard University Press, 1971): pp. 126ff.

8. These remarks obviously assume a particular reading of Kant's Formula of Humanity, according to which what is involved in treating someone as an end-in-itself is respecting her as a rational being, whose choices confer value on their objects, and whose actions must be left to her own autonomous decision. I defend this reading in two articles, "Kant's Formula of Humanity" *Kant-Studien*, Band 77, Heft 2 (April 1986): pp. 183-202, especially pp. 197-200; and "The Right to Lie: Kant on Dealing with Evil" *Philosophy and Public Affairs*, Volume 15, Number 4 (Fall 1986): pp. 325-349; especially pp. 330-337.

9. See note 15 for some remarks on this point.

10. Here, as several readers have pointed out to me, I am obviously discussing very close and intimate friendships, and saying things that do not hold of less personal but still particular relationships. In these cases perhaps the right thing to say is that reciprocity is heightened, but only in a certain sphere of activity. The members of a committee or a department, for example, must take action and make decisions together, and this involves a commitment to treating each another's contributions to these decisions as responsible ones and each other's wishes about them as

having weight. This is a heightened form of reciprocity, although only within a delimited sphere. But within this sphere what is involved is like friendship. The comparison of factionalized departments to unhappy marriages is a good one. When reciprocity breaks down, and the entity is held together only by formal institutional mechanisms, not only its pleasantness but also its moral character deteriorates.

11. Sometimes Kant unfortunately changes his ground and says the problem is precisely that we don't want the other person *qua* that person, but only *qua* member of a particular gender. (LE 164) This is nonsense, and spoils what I take to be of interest in his point.

12. In the *Groundwork*, Kant suggests that in the Kingdom of Ends everything either has a market price, an affective price, or a dignity. Ordinary commodities have market prices, art objects have affective prices, and human beings have dignity. (G 434-435/40) Thus my suggestion in the text is that Kant is not worried that sexual desire reduces its object to something with a market price, but to something with an affective price. This suggests two further reflections. The first is interpretive. Whatever has a price, Kant claims, can be replaced by something else as its equivalent. This is already an odd thing to say about art objects, but it may explain why he was driven to make the bizarre claim mentioned in note 11 above: that we do not desire another as a person but as a member of a gender. The second is more general. Many people seem to be more skeptical about the respectability of offering yourself as a direct object of enjoyment than about the respectability of offering your services; especially, of course, if you are a woman. Actresses, entertainers, and models have often been regarded as disreputable characters; while cleaning ladies, nurses, and sales clerks are not thought thereby to degrade themselves. People may even have the obscure feeling that the character actor is more respectable than the movie star, and in this case Kant's analysis fits; for what the movie star offers for our delight is not her talents but simply herself. The view, perhaps surprising but not completely at odds with our intuitions, is then this: being useful is no threat to your dignity, but being delectable is. I do not say this to criticize movie stars, of course, but rather to urge that they are unusually dependent upon the good will and delicacy of their audiences.

13. Again Kant spoils his point, by making an oddly metaphysical-sounding argument that the lover only wants your sexuality but that "It is not possible to have the disposal of a part only of a person without having at the same time a right of disposal over the whole person, for each part of a person is integrally bound up with the whole." (LE 166) But perhaps the argument that sexual love wants its object to be entirely at its disposal can still be made, and made on more interesting grounds than the ones Kant appeals to here. Pursuing this line of thought might have forced Kant to admit that the problem he is concerned with here is more of a problem about sexual love than about casual sexual encounters.

14. It is clear from the way Kant sets the problem up in the *Lectures on Ethics* that he sees the problem as arising, so to speak, from the point of view of the sexual object. (LE 164) This point should be detachable from the familiar view, which he also sometimes seems to have in mind, that this fact makes the morality of sexuality more of a problem for a woman.

15. In public discussions of this paper, several people pointed out that more needs to be said about the sense in which one is restored to oneself in these relationships. Lawful freedom is not the same as lawless freedom; the condition to which one is restored is not the same. Kant makes this clear in a rather forceful way when he says that marriage produces a unity of will. The kind of reciprocity I am discussing here is not mere exchange, from which one can walk away. What is

exchanged is a part of one's practical identity, and what results is a transformation of that identity. Kant's account of marriage is clearly based on Rousseau's account of the social contract, in which "each person gives himself whole and entire" and "in giving himself to all, each person gives himself to no one. And since there is no associate over whom he does not acquire the same right that he would grant others over himself, he gains the equivalent of everything he loses..." Rousseau certainly thinks that this produces a change of identity, since he says it is what transforms a human being from "a stupid, limited animal into an intelligent being and a man." (Rousseau, *On the Social Contract*, trans. Donald A. Cress. Indianapolis: Hackett, 1983: pp. 24-27) This aspect of Kant's view of personal relations has a number of striking implications, among them some that address contemporary criticisms of Kant. From a feminist perspective, Kant has sometimes been accused of denying that personal relationships can be constitutive of identity. See for instance Sally Sedgwick, "Can Kant's Ethics Survive the Feminist Critique?" (*Pacific Philosophical Quarterly* 71 (1990): pp. 60-79, especially p.74) And it has also been argued that his ethics requires that the moral agent be completely impartial among persons in some undesirable way. See for instance, Bernard Williams, "Persons, Character and Morality" in *Moral Luck* (Cambridge: Cambridge University Press, 1981): pp. 1-19, especially pp. 16-18. In my view Kant's theory of personal relations provides grounds for challenging both of these views. I hope to pursue these points sometime.

16. Not translated in Ladd. Kant does not draw *this* conclusion, of course. But he comes close. For he goes on to raise the obvious question whether the marriages of his time, which declare the husband to be master, are real marriages, and to assert absurdly that so long as the inequality is really only based on the natural superiority of the man's faculties it is no inequality at all. Both the feebleness and the moral irrelevance of this excuse for inequality suggest the conclusion in the text.

17. In *The Possibility of Altruism* (Princeton: Princeton University Press, 1970: 83), Thomas Nagel argues that resentment, for instance, involves the thought that the person resented had a *reason* to act differently than he did. If this is right, and personal relations essentially involve the sharing of reasons, it is clear why personal relations especially involve such reactive attitudes.

18. See Strawson, *Freedom and Resentment and Others Essays* (London: Methuen & Co., 1974), p. 4.

19. In his discussion of Gauguin in "Moral Luck," Bernard Williams suggests that, even if we accept Gauguin's success in painting as a justification for his desertion of his family, his family need not do so. Williams thinks that this is because you can do something justified and yet leave some people with a justified complaint. Leaving aside that question, on my view we may at least say this: given Gauguin's belief in his vocation, *we* may find his desertion of his family understandable and forgivable—just another instance of the strains which the institution of marriage places on the moral life—while *his wife* certainly need not find in this a reason for forgiveness at all. See Williams, "Moral Luck" in *Moral Luck* (Cambridge: Cambridge University Press, 1981): pp. 20-39; and especially pp. 36-37.

20. There are others, of course. For instance, one who knows you well may use his knowledge to manipulate you psychologically. And there is also the simple risk that while you are opening your heart, the other is holding back. Few things are as disconcerting as the discovery that someone in whom you have confided a certain kind of secret or thought or feeling has secrets or thoughts or feelings of a similar kind, which she has not in turn shared with you. This may make you feel exposed, watched, or objectified. You do not need to think that she was

spying on or judging you in order for this to hurt; the bare failure of reciprocity is enough.

21. We must suppose this, more specifically, to avoid falling into the third antinomy. (C1 A444 & B472-A452 & B480/409-415)

22. In this sketch of Kant's view I skate over the differences between Kant's accounts of how we arrive at the idea of our own freedom in the Third Section of the *Groundwork for the Metaphysics of Morals* and in the *Critique of Practical Reason*. In the *Groundwork*, Kant's emphasis is on our consciousness of the spontaneity of reason in the production of ideas in general; in the *Critique of Practical Reason*, it is on our awareness of the moral law and of our ability to act from it (the Fact of Reason), which he says reveals our freedom to us. (See the references in the text and C2 30-31/30-31) I believe that Kant revised his argument because the spontaneous production of ideas only places us among the noumena as thinkers. To be among the noumena as *agents*, we must be able to *act from* pure ideas, and for this, the positive conception of freedom which is found only in the categorical imperative, as well as our ability to act from that conception, are necessary.

23. This account, which of course is not Kant's, resembles the more traditional rationalist account: incentives incline but do not determine the will. Kant does think that this is how we must regard our own incentives from the practical point of view.

24. It is important to say that the claim is only that it is crazy to regard *Marilyn's* noumenal will, taken by itself, as standing behind the laws of nature. Whether Kant thinks that all rational wills taken together should be regarded as standing behind the laws of nature is a different question altogether.

25. Kant's language in *Groundwork III* could certainly lead one to believe that he holds this view; and it is this same language which gives rise to the paradoxes mentioned. If we always choose morally in the noumenal world, and if our noumenal choices govern our phenomenal ones, how do bad actions ever occur? And if they do occur, since they cannot be attributed to our noumenal will, how can we be held responsible for them? It is possible that at the time of writing the *Groundwork* Kant had not sufficiently distinguished (what I take to be) his own view from the one under discussion here. I discuss this further in note 29. I discuss the paradoxes about the possibility of evil and responsibility for evil in "Morality as Freedom" in *Kant's Practical Philosophy Reconsidered*, ed. Y. Yovel (Kluwer Academic Publishers, 1989), especially pp. 35-40.

26. The knowability of pure activity or power is an important theme in modern philosophy, taken up by thinkers as diverse as Descartes and Hume. In the *Second Meditation*, Descartes argues that although we cannot "imagine" ourselves as pure thinkers, that is the role in which we *know* ourselves best (i.e., most free from skeptical doubt). (*Meditations on First Philosophy,* trans. Elizabeth S. Haldane and G.R.T. Ross. in *The Philosophical Works of Descartes*, Volume I. Cambridge: Cambridge University Press, 1911, p. 153) Hume, who thinks we get all of our ideas from the senses and therefore cannot have ideas of what we cannot imagine or envision, supposes that we do *not* know ourselves as active thinkers. He tells us that "The uniting principle among our internal perceptions is as unintelligible as that among external objects, and is not known to us any other way than by experience." (*A Treatise of Human Nature*, cited in note 4 above, p. 169) But the view comes out most clearly in the *Dialogues Concerning Natural Religion*, in remarks like "But the ideas in a human mind, we see, by an unknown, inexplicable economy, arrange themselves as to form the plan of a watch or a house..." (Part II, p. 146) and "We have indeed, experience of ideas, which fall

into order, of themselves, and without any known cause..." (Part IV, p. 162; quoted from the edition by Norman Kemp Smith, Macmillan Library of Liberal Arts, 1947). Kant's move here as everywhere is to find a path between empiricism and rationalism, using what is right in both positions. Hume is correct in tying what we can know to what can be represented. The world must show itself to us before we can apply the concepts that give us understanding. But he is wrong in thinking we can only *have ideas* of the sorts of things we can know. What we can think is not exhausted by what we can know: our concepts do not all come from sensible intuition. Descartes is right in insisting that we can *think* about our activity. But he is wrong to suppose that we *know* ourselves as thinkers and agents. Our agency, although not knowable, is *intelligible*, and we must think of it. (C1 A538 & B566/467)

27. These remarks apply to the moral law, on the practical side, and to the regulative principles of reason, on the theoretical or speculative side. Something more complex must be said about the constitutive principles of the understanding, an issue which I here leave aside.

28. Including, in the theoretical or speculative realm, deciding how to proceed with our investigation or theory construction. In fact, when describing and explaining our behavior we must view ourselves both ways, since we appear in the role of thinker as well as that of object thought about.

29. The reader may wonder whether I am suggesting that Kant was simply wrong in the *Groundwork* when he said that insofar as we are members of the intelligible world we necessarily will according to the moral law, and that if we were only members of that world we would will always according to that law (G 453/54). The answer is no, but here I think it is significant that in the *Groundwork* Kant uses the language of "intelligible" and "sensible" rather than that of "noumenal" and "phenomenal"; and also that he changes his language in the *Critique of Practical Reason*. As I understand these terms, the noumenal world is the intelligible world insofar as it is thinkable. If we think of noumena at all, we must think of them as acting in the only way that is intelligible to us, which is according to the laws of freedom. But at the same time we must always admit the possibility that the noumenal world is unintelligible to us. The trouble with the way Kant phrases the argument in *Groundwork III* is that it can make it sound as if the normative force of the moral law followed from its descriptive application in the noumenal world: "Now if I were a member of only that world [the intelligible world], all my actions *would* always accord with autonomy of the will. But since I intuit myself at the same time as a member of the world of sense, my actions *ought* so to accord." (G 454/55) If we suppose, naturally but incorrectly, that the normativity of morality enters the scene with the "ought", Kant seems to be deriving a normative sensible "ought" from a descriptive intelligible "is". But he is not, for the laws of the intelligible world are normative through and through. The moral law characterizes noumena insofar as they are intelligences (insofar as we can think of them) because acting according to it is the only thing it makes sense for them to *do*; and this is already a normative point.

30. This is slightly overstated, since Kant does think that insofar as we are free we think of ourselves as the causes of our action; and this idea plays an important role in his ethics at various crucial moments. But since he insists that free causality is an idea without a theoretical employment, the point still holds. (C2 49/50; 56/57-58; 133-136/137-142)

31. Perhaps I should make it clear that the question I am asking here concerns the way we make this decision in a case where it is *already* clear that we *can* view the creature and its actions in either of these two ways. Kant thinks we can do

this whenever the actions are performed by a human being. I am not concerned here with what justifies that view—that is, I am not discussing the question why we think that human beings are candidates for being held responsible while the other intelligent animals, who make some use of reason and with whom we may enter into some forms of relationship, are not. This is an important question, but it requires a separate treatment.

32. This remark again straddles the accounts in the *Groundwork* and in the *Critique of Practical Reason*, since I think that both elements are involved in Kant's best explanation of how we come to think of our own freedom. See my "Morality as Freedom," pp. 39-40, cited in note 25 above.

33. See Derek Parfit, "Later Selves and Moral Principles" in A. Montefiore, ed. *Philosophy and Personal Relations* (London: Routledge & Kegan Paul, 1973, pp. 145ff.; and *Reasons and Persons* (Oxford: Oxford University Press, 1984) pp. 327-328.

34. I discuss the practical construction of our own identities in "Personal Identity and the Unity of Agency: A Kantian Reply to Parfit" *Philosophy and Public Affairs*, Volume 18, Number 2 (Spring, 1989): 101-132. The issue of whether relationships can be constitutive of identity is touched on in note 15 above.

35. "This commitment ['the natural human commitment to ordinary inter-personal attitudes'] is part of the general framework of human life, not something that can come up for review as particular cases can up for review within this particular framework." Strawson, "Freedom and Resentment", cited in note 18 above.

36. Kant's theory is spelled out in the "Methodologies" of the *Metaphysical Principles of Virtue* (477-484/145-153) and of the *Critique of Practical Reason* (151-163/155-168), as well as in his book *Education*. (1803, trans. Annette Churton. Ann Arbor: University of Michigan Press, 1971).

37. Kant denies that we can have a duty to promote the moral perfection of others, on these grounds: "For the perfection of another man as a person consists precisely in his being able to set his end for himself according to his own concepts of duty. And it is a contradiction to require (to make it a duty for me) that I ought to do something which no one except another himself can do." (MMV 387/44) But this, again, is overstated. Granted, that it would be both disrespectful to you, and unfair to me, to hold me responsible in a general way for your moral character. Yet it is clear that we have a duty to provide for the moral education of our children, and, Kant himself insists, our intimate friends. (MMV 470/136) Choosing ends on another's behalf is as impossible as it would be disrespectful, but putting others in a good position to choose ends for themselves, and to choose them well, is the proper work of parents, teachers, friends, and politicians; providing for someone's moral education as well as nurturing her self-respect is an important part of the way we do this.

38. Nor is Kant unaware of the more direct educational benefits of holding others responsible, for he reminds us that "Examples of respect shown to others may also incite in them an endeavor to deserve it." (MV 466/132) In *Ethics and the Limits of Philosophy* (Cambridge: Harvard University Press, 1985), Bernard Williams writes, "The institution of blame is best understood as involving a fiction, by which we treat the agent as one for whom the relevant ethical considerations are reasons. ...This fiction has various functions. One is that if we treat the agent as someone who gives weight to ethical reasons, this may help to make him into such a person." (p. 193) It is presumably this form of "recruitment into the deliberative community," to use Williams's phrase, that he has in mind when he writes "The purity of morality conceals not only the means by which it deals with

deviant members of its community, but also the virtues of those means." (p. 195) Williams thinks that "the fiction of the deliberative community is one of the positive achievements of the morality system" but adds "As with other fictions it is a real question whether its working could survive a clear understanding of how it works." (193-194) I want to make two comments about these remarks. First, the view of persons we adopt from the practical point of view will seem "fictional" (if that is supposed to suggest some form of inferiority) only to those who privilege the theoretical standpoint and its concepts, or at least believe that all our concepts should be congruent with those. This suggests a certain view of what concepts in general are for. No doubt theoretical concepts are more firmly aimed at tracking the truth, but tracking the truth is not the primary business of ethical concepts, as Williams would certainly agree. In any case the term "fiction" is one adopted from the theoretical standpoint, and relativized in an obvious way to the purposes of theoretical reason. My second point concerns recruitment into the deliberative community. Kant himself apparently thought that we *can* understand how holding people responsible works—and even, as the quotation above suggests, that we can take notice of its more strategic benefits—and yet go on doing it. Of course it is a delicate business to manipulate someone into morality while maintaining the essentially non-manipulative attitude that morality demands. But, as Kant's remarks about error at MMV 463/129 (quoted in Section V) show, he rightly perceives this to be a quite general problem about education.

Philosophical Perspectives, 6, Ethics, 1992

HOBBES AND ETHICAL NATURALISM

Jean Hampton
University of Arizona

In his book *Ethics: Inventing Right and Wrong*, John Mackie puts his finger on the reason many contemporary moral theorists have repudiated much of the moral language of the Aristotelian, Kantian, rights-based, and utilitarian traditions: it is, in their view, a language that refers either to metaphysically "queer" objects that are supposed to be inherently prescriptive, or to what seem like the magical powers of something called "practical reason" to discover and motivate other-regarding action. Mackie and other contemporary moral theorists, among them, Gauthier and Harman, have argued for what I call a "no-nonsense" moral theory, exemplifying what is called "naturalism" in ethics.[1] Such a theory refers to no queer objects, attributes no strange powers to human reason, and is entirely consistent with a physicalist metaphysics. But this approach to ethics isn't new: in early modern times the most famous and sophisticated exponent of this approach was Thomas Hobbes. Attacking what he called the "filth and fraud" in Greek philosophy, (DC, EW i, Ep. Ded., ix), Hobbes dismissed the existence of any *Summum Bonum*, the prescriptive entity that his academic contemporaries were most likely to embrace, and constructed what he called a "science" of moral philosophy that he viewed as the equal of scientific theories in the physical sciences advanced by Galileo, Kepler and Harvey. And the broad outlines of this approach have recently been followed by a number of ethical naturalists.

The aim of this article is to evaluate the success of the Hobbesian version of ethical naturalism. After outlining and evaluating Hobbes's moral theory, and noting why its broad outlines have appealed to so many both in his day and in our own, I shall argue that the plausibility of this approach depends upon the covert importation of the very metaphysical nonsense it claims to eschew. So my intention is not only to provide an interpretation of the Hobbesian texts, but also to explore the structure and weaknesses of a version of a presently popular approach to ethics. I hope to show that certain contemporary moral theorists who share Hobbes's metaphysical scruples as they promulgate this type of moral theory are just as misled as he was about the extent to which it avoids importing what they take to be illicit metaphysical content. While the arguments of the paper are not against ethical naturalism per se but only against the Hobbesian brand of this approach, nonetheless I will explain how the problems with Hobbes's approach are serious enough to worry any ethical naturalist.

This article also has a scholarly as well as a theoretical point: I shall argue that once the metaphysical problems of Hobbes's type of moral theory are understood, it is possible to reconcile two divergent interpretations of the Hobbesian moral texts. Whereas some Hobbes scholars have followed Howard Warrender in thinking that Hobbes should be interpreted as a natural law theorist, propounding moral obligations that hold regardless of our desires and a conception of rationality that is non-instrumental, others have insisted that Hobbes was a thorough-going ethical subjectivist, who attempts to derive moral obligations from enlightened self-interest and who holds an entirely instrumental understanding of reason. It ought to be a source of amazement to Hobbes scholars that two such different interpretations could be generated from the same texts. I hope to show how both these divergent views are possible and partially correct: the latter camp, I will argue, correctly understands the view Hobbes intended to put forward; the former camp, however, appreciates the view that he is forced to fall back upon given the theoretical problems with his intended view and the way in which those problems undercut his political agenda.

I. Hobbes's Science of Moral Philosophy

Hobbes maintains that the key to the scientific penetration of the world is the proper use of reason. (See De Corp, EW i, I ,1, 1) Mental activity, he claims, is always regulated "by some desire or design" (Lev, 3, 4, 9). When such thinking is done "rightly" we are determining as effectively as possible means to our ends; nonetheless Hobbes distinguishes true reasoning from mere prudential calculation by insisting that reason is

> not gotten by experience only; as Prudence is; but attayned by Industry; first
> in apt imposing of Names; and Secondly by getting good and orderly
> Method in proceeding from the Elements, which are Names, to Assertions
> made by Connexion of one of them to another; and so to Syllogisms, which
> are the Connexions of one Assertion to another, till we come to a
> knowledge of all the Consequences of names appertaining to the subject in
> hand; and that is it, men call SCIENCE. (Lev, 5, 17, 21)

One point Hobbes is certainly trying to make in this passage is that a language-user has the capacity to reason syllogistically and thus to arrive at conclusions that are "logically necessary"—i.e. necessary in the sense that they are logical implications, and that are true provided that the premises of the (valid) syllogism are true. (e.g. see De Corp, EW i, I 6, 16, 86)

However, not only does Hobbes perceive science as a discipline that follows a logical method to yield logically necessary truths, he also sees it as having a certain *content*, in which necessity of a very different and *causal* sort is made manifest. He insists in *Leviathan* that "Science is the knowledge of Consequences" (Lev, 5, 17, 21), which seeks to understand a world that is experienced by us as filled with change. Hobbes argues in *De Corpore* that the foundation of such a world can be revealed to us "without method," for the causes of such changes "are manifest of themselves, or (as they say commonly) known to nature"—and he contends that the cause of all change is *motion* (De Corp, EW i, I, 6, 5, 69). Hence, the first principles of science must explain and reveal the causal connection of objects in the world by appeal to certain *laws of motion*, one of which he takes to be Galileo's law of inertia. (De Corp, EW i, II, 9, 7, 124-5; see also I, 6, 6, 70-73.)

Hobbes does not think that we engage in scientific inquiry solely or even primarily because we value the acquisition of truth about the world for its own sake. Instead he believes, with Bacon, that "the *end* or *scope* of philosophy is, that we may make use to our benefit of effects formerly seen...*for the commodity of human life*." (De Corp, EW i, I, 1, 6, 7; emphasis added) Hence, science, for Hobbes, has a prescriptive role as well as a descriptive role. It not only describes the world but also directs us in efficacious ways of behavior based on its discoveries about the structure and operation of the world. If we want to shoot a cannonball to destroy our enemy in battle, or if we want to change our body chemistry to cure a disease, science tells us what to do by giving us the causal information we need to achieve these aims.

Given this distinctive understanding of science, it is significant that Hobbes calls his body of ethical and political arguments a "science" at the end of chapter 15 of *Leviathan*. After completing his definition of nineteen moral laws of nature, the second of which contains the directive to institute an absolute sovereign, he maintains that "the science of them is the true and only moral philosophy." (Lev, 15, 40, 79) If science is "knowledge of consequences," then do these nineteen laws of nature give us causal knowledge of the world?

Indeed they do, as Hobbes goes on to explain. First, he repeats his subjectivist definitions of 'good' and 'evil' from chapter 6. Those definitions go as follows:

> whatsoever is the object of any mans Appetite or Desire; that is it, which he for his part calleth *Good*: And the object of his Hate, and Aversion, *Evill*; And of his Contempt, *Vile* and *Inconsiderable*. For these words of Good, Evill, and Contemptible, are ever used with relation to the person that useth them: There being nothing simply and absolutely so; nor any common Rule of Good and Evill, to be taken from the nature of the objects themselves...(Lev, 6, 7, 24).

This subjectivism is, in essence, a position on human value that eschews metaphysical "nonsense". That which is responsible for our evaluations and which moves us to act is not some kind of mysterious intrinsic good "out there," but our desires, whose satisfaction is accomplished by securing objects which, in virtue of their power to satisfy desire, we call good. Hobbes does not explicitly put forward a projection theory of value, i.e. one in which positive or negative evaluation is projected on to objects in virtue of our perception of them as objects which satisfy or impede desire (and which are therefore experienced as pleasure-producing or pain-producing). But his remarks are certainly suggestive of, and consistent with, such a theory (so that these remarks must surely have had an influence on Hume).[2]

After taking this naturalistic approach to value, Hobbes goes on to declare:

> Morall philosophy is nothing else but the Science of what is *Good* and *Evill*, in the conversation, and society of mankind. *Good* and *Evill*, are names that signifie our Appetites, and Aversions; which in different tempers, customes, and doctrines of men, are different...(Lev, 15, 40, 79)

At this point, Hobbes's moral philosophy sounds like little more than an anthropological study—it certainly would appear to be a wholly descriptive rather than a prescriptive enterprise.

But this is a premature conclusion. Next he says that, although men differ greatly in what they desire, "all men agree on this, that Peace is good." (Lev, 15, 40, 80) In *De Homine*, Hobbes calls this type of good (i.e. one that all human beings want and that they can all share) a "common good."(chapter 11) But Hobbes also distinguishes between two sorts of desired goods: real and apparent. The former is what a person would desire if he had true beliefs as well as a physiologically healthy reasoning and desire-formation system; the latter is what a person actually desires given the beliefs that he has and the physiological state he is in. Therefore, when Hobbes speaks about moral philosophy as the science of what is good in the conversation of mankind, he is not being completely clear. He is not interested merely in what people actually seek, given their desires, as means to achieving those desires; he is also interested in what they *should* seek as means to achieving them (i.e. as the correct or most effective way to realize the object they are pursuing). Peace is, in his eyes, a "real" common good insofar as it actually does lead to the furtherance of what people desire most—their self-preservation. Moreover, he also believes that peace is actually perceived by all men as a good—the apparent and the real coincide in this case. But what is not so manifest to all men is that if peace is good, then also

> the way, or means of Peace, which (as I have shewed before) are *Justice, Gratitude, Modesty, Equity, Mercy*, and the rest of the Laws of Nature, are good; that is to say *Morall Vertues*; and their contrarie *Vices*, Evill. (Lev, 15, 40, 80)

The laws of nature assert a causal connection between these cooperative forms of behavior and self-preservation because these forms of behavior effect peace and peace in turn helps to effect longer life (although he specifies later on that they do so only in circumstances where others also are willing to perform these actions). Therefore, on Hobbes's view the ingredients of a moral imperatives are certain cause-and-effect statements connected with appeals to certain kinds of desire. As I shall now discuss, such a theory at least appears to be one that entirely satisfies the metaphysical scruples of the naturalist.

II. Value and Reason

There are a number of ways to measure the success of the Hobbesian moral theory. One can, for example, worry about the extent to which it really succeeds in capturing the concepts and content that many of us intuitively believe morality must involve. I want, however, to try a different evaluative strategy: I want to see whether or not this moral theory is really free of the metaphysical nonsense it claims to renounce.

Consider that Hobbes's moral science is only successful if it offers a naturalistic explanation of norms. As I will understand it, *a norm is something that is taken to have authority over our decision-making in the sense that it gives us a reason to act, choose, or believe as the norm directs, no matter what other reason or motives we have, where this reason is supposed to be decisive in some circumstances.* The authority of a norm can be understood in an internalist or externalist way, and there can be all sorts of norms; e.g. norms of morality, norms of rationality, even norms of linguistic competence.

Now it seems plausible to explain norms of linguistic competence as, in some sense, social constructs, and many contemporary theorists believe rational and moral norms can be successfully explained in the same way. If the theorist is careful, such an explanation can be entirely naturalistic.[3] But no self-respecting Hobbesian can take seriously a societal explanation of *all* rational and moral norms (even if it might do for some of them), given that, for a Hobbesian, our sociality is tenuous at best and not fundamental to our nature as persons.[4] Indeed, Hobbes believes he has to give a naturalistic explanation of one norm, mandating the establishment of the absolute sovereign, in order to explain how any cooperative human society is even possible. But if there are rational and moral norms that are not in any fundamental way social constructs (even if they might eventually become socially recognized, taught and reinforced), then they are metaphysically problematic for anyone impressed by the fact that the physical sciences recognize no object like them.

Philosophers such as John Mackie with metaphysical scruples have therefore suggested that terms referring to these sorts of norms in fact denote non-existent entities, amounting to an "error theory" of normative discourse.

Hobbes's moral science attempts to do something harder and to my mind more exciting: it attempts to recognize the existence of norms, including moral norms, without explaining them as social constructs, while nonetheless explaining them naturalistically.

Like Aristotle, Hobbes accepts the standard definition and authority of the traditional virtues; his nineteen laws of nature are really norms of cooperative behavior and individual human excellence. However, what Hobbes does not accept is Aristotle's objectivist way of defining them or justifying their authority.[5] Instead, he believes that we ought to act morally in the same way that we ought to take our medicine when we are sick; both actions are necessary causes of desired effects. So, the amazing authority of the norms of behavior and character that we call virtues is explained in an entirely naturalistic way, as a function of two things: first, the causal connection between the virtuous behavior or characteristic and the state of peace; and second, the desire that virtually all of us have to achieve peace in view of the fact that it promotes our self-preservation. A moral imperative is the assertion of this causal connection, and it has authoritative power over our decision-making if (but only if) the person to whom it is addressed desires the object which the imperative tells him how to effect or achieve. So Hobbes would appear to be proposing a moral theory that succeeds in offering pre-scriptions that are entirely reducible to non-prescriptive, scientifically acceptable components. *It is a theory that would preserve the normativity of moral imperatives, but explain that normativity as something constructed entirely out of non-normative ingredients.*

This explanation of normative authority clearly meets the metaphysical standards of the naturalist. Moreover it also yields what seems a very success-ful explanation of moral motivation. We should act cooperatively and display the traditional virtues of character because it is in our interest to do so (albeit only when others are similarly disposed). We need only appeal to our fundamental desires as human beings in order to explain what can and should move us to act morally.

Hobbes can even explain how moral imperatives can be judged true or false. To make such a judgement one does not need to posit strange moral objects, prescriptive properties or a divinely-revealed truth; instead one explains these laws as true in the same way that any conditional cause-and-effect proposition in a physical science is true. Indeed, Hobbes can regard himself as a moral objectivist of sorts, because he insists that moral proposi-tions are objectively true insofar as they are assertions of causal connections between certain actions and a commonly desired goal. Of course, this is not the sort of 'objectivity' that a Kantian or an Aristotelian wants, but this only shows that we should beware of the terms 'subjective' and 'objective' in moral theory since they do not necessarily mark the right distinctions. Critical to Hobbes's project is a subjectivist theory of value, but in virtue of the fact that there can be true and false propositions in regard to achieving what one values, Hobbes can insist that moral propositions are capable of being objectively assessed for their truth.

However, the key to Hobbes's no-nonsense theory is his subjectivist theory of value; it is this theory which provides the non-normative building blocks for the theory. By insisting that value and disvalue are either equivalent to or projections of what we desire and what we are averse to, Hobbes has an entirely naturalistic explanation of why and how objects are taken by us to be 'good' and 'bad'. This notion of value is then used to explain the authority and motivating force of the laws of nature. But if, upon examination, the selection or definition of what counts as value-defining turns out to presuppose a norm either directly (i.e. that which does the selection or defining is a norm) or indirectly (i.e. a norm motivates the requirement that does the selecting or defining), then Hobbes's no-nonsense theory fails because it presupposes the existence of the sort of metaphysically queer object it was supposed to be explaining.

Thus it is interesting that certain critics of Hobbes's work have located and discussed passages from the Hobbesian texts that do not seem to be in accord with the subjectivist theory of value and which even have an Aristotelian flavor to them. Aristotle posited the existence of an objective value, the *Summum Bonum*, which is good for its own sake and which one ought to desire. The *Summum Bonum* is supposed to be accessible through the use of reason, so that reason has an end of its own, which may conflict with the ends of our desires. Accordingly, if someone pursues an end set by desire that is in conflict with the end set by reason, he is rightly criticized as irrational.

Now when Hobbes labels as irrational those people who do not pursue their self-preservation (especially the glory-prone among us) he sounds very Aristotelian. How can a subjectivist say that the effective pursuit of any good defined by desire is contrary to reason? As Hume puts it, "'Tis as little contrary to reason to prefer the destruction of the whole world to the scratching of my little finger..." (Treatise, II, iii, iii, 1978, 416) A true subjectivist is barred from attributing to reason a goal that is taken to be objectively valuable and which can be opposed to the goals of desire.

Some critics[6] maintain these passages show that Hobbes embraces a highly Aristotelian theory about the role of reason in defining value. This conclusion in my view cannot be right, not only for textual reasons but also for philosophical ones. The constant disparaging of Aristotelian ethics in Hobbes's writings shows that he didn't intend an Aristotelian theory, and the scientific approach to moral imperatives developed in these writings requires an instrumental (and thus non-Aristotelian) conception of reason and a subjective conception of value. But these Aristotelian passages may very well be evidence for what I think is a more interesting and important conclusion:

i.e. that Hobbes cannot sustain a purely naturalistic, no-nonsense moral theory in his writings.

To find out whether or not this conclusion is right, we need to examine the Aristotelian passages to determine, first of all, whether or not they really must be interpreted in a way that is inconsistent with Hobbes's subjectivist approach to value. Elsewhere I argued that there was no inconsistency between these passages and that theory of value.[7] But now I have second thoughts.

III. The Irrationality of Desires

The adjective 'irrational' can be applied by us to a person, action, belief, or desire. One appears to apply the label anti-subjectively if one applies it to any desire, because calling a desire irrational appears to presuppose, in Aristotelian fashion, that they are rightly judged with reference to an objective, normative evaluative standard of reason, meaning that they cannot play the role of a non-normative foundation for a naturalistic ethical theory. So if desires define value, and rationality is understood instrumentally as the person's effective pursuit of the satisfaction of his desires, then only the incorrect actions he takes to satisfy his desires, or else the incorrect beliefs that lead him to take these actions, or else he himself—the person who chose those incorrect actions, can appropriately be labelled 'irrational'.

However, this is not quite correct: subjectivists do have the conceptual room to make *one* kind of criticism of desire. Let me make a (Nagel-like) distinction between "basic" and "motivated" desires, a distinction which individuates desires by reference to their objects. Basic desires are what Hume might call "original existences"; the object of the desire is desired for its own sake, whereas the object of a motivated desire is desired, at least in part, as the means to the satisfaction of some other desire.[8] To be precise: desire $d1$ is motivated by desire $d2$ if attaining the object of $d1$ is required in the circumstances to attain the object of $d2$. Hobbes himself would give a substantive characterization of the difference between the two types of desires as follows: the object of a basic desire is perceived as pleasure-producing or pain-avoiding in and of itself, whereas the object of a motivated desire is entirely or in part a means to achieving some other object or state of affairs that is directly pleasure-producing or pain-avoiding. A motivated desire can itself motivate a further desire. My motivated desire for fresh trout, which I desire in order to satisfy my basic desire to alleviate pangs of hunger, motivates my desire to construct a fishing pole. By the phrase "more basic desire" I will mean any desire, either basic or motivated, whose satisfaction in the circumstances requires obtaining the object of a motivated desire.

But what if I believe that attaining the object of $d2$ will allow me to achieve the object of $d1$, and my belief is false? We can distinguish between desires that are subjectively motivated by my beliefs about means-ends connections, and objectively motivated desires—i.e. desires that ought to be motivated given the facts about means-ends connections. Subjectively motivated desires may or may not match their objective counterparts; when they do not, the reasoner has made a mistake.

So on this line of reasoning, one can be a thorough-going subjectivist and still criticize desires as irrational, if those desires are motivated and they are informed by factual error. In particular, if the agent is mistaken about how to achieve either a basic desire or another motivated desire, such that the object of his motivated desire is not in fact a means to the satisfaction of the more basic desire, then criticizing that motivated desire as irrational amounts to saying that reason has motivated a desire for the wrong object and has therefore failed to be an effective servant to the more basic desire.

In fact, Hobbes's distinction between 'real' and 'seeming' goods seems to be prompted at least in part by his wish to make exactly this kind of criticism of motivated desires. Consider that the desire for peace is a motivated desire; we are supposed to want peace as a means to achieving the object of a basic desire, i.e. self-preservation. So when certain behaviors or objects appear to us as good because they appear to us as means to furthering our self-preservation, but turn out nonetheless to impede rather than further the achievement of peace (in a situation where cooperative interaction was really possible)[9] Hobbes can call the objects of these desires "seeming" rather than "real" goods, and criticize the (motivated) desires for them as irrational, consistent with his subjectivism. Those labels simply tell us that the positive valuation of these objects was contrary to the facts about how to satisfy a more basic desire, a fact which (as I'll discuss by the end of the paper) the person criticized is considered to be in a position to have known through the use of her reason. So consistent with Hobbesian terminology, we may call objectively correct motivated desires 'real' motivated desires, where, in virtue of their correctness, these will always be rational desires. Moreover, we may label subjectively generated motivated desires 'apparent' motivated desires, and evaluate them as rational or irrational depending upon whether or not their objects are effective means for attaining the object that will allow for the satisfaction of the agent's more basic desire (which must itself be either an objectively correct motivated desire or else a basic desire).

Unfortunately Hobbes's use of the notion of irrationality doesn't always fit this analysis. Often he criticizes as irrational a person who acts to achieve one basic desire, i.e. the desire for glory, insofar as this pursuit impedes the satisfaction of another basic desire, i.e. the desire for self-preservation. Such criticism appears to be motivated by the Aristotelian thought that self-preservation is the "right" good for people to pursue, regardless of what they actually desire.

Nonetheless there is still a subjectivist reason for making this criticism.

Imagine a person whose desires are hierarchically ordered in respect to something we'll call "importance". If basic desire x is more important than basic desire y, and if the person acts on basic desire y in such a way that he impedes the satisfaction of basic desire x, then once again he can be called irrational, given the importance *he* attaches to x, and not the importance we attach to it. We criticize him for acting in such a way as to fail to satisfy what *he* takes to be good, and in particular we call him irrational if we believe that he could have used his reason beforehand to recognize his mistake.

Hobbes's criticism of glory-prone people as irrational insofar as they act so as to threaten their self-preservation nicely fits this last analysis. He believes that for virtually all of us, achieving glory is less important than forestalling death, so that, given the structure of *our own desires*, we are making a mistake if we persist in the pursuit of glory in a way that involves a significant risk of death.

Note that this last use of irrationality is, properly speaking, only a criticism of either the actions taken to satisfy the less important desire or the person who has chosen to satisfy the less important desire. That less important desire is not *itself* irrational. *It* doesn't impede the satisfaction of the more important desire; only action from it does so. And a person cannot be irrational insofar as she has the desire, but only insofar as she chooses to act on it. (Consider a desire whose satisfaction impedes the satisfaction of more important preferences, but which the agent finds herself inexplicably acting on: e.g. a smoker's preference for cigarettes impeding action to insure her survival. Does it make sense to call these preferences irrational? A good value-subjectivist can and should say no. There is nothing wrong with such preferences per se; what is wrong is the agent's acting upon them given her motivational set. If she cannot avoid acting upon them, she should strive to remove them, but this is because of a defect in her ability to act rationally. *She* is what is irrational, not the preference.)

However, Hobbes does appear to criticize certain basic desires themselves, and not merely action from them, as irrational, in apparent violation of his subjectivist position. Consider what he must mean when he calls those who desire glory 'madmen':

> the Passion, whose violence, or continuance maketh Madnesse, is either great *vaine-Glory*; which is commonly called *Pride*, and self-conceipt; or great *Dejection* of mind. (Lev, 8, 18, 35)

and also in *De Homine*:

> Excessive self-esteem impedes reason; and on that account is a perturbation of the mind, wherein a certain swelling of the mind is experienced because the animal spirits are transported. (DH, xii, 9, 60)

And after saying this Hobbes adds a remark that appears blatantly normative: "Proper self-esteem, however, is not a perturbation, but a state of mind that ought to be." (DH, xii, 9, 60-1)

In this passage and others[10] Hobbes seems to be criticizing a basic desire as itself irrational or as "impeding reason" not because action from it impedes the satisfaction of a more important desire, but because the desire is "wrong" in and of itself. The physiological remarks seem to present the position that, while value is defined by desires, it is only by desires formed normally in a healthy human body—a body that "ought to be". Those desires whose generation is indicative of diseases such as madness are to be discounted, and action on them is to be criticized as irrational.[11]

Can this position be consistent with subjectivism? The problem with making it so is that Hobbes is not merely criticizing the actions of "crazy" people that prevent them from satisfying a desire (plausibly attributed to them) to get well. It is also that *what* they desire, and take action to achieve, is 'wrong', 'nuts'—manifesting a failure of reason. When Lady MacBeth desires to wash her hands continually, she is displaying a failure of reason simply in virtue of having that very desire. If this is what Hobbes wants to say, then he must admit that not every desire we have can be taken to define value, but only desires that are "normal", arising from a healthy body chemistry.

Critics of Hobbes's writings have plenty of material to use to sustain for years a quarrel over whether or not Hobbes really wants to make this kind of criticism of certain desires. But I want to put this highly disputable interpretive matter aside for the moment and consider a different question: *should* Hobbes be interested in making this kind of criticism? I want to argue that while it is clear that he shouldn't if he wants to remain a theoretically consistent subjectivist, nonetheless he *must* be able to criticize desires in this way, in violation of his value-subjectivism, if his moral theory is going to be at all plausible.

IV. The Inescapable Normative Assessment of Our Desires

Consider the following (real) story of someone who has what we would normally call an irrational desire: a World War II soldier who has served in Asia returns home after the war still not fully recovered from malaria. He suffers occasional bouts of high fever during which people say he is "not himself." Upon arriving home, he tells his brothers, "when I start getting a fever, take me directly to the hospital for treatment, because as the fever gets higher I will refuse to go and fight your efforts to take me." When the fever hits, the brothers quickly get the soldier into a car to take him to the hospital, and find that, on the way, he demands that they take him home, expressing deep aversion to medical treatment. But they do not take these desires or aversions seriously, since on their view, the fever has made him "out of his mind."

Our pre-theoretical intuitions are certainly the same as the brothers': we would naturally characterize the fevered soldier's desire not to go to the hospital as an irrational desire, one that is spurious rather than real insofar as it is generated by a sick body. But if Hobbes is a value-subjectivist, does he have the conceptual room he needs to be able to say this?

He might claim that he can do so as long as the characterization rests on the belief that the sick person's desires were generated by a physiological state that "ought not to be" given that person's earlier expression of a desire for a different bodily chemistry. If I form a desire to have a chemistry associated with what are called "normal" desires, then it seems that if I later develop desires that are generated by the deviant chemistry, other people can criticize those desires assuming what they rightly take to be my preference for a normal body chemistry and my consequent aversion to the deviant desires generated by the abnormal chemistry.

Note that, on this view, one could only criticize sick desires if the sick person happened to have a previous desire not to be sick. So if our fevered soldier never formed a preference for one kind of bodily state over another, and is now in a physiological state that we describe as mad or diseased, Hobbes could not say that it was irrational for the soldier to return home. The fact that nearly all of us would want to call him irrational anyway (and here our criticism looks for all the world as if it rests on an objective evaluation of what constitutes a rational desire) should make us uneasy with the limitations of this view.

But the view has an even more serious problem. Even if such individuals used to have a preference for one kind of bodily chemistry over another (as one might believe the soldier implicitly did when he instructed his brothers about how they should treat him during his fever), nonetheless when they are in a mad or diseased state they may no longer have a preference for what we call a healthy bodily chemistry. And if they don't, and express aversion to treatment designed to make them healthy, why should we discount their present preferences based upon a preference they used to have? If I used to want to be a ballerina, and I no longer have that preference, then it seems entirely incorrect for a subjectivist to criticize me as irrational *now* for failing to do my exercises at the barre.

But, someone might say, the fevered soldier isn't really "himself" and so we must discount the preferences he has in his diseased state insofar as they are not really *his* preferences. Yet on what basis do we make the judgement that his "real" self is the one we associate with what *we* take to be a normal body chemistry? Doesn't that judgement presuppose our acceptance of some kind of ideal of a human being of the sort Aristotle is always commending to us? We are implicitly considering the person's changed bodily chemistry as not only bad for him but also obscuring (maybe even damaging or destroying) the "real" him given what we consider to be a physiologically and psychologically successful human being. And it is this ideal which allows us to identify, given the various states he can be in, which chemical state constitutes his "real" self, and thus which desires are real and not spurious.

I am essentially arguing here that our concepts of health and madness are shot through with norms: to judge someone as sick or well, sane or mad, is to judge him using an ideal as one's yardstick. Hence we cannot use these concepts to select which of our desires is value-defining without importing the normativity we had hoped the desires themselves would explain.

So, returning to interpretive matters, by calling a glory-prone person mad, Hobbes gives himself away as a man who cannot completely eschew Aristotelianism; by using this word he is illicitly relying on a norm to criticize this kind of human being, where this norm also justifies him in using only the desires of a person in a healthy and sane state to define value. But if a norm indirectly picks out what is supposed to be the "non-normative" building blocks of Hobbes's normative theory, then his building blocks are normatively loaded from the start. His no-nonsense moral theory smuggles in at the ground level the nonsense it was supposed to be explaining, and so the theory fails. I have denied this claim elsewhere,[12] but I now think I was wrong.

A Hobbesian subjectivist might try to resist this conclusion by arguing that, for reasons that have *nothing* to do with some sort of objective ideal, preferences that could be taken to define value have to be generated in a certain physiological way, so that because certain (or all) preferences of mad people are not so generated, these cannot count as value-defining. But I confess to being unable to see how to generate such an account. Indeed, what plausible non-normative reason could one have for linking value only with one kind of desire-generation mechanism? It looks for all the world as if that linkage rests upon an implicit judgment that this mechanism is "better" than the "sick" one, and thus presupposes a normative evaluation.

We now have our answer to the puzzle of how Hobbes interpretation came to diverge into subjectivist and objectivist camps over the years. The subjectivists are right to find subjectivist ideas explicitly defined and promulgated in Hobbes's work. But given that a subjectivist must covertly be able to use at least some normative notions to criticize desires in order to sound plausible, then we have a nice explanation for why Hobbes, despite his virulent anti-Aristotelian sentiments and his dismissal of inherently prescriptive objects as metaphysical nonsense, should nonetheless say things that presuppose a non-subjectivist theory of value and a non-instrumental role for reason. These are the passages to which Warrender and others have been sensitive. So the subjectivists are right that Hobbes intended a proto-Humean position on the role of reason and the non-normative status of desires; and the objectivists are right that this position is not sustained in his writings and that there are persistent (albeit often subtle) appeals to the non-instrumental irrationality of certain desires.

If Hobbes could not resist the nonsense he persistently ridicules, then who can? Hobbes's inability to sustain a pure value-subjectivism raises an important question: must a plausible subjectivism rest on a distinction between good and bad desires which is taken to be objectively based? If so, then any moral theory that seeks to "build up" morality using non-normative material such as desires or preferences as fundamental building blocks seems doomed, because if it eschews normative evaluation of desires it is implausible, and if it admits such evaluations, then the building blocks are already infected with normative content that cannot be explained away by reference to what we desire or prefer.

As long as they are determined to be free of all normative nonsense at the foundations of their theory, Neo-Hobbesians have to choose the first option and take people and their desires as they come, maintaining that, "sick" or "well", the desires they have define value for them. But Hobbes's own choice of pejoratives shows this position was not attractive to him. Having no wish to sound implausible to his readers, Hobbes dismisses the desires of madmen as irrational (although many of us will not agree with him about who counts as mad—which is a disagreement over the nature and application of a normative notion). However, this very sensible position, which would also allow Hobbes to dismiss the fevered soldier's aversion to medical treatment as spurious, turns out to be incompatible with a purely subjectivist position on value. Contemporary neo-Hobbesians show signs of being just as ready to dismiss as spurious what they take to be "crazy" desires as Hobbes. For example, Jon Elster takes it for granted that Ulysses' desire to steer toward the rocks while he listens to the sirens' song is irrational, and commends as rational Ulysses's plan to prevent himself from satisfying the desire.[13] But such a dismissal has to rest on some kind of normative evaluation, either of the content of the desire itself or of the mental state of Ulysses when the desire was formed, such that the desire can be branded in some way 'wrong' or spurious. The fact that so few philosophers have even noticed the anti-subjectivist force of Elster's treatment of the Ulysses case demonstrates that contemporary thinkers are just as inclined as Hobbes to underestimate the extent to which our linguistic practices commit us to various normative evaluations of desires and preferences. To the extent that we find those linguistic practices irresistible, then to that extent we are giving up on the project of finding a norm-free desire-based foundation for a Hobbesian naturalistic moral theory.[14]

V. Instrumental Rationality

Suppose Neo-Hobbesians decided to bite the bullet, and tried to restructure their theories in order to purge them of any foundational normative notions whatsoever, fully prepared for the consequence that the resulting view may not be suitable for use by economists or game theorists, and ready to stomach what may be the highly counter-intuitive results of such an approach.

But is such an implausible, largely useless theory even possible? There is an important reason why I doubt that it is. Any such theory must still rely on an instrumental conception of reason, and I will now argue that this conception of reason is inescapably normative, and cannot be naturalistically reduced to non-normative components.

Consider what we are doing when we criticize *persons* as irrational. We believe there is a distinction between criticizing someone's preferences as incorrect given that they rest on faulty belief, and criticizing that person as *irrational* when she acts on her incorrect preference. Queen Gertrude's preference for (what she does not know to be) the poisoned cup of wine is incorrect—the cup is only an apparent and not a real good. But if she did not and could not know it was poisoned, how can she be criticized as irrational if she drinks from it? On the other hand, if she had reason to believe there was poison in the cup but refused to investigate further, then it seems appropriate to call her behavior irrational. The criticism of someone who has faulty beliefs as irrational therefore seems to depend upon whether or not she could and should have known that one or more of the beliefs upon which she relied in her reasoning process was incorrect, such that we can hold her "culpably negligent" for failing to reach the right conclusion.

But such an assessment of culpability is clearly made relative to some norm or standard of behavior to which we think people should be held regarding when and how information relevant to choices should be collected. And an ethical naturalist cannot covertly rely on such a standard if he is supposed to be offering a no-nonsense explanation of how norms and standards of behavior are generated. Such a theorist is barred from using the word 'irrational' in this sense, and must therefore use it merely to mark a mistake made by the reasoner in what he chooses to do or desire in the face of other more important or more basic desires. But this means he has to conflate irrationality and incorrectness, in a way that flies in the face of our linguistic practice.

But not only must he conflate what seem to be two distinct kinds of error, one "innocent" and the other "culpable", more worryingly he must also misrepresent another kind of failure in order to avoid making ground-level normative judgements in violation of his subjectivist theory. A Hobbesian ethical naturalist is going to find it problematic to characterize akratic phenomena, in which the agent seems for all the world to *know* that what she is doing or desiring impedes her ability to satisfy another more important or more basic desire. Such people appear to *flout* or *defy* a hypothetical imperative. How should such people be understood and evaluated?

Consider that a hypothetical imperative tells you what you ought to do if you wish to satisfy a desire that you have. Now what is the force of the 'ought' in the imperative? As a solely descriptive statement, it identifies what is required for the satisfaction of a preference. But hypothetical imperatives are supposed to be more than descriptive statements; they are supposed to have normative force. Accordingly people who flout hypothetical imperatives are *criticized*: they are called wrong, imprudent, irrational. They have, we say, made a certain kind of mistake. But exactly how are they mistaken? Yes, they have failed to do that which would have allowed them to satisfy a desire; that is a description of what happened. But by calling them 'wrong' we appear to be evaluating them and not merely describing some way in which they have failed. From where does this normative judgement come?

Well, you might say, it comes from the desire itself in the sense that, if I fail to follow the imperative I fail to satisfy the desire. But that response merely reduces the criticism to description again: given that desire, they failed to act to satisfy it. Yes, you say, but not only did they fail to satisfy the desire, they also acted irrationally. But now it seems that in addition to the desire providing a reason for them to follow the imperative, there is something called rationality—some kind of standard of reasoning and choice—which is violated if they don't follow it and that also requires them to follow it. To put it another way, rationality appears to be a standard that is providing a reason for following the imperative, so that if I don't act so as to satisfy the desire, I have not only failed to secure what I desire but have also failed to act from this reason-giving standard. So my failure consists in my falling short of a norm of human thought and action, such that calling me irrational in this sense involves presupposing the sort of prescriptivity the neo-Hobbesians had wanted to explain rather than assume.

There is another way to make this point. We believe that if action a is a means to some end b, then if I want a, I should want b. Suppose, however, that I don't want b. But you say to me that I *ought* to want b. Where does this 'ought' come from? In fact I don't want b, so in fact I won't get a. But calling me irrational because I *ought* to want b in virtue of its causal efficacy is presupposing a normative ideal of human reasoning and choice. Small children are constantly in violation of this ideal. When a child declares that he wants to see Grandma but refuses to get into the car that must take him to Grandma, we see this failure in action. Parents who are philosophers call the child irrational; parents who are not philosophers have different and sometimes more colorful descriptions of the failure. The point is that they are all making a normative evaluation of the child.[15]

Finally, let me construct the argument in a third way. Consider Bernard Williams' distinction between internal and external reasons: the former are reasons an agent is actually motivated by and the latter are reasons that one believes should be attributed to her but which she has no motive to follow. Williams argues that, from the standpoint of the agent, a reason that is purely external is no reason at all. If the agent has no motivation to follow it, then for her it cannot constitute a reason to do anything. But what if an instrumental reason is a purely external reason for an agent? If you say to her, "But b is a way to get a, so of course you have to do b," and she replies, "I understand the means-end connection between b and a, but it does not move me to want to do b," then the instrumental reason you give her is not an internal reason. "But it ought to be!" you cry. And if you take that view, then you are judging this agent's motives by reference to a norm that you take to be authoritative over her decision-making in this situation. In particular, you are saying that, regardless of whether or not she endorses it, the norm governs her (and everyone's) decision-making process, and that using it you can attribute to her a reason even if she won't recognize it herself. *Contra* Williams' thesis, this is a nice example of what I regard as a highly plausible attribution to an agent of an external reason. But the point I want to emphasize is precisely that an instrumental reason can indeed be external, in which case any appeal to such a reason on our part is precisely not an appeal to the agent's set of desires, but to a normative conception of rationality which we take to be authoritative over her actions, whether or not she agrees.

Of course, the appeal to the authority of a norm of instrumental rationality is mysterious—as all normative appeals are. In an influential article, Philippa Foot called upon philosophers to think of moral imperatives as hypothetical rather than categorical, in order that their prescriptive force be understandable and the "mystery" of their validity solved.[16] But the preceding discussion is meant to show that the force of hypothetical imperatives is just as mysterious as the force of categorical imperatives. Granted, we are more often disposed to follow hypothetical imperatives than we are categorical imperatives. One might say that the authority of the former is generally seen as more inescapable and more congenial (or at any rate, less objectionable) than the latter. But this isn't always true, as anyone knows who puts off timely dentist visits, resists eating oat bran for breakfast, or leaves studying for her exams until the last moment.

Even if he accepts the preceding argument, an ethical naturalist may still believe he can salvage his no-nonsense theory by insisting that henceforth any use of the word 'irrational' in his no-nonsense theory is only descriptive, signifying only that the agent has failed to act so as to satisfy the desires he has, given the information that he either did have or could have had about how to satisfy them (where care is taken to spell out precisely what we mean by this last counterfactual, and where we spell it out in an entirely descriptive fashion). Note that such a theory would imply an error theory of our normative discourse. The only true discourse would be entirely descriptive. But we are now left with a moral theory devoid of any normative power: Its "imperatives" are mere causal connections, its criticisms only descriptions of agents who have not acted so as to satisfy their desires. But a moral theory without prescriptions seems to have lost precisely what it was supposed to explain.

If this is all that a Hobbesian naturalistic moral theory can be, many of us will conclude that it fails to be a moral theory at all.

VI. Conclusions

What conclusions should one draw from these arguments regarding both Hobbes's moral theory and the position of ethical naturalism itself? The disappointing results of Hobbes's ethical naturalism prompt the following conclusions about his theory: First, like it or not, the long shadow of Aristotle is cast upon Hobbes, who found it impossible to sustain a pure value-subjectivism and who was therefore driven to smuggle normative ideals into his discussion of value as a way of ensuring the plausibility of his theory. Second, like it or not, Hobbes appeals to a notion of rationality whose prescriptive force is no less mysterious (albeit perhaps more congenial) than the prescriptive force of categorical imperatives (a conclusion any Kantian will enjoy). Indeed, we must conclude that what appeared earlier in the paper to be permissible naturalistic criticisms of motivated and basic desires by a Hobbesian naturalist are not permissible at all. To call a motivated desire irrational because its object is not an effective means to satisfying a more basic desire, or to call an action taken to satisfy a basic desire irrational because it precludes the satisfaction of a more important basic desire, is to make evaluations using the norm of instrumental rationality, contrary to Hobbes's subjectivist and naturalist commitments.

And third, the fact that, despite his best efforts, Hobbes cannot keep normative standards of value and reasoning out of his theory raises the possibility that these standards may not be nonsense after all. Why dismiss as nonsense what you cannot resist? While it certainly doesn't lend justification to normative discourse, Hobbes's secret penchant for some of this discourse is good news to contemporary Aristotelian and Kantian moral objectivists weary of defending their use of it against present-day neo-Hobbesian attacks.

Why is it good news? Consider the fact that many neo-Hobbesians (indeed, many philosophers generally) take it for granted that there is nothing problematic about using hypothetical imperatives in logic or philosophy of language or decision theory, even while criticizing the use of categorical imperatives by moral theorists. But if, as I have argued, there is an appeal to norms implicit in hypothetical imperatives, than that appeal must be explained, and a naturalist metaphysics would demand that such an explanation be consistent with what we understand to be the natural facts. What would such an explanation look like? A naturalist might explain these and other norms in her theory, whether rational, scientific or moral, as something generated by certain social traditions or practices, or as something generated in us as a result of certain psychological developments which psychoanalysts or psychologists study.[17] So understood, norms might be thought to contain words that may or may not be descriptive of the world, but in any case, only move us to act because of contingent facts about our psychology and the effects of these words upon it.

But this means that even the prescriptive power of hypothetical imperatives must be understood merely as the contingent effect of the imperative on human psychology. This includes imperatives that tell one not to violate the principle of non-contradiction, or not to take poison if one wants to stay healthy, or to include a control group if one intends to design a sound scientific experiment. Yet such a position seems intuitively wrong: we take it for granted that something more than mere human psychological or social facts explains why it is, for example, a good idea not to deny De Morgan's laws. The rules of logic, the prescriptions for attaining good health, and the norms of scientific investigation appear to have an authority that isn't just reducible to contingent facts.

Suppose a naturalist admitted this but argued that a certain *minimal* objective normative authority in any theory is acceptable, so that, for example, it is alright to have as objective normative standards such things as instrumental rationality and coherent, healthy preferences, but that any other normative standards (e.g. moral standards) used to define correct values or moral reasoning procedures cannot be defended. I confess to having no idea how one is supposed to tell a "good" norm from a "bad" one, and since most post-Hobbesian naturalists have been rather fond of dismissing all objective normative authority as metaphysical nonsense, they have thus far given us no way to make the distinction that this modified theory would require.

So I would submit that the best lesson contemporary theorists can learn from Hobbes's early attempt to propound an ethical naturalism is that the problems dogging his theory have yet to be satisfactorily solved in our own day. And that should, I think, be grounds for worrying about the viability of the position itself. If a naturalized ethics must be devoid of objective normative authority, then we have good reason to ask whether "naturalization" has ripped the guts out of morality, or for that matter, any theory—such as rational choice theory, or philosophy of science or language—that relies on prescriptions of any kind, including hypothetical imperatives.

Notes

1. For a nice example of this thesis, see Peter Railton's discussion of naturalism in ethics in his, "Preferences and Goodness," in E. Paul, F. Miller and J. Paul, eds. *The Foundations of Morality*, Blackwell, 1989. And see the papers by R. Boyd and N. Sturgeon in *Essays on Moral Realism*, ed. G. Sayre-McCord (Cornell, 1988).
2. See J. L. Mackie, *Ethics: Inventing Right and Wrong* (Harmondsworth: Penguin, 1977).
3. For a suggestion of how this type of explanation would go in the context of a discussion of linguistic norms, see Robert Brandom, "Freedom and Constraint

by Norms", *American Philosophical Quarterly*, Vol. 16, no. 3, July 1979, pp. 187-196. ·

4. Hobbes might even reject an entirely societal explanation for linguistic norms, given the rather extraordinary way in which he makes the development of language an individualistic affair. For a discussion of this, see J. W. N. Watkins, *Hobbes's System of Ideas* (London: Hutchison, 1965), pp. 101ff, and Hampton, *Hobbes and the Social Contract Tradition* (Cambridge: Cambridge University Press, 1986), pp. 9-10.

5. He says in *Leviathan*:

> there is no such *finis ultimus,* (utmost ayme,) or *Summum Bonum,* (greatest Good,) as is spoken of in the books of the old Morall Philosophers. (Lev, 11, 1, 47)

and later in the same work:

> the Writers of Morall Philosophie, though they acknowledge the same Vertues and Vices; Yet not seeing where in consisted their Goodnesse; nor that they come to be praised, as the meanes of peaceable, sociable, and comfortable living; place them in a mediocrity of the passions: as if not the Cause, but the Quantity of a gift, made Liberality. (Lev, 15, 40, 80)

6. e.g. Bernard Gert, Preface to *Man and Citizen* (Atlantic Highlands, N. J.: Humanities Press, 1978).

7. See *Hobbes and the Social Contract Tradition*, (Cambridge: Cambridge University Press, 1986), especially chapter 1.

8. Note that I am individuating desires by their objects. Don Hubin has pointed out to me that it is possible to individuate them in other ways; e.g. by their role in a person's conative structure. Individuation via objects seems to fit Hobbesian ways of talking.

9. Such a situation is one in which others are also disposed to cooperate; unilateral cooperation is neither required nor encouraged by Hobbes insofar as it is futile to achieving peace and destructive of self-preservation.

10. Consider, for example, the following passages:

> Pride, subjecteth a man to Anger, the excesse whereof, is the Madness called RAGE, and FURY...
> Though the effect of folly, in them that are possessed of an opinion of being inspired, be not visible always in one man, by any very extravagant action, that proceedeth from such Passion; yet when many of them conspire together, the Rage of the whole multitude is visible enough. For what argument of Madnesse can there be greater, than to clamour, strike, and throw stones at our best friends? Yet this is somewhat less than such a multitude will do. For they will clamor, fight against, and destroy those, by whom all their life-time before, they have protected, and secured from injury. And if this be Madnesse in the multitude, it is the same in every particular man...so also, though wee perceive no great unquietnesse, in one, or two men; yet we may be well assured, that their singular Passions, are parts of the Seditious roaring of a troubled Nation. And if there were nothing else that be[t]rayed their madness; yet that very arrogating such inspiration to themselves, is argument enough. (Lev, 8, 19, 35 and 8, 21, 36)

The passage betrays not just Hobbes's disapproval but also his disgust for the glory-prone rebels of his day. Moreover, when discussing how the glory-prone jeopardize their future well being for the sake of attaining glory he writes in *De Cive*:

> men cannot put off this same irrational appetite, whereby they greedily prefer the present good (to which, by strict consequence, many unforeseen evils do adhere) before the future...(DC, EW ii, 3, 32, 48)

and in the same work

> most men, by reason of their perverse desire of present profit, are very unapt to observe these laws, although acknowledged by them...(DC, EW ii, 3, 27, 45)

Note the linkage of irrationality with "greedy" and "perverse" desires.

11. One might worry that Hobbes is linking the notions of rational action and sanity too closely; this issue does not affect the following discussion, which only aims to establish that when Hobbes dismisses certain "crazy" passions as spurious, he is appealing to a norm (which may or may not be a norm of rational action).
12. In Hampton (1986), chapter 1.
13. See Jon Elster, *Ulysses and the Sirens*, (Cambridge: Cambridge University Press, 1979).
14. I discuss this point further in my "Naturalism and Normativity" (unpublished manuscript) which reviews contemporary neo-Hobbesian ideas appearing in the work of Gauthier, Mackie, Harman, and Brandt, among others.
15. Indeed, raising children involves teaching them to respect the norm of prudential action. In small children this respect is virtually non-existent. If one tries arguing with the child, one might get somewhere by attempting to enliven and strengthen the motivational efficacy of the desire to see grandma, so that it can defeat the aversion to get into the car. (For example, one might try, "Grandma has new toys at her house! Let's get in quick and see them!) But an appeal to rationality is largely useless. Hence the frequent use of negative sanctions in such situations—sanctions which may not only get the child in the car but play a role in teaching him respect for the norm of rationality.
16. "Morality As A System of Hypothetical Imperatives" in her *Virtues and Vices* (Berkeley: University of California Press, 1978) pp. 157-93.
17. Something like this position has been suggested by Richard Boyd, who has written a great deal about the plausibility of ethical naturalism and who believes that the denotation of moral terms is no more problematic than other terms admitted by science. However, Boyd appreciates that ethical naturalism cannot admit the existence of any objective authority of a norm, arguing that naturalism has to reject the idea of such authority, which means rejecting the idea that "the recognition that one course of action is morally preferable to another *necessarily* provides a reason (even if not a decisive one) to prefer the morally better course of action." From Boyd, "How to be a Moral Realist," in Sayre-McCord, Op. Cit., p. 214.

Philosophical Perspectives, 6, Ethics, 1992

ETHICS NATURALIZED

Michael Slote
University of Maryland at College Park

Philosophers who have discussed or advocated naturalized epistemology have often called attention to analogies between ethics or moral theory, on the one hand, and epistemology or theory of knowledge, on the other. And utilitarianism in particular has been singled out as an ethical analogue of a naturalistic or naturalizing approach to questions of epistemic justification.[1] Both BonJour and Firth make the latter point, and since both also regard utilitarianism as ethically unacceptable, they make use of the epistemic/ethical parallelism to cast doubt on naturalizing epistemology.

It is certainly possible, however, to doubt that utilitarianism can readily be dismissed simply on the basis of counterintuitive implications of the sort Firth and BonJour allude to; for it has (for one thing) become increasingly recognized that our intuitive moral thinking can lead to counterintuitive results quite on its own—we have reason to believe, in other words, that common-sense moral intuitions conflict with one another, are incoherent as a class.[2] And this seems to give new life to the philosophical impulse toward theory and system that has been so clearly exemplified in utilitarian ethics. But quite apart from the merits of utilitarianism or naturalistic epistemology, recent discussions connecting these two may give a false impression of that connection by seeming to imply that any epistemological naturalist will inevitably want to adopt some form of utilitarianism if she seeks a coherent overall philosophical view. Utilitarianism naturally lends support to and gains support from naturalized epistemology. But utilitarianism is not the only ethical view that naturally "goes" with a naturalizing approach in epistemology, and in this paper my main purpose will be to point out another, less familiar ethical approach that goes well with naturalized epistemology and show how differences between the less familiar approach and utilitarianism correspond to interesting differences in the ways we can seek to naturalize epistemology. It would not be correct to claim that virtue ethics in general harmonizes with a naturalizing approach to epistemology: quite the contrary, there are standard forms of virtue ethics that seem most plausibly associated with traditional, internalist epistemology. But there is another, less familiar kind of virtue ethics that can very plausibly be seen as analogous to epistemological naturalism in one of its guises, one whose present-day relevance and importance is further underscored by its ability to deal in a coherent fashion with the exasperating problem of moral/ethical luck. But Utilitarianism also has an interesting way of dealing with this problem, and I propose to begin our discussion by saying something about the paradoxes involved in our ordinary thinking about moral luck.

1. Moral Luck, Kantian Ethics and Reductionist Utilitarianism

One of the unnerving accomplishments of recent discussions of moral luck is to point to a nest of inconsistencies at the heart of our intuitive moral thinking. Consider, for example, our everyday moral reactions to the unforeseen consequences of people's actions. Ordinary moral thinking distinguishes the moral status of attempted murder from that of murder, for example, and quite apart from legal distinctions between murder and attempted murder, we think much worse of someone who has killed an innocent victim than of someone who accidentally fails to kill an intended innocent victim. And we are inclined to heap greater blame on an actual murderer than on an unsuccessful one.

To that extent common-sense morality allows actual unforeseeable consequences a role in determining moral judgment, thus making room for a certain kind of "moral luck". But as has been frequently pointed out, the very idea of moral luck affronts our common-sense moral intuitions. So our moral intuitions about cases taken singly are in conflict with a general common-sense conviction that judgments of morally better and worse, or greater or less culpability or blameworthiness, cannot properly be subject to luck or accident. And the cases where such inconsistency arises are quite numerous and varied.

To take an even clearer example, imagine someone driving a car along a country road and pointing out noteworthy sights to his passengers. As a result of his preoccupation, the car suddenly swerves to the middle of the road; fortunately there are no cars coming in the opposite direction and no accident occurs. However, in another scenario the person is similarly preoccupied, and because a truck happens to be coming, has a major accident. He is then responsible for a great deal of harm to others and would normally be accounted blameworthy or culpable in a way that he would not be thought blameworthy or culpable in the first-mentioned case. This example is borrowed from Thomas Nagel's paper "Moral Luck". But as Nagel also points out, something in us revolts against the idea of moral luck, inclining us to the view that the driver must have the *same* degree of culpability in the two cases mentioned above.[3] There is something repelling in the idea that one can be more or less culpable depending on events outside one's ken or control. And in regard to the just-mentioned pair of examples, therefore, it may seem as if we should be able to insert some kind of probability estimate into the example, so that whether the driver who swerves is culpable and the degree, if any, of his culpability would depend solely on whether he was sufficiently aware of the likelihood of an accident and on how likely an accident was, given his preoccupation with the scenery—judgments that are constant between the two imagined cases and that might allow us to say the man was culpable (or not culpable) in both cases to the same extent for having paid attention to the scenery while driving.

But (following Nagel) I think that no such solution really squares with the moral judgments we make in the ordinary course of events, before we begin to worry about moral luck in a self-conscious way. I think no matter how constant one imagines the (awareness of) probability in the two situations, common-sense morality sees some difference in the culpability, blame-worthiness, or reprehensibleness of the agent. (Actually, it doesn't matter whether the two situations are viewed as counterfactually possible relative to one another or are viewed as involving similar persons—or one person at different times—facing relevantly similar situations.) Common sense appears to subscribe to a mutually contradictory set of assumptions with regard to putative cases of inattention, carelessness, or negligence, and we therefore need to go beyond our ordinary moral thinking.

We have just spoken of one particular form of moral luck: luck with respect to results or consequences of one's actions or inactions. But moral luck can also come about in other ways. Thus if some of us would have done nothing to stop the Nazis, had we been living in Germany before and during the Second World War, then arguably any lesser or negligible guilt we have through not having in fact been in Germany during that period is attributable to moral luck in our *circumstances*. And such assumptions of circumstantial luck lead to inconsistencies that resemble those uncovered in connection with luck in *results* or *consequences*, though I don't want at this point to dwell on these difficulties.

The issue of blameworthiness (or culpability or reprehensibility) is at the very heart of the issue of moral luck, because it is the idea that luck or accident can make a difference to blameworthiness, etc., that most grates against our antecedent moral intuitions. If we concentrate on praiseworthiness the clash of intuitions is less evident, because there is such a thing as non-moral praiseworthiness—we can praise an artistic performance or work that it would make no sense to regard as culpable or blameworthy—and because it is therefore not odd at all to suppose that non-moral praiseworthiness can sometimes depend on accident. Of course, we could distinguish moral praiseworthiness from praiseworthiness in general and claim that it grates on our intuitions to suppose that moral praiseworthiness can be subject to luck; but it is just easier to focus on blameworthiness, where ambiguity seems less capable of misleading us because all blameworthiness seems to be moral blameworthiness. And so in what follows I shall frame the issues of moral luck largely in terms of the notion of blameworthiness.

The two dominant ethical traditions of recent times—Kantianism and utilitarianism—have different and indeed distinctive ways of avoiding the paradox and inconsistency our intuitive thinking gets into in the area of moral luck. (That is not to say that all, or even most, utilitarians and Kantians have been *self-consciously aware* of the problem of moral luck or that they have adopted their main views in *response* to that problem.) It is fairly clear that Kant wishes to preclude the possibility of moral luck and thus to avoid those judgments about individual cases that jointly imply that someone's (degree of) blameworthiness can depend on factors of luck or accident. The utilitarians, by contrast, make room for the phenomenon of moral luck, but enunciate a theory or conception of praise- and blameworthiness which, if correct, takes the sting from moral luck, i.e., makes it seem unproblematic (despite our ordinary intuitions) that differences in blameworthiness should depend on accidental factors. Let me therefore say a bit more about the ways in which Kantians and utilitarians respectively elude, or seek to elude, the intuitive tangle known as the problem of moral luck.

Kant, as I said, denies the possibility of moral luck, but he has recourse to the metaphysics of noumenal will(ing) in his effort to establish conditions of moral evaluation entirely free from contamination by luck or accident. Nowadays most of us, even many Kantians among us, would tend to resist a noumenal metaphysics—even one in which the noumenal is regarded merely as an inevitable *postulate* of the moral point of view—as the price to be paid for luck-free moral judgment. But if the idea of the noumenal is left to the side, it is difficult to see how the this-worldly determinants of moral evaluation—the factors of circumstance, constitution, and causation that give actuality and substance to moral thought—can reasonably be conceived independently of all luck and accident. And in that case the Kantian still owes us an account of how morality *without* luck is possible.

Utilitarianism, on the other hand, makes the entirely different move of *allowing* for moral luck by conceiving moral predicates in such a way as to make the possibility of moral luck seem less problematic. For the utilitarian, an act is right if it has overall better, happier consequences than any of its alternatives, and an act counts as blameworthy if the further act of blaming it is right in the aforementioned utilitarian terms. (Praiseworthiness is treated in parallel fashion.) In that case the blameworthiness of a person's act amount to nothing more than (reduces to) the fact that blaming it would have better consequences that not blaming it, and since the goodness of consequences is one of the things in this world and this life which are most subject to luck or accident, such a view makes it easy to see how blameworthiness can depend on factors of luck, if only (or once) the view itself is accepted. Of course, the utilitarian conception of blameworthiness is far from our intuitive ideas about blameworthiness (however muddled the latter may be—for the utilitarian conception is at least not *muddled*). But relative to the acceptance of utilitarian views at least, moral luck becomes fairly unproblematic.

Let us then dwell for a moment on the differences between Kantianism and utilitarianism viewed as attempts to evade the incoherence/paradoxes endemic to our ordinary thinking about moral luck. Kant seeks, in effect, to avoid (our) having to assume the existence of moral luck through the idea of a noumenal realm where human reason and activity are purified of all those empirical factors that so clearly connect with matters of luck or accident. Morality is thereby taken out of the empirical world and construed as pure (inner?) rational willing that bears only an indirect or non-constitutive relation to things and events in the external or phenomenal world. Such a move is clearly reminiscent of and is arguably analogous to the way traditional internalistic/Cartesian epistemology treats epistemic rationality and justification as a function solely of the inner states of the would-be knower.

By contrast, the utilitarian solution to the problem of moral luck is to treat the crucial notions of blameworthiness and culpability as understandable in "externalistic" or naturalistic terms in the light of which the idea of moral luck loses its intuitive unacceptability. We ordinarily think of blameworthiness or culpability as in some sense attaching deeply rather than through luck or accident to moral agents, but a utilitarianism that regards blameworthiness and culpability as matters, respectively, of what it has good/optimal consequences to blame and to treat as guilty considers such matters to be largely *extrinsic* and *accidental* to the agent/act thus deemed blameworthy or culpable. And if, e. g., a person's blameworthiness (for doing x) is a matter of its being the case that blaming the person (for doing x) will have better results for overall human (sentient) happiness than not doing so, then blameworthiness treated as an external property of this kind will also be reducible to non-evaluative empirical terms (assuming that happiness is cashed out in terms of empirically measurable preference satisfaction or pleasure, etc.).

In fact, standard utilitarianism reduces all its ethical vocabulary to supposedly empirical notions/terms—e.g., rightness is just a matter of having consequences for human happiness as good as those of any alternative action—and those who have compared utilitarianism with naturalistic accounts of epistemic terms have seen or come close to seeing that both involve a form of naturalistic *reductionism*. Thus a naturalizing approach that construes epistemic justification in terms of the use of some type of reliable belief-forming process reduces the evaluative epistemic notion of justification to non-evaluative natural/empirical terms, and this is clearly parallel to the way in which utilitarianism reduces all ethical evaluative notions to natural/empirical ones.[4] But reduction of this sort is not the only procedure open to an epistemological naturalizer, and that fact has, in ways to be discussed shortly, been well known to various recent participants in epistemological debates over the merits of the naturalizing tendency. What has not, however, been known or mentioned is the fact that an ethics aware of the problems of moral luck and conceiving itself as intellectually allied or associated with naturalized epistemology need not assume a utilitarian form. Perhaps it will be easier to see how this is possible, if we now consider an epistemic phenomenon that has received some attention in the literature, but not nearly as much as its ethical analogue: the problem, namely, of epistemic luck.

2. Epistemic Luck and Eliminative Utilitarianism

Many of those who have written on the nature and prospects of naturalized epistemology have pointed out that reductions of epistemic warrant or justification to non-evaluative "natural" concepts introduce a kind of unfairness and/or arbitrariness into attributions of warrant or justification. If, for example, epistemic justification is a matter (very roughly) of arriving at certain beliefs via a reliable (e. g., a typically truth-producing or truth-preserving) cognitive process, then whether or not a given person is (epistemically or rationally) justified in holding a certain belief may depend on factors he has no way of knowing about, on facts beyond his ken and unavailable to him. Thus in two different possible worlds there may be two people making the same inference about their environment on the basis of exactly similar perceptual data; but if the inference is generally reliable in one of the worlds, but not in the other, then on a reductive account of justification, the two individuals differ in the justification of their inferential beliefs. One of them will be justified in believing what he does about his environment, and the other will not be, even though neither has any view about the reliability of the process that underlies his own belief-acquisition. And it seems epistemically unfair and, from an epistemological standpoint, implausible to suppose that the individuals should thus differ in epistemic warrant, when from the standpoint of their mental activity they are (we may assume) exemplifying exactly similar perceptual and inferential processes.

Reductive, naturalizing reliabilist (or related) accounts of epistemic rationality or justification have frequently been objected to in terms like these,[5] and if we may put matters in terms closer to those we have been using here, but quite naturally invoked in regard to the example just mentioned, we can say that the idea that epistemic rationality or justification can depend on factors of luck or accident totally outside the ken of those being epistemologically evaluated is counterintuitive. Just as it is intuitively repellent to have to suppose that the moral justification of an agent's performing some act can depend on factors of luck or accident outside the ken or control of the agent, it at least initially seems implausible to hold that someone's epistemic justification should depend on factors outside her ken or control. And that explains some of the reluctance to adopt a reliabilist or any similarly externalistic naturalist account of epistemic evaluations.

However, the matter is somewhat more complicated than anti-reliabilists and anti-naturalists seem to have realized. We have seen that our intuitions about moral luck are not all on the side of denying the possibility of such luck, and something similar seems to be the case with regard to epistemic evaluations generally and most particularly with regard to claims about epistemic or rational justification.

Thus imagine a pair of examiners who have just had the unenviable task of telling a dissertation candidate that his dissertation is unacceptable and requires the most extensive revision. We may imagine that at the dissertation interview, the examiners were in substantial agreement about the defects of the dissertation, and that the candidate himself, when told of their objections, admitted their force and validity with a rather dejected air of resignation. At the point, however, when the examiners emerge from this meeting, one of them says to the other: I wonder whether he'll appeal the decision to higher university authorities. And the other immediately counters by pointing out that there is no reason for the candidate to appeal, since he himself agreed with the strong and shared objections of both examiners. Hearing this reply, the examiner making the original conjecture about an appeal may well feel that he was being irrational, possibly somewhat paranoid, to suggest the possibility of an appeal. But what happens if out of the blue, a few weeks later, it turns out that the student has gone on to appeal—totally unreasonably, let us assume—the examiners' decision on his dissertation? I think the examiner who originally conjectured that he might do so will tend to revise his view about the irrationality or paranoid quality of his own original conjecture. He will feel, instead, that the course of events has in some measure (perhaps completely) *vindicated* his original opinion about the real possibility of an appeal.

However, this is a case of rational luck only if we imagine that the conjecturing examiner does not attribute his vindication to some sort of intuitiveness on his part in the original situation where he made his conjecture. If he, or we, imagine that in the original situation he had some clue about the possibility of an appeal from the way the student was behaving (from the peculiar quality of his dejectedness, for example), a clue which he received subliminally but which was nonetheless functioning *as evidence* affecting the conjectures he was willing to make, then we do not have a putative case of rational luck so much as one of subliminal evidence only subsequently recognized as such.

But I don't think there is any need for the conjecturing examiner, or for us, to see his situation, and his subsequent loss of a sense of being slightly paranoid and irrational, as reflecting the existence of subliminal evidence and the subsequent recognition of its presence. The man himself may be led to revise his estimation of his own earlier rationality or irrationality by the mere fact that his conjecture turned out to be correct. His fears may seem to be (somewhat) justified *by subsequent events*, rather than by a subsequently acknowledged earlier bit of evidence, and this description may indeed be the best expression of the man's own sense of how he is (turns out to be) justified (or less unjustified and certainly not paranoid) in his original assumption. Certainly we ourselves, looking at his situation from the outside, have a tendency to withhold the judgment of paranoidness and irrationality with regard to his original conjecture in a way we would not have been inclined to do if we had simply imagined a case in which no appeal was ever lodged. Even assuming that the candidate provided no subliminal clues to his subsequent behavior, our judgment as to (degree of) irrationality and paranoidness is commonly affected by how we imagine things actually turning out, and this provides for a possibility of (epistemic) rational luck that is quite similar to what we said earlier about the common-sense possibilities of moral luck.

On the other hand, something in us recoils at the idea that epistemic or rational justification (or vindication) in cases like that just mentioned can hinge on subsequent events. And so it would seem that as with moral luck, our initial intuitions and judgments in the area of epistemic or rational luck are not entirely consistent with one another; in that case, again as with moral luck, we cannot simply remain on the level of intuitions, but are in need of theory to tell us which intuitions ought to be abandoned. Since *some* intuitions must be dropped, it cannot be a decisive objection to reliabilist and other naturalistic, reductionist accounts of epistemic justification that they go against some of our intuitions. Rather, the question must be whether, with due weight given to overall considerations of intuitiveness, the total theory arrived at by one or another naturalizing tendency or project is superior to our best internalist, anti-naturalistic, anti-reductionist epistemologies, and this question presumably cannot and should not be closed prematurely.

However, epistemological naturalizers need not end up being reductionists. Some, instead, have advocated that epistemology should be replaced by or turn into a form of psychology (or psychology-cum-neuroscience-cum-biology, etc.). And under such a development epistemic evaluations would presumably be eliminated altogether, rather than reduced to other terms. In explaining human thought and action, we might still be interested in questions of reliability and the like, but an eliminative naturalistic epistemology or psychology would have no (further) interest in whether certain cognitive mechanisms yielded or allowed for rational or justified beliefs or inferences.

A thoroughgoing eliminativism would permit of no such epistemic evaluations (let us assume it would eliminate claims about knowledge along with claims about justification) and would presumably hold that there is no good *theoretical* reason to countenance the making of such evaluations (though there might be no reason to forbid them to every-day life).

I have mentioned the possibility of eliminativism, not because I wish to defend it against naturalistic reductionism or anti-reductionism in epistemology, but because its very possibility can give us a clue to some previously unsuspected ways in which ethics can be naturalized. Standard utilitarianism is the only form of naturalized ethics that (to my knowledge) has been recognized as analogous to a naturalizing trend in epistemology. But once we see that eliminativism is a possible direction for the naturalizer in epistemology, we may be encouraged to look for similar possibilities in (naturalizing) ethics.

Utilitarianism as standardly formulated is a reductionistic form of ethical naturalism, but it is also possible for utilitarianism to present itself in an eliminativist mode, and as such it represents a new and, I believe, interesting way in which ethics can seek to naturalize itself. Moreover, once we see how a thoroughly eliminativist ethical naturalism parallel to eliminativist epistemological naturalism is possible, it will be easier to recognize the possibilities of a naturalistically eliminativist virtue ethics, and the possibilities for naturalizing epistemology will in turn be enriched. But let us begin this process with an account of utilitarianism as a form of eliminativist ethical naturalism.

Eliminative utilitarianism stands to familiar reductive utilitarianism as, say, eliminative materialism stands to reductive materialism (I shall not try to respond to those, like Quine, who hold that the theoretical difference between elimination and reduction is nil or negligible). So just as an eliminative materialism claims there are no mental entities or (realized) mental properties, only physical entities and properties functioning in certain complex ways, an eliminative utilitarianism will deny that anything is right or obligatory or intrinsically good, will deny that there are any exemplified ethical (or evaluative) properties or facts. And the reasoning behind such conclusions will in fact, as in other cases where there is a choice to make between reduction and elimination, follow the reasoning for reductive utilitarianism till it reaches an ultimate parting of the ways with it. Like reductionist utilitarians, the eliminative utilitarian will point out the incoherent, or at least intellectually unsatisfactory, thinking that lies, for example, behind our ordinary moral thinking. She will hold that when one properly strips away or otherwise removes the irrational or unjustified elements in our ordinary usage of "right" and "wrong", one will be left with the clear and humanly significant core idea of producing (a net balance of) pleasure or satisfaction for sentient beings. But here, parting ways with ordinary reductive utilitarianism, the eliminativist will argue that the sheer enormity of the error and confusion in our ordinary beliefs about moral rightness justifies us in claiming that there is no such thing as moral rightness, etc. By contrast, the reductivist utilitarian holds that rightness turns out to be conduciveness to pleasure or desire-satisfaction and that ordinary moral thinking is simply very much in error about (what) rightness (is).

Clearly, the issue here between eliminative and reductive utilitarianism is familiar from our experience of other disputes regarding the respective merits of an eliminative and a reductive approach. And since the most familiar of these, probably, is the long-standing debate between eliminative and reductive materialism, it is perhaps worth mentioning one possible advantage that eliminative utilitarianism (or eliminative ethics more generally) has over eliminative materialism. It is not obvious that sense experience and thinking are merely posited hypothetical entities, and there may be some force to the claim, therefore, that what eliminative materialism eliminates (among other things) are some of the very data which reasonable abductive thinking must seek to account for. But the idea that we immediately experience certain ethical data or properties is, I believe, an (even) harder thesis to defend than what we have just allowed as a possibility in the area of mind and body, and to the extent, therefore, we have better or more immediate knowledge of our own experience(s) than of ethical facts and properties, utilitarian eliminativism may well be in better shape than (or have at least one advantage over) eliminative materialism.

But even apart from this consideration, it seems difficult to find any reason to prefer reductive to eliminative utilitarianism *as a form of naturalism*. If the traditional, reductive utilitarian protests, for example, that the eliminative approach does away with ethics altogether and therefore with utilitarianism itself as a form of ethics, it can be pointed out that this pair of claims is either simply false or altogether begs the issue against eliminativism. After all, eliminative utilitarianism, like eliminative materialism, makes a distinctive claim of its own. It doesn't remain silent or somehow render it impossible for claims to be made, but rather comes out openly and asserts that nothing is good or virtuous or obligatory—or, if you prefer, that "good", etc., do not denote any properties of things. To be sure, problems can arise here about how the negative claims of eliminative utilitarianism are most properly formulated, but there are similar problems about how to express eliminative materialism, and there is no reason, in either case, to say that the eliminativist eliminates the philosophical field he or she is supposed to be working in. Just as the eliminative materialist holds a metaphysical position and is naturally regarded as a materialist of one particular stripe, the eliminative utilitarian subscribes to a particular ethical view, and one, moreover, that is for similar reasons naturally regarded as a form of utilitarianism.

On the other hand, what one may mean by saying that the eliminativist does away with ethics is that the eliminativist does away with, in the sense of denying the existence of, ethical properties or facts. But even granting that there is a sense in which this charge is true, it hardly seems to constitute an intelligible reason for preferring reductive utilitarianism over eliminative. In the sense presumably intended, the claim that the latter does away with ethical facts or properties simply points out the essential difference between the two forms of utilitarianism. And one cannot treat that as an argument against eliminativism without essentially begging the question against it.

Certainly, if one denies the existence of good things or right acts in favor of the (mere) existence of pleasure and things conductive to it, that may have an effect on those who hear the denial(s), an effect which the reductivist may wish to call bad and that even the eliminativist can say goes against overall human happiness or pleasure. But because the eliminativist may care as much about the advancement of human happiness as any reductionist, he may have equal reason or motive to keep his theoretical views from becoming known. If, as so often happens, a reductive utilitarian can defend the validity of his views while disavowing their practical usefulness and recommending that they remain esoteric, the eliminativist can do something entirely analogous even without making use of specifically ethical or evaluative notions. And so eliminative utilitarianism cannot readily be undercut as a theoretical option by pointing to the consequences of its being adopted by people generally.

The choice between reductionist and eliminationist utilitarianism is not an easy one. And likewise it is unclear for naturalizing epistemology whether it is better to reduce terms like "justified" and risk the consequent unintuitiveness of certain judgments that then have to be made about particular examples[6] or to eliminate such intuitive judgments by the draconian method of forbidding or deeming false all epistemic value claims. At least there is considerable diversity of opinion on this question among naturalizing and even anti-naturalist epistemologists. And by the same token I don't know how to say anything definitive about the choice between reductionistic and eliminativistic utilitarianism. To be sure, accepting the former guarantees a commitment to counter-intuitive moral judgments and, in particular, to the possibility of moral luck, but eliminative utilitarianism makes its own counterintuitive judgments, and in any event both forms of utilitarianism avoid the *inconsistencies* involved in our intuitive judgments concerning moral luck.

However, another way of avoiding the problems of moral luck needs to be mentioned at this point. This alternative ethical approach is very different from any form of utilitarianism, though it resembles eliminative utilitarianism at least to the extent of advocating the elimination of certain ethical properties/epithets from our ongoing ethical theorizing. What I have in mind is a form of virtue ethics that seeks to avoid the paradoxes of moral luck by being *selectively* eliminative in regard to ethical properties/terms. It will turn out that selective eliminativism is also an attractive possibility in naturalizing epistemology, and our brief sketch of the virtue-ethical approach I want to bring to your attention may help to bring to light some previously neglected possibilities in naturalizing epistemology.

3. Naturalizing Virtue Ethics

Some paradigmatic forms of virtue ethics seem totally opposed to any naturalizing approach to ethical theory. It is sometimes said that an emphasis on inner motivations/dispositions and a primary reliance on aretaic, as opposed to deontic, ethical terms typify any virtue ethics worthy of the name, and given these criteria an ethical view like James Martineau's, which defines a hierarchy of morally better and worse motives and claims that actions are to be evaluated solely in terms of their (previously or independently evaluated) motives, is paradigmatically a form of virtue ethics. Yet its primary and exclusive emphasis on inner motivation seems to ally it with epistemological Cartesianism and the latter's "subjective turn" rather than with the kind of naturalizing epistemology that refuses to base its evaluations solely on accessible and inner mental factors. Indeed, an ethical theory like Martineau's—and I mention this unfamiliar view because it is so simply formulated and such a clear-cut instance of virtue ethics—seems to lie at the opposite end of the ethical spectrum from utilitarianism, and if all virtue ethics had to resemble Martineau's view in the relevant respects, it would make no sense to mine the field of virtue ethics for a naturalizing example.[7]

But whereas Martineau's virtue ethics seems capable of making use, in its distinctive way, of all the main concepts/terms of standard ethical theory, there is another, quite different form of virtue ethics—historically familiar from Spinoza's *Ethics*—which *restricts* its ethical terminology in the light of problems raised by a more extensive ethical vocabulary. Spinoza denies the possibility of metaphysical human freedom and on that basis refuses to allow attributions of moral praise- or blameworthiness into his theoretical account of ethical phenomena. But he is willing to speak of certain character traits as virtues or vices, and as admirable or not admirable, because he assumes we can make sense of these notions independently of any assumptions about metaphysical freedom of will.

For Spinoza some people can be better or more excellent than others in various respects—e.g., one person might be a lovely person, another a vicious human being—though those judged worse in these ways are not thereby be deemed blameworthy or more blameworthy than those judged to be better. The absence of freedom undercuts moral evaluations that inherently assume some sort of metaphysical freedom on the part of human beings, but other sorts of evaluation do not entail such freedom and thus, according to Spinoza, apply to the sort of metaphysically determined but rational creatures we humans are or can be. A person who frequently turns on people un-expectedly—someone who acts angrily and aggressively toward people, without having been given any provocation—can be regarded as vicious and be avoided as such independently of any commitment to blame the person for being vicious and acting or interacting badly with others (after all, a dog can be called vicious for similar reasons). So Spinoza holds, and we can follow him in holding, that ethical evaluations need not commit us to freedom of will or (therefore) to ascriptions of moral blameworthiness, moral praise-worthiness, or moral responsibility generally.

Nowadays, we are less confident than Spinoza was that causal/metaphysical determinism makes human free will impossible, but we have another motive for wanting to avoid moral/ethical language that commits us to ascriptions of moral praise—and blameworthiness that Spinoza lacked. For we have seen that it is precisely with respect to ascription of blameworthiness and the like that ordinary intuitive thinking ties itself up into knots; the paradoxes of moral luck most closely concern such ascriptions, and so one way to avoid the paradoxes is simply to avoid ascribing blameworthiness, etc., altogether. An ethics of virtue that speaks of admirable and deplorable traits of character and of virtues and vices (or anti-virtues) in the manner indicated by Spinoza can avoid the paradoxes of moral luck by simply eliminating those ethical/ moral terms whose ordinary use gives rise to the paradoxes. And this way of dealing with moral luck is quite different both from eliminative and from reductive utilitarianism.

Unlike eliminative utilitarianism, Spinoza-like virtue ethics is only selectively eliminative of moral/ethical concepts/terms, and the concepts/ terms it eliminates are (among) those utilitarianism retains, but (re)interprets, reductionistically, in empirical, naturalistic terms. We have thus uncovered three different ways in which naturalizing ethical views can seek to take the sting out of the problem of moral luck. But since it may not yet be clear why I want to hold that virtue ethics of the sort just described should be viewed as a *naturalizing* alternative to utilitarianism, we have some more explaining to do, and the further explanation will help us, in turn, to identify a promising form of naturalizing epistemology that has not yet received the attention it deserves.

One of the most important aspects of naturalizing epistemology has been its typical commitment to externalism in regard to epistemic/evaluative attributions. For the Cartesian epistemologist epistemic rationality and/or justification is a matter of the thoughts, perceptual experiences, and inferences of the would-be knower, and thus concern only the internal mental states of that knower. But an externalist will treat rationality and/or justification as at least partly involving matters external to the mind or subjectivity of the person whose rationality/justification is in question. And a form of externalism like reliabilism with respect to epistemic justification, by making such justification depend in part on how reliable certain inferential processes actually are in representing our environment to us, makes epistemic justification depend on relations between the mind and the (rest of) the natural world. By contrast, internalism may or may not locate the mind at a point in the natural world but it leaves epistemic justification having nothing to do with (the rest of) the natural world, and this illustrates, I think, the clear sense in which externalism is a typical and exemplary feature of naturalizing epistemology.

But one of the thoughts that help to give rise to the paradoxes of moral luck is our ordinary belief that moral blameworthiness, badness, and goodness are a matter of inner willing or intention, not of possibly accidental and/or unforeseeable extra-subjective effects or circumstances. And to the extent, for example, that a Kantian or intuitionist places a primary emphasis on moral evaluation and sees such evaluation as based in the inner or mental life of rational agents, such an approach to ethics seems highly analogous to Cartesian epistemological internalism, and it is not surprising, therefore, that Kantian epistemology is a paradigmatic (though of course highly distinctive) example of Cartesian epistemological subjectivism.

So an ethical emphasis on the moral as inner parallels Cartesian epistemological internalism, but both these positions emphasize only one side of our ordinary ethical and epistemic evaluations. As we have seen, another part of our thinking seems to want to allow for luck, and both reductionist utilitarianism and reductionist naturalizing epistemology rely on and develop this other side of our ethical and epistemic thinking. Each of the latter focuses on extra-subjective factors that may be thought relevant to ethical or epistemic evaluation(s), and so reductionist naturalizing epistemology and standard reductionist utilitarianism represent antitheses to anti-naturalistic epistemological and ethical internalism.

But there is another way of dealing with the tensions and contradictions in our evaluative thinking than by emphasizing one element of the contradiction or paradox at the expense of the other(s). One may find reasons in the contradiction and paradox to drop the terms that give rise to them, and this, we have seen, is how a naturalistic but eliminative utilitarianism and an eliminative naturalizing epistemology-as-psychology both think we should proceed. Or, as a virtue ethics influenced by Spinoza would urge, we can be selectively eliminative: eliminating the (moral) terms whose dependence on luck seems (to some of our strong intuitions) so objectionable in favor of ethical terms/concepts whose dependence on luck or accident or the unforseen seems much less problematic and which (therefore) are less problematically understood in externalist fashion than such specifically moral terms as "blameworthy," "reprehensible," and "morally good."

Thus a person who was maltreated as a child and who (let us assume) became subsequently incapable of getting along well with others can be regarded as being the way he is as a result, in large part, of external, unlucky factors outside his control or ken. But that is no reason to deny that the person gets on badly or poorly with others if the latter notion is understood—as it seems quite natural to do—as entirely independent of the supposition that the person in question is morally blameworthy or reprehensible or responsible for being as he is. And so a Spinoza-inspired ethics of virtue can make use of evaluations that clearly and unproblematically depend on factors external to the agent (her will and knowledge).

Consider a further example. One component of being a good father and, as we may now assume, a good mother as well is to be a good provider for one's family. Imagine, therefore, a father who is laid off work after many years on the job, but who, after several weeks of vain searching for another, comparable position, finds such a position through the sheerest luck (imagine, if you will, that thousands of people with his skills have been laid off and that they are in competition for the small number of positions requiring those skills that are available or opening up). In that case, if he takes the position and is again able to provide for his family in the manner to which they had been accustomed, he will eventually be considered to have been a good provider. But if, on the other hand, he had failed to find any good job and were never again able to provide his family with any sort of comfort, then the overall claim that he is or has been a good provider would be irremediably undercut. Circumstances of the sort just described are familiar from the historical example of the Great Depression of the 1930's, and in regard to such a period it seems in no way odd or problematic to claim that factors of luck played a (considerable) role in determining who was and who was not (able to be) a good provider for his family. (Similar points can be made about the notion of taking good care of one's children/spouse/family.)

The people who were unable to find jobs in the Depression through no fault of their own cannot be considered to have been good providers, but in evaluating them thus we need not condemn or blame them, in fact it is difficult to see how anyone *could* blame them for failing, in such circumstances, to provide well for their families. (It is tragic that a whole generation of men and women should so largely have lacked access to this kind of normal human role-ethical attainment, but that is another matter.) And it is the absence of any implication of blameworthiness or reprehensibility here that allows judgments of good providerhood to depend so plausibly and unproblematically on extra-subjective factors external to the (consciousness of) the evaluated agent. So a Spinoza-inspired ethics of virtue (and in the next section we shall see, as is perhaps already obvious, that such an ethics need not be fundamentally egoistic like Spinoza's) removes those ethical concepts that push one toward internalism and relies on other concepts (at least some of) which are understandable in an externalist manner similar to (though not exactly the same as) what we find in reductionistic utilitarianism. And though such virtue ethics doesn't propose to reduce the terms it uses to purely naturalistic terminology, its freedom from internalism and frequent emphasis on external factors of luck give it a definite and substantial resemblance to naturalizing epistemology.[8] What will make the attribution of naturalizing to virtue ethics more plausible, however, will be the fact that naturalizing epistemology allows for an almost exact analogue of the virtue ethics I have just been discussing.

The dispute in the recent epistemological literature between internalists/ anti-naturalists and externalists/naturalists largely centers around terms like "justified" and "warranted" which, as we have seen, have aspects favorable to both sides of the dispute. This can lead one to reject all evaluative epistemic terms and move into pure psychology-biology, etc. But, as we saw with ethics, a selective elimination may be possible in which one rejects the terms which underlie and are the source of recent disputes in favor of other evaluative terms that give rise to no similar difficulties, but are less frequently used by epistemologists than the controversial terms "justified," "vindicated," "warranted," etc.

Instead of using the latter, why shouldn't we talk of cognitive mechanisms or strategies or habits that allow or cause *better or worse adaptation* to a creature's (or a person's or a species's) environment or talk of *better or worse cognitive functioning* (of functioning well or poorly)? Such notions/terms take in extra-subjective factors and are clearly relational and externalist; but unlike the terms that are presently the cause of so much epistemological controversy, these notions wear their relationality on their sleeve. Talk of functioning and of adaptation clearly has to do with more than what is inside the mind (or even the body, in most cases) of the individual whose functioning or adaptation is being evaluated as better or worse. And if internalism has no plausibility whatever in regard to such notions, then there is no reason to deny that luck or accident or the unforseeable can play a role in their applicability. So if we are selectively eliminative in epistemology, we can undercut the problems of rational or epistemic luck analogously to the way in which virtue ethics can undercut the problems of moral luck.

Thus a naturalizing epistemology that seeks to get beyond the opposing positions in recent disputes about epistemological naturalizing need not go all the way to psychology and biology. Or, since much psychology would be willing to talk about cognitive dysfunction and much biology about maladaptiveness, perhaps I should say, rather, that leaving internalism or naturalizing reductionism for science does not, as one might suppose, force one to give up all epistemic or cognitive evaluation(s). Talk about how well and adaptively one's cognitive mechanisms are functioning seems non-committal on the questions of justification and rationality that have been the focus of recent and traditional epistemological debate. And an epistemology that makes use of the former notions and avoids the latter is indisputably a version or example of naturalizing epistemology.[9] Since, by dint of its Spinozistic talk of better and worse or more and less excellent, the virtue ethics we have been talking about seems a very close analogue of the just-mentioned form of naturalizing epistemology, it may also now be clearer why I have spoken of such an approach to virtue ethics as naturalized or naturalizing. However, I would like at this point, and finally, to consider one further familiar aspect of the naturalizing tendency in epistemology. It too has an analogue in ethics, and in this case I think ethics, and in particular the virtue ethics we have been describing so sketchily, has a great deal to learn from its counterpart in epistemology.[10]

4. Ethics in Mid-Voyage

In our discussion so far of the naturalizing tendency in epistemology and its ethical counterparts, we have not mentioned what is perhaps the historically most important and currently most familiar aspect of naturalizing epistemology. The idea that in philosophy as in science, we must proceed with our actual beliefs and doubts, rather than base our thinking on some isolated set of pure certainties arrived at through some methodological ideal of absolute indubitability, goes back at least to Peirce and is perhaps most forcefully and famously expressed in Neurath's image of sailors who must repair their ship in mid-voyage.[11] In "Epistemology Naturalized," Quine refers to the Neurath simile in describing what he clearly takes to be an essential element of epistemological naturalizing: the commitment to working what one has and already accepts in order to improve the latter and learn more about the world.[12] But although this methodological conservatism has been typical of inquiry in the natural sciences, it has been notably absent from Cartesian-influenced attempts to reconstruct all knowledge on the basis of idealized and absolute certainties. And according to Quine epistemology should change its stripes and, by adopting a similar attitude of methodological conservatism, become properly scientific and naturalistic.

Note, however, that it is hardly clear that methodologically conservative natural science must ipso facto commit itself to reducing or eliminating certain (ordinary) terms. In letting our critical and inventive faculties loose on the corpus of what we already accept, we needn't perhaps prejudge the issue of whether the progress to be made thereby must inevitably occur through the reduction/elimination of various terms/concepts. So Quine and Peirce and Neurath's sober ideal of epistemology done in mid-voyage seems both more fundamental than and at the same time logically independent of the aspects of naturalizing discussed in earlier sections of the present essay. As such, moreover, it has an analogue in ethics that we have so far left unmentioned. If, given the history of ethical theory, anything has a right to be considered the most fundamental task of ethics, surely it is the task of showing that justice pays—or, more generally, that morality and a concern to do well by other people can be justified. Typically, attempts to show the validity of morality in this fashion have centered around arguments intended to refute egoism, the attitude of pure or fundamental selfishness. And what seems interesting here in connection with the issue of naturalizing is the resemblance this traditional ethical enterprise bears to Cartesian epistemology.

The Cartesian/Kantian epistemologist starts with the subjective data or consciousness of a single individual in isolation and seeks by argument to bridge the putative gap between the subject and the world. Such epistemology starts with what it takes to be the indubitable or more certain and attempts to justify belief in what it takes to be initially less certain and more in need of epistemic/epistemological validation. As such it clearly falls under Quine's strictures, and even without committing ourselves here either to agreeing or to disagreeing with those strictures, we should at this point be able to recognize the possibility of a similar move in a methodologically naturalizing ethics.

Why should an ethics that is properly sure itself, that wishes to proceed as far as possible in the manner of natural or other science, treat the standpoint of self-concern or self-interest not only as more secure than concern for others, but as a theoretically necessary point of departure for any attempt to justify or vindicate the latter? Why does (basic) concern for others need this kind of justification? Why can't we say, rather, that (almost) everyone in recent ethics has rejected (basic) egoism, and that current ethical theory has a perfect right to assume the validity and ethical justification of concern for other people until and unless our accumulating ethical ideas and theories give us reason to reject this fundamental assumption? There were notable egoistic theories (e.g., Stoicism and Epicureanism) in the ancient world, but that need not and should not disturb our own long-standing and on-going assumption of the validity of (non-egoistic) concern for others, any more than the existence of epistemological skeptics in the ancient world and in some cases more recently is a sufficient reason to go in for Cartesian epistemology. If a proper naturalizing methodology undercuts any need in epistemology to vindicate our beliefs about the world and others on the basis of assumptions about the subject in isolation, then a similarly naturalistic attitude in and toward ethical thought and theory should allow us to accept the ethical validity of a fundamental concern for others without (successfully) attempting to show how concern for others can be based in sheer self-concern or self-interest.[13] Both epistemological Cartesianism and the traditional task of defending altruism to the egoist treat the individual or individualistic standpoint as more fundamental than and necessarily involved in the justification of some larger or more inclusive picture of things, and, again, even if we remain neutral or uncertain about the relevance of scientific methodological conservatism to these areas of philosophy, we can surely see that ethics contains a plausible analogue to the naturalizing epistemological attitude of a Peirce, or Quine, or Neurath. An ethics or an ethical theory that adopts for itself the same methodological attitude as these philosophers recommend for epistemology—though clearly they wouldn't have wanted to limit its application just to one area of philosophy—deserves to be called a naturalizing or naturalized ethics, and I think ethical theory therefore needs at this point to recognize the possibility of such an approach and consider its merits and demerits. And it may be worth our while to consider in particular whether some philosophers who accept the validity of basic concern for others have recently been too concerned about finding a way to refute egoism.

However, I also want to point out that a methodologically naturalizing approach in ethics is perfectly compatible (at least on the face of it) with the alterations in our ordinary ethical thinking that utilitarianism and Spinozistic virtue ethics urge on us for their respective theoretical reasons. As I mentioned earlier, utilitarians believe various elements in our common-sense moral thinking to be incoherent or without adequate foundation, and it is largely on that basis that they propose some version of the principle of utility as the ultimate criterion of right and virtuous action. But the principle of utility retains the concern for others that is fundamental to common-sense morality; it merely gerrymanders it—in some ways shrinking, in others ways enlarging it—in the light of the difficulties and confusions it claims to find in our ordinary morality. This procedure seems in no way out of keeping with the ethical instantiation of methodological conservatism, and given the obvious connection between utilitarianism and the naturalizing tendency, this should come as no surprise. So utilitarianism in appropriate methodological fashion retains concern for others while rejecting other elements in ordinary moral thought, and a naturalizing methodological approach to ethics generally would then insist that utilitarianism has every reason to retain its commitment to a concern for other people and needn't feel any need to present a refutation of egoism.

By the same token, anyone nowadays who starts with the assumption—either theoretically or in daily living—that we should be concerned with other people and who decides, on the basis of their inherent difficulties, that we should abandon Kantian, common-sense, or utilitarian moral theory for an ethics of virtue, should favor an altruistic over an egoistically Spinozan ethics of virtue. We saw earlier that what distinguishes an ethics of virtue that seeks to handle the paradoxes of moral luck (and other theoretical problems that we have no space to mention here)[14] is the absence of those concepts of morality that give rise to the paradoxes. Such an ethics eliminates the notions of moral blameworthiness or moral goodness in favor of talk about what is better or worse, excellent or poor, admirable or criticizable in human conduct or motivation, and though it is true that Spinoza eliminates the former notions for the latter in a fundamentally egoistic manner, there is absolutely no reason, given methodological conservatism, why we should follow him in this respect.

An adherent of the naturalizing approach to ethics can therefore claim that we can and should formulate any virtue ethics we may wish to defend without assuming that we need to show how such an ethics can refute egoism. In other words, a virtue ethics that avoids (certain) specifically moral categories can fundamentally deplore attempts to harm or failures of concern for other people, and in the light of methodological conservatism has every right and reason to do so until and unless something turns up to cast substantive doubt on such non-egoistic terms of criticism.

Does that mean that we have no motive to show how other-regarding reasons/virtues can be derived from self-regarding (or non-other-regarding) reasons/virtues unless we reject naturalizing in ethics? Not at all.

To be sure, I have only analogized between naturalizing ethical and epistemological ideas and structures, rather than seeking to defend naturalizing across the board in any definitive way, and anyone who feels a pressing philosophical need to defend ethical concern for others might stand the present discussion on its head and reject ethical naturalism or naturalizing for its inability to comprehend the philosophical force of egoism. But, perhaps more significantly, even a naturalizer in ethics or elsewhere has reason to encourage attempts to argue from non-other-regarding virtues/reasons to other-regarding virtues/reasons or at least to welcome such an argument if one is ever successfully produced. The reason, however, has more to do with the metaphysical/reductionist naturalism mentioned earlier than with doubts about the appropriateness of methodological conservatism in science, epistemology, or even ethics.

If (all) other-regarding virtues/reasons can be derived from non-other-regarding virtues/reasons, then the latter can be reduced to the former and this opens up the possibility of an ethics of reasons or virtues that is fundamentally simpler and more systematically unified that an ethics that cannot effect such reductions. So a reduction of other-regarding values to egoistic or neutral coinage helps to achieve the scientific methodological desideratum of systematic unity in theory. There is thus reason even in a naturalistic or naturalizing ethics to applaud the reduction of the other-regarding to self-regarding terms, if such a thing ever turns out to be possible, but such an attitude is in no way incompatible with the naturalizing methodological belief that we can be and presently are justified in accepting certain other-regarding virtues and/or reasons without being able to produce such a reduction. Compare for example, Smart's version of central-state materialism. On his view we can reduce the mental to the physical or neurophysiological without having to presuppose, as clearly Smart does not, that our beliefs about mental states and processes are made more secure or stand in need of justification by such a unifying philosophical/scientific reduction. A similar view can be taken of the relation between ethical concern for others and egoism or self-interest.

If what we have been saying above is correct, there have been naturalizing tendencies in ethics—e.g., utilitarianism—for a long time now.[15] But they have not been conscious of themselves in relation to the wider spectrum of naturalizing possibilities explored in this paper. It will be interesting to see how ethics can accommodate itself to the broader picture.

Notes

1. See, e.g., Laurence BonJour, "Externalist Theories of Empirical Knowledge," in *Midwest Studies in Philosophy* V (*Studies in Epistemology*), 1980, pp. 53-73; Roderick Firth, "Epistemic Merit, Intrinsic and Instrumental," *Proceedings and Addresses of the American Philosophical Assn*. 55, pp. 5-23; and Hilary Kornblith's Introduction to *Naturalizing Epistemology*, Cambridge, Mass.: Bradford/MIT, 1985, pp. 1-29.
2. Arguments to this effect can be found in Thomas Nagel's "Moral Luck," in *Mortal Questions*, Cambridge University Press, 1979, pp. 24-38; in Samuel Scheffler's *The Rejection of Consequentialism*, Oxford, 1982; and in my "Utilitarian Virtue," in *Midwest Studies in Philosophy* XIII (Ethical Theory), 1989, pp. 393 ff. These discussions focus on different aspects of common-sense morality's incoherence or self-conflict.
3. See Nagel, *op. cit.* The first discussion of the problem of moral luck I am aware of occurs in Adam Smith's *Theory of the Moral Sentiments*.
4. I am assuming—with Putnam, Hempel, and many others—that the reduction of terms/properties can occur non-analytically, as, for example, when we say that water is nothing more than H2O. One can most plausibly equate epistemic justification with the use of some appropriately reliable belief-forming process if one doesn't insist that this equation/reduction obtains *ex vi terminorum*. And, similarly, utilitarian reductionism needn't commit any sort of naturalistic/definist fallacy. For further comparison of the role of reductions in science and ethics, see my *From Morality to Virtue*, Oxford University Press forthcoming, Chs. 4, 11, 13.
5. See, e.g., Hilary Kornblith, "The Psychological Turn," *Australasian Journal of Philosophy* 60, 1982, esp. p. 244, and Alvin Goldman, "Strong and Weak Justification," in J. Tomberlin, ed., *Philosophical Perspectives* 2, 1988, esp. pp. 64f.
6. Note that a reliabilist view of justification will hold that in possible worlds (assuming they are possible) where a solitary person is given some totally illusory set of experiences that is exactly like someone's experiences in our actual world the former will lack the latter's *justification(s)* for belief in external things, not merely her *knowledge* of such things.
7. For Martineau's views, see his *Types of Ethical Theory*, 2 volumes, 3rd edit., 1891. Given Martineau's comparative obscurity, it is perhaps worth noting that Sidgwick devoted more space in *Methods of Ethics* to Martineau's ideas than to those of any other of his contemporaries.
8. Cf. Ernest Sosa, "The Raft and the Pyramid: Coherence versus Foundations in the Theory of Knowledge," in *Midwest Studies in Philosophy* V, esp. p. 23.
9. Unless it brings in God's purposes as the basis for understanding "functioning well," etc. In "Positive Epistemic Status," *Philosophical Perspectives* 2, 1988, pp. 1-50, Alvin Plantinga makes this sort of notion central to his epistemological view

without committing himself on the necessity of relying on theism. Plantinga also doesn't point out the analogy with Spinoza's ethics, and I should perhaps mention that non-egoistic naturalistic virtue ethics need have nothing to do with theism or Spinoza's pantheism.

10. The just-sketched form of virtue ethics is described and defended at length in *From Morality to Virtue*.
11. See Otto Neurath, "Protokollsaetze," *Erkenntnis* 3, 1932, p. 206; and C. S. Peirce, "The Fixation of Belief," in J. Buchler, ed., *The Philosophical Writings of Peirce*, N. Y.: Dover, 1955.
12. See Kornblith, ed., *Naturalizing Epistemology*, pp. 15-29.
13. This point is, in effect, a naturalized version of Prichard's intuitionistic thesis that other-regarding moral claims present themselves as binding on us quite independently of any eudaimonistic assumptions we may or may not make. See his "Does Moral Philosophy Rest on a Mistake?" in *Moral Obligation*, Oxford, 1949.
14. See the works referred to in footnote 2.
15. Some recent naturalizing trends in ethics that I have not mentioned here include: the use of ethical claims as (best) explanations of historical phenomena by Nicholas Sturgeon and others; attempts by Georges Rey, Daniel Dennett and others to reduce moral-psychological notions like weakness of will and free will to computational/naturalistic categories; and, of course, continuing attempts to give naturalistic *analyses* of ethical terms.

I would like to thank Michael Devitt for extremely helpful comments on the present paper.

Philosophical Perspectives, 6, Ethics, 1992

PREROGATIVES WITHOUT RESTRICTIONS

Samuel Scheffler
University of California, Berkeley

Consequentialists hold that the right act in any situation is the one that will produce the best overall outcome, as judged from an impersonal point of view. By contrast, many non-consequentialists maintain that, given any impersonal principle for ranking overall outcomes from best to worst, there will be some circumstances in which one is forbidden to produce the best available outcome so characterized, and still others in which one is permitted but not required to do so. They accept, in other words, both what I call *agent-centered restrictions* and what I call an *agent-centered prerogative*.[1]

In *The Rejection of Consequentialism*,[2] I argued that an agent-centered prerogative is easier to explain and defend than are agent-centered restrictions. For, I suggested, whereas it is possible to identify an underlying principled rationale for such a prerogative, a comparable rationale for agent-centered restrictions is surprisingly elusive. In consequence, I argued, "hybrid theories", which depart from consequentialism to the extent of incorporating an agent-centered prerogative, but which do not include agent-centered restrictions, deserve our attention.

In the ensuing discussion, a number of writers have argued that hybrid theories have radically counterintuitive implications and cannot be accepted. However, these writers have disagreed among themselves about what conclusion to draw from this. Some have seen the criticism of such theories as helping to vindicate a version of commonsense morality, which is taken to include both prerogatives and restrictions, while others have treated the criticism as casting doubt on the advisability of any departure from consequentialism. The former, in effect, see the alleged defects of hybrid views as helping to supply the missing rationale for agent-centered restrictions. The latter regard the indefensibility of the restrictions as a fixed point, and treat the supposed unacceptability of hybrid views as serving to eliminate another potential rival to consequentialism. In this paper, I will explore the force and significance of some of the objections that generate these divergent responses.

I.

In *The Rejection of Consequentialism* I made the following suggestion about the structure of an agent-centered prerogative:

> ...a plausible agent-centered prerogative would allow each agent to assign a certain proportionately greater weight to his own interests than to the interests of other people. It would then allow the agent to promote the non-optimal outcome of his choosing, provided only that the degree of its inferiority to each of the superior outcomes he could instead promote in no case exceeded, by more than the specified proportion, the degree of sacrifice necessary for him to promote the superior outcome. If all of the non-optimal outcomes available to the agent were ruled out on these grounds, then and only then would he be required to promote the best overall outcome.[3]

Suppose, in other words, that each agent were allowed to give M times more weight to his own interests than to the interests of anyone else. This would mean that an agent was permitted to perform his preferred act (call it *P*), provided that there was no alternative A open to him, such that 1) A would produce a better overall outcome than P, as judged from an impersonal standpoint which gives equal weight to everyone's interests, and 2) the total net loss to others of his doing P rather than A was more than M times as great as the net loss to him of doing A rather than P. As this implies, the agent would always be *permitted* to perform the act that would have the *best* overall outcome from an impersonal standpoint if he wished to do so. But he would be required to perform the act that would have optimal results in impersonal terms just in case *each* alternative would involve a total net loss to others more than M times as great as the net loss to him of performing the optimal act instead of that alternative.

This proposal was intended as a very rough gesture at specifying the shape of an acceptable agent-centered prerogative. Obviously, the suggestion of mathematical precision is wholly artificial, and the proposal is in various respects insufficiently fine-grained. On the other hand, commonsense morality seems implicitly committed, both to an agent-centered prerogative of some form, and to at least some rough weightings along more or less the lines I suggested. And it is difficult to see how an acceptable non-consequentialist view could altogether dispense with such weightings. Thus my proposal was meant to provide a working basis, admittedly oversimplified but with roots in ordinary moral thought, for the discussion of agent-relative permissions.

Now a number of critics have argued that, when taken by itself, a prerogative of the kind I have described "will not only permit agents to *allow* harm, it will also permit agents to *do* harm in pursuit of their nonoptimal projects.... . For the prerogative is only sensitive to the *size* of the loss to others, and not to whether the loss is caused by the agent's act."[4] This problem will not arise if the prerogative is accompanied and constrained by an agent-centered restriction against harming, as it appears to be in commonsense morality. For such a restriction will forbid harming people even in order to produce an optimal outcome overall, let alone to secure some advantage for oneself. But, critics charge, a theory that includes a prerogative unaccompanied by agent-centered restrictions will permit far too much. Or, more precisely, the only way it can avoid permitting too much is by permitting too little. Thus, for example, Shelly Kagan claims that, on such a view,

> it will apparently be permissible to kill my rich uncle in order to inherit $10,000. Lest it be suggested that a plausible M will avoid these results, bear in mind that most of us believe that we would not be required to *pay* $10,000 in order to *save* the life of some stranger; any M large enough to save such results will obviously work in the former case as well.[5]

Kagan's argument is that a hybrid theory must treat cases of murdering one's uncle in order to gain $10,000 for oneself in just the same way that it treats the case of keeping $10,000 that one already has rather than spending it to prevent a stranger's death. For in each case one must choose a cost of $10,000 for oneself or death for someone else, and, Kagan suggests, there are no differences between the two choices that would lead a hybrid theory to say different things about them. So if the theory allows a person to give *enough* extra weight to his own interests that he is not required to pay $10,000 to save a stranger's life, it will also be committed to allowing him to kill his uncle for a $10,000 gain. And, on the other hand, if it does not allow him to give enough extra weight to his own interests that he can permissibly kill his uncle for a $10,000 gain, it must also require him to pay $10,000 to save a stranger's life. Thus, it seems, the theory either permits too much or requires too much.

In the next section, I will explore Kagan's example in greater detail. I will argue that his discussion of that example is misleading in at least two important respects. I will also argue that seeing why this is so enables us to identify considerations which, at the very least, support a significantly reduced estimate of the extent to which hybrid views are committed to tolerating harms inflicted in pursuit of one's nonoptimal ends, and which may even militate in favor of an absolute hybrid prohibition against such harms. In Section III I will discuss a different kind of argument in support of a hybrid prohibition against nonoptimal harming.[6] If the arguments of these two sections are correct, hybrid views need not have the radically counterintuitive implications that Kagan's example is meant to suggest they have. Nevertheless, such views are almost certainly counterintuitive in various other respects, and I will conclude, in Section IV, by considering the implications of this fact.

II.

The agent-centered prerogative as I described it says that an agent may do what he prefers to do, P, provided there is no impersonally superior alternative A, such that the total net loss to others of his doing P rather than A is more than M times as great as the net loss to him of doing A rather than P. From this it seems to follow that if it is permissible for a person to allow an n-sized harm to befall someone else in order to avoid a q-sized cost to himself, then it must, everything else equal, also be permissible for the person to inflict an n-sized harm directly in order to avoid a q-sized cost to himself. This "symmetry condition" is the troubling feature of hybrid views to which Kagan's example is meant to call attention. Care must be taken in interpreting the implications of this condition, however. For the cost to me of preventing an n-sized harm from befalling someone else will typically be much greater than the cost to me of failing to inflict such a harm directly myself. To use an example familiar from the literature, the cost to me of preventing deaths by starvation in far-away lands will typically be much greater than the cost to me of not mailing poisoned food packages to people in those lands. It will involve a greater drain on my resources, and a greater narrowing of the morally acceptable options available to me. Thus the symmetry condition will typically not imply that *if* it is permissible for me to allow death by starvation in far-away lands, it must also be permissible for me to mail poisoned food packages. More generally, what this example suggests is that the symmetry condition will not license as much harmful behavior as it may originally have seemed to. That it will nevertheless license an intolerable amount of such behavior is what Kagan's example is meant to show. But that example, or what Kagan says about it, seems to me misleading in a number of respects, of which two seem particularly important.

Before discussing these, we may first note that the scenarios we are invited to compare in Kagan's example are actually asymmetrical in two obvious ways. First, we are asked to compare a killing in one case with a death of some unspecified kind in the other. Second, we are asked to compare the demise of one's uncle with the death of a stranger. A more symmetrical version of Kagan's example might have read:

> it will apparently be permissible to kill my rich uncle in order to inherit $10,000. Lest it be suggested that a plausible M will avoid this result, bear in mind that most of us believe we would not be required to *pay* $10,000 to prevent someone from murdering our uncle; any M large enough to save such results will obviously work in the former case as well.

If this revised example has less apparent force than Kagan's original, that is presumably because it is less than obvious that one would not be required to pay $10,000 to prevent the murder of one's uncle if one were in a position to do so. Although this suggests that the asymmetries in Kagan's example contribute to its impact, I will ignore them in the remainder of my discussion, on the assumption that Kagan could have produced cases which were symmetrical in the two relevant respects, and which served his purposes about as well as the pair he actually used.

So let us turn to the first of the two major respects in which Kagan's example, and his discussion of it, are misleading. Kagan tacitly assumes that because in his example not killing and preventing death both involve $10,000 disadvantages, the relevant costs to the agent of the two courses of action are equal. But this simple identification of cost and financial disadvantage is unwarranted. When considering the cost to an agent of a given course of action, the relevant issue is the extent to which the agent's interests will be damaged if he pursues that course of action. And although financial disadvantage represents one important dimension of damage, it is not the only one. Thus, in considering Kagan's example, we may begin by reminding ourselves of the general empirical observation that the psychological costs of surrendering a benefit one already has tend to be greater than the psychological costs of doing without a comparable benefit that one has not yet acquired. This by itself provides some reason for thinking that the cost of preventing death, in Kagan's example, would be greater than the cost of not killing. This conclusion is substantially reinforced if one reflects on the putatively identical benefits that are forgone in the two cases Kagan compares. For, leaving aside psychopaths and the stick-figure characters who sometimes inhabit philosophical examples, it is wildly implausible to suggest that the net benefit to a typical agent of killing a relative so as to inherit $10,000 is likely to be just as great as the net benefit to him of retaining $10,000 he already possesses rather than using it to prevent a stranger's death. It is true that in each case he ends up with $10,000 he would otherwise have done without. But there the similarity ends. In the first case, the $10,000 is obtainable only by killing. If he gets it, he gets it as part of a package that may, depending on the specific circumstances, include everything from fear, horror, shame, humiliation, disgust, self-loathing, and punitive attacks of conscience, to the risk of social ostracism, alienated love, imprisonment, and economic ruin, to profound distortions of personality and of the capacity to lead a fulfilling life. In the second case, the $10,000 is, as Kagan presumably wishes us to suppose, a sum that the agent has obtained legally and that he is legally entitled to keep. Depending again on the specific circumstances, which Kagan does not describe, retaining this money might, if the agent is morally sensitive, cause him some more or less serious pangs of guilt, but it is very unlikely to involve any of the severe penalties associated with the acquisition of the first $10,000.

In view of these considerations, it seems fair to say that the costs to the agent of doing without the two sums of money are likely to be very different. In forgoing the first $10,000 he is, given the severity of the penalties attached to it, arguably *better* off than he would be with the money. In giving up the second $10,000, he avoids no such penalties; he simply suffers an economic loss plus, perhaps, the associated psychological costs of surrendering a benefit that is already in his possession. Since the net cost to the agent of doing without the second $10,000 thus appears to be significantly greater than the net cost to him of doing without the first $10,000, it would seem that an agent-centered prerogative could, contrary to what Kagan suggests, allow him to keep the second $10,000 without permitting him to kill his uncle so as to inherit the first $10,000.

It may be objected that all that has been established is that, given certain common but not invariant patterns of emotion and motivation, an agent-centered prerogative could permit an agent to fail to prevent a death without being committed to letting him kill. In other words, given that the agent is a normally motivated person in normal circumstances, and given that for such people murdering relatives for profit involves substantial emotional and psychological penalties which failing to spend one's money saving the lives of strangers does not, an agent-centered prerogative could treat those two courses of action differently. But the possibility of differential treatment depends on the presence of the "normal" pattern of emotion and motivation, and on the asymmetrical attitudes toward killing and letting die that are characteristic of that pattern. Where there was a symmetry of attitude, the agent-centered prerogative would no longer have any basis for differential treatment. Such a symmetry of attitude could take a variety of forms. Consider two extreme cases. In the first case, *both* the emotional cost to the agent of killing his uncle so as to inherit $10,000 *and* the emotional cost of letting the stranger die rather than paying $10,000 to save him would be so great that it would be in the agent's own interest to avoid doing either. In the second case, neither killing nor letting die would involve any emotional cost to the agent, so that each course of action would simply represent to him a net advantage of $10,000. In both of these cases, the objection might run, an agent-centered prerogative would have to treat killing and letting die symmetrically; in neither case could it allow the agent to keep the $10,000 he already had unless it also permitted him to kill for his inheritance.

The first of these cases does not pose a clear difficulty for a hybrid theory. For such a theory allows a person to give more weight to his own interests than to the interests of other people. But if, *ex hypothesi*, killing and letting die would both be very costly for the agent, then his interests and the interests of other people would coincide; it would be better from both points of view if he neither killed his uncle nor let the stranger die. So a hybrid view could satisfy the symmetry condition in this case by forbidding the agent either to kill his relative or to allow the stranger's death, thereby requiring him to act in a way that would be best both for himself and for everyone else. (More generally, whenever the net costs to an agent of preventing death and avoiding killing are equalized, not by increasing the cost of the latter but by decreasing the cost of the former, a hybrid view can, plausibly enough, satisfy the symmetry condition by requiring prevention rather than by permitting killing.)

The second case, however, seems much more troublesome for a hybrid view. In this case, *ex hypothesi*, neither killing nor letting die would be costly for the agent, so that his interests and the interests of others would conflict. In order to prevent the death of a stranger, he would have to pay $10,000 without receiving any compensating benefit for himself. Since the agent-centered prerogative allows him to give more weight to his own interests than to the interests of others, a hybrid view would, it seems, permit him to keep his $10,000. Or if not, there must be *some* sum large enough that the agent would be allowed to keep it for himself rather than spend it to save the stranger's life. But then it seems that the prerogative must also, by the symmetry condition, permit him to kill his uncle to inherit the same sum of money, which is outrageous. In this instance, the hybrid view seems to reward psychopathy. The person who can kill for profit without any qualms is permitted to do so; only those who have scruples are prohibited from killing.

This objection might be augmented in the following way. An agent-centered prerogative can permit normally motivated people to fail to save lives without permitting them to kill because normally motivated people have asymmetrical attitudes toward killing and letting die, as a result of which there are differential emotional costs for them associated with these two ways of behaving. But normally motivated people have these asymmetrical attitudes only because they have internalized commonsense morality, which says that it is intrinsically worse to kill than to let someone die. Hybrid views, by contrast, do not say this. So if hybrid views ever became generally accepted, agents would have symmetrical attitudes toward killing and letting die in cases where the costs to them *apart* from emotional costs were equal, and as a result the emotional costs in such cases would be equal too. And that means that if hybrid views were generally accepted, then such views would no longer have any basis for permitting normally motivated people to fail to save lives without also permitting them to kill. Thus, to put the augmented objection in its strongest form, as long as the moral view that normally motivated people have internalized is commonsense morality, then hybrid views will by and large allow only psychopaths to kill for personal advantage. But if there were ever a time when normally motivated people had internalized hybrid views, then those views could no longer allow even normally motivated people to let others die without at the same time permitting them to kill.

This objection may be challenged at a number of points. For one thing, it is not clear that the asymmetry of our ordinary attitudes toward killing and letting die really is dependent on our internalization of commonsense morality. It seems at least as plausible to maintain that the reverse is true: that commonsense morality appeals to us in part because it endorses an asymmetrical attitude toward doing and letting happen that we find natural independently of moral considerations. In addition, the objection depends on the idea that the penalties associated with killing one's uncle for profit are all psychological, so that they could be avoided by someone with a non-standard psychology. But the penalties I enumerated were not all emotional or psychological, and it is not clear that a non-standard psychology would be sufficient to avoid them. More generally, the fact that an agent had no qualms about such a killing would not suffice to show that it was really in his interest to kill, that it really advanced his good.

These points suggest that the differential costs to the agent of not killing and of preventing death may be more deeply rooted than the objection would have it. But there is also another difficulty with the objection. At the beginning of this section I said that Kagan's example, or his presentation of it, was misleading in two respects. I have so far mentioned only one of these: namely, the identification in that example of the cost to the agent with his financial disadvantage. This, I have suggested, helps to create the misleading impression that avoiding killing will quite often be just as costly for agents as preventing death. However we should now take note of the second thing that is misleading about Kagan's example. This has to do, not with what the example suggests about the relative costs to the agent of killing and letting die, but with what it suggests about the costs to everyone else. In particular, the example creates the impression that the overall consequences from an impersonal point of view of killing for personal gain will typically be no worse than the overall consequences of allowing death. For, in the example, the costs to everyone but the agent of killing and letting die are supposed *ex hypothesi* to be equal (despite the potentially complicating and therefore unhelpful fact, earlier noted, that we are asked to compare an avoidable killing in one case with a preventable death of some unspecified kind in the other). In real life, however, the situation will typically be very different. Consider first a related case. Defenders of consequentialism often argue that their theory provides strong reasons for not killing the innocent even if, in certain types of circumstances, doing so would seem to be the way to promote the best outcome overall. For, they argue, the long-term consequences of people killing each other in order to promote the overall good must also be taken into account. And these consequences, it is argued, would be disastrous; violence only begets more violence, and the inevitable effect of such killings would be to create fear, conflict, and mistrust, and to undermine the fragile structures of civility, civic order, and social harmony. So initial appearances to the contrary notwithstanding, it is claimed, consequentialism would generally forbid the killing of innocent people as a way of promoting the overall good.

Most people would agree that these considerations have at least some force. Now consider again the kind of case raised by Kagan against hybrid theories. However disastrous the long-term consequences might be of people killing each other in order to advance the overall good, they surely pale by comparison to the consequences of people killing each other in order to advance their own interests. We cringe at the very idea of a world in which individuals routinely form, develop, and pursue personal projects that require them, even within limits, to kill or injure others. By contrast, the consequences of a practice according to which people typically do not expend great portions of their own resources to save the lives of strangers, while certainly far from optimal, are not likely to be nearly as catastrophic. The difference may amount only to the advantage that the present miserable condition of the world enjoys in comparison with a Hobbesian war of all against all, but that advantage, as limited, intermittent, and insecure as it is, is not one that many sane people would be prepared to forgo. Thus there is, in general, an asymmetry between the consequences of people killing the innocent for profit, and the consequences of their failing to expend large sums of money in order to save innocent lives. Failure to reflect this point constitutes the second respect in which Kagan's example is misleading. When it is taken into account, we can see that hybrid views do, contrary to the claim of the "augmented objection", have a basis for treating killing and letting die differently, even when the costs to the agent of avoiding each one are identical. For the cost to the agent is not the only factor that determines what an agent-centered prerogative will allow. The costs to everyone else must also be considered. And when it comes to cases of killing and letting die such as those we have been discussing, these costs are not identical.

It will be observed, however, that the asymmetry I have identified derives from the presumably catastrophic consequences of a general practice of killing to advance one's own good. It has not been suggested, nor is it true, that there is any single act to which these consequences would all attach. But the agent-centered prerogative as I have described it is sensitive precisely to the consequences of individual actions. It remains unclear, therefore, to what extent and *via* what mechanism the catastrophic consequences I have spoken of could qualify as relevant from the perspective of the prerogative, and result in a prohibition of harmful activity designed to advance the individual good.

Similar questions arise, of course, with regard to consequentialist claims about the undesirable effects of a general practice of harming others for the overall good. In that case, such questions have provided one motivation for a move to "two-level" views, in which consequential assessment is applied to competing rules, policies, or motives rather than to individual acts. It might therefore be suggested that if the disastrous consequences of a general practice of nonoptimal harming cannot be fully taken account of in a hybrid theory's act-by-act assessment of individual harms, then this constitutes an argument for a "rule-hybrid" prohibition against all such harming.[7] Of course, overall consequences do not carry as much weight in a hybrid theory as they do in a consequentialist theory. In a consequentialist theory, the overall consequences are all that matter. In a hybrid theory, they must be balanced against the agent's interests. Thus, whereas two-level consequentialist restrictions are defended by appeal to consequential considerations alone, a hybrid prohibition against nonoptimal harming would have to be defended by appeal to what might be called "adjusted consequential considerations": that is, to the net effect of taking into account both the relevant considerations of overall consequences and the relevant agent-centered considerations. The argument would have to be that the impersonal advantages of an absolute prohibition against nonoptimal harming are great enough to outweigh the costs to agents of having such conduct ruled out.

This does not seem like an implausible thing to claim, but the argument would have to be spelled out in greater detail in order to be persuasive. In particular, a fuller explanation would have to be provided of how, at the level of rules, impersonal and agent-centered considerations were to be balanced against one another. And even if the argument were presented more fully, it would undoubtedly remain controversial. Some might argue instead that what the appeal to adjusted consequences supports is a rule of thumb which prohibits nonoptimal harming in general, but which fails to apply to individual harms whose adjusted consequences are, by themselves, clearly insufficient to render those harms impermissible. Others might argue that what such an appeal demonstrates is that beyond a certain threshold, nonoptimal harms will have sufficiently bad consequences that they will be disallowed by the prerogative as originally described on the basis of the usual kind of act-by-act assessment.

It is evident from this that there is room for considerable disagreement about the way in which the relevant consequential considerations are most appropriately to be accommodated within a hybrid theory. But however this disagreement may be resolved, the importance of those considerations for such a theory seems undeniable. Whether or not they provide support for an absolute hybrid prohibition against all nonoptimal harming, they clearly serve in one way or another to attenuate the degree of a hybrid view's toleration of such harms.

Thus, to sum up the argument of this section, Kagan's example is misleading because it encourages us to overlook two important points. Harming others for profit will in general be both less advantageous for the agent, and more costly for everyone else, than failing to pay to prevent harm. Taken together, these two points may be thought by some to support an absolute hybrid prohibition against harming others in pursuit of one's nonoptimal ends. At the very least, however, they call for a substantially reduced estimate of the extent to which hybrid views are committed to tolerating such harms.

Nevertheless, if one doubts whether adjusted consequential considerations actually do support an absolute prohibition against nonoptimal harming, and if one regards anything less than an absolute prohibition as insufficient, then one is bound to conclude that hybrid theories remain excessively tolerant of this type of behavior, even if they are less tolerant than Kagan implies. The basic problem, one is likely to feel, is that the purely quantitative structure of the agent-centered prerogative renders it incapable of assigning sufficient importance to the qualitative distinction between harming and failing to prevent harm. In the next section, I will discuss a different kind of argument for an absolute hybrid prohibition against nonoptimal harming: or, as I shall put it, for replacing the "pure-cost" version of the agent-centered prerogative with a "no-harm" version. If this argument is persuasive, then the prerogative need not have a purely quantitative structure.

III.

We may begin by recalling the claim that it is difficult to identify an underlying principled rationale for agent-centered restrictions. Briefly, the difficulty arises because the restrictions may not ordinarily be violated even to produce optimal outcomes overall. This means that there are circumstances in which they may not be violated, even though a violation would serve to minimize total overall violations of the very same restriction, or other events at least as objectionable, and would have no other morally relevant consequences. And it is very hard to explain how it can be rational to forbid the performance of a morally objectionable action that would have the effect of minimizing the total number of comparably objectionable actions that were performed, and would have no other relevant effects.[8]

Thus the difficulty in providing a satisfactory rationale for agent-centered restrictions derives from the fact that the restrictions prohibit acts of certain kinds even when they would produce optimal outcomes overall. At the same time, the objection to hybrid views that we have been considering arises from their apparent *failure* to prohibit acts of certain kinds even when they would produce *nonoptimal* outcomes. A modified hybrid view, which included a no-harm version of the prerogative instead of a pure-cost version, would avoid both difficulties. Like the original hybrid view, it would avoid the first difficulty because it would always permit the production of the best available outcome overall. And, by expressly prohibiting all nonoptimal harms, it would avoid the second difficulty as well.[9] Thus it would not give agents unqualified permission to devote proportionately greater weight to their own interests than to the interests of other people. Rather, it would only permit agents to do this provided they did not harm others in pursuit of their nonoptimal ends.[10]

In my book, I argued that it was possible to identify a rationale for an agent-centered prerogative, but I also argued that the rationale in question underdetermines the specific form taken by the prerogative.[11] It is therefore tempting to reason as follows. If the pure-cost version of the prerogative is subject to an objection that the no-harm version avoids, and if the rationale for an agent-centered prerogative underdetermines the choice between the two versions, then, other things equal, the fact that only the no-harm version avoids the objection constitutes a reason for accepting that version in preference to the pure-cost version. Reasoning in this way, we would conclude that the force of Kagan's example is not to cast doubt on hybrid theories in general, but rather to provide support for those hybrid theories that include a no-harm prerogative as against those that include a pure-cost prerogative.

Before this simple solution can be accepted, however, there is an objection to it that must be answered. The objection may be put as follows.[12] The rationale for a prerogative is a rationale for allowing people to devote some proportionately greater weight to their own interests than to the interests of other people. This rationale in itself provides no basis for distinguishing between a case in which one directly harms another in pursuit of one's own nonoptimal ends, and a case in which one merely fails to prevent a harm of comparable magnitude because of one's devotion to the pursuit of those same ends. That is, it provides no basis for distinguishing between such cases provided the size of the loss in aggregate well-being and the size of the advantage to the agent each remains the same in the two cases. The modified hybrid view, however, treats at least some such pairs of cases differentially. There are times when it prohibits an agent from harming an innocent person in order to secure some advantage for himself, but permits him to secure the same advantage in some other way, even at the cost of failing to prevent a harm just as great as the first one from befalling the same innocent person. The modified hybrid view is thus committed to the claim that it is (sometimes) worse to inflict a harm oneself in order to obtain some personal advantage than it is to allow a comparable harm to occur in order to obtain the very same advantage. And it is hard to see how there could be considerations that supported this claim without implying that harming is in general worse than allowing harm. But this is just to say that any considerations capable of supporting prohibitions against harming in pursuit of one's nonoptimal ends would also support agent-centered restrictions that prohibit harming even when it is necessary to prevent still greater harm and so to achieve a better outcome overall. And, contrapositively, any doubts there may be about the rationale for agent-centered restrictions must also be doubts about the rationale for prohibitions against nonoptimal harming. Thus the modified hybrid view is not a stable theoretical option, for one cannot consistently accept a no-harm version of the agent-centered prerogative without also accepting agent-centered restrictions, and one cannot reject the restrictions without also rejecting the no-harm version of the prerogative.

At one time I was inclined to regard this objection as decisive. As a result, I was led away from the no-harm version of the prerogative I had originally formulated,[13] to the pure-cost version sketched in my book. (Thus, purely as a matter of autobiography, what I am now calling the "modified" hybrid theory was really the original version, and what I am now calling the "original" hybrid theory—that is, the one sketched in my book—was in fact a later modification.) However, the objection no longer seems to me conclusive, for the following reasons.

The objection derives its force from the suggestion that there could not, in principle, be a reason for prohibiting nonoptimal harms more strenuously than nonoptimal failures to prevent harm which did not constitute an equally good reason for holding that harming is in general more objectionable than failing to prevent harm. However, the discussion in the previous section has already given us some reason to reject this suggestion. For, as that discussion made clear, it would be perfectly consistent for someone to hold that adjusted consequential considerations support a hybrid restriction on nonoptimal harming, while denying that harming is in general worse than failing to prevent harm, or that it is wrong to inflict a harm when doing so will produce optimal results overall. Such a position may or may not be correct. Even if one does not regard it as correct, however, the fact that it is a consistent position, and one which is not obviously unreasonable, suffices to cast doubt on the suggestion that there could not, in principle, be a reason for prohibiting nonoptimal harms more strenuously than nonoptimal failures to prevent harm which was not also a reason for agent-centered restrictions. Right or wrong, the position offers us one example of something that would count as such a reason.

Here is a second example. There are, it might be said, certain quasi-practical advantages that prohibitions against harming have in comparison with requirements to prevent harm. The former are more easily taught, internalized, and obeyed than are the latter. Moreover, prohibitions against harming help to demarcate a conception of moral responsibility that coheres smoothly with our natural conceptions of agency and causal responsibility. These considerations, it might be claimed, make it reasonable that a hybrid view should prohibit nonoptimal harms more strenuously than nonoptimal failures to prevent harm. For, given that some but not all nonoptimal conduct is, for independent reasons, to be permitted, such considerations provide a plausible rationale for what is, in effect, one way of drawing the line between permissible and impermissible types of nonoptimal behavior. (Adjusted consequential considerations might be said to be provide an additional rationale for the same way of drawing that line.) By themselves, however, these quasi-practical considerations provide no support for prohibitions against harms that will produce optimal results overall, for they do not themselves give us any reason to think that such harms are, on balance, morally undesirable.

Again, whether or not one finds this argument persuasive, it is in any case consistent and not obviously unreasonable. And the mere availability of such an argument provides additional evidence against the claim that there could not, in principle, be a reason for prohibiting nonoptimal harms more strenuously than nonoptimal failures to prevent harm which did not constitute an equally good reason for agent-centered restrictions. It suggests that there is plenty of conceptual space available in which such a reason might be located.

In short, the two examples I have given may convince some people that there *are* considerations which support a no-harm version of the prerogative without also supporting agent-centered restrictions. But it is sufficient for my purposes if those examples are taken only to establish that there *could* be such considerations. For that weaker conclusion suffices to rebut arguments which deny the possibility of such considerations, and which seek thereby to challenge the modified hybrid view's status as a consistent theoretical option.

Where does this leave us? At the beginning of this section I acknowledged a temptation to argue that if the pure-cost version of the prerogative is subject to an objection that the no-harm version avoids, and if the rationale for an agent-centered prerogative underdetermines the choice between the two versions, then, other things equal, the fact that the no-harm version avoids the objection constitutes a reason for incorporating that version into a hybrid theory in preference to the pure-cost version. The claim that acceptance of a no-harm prerogative would commit one to agent-centered restrictions posed a threat to this line of thought, for it cast doubt on the idea that a hybrid theory thus modified would be a stable theoretical position. Although that claim has now been rebutted, the line of thought it threatened has not been fully vindicated, because the reason for accepting a no-harm prerogative which is suggested by that line of thought is inadequate. The putative reason amounts to saying that we should accept a no-harm prerogative because there is a rationale for a prerogative of some form, and because a pure-cost version has unacceptably counterintuitive implications. But although, as I have argued, there may in principle be considerations that provide support for a no-harm version of the prerogative without supporting agent-centered restrictions as well, this does not seem like a good example of such a consideration, since the appeal of agent-centered restrictions on the intuitive level is also considerable. Moreover, the very enterprise in which I have been engaged consists in looking past the intuitive appeal of various moral doctrines, in an attempt to discover whether deeper rationales for them can be identified. I have argued, for example, that agent-centered restrictions seem paradoxical despite their intuitive appeal, and that their underlying rationale remains obscure. Again, therefore, I can hardly maintain that the intuitive appeal of a no-harm prerogative suffices to establish its acceptability. So the line of thought sketched above has not been fully vindicated. On the other hand, neither has it been entirely discredited. A better reason is required for accepting a no-harm prerogative than the one it advances. However, we have now had occasion, in the course of discussing the objection that threatened that line of thought, to identify two possible candidates for such a reason, one or both of which will be found persuasive by some. And, as we have seen, even people who find both of those reasons unpersuasive should agree that we have been given no principled grounds for thinking that a satisfactory reason cannot be found. Nor do prohibitions against nonoptimal harming seem paradoxical in the way that agent-centered restrictions do. Thus if one believes that no satisfactory reason for accepting a no-harm prerogative has yet been identified, what can nevertheless be said to have been established is that there is a rationale for an agent-centered prerogative of some kind, and that such a prerogative *need* not take a pure-cost form.

Put this way, the point is parallel to a point about egoism that I made in my book. There I noted that the choice between a pure-cost version of the prerogative and an egoist version allowing each agent always to advance his own interests was underdetermined by the rationale for the prerogative that I had identified. What I nevertheless claimed to have shown was that there was a rationale for a prerogative of some kind, and that such a prerogative need not take an egoist form. The question of why the prerogative *should* not take an egoist form—the question what is wrong with egoism—was said to be beyond the scope of my inquiry, and was therefore left open.[14] In a similar spirit, what can be said in the present context, by those who believe that no adequate reason for accepting a no-harm prerogative has yet been identified, is that there is a rationale for an agent-centered prerogative, and that such a prerogative need not take a pure-cost form. It can take a no-harm form instead. The question of why, ultimately, it should take a no-harm form, if it should, remains open, on this view. Even on this view, however, we need not feel that if we believe there to be a rationale for an agent-centered prerogative, we are then faced with a choice between a pure-cost version on the one hand, and a version that commits us to agent-centered restrictions on the other.

IV.

If the arguments of the preceding two sections are correct, hybrid views need not have the radically counterintuitive implications that Kagan's example is meant to suggest they have. However, even if those arguments are correct, that does not show that hybrid views are wholly congenial to moral commonsense. On the contrary, even a modified hybrid view with a no-harm prerogative will almost certainly be counterintuitive in various significant respects. For one thing, since hybrid views permit whatever consequentialist views require, the former will presumably share some of the counterintuitive features of the latter. In addition, however, hybrid views appear to have some counterintuitive implications which derive from their own idiosyncratic structure, and which consequentialism accordingly lacks. Most notably, as I pointed out in my book,[15] hybrid views seem to imply that it may sometimes be legitimate to force someone to do something that he would not be required to do voluntarily. Imagine a situation in which agent A was permitted by the agent-centered prerogative to refrain from performing that act (call it X) that would produce the best overall outcome of any option available to him, but in which the best overall outcome agent B could produce would involve his forcing A to do X. Since it does not include agent-centered restrictions, even a modified hybrid view would appear to say that B could permissibly force A to do X, despite the fact that A would not be required to do X voluntarily.

In assessing the significance of this point, three things need to be kept in mind. First, as I also pointed out in the book, we should guard against the erroneous assumption that, merely from the fact that X would produce the best overall outcome of any act available to A, it *follows* that the optimal course of action for B would be to force A to do X.[16] Quite apart from the fact that the array of options facing B might include some unrelated act that would have better results even than A's doing X voluntarily would, we must remember that the results of B's coercive act would not be identical to the results of A's uncoerced performance of X. And since coercion almost always has costs, the net good that would result from B's forcing A to do X would be unlikely to equal the net good that would result from A's voluntarily doing X. So it is important to remember that, on a modified hybrid view, B could permissibly force A to do X only if nothing else B could do would lead to better results overall, and, moreover, that this condition might well fail to be met despite the fact that X represented A's optimal choice.[17] The second thing to bear in mind is that what is distinctive about hybrid views, as contrasted with consequentialist views, is not that they would allow B to force A to do X if B's doing that would have better overall results than anything else B could do. For consequentialism would also allow this; indeed, consequentialism would require it. What is distinctive about hybrid views is that they would, it seems, allow B to do this despite their not requiring A to do X voluntarily. Consequentialism, by contrast, seems to require *both* that A do X, and that B force A to do X should A fail to do X voluntarily. Finally, we may observe that it is unclear exactly how a hybrid view is to be thought of as applying on the governmental level, but that the possibility is by no means excluded that considerations of a broadly consequential or contractarian character might lead hybrid views to endorse a system of legal protections that mimicked many of the effects of agent-centered restrictions, in which case such views might not tolerate the type of coercion under discussion after all.[18]

Having made these points, however, I do not wish to deny that even modified hybrid views will very likely remain seriously counterintuitive in the end. Let us proceed on the assumption that this is so, and ask what it shows. Those sympathetic to consequentialism might argue that if no plausible rationale for agent-centered restrictions can be found, and if an agent-centered prerogative without agent-centered restrictions has disturbingly counter-intuitive implications, then that leaves consequentialism as the preferred option. This argument is fallacious, for it depends on the application of a double standard in assessing consequentialist and hybrid theories respectively. It urges us to reject hybrid views because of their counterintuitive implications, and despite their underlying rationale. But if we were to do that, we would then have no reason to accept consequentialism as an alternative, for consequentialism is also a theory with a comprehensible underlying rationale and many counterintuitive implications. The argument achieves the appearance of plausibility unfairly, by applying the test of intuitive adequacy to hybrid theories but then suspending it for consequentialism.

Those sympathetic to commonsense morality might instead argue that if it is indeed possible to identify a rationale for an agent-centered prerogative, and if a moral theory that includes a prerogative but no restrictions is unacceptable, then perhaps the rationale for such restrictions is that they are essential to the design of an acceptable prerogative. This initially surprising thought, that agent-centered restrictions may depend for their rationale on the agent-centered prerogative, is not altogether unappealing. However, the argument that purports to lead to this conclusion is no more persuasive as it stands than the argument for consequentialism that preceded it, and if it is to be made more persuasive, the idea that a prerogative without restrictions is "unacceptable", or that restrictions are "essential" to the design of an "acceptable" prerogative, will have to be given a different kind of content than it has been so far. All that has so far been said is that a prerogative without restrictions has some implications which are disturbingly counter-intuitive and which could be avoided by the inclusion of restrictions. But there was never any doubt about the intuitive appeal of agent-centered restrictions. The question was whether, in addition to their intuitive appeal, they could be seen to have a plausible underlying rationale, and that question is not answered by simply calling attention once again to their intuitive appeal. This is of course the same point as the one that I made a little earlier about the no-harm version of the prerogative. The fact that there is a rationale for an agent-centered prerogative of some kind, and that such a prerogative would be seriously counterintuitive if it did not take a no-harm form, or if it were unaccompanied by agent-centered restrictions, does not by itself amount to a rationale either for the no-harm version of the prerogative or for the restrictions. Rather, it provides us with an even greater incentive to identify such rationales if we can. Moreover, in the case of the restrictions there is the additional problem that they seem paradoxical despite their intuitive appeal, and that persistent difficulties have plagued efforts to provide a rationale for them which is capable of dispelling this air of paradox. If it is true that a prerogative without restrictions would have seriously counter-intuitive implications, that fact certainly does not solve this problem or make it go away. On the contrary, it makes it appear even more urgent, because it emphasizes the centrality and importance to us of the seemingly paradoxical moral idea that agent-centered restrictions embody.

This brings me to the main point I want to make about the counter-intuitiveness of hybrid theories, and it is also a point about what I take the significance of my book's central themes to be. What the two opposing arguments just considered have in common is the assumption that, if hybrid views could be shown to be radically counterintuitive, the primary effect would be to eliminate such views as candidate accounts of the content of morality. However, this presupposes that the main interest of hybrid views is as "accounts" of this kind. My own opinion, by contrast, is that the most important role of hybrid theories is in helping to frame two challenges: one to consequentialism, and one to commonsense morality. The challenge to consequentialism is to articulate a more compelling reason why we should accept the hegemony of agent-neutral considerations in ethics, in view of the fact that it is possible to provide a plausible rationale for one major agent-relative principle, and in view of the fact that the main objection to departing from consequentialism to the extent of accepting such a principle, namely the counterintuitiveness of the results, is one that consequentialism itself appears unable consistently to advance. The challenge to commonsense morality is different. Since the commonsense view includes both an agent-centered prerogative and agent-centered restrictions, and since the former appears to be better motivated than the latter, the challenge is to identify a plausible rationale for the restrictions, or else to show why the absence of such a rationale is not troubling.

In this paper, I have suggested that hybrid views may be less drastically counterintuitive than some have claimed. At the same time, there has never been much doubt that they were counterintuitive to one degree or another. After all, one of their defining features is that they dispense with agent-centered restrictions, despite the intuitive appeal of such restrictions. What is important to note, however, is that the effectiveness of hybrid views in helping to frame the challenges I have described does not depend on their intuitive appeal. Indeed, the less comfortable we are with hybrid views when they are conceived of as embodying an alternative moral outlook in their own right, the more pressing it becomes to find some way of meeting the challenges they present. As I have suggested, this is especially true for those of us who are sympathetic to commonsense morality. The less comfortable we are with hybrid views, the more important it becomes for us to solve the puzzle of agent-centered restrictions, and thereby to convince ourselves that the principles we accept can be explained to our own satisfaction. In effect, hybrid views challenge us to undertake an exercise in moral self-understanding: to excavate the sources of the commonsense principles we find congenial, in the hope of discovering a more satisfactory way of explaining them, and our allegiance to them, than has hitherto been identified. To the extent that hybrid views remain counterintuitive despite my arguments in this paper, the need to meet this challenge becomes that much more acute.[19]

Notes

1. I interpret such non-consequentialist views as holding that each individual has a single general prerogative to devote disproportionate attention to his or her own interests, within certain limits, but that there are many different restrictions that apply to each agent, with each restriction specifying some type of prohibited act. That is why I typically speak of *an agent-centered prerogative* (singular), but of *agent-centered restrictions* (plural). Of course, there are contexts in which it is appropriate to use the plural for the former as well; since each agent has a prerogative, what groups of agents have are prerogatives. Hence the title of this paper.
2. Oxford: Clarendon Press, 1982. Abbreviated in subsequent notes as *RC*.
3. *Ibid.*, p. 20.
4. Shelly Kagan, "Does Consequentialism Demand Too Much?", *Philosophy and Public Affairs* 13(1984): 239-54, at p. 251. The same argument is made by Frances Kamm in "Supererogation and Obligation," *Journal of Philosophy* 82(1985): 118-38, and by David Schmidtz in his review of *RC* in *Noûs* 24(1990): 622-7. Kagan's formulation is endorsed by Larry A. Alexander in "Scheffler on the Independence of Agent-centered Prerogatives from Agent-centered Restrictions," *Journal of Philosophy* 84(1987): 277-83. Kagan develops the same point in a more general context in his book *The Limits of Morality* (Oxford: Clarendon Press, 1989), pp. 19-24.
5. Kagan, "Does Consequentialism Demand Too Much?", p. 251.
6. I am treating a hybrid prohibition against harming others in pursuit of one's nonoptimal ends as equivalent to a hybrid prohibition against nonoptimal harming. My reasons for doing so are explained in note 7 below.
7. Notice that a hybrid prohibition against all nonoptimal harming would forbid such harms even when they would produce better overall results than some other acts that the agent could permissibly perform. For example, suppose that Edward has three options. Option A is what he would most like to do, and although it would have the worst overall results of the three options, it would not involve Edward's harming anyone, nor would it require the assignment of so much extra weight to Edward's own interests as to render it impermissible from the standpoint of a hybrid theory. Option B would have better overall results than option A, but it would require Edward to inflict a harm, and, since it is not what he would most like to do, it would also represent a sacrifice for him relative to A. Option C would

have the best overall results of any act available to Edward, and it would not require him to harm anyone, but it would require him to sacrifice his own interests to an extraordinary degree. A hybrid theory whose agent-centered prerogative included a prohibition against nonoptimal harming would permit Edward to take either Option A or Option C, but it would prohibit Option B. Nor would these verdicts be different if C also required Edward to inflict a harm.

Since it may not seem natural to think of B as a case of harming someone in pursuit of one's own nonoptimal ends, or as a way of advancing one's own good, it may seem that B is not the type of act to which the consequential considerations I have been discussing above apply. And since a general hybrid prohibition against nonoptimal harming would rule out acts like B, it may seem that such a prohibition is too broad to consider as a candidate response to those considerations. It may seem that a restriction against harming in pursuit of one's nonoptimal ends should be considered instead. However, for Edward to take Option B, when an act with better overall results was available, would be for him to inflict a harm which served to secure a relative advantage for himself and his purposes at the expense of a worse outcome overall. That is sufficient, in my view, for B to count as a harm inflicted in pursuit of Edward's nonoptimal ends, and to fall within the scope of the consequential considerations in question. Thus, when I speak of harms inflicted to advance one's own good, or in pursuit of one's nonoptimal ends, these expressions (and others like them) should be understood broadly to include harms like B. Given this usage, a hybrid prohibition against harming others in pursuit of one's nonoptimal ends is equivalent to a hybrid restriction against nonoptimal harming.

8. I have developed this argument more fully in Chapter Four of *RC* and in "Agent-Centered Restrictions, Rationality, and the Virtues," *Mind* 94(1985): 409-419 (reprinted in *Consequentialism and Its Critics* [Oxford University Press, 1988], pp. 243-260).

9. Here, and throughout most of this paper, I make the simplifying assumption that the second objection is concerned exclusively with the nonoptimal *harms* that an unmodified hybrid theory appears to allow. Since this is in fact the way Kagan formulates the objection, this assumption is a reasonable one to make in the context of a reply to his particular formulation. However, the same sort of objection might equally well focus on a hybrid theory's apparent failure to prohibit nonoptimal acts of other morally abhorrent types, e.g. lies, theft, etc. Although, for the most part, it is only nonoptimal harms that I explicitly discuss in this paper, I believe that my arguments apply, *mutatis mutandis*, to these other types of act as well. If this is correct, then the term 'no-harm prerogative' is something of a misnomer, for such a prerogative, fully characterized, would prohibit more than just harming.

10. A modified hybrid theory with a no-harm prerogative would differ from the system Kagan describes in his book as "neo-moderate" (*The Limits of Morality*, pp. 186-94). For the latter includes, instead of a prohibition against all nonoptimal harming, a prohibition against harming "in those cases where this leads to a decline in overall good" (p. 188); and, instead of a permission to inflict optimal harms only, it includes a permission to inflict any harm "that leads to better consequences overall" (p. 192). Kagan refers to these neo-moderate features as a "zero threshold constraint" against harming and a "zero threshold option" to harm respectively. The way in which the modified hybrid view differs from the neo-moderate system, however, is not by imposing any absolute non-zero thresholds, but rather by maintaining that harms must be optimal—relative to the options available—in order to be permissible.

11. For the rationale itself, see Chapter Three of *RC*. For the point that the rationale underdetermines the form of the prerogative, see pp. 41 and 69-70.
12. In Chapter Four of his Ph.D. dissertation (*The Limits of Morality*, Princeton University, 1982), Kagan directs an objection of this kind against "neo-moderate" views. However, in his recent book of the same title, which is based on his dissertation, Kagan has eliminated this objection from his discussion of the neo-moderate position (*The Limits of Morality*, Clarendon Press, Chapter Five).
13. In my Ph.D. dissertation, *Agents and Outcomes* (Princeton University, 1977).
14. *RC*, p. 70.
15. *RC*, p. 37.
16. Larry Alexander seems to rely on just such an assumption at several points in the paper cited in Note 4, as for example when he asserts that the state, operating as a consequentialist agent, "would be obligated to prevent all non-consequentialist-justified exercises of the agent-centered prerogative, perhaps even to the extent of denying the existence of such a prerogative and inculcating a purely consequentialist morality" (p. 283). Note that, in this passage, Alexander also assumes that hybrid views would, when applied to the state rather than to individuals, be equivalent to consequentialism. This is by no means obvious, as I argued at pp. 33-5 of *RC*.
17. Here I am assuming that a modified hybrid view would rule out nonoptimal coercion as well as nonoptimal harming. See note 9 above.
18. See note 16 above, and the discussion in *RC* referred to in that note.
19. Earlier versions of this paper were presented to a number of audiences, and many people offered valuable criticisms and suggestions. I am especially grateful to G.A. Cohen, Frances Kamm, and Jeremy Waldron, each of whom provided very helpful written comments on one draft or another.

Philosophical Perspectives, 6, Ethics, 1992

AN ARGUMENT FOR CONSEQUENTIALISM

Walter Sinnott-Armstrong
Dartmouth College

The most common way to choose among moral theories is to test how well they cohere with our intuitions or considered judgments about what is morally right and wrong, about the nature or ideal of a person, and about the purpose(s) of morality.[1] Another kind of intuition is often overlooked. We also have intuitions about principles of practical and moral reasoning, such as those captured by deontic logic. In order to be principles of reasoning rather than substance, these principles must be consistent with all substantive moral theories. But consistency is not enough. We want the deeper kind of coherence that comes only with explanation. A moral theory that simply reports the principles behind common moral reasoning but cannot explain why these principles are so common or so plausible is inferior in this respect to another moral theory which not only includes the principles but also explains why they are true. Why is the explanatory theory better? Because we want a moral theory to help us understand moral reasoning, and such understanding is gained only when our principles are explained. Without such understanding, our intuitions do not seem justified, and we cannot know whether or how to extend our principles to new situations. These are reasons to prefer a moral theory that explains our principles of moral reasoning.

This preference for explanation provides a new method for choosing among competing moral theories. I will illustrate and apply this method in this paper. First, I will argue that a certain principle holds for reasons for action in general and for moral reasons in particular. Next, I will argue that this principle of moral reasoning cannot be explained by deontological moral theories or by traditional forms of consequentialism. Finally, I will outline a new kind of consequentialism that provides a natural explanation of this principle of moral reasoning. Its explanatory power is a reason to prefer this new version of consequentialism.

1. General Substitutability

My principle can be introduced by a non-moral example from everyday life. I have a cavity, and cavities become painful when they are not filled, so I have a reason to get my cavity filled. I can't get my cavity filled without going to a dentist, so I have a reason to go to a dentist. Arguments with this form are very common.[2]

They are also incomplete. Suppose that no dentist will fill my cavity without an appointment, and I don't have an appointment. Then I don't have any reason to go to a dentist. Why not? Going to a dentist would be a waste of time, since it would not enable me get my cavity filled. Of course, going to a dentist is never sufficient by itself to get my cavity filled, since I also must stay there long enough, promise payment, etc. Nonetheless, going to a dentist often enables me to get my cavity filled in the sense that, if I go to the dentist, I can do other things which will together be sufficient for me to get my cavity filled. In general, I will say that doing Y *enables* an agent to do X if and only if Y is part of a larger course of action that is sufficient for the agent to do X, and the agent can do the other acts that make up what is sufficient for X. Now, when going to a dentist both enables me to get my cavity filled and also is necessary to get my cavity filled, then a reason to get my cavity filled does generate a reason to go to a dentist.

It is crucial not to overestimate this claim. Although I have *some* reason to go to a dentist, this reason still might be overridden. I might have an overriding reason to leave for Australia. Also, my reason to go to a dentist and my reason to get my cavity filled need not be distinct in any way that would allow me to add the force of two reasons. Even if these reasons are the same, I still have *a* reason to go to a dentist. That is all the above argument claims.

It is also important that this argument does not require logical impossibility. It is logically possible for me to get my cavity filled without going to a dentist. My wife might know how and be willing to fill my cavity, but she doesn't and isn't. So my particular situation makes it *causally* impossible for me to get my cavity filled except by going to a dentist. That kind of causal impossibility is enough for the above argument to be valid.

The most general principle that warrants arguments of this form is this:

> (GS) If there is a reason for A to do X, and if A cannot do X without doing Y, and if doing Y will enable A to do X, then there is a reason for A to do Y.

I will call this 'the general principle of substitutability' (or just 'general substitutability'), since it specifies conditions when 'Y' can be substituted for 'X' within the scope of the operator 'there is a reason'. I will also call Y a 'necessary enabler' of X. Some more conditions might be needed,[3] but some principle along these lines must be accepted in order to explain why the above argument is valid.

It might seem that a stronger principle is true. Suppose I get another cavity, and two dentists are equally good and available. Going to the first dentist will enable me to get my cavity filled, but it is not necessary, since the other dentist is also available. Do I have a reason to go to the first dentist? This question is hard to answer because reasons are relative to a set of alternatives. If the question is whether I have a reason to go to the first dentist as opposed to going to no dentist at all, the answer is that I *do* have a reason of this kind. However, if the question is whether I have a reason to go to the first dentist as opposed to the other dentist, then I do not have any reason of this kind (since the dentists are equal). It is this latter, stronger kind of reason that is most accurately called a reason to go to *the first* dentist, and I will discuss this kind of reason. In general, I will say that there is a reason to do X only if there is a reason to do X as opposed to all relevant alternatives to X. When we consider reasons of this kind, (GS) is the strongest principle that is plausible.[4]

(GS) can be supported by several arguments. First, (GS) is confirmed when we can apply it again to the same example. If I have a reason to go to a dentist, and I can't go to a dentist without getting in my car, and getting in my car will enable me to go to a dentist, then I have a reason to get in my car. It might seem more natural to say, 'You ought to get in your car' or just 'Get in the car. We have to get going.' But what justifies these utterances is that I have a reason to get in the car.

More confirmation comes from reasons with different *sources*. I have an aesthetic reason to play a certain note at a certain time, for I am playing a piece of music that will be ugly if I don't play that note then. I can't play the right note without moving my fingers just so. Moving my fingers just so will enable me to play the right note, since I do have the right instrument in my hands. Therefore, I have a reason to move my fingers just so. Similarly, if I have a religious reason to go to church, and getting out of my chair is necessary and will enable me to go to church, I have a reason to get out of my chair. It need not be imprudent or ugly or immoral for me to stay in my chair, but religious truth or belief can still give me a reason to get out of my chair.

General substitutability also works for *negative* reasons. For example, I have a reason *not* to work all day, because I have a reason to get my cavity filled today, I cannot do so if I work all day, and not working all day would enable me to get my cavity filled. This argument is valid, so the above principle remains true when we replace 'Y' with '~Y'.

The principle also holds when we replace 'X' with '~X'. If I have a reason *not* to anger my boss, and not leaving early is necessary and will enable me to avoid angering my boss, then I have a reason not to leave early (even if this reason is overridden). Similarly, if I have a reason not to anger my boss, going to my boss's party is necessary and will enable me to avoid angering her, then I have a reason to go to her party. These arguments remain valid throughout these variations in the source and structure of reasons, and this confirms the general principle of substitutability.

Additional justification comes from a theory of reasons for action. In my view, a reason for an action is a fact about that action. Others deny that there is a reason when the relevant fact is not known. But suppose that both the high road and the low road lead to my house. A bridge is out on the low road, and I do not know this. I might not *have* any reason not to take the low road, but there still *is* a reason for me not to take the low road. That is why someone who knows about the bridge can tell me that I *ought* to take the high road. This suggests that there is a reason for an action when there is the right kind of fact about the action.

But what is the right kind? What makes certain facts reasons? It is hard to say anything very informative here, but one formula does provide some guidance for our intuitions. A fact is a reason when it has rational force in the sense that it can have an effect on what is rational or irrational. Some facts are reasons to do what there would otherwise be no reason to do. They make rationally neutral acts rationally required. I will identify reasons by another effect: a fact is a reason for action if it can make rational an action that would otherwise be irrational.[5] For example, it would be irrational to pay a dentist to drill a hole in your tooth if you had no reason to do so, but this act is not irrational when it is necessary and enables you to avoid greater future pain. This ability to make otherwise irrational acts rational is what makes this fact a reason to get your cavity filled.

A reason for an act does not always make the act rational, since the reason is sometimes overridden. Nonetheless, even if a reason is overridden in a particular case, it is still a reason if it has enough force to make an irrational act rational in some other case where the opposing reasons are weaker. If this kind of fact has this force in other cases, it also needs to be weighed along with other reasons in order to determine whether the present act is rational. This force and this need are captured by defining a reason as a fact that *can* affect rationality in some cases.

This use of 'can' might seem to make every fact a reason. If the fact that the wall is blue *can* make it rational to repaint the wall, this is a reason to paint the wall even if I like the color blue. However, all this really shows is that it is not the color of the wall that makes it rational to paint the wall. The color of the wall cannot be the real reason to paint the wall because it would still be irrational to paint the wall if I did not dislike or suffer some harm because of its color or condition. Thus, there are many facts that do not count as reasons on this theory.

This partial theory of reasons for action supports the general principle of substitutability. When there is a reason for me to get my cavity filled, the fact that going to a dentist is necessary and enables me to get my cavity filled makes it rational to go to a dentist even if this act would otherwise be irrational, so that fact is a reason for me to go to a dentist. Thus, the ability to make irrational acts rational transfers from acts to their necessary enablers, just as general substitutability claims.

2. Moral Substitutability

Since general substitutability works for other kinds of reasons for action, we would need a strong argument to deny that it holds also for moral reasons. If moral reasons obeyed different principles, it would be hard to understand why moral reasons are also called 'reasons' and how moral reasons interact with other reasons when they apply to the same action. Nonetheless, this extension has been denied, so we have to look at moral reasons carefully.

I have a moral reason to feed my child tonight, both because I promised my wife to do so, and also because of my special relation to my child along with the fact that she will go hungry if I don't feed her. I can't feed my child tonight without going home soon, and going home soon will enable me to feed her tonight. Therefore, there is a moral reason for me to go home soon. It need not be imprudent or ugly or sacrilegious or illegal for me not to feed her, but the requirements of morality give me a moral reason to feed her. This argument assumes a special case of substitutability:

> (MS) If there is a moral reason for A to do X, and if A cannot do X without doing Y, and if doing Y will enable A to do X, then there is a moral reason for A to do Y.

I will call this 'the principle of moral substitutability', or just 'moral substitutability'.

This principle is confirmed by moral reasons with negative structures. I have a moral reason to help a friend this afternoon. I cannot do so if I play golf this afternoon. Not playing golf this afternoon will enable me to help my friend. So I have a moral reason *not* to play golf this afternoon. Similarly, I have a moral reason *not* to endanger other drivers (beyond acceptable limits). I can't drink too much before I drive without endangering other drivers. Not drinking too much will enable me to avoid endangering other drivers. Therefore, I have a moral reason not to drink too much before I drive. The validity of such varied arguments confirms moral substitutability.

We can also extend the above theory of reasons. Since a reason for action is a fact that can affect the rationality of an act, a moral reason is a fact that can affect the morality of an act, either by making an otherwise morally neutral act morally good or by making an otherwise immoral act moral. As above, a moral reason need not be strong enough to make its act moral in every case as long as it has that ability in some cases. For example, if I promised to meet a needy student later this afternoon, it is immoral for me to go home now if I have no morally relevant reason to go. Nonetheless, it is not immoral for me to go home now if this is necessary and enables me to feed my child when I have a moral reason to feed her. Thus, this fact about going home now can make an otherwise immoral act moral, so this fact is a moral reason. This supports moral substitutability. When there is a moral reason for me to feed my child, and going home now is necessary and enables me to feed my child, this fact makes it moral for me to go home now even in a situation where this would otherwise be immoral, so this fact is a moral reason for me to go home now. Thus, the ability to make immoral acts moral transfers from acts to their necessary enablers, just as moral substitutability claims.

Despite these arguments for moral substitutability, critics will raise several objections. I will consider only three kinds of objections, but they set the basic patterns for most others.

The first kind of objection claims that some necessary enablers of what I have a moral reason to do seem morally *neutral*. For example, I promised, so I have a moral reason to cook dinner. I cannot cook dinner without moving some air molecules, and moving some air molecules does enable me to cook dinner. Moral substitutability warrants the conclusion that there is a moral reason for me to move some air molecules. This seems at least odd.

My response is that this conclusion is still true. Its oddness can be explained by pragmatic principles.[6] My moral reason to move some air molecules is very weak and general, since I can move air molecules in many different ways, but only some of these count as cooking dinner. Thus, when one can make the stronger and more specific judgment that I have a moral reason to cook dinner, it is misleading to say only that there is a moral reason to move some air molecules. This weaker judgment suggests that this is all I have a moral reason to do, since, if I have a moral reason to do more, why not say so? Furthermore, if the purpose of the conversation is to direct my action, then it is irrelevant to say that I have a moral reason to move some air molecules, since this judgment fails to tell me *how* to move them. This judgment also fails to help others determine whether I have done *all* that I have a moral reason to do, or whether I am blameworthy. The failure to achieve such purposes explains why it is odd to say that I have a moral reason to move some air molecules. But this explanation is purely pragmatic, so it can still be *true* that I have a moral reason to move some air molecules. And it *is* true, because my act will move some air molecules if I do what I have a moral reason to do. The truth of this consequence is all that is needed to defend moral substitutability.

The second objection is that some necessary enablers of what I have a moral reason to do are morally *wrong*. Philippa Foot gives an example:

Suppose, for instance, that some person has an obligation to support a dependent relative, an aged parent perhaps. Then it may be that he ought to take a job to get some money. ...But what if the only means of getting money is by killing someone? ...It is not the case that the son or daughter ought to kill to get the money.[7]

If we change 'obligation' and 'ought' into 'moral reason', Foot seems to claim that the child does not have any moral reason to kill, even though the child has a moral reason to get the money, the child cannot get the money without killing, and killing would enable the child to get the money. This would refute moral substitutability.

However, the child does have *some* moral reason to kill. This moral reason is vastly overridden by the moral reason not to kill, but, if the child kills, it will not be for no reason at all or for a selfish reason. Moreover, the fact that an act is necessary and enables the child to support the parents can make an otherwise immoral act moral in other cases, even if it is not strong enough to remove the immorality in this case. It still would be odd to say *only* that the child has a moral reason to kill, but what makes this utterance odd is just that it leaves out some very important information: the reason is vastly overridden. Nonetheless, it is still *true* that the child has *some* moral reason to kill, so moral substitutability stands.

Foot does make another suggestion that deserves a response. In place of moral substitutability, she says in effect that there is a moral reason to do what is a necessary *means* of doing what there is a moral reason to do. This weaker principle is supposed explain the validity of arguments like those above. Foot also claims that this principle does not yield any moral reason to kill in her example, because a means must be possible, but here killing is not a 'moral possibility', because it is wrong. I am not convinced, however, that what is morally impossible in this way čannot be a means. More importantly, Foot's principle is too weak to explain the validity of many common arguments. Getting in my car does not seem to be a *means* of getting my cavity filled, since I do not get my cavity filled by (means of) getting in my car. Other examples are even clearer. Suppose I have a moral reason to go home, but I cannot go home without waking the dog that is sleeping outside my office. Waking the dog does *enable* me to go home in my sense that it is part of a larger course of action that is sufficient for me to go home, where I can do the rest of what is sufficient. Therefore, I have a moral reason to wake the dog (even if it is odd to describe the reason in this way). However, waking the dog is not a *means* of going home. Thus, Foot's principle cannot explain why *this* argument is valid. We need a principle as strong as moral substitutability in order to explain the validity of all of the arguments that are valid.

A final objection asks which reasons are moral. Even if I have a moral reason to feed my child, and even if this gives me *a* reason to go home, a critic still might deny that my reason to go home is *moral* in nature. However, my reason to go home seems moral, both because its source is a moral reason, and also because its role is to affect what is moral or immoral. Furthermore, if it is not a moral reason, what kind of reason is it? My reason to go home is derived by substitutability from a moral reason (my reason to feed my child). This chain of reasons need not have any source apart from morality, and, if it does not, my reason to go home is not aesthetic or religious or prudential or legal. Opponents might respond that my reason to go home is a 'practical' or 'instrumental' reason. However, this is just another way of saying that it is derived by substitutability, and this does not show that it is not *also* a moral reason. Instrumental moral reasons must still count as moral reasons, since otherwise we could not explain how they differ from instrumental religious reasons, instrumental aesthetic reasons, and so on. My reason to go home is stronger and different in character if it derives from a moral reason to feed my child than if it derives from a prudential reason to take a nap. The differences between my reasons to go home in these two cases would be hidden if both reasons were described solely as 'instrumental' without recognizing that the first is moral and the second is prudential. That is why we need to count reasons derived from moral reasons via substitutability as moral reasons themselves. Finally, we can also argue more positively for the moral nature of my reason to go home. This reason meets every necessary condition in every plausible definition of morality. Morality is usually defined by its form, content, or force. Regarding form, my reason to go home is universalizable, since anyone in similar circumstances would also have a reason to go home. My reason to go home also has the content essential to morality, since it concerns social relations and harm to others. Even if morality must be supreme in force (which I doubt), my reason to go home is just as likely to be supreme as my reason to feed my child, since my reason to go home is not overridden in this situation unless my reason to feed my child is also overridden. This leaves no reason to deny that my reason to go home is moral in nature.

There are, of course, many other possible objections to moral substitutability, and I cannot answer all of them here.[8] Nonetheless, we already have several arguments for moral substitutability. It is confirmed by numerous and varied examples. It coheres well with a general theory of reasons for action. And the main objections have been met. So I conclude that the principle of moral substitutability is true.

3. Why and How to Explain Substitutability

If moral substitutability is so obvious, why does it need to be explained? The answer lies in its unusual features. Moral substitutability relates a moral operator ('there is a moral reason') to a non-moral operator ('can'). Moreover, the non-moral operator ('can') represents contingent facts and not just necessary relations, such as logical impossibility or act identity. Thus, moral substitutability takes us from a moral judgment about one action to a moral judgment about a different action that is only contingently related.

Similar inferences are not allowed for many other properties. For example, even if I cannot chop vegetables without taking a knife out of a drawer, and even if taking out a knife does enable me to chop vegetables, my taking out a knife still might be quick when my chopping vegetables is slow. Thus, quickness and many other properties of acts do not transfer to necessary enablers of those acts. This makes it odd that moral and other reasons for acts do transfer to necessary enablers of those acts. This oddity creates the need to explain moral substitutability.

How can a moral theory explain moral substitutability? The most direct way is if moral substitutability follows from the substantive principles in the moral theory. Moral theories present basic moral principles about what morally ought or ought not to be done, or about what is morally right or wrong, etc. Regardless of terminology, these substantive principles tell us in effect what moral reasons there are. For example, if the rule 'Keep your promises' or the principle 'You ought to keep your promises' is basic to a moral theory, then the fact that an act is an act of keeping a promise is a moral reason to do that act according to that theory. In such basic rules or principles, each moral theory specifies which properties of acts constitute moral reasons to do or not to do acts with those properties.

Moral theories can then explain moral substitutability by picking out the right kinds of properties as moral reasons. Suppose a moral theory implies that an agent has a moral reason to do act R because act R has a property P. Now suppose that act N is a necessary enabler for act R. Moral substitutability implies that there is also a moral reason to do act N, but the question is: why? If act N also has property P, this makes it clear why there is also a reason to do act N. However, if act N does not have property P, this moral theory does not explain why the agent has any reason to do act N. Schematically,

$$P? \quad P$$
$$| \quad\ \ |$$
$$N \leftarrow R$$

Thus, a moral theory can explain why moral substitutability holds if its basic substantive principles imply that all moral reasons are or are due to properties such that, if one act has such a property, then any act which is a necessary enabler for the first act also has such a property. Moral substitutability then follows from the substantive principles of the moral theory.

It might seem that this kind of explanation is not needed, because another explanation is readily available.[9] Moral substitutability can be derived from general substitutability. Doesn't that explain moral substitutability? Not really. General and moral substitutability set abstract constraints on reasons and moral reasons. We still need to know whether and why these constraints are actually met by the moral reasons picked out by each moral theory. Suppose a substantive moral theory implies that there are moral reasons to do acts of types A, B, C, and D, but no more. Moral substitutability, however, implies that there are also moral reasons to do acts of type E, F, G, and H, since these are necessary enablers for A-D. The substantive moral theory itself cannot explain why there are these additional moral reasons to do E-H. General substitutability still implies moral substitutability, but neither of these principles stands in any explanatory relation to the substantive moral theory itself. We could just add the principle of moral substitutability to the original theory, and the new, extended theory would imply moral reasons to do acts of type E-H. However, the original, substantive principles would still give us no understanding of why the extension is needed. The substitutability principles were just tacked on in an ad hoc fashion, so they are still not connected in any significant way to the substantive part of the theory. This lack of coherence and explanatory value makes this extended theory inferior to another moral theory whose substantive moral principles imply and thus explain moral substitutability.

The same burden arises outside morality. General substitutability applies to prudential reasons, aesthetic reasons, etc., so a substantive theory of prudence, aesthetics, etc., also needs to specify the content of its reasons in such a way that we can understand why those reasons obey the constraints of general substitutability. Although this explanatory burden is general, this does not make it any easier to carry. Each theory in each area will lack coherence unless its particular substantive principles bear some explanatory relation to the relevant principles of substitutability. This general requirement has important implications in all of these areas, but I will focus on moral reasons.

4. Kinds of Moral Reasons

In order to determine which moral theories can explain moral substitutability, we need to distinguish two kinds of moral reasons and theories: consequential and deontological. These terms are used in many ways, but one particular distinction will serve my purposes.

A moral reason to do an act is *consequential* if and only if the reason depends *only* on the consequences of either doing the act or not doing the act. For example, a moral reason not to hit someone is that this will hurt her or him. A moral reason to turn your car to the left might be that, if you do not do so, you will run over and kill someone. A moral reason to feed a starving child is that the child will lose important mental or physical abilities if you do not feed it. All such reasons are consequential reasons.

All other moral reasons are non-consequential. Thus, a moral reason to do an act is non-consequential if and only if the reason depends even partly on some property that the act has independently of its consequences. For example, an act can be a lie regardless of what happens as a result of the lie (since some lies are not believed), and some moral theories claim that that property of being a lie provides a moral reason not to tell a lie regardless of the consequences of this lie. Similarly, the fact that an act fulfills a promise is often seen as a moral reason to do the act, even though the act has that property of fulfilling a promise independently of its consequences. All such moral reasons are non-consequential. In order to avoid so many negations, I will also call them 'deontological'.

This distinction would not make sense if we did not restrict the notion of consequences. If I promise to mow the lawn, then one consequence of my mowing might seem to be that my promise is fulfilled. One way to avoid this problem is to specify that the consequences of an act must be distinct from the act itself. My act of fulfilling my promise and my act of mowing are not distinct, because they are done by the same bodily movements.[10] Thus, my fulfilling my promise is not a consequence of my mowing. A consequence of an act need not be later in time than the act, since causation can be simultaneous, but the consequence must at least be different from the act. Even with this clarification, it is still hard to classify some moral reasons as consequential or deontological,[11] but I will stick to examples that are clear.

In accordance with this distinction between kinds of moral reasons, I can now distinguish different kinds of moral theories. I will say that a moral theory is consequentialist if and only if it implies that all basic moral reasons are consequential. A moral theory is then non-consequentialist or deontological if it includes any basic moral reasons which are not consequential.

5. Against Deontology

So defined, the class of deontological moral theories is very large and diverse. This makes it hard to say anything in general about it. Nonetheless, I will argue that no deontological moral theory can explain why moral substitutability holds. My argument applies to all deontological theories because it depends only on what is common to them all, namely, the claim that some basic moral reasons are not consequential. Some deontological theories allow very many weighty moral reasons that are consequential, and these theories might be able to explain why moral substitutability holds for some of their moral reasons: the consequential ones. But even these theories cannot explain why moral substitutability holds for *all* moral reasons, including the non-consequential reasons that make the theory deontological. The failure of deontological moral theories to explain moral substitutability in the very cases that make them deontological is a reason to reject all deontological moral theories.

I cannot discuss every deontological moral theory, so I will discuss only a few paradigm examples and show why they cannot explain moral substitutability. After this, I will argue that similar problems are bound to arise for all other deontological theories by their very nature.

The simplest deontological theory is the pluralistic intuitionism of Prichard and Ross. Ross writes that, when someone promises to do something, 'This we consider obligatory in its own nature, just because it is a fulfillment of a promise, and not because of *its* consequences.'[12] Such deontologists claim in effect that, if I promise to mow the grass, there is a moral reason for me to mow the grass, and this moral reason is constituted by the fact that mowing the grass fulfills my promise. This reason exists regardless of the consequences of mowing the grass, even though it might be overridden by certain bad consequences. However, if this is why I have a moral reason to mow the grass, then, even if I cannot mow the grass without starting my mower, and starting the mower would enable me to mow the grass, it still would not follow that I have any moral reason to start my mower, since I did *not* promise to start my mower, and starting my mower does *not* fulfill my promise. Thus, a moral theory cannot explain moral substitutability if it claims that properties like this provide moral reasons.

Of course, this argument is too simple to be conclusive by itself, since deontologists will have many responses. The question is whether any response is adequate. I will argue that no response can meet the basic challenge.

A deontologist might respond that his moral theory includes not only the principle that there is a moral reason to keep one's promises but also another principle that there is a moral reason to do whatever is a necessary enabler for what there is a moral reason to do. This other principle just is the principle of moral substitutability, so, of course, I agree that it is true. However, the question is *why* it is true. This new principle is very different from the substantive principles in a deontological theory, so it cries out for an explanation. If a deontologist simply adds this new principle to the substantive principles in his theory, he has done nothing to explain why the new principle is true. It would be ad hoc to tack it on solely in order to yield moral reasons like the moral reason to start the mower. In order to explain or justify moral substitutability, a deontologist needs to show how this principle coheres in some deeper way with the substantive principles of the theory. That is what deontologists cannot do.

A second response is that I misdescribed the property that provides the moral reason. Deontologists might admit that the reason to mow the lawn is not that this fulfills a promise, but they can claim instead that the moral reason to mow the lawn is that this is a necessary enabler for keeping a promise. They can then claim that there is a moral reason to start the mower, because starting the mower is also a necessary enabler for keeping my promise. Again, I agree that these reasons exist. But the question is *why*. This deontologist needs to explain why the moral reason has to be that the act is a necessary enabler for fulfilling a promise instead of just that the act does fulfill a promise. If there is no moral reason to keep a promise, it is hard to understand why there is any moral reason to do what is a necessary enabler for keeping a promise. Furthermore, deontologists claim that the crucial fact is not about consequences but directly about promises. My moral reason is supposed to arise from what I said before my act and not from consequences after my act. However, what I said was 'I promise to mow the grass'. I did *not* say, 'I promise to do what is a necessary enabler for mowing the grass.' Thus, I did *not* promise to do what is a necessary enabler for keeping the promise. What I promised was only to keep the promise. Because of this, deontologists who base moral reasons directly on promises cannot explain why there is not only a moral reason to do what I promised to do (mow the grass) but also a moral reason to do what I did not promise to do (start the mower).

Deontologists might try to defend the claim that moral reasons are based on promises by claiming that promise keeping is intrinsically good and there is a moral reason to do what is a necessary enabler of what is intrinsically good. However, this response runs into two problems. First, on this theory, the reason to keep a promise is a reason to do what is itself intrinsically good, but the reason to start the mower is *not* a reason to do what is intrinsically good. Since these reasons are so different, they are derived in different ways. This creates an incoherence or lack of unity which is avoided in other theories. Second, this response conflicts with a basic theme in deontological theories. If my promise keeping is intrinsically good, your promise keeping is just as intrinsically good. But then, if what gives me a moral reason to keep my promise is that I have a moral reason to do whatever is intrinsically good, I have just as much moral reason to do what is a necessary enabler for you to keep your promise. And, if my breaking my promise is a necessary enabler for two other people to keep their promises, then my moral reason to break my promise is stronger than my moral reason to keep it (other things being equal). This undermines the basic deontological claim that my reasons derive in a special way from *my* promises.[13] So this response explains moral substitutability at the expense of giving up deontology.

A fourth possible response is that any reason to mow the grass is also a reason to start my mower because starting my mower is *part* of mowing the grass. However, starting my mower is *not* part of mowing the grass, because I can start my mower without cutting *any* grass. I might start my mower hours in advance and never get around to cutting any grass. Suppose I start the mower then go inside and watch television. My wife comes in and asks, 'Have you started to mow the lawn?', so I answer, 'Yes. I've done part of it. I'll finish it later.' This is not only misleading but false. Furthermore, mowing the grass can have other necessary conditions, such as buying a mower or leaving my chair, which are not parts of mowing the grass by any stretch of the imagination.

Finally, deontologists might charge that my argument *begs the question*. It would beg the question to assume moral substitutability if this principle were inconsistent with deontological theories. However, my point is *not* that moral substitutability is *inconsistent* with deontology. It is not. Deontologists can consistently tack moral substitutability onto their theories. My point is only that deontologists cannot *explain* why moral substitutability holds. It would still beg the question to assert moral substitutability without argument. However, I *did* argue for moral substitutability, and my argument was independent of its implications for deontology. I even used examples of moral reasons that are typical of deontological theories. Deontologists still might complain that the failure of so many theories to explain moral substitutability casts new doubt on this principle. However, we normally should not reject a scientific observation just because our theory cannot explain it. Similarly, we normally should not reject an otherwise plausible moral judgment just because our favorite theory cannot explain why it is true. Otherwise, no inference to the best explanation could work. My argument simply extends this general explanatory burden to principles of moral reasoning and shows that deontological theories cannot carry that burden.

Even though this simple kind of deontological theory cannot explain moral substitutability, more complex deontological theories might seem to do better. One candidate is Kant, who accepts something like substitutability when he writes, 'Whoever wills the end, so far as reason has decisive influence on his action, wills also the indispensably necessary means to it that lie in his power.'[14] Despite this claim, however, Kant fails to explain moral substitutability. Kant says in effect that there is a moral reason to do an act when the maxim of not doing that act cannot be willed as a universal law without contradiction. My moral reason to keep my promise to mow the grass is then supposed to be that not keeping promises cannot be willed universally without contradiction. However, not starting my mower *can* be willed universally without contradiction. I can even consistently and universally will not to start my mower when this is a necessary enabler for keeping a promise. The basic problem is that Kant repeatedly claims that his theory is purely a priori, but moral substitutability makes moral reasons depend on what is empirically possible. Kantians might try to avoid this problem by interpreting universalizability in terms of a less pure kind of possibility and 'contradiction'. On one such interpretation, Kant claims it is contradictory to will universal promise breaking, because, if everyone always broke their promises, no promises would be trusted, so no promises could be made or, therefore, broken. There are several problems here, but the most relevant one is that people could still trust each other's promises, including their promises to mow a lawn, even if nobody ever starts his mower when this is a necessary enabler for keeping a promise. This might happen, for example, if it is common practice to keep mowers running for long periods, so those to whom promises are made assume that it is not necessary to start one's mower in order to mow the lawn. This shows that there is no contradiction of this kind in a universal will not to start my mower when this is a necessary enabler for keeping a promise. Thus, this interpretation of Kant also fails to explain why there is a moral reason to start the mower. Some defenders of Kant will insist that both of these interpretations fail to recognize that, for Kant, certain ends are required by reason, so rational people cannot universally will anything that conflicts with these ends. One problem here is to specify which and why particular ends have this special status. It is also not clear how these rational ends would conflict with universally not starting mowers. Thus, Kant can do no better than other deontologists at explaining why there is a moral reason to start my mower or why moral substitutability holds.

Of course, there are many other versions of deontology. I cannot discuss them all. Nonetheless, these examples suggest that it is the very nature of deontological reasons that makes deontological theories unable to explain moral substitutability. This comes out clearly if we start from the other side and ask which properties create the moral reasons that are derived by moral substitutability. What gives me a moral reason to start the mower is the *consequences* of starting the mower. Specifically, it has the consequence that I am able to mow the grass. This reason cannot derive from the same property as my moral reason to mow the lawn unless what gives me a moral reason to mow the lawn is *its* consequences. Thus, any non-consequentialist moral theory will have to posit two distinct kinds of moral reasons: one for starting the mower and another for mowing the grass. Once these kinds of reasons are separated, we need to understand the connection between them. But this connection cannot be explained by the substantive principles of the theory. That is why all deontological theories must lack the explanatory coherence which is a general test of adequacy for all theories.

I conclude that no deontological theory can adequately explain moral substitutability. I have not proven this, but I do challenge deontologists to give a better explanation of moral substitutability. Deontologists are very inventive, but I doubt that they can meet this challenge.

6. Against Sufficient Consequentialism

The failure of deontological theories to explain moral substitutability might seem to support the alternative: consequentialism. However, this does not follow unless consequentialists themselves can explain moral substitutability. And many traditional consequentialists cannot explain moral substitutability any better than deontologists can.

Many consequentialists claim that there is a moral reason to do what is sufficient to cause or maximize the good. For example, Smart formulates act utilitarianism as the claim that 'the only reason for performing an action A rather than an alternative action B is that doing A will make mankind (or, perhaps, all sentient beings) happier than will doing B.'[15] We often say that an action makes something happen when the action is sufficient for the result, even if it is not necessary. This makes it natural to read Smart's principle as ascribing moral reasons on the basis of sufficient conditions. His theory is then a version of 'sufficient consequentialism', which in general is the claim that there are moral reasons for what causes or maximizes happiness or any other good.

Sufficient consequentialism fails when it is applied to examples. Suppose I can give a surprise birthday party for Susan, and this will make her happy. Telling the guests about the party is necessary and enables me to have the party. Moral substitutability then implies that, if there is a moral reason to have the party, there must also be a moral reason to tell the guests about it. However, the act of calling guests is not sufficient to make Susan happy, since she does not even know that I am calling the guests. In general, even if an act is sufficient for some good, the necessary enablers of the act need not be sufficient for the good. If they are not, and if moral reasons depended on what is sufficient for the good, then there would not be any moral reason to do the acts that are necessary enablers. That is why sufficient consequentialists cannot explain moral substitutability.

Defenders of sufficient consequentialism might respond that this argument depends on too narrow a view of what is sufficient. Telling the guests about the party really is sufficient *in the circumstances*, since these include the facts that the guests will come and I will get Susan to the party and do whatever else is necessary for the party. They might even add that, if I know I will not get Susan to the party, then I do not have any reason to call the guests. But this is not right. I do have *a* moral reason to call the guests even if I will not get Susan to the party. What makes it seem otherwise is only that the gathering will be a disaster or at least a waste if the guest of honor, Susan, does not show up. This gives me a much stronger reason not to call the guests. But I still have *some* moral reason to call the guests, because calling them is a necessary enabler for making Susan happy, and that fact can make an immoral act moral. This comes out clearly if we imagine a case where there is no cost to calling the guests even if Susan does not show up. Maybe the guests would not mind at all coming to my house for a surprise party even if Susan does not show up. Then I have a reason to call the guests, because this keeps me in a position to make Susan happy if it turns out that she can come. It keeps my options open at no cost. Thus, I have a reason to call the guests, even when doing so is not sufficient in the circumstances for making Susan happy, as long as doing so is a necessary enabler for keeping Susan happy. This reason cannot be explained by sufficient consequentialism.

Another problem for sufficient consequentialism is that it implies that an agent has a moral reason to do whatever is a sufficient condition of what she has a moral reason to do, since the sufficient conditions of an act are sufficient for whatever the act is sufficient for. However, a single act can have many sufficient conditions, and the agent might be allowed to choose among them. Then the agent does not have a reason to do one particular sufficient condition, even if the agent does have a reason to do the disjunction. For example, suppose it would make Susan happy to have a surprise party at my house, but it would also make her just as happy to have a surprise party at Mark's house. Then I do not have a reason to have a surprise party at my house as opposed to Mark's house. I do not even have a reason to have the party at my house, since, as I said, I am concerned with reasons to do an act as opposed to all of its relevant alternatives, and having the party at Mark's house is a relevant alternative to having the party at my house.

Defenders of sufficient consequentialism might respond that, if I had the party at my house, I would not have acted for *no* reason. But all this shows is that I have a reason to have the party at my house as opposed to not having any party at all. I might also have a disjunctive moral reason to have a party *either* at my house or at Mark's house. But neither of these amounts to a reason to have a party *at my house*, even though having it at that particular location would be sufficient for Susan's happiness. Thus, sufficient conditions of the good do not always yield moral reasons. So sufficient consequentialism fails.[16]

7. For Necessary Enabler Consequentialism

All of this leads to necessary enabler consequentialism or NEC. NEC claims that all moral reasons for acts are provided by facts that the acts are necessary enablers for preventing harm or promoting good. All moral reasons on this theory are consequential reasons, but there are two kinds. Some moral reasons are *prevention* reasons, because they are facts that an act is a necessary enabler for preventing harm or loss. For example, if giving Alice food is necessary and enables me to prevent her from starving, then that fact is a moral reason to give her food. In this case, I would not *cause* her death even if I let her starve, but other moral prevention reasons are reasons to avoid causing harm. For example, if turning my car to the left is necessary and enables me to avoid killing Bobby, that is a moral reason to turn my car to the left. The other kind of moral reason is a *promotion* reason. This kind of reason occurs when doing something is necessary and enables me to promote (or maximize) some good. For example, I have a moral reason to throw a surprise party for Susan if this is necessary and enables me to make her happy. Because of substitutability, these moral reasons *for* actions also yield moral reasons *against* contrary actions. There are then also moral reasons *not* to do what will cause harm or ensure a failure to prevent harm or to promote good.

What makes these facts moral reasons is that they can make an otherwise immoral act moral. If I have a moral reason to feed my child, then it might be immoral to give my only food to Alice, who is a stranger. But this would not be immoral if giving Alice food is necessary and enables me to prevent Alice from starving, as long as my child will not starve also. Similarly, it is normally immoral to lie to Susan, but a lie can be moral if it is necessary and enables me to keep my party for Susan a surprise, and if this is also necessary and enables me to make her happy. Thus, NEC fits nicely into the above theory of moral reasons.

NEC can provide a natural explanation of moral substitutability for both kinds of moral reasons. I have a prevention moral reason to give someone food when doing so is necessary and enables me to prevent that person from starving. Suppose that buying food is a necessary enabler for giving the person food, and getting in my car is a necessary enabler for buying food. Moral substitutability warrants the conclusion that I have a moral reason to get in my car. And this act of getting in my car does have the property of being a necessary enabler for preventing starvation. Thus, the necessary enabler has the same property that provided the moral reason to give the food in the first place. This explains why substitutability holds for moral prevention reasons. The other kind of moral reason covers necessary enablers for promoting good. In my example above, if a surprise party is a necessary enabler for making Susan happy, and letting people know about the party is a necessary enabler for having the party, then letting people know is a necessary enabler for making Susan happy. The very fact that provides a moral reason to have the party also provides a moral reason to let people know about it. Thus, NEC can explain why moral substitutability holds for every kind of moral reason that it includes. Similar explanations work for moral reasons *not* to do certain acts, and this explanatory power is a reason to favor NEC.[17]

Of course, this should come as no surprise. NEC was intentionally structured so that it would explain moral substitutability. But this does not detract from its explanatory force. The point is that moral substitutability remains a mystery unless we restrict our substantive theory to moral reasons that obey moral substitutability by their very nature.

The crucial advantage of NEC lies in its unity. Other theories claim that my reason to do what I promised is just that this fulfills my promise or that promise keeping is intrinsically good. However, I did not promise to start the mower, and starting the mower is not intrinsically good. Thus, my reason to start the mower derives from a different property than my reason to keep my promise. In contrast, NEC makes my reasons to keep my promise, to mow the lawn, and to start the mower derive from the very same property: being a necessary enabler of preventing harm or promoting good. This makes NEC's explanation more coherent and better.

A critic might complain that NEC just postpones the problem, since NEC will eventually need to explain why certain things are good or bad, and some will be good or bad as means, but others will not. However, if what is good or bad intrinsically are *states* (such as pleasure and freedom or pain and death) rather than *acts*, then they are not the kind of thing that can be done, so there cannot be any question of a reason to do them. This makes it possible for all reasons *for acts* to have the same nature or derive from the same property. NEC will still have to explain why certain states are good or bad, but so will every other moral theory. The difference is that other theories will *also* have to explain why there are two kinds of reasons for acts and how these reasons are connected. This is what other theories cannot explain. This additional explanatory gap is avoided by the unified nature of reasons in NEC.[18]

8. Two Puzzles Solved

Another advantage of NEC is that it can solve two puzzles. The first example is modified from Parfit[19] and concerns how we weigh moral reasons. Suppose that I can feed either Ann or Beth but not both. If I feed Beth, this will be sufficient to prevent her death. If I feed Ann, this will be sufficient to prevent the pain of hunger but not to prevent death, because Ann is not starving. This makes my reason to feed Beth seem stronger, since death is worse than the pain of hunger. However, suppose I know that, if I do not feed Beth, someone else certainly will, but, if I do not feed Ann, nobody else will. Now my reason to feed Ann is stronger. Why? Because feeding Beth now is *not* necessary to prevent any harm, but feeding Ann *is* a necessary enabler for preventing harm. This shows that the strength of a moral reason for an act depends on what the act is a necessary enabler for, rather than on what the act is sufficient for. This is exactly what NEC would predict.

NEC also solves a puzzle that bothers Feldman.[20] Feldman has to decide between working in his garden and going to the dump. Working in his garden is sufficient for 12 units of utility, and going to the dump is sufficient for only 8 units of utility. Each of these alternatives has a certain prerequisite. Feldman cannot work in the garden without gathering his garden tools, which is sufficient for -1 unit of utility, and he cannot go to the dump without loading his truck, which is sufficient for +1 unit of utility. (It is not clear why Feldman likes to load his truck!) Now sufficient consequentialism implies both that he has a reason to work in the garden (because this is sufficient for more utility than its alternative) and also that it is not true that he has a reason to gather his garden tools (because that act has an alternative that is sufficient for more utility). But this conflicts with substitutability. This result is easily avoided if we turn to NEC. Gathering his garden tools is a necessary enabler for more utility than is loading and starting his truck, since gathering his gardening tools is a necessary enabler for working in his garden (and we are assuming that all else is equal). That is why he has more reason to gather his garden tools, even though that act is sufficient for less utility than its alternative. Thus, NEC again coheres with our intuitions and saves us from the absurdities of sufficient consequentialism.

9. Conclusions

Let's review what has been accomplished. I argued first for principles of substitutability in general and moral substitutability in particular. I argued next that deontological moral theories and sufficient consequentialism cannot explain why moral substitutability holds. My positive conclusion was that necessary enabler consequentialism can easily explain why moral substitutability holds for all of its moral reasons. Since, as I also argued, a moral theory should not only describe but also explain principles of moral reasoning, my conclusions give us a reason to prefer some kind of necessary enabler consequentialism. The reason is that it provides a simple explanation of an obvious principle that cannot be explained as well by contrary theories.

Although I focussed on moral reasons, my conclusions can be extended to non-moral reasons for action. Reasons of prudence, aesthetics, etc., also obey general substitutability. My argument suggests that this cannot be explained by theories of prudence, aesthetics, etc., unless these theories identify these reasons with necessary enablers. The differences among various kinds of reasons for action can still be explained by differences among the goods or harms for which actions are necessary enablers. Prudential reasons concern good and harm only to oneself, and aesthetic reasons concern specifically aesthetic goods, such as beauty or aesthetic pleasure. Despite these differences, all reasons for action share a reference to necessary enablers, since they all obey general substitutability. In this way, necessary enabler consequentialism can be extended to yield a theory about reasons for action in general, and this wider coherence provides even more support for necessary enabler consequentialism.[21]

None of this proves that necessary enabler consequentialism is true or even that it is preferable overall to its competitors. Other theories still might be preferable in other respects, so we need to consider the many objections to consequentialism in order to determine whether the idea of necessary enablers can help to avoid those objections. We also need to specify a theory of value[22] and a theory of how the distribution of goods and harms affects moral reasons and their weights. All of these details need to be worked out before necessary enabler consequentialism can be assessed overall. Nonetheless, I do hope to have shown why this kind of theory meets one general test of adequacy and why other theories need to show how they can meet this test.[23]

Notes

1. Cf. Norman Daniels, 'Wide Reflective Equilibrium and Theory Acceptance in Ethics', *Journal of Philosophy*, 1979, pp. 256-282. My method is an even wider reflective equilibrium including principles of moral reasoning. None of these 'intuitions' requires a special faculty or is supposed to be infallible.
2. It might be more common to argue in terms of 'ought': I ought to get a cavity filled, and I can't get it filled except by going to a dentist, so I ought to go to a dentist. Although this argument also is valid and needs to be explained, it is not clear whether I ought to do something when there are overriding reasons not to do it. That is why I write about reasons, which clearly can be overridden.
3. Cf. my *Moral Dilemmas*, Oxford, Basil Blackwell, 1988, pp. 152-4. Since (GS) refers to 'doing' X and Y, this principle is restricted to acts. What I have a reason to do is usually not a particular act but some act of a relevant kind. Cf. Donald Davidson, *Essays on Actions and Events*, New York, Oxford University Press, 1980, esp. essay 6. This complication does not affect my argument, so I will sometimes write as if 'X' and 'Y' refer to acts.
4. Even if some stronger principle were defensible, (GS) would still be true, and its truth would still need to be explained, so my main argument would not be affected.
5. Cf. Bernard Gert, *Morality*, New York, Oxford University Press, 1988, p. 34.
6. My explanations use the rules of quantity and relevance from Paul Grice, 'Logic and Conversation', in *Studies in the Ways of Words*, Cambridge, Harvard University Press, 1989, pp. 26-7. Others might respond that moving air molecules is not an act, but I do not want to depend on that claim.
7. Philippa Foot, 'Moral Realism and Moral Dilemma', *Journal of Philosophy*, 1983, p. 384.
8. I respond to some more objections in *Moral Dilemmas*, sec. 5.2.
9. Yet another way to explain moral substitutability would be to show that it is analytic. However, I have never seen any way to derive this principle from any definition of moral reasons.
10. I assume here that acts are identical when they are constituted by or done by means of the same bodily movements. Cf. Donald Davidson, *Essays on Actions and Events*, New York, Oxford University Press, 1980, esp. essay 3. This claim is controversial, but those who reject it can avoid all reference to identity by saying

simply that an act and its consequences cannot be constituted by the same bodily movements. There are also other ways to define consequences so that fulfilling a promise is not a consequence of the act that fulfills the promise.

11. On this account, a moral reason to do an act because the act is good in-itself or intrinsically is deontological, so some kinds of perfectionism or eudaemonism are deontological. This is probably not common usage, but it is what I want, because my argument against deontological theories will apply to these kinds of perfectionism, since the reason to do an act that is intrinsically good will be different in nature from the reason to do a necessary enabler of the act.

12. W. D. Ross, *The Right and the Good*, Indianapolis, Hackett, 1988, p. 44. See also p. 17, and H. A. Prichard, *Moral Obligation*, New York, Oxford University Press, 1968, pp. 6-7. It might seem that what makes Ross and Prichard unable to explain moral substitutability is just that they see rightness and wrongness as non-natural properties, and these need not transfer across natural causal connections. However, my argument will apply to deontologists even if they are naturalists, and some non-naturalistic consequentialists can explain moral substitutability. Thus, the issue of naturalism cuts across the issue of how to explain moral substitutability.

13. Cf. Samuel Scheffler, *The Rejection of Consequentialism*, New York, Oxford University Press, 1982, pp. 87-90.

14. *Foundations of the Metaphysics of Morals*, trans. L. W. Beck, p. 417 of the Akademie edition. Kant's principle is not the same as moral substitutability, since his principle is about willing, and he applies it only to imperatives of skill, which lie outside morality. Kant says that his principle is analytic, but his argument for its analyticity is hardly persuasive.

15. J. J. C. Smart, 'An Outline of a System of Utilitarian Ethics' in *Utilitarianism: for and against*, by J. J. C. Smart and Bernard Williams, Cambridge, Cambridge University Press, 1973, p. 30. Bentham also suggests sufficient conditions when he refers to whether acts 'augment or diminish' or 'promote or oppose' happiness. Mill uses the words 'produce' and 'promote'. I do not deny that these quotations can be read in terms of necessary enablers, but the most natural reading refers to sufficient conditions. Anyway, I am more interested in the plausibility of sufficient consequentialism than in the question of who actually held this position.

16. Even if my arguments do not refute sufficient conseqentialism, this would not affect my arguments against deontological moral theories.

17. NEC is a version of act consequentialism. It seems harder for rule consequentialists to explain moral substitutability because moral substitutability generates reasons from the facts of particular situations that might not be shared by other acts that fall under the same general rules. It might be disastrous for everyone to break their promises, but it would not be disastrous for everyone not to start their mowers. Some rule consequentialists have responses, but there are too many varieties of rule consequentialism for me to discuss the possibilities here.

18. This also applies to perfectionists and eudaemonists who claim that certain types of action are intrinsically good and that that is what gives us a reason to do them. See footnote 11.

19. Derek Parfit, *Reasons and Persons*, New York, Oxford University Press, 1984, pp. 69-70.

20. Fred Feldman, *Doing the Best We Can*, Boston, D. Reidel, 1986, pp. 5-7. See also pp. 8-11. I have simplified Feldman's example somewhat. It is not clear that the reasons in his example are moral, but that does not affect my point.

21. The coherent package becomes even larger if it is extended to reasons for *belief*. A reason for a belief can be seen as a fact about the belief which can make an otherwise irrational belief rational. There are two kinds of reasons for belief: reasons for the truth of belief contents and reasons for forming and maintaining belief states. Substitutability seems to work in both cases. First, if there is a reason for the truth of a belief content, there is also a reason for a belief content whose truth is a necessary enabler for the truth of the former belief content. (Notice that the 'enabler' clause helps avoid paradoxes of implication.) Second, if there is a reason to form or maintain a belief state, there is also a reason to form or maintain any belief state whose existence is a necessary enabler for the former belief state. All of this adds even more support for NEC.

22. Some help in value theory might come from another kind of substitutability. If the necessary enablers of what is good are also good (to some extent), this might be inexplicable on desire-based theories of value, because a desire for something does not ensure a desire for its necessary enablers. I can desire to play golf without desiring to pay for it. To develop this additional argument would be beyond the scope of this paper.

23. For constructive criticisms, I thank Jonathan Bennett, David Cummiskey, Robert Fogelin, Bernard Gert, David McNaughton, Jim Moor, Igor Primoratz, Mark Sainsbury, Geoff Sayre McCord, Dore Scaltsas, Sally Sedgwick, Holly Smith, and Timothy Sprigge, as well as audiences at Bates College, Dartmouth College, Johns Hopkins University, the Northern New England Philosophy Association, and the Universities of Aberdeen, Edinburgh, Glasgow, Leeds, St. Andrews, York, and North Carolina at Chapel Hill.

Philosophical Perspectives, 6, Ethics, 1992

WHEN THE WILL IS FREE

John Martin Fischer and Mark Ravizza
University of California, Riverside

Incompatibilists usually direct their attention to the following worry: if the thesis of causal determinism is true, then none of us is free to do other than what he actually does. But although causal determinism poses the most frequently discussed threat to freedom for incompatibilists, it may not be their only source of worry, at least not for those incompatibilists who also accept the common intuition that most of us, most of the time, are free to do otherwise.

In his article "When Is The Will Free?"[1] Peter van Inwagen offers a creative and systematic development of this less often discussed side of incompatibilism. He maintains (1) that anyone who is an incompatibilist should accept a rule of inference which he calls 'Beta,' and (2) that "anyone who accepts Beta should concede that [even if causal determinism is false] one has precious little free will, that rarely, if ever, is anyone able to do otherwise than he in fact does" (p. 405).[2] We will call the position suggested by van Inwagen's arguments 'restrictive incompatibilism' or 'restrictivism' for short. This name seems appropriate because restrictive incompatibilists hold both that incompatibilism is true, and that anyone who accepts the truth of incompatibilism must also (in virtue of accepting Beta) accept radical restrictions on one's ability to do otherwise.[3] According to this position, if causal determinism is true, we never are free to do otherwise, and if causal determinism is false, we "rarely, if ever" are free to do otherwise.

The conclusion that all incompatibilists allegedly must accept—that we, at best, are only rarely free to do otherwise—will come as a shock to many. However, this conclusion becomes even more disquieting when it is combined with another assumption of the "classical tradition" which van Inwagen and many other incompatibilists embrace. This is the assumption that freedom to do otherwise is a necessary condition of moral responsibility. Accept this premise and the following worry quickly arises: If the restrictivist is right—if incompatibilists are committed to a severe restriction on one's ability to do otherwise—then must they not also accept a similar limitation on the range of states of affairs for which one can be held morally responsible? And if this is the case, then would not incompatibilism itself seem to be incompatible with many of our most deeply held beliefs about the type of respect, praise and blame merited by persons?

In what follows we will address these issues by outlining the arguments for restrictive incompatibilism and then by discussing some responses to this position. In particular, we will argue that one can accept incompatibilism without a *fortiori* being committed to the restrictivist position. That is, we will maintain that one can accept the thesis that freedom to do otherwise is incompatible with causal determinism without implicitly being committed to the further conclusion that "rarely, if ever, is anyone able to do otherwise than he in fact does" (p. 405). In taking this position, we do not intend to argue *for* the truth of causal determinism or incompatibilism, but rather to argue *against* the restrictivists' claim that the logic behind the incompatibilist position requires that any incompatibilist also accept severe restrictions on freedom to do otherwise. Finally we will argue that, irrespective of our earlier criticisms, restrictive incompatibilists cannot (as van Inwagen suggests they can) provide a satisfying theory of moral accountability while still remaining within the classical tradition (which accepts that such accountability requires freedom to do otherwise).

I. From Incompatibilism to Restrictive Incompatibilism

Let us begin by considering why incompatibilists purportedly must find themselves with little, if any, freedom to do otherwise. The restrictivist argues that the incompatibilist position rests upon a rule of inference termed 'Rule Beta'. Beta says that "from Np and N(p ⊃ q) deduce Nq" (where "'Np' stands for 'p and no one has or ever had any choice about whether p'") (pp. 404-5). To appreciate the reason for this stress on Rule Beta we need only digress for a moment to consider one form of the Consequence Argument which persuades the restrictive incompatibilist that free will is not compatible with causal determinism:[4]

Rule Alpha: From □p deduce Np.

('□' represents "standard necessity": truth in all possible circumstances.)

Rule Beta: From Np and N(p ⊃ q) deduce Nq.

Now let 'P' represent any true proposition whatever. Let 'L' represent the conjunction into a single proposition of all laws of nature. Let 'Po' represent a proposition that gives a complete and correct description of the whole world at some instant in the remote past—before there were any human beings. If determinism is true, then □(Po & L. ⊃ P). We argue from the consequence of this as follows.

1. $\Box(\text{Po \& L.} \supset \text{P})$
2. $\Box(\text{Po} \supset (\text{L} \supset \text{P}))$ 1; modal and sentential logic
3. $\text{N}(\text{Po} \supset (\text{L} \supset \text{P}))$ 2; Rule Alpha
4. NPo   Premise
5. $\text{N}(\text{L} \supset \text{P})$ 3,4; Rule Beta
6. NL   Premise
7. NP   5,6; Rule Beta

If the above argument is sound, then determinism entails that no one has a choice about what she does; hence, determinism is incompatible with freedom to do otherwise. Since the restrictive incompatibilist insists that no one reasonably could take issue with either of the premises or Rule Alpha, he concludes that the soundness of the incompatibilist argument depends upon the validity of Beta. Indeed van Inwagen goes so far as to say that "if one accepts Beta, one should be an incompatibilist, and if one is an incompatibilist, one should accept Beta" (p. 405).

The next step in the restrictivist argument is to claim that any person who accepts Beta should also accept a similar rule of inference termed 'Beta-prime'. Beta-prime tells us that "from Nx,p and Nx,(p $\supset$ q) deduce Nx,q" (where the two-place operator 'N' is used as follows: 'Nx,p' abbreviates 'p and x now has no choice about whether p') (p. 408). When an agent has no choice about whether a proposition (or statement) obtains we will say that that proposition is "power necessary" for him.

Finally the restrictivist presents three arguments to show that if Beta-prime is valid then (even if causal determinism is false) we are not able to do otherwise in three types of cases which represent the majority of all actions. We will discuss the details of these arguments in section III; here we need only note the three cases. The first is one of duty unopposed by inclination; that is, "no one is able to perform an act he considers morally reprehensible" (p. 405). The second case is one of unopposed inclination; thus, "no one is able to do anything that he wants very much *not* to do and has no countervailing desire to do it" (p. 406). The third case is one in which we act without reflection or deliberation; thus "if we regard an act as the one obvious thing or the only sensible thing to do, we cannot do anything but that thing" (p. 406). Given these points, the restrictivist concludes that the only times an agent *is* free to do otherwise are times in which the agent is confronted with conflicting alternatives such that, even after reflection, it is not obvious to him what to do. Such conflict situations, van Inwagen tells us, occur *rarely* and can be divided into three general categories: (1) "Buridan's Ass" cases,[5] (2) cases in which duty or general policy conflicts with inclination or momentary desire, and (3) cases in which one must choose between incommensurable values.[6]

Since the restrictivist holds that all incompatibilists must accept Beta and hence Beta-prime, and that anyone who accepts Beta-prime must concede that we cannot do otherwise in the cases which make up the majority of all our actions, he therefore concludes that "the incompatibilist must hold that being able to do otherwise is a comparatively rare condition, even a *very* rare condition" (p. 404).

II. Who Needs Beta?

Before getting involved in the details of the restrictivist's individual arguments, we should note that an immediate way to circumvent his conclusion is simply to deny the initial contention that "... if one is an incompatibilist, one should accept Beta."[7] To support this denial a non-restrictive incompatibilist could simply refer to any of a number of formulations of the Consequence Argument for incompatibilism which do not explicitly make use of modal principles akin to Beta.[8] If valid, these arguments apparently would give one reason to accept incompatibilism without also requiring one to accept Beta or Beta-prime. Then, even if all of the restrictivist's remaining arguments should prove to be valid, one could accept incompatibilism without having any corresponding commitment to accept the restrictivist's conclusion that we rarely, if ever, have free will.

In response to this type of objection the restrictive incompatibilist might insist that all formulations of the Consequence Argument, even those which aren't explicitly formulated using Beta, must implicitly depend upon *some* rule of inference similar to Beta. Such a response is suggested by van Inwagen's own claim that all three of his formulations of the Consequence Argument in *An Essay On Free Will* should "stand or fall together."[9] This claim is particularly germane to our discussion, because only van Inwagen's third argument explicitly depends upon Beta. Nevertheless, he writes: "I am quite sure that any specific and detailed objection to one of the arguments can be fairly easily translated into specific and detailed objections to the others; and I think that any objection to one of the arguments will be a good objection to *that* argument if and only if the corresponding objections to the others are good objections to *them*."[10]

Van Inwagen is not alone in holding this view. Even some compatibilists, who in other respects want to take issue with van Inwagen's reasoning, agree with his intuition that any respectable form of the argument for incompatibilism must depend upon some type of inference akin to Beta. Pursuing this intuition, such compatibilists have sought to attack the incompatibilist's position by blocking the modal inference on which it purportedly rests. One such "beta-blocker," Michael Slote, writes: "I want to argue, in particular, that the arguments of GLVW [Carl Ginet, James Lamb, Peter van Inwagen, and David Wiggins] all rest on the questionable form of inference, the very inference from the double modality of 'Np' and 'N(p $\supset$ q)' to 'Nq' which marks the superiority of the new kind of argument to earlier defenses of incompatibilism."[11] Further support for this position is found in Terence Horgan's comment that "Slote has described well the deep family resemblances among the various formulations [of the Consequence Argument for incompatibilism], and he too has suggested that the different versions probably stand or fall together."[12] This shared opinion on the part of compatibilists and incompatibilists alike, along with the debate over the validity of Beta to which it has given rise, support the restrictivist's contention that anyone who accepts any formulation of the Consequence Argument implicitly is committed to accepting Beta. Thus, the restrictivist might seem to be on firm ground when he insists that "if one is an incompatibilist, one should accept Beta" and with it (assuming the soundness of his subsequent arguments) restrictive incompatibilism.

Nevertheless, we want to argue that this claim is false. Admittedly, many formulations of the Consequence Argument do depend upon intuitions similar to those which underlie Beta. However, the argument for incompatibilism can be formulated in such a way that it does not explicitly make use of Beta, and hence the onus remains on the restrictivist to show how such arguments do, in fact, commit their proponents to accepting Beta.[13]

To illustrate this point consider the following sketch of an argument which is adapted from a parallel argument concerning the incompatibility of God's foreknowledge and free will.[14] The argument rests upon two principles which are controversial though not implausible. The first principle expresses the fixity of the past; it says not only that one cannot causally affect the past, but also that one cannot so act that the past would have been different from what it actually was. The fixity of the past principle can be formulated as follows:

> (FP) For any action Y, agent S, and time T, if it is true that if S were to do Y at T, some fact about the past relative to T would not have been a fact, then S cannot at T do Y at T.

The second principle expresses the fixity of the laws; in a manner similar to FP it says not only that one cannot causally change the laws, but also that one cannot so act that the laws of nature would have been different from what they actually are.[15] The fixity of the laws principle can be formulated as follows:

> (FL) For any action Y, and agent S, if it is true that if S were to do Y, some natural law which actually obtains would not obtain, then S cannot do Y.

Now consider some act X which agent A actually refrains from doing at T_2. Taking determinism to be the thesis that a complete description of the world at T in conjunction with a complete formulation of the laws entails every subsequent truth, then if determinism is true, and S_1 is the total state of the world at T_1, one of the following conditionals must be true:

(1) If A were to do X at T_2, S_1 would not have been the total state of the world at T_1.

(2) If A were to do X at T_2, then some natural law which actually obtains would not obtain.

(3) · If A were to do X at T_2, then either S_1 would not have been the total state of the world at T_1, or some natural law which actually obtains would not obtain.

But if (1) is true, then (via FP) A cannot do X at T_2; similarly, if (2) is true, then (via FL) A cannot do X at T_2. Finally, if (1)'s truth implies that A cannot do X at T_2 and (2)'s truth implies that A cannot do X at T_2, then it follows that if (3) is true, then A cannot do X at T_2. The conclusion of this argument is that if determinism is true, then A cannot do anything other than what he actually does at T_2. Generalizing this result, the incompatibilist claims that if determinism is true none of us is free to do other than what he does.

The importance of the argument for our purposes, however, it not to raise yet one more banner for incompatibilism.[16] Rather, the argument serves to illustrate that the debate over incompatibilism should not be reduced to a discussion about the validity of Beta. Incompatibilists share basic beliefs about the relationships between free will, determinism, the fixity of the past and the fixity of the laws. But these beliefs can find expression in different forms of argument, not all of which necessarily involve the same commitments. Such arguments show that an incompatibilist can consistently adhere to her position without automatically being committed to Beta or restrictive incompatibilism.[17]

As we pointed out above, van Inwagen claims that incompatibilism depends upon Beta, but we have presented an argument for incompatibilism which does not appear to depend in any way upon Beta. We thus conclude that van Inwagen's claim is false. Further, if we are correct, then Slote's strategy (in what has been described by Dennett as a "pioneering article") is not nearly so promising as it might have been supposed to be.[18] Slote alleges that there are counterexamples to modal principles structurally analogous to Beta, and he suggests that Beta is similarly flawed. He concludes that incompatibilism should be rejected. We take issue with Slote's claim that Beta is flawed.[19] But what is relevant to our discussion here is that *even if Slote were correct and Beta were invalid*, one could generate versions of the troubling argument for incompatibilism. Thus, a Beta-blocking strategy cannot easily assuage the panic that might issue from the incompatibilist's argument.

There is another approach which claims that Beta is not necessary in order to generate the incompatibilist's argument. Bernard Berofsky has recently argued that one can develop the argument without the use of Beta.[20]

Berofsky presents what he calls a 'system of contingent necessity'. This sort of system validates the following kind of principle, with certain restrictions:

P

N(P ⊃ Q)

hence, N(Q)

Whereas it is often alleged that this sort of move involves a modal fallacy, Berofsky attempts to justify this inference (with suitable restrictions on the substitution-instances of the propositional variables), and he claims that it provides a way of formulating the incompatibilist's argument in a valid fashion. We share with Berofsky the claim that the incompatibilist's argument does not require Beta. But if we are correct, then the incompatibilist's argument does not even require the validity of Berofsky's principle and his system of contingent necessity.[21] It is useful to see that the incompatibilist's argument does not require *any* modal principle similar to Beta.

Clearly, the above considerations—that the incompatibilist's argument can be formulated in various ways without the use of Beta—do not in any way bear on the validity of Beta.[22] We, in fact, are of the opinion that Beta might well be one of those intractable principles which seems valid but which can neither be easily proved nor disproved. Recognizing this, the restrictive incompatibilist might contend that, independently of its decisive role in many arguments for incompatibilism, Beta should be accepted by all incompatibilists simply because Beta is valid. And these grounds alone would be sufficient to confirm the restrictivist's position.

For the sake of argument, let us entertain this claim. Let us consider that Beta may well be valid, or at the very least that incompatibilists of the van Inwagen sort are committed to its validity. Does it now follow that such incompatibilists must also be restrictive incompatibilists? To evaluate this question, we turn to van Inwagen's three arguments that purportedly establish that if Beta is valid, then rarely, if ever, is one free to do otherwise.

III. Free to Ignore the Obvious

In order to show that most of the time one is not able to do otherwise, the restrictivist presents a series of three arguments. In the first, he argues that no one is able to act in a manner that he considers morally indefensible. The argument runs as follows:

(1) N I, (I regard A as indefensible).

(2) N I, (I regard A as indefensible ⊃ I am not going to do A).

Hence (via Beta),

(3) N I, (I am not going to do A) (p. 409).

The intuitive idea behind the argument is that at this moment I don't have any choice about the fact that I now consider some action A indefensible, and I also don't have any choice about its being the case that if I regard an action as being morally indefensible then I am not going to do it; these two premises being true, it follows that at this moment I'm not going to do A and I don't have any choice about this. In short, it is power necessary for me that I am not going to do A. Generalizing the results of this argument the restrictivist concludes that "no one is able to perform an act he considers morally reprehensible" (p.405).

Van Inwagen (our model restrictive incompatibilist) then extends the type of reasoning used in this argument about morally indefensible actions to two other cases which, he claims, constitute the majority of all actions: (1) cases of unopposed inclination in which we want very much to do one thing and have no opposing desires; and (2) cases of unreflective action in which we know what the obvious thing to do is after little if any deliberation. In the case of unopposed inclination, we are asked to consider an example in which a person, Nightingale, is anxiously awaiting a phone call which he very much desires to receive. Nightingale has a very strong desire to answer the phone, and no countervailing desires not to do so. The question is: Can Nightingale refrain from answering the phone? The restrictivist reasons that he cannot, and in support of this conclusion he offers the same argument-form used above. Skipping the formalization, the rough idea behind the argument is as follows: (1) At this moment Nightingale does not have any choice about the fact that he very much desires to answer the phone, and (2) he also has no choice about its being the case that if he very much desires to answer the phone (and he has no countervailing desire to refrain from doing so), then he is going to answer the phone; these two premises being true, it follows that at this moment Nightingale is going to answer the phone and he doesn't have any choice about this. Van Inwagen concludes that "no one is able to do anything that he wants very much *not* to do and has no countervailing desire to do it" (p. 406).

In the last argument, which is supposed to cover the broadest range of actions, the restrictivist turns to actions which "with little or no deliberation...just seem—or would seem if we reflected on them at all—to be the obvious thing to do in the circumstances" (p. 412). Again we are asked to consider a situation in which a phone rings and a person immediately answers it without giving the matter a second thought. Following the same style of reasoning as in the Nightingale example, the argument claims that the agent is not free to refrain from answering the phone. Roughly the argument runs as before: (1) At the moment the phone rings, the person has no choice about the fact that he has no reason not to answer the phone immediately or to deliberate about answering it; (2) furthermore, he has no choice about its being the case that if he hasn't any reason not to answer the phone then he is going to answer it. From these two premises it follows that at the moment the phone rings, the agent is going to answer it and he has no choice about this. Generalizing this conclusion and that of the preceding argument van Inwagen concludes:

> There are therefore, few occasions in life on which—at least after a little reflection and perhaps some investigation into the facts—it isn't absolutely clear what to do. And if the above arguments are correct, then an incompatibilist should believe that on such occasions the agent cannot do anything other than the thing that seems to him to be clearly the only sensible thing to do" (p. 415).

Does an incompatibilist have to accept this conclusion? We think not. To challenge these arguments, we want to take issue with the second premise in each. The most detailed defense of premise (2) is offered in the first argument; here van Inwagen maintains that the second premise is true because the following conditional is a necessary truth and no one has a choice about a necessary truth.

(C1) If X regards A as an indefensible act, given the totality of relevant information available to him, and if he has no way of getting further relevant information, and if he lacks any positive desire to do A, and if he sees no objection to *not* doing A (again, given the totality of relevant information available to him), then X is not going to do A (p. 407).[23]

Van Inwagen claims that the restrictivist's three arguments are similar, and thus we assume that van Inwagen imagines that there are conditionals parallel to (C1) which are supposed to support the parallel premises of the latter two arguments. Here, we will begin by discussing the latter two arguments— pertaining to unopposed inclination and unreflective action. We will deny the claim that the relevant conditionals successfully support the second premises of these arguments. We shall focus our remarks on the argument concerning unopposed inclination; this argument appears to us to be the stronger of the latter two restrictivist arguments, and the considerations adduced against it can readily be applied to the third argument. Then we will turn to van Inwagen's first argument—concerning indefensible actions. Although we are departing from van Inwagen's order of presentation, our criticism can be developed more naturally in this fashion.

In his second argument, the restrictivist argues that in cases of unopposed inclination the agent cannot do other than what he actually does (despite the intuitive impression that he can so act). The argument has the same form as the argument concerning indefensible actions sketched above, but now the second premise (upon which we shall concentrate) is:

(2) N X, (X has an unopposed inclination to do A $\supset$ X is going to do A).

And parallel to the conditional which allegedly supports the second premise of the argument about indefensibility, we have:

> (C2) If X very much desires to do some act A given the totality of relevant information available to him, and if he has no way of getting further relevant information, and if he lacks any positive desire to perform any act other than A, and if he sees no objection to doing A and refraining from doing anything else (again, given the totality of relevant information available to him), then the person is not going to do anything other than A.

Now, the only way in which (C2) can support premise two of the argument is if (C2) is *power necessary* for the relevant agent. That is, (C2) must be true and X must have no choice about whether C2 is true. (This is parallel to the point made above that it is in virtue of the fact that no one has any choice about the truth of (C1) that premise (2) of the first argument is supported.)

The problem with the argument can be made clear by employing the following rather familiar sort of strategy. (C2) admits of two interpretations. On one interpretation, (C2) is plausibly thought to be true and power necessary, but it does not support the second premise of the argument. And on the other interpretation the second premise is supported but (C2) is not plausible. Thus, there is *no* interpretation according to which it is the case that both (C2) is plausibly thought to be power necessary and the relevant premise of the argument is true.

Let us first consider the interpretation according to which (C2) is plausibly taken to be true and power necessary. This interpretation is motivated by the basic idea that action requires some sort of "pro-attitude"—say, a desire. That is, it might be argued that actions are distinguished from mere events in virtue of being preceded (in a suitable way) by special sorts of events: "volitions." Further, it might be claimed that a volition must be based (in a suitable way) on at least *some* desire. If these claims were true, it would follow that it would be impossible for an agent to perform an *action* without having some desire to do so. We suppose that the necessity of desire for action could be posited even by a theorist who does not believe in volitions. In any case, it is a plausible conceptual claim that it is impossible for an agent to perform an action without having some desire to perform the action in question.[24]

The key point is that the alleged conceptual truth cannot support premise two of the argument. Note that the alleged conceptual truth can be regimented as follows:

> (C2*) It is not possible that the following state of affairs obtain: that X performs an act other than A without having any desire to perform such an act.

And note further that (C2*) does *not* imply

(2) N, X (X has an unopposed desire to do A ⊃ X is going to do A).

As long as there is no *obstacle* to the agent's having the desire to do other than A during the relevant temporal interval, we believe that (2) can be false compatibly with the truth of (C2*). (2) would be false if, despite the fact that X has an unopposed desire to do A, he *could* refrain from doing A; and, given that (during the relevant temporal period) X *can* acquire this sort of desire, we believe that it is reasonable to suppose that X can do other than A. (We will argue for this below.)

That (C2*) fails to imply (2) can be seen by considering this simple analogy. It is uncontroversially true that it is not possible that the following state of affairs obtain at all points in some temporal interval: Jones is sitting and Jones is standing up. But this conceptual truth does *not* imply that, if Jones is sitting at some point in some temporal interval, then Jones cannot stand at some point in that interval. Thus, even if (C2*) were true—and it does seem plausible to us—it would not successfully secure the truth of the second premise of van Inwagen's argument.

Now let us interpret (C2) such that it does entail (2):

(C2**) If X does not desire to do other than A, X cannot do other than A.

We concede that (C2**) supports (2), but at the price of plausibility. This is because, even if an agent does not actually desire to do other than A, he might well have the ability (during the relevant temporal interval) to generate such a desire, and to act on this desire. And it is extremely implausible to suppose that agents quite generally lack the *power* to generate the relevant sorts of desires.

We elaborate. Just about anybody can summon up the worry that he is not free to do otherwise. That is, one can worry that, despite the pervasive intuitive feeling that frequently we have genuine freedom to do various things, we do not in fact have such freedom. (Indeed, anyone who thinks about the restrictivist's argument certainly has reason to worry that he might not be free to do otherwise in many contexts.) This worry can then generate *some* reason (perhaps, a desire) to do otherwise simply to prove that one can do so.[25] Thus, barring special circumstances—to which the restrictivist does not allude in his arguments—even an agent who actually does not have any desire to do other than A can have the power to generate such a desire (during the relevant temporal interval). And insofar as: (i) the agent *can* generate the desire to do other than A, (ii) the agent can try to act on this desire, and (iii) if he were to try to act on this desire, he would succeed, then we believe that the agent *can* (during the relevant temporal interval) do other than A.[26] The leading idea here is that there is no reason to suppose that agents *generally* lack the power to generate (in some way or another) reasons to do otherwise, the power to try to act on those reasons, or the power to succeed in so acting.

Consider van Inwagen's own example in which Nightingale wants very much to answer the phone as soon as it rings. If Nightingale can call to mind the doubt that he is able to do otherwise in such situations, this very doubt can give him a reason to pause before picking up the receiver. (Perhaps he simply does not answer the phone on the first ring, but waits until it rings five times; this suffices, he might feel, to prove he was free to do otherwise.) In this scenario, Nightingale's worry has transformed a normally routine phone call into a situation in which Nightingale must decide between two conflicting desires: (1) a desire to answer the phone as soon as it rings, and (2) a desire to prove to himself that he doesn't have to answer it as soon as it rings. We claim that insofar as: (i) the agent can generate a desire of the second sort, (ii) he can try to act on this desire, and (iii) if the agent were to try to act on this sort of desire, he would succeed in doing other than A, then the agent *can* (during the relevant temporal period) do other than A, even though he actually lacks any desire to do other than A.[27]

We believe that the above considerations show that, even if an agent actually lacks any desire to perform a given act, he *can* perform that action, insofar as certain conditions are met. These conditions involve the ability to generate certain reasons and to translate these reasons into action. Further, we suggested that it is extremely plausible to suppose that (absent special assumptions about causal determinism or particular psychological or physical impairments) these conditions are frequently met.[28] Thus, we believe that (C2**) is not in general true. We have argued, then, that whereas (C2*) is plausible, it does not imply (2); and whereas (C2**) implies (2), it is not plausible.

In order more clearly to highlight our position, it is useful to consider the complaint that we have simply missed van Inwagen's point.[29] Van Inwagen's claim is that if in some possible world, W1, Nightingale has a strong, unopposed inclination to answer the phone as soon as it rings, then, Nightingale is going to answer the phone as soon as it rings and he is not able in W1 to do otherwise. But—the objector continues—all your reconstruction of the example shows is that if in some other possible world, W2, Nightingale's motivational set is changed so that he has two conflicting inclinations, then Nightingale in W2 is able to refrain from answering the phone as soon as it rings. Nightingale's ability in W2, however, is a function of his having opposing inclinations, and in itself this doesn't show that Nightingale in W1, without the opposing inclinations, is able to do otherwise. The issue, then, is not what Nightingale can do in W2 with a different motivational set, but rather what Nightingale can do in W1 given that his motivational set is just as van Inwagen stipulates.

We reply that, as long as Nightingale is genuinely *able* (during the relevant temporal interval) in W1 to generate a desire to answer the phone, then he is *able* in W1 to answer the phone. Insofar as W2 is *genuinely accessible* to Nightingale, then W2 is relevant to what Nightingale *can* do in W1. It is only if W2 is not so accessible that it is irrelevant to Nightingale's abilities in W1. Of course, we rely here on the fact, if some world W2 is in the appropriate sense accessible to W1, then W2 may be relevant to the modal properties of individuals in W1.

IV. Free To Act Indefensibly, Free To Act Crazily

Thus far we have argued against the restrictivist's argument that in cases of unopposed inclination the agent is not free to do otherwise. We believe that the same considerations apply, *mutatis mutandis*, to the argument concerning unreflective actions. Thus, we believe that we have pointed to a way of salvaging the intuition that, even if Beta were true, individuals are often free to do otherwise in contexts of unopposed desire and unreflective action. Now let us turn to van Inwagen's parallel argument concerning indefensible actions.

Having developed the criticism of the argument pertaining to unopposed desire, it is now extremely simple to explain what is wrong with the argument concerning indefensible actions. In fact, our objection to the argument concerning indefensible actions is precisely the same as the objection to the argument concerning unopposed desires.

Recall that van Inwagen adduces (C1) in support of premise (2) of the argument:

(C1) If X regards A as an indefensible act, given the totality of relevant information available to him, and if he has no way of getting further relevant information, and if he lacks any positive desire to do A, and if he sees no objection to *not* doing A (again, given the totality of relevant information available to him), then X is not going to do A (p. 407).

Given that van Inwagen adduces (C1) in support of (2), it is clear that he is interpreting the second premise of the argument in the following way:

(2) N, X (X regards A as an indefensible act and X lacks any desire to do A ⊃ X does not do A).

To proceed as above. (C1) can be interpreted so as to claim that the following state of affairs is not possible: that X regards A as indefensible, has no desire to perform A, and performs A. But (C1), so interpreted, does not imply (2). Alternatively, (C1) could be interpreted so as to claim that if X regards A as indefensible and X lacks any desire to do A, then X cannot do A. But, so interpreted, (C1) is false, insofar as X can (in the relevant temporal interval) generate the desire in question.

But in the context of unopposed desire discussed above, it is not supposed that the agent believes that the act in question is *indefensible*. Might this belief constitute an obstacle to generating a reason (or desire of the sort discussed above) to perform the act? That is, is the context of indefensible acts relevantly different from the contexts of unopposed desire and unreflective action?

The examples adduced by van Inwagen in support of (C1) suggest that morally indefensible actions *do* have some special status such that one literally is unable to bring oneself to desire to do (and to do) them.[30] To make this point, van Inwagen begins with an example presented by Daniel Dennett in which Dennett makes the claim that he is unable to torture innocent victims for small sums of money.[31] Van Inwagen observes that the point of the example is not so much that Dennett would not be able to torture these innocents if he so chose, but rather that, given Dennett's character, he simply is *unable to make such a choice* (and, presumably, unable to generate the relevant desire). Van Inwagen wishes to extend this line of reasoning to show that he also could not slander a colleague to prevent that colleague's appointment to Chairman of the Tenure Committee, and similarly that none of us could do anything that he considers indefensible.

Now, we certainly grant that there may be *some* actions—call them "unwillable" actions—which a particular agent literally cannot bring himself to choose to do (and to do); and some (although not necessarily all) of these unwillable actions may be ones that are morally indefensible.[32] Indeed, Dennett's example of torturing innocents seems to be just such a case. We wish to emphasize, however, that it does not follow from an action's being morally indefensible that it is *unwillable*. That is, we suggest that the Dennett/van Inwagen point here gains plausibility from their focusing on a proper subset of the relevant cases: those morally indefensible actions which are *also* unwillable. But an indefensible action is not *eo ipso* unwillable. Thus, we wish to block the move from the specific case of one's not being able to torture innocents to the general claim that "no one is able to perform an act he considers morally reprehensible" (p. 405).

We believe that there *can* be cases in which an agent believes that an act is morally indefensible and nevertheless has a desire to perform it (of the sort mentioned above) and indeed successfully acts on this desire. And it is in general plausible to suppose that agents have the *power* to generate this sort of desire. In order to support our claim that the context of indefensible action is not relevantly different from the other two contexts, we present the following examples in which an individual believes that the act in question is indefensible but nevertheless has a desire to perform it and does indeed perform it.

Consider first Augustine's famous account of the theft of pears in his boyhood. Shortly before this passage, Augustine is wondering about the reason for his stealing pears for which he had no desire, and after acknowledging the view that all action must be for the sake of some apparent good, he dismisses this explanation in his own case:

> ...now that I ask what pleasure I had in that theft, I find that it had no beauty to attract me.... It did not even have the shadowy, deceptive beauty which makes vice attractive" (*Confessions* II, vi, Pine-Coffin translation). ...Let my heart now tell you what it sought when I was thus evil for no object, having no cause for wrongdoing save my wrongness. The malice of the act was base and I loved it—that is to say I loved my own undoing, I loved the evil in me—not the thing for which I did the evil, simply the evil...(*Confessions* II, iv, Sheed translation).

Augustine's reflections are disturbing precisely because they exemplify one man's ability not only to do something he takes to be morally indefensible, but to be drawn to the action precisely because it is so indefensible. This is not to say that Augustine did not see the robbery as having some desirable consequences. He himself admits that he would not have committed the crime had it not been for his companions and the "thrill of having partners in sin" (*Confessions* II, viii). However, simply because Augustine wanted something from his thieving, this does not show that he saw the thieving as good, or that he believed it conformed to an overall system of values he was willing to defend. A person might see the pilfering of pears as wholly indefensible and still desire to do it, if for no other reason than to assert one's ability to act against moral value. Indeed Augustine's comments suggest that he saw his attraction to evil as being intimately connected to this desire for a perverse sort of freedom and power—a freedom to ignore the Good:

> What was it, then, that pleased me in that act of theft? Which of my Lord's powers did I imitate in a perverse and wicked way? Since I had no real power to break his law, was it that I enjoyed at least the pretence of doing so, like a prisoner who creates for himself the illusion of liberty by doing something wrong, when he has no fear of punishment, under a feeble hallucination of power? Here was a slave who ran away from his master and chased a shadow instead! What an abomination! What a parody of life! What abysmal death! Could I enjoy doing wrong for no other reason that that it was wrong?...
> ...I loved nothing in it except the thieving, though I cannot truly speak of that as a 'thing' that I could love, and I was only the more miserable because of it (*Confessions* II, vi-viii, Pine-Coffin Translation).

A different type of rebellion, but one which expresses a related yearning to flout moral prohibitions, is found in the story of a character quite distinct from St. Augustine: Dostoevsky's Raskalnikov. Recall that at the outset of the story, Raskalnikov is contemplating killing and robbing the old pawnbroker, Alena Ivanovna, and as he does so, he is keenly aware of the evil at hand; he knows such acts are morally reprehensible and he is repulsed by his own musings:

"Oh God, how repulsive! Can I possibly, can I possibly...no, that's nonsense, it's ridiculous!" he broke off decisively. "How could such a horrible idea [i.e., to rob and murder Ivanovna] enter my mind? What vileness my heart seems capable of! The point is, that it is vile, filthy, horrible, horrible!" (*Crime and Punishment*, I.1).

In spite of this moral aversion, Raskalnikov nonetheless finds that he is able to do the indefensible: he takes a borrowed axe to the head of not only Alena Ivanovna but her sister as well. Later, as he thinks back on the murder and robbery, Raskalnikov dismisses the only reasonable motive for the crime: "If it all has been done deliberately and not idiotically," he ponders, "if I really had a certain and definite object, how is it I did not even glance into the purse and don't know what I had there, for which I have undergone these agonies and have deliberately undertaken this base, filthy, degrading business?" (*Crime and Punishment*, II.2). Raskalnikov knows that he did not kill the old woman, as a more typical criminal might have, for her money. And later, as he confesses to Sonya, the deeper motivation behind the crime comes out:

"I realized then, Sonya," he went on enthusiastically, "that power is given only to the man who dares stoop and take it. There is only one thing needed, only one—to dare...I wanted to *have the courage*, and I killed...I only wanted to dare, Sonya, that was the only reason!"
..."what I needed to find out then, and find out as soon as possible, was whether I was a louse like everybody else or a man, whether I was capable of stepping over the barriers or not. Dared I stoop and take the power or not?"...
..."Listen: when I went to the old woman's that time, it was only to *test myself*...Understand that!" (*Crime and Punishment*, V.5).

Raskalnikov's remarks are of interest to us because they give an example of a man who (1) knows that robbery and murder are morally indefensible, (2) is not driven to perform these acts in the pursuit of some good which can be separated from the crime itself, and (3) nonetheless does rob and murder two people. Indeed, what is most important about Raskalnikov for our purposes, is that, given a straightforward reading, he seems drawn to murder the aging pawnbroker, precisely to see if he *can* do it: He wants to discover if he has the power to ignore moral prohibitions; he wants to know if he is free to do the morally indefensible.[33]

What is striking about the crimes of both Augustine and Raskalnikov is that, unlike a more mundane robbery in which the wrongdoing is merely a means to material gain, the motive behind their crimes is inextricably bound up with a desire to do wrong and to flout moral constraints. This is not to say that the motivations of Augustine and Raskalnikov can be assimilated in every respect. Whereas Augustine seeks the freedom to do evil in order to rebel against the good, Raskalnikov seeks this freedom to show that he is beyond good and evil. But the crucial point for our discussion is that both men claim to do what the restrictive incompatibilist says they cannot—freely perform an act that is perceived by the agent to be morally indefensible.

We have argued, then, that the context of indefensibility is not relevantly different from the context of (say) unopposed desire: an agent can generate a certain sort of desire to perform an action even though he believes that the action is morally indefensible. Thus, our critique of van Inwagen's argument about contexts of unopposed desire (and unreflective action) can be extended to apply to his argument about contexts of indefensible actions. Someone might object that our examples only pertain to contexts in which agents believe that the relevant actions are *morally* indefensible, rather than indefensible from some broader (perhaps "all-things-considered") perspective.[34] But it is clear that van Inwagen has in mind the notion of moral indefensibility. Further, if the broader notion of indefensibility were employed, this would substantially reduce the incidence of contexts of indefensibility (thus vitiating the restrictivist's claim that we are rarely free to do otherwise). Finally, we do not see why individuals cannot generate desires (perhaps they would be "weak-willed desires") to do things which they consider to be indefensible, all things considered.

Before leaving the question of whether or not we are free to act indefensibly, we want to consider a final worry about such freedom which is suggested by two interesting examples recently formulated by Susan Wolf. Wolf asks us to consider what it would mean for an agent to have the ability to act against everything he believes in and cares about:

> It would mean, for example, that if the agent's son were inside a burning building, the agent could just stand there and watch the house go up in flames. Or that the agent, though he thinks his neighbor a fine and agreeable fellow, could just get up one day, ring the doorbell, and punch him in the nose. One might think that such pieces of behavior should not be classified as actions at all—that they are rather more like spasms that the agent cannot control. If they are actions they are very bizarre, and an agent who performed them would have to be insane. *Indeed, one might think he would have to be insane if he had even the ability to perform them.* For the rationality of an agent who could perform such irrational actions as these must hang by a dangerously thin thread.[35]

Before directly discussing these examples, a word of qualification is in order. Wolf originally presents these examples to illustrate what it would mean for an agent's actions not to be determined by any interests whatsoever. One of the points she is making, if we have understood her properly, is that a person whose actions weren't determined by *any* interests could hardly be said to be acting at all. Rather his behavior, since it did not reflect any interests or intention, would seem more like spasms or the bizarre movements of an insane person. Understood in this fashion Wolf's claim is certainly unobjectionable; indeed, this insight seems merely to reflect the (alleged) conceptual truth discussed above that all behavior, if it is to be considered action at all, must reflect some pro-attitude.

Our interest in Wolf's examples comes from another more substantive claim which is also suggested by her examples and subsequent comments; this is the suggestion that anyone who even had the *ability* to perform indefensible acts (like allowing her children to burn, or punching her neighbor in the nose for no good reason) would have to be insane. This claim is not the trivial one that anyone whose bodily movements did not reflect her interests would be insane; rather it is the more interesting and substantive claim that anyone who even had the ability to act against all seemingly good interests would be insane. A similar sentiment is found in the following passage by Daniel Dennett: "But in other cases, like Luther's, when I say I cannot do otherwise I mean I cannot because I see so clearly what the situation is and because my rational control faculty is *not* impaired. It is too obvious what to do; reason dictates it; I would have to be mad to do otherwise, and since I happen not to be mad, I cannot do otherwise."[36] Both Wolf and Dennett seem inclined to slide from the claim that 'doing X would be crazy' to a stronger claim that 'anyone who had the ability to do X would be crazy'. If this "Wolf/Dennett slide" were correct, then, since most of us are not crazy, it would seem to follow that most of us are not able to act in a crazy, indefensible manner—a conclusion which the restrictive incompatibilist would of course welcome.

We think the conclusion reached via the Wolf/Dennett slide is false. In fact, a strategy similar to the one used earlier to expose the fallacy in van Inwagen's arguments also can be deployed here to make clear the problem with this slide. The conclusion that sane people are not free to do insane things is supposed to follow from the claim that it is not possible for someone to do something that is crazy without actually being crazy. But there are two ways to interpret this claim. On one interpretation, the claim is true, but it fails to support the desired conclusion; on the other interpretation, the conclusion does follow, but the claim is false.

On the first interpretation, the initial claim is construed to mean that the following state of affairs is not possible: that an agent be sane and perform a crazy action. So interpreted the claim may be true, but it certainly does not imply the conclusion that no sane person has the *ability* to act crazily. In order to reach this conclusion, the initial claim needs to be strengthened so as to claim that if an agent is sane then it is not possible for her to do crazy things. But so interpreted the claim seems false. After all, what reason is there to think that the mere *ability* to act crazily should call one's rationality into question?

With respect to other vices, it is customary to accept a distinction between having an ability and exercising it. For example, having the ability to eat and drink to excess does not imply that one is intemperate; nor does having the ability to flee from the battlefield, a coward make. Indeed this distinction seems applicable to a wide range of character traits—having the ability to act generously does not make one generous, having the ability to act dishonestly does not make one a liar, and so forth. The point here is simply that having the power to act in a certain way does not entail that someone is the type of person who will act that way. And given this general fact, why should we expect the case to be otherwise with indefensible actions like punching one's neighbor for no good reason?[37] Why should simply having the ability to act crazily render one crazy? Why should there be this asymmetry between the "ability to act crazily" and other dispositional notions?

An example might be helpful here. A traditional view has it that if we have a free will at all, we must have a perfect, God-like free will. Roughly the idea behind the view is that whereas there can be impediments to action—i.e., one can be unable to act in accordance with one's will—there cannot be any impediments to willing.[38] We raise this view not to defend it, but rather to assume, for the purposes of this example, that it is true. (If one prefers science fiction and fantasy to tradition, then simply imagine that you happen upon a magical ring, and after placing it on your finger, you discover that it has bestowed upon you the infinitely free will described by the traditional view above: a will that enables you to choose or not choose any option you desire irrespective of your morals or best interests). Now one thing should be clear: simply because the range of your choices has been increased (thanks to the ring), your ability to listen to reason has not been decreased. Having this freedom does not somehow mute the voice of conscience, or leave you with no way to know which course of action is the most rational; it merely gives you the ability to pick a less optimal path if you so will. Like the motorist who reaches a junction from which she can take either a scenic parkway heading directly toward her destination, or a one-lane dirt road that crawls through acres of sanitary landfill in the wrong direction, you more than likely will pick the most reasonable alternative. But surely we won't judge the motorist to be crazy simply because she is at a junction were she can choose a route which is not in her interests, and neither should we judge you crazy simply because you have the power to choose against your interests.

"Still"—one might complain—"being at a crossroads scarcely shows that one is free to turn as she pleases. After all, no sane motorist ever *will* take the dirt path, and similarly no sane person ever *will* knowingly act against her interests. Indeed having the freedom to act this way would appear to be less a blessing than a curse; for why would anyone ever want the ability to behave in such a contrary fashion? It short it would seem that the power to act both irrationally and immorally, if we have it at all, is hardly as much of an ability, as it is a *dis*ability—a character flaw which needs to be overcome."[39]

Two points are raised by this worry. One is easily dealt with; the other broaches a broader issue which we can only touch upon in the context of this discussion. As to the first point—that a sane motorist will never actually choose the dirt road, and a sane person will never actually act against her best interests—we can agree that in most cases this is true.[40] Nevertheless, as we saw above, the fact that someone never *will* act against her interests does not entail that she *cannot* do so. For surely there is nothing incoherent about a person having a power which she never exercises. Having given this response, however, we are lead straightaway to the second, more complicated worry: why would a sane person ever want to have a power that she will never exercise, especially a power to act against all of her morals and best interests?[41]

But, lamentably, to ask whether we would *want* to have something is, of course, not the same as asking whether we *have* it, for it might turn out that we have the freedom to act indefensibly even though this is hardly a freedom we *would like* to have. Hence, this worry cannot aid the restrictive incompatibilist in securing his position.[42]

The Wolf/Dennett slide *is* a slide, and it is not well-motivated; the fact that doing X would be crazy does not (in itself and without further argumentation) imply that anyone who had the *ability* to do X would be crazy. Just as agents with the *power* to be gluttonous need not *be* gluttons, agents with the *power* to act crazily need not be considered crazy.

V. Restrictive Incompatibilism and Moral Responsibility: Tracing

Thus far we have argued that incompatibilists need not accept the restrictive incompatibilist's claim that "rarely, if ever, is anyone able to do otherwise than he in fact does." But what if our criticisms have not persuaded? What if incompatibilists still believe that they are conceptually committed to the thesis of restrictive incompatibilism? In closing we want to entertain this possibility and in particular to direct our attention to the following question: how would an incompatibilist account of moral responsibility be affected if one were convinced that most of the time we are not able to do otherwise? Answering this question will show that, even if incompatibilists did not find our previous objections compelling, they should wish they had.

As we mentioned at the outset of this paper, the restrictive incompatibilist identifies himself with what van Inwagen terms the 'classical tradition.' This tradition holds that there is an intimate connection between free will and moral responsibility, such that if there were no free will—if nobody were ever able to do otherwise—then there would be no moral responsibility. This requirement does not, of course, mean that there aren't particular instances in which a person might still be held accountable even though at the time of the action he was unable to do otherwise. (Van Inwagen's example of the drunk driver is such a case). However, it does suggest that any state of affairs for which we are responsible must be able to be traced back to some prior free action. To capture this "tracing" principle van Inwagen offers the following rule:

> An agent cannot be blamed for a state of affairs unless there was a time at which he could so have arranged matters that that state of affairs not obtain (p. 419).

This type of principle does not bode well for any incompatibilist who feels compelled to accept the restrictivist's conclusions, but still hopes to remain within the classical tradition. Remember the restrictive incompatibilist must hold that there are only three situations in which we are able to do otherwise: Buridan cases, cases in which duty conflicts with inclination, and situations of conflict between incommensurable values. Conjoin this premise with the above tracing principle, and now the restrictive incompatibilist is committed to showing that all states of affairs for which we are responsible can be traced back to one of these three kinds of situations. But why should we think that everything for which we are responsible can be traced back to some free choice between equally attractive alternatives, duty and inclinations, or incommensurable values?

The most promising strategy for the incompatibilist to adopt at this point is to argue that these kinds of conflict situations are precisely the ones through which our characters are formed; hence, we can accept his theory and still be responsible for all states of affairs which come about as a result of actions that are produced by our characters. In the end, however, even this strategy must fail. Much of our character results from the habituation we receive in early life, and these portions of our character don't seem to be necessarily connected with situations of conflict between duty, inclinations, or incommensurable values.

Consider a young woman, call her Betty, who has spent all of her life in a small, rural community. Like most of the citizens of her town, Betty's family is still proud to be American, and over the years Betty has gradually, almost imperceptibly, internalized a certain degree of patriotism. Being raised mostly during the apathy of the Reagan years, Betty has never been in any situation where her mild patriotism has come into conflict with any of her short-term inclinations or other values. Indeed she has never given the matter much thought—for Betty, being a loyal American has come as naturally as flying the flag on Independence Day. Even though this mild patriotism is a fixed feature of Betty's character, the restrictivist must hold that she is not yet responsible for it; he is committed to this view because Betty has not yet been in a conflict situation in which she was able to make a free choice that would have prevented her from having her patriotic disposition. Imagine now that Betty travels abroad for the first time, and through a series of strange coincidences, a singularly incompetent foreign agent mistakes her for a young American soldier who has expressed an interest in selling government secrets. He approaches Betty and asks her, in so many words, to betray her country.

Of course, Betty thinks that treason is morally indefensible; she has a strong desire not to do it, and with scarcely a moment's deliberation she turns down the agent's offer without waiting for any further explanation. For the restrictive incompatibilist, Betty clearly was not able to do anything but what she did. Moreover given that her action resulted from features of her character which in turn could not be traced back to some earlier free decision, it seems that he should say that Betty is not responsible for the ensuing state of affairs that Betty declined to betray her country. But such a conclusion runs directly counter to our actual practices of holding people responsible. Indeed if Betty is not responsible in this case, then it would appear that the restrictivist's position requires that he severely limit the domain of moral responsibility, for a great many of our everyday actions result from other character traits and dispositions which, like Betty's patriotism, are not able to be traced back to one of these situations of conflict between duty and inclination or between incommensurable values.

Of course, the restrictive incompatibilist might object that Betty really is responsible for her disposition to patriotism. "Undoubtedly"—the argument goes—"there must have been many more small conflict situations in her life than you have allowed for (or she is even aware of), and these situations taken together account for her present disposition." However, to make such a concession would prove fatal to the restrictivist's position, for it would undermine his central thesis that rarely, if ever, are we in one of these situations in which we are free to do otherwise. Thus, we leave the restrictive incompatibilist with a dilemma: either accept a severe restriction on the range of states of affairs for which we can be held morally accountable, or else reject the claim that most of the time we are unable to do otherwise. Van Inwagen claims that restrictive incompatibilism can be embedded within a traditional approach to moral responsibility via a tracing theory; we have argued this claim is false.

VI. Conclusion

We have not in this paper intended to argue for incompatibilism, nor have we attempted to explain how the will can be free in an indeterministic world. Rather, we have tried to make several more minimal points. First we sought to undermine the restrictive incompatibilist's position by challenging van Inwagen's initial claim that "if one accepts Beta, one should be an incompatibilist, and if one is an incompatibilist, one should accept Beta" (p. 405). In particular we presented an argument to show that accepting Beta is not a necessary condition of incompatibilism. (In passing we also cited several compatibilist strategies which allege that accepting Beta is not a sufficient condition of incompatibilism.) The argument that one can be an incompatibilist without having to accept Beta has ramifications beyond the scope of our discussion of restrictive incompatibilism. If incompatibilism can be secured without explicitly using Beta, then a recent trend—exemplified by Slote—which sees a deep family resemblance among various formulations of the argument for incompatibilism and which hopes to undermine them all by questioning the validity of Beta must be seen to have a more limited scope than its proponents might previously have hoped.

Second, we argued that even if an incompatibilist does accept Beta, he need not accept the restrictivist's thesis that one rarely, if ever, is free to do otherwise. Specifically we challenged the restrictivist's claim that persons are unable to (1) perform actions they consider morally indefensible, (2) refrain from performing actions which they strongly desire to perform, and (3) refrain from performing actions which they take to be the only sensible thing to do. In connection with these arguments we questioned a slide (suggested in the writings of Wolf and Dennett) which sought to move from the claim that 'doing X would be crazy' to the stronger conclusion that 'anyone who can do X must be crazy'.

Finally we examined the consequences that restrictive incompatibilism would have for a traditional theory of moral responsibility. We concluded that if incompatibilists were indeed committed to the thesis that we rarely are able to do otherwise, such a commitment would bode ill for any incompatibilistic theory of responsibility which still hoped to remain within the classical tradition. [43,44]

Notes

1. Peter van Inwagen, "When Is The Will Free?" in *Philosophical Perspectives, 3, Philosophy Of Mind And Action Theory*, ed. James Tomberlin (Atascadero, California: Ridgeview Publishing Co., 1989), pp. 399-422. All subsequent page references will be to this article unless otherwise noted.
2. We will follow van Inwagen's usage and treat 'free will' as "a philosophical term of art." According to van Inwagen to say of someone that she "has free will" means roughly that she sometimes is free to do other than what she, in fact, does.
3. In "When Is The Will Free?" van Inwagen primarily argues for the second half of this thesis; he doesn't purport to offer a detailed defense of the argument that free will is incompatible with causal determinism. He does, however, provide such a defense in his excellent book *An Essay On Free Will* (Oxford: Clarendon Press, 1983). Hence we believe that when taken together "When Is The Will Free?" and *An Essay On Free Will* can reasonably be construed as a defense of the position we are calling 'restrictivism'.
4. The following formulation of the Consequence Argument is quoted from "When Is The Will Free?" p. 405. See also *An Essay On Free Will*, pp. 55-105, and Carl Ginet, "In Defense of Incompatibilism," *Philosophical Studies* 44 (November 1983), pp. 391-400.
5. Van Inwagen uses this term broadly to include both standard Buridan cases in which "one wants each of two or more incompatible things and it isn't clear which one he should (try to) get, and the things are interchangeable" (p. 415), and cases which he calls "vanilla/chocolate cases." These are situations in which "the

alternatives are not really interchangeable (as two identical and equally accessible piles of hay) but in which the properties of the alternatives that constitute the whole difference between them are precisely the objects of the conflicting desires" (p. 415).

6. Because the central thrust of our criticisms lies elsewhere, we will not directly take issue with this claim. However, it is worth noting that van Inwagen's contention that these sorts of cases (i.e. cases in which we are free) occur only *rarely* is highly debatable. Indeed it seems more plausible to suppose that these cases occur as often, if not more often, than the three types of cases in which van Inwagen claims we are *not* free. We are grateful to Carl Ginet and Nancy Schauber for calling this point to our attention.

7. Van Inwagen claims that "if one accepts Beta one should be an incompatibilist, and if one is an incompatibilist, one should accept Beta" (p. 405). In what follows we discuss how certain *incompatibilists* would take issue with the latter half of this claim—i.e., "if one is an incompatibilist, one should accept Beta." However, it is worth noting that the former half of the claim—"if one accepts Beta, one should be an incompatibilist"—would also be contested by certain *compatibilists*. Such compatibilists argue that one can accept Beta and still take issue with the basic argument for incompatibilism; they do so either by challenging the fixity of the past (van Inwagen's premise 4) or by challenging the fixity of laws (van Inwagen's premise 6). (For a discussion of former type of compatibilism which might be called "multiple-pasts" compatibilism see Jan Narveson, "Compatibilism Defended," *Philosophical Studies* 32 (July 1977), pp. 83-87; André Gallois, "van Inwagen On Free Will And Determinism," *Philosophical Studies* 32 (July 1977), pp. 99-105; Richard Foley, "Compatibilism And Control Over The Past," *Analysis* 39 (March 1979), pp. 70-74; Keith Lehrer, "Preferences, Conditionals, And Freedom," in *Time And Cause* ed. Peter van Inwagen (Dordrecht: D. Reidel Publishing Co., 1980); John Martin Fischer, "Incompatibilism," *Philosophical Studies* 43 (January 1983), pp. 127-37. For a discussion of the latter type of compatibilism, which might be called "'local-miracle" compatibilism', see David Lewis, "Are We Free To Break The Laws," *Theoria* 47 (1981, Part 3), pp. 113-121; Carl Ginet, "In Defense of Incompatibilism"; John Martin Fischer, "Incompatibilism"; and Fischer, "Freedom And Miracles," *Noûs* 22 (June 1988), pp. 235-252; and Kadri Vihvelin, "How Are We (And Are Not) Free To Break The Laws Of Nature" (manuscript).

8. Indeed van Inwagen himself offers two formulations of the argument for incompatibilism that do not depend on any rule of inference like Beta. See van Inwagen's presentation of his First Formal Argument and his Second "Possible Worlds" Argument in *An Essay On Free Will* pp. 55-93. For another example see Carl Ginet, *On Action* (Cambridge: Cambridge University Press, 1990), pp. 90-123.

9. *An Essay On Free Will*, p. 57.

10. *Ibid.*

11. Michael Slote, "Selective Necessity and the Free-Will Problem," *Journal of Philosophy*, 79 (January 1982), p. 9.

12. See Terence Horgan, "Compatibilism and The Consequence Argument," *Philosophical Studies*, 47 (1985), p. 339.

13. *Pace* van Inwagen, Slote, and Horgan, we want to argue that a "finer-grained" approach to the various arguments for incompatibilism is needed which recognizes that not all formulations make use of the same inference rules or involve the incompatibilist in the same commitments. For example, whereas van Inwagen's

modal argument makes use of principle Beta (*Essay On Free Will*, p. 94), his First Formal Argument uses a different "entailment" principle: "If s can render r false, and if q entails r, then s can render q false" (*Essay On Free Will*, p. 72). Other arguments for incompatibilism rely on still a different type of "transfer" principle: "S cannot do X; In the circumstances doing X is doing Y; Therefore, S cannot do Y." (See Fischer's discussion in "Scotism," *Mind*, 94 (April 1985), pp. 231-243). Other philosophers also employ similar principles. For discussions of such principles and their roles in incompatibilistic arguments see: Philip L. Quinn, "Plantinga On Foreknowledge And Freedom," in *Alvin Plantinga*, eds. James E. Tomberlin, and Peter van Inwagen (Dordrecht: D. Reidel Publishing Co., 1985); Thomas B. Talbott, "Of Divine Foreknowledge And Bringing About The Past," *Philosophy And Phenomenological Research* 46 (March 1986), pp. 455-469; David Widerker, "On An Argument For Incompatibilism," *Analysis* 47 (January 1987), pp. 37-41; and Widerker, "Two Forms Of Fatalism," in *God, Foreknowledge, And Freedom*, ed. John Martin Fischer (Stanford: Stanford University Press, 1989); and Ginet *On Action*. Although all of these Beta-like principles bear some resemblance to one another, it is clear that (on the surface at least) they are not identical. Moreover, as we argue below, the incompatibilist's argument can be formulated in such a way that it makes use of neither Beta, van Inwagen's entailment principle nor any transfer principle. In addition to the argument we shall present, van Inwagen's second argument—the "possible worlds" argument—is an example of an incompatibilist argument which does not depend on any principles of this sort.

14. For a detailed presentation and discussion of this argument see Fischer, "Scotism."
15. The issues here are complex and delicate: see Lewis, "Are We Free to Break the Laws?"; Ginet, "In Defense of Incompatibilism"; Fischer, "Incompatibilism" and "Freedom and Miracles"; and Vihvelin, "How We Are (And Are Not) Free To Break The Laws."
16. In fact, we do not take this argument to be a definitive proof of incompatibilism. For one type of compatibilist response to this argument, see John Martin Fischer, "Power Over The Past," *Pacific Philosophical Quarterly*, 65 (1984), pp. 335-350. The criticisms in this article suggest that a stronger version of the argument for incompatibilism might well be something like the "possible worlds" argument which van Inwagen develops in *An Essay On Free Will*. This argument has the advantage that it relies on neither Beta nor on an overly strong fixity of the past claim which denies one even non-causal power over the past.
17. One might object that although the above argument does not explicitly employ Beta, it would not be sound unless Beta were valid because some principle like Beta is what leads one to accept FL and FP. We, however, do not see how this objection could be developed to show that FP or FL is indeed formally dependent on Beta, nor do we see how the alleged counterexamples to Beta could be successfully translated into criticisms of the above argument. Rather it seems to us that such principles about the fixity of the past and the laws have an independent appeal, and hence one could accept FP and FL without having to accept anything like Beta as a general rule of inference.
18. See Daniel C. Dennett, *Elbow Room: The Varieties Of Free Will Worth Wanting* (Cambridge: The MIT Press, 1984), p. 148; and Slote, "Selective Necessity and the Free-Will Problem."
19. John Martin Fischer, "Power Necessity," *Philosophical Topics*, 14 (Fall 1986), pp. 77-91.
20. Bernard Berofsky. *Freedom from Necessity: The Metaphysical Basis of Responsibility*. (New York: Routledge and Kegan Paul, 1987).

21. Indeed, recognizing that the incompatibilist's argument can be formulated without either Beta or Berofsky's principle calls into question much of the motivation for developing such a system of contingent necessity. The machinery of the system of contingent necessity developed by Berofsky is useful insofar as one wishes to have a modal version of the incompatibilist's argument; but it is important to see that this machinery is not necessary in order to generate the incompatibilist's argument.

22. For further discussion concerning the validity of Beta see John Martin Fischer, "Introduction: Responsibility And Freedom," in *Moral Responsibility*, ed. Fischer (Ithaca: Cornell University Press, 1986), pp. 9-61; and Fischer "Power Necessity."

23. Although van Inwagen calls this conditional, '(C)', it will be useful for our purposes to call it, '(C1)'.

24. It is of course not clear that this conceptual claim is true. A Kantian theorist of action might argue that actions can be motivated by reason alone and that desire is not a necessary precursor of genuine action. Thus, we do not wish to suggest that the (Humean) conceptual claim is obviously true; rather, we only suggest that it has a certain plausibility. Further, it is clear that if the Humean conceptual point is indeed false, then van Inwagen's argument is even in worse shape: in this case even the weaker interpretation would issue in a falsehood and thus no support for (2).

25. In *De Fato* Alexander suggests that when one's freedom is called into question it can be reasonable to do something (that might on other occasions be seen as irrational) simply in order to demonstrate one's ability to do otherwise: "Next it is not by compulsion that the wise man does any one of the things which he chooses, but as himself having control also over not doing any one of them. For it might also sometimes seem reasonable to the wise man *not* to do on some occasion what would reasonably have been brought about by him—in order to show the freedom of his actions, if some prophet predicted to him that he would of necessity do this very thing" (*De Fato* 200.2-7).

26. The notion of successfully acting on a desire is ambiguous between being moved by the desire and actually succeeding in getting the object of one's desire. We mean to adopt the latter interpretation.

27. Of course, a critic might object that this scenario presupposes that we always do have the ability to call such a worry to mind. However, nothing the restrictivist has said suggests that an incompatibilist must deny that we have *this* ability, and until such an argument is given it seems reasonable to adhere to the common wisdom that we are free to think as we will. And one cannot here point out that *if* causal determinism were true—together with incompatibilism—it would follow that we would not have the power in question. This is because the restrictivist's argument is supposed to show that Beta implies that we are rarely free to do otherwise, even if determinism were false.

28. Admittedly van Inwagen does want to construe his example in such a way that the incompatibilist must agree that the person is unable to call to mind any reason for not answering the phone. To ensure this condition, he writes: "But we might also imagine that there exists no basis either in my psyche or my environment (at the moment the telephone rings) for any of these things [i.e., things that would give me a reason not to answer the phone or that would keep me from answering it]. We may even, if you like, suppose that at the moment the telephone rings it is causally determined that no reason for not answering the phone will pop into my mind in the next few seconds..." (p. 413). We will agree that if a person's motivational set is such that he has no reason to or pro-attitude toward answering

the phone, then he will not answer the phone. This is simply an instance of the sort of consideration which supports the alleged Humean conceptual point. However, what is at issue is whether a person with such a motivational set *can* answer the phone. As far as we can tell, the restrictivist has not presented any argument to show that a person with this motivational set lacks the power to call to mind the worry that he might be unable to refrain from answering the phone. If a person has this power, then (even if he actually has no reason or desire to refrain from answering the phone) he does have the power to call to mind a reason not to answer the phone. Given that certain other conditions are satisfied, it is plausible to suppose that he has the power to refrain from answering the phone.

Of course, if it is supposed that causal determinism obtains, then the incompatibilist must say that the agent does not have the power to generate the relevant reasons and thus lacks the power to refrain from answering the phone. But in the context of an assessment of restrictivism, it is not fair to assume causal determinism; after all, the restrictivist's claim is that, even if causal determinism were false, we would rarely be free to do otherwise.

29. We are grateful to Sarah Buss, Nancy Schauber and Eleonore Stump for each calling this objection to our attention.

30. See pp. 406-407.

31. Dennett, *Elbow Room*, pp. 133ff.

32. Harry Frankfurt uses the term "unthinkable" to describe actions which an agent cannot bring himself to will to perform. According to Frankfurt some acts will be unthinkable for an agent because of his moral inhibitions, but "on the other hand, the considerations on account of which something is unthinkable may be entirely self-regarding and without any moral significance." See Harry G. Frankfurt, "Rationality And The Unthinkable," chap. in *The Importance Of What We Care About* (Cambridge: Cambridge University Press, 1988), p. 182. Another reason why an agent may be unable to will something is given by Lehrer's examples of agents who cannot bring themselves to choose to do something because they suffer from a pathological aversion. See Keith Lehrer, "Cans Without Ifs," *Analysis* 29 (October 1968), pp. 29-32; and Lehrer, "'Can' In Theory And Practice: A Possible Worlds Analysis," in *Action Theory*, ed. Myles Brand and Douglas Walton (Dordrecht: D. Reidel Publishing Company, 1976), pp. 241-270.

33. We do not mean to suggest that this is a complete analysis of Raskalnikov's complex character; rather for the sake of brevity we want to limit our comments about his motivations to those which emerge from the passages cited. A more complete analysis would undoubtedly have to consider among other things: (1) the fact that Raskalnikov claims to have felt *beforehand* that he would know *after* the crime that he was only a louse and not an extraordinary man (III.6) and his later demise which seems to confirm this suspicion; (2) his later insistence which challenges the previous claim and suggests that he now, like the extraordinary man, feels no guilt for his crime (Epilogue.2); (3) his claim to have suffered his downfall through "some decree of blind fate" (Epilogue.2); (4) the promised repentance at the end of the book. All these facts point to the need further to refine and revise our abbreviated sketch of Raskalnikov; however, we leave this task to more capable literary critics. For an interesting discussion of these issues, see the collection of critical essays on Raskalnikov in the *Norton Critical Edition of Crime and Punishment*, ed. George Gibian (New York: W. W. Norton & Company, 1975).

34. For example, one might object that Raskalnikov commits his crime in order to

show that he is the "extraordinary man" for whom all things are permitted, and therefore he must view his act as being defensible from the broader perspective available to such a person. Even on this reading, however, Raskalnikov still must be seen as doing something he takes to be indefensible given the constraints of conventional morality, for to want to be the "extraordinary man" is to want nothing less than to be free to ignore such moral imperatives.

35. Susan Wolf, "Asymmetrical Freedom," in *Moral Responsibility* p. 206 emphasis added. Watson outlines this worry in his excellent article "Free Action and Free Will," *Mind* 96 (April 1987), pp. 145-172.

36. *Elbow Room*, p. 133.

37. It is interesting to note that Wolf, like van Inwagen, begins with an example—that of allowing one's children to be incinerated—which is an action most people would find both indefensible and unthinkable, and then moves to an example—that of punching ones' neighbor—which most people would just find indefensible. Since we want to focus on the question of whether the mere ability to do indefensible things does indeed make one crazy, we will concentrate on her second example.

38. For example, Descartes in his Fourth Meditation claims: "It is free will alone or liberty of choice which I find to be so great in me that I can conceive no other idea to be more great; it is indeed the case that it is for the most part this will that causes me to know that in some manner I bear the image and similitude of God." For a modern defense of the view that idea of an unfree will is inconceivable see Brian O'Shaugnessy, *The Will: A Dual Aspect Theory* (Cambridge: Cambridge University Press, 1980); and Rogers Albritton, "Freedom of Will and Freedom of Action," Presidential Address, *Proceeding of the American Philosophical Association* (November 1985). As Watson points out the truth behind such claims seems to be that "our concept of the will is such that there is no such thing as failing to will; willing is necessarily successful"; from this point, however, "it does not follow that one cannot be prevented from willing, not by having obstacles placed in the path, but by having one's will pushed as it were toward one path or another"—see Gary Watson, "Free Action and Free Will," *Mind*, 96 (April 1987), p. 163.

39. Watson raises this worry in "Free Action and Free Will," p. 164.

40. Although we have suggested that examples like those of Augustine challenge even this intuition: for if we take Augustine at his word, he seems to be a case of someone who did act against his best interests, in a manner he believed to be indefensible, and still was not crazy. And if this true, if one can exercise this freedom and not be insane, then surely one can simply possess this freedom without being crazy.

41. Wolf puts this latter point well when she asks: "Why would one want the ability to pass up the apple when to do so would merely be unpleasant or arbitrary? Why would one want the ability to stay planted on the sand when to do so would be cowardly and callous?...To want autonomy in other words, is to want not only the ability to act rationally but also the ability to act *ir*rationally—but this latter is a very strange ability to want, if it is an ability at all." (Wolf, *Freedom Within Reason* (Oxford: Oxford University Press, 1990), pp. 55-56.)

42. Although authors like Dennett and Wolf have argued that the freedom to act indefensibly is not only not wanted by rational agents, but further that it may even be a liability to them, other writers have viewed this freedom in quite an opposite fashion; they have pointed to it as a primary source of human dignity. Jeffrie Murphy asks: "Does not each person want to believe of himself, as a part

of his pride in his human dignity, that he is *capable* of performing, freely and responsibly performing, evil acts that would quite properly earn for him the retributive hatred of others? And shouldn't he at least sometimes extend this compliment to others?" (See Jeffrie G. Murphy and Jean Hampton, *Forgiveness And Mercy* (Cambridge: Cambridge University Press, 1988), p. 102.) Presumably, part of the intuition here is that our respect for others stems from seeing them as responsible agents who, even though they are able to do the bad, refrain from doing so and choose instead to act in accord with morality. Indeed Watson suggests (in his article "Free Action And Free Will") that a Kantian conception of moral agency which emphasizes an ability to set ends requires this type of freedom. On this view, we want the freedom to act indefensibly, not because we want to be irrational, but rather because this freedom underlies our unique status as moral agents; it gives us the ability to reorder our values and to change radically the ends which govern our actions.

43. With respect to this last point, it is worth noting that there are good reasons for abandoning this tradition. For a representative sample of articles discussing this position, see Fischer, *Moral Responsibility*, pp. 143-249. Also see John Martin Fischer, "Responsiveness and Moral Responsibility," in *Responsibility, Character, and the Emotions*, ed. Ferdinand Schoeman (Cambridge: Cambridge University Press, 1987), pp. 81-106; Mark Ravizza, "Is Responsiveness Sufficient For Responsibility" (manuscript); and Fischer and Ravizza, "Responsibility And Inevitability" *Ethics* 101 (January 1991).

44. We are grateful to Sarah Buss, David Copp, Carl Ginet, Jonathan Lear, Nancy Schauber, and Eleonore Stump for their helpful comments on a previous draft of this paper. Previous versions of this paper were read at the UCLA Law and Philosophy Discussion Group, and at the University of California, San Diego.

Philosophical Perspectives, 6, Ethics, 1992

WHO DISCOVERED THE WILL?

T. H. Irwin
Cornell University

1. Approaches to the Question

Many modern critics regard the concept of the will as an anachronism that ought to be excluded from our account of Greek philosophers. Ross remarks: 'It has often been complained that the psychology of Plato and Aristotle has no distinct conception of the will.'[1] Gauthier insists that 'in the psychology of Aristotle the will does not exist'.[2] According to MacIntyre, 'Aristotle, like every other ancient pre-Christian author, had no concept of the will and there is no conceptual space in his scheme for such an alien notion in the explanations of defect and error.'[3] Different candidates have been proposed for the title of discoverer of the will. Sometimes the introduction of the will into accounts of choice and action is attributed to the Romans.[4] Sometimes Augustine is regarded as the pioneer, under Hebraic and Christian influence.[5] Sometimes the honour (if that is the right word) goes to Maximus the Confessor.[6]

A proper discussion of this question requires a wide-ranging historical and philosophical inquiry. It is particularly important to identify and to examine the relevant philosophical issues, if we are to see which questions need to be answered in deciding whether or not a philosopher has a concept or theory of the will.[7] I do not intend to survey all the relevant evidence and issues. I will simply pick out some issues that are relevant to one dispute about the will.

Those who deny that Greek philosophers have any concept of the will recognize that Greek theories explain choice and action by reference to beliefs and desires. But they argue that the features ascribed to beliefs and desires in these theories fall short of the characteristic features of the will.[8]

Some Greek theories, and in particular the Socratic and Stoic theories, are intellectualist. According to an intellectualist view, all that affects our choice between doing A and doing B is our belief about whether A or B is, all things considered, better. No non-cognitive element in the agent determines the choice between A and B. This does not mean that belief by itself moves us to action. An intellectualist might agree that a non-cognitive element is present, but deny that it makes a difference between one agent's choices and another's. This is the view Socrates seems to take in the *Hippias Minor* and *Euthydemus*. He assumes that we all have the fixed desire for our own happiness and differ only in our beliefs about what promotes happiness; we cannot reject this desire for happiness in favour of some other aim and we do not decide to pursue happiness in preference to something else.

Not all Greek theories claim that only ignorance can explain failure to choose the apparent good. Plato's and Aristotle's doctrine of the divided soul recognizes that both rational and non-rational desires influence action.[9] They argue against Socrates that our doing or not doing what we believe to be best depends not only on our beliefs about the good, but also on the comparative strength of our desires; if we want the immediate satisfaction more strongly than we want our overall good, we choose the action promising the immediate satisfaction.

Both these views seem to treat agents as passive subjects of their desires and in doing so they seem to leave out an important aspect of human agency. The intellectualist view recognizes one constant motivational force, our desire for the good; the anti-intellectualist view, recognizing conflicts of motives, allows other forces besides the desire for the good, but it treats the agent as a mere victim and spectator of possible conflicts. Both accounts seem to overlook our capacity to reflect on our desires and to choose between them. We are inclined to say that we need not simply contemplate our desires; if we reflect on them, we can decide whether or not to regard a desire as expressing our will, and we can act accordingly.

If we must recognize this reflective decision between desires, then, it seems we must recognize the will as a third element in rational choice besides mere belief and mere desire. If we recognize this third element, we will readily infer that it must be important, even decisive, in character, virtue, and vice, for our actions, plans, and effective preferences will reflect not our mere desire, but the results of our reflexions on these desires and our choices about which desires to follow.

This conception of the will and its moral importance is prominent in the moral psychology of St Augustine. Rejecting the view that we are passive in relation to our choices, he identifies the will with the unforced movement of the mind towards getting or keeping something.[10] Our consciousness of our will is inseparable from consciousness of ourselves, and we attribute an action to ourselves precisely in so far as we attribute it to our will.[11] The will, rather than any external influence or internal force, is both the cause of our being subject to sin and the cause of our turning towards virtue.[12]

determines whether our passions are good or bad; indeed, when the will is good, the passions themselves are expressions of the good will.[13]

Virtue, as Augustine conceives it, is precisely the good use of free choice.[14] The overriding direction of people's will is expressed in their love,[15] and virtue is the proper ordering or direction of people's love.[16] If the will correctly aims at the right ultimate end, and the expressions of will towards the means are rightly connected with it, then the agent is virtuous.[17] The will orders and directs not only our desires, but also our perceptions, memories, and beliefs, in the direction it has chosen.[18]

If we compare these remarks of Augustine's about the will with Plato, or Aristotle, or the Stoics, we find no earlier parallels for this pervasive and explicit appeal to the will. We ought not to infer, however, that the earlier philosophers have no concept of the will. To see whether or not they have this concept, we ought to see whether the intellectualist and anti-intellectualist views that I described provide an accurate account of what Greek philosophers have to offer. If these views fail to do justice to Greek moral psychology, then it may be reasonable to attribute a concept of the will to Greek philosophers.

I will pursue this question with special reference to Aristotle. Though he does not necessarily provide the clearest evidence for the presence of a concept of the will in Greek philosophy, it is particularly instructive to consider him, for reasons that I will now explain.

2. Aquinas and Aristotle

St Thomas Aquinas's treatment of Aristotle holds a special place in the history of treatments of the will. For St Thomas clearly comes well after the discovery of the will, whenever that was; he unambiguously recognizes the will as a distinct faculty of the soul (*Summa Theologiae* 1a q80 a2; *De Veritate* q22 a3-4). His account of the will is influenced by Augustine, and by the Greek Christian writers Nemesius and John Damascene, who summarize a composite account of moral psychology derived from different sources in Greek philosophy.

Despite all this influence from the Greek and Latin Fathers, however, Aquinas takes himself to be expounding Aristotle's view. He regards Augustine's remarks about the will not as a description of something unknown to Aristotle, but as an elaboration of something that was already familiar to Aristotle. Augustine does not say what it is that could have all the functions that he ascribes to the will. Aquinas seeks to answer that question; in his view, Aristotle recognizes something that can do what Augustine says the will does, and therefore Aristotle has a concept of the will. It would be unfair to Aquinas if we were to assume that since we know Aristotle has no concept of the will, we know Aquinas must be wrong. We ought instead to see why he believes that Aristotle's remarks apply to the will.

If Aquinas has a concept of the will, then we can try to answer our original question about whether Aristotle has a concept of the will, by answering a more precise question. If Aquinas interprets Aristotle correctly, then Aristotle has a concept of the will. If, on the other hand, we believe that Aristotle has no concept of the will, then we must show where Aquinas's interpretation of him is wrong.

In attributing a concept of the will to Aristotle, Aquinas makes two claims. First, he claims that Aristotle's concept of 'wish' (*boulêsis*) is really a concept of the will. Second, he claims that Aristotle's remarks about 'voluntary' (*hekousion*) action are about the role of the will. These are his general interpretative claims about Aristotle; but the Aristotelian passages he cites raise their own difficulties of exegesis, and it is not easy to decide for or against Aquinas. Aquinas's exegesis is careful and fair; he cannot be accused of simply forcing his general interpretation into his exegesis of individual passages. Indeed, I will sometimes suggest that Aquinas's exegesis is wrong, and that the right exegesis would actually support his general interpretation better than his own exegesis supports it. On the other hand I will not try to answer all the exegetical questions that would need to be answered if we were trying to vindicate Aquinas's general interpretation. I will simply argue that a reasonable case can be made for some of Aquinas's claims, and that he focusses on an important aspect of Aristotle's theory that receives too little attention from Aristotle himself. If this is true, then Aquinas is justified in his claim that Aristotle has a concept of the will.

3. Will as Rational Desire

Aquinas's term 'will' (voluntas) is the standard Latin translation of '*boulêsis*'.[19] The translation is justified by the fact that 'velle' and 'voluntas' in Ciceronian Latin correspond fairly well in their non-technical uses to '*boulesthai*' and '*boulêsis*' in Greek. Aristotle's term is not his own invention; *boulêsis* is the sort of wanting, or wishing, or preferring, or aiming, that need not be an urgent desire resulting from some immediate felt need or passion.[20] 'Velle' and 'voluntas' capture this aspect of '*boulesthai*' and '*boulêsis*' quite well in Latin. It is a different question, however, whether Aristotle's remarks about *boulêsis* reveal a concept of the will that matches Aquinas's particular philosophical account of the will.

In Aquinas's view, 'will' is the name for essentially rational desire.[21] It is 'a desire following the apprehension by the one who desires in accordance with free judgment. And of this sort is rational or intellectual desire, which is called the will' (*ST* 1-2 q26 a1). Aquinas appeals to the rational character of the will to contrast it with sensory desire, 'which follows apprehension by the one who desires, but from necessity, not from free judgment. And of this sort is sensory desire in beasts; in human beings, however, it has some share in freedom, to the extent that it obeys reason' (1-2 q26 a1). Since human beings have essentially rational desires, they are not simply passive in relation to their desires; and so essentially rational desire gives us the reflective control that seems to be missing in accounts of choice that omit the will.

Aquinas believes that Aristotle also regards the will as essentially rational desire, realizing a capacity distinct from sensory desire (*De Ver* q22 a4). He recognizes that in Aristotle's list of the different types of capacities of the soul, desire is mentioned without distinction (*De Ver* q24 a4 obj 4), but he appeals none the less to Aristotle's division in *De Anima* iii (432b5) between *boulêsis* and the other desires (*in DA* §802-3; *ST* 1a q82 a1 obj 3; q87 a4; *De Ver* q22 a4 sc 1). Aquinas argues that the difference between the ways in which we grasp the objects of rational and non-rational desires makes it clear that Aristotle regards them as constituting different capacities (*ST* 1a q80 a2).

Some readers reject Aquinas's interpretation of Aristotle's tripartition of desire. While Aristotle sometimes distinguishes *boulêsis* from spirit and appetite, we might argue that this distinction does not imply recognition of an essentially rational form of desire. We might understand *boulêsis* as simply the desire that is not formed under the stimulus of some immediate pain, need, or provocation of the sort that produces the desires of *epithumia* and *thumos*.[22] This sort of desire can be trained to conform to reason, since it can more easily be trained to focus on more remote objects and is less tied to immediate satisfactions. Still, it belongs, as the other desires do, to the desiring part, which is inherently non-rational, though it is capable of following reason (cf. *Nicomachean Ethics* 1102b13-1103a2).

If this is the right account of Aristotle's view of *boulêsis*, then Aquinas has gone wrong by imposing an inappropriately rationalist interpretation. The rationalist interpretation recognizes a sort of desire that is peculiar to the rational part of the soul and is distinct from non-rational desire. Aquinas, we might argue, commits an anachronism in claiming to find this rationalist view in Aristotle.[23] An 'anti-rationalist' view denies that the relation of different desires to reason constitutes an essential difference between them. Can we decide between these two views?

Aristotle describes *boulêsis* as rational desire aiming at the good (*Rhetoric* 1369a2-7), and he assumes that the only way we can be moved in accordance with reason is to be moved in accordance with *boulêsis* (*DA* 433a22-5). He even describes incontinence as the overcoming of *boulêsis* by non-rational desire (434a11-14).[24] What could Aristotle mean by claiming that all action in accordance with reason is action on *boulêsis*?

A difficulty for his claim arises from the role that he assigns to decision (*prohairesis*). For he distinguishes *prohairesis* from *boulêsis*, and claims that when we act on a specific rational desire for some achievable object here and now we act on a *prohairesis*.[25] If *prohairesis* is to fit into the threefold classification of desire, it must count as *boulêsis*. In that case, we must not take Aristotle's division between *boulêsis* and *prohairesis* to imply that a *prohairesis* is not a *boulêsis*, in the sense of '*boulêsis*' that makes it coordinate with *thumos* and *epithumia*. When Aristotle compares *boulêsis* with *prohairesis*, he has already excluded the two non-rational forms of desire (1111b10-19); and when he says that *prohairesis* is not to be identified with *boulêsis*, he remarks that it none the less appears close to it (1111b19-20). The close connexion between *boulêsis* and *prohairesis* is emphasized in Aspasius' commentary:

> *Boulêsis* appears close to *prohairesis*, since, first of all, it is in the rational part of the soul, where what most controls *prohairesis*[26] is, and, second, because it is a part of *prohairesis*. For whenever intellect after having deliberated approves and chooses, *boulêsis*, being a desire, goes forward with it. And in fact we are in the habit of treating *bouulesthai* and *prohaireisthai* as signifying the same thing. For instead of saying 'I decide to farm my land' we say 'I wish (volo) to farm my land', and we say 'he has a good will (voluntas)', that is to say a good *prohairesis*.[27]

Aristotle, then, acknowledges, indeed insists, that *prohairesis* and *boulêsis* are both desires belonging to the rational part.

If this is right, then Aristotle's remarks about the character of *prohairesis* may help us to see whether *boulêsis* is an essentially rational desire. If acting on *boulêsis* is simply acting on a desire that has been causally influenced by some sort of reasoning, then any action resulting from deliberation should be action on *boulêsis*. But Aristotle denies this. For he insists that a *prohairesis* cannot result simply from deliberation about the satisfaction of a non-rational desire; the deliberation of an incontinent person about how to satisfy his appetites does not produce a *prohairesis*, and hence does not arise from *boulêsis*.[28] Action on *boulêsis* must be rational in some sense that goes beyond simply acting on deliberation about a non-rational desire; and so a *boulêsis* must be rational in some sense that goes beyond simply being influenced by deliberation. Aristotle's claims about the connexion between *prohairesis* and *boulêsis* tend to support Aquinas's view that Aristotle recognizes an essentially rational form of desire; and so Aquinas is justified in supposing that Aristotle recognizes the will.

The case against Aquinas rests especially on an interpretation of *EN* i 13 and a claim about its connexion to *De Anima* iii 9. In this chapter of the *EN* Aristotle distinguishes a part of the soul that 'has reason fully and within itself' (1103a2) from a part that is 'non-rational, but shares in a way in reason' (1102b13-14). This second part is also called 'appetitive, and in general desiring' (*epithumêtikon kai holôs orektikon*, 1102b30). Two interpretations of this remark have been suggested. (1) According to the anti-rationalist interpretation, Aristotle means to include all the desires mentioned in *De Anima* iii 9, including *boulêsis*, within the non-rational part; hence he recognizes no essentially rational desires.[29] (2) According to the rationalist interpretation, 'desiring' must indicate not that all desire is included in the non-rational part, but that the non-rational part is simply a desiring part (*haplôs orektikon*, as Aristotle might have put it), whereas the rational part is not simply a desiring part, but has distinctively rational desires. We need not, on this view, suppose that desire is confined to the non-rational part.[30] If the anti-rationalist interpretation of this chapter is correct, then Aristotle, at least sometimes, describes desire in terms that exclude any essentially rational desire of the sort that is required by Aquinas's conception of the will.

The anti-rationalist interpretation, however, cannot explain the argument of this chapter. For Aristotle takes incontinence as an example of conflict between the rational and the non-rational parts, remarking that in the incontinent person there is something that fights against and resists reason (1102b17-18). He sums this up by saying that 'the impulses (*hormai*) of incontinent people go in contrary directions' (1102b21).[31] Now one of these contrary impulses belongs to the non-rational part that is capable of obeying reason but fails to obey reason in the incontinent person. But the other impulse cannot also belong to the non-rational part that is capable of obeying reason; it must belong to the part that is rational in its own right. In recognizing an impulse proper to the rational part, Aristotle seems to recognize essentially rational desire.[32]

The difficulty of maintaining an anti-rationalist view of this chapter becomes especially clear if we consider Aquinas's own account of it; for, surprisingly, he accepts the anti-rationalist view, assuming that all desire belongs to the non-rational part that 'participates in a way in reason' (1102b13-14). Aquinas often appeals to this passage in support of his claim that the will is rational 'by participation' (*ST* 1-2 q56 a6 ad 2; q59 a4 ad 2; q61 a2c, ad 2; 2-2 q58 a4 ad 3). This claim is consistent with the claim that desires belonging to the will are essentially rational; in saying that the will is rational by participation Aquinas need only mean that it is rational in so far as it depends on rational beliefs and judgments, which are themselves rational in a more basic sense ('per essentiam', 1-2 q61 a2). Aquinas supposes that this conception of the will as rational by participation explains how Aristotle in *EN* i 13 could attribute all desire to the non-rational part.

This explanation, however, does not work. First Aquinas claims that 'the appetitive (*concupiscibilis*) power, and every desiring power, including the irascible power and the will, participate in some way in reason' (*in EN* §240). But at once he seems to contradict this claim. After remarking that the intellect is not subject to the actions of any bodily power, he says that the same is true of the will, 'which is in reason, as is said in *De Anima* iii' (§241). Having said this, however, he reverts to his first view, saying that one part of the soul, including both sensory desire and the will, is non-rational in its own right, but rational by participation (§242). It is difficult to see how the will can both be in the rational part and be non-rational in its own right.

Aquinas's attempt to understand the non-rational part as including the will is especially difficult to reconcile with his account of Aristotle's remarks on incontinence. For he sees that Aristotle means to attribute a correct decision to the rational part of both the continent and the incontinent person, and that the non-rational part 'obstructs reason, that is to say, impedes it in carrying out its decision (electio = *prohairesis*)' (§237); the obstructing element is sensory desire. Now Aquinas recognizes that decision is an act of the will (§486; *ST* 1a q83 a3; 1-2 q13 a1), and so he must agree that the incontinent person's sensory desire obstructs his will. If this is true, then one of the conflicting parts of the soul must include the will and the other must include sensory desire; hence Aristotle must take the rational part to include the will, and therefore to include rational desires. Aquinas's account of Aristotle's remarks on incontinence is quite correct, and it fits the rationalist rather than the anti-rationalist interpretation; and so it shows why the anti-rationalist interpretation of the division between the rational and non-rational parts is wrong, and why Aquinas should not have accepted it.

We must reach the same conclusion if we try to reconcile this passage with Aristotle's other remarks about psychic conflict and the virtues. He remarks elsewhere that decision is contrary to appetite (*epithumia*), but appetite is not contrary to appetite (1111b15-16), and that incontinent people act on appetite, but not on decision (1111b13-14), even though they make the correct decision (1151b6-7). In the incontinent person, then, appetite conflicts with decision, which is a desire based on *boulêsis*. Now in i 13 Aristotle describes the conflict in the incontinent person as a conflict between the rational and the non-rational part. This description is inconsistent with his view that the conflict is between appetite and decision, unless he claims that some desire (i.e. *boulêsis*) belongs to the rational part. The rationalist view, then, gives a better account of this chapter in relation to Aristotle's other remarks.

Moreover, the anti-rationalist view forces on Aristotle a conception of *boulêsis* that raises far-reaching difficulties for his theory of virtue. For if the anti-rationalist view recognizes no essentially rational desires, it must explain what makes a desire into a *boulêsis*. It must apparently say that we come to form desires that are attached to objects that we believe to be good. First, (we might suppose) we pursue things that seem to offer pleasure or reward rather than pain or punishment, but gradually we are habituated to pursue things that seem to be good rather than bad. Such a desire, however, may still be non-rational. If we have been correctly trained, we will be pleased with the thought that an action is good and fine; in fact this is how the temperate or brave person's non-rational desires react to the appropriate information. But these non-rational reactions do not count, in Aristotle's view, as expressions of *boulêsis* and *prohairesis*. For while he certainly agrees that we ought to form non-rational desires for things we believe to be good (1111a29-31), he does not suggest that every such desire is a *boulêsis*. The anti-rationalist view seems to oversimplify Aristotle's conception of the different sorts of desires that are present in a well-trained person.

The anti-rationalist view might be defended by appeal to the last part of *EN* i 13, where Aristotle uses his division of parts of the soul to mark the division between virtues of character and virtues of intellect (1103a3-10). The virtues of intellect clearly belong to the rational part, and do not essentially consist in well-ordered desires; well-ordered desires belong to the virtues of character. Does this not imply that all well-ordered desires, including those belonging to the will, belong to the non-rational part?[33]

We ought not to draw this conclusion; for Aristotle neither says nor implies that the virtues of character belong exclusively to the non-rational part. He believes that none of them is exclusively a virtue of the rational part, since all of them essentially include some appropriate training of non-rational desires (those belonging to spirit and appetite). But to say this is quite consistent with saying that the virtues of character are also virtues of the rational part, in so far as they include the right decision. There is no reason to deny that Aristotle ascribes the rational desires characteristic of right decision to the rational part. And so this passage does not after all suggest that Aristotle assigns all desires to the non-rational part.

I have discussed *EN* i 13 because it may appear to suggest that Aristotle attributes all desire to the non-rational part, and hence recognizes no essentially rational desire. If this is his view, then the rationalist interpretation that identifies *boulêsis* with the will is open to severe objection. I have tried to show, however, that the rationalist interpretation is quite defensible as the best account of Aristotle's various remarks about desire and action. Aquinas provides us with a good argument for attributing a concept of the will to Aristotle.

4. Voluntary Action and the Will

If we agree with Aquinas so far, we will agree that Aristotle attributes to *boulêsis* the properties that belong to the will, and hence that 'voluntas' is a good translation of '*boulêsis*'. It is a further question, however, whether Aquinas is right to claim that Aristotle regards the will as the source of 'voluntary' (*hekousion*)[34] actions, those that deserve praise and blame. If we disagree with Aquinas on this point, we need not reject his whole case for believing that Aristotle has a concept of the will; for the case rests primarily on Aquinas's view that *boulêsis* is essentially rational desire, and we have seen reasons for agreeing with that view. Still, it is worth seeing whether Aquinas is right in his claim about the role of the will in Aristotle's account of voluntary action; for it is often supposed that we must recognize the will if we are to understand free and responsible agency, and it is worth asking whether Aristotle appeals to the will for this purpose.

Aquinas's account of Aristotle on the will seems to raise a special difficulty for his account of Aristotle on the voluntary. For in identifying *boulêsis* with the will, he assumes a strict conception of the will as essentially rational desire, and in claiming that voluntary action involves the will he assumes the same strict conception of the will. He must show, then that Aristotle regards voluntary action as the product of essentially rational desire. If we suppose that Aquinas is right about the nature of *boulêsis* in Aristotle, ought we also to agree with his view that voluntary action essentially involves *boulêsis*?

It would be easy to agree with Aquinas, if we found that Aristotle takes *prohairesis* to be necessary for voluntary action; for *prohairesis* requires *boulêsis*, and (in the sense explained above) actually counts as *boulêsis* in contrast to non-rational desires. Aristotle, however, seems to deny that *prohairesis* is necessary for voluntary action. He describes voluntary action as what is done neither by force nor because of ignorance, where the origin of the action is in the agent (*EN* 1111a22-4). This description seems to cover many actions that are not produced by deliberation and decision. Indeed Aristotle remarks that animals and children act voluntarily, because they act on their desires neither by force nor because of ignorance; and so voluntariness is not confined to rational agents (1111a24-6, b8-9).

Aquinas, however, applies his strict conception of the will to his account of Aristotle on voluntary action. He analyses a voluntary action as the product of the will (*ST* 1-2 qq 8-17), so that his account of all voluntary action includes deliberation and decision among the mental antecedents of action. He does not abandon or modify these conditions to allow animals to act voluntarily; instead he claims that they act voluntarily only to a lower degree (q6 a2). This claim about two degrees of voluntariness is not present in Aristotle.[35]

Aquinas assumes that the voluntary is so called by reference to the will (voluntas) (q6 a2 obj 1), and so he infers that Aristotle takes voluntary action to involve the will. But this argument does not proceed as smoothly in Greek as it may seem to in Latin. For there is a clear apparent connexion in Aquinas's Latin between 'voluntarium' and 'voluntas', but there is no parallel connexion between '*hekousion*' and '*boulêsis*' in Aristotle's Greek; and so there is no reason to suppose that Aristotle must have assumed the connexion that leaps to Aquinas's eye. In fact Aristotle seems to take rational wish to be only one sort of desire that may initiate voluntary action.

Is Aquinas simply misled by Latin translations of Aristotle? This would not be a fair verdict on his claim that Aristotle's concept of *boulêsis* is a concept of the will; for Aquinas has good reasons for believing that the conventional translation conveys the right philosophical point. The same is true of his claims about the voluntary; he argues that Aristotle is committed to assuming some connexion between voluntary action and the will.

First, Aquinas assumes that voluntary actions are the proper focus of praise and blame (q6 a2 obj 3). Aristotle agrees with this, since he thinks voluntariness is sufficient for being open to praise or blame. Aquinas claims, however, that 'praise and blame follow on a voluntary action that is in accordance with the complete form (perfecta ratio) of the voluntary, the sort that is not found in beasts' (q6 a2 ad 3). He infers that non-rational agents do not have the complete form of voluntary action, since they are not open to praise and blame, and that when Aristotle attributes voluntary action to these agents, he must intend only an incomplete form of voluntary action (q6 a2).

How much of this must Aristotle accept? He apparently agrees that the actions of non-rational agents are not open to praise and blame in the same way as the actions of rational agents are.[36] To avoid saying that their acting voluntarily makes them candidates for praise and blame, he must either deny that voluntary action is sufficient for praise and blame or agree with Aquinas's claim that non-rational agents lack the complete form of voluntary action that is necessary for praise and blame. Since he does not suggest that voluntariness is insufficient for praise and blame, he has good reason to accept Aquinas's interpretation of him.

Why, then, does the 'complete form of the voluntary' that is necessary for praise and blame involve the will? The complete form of the voluntary requires the complete knowledge of the end, in which 'not only does one grasp the thing that is the end, but one also grasps the character (ratio) of the end and how the thing directed to the end is related to the end' (q6 a2). If we have this grasp of the end and the means, we can deliberate about the means, and as a result of deliberation we can pursue or refrain from pursuing the end. In claiming that praise and blame require this complete knowledge of the end, Aquinas assumes that they require the deliberative choice that is characteristic of the will. This is the sort of choice that is necessary if we are to be in control (domini) of our actions (q6 a2 ad 2).

How far does Aristotle accept these connexions between the voluntary, control, and deliberation? He believes that actions we are praised or blamed for are 'up to us' (eph'hêmin), and does not suggest that anything further besides voluntariness is necessary if an action is to be up to us. Indeed he argues that an action is up to us if the origin is in us (1110a15-18);[37] and he supposes that when we do an action voluntarily, we are in control (kurioi) of that action (1113b30-1114a3).

What, then, constitutes our control over our actions? Aquinas believes we have control to the extent that we can deliberate about our actions: 'for from the fact that deliberating reason is related to contraries, the will is capable of going in both directions' (q6 a2 ad 2). Praise and blame are appropriate for agents who deliberate, because their capacity to deliberate gives them control over their actions, and so allows them to modify their actions in response to praise and blame. Aquinas has a good reason, then, for claiming that the capacity for deliberation is an important condition for praise and blame, and therefore ought to be closely connected with voluntariness.

In marking this connexion between deliberation and control Aquinas follows Nemesius.[38] Aristotle says nothing so explicit; but he agrees in connecting deliberation with what is up to us (1112a30-1). He claims that it is reasonable to blame people who act wrongly because they are drunk and people who behave carelessly, even though they cannot help what they do when they are drunk and cannot help their careless behaviour. These people cannot plead that their inability to avoid what they did exempts them from blame; for, Aristotle insists, they were in control of not getting drunk and not becoming careless (1113b30-1114a7). Aristotle does not say that control consists in deliberative control; but it is reasonable to infer from the context that this is what he means.[39] For at the beginning of this discussion he refers back to his account of deliberation about means to ends, and of *boulêsis* for the end, and says that actions about means to ends are in accordance with decision and voluntary.[40] He infers that since the activities of the virtues are about means to ends, virtue and vice are up to us (1113b3-7). Here he answers in advance the question that arises later about why we are in control of not getting drunk or not being careless; he implies that it is because we can deliberate about the actions leading to these results. It is therefore difficult for Aristotle to resist Aquinas's claim that voluntary action requires deliberation and decision.

On the other hand, Aquinas's view does not seem to be Aristotle's unambiguous position. Both Aristotle and Aquinas believe that having the origin of x in me, having x up to me, doing x voluntarily, and being in control of x all seem to imply each other. But since Aristotle also believes that non-rational animals act voluntarily, he should infer that their actions are up to them; and elsewhere he suggests they this is indeed his view (*Phys.* 255a5-10). In that case they should also be in control of their actions; but Aquinas denies this. His denial does not contradict anything Aristotle actually says; for Aristotle never actually says that non-rational animals are in control of their actions. Still, Aquinas's view seems to conflict with the implications of Aristotle's remarks about the connexion between control and the other concepts used to describe voluntary action.

We have some reason to revise Aristotle's view in the direction taken by Aquinas, if we focus on the fact that Aristotle believes that control over our action is sufficient for being open to praise or blame for it. For he apparently ought to agree that if the source of our action were merely internal to us in the same way as it is internal to a non-rational animal, that would be insufficient for praise and blame; if it were sufficient for praise and blame, why would non-rational agents not be open to praise and blame?

Aristotle recognizes that there is no reason to blame people for actions caused by defects that result from nature or illness or injury, since these defects are not up to the agents (1114a21-31). It is not clear how many defects are excluded by this test.[41] But Aristotle ought to admit that some of the actions he means to exclude result from the agent's desires and not from external force, and so are no less voluntary than the actions of non-rational agents; actions resulting from insanity or sudden panic provide examples. If this degree of voluntariness is insufficient to warrant praise and blame, Aristotle ought to explain what further sort of control praiseworthy and blameworthy agents must have over their actions. He does not answer this question in general terms; but we have seen that when he defends his claim that virtue and vice are up to us, he appeals to the fact that the actions resulting in virtue and vice are open to deliberation. If we generalize this answer, Aristotle must say that praiseworthy and blameworthy agents have the relevant sort of control over their actions to the extent that they can deliberate about their actions. He must infer that non-rational animals lack this sort of control over their actions.

If Aristotle agrees with this, how ought he to modify his view about the connexions between control, being up to the agent, having the origin in the agent, and being voluntary? Aquinas suggests that non-rational agents act 'on their own initiative' (sua sponte) without being capable of the sort of voluntary action that depends on the will (*ST* 1-2 q6 a2; *in EN* §427; *De Ver* q24 a2 ad 1). Hence Aquinas apparently cannot believe that having an internal origin is sufficient for voluntary action. But Aristotle cannot reasonably believe this either. For the movements of plants and the purely nutritive movements of animals have an internal origin in so far as they are not the product of external force, but they are not voluntary movements. To argue that actions that have their origins in us are our voluntary actions, Aristotle must say that they have their origin properly in ourselves in so far as they have their origin in our will; these actions satisfy Aquinas's conditions for voluntariness.

Even if these are good reasons for agreeing with Aquinas's view that an Aristotelian account must regard the will as the source of voluntary action, there also seem to be good reasons for rejecting this view. Aristotle mentions 'sudden' actions as examples of voluntary actions that do not involve any decision (1111b9-10; see Aquinas, *in EN* §436; cf. Nemesius, *NH* 33.278); we just do them on the spur of the moment without any deliberation. Moreover, the incontinent person acts on appetite, but not on decision (*in EN* §439). This remark suggests, and Aristotle's account of incontinence explains further, that the incontinent acts voluntarily, but not on his decision. In these cases Aristotle clearly recognizes voluntary actions by rational agents, but insists that these actions are not products of decision. He does not explain why they are open to praise and blame, but he clearly assumes that they are.

It is important, then, for Aristotle to explain how we can be responsible for these actions that are not themselves the immediate product of a decision.

If he connects responsibility with the will, then he ought to be able to show how the will is engaged in these actions, even if they are not preceded by the most characteristic operations of the will. Aristotle does not take up this question directly, but Aquinas takes it up. His answer is too elaborate to be described fully here, but a few points will suggest the issues that it raises about Aristotle.

Aquinas recognizes a role for the will beyond actions produced by deliberation, by introducing some indirect effects of the will:

1. He remarks that we can be acting for the sake of an end without thinking about it all the time; 'for the power of the first aiming remains', even if we are not explicitly thinking about it (*ST* 1-2 q1 a6 ad 3).

2. He distinguishes directly voluntary from indirectly voluntary actions (q77 a7). A directly voluntary action is one towards which the will is moved; an indirectly voluntary action is one 'that the will was able to prohibit but does not prohibit'.

3. Voluntary action on passions requires the consent of the will (q15 a2; a4 ad 2), passions can influence the will in the direction of consenting (q9 a2; q77 a1). The incontinent person's will is engaged because he consents to the course of action favoured by his non-rational desires; hence he abandons his previous decision under the influence of passion.[42]

More needs to be said to clarify Aquinas's account, and to see how well it might fit Aristotle. But the account is relevant to our general question, since it shows how an appeal to the will helps to explain how these actions are indeed, as Aristotle claims, voluntary actions for which the agent can reasonably be praised or blamed. Aristotle remarks that instead of holding pleasant or fine things responsible for our actions, we should regard ourselves as the causes, as being 'an easy prey' to such things (1110b13-14). Aquinas paraphrases:

> ...it is ridiculous...not to accuse oneself on the ground that one makes oneself an easy prey, that is to say, permits oneself to be overcome by pleasant objects of this sort. For our will is not moved of necessity by such objects of desire, but it is capable of attaching itself to them and of not attaching itself to them. (*in EN* §403).

Aquinas takes the same view about Aristotle's claim that action on non-rational desires is voluntary (1111a29-31):

> For no matter how much anger or appetite grows, a human being does not rush into action, unless the consent of rational desire is added. Further, the first claim seems inappropriate in the same way, namely someone's saying that goods that one ought to desire in accordance with passion as well [as rational desire] are not voluntary. For reason leads us through will to desire

those things that we ought to. (*in EN* §428)

In both cases Aquinas's paraphrase implies that Aristotle's argument is really about the will.

Aristotle says nothing here about the role that Aquinas ascribes to the will. But unless he assumes something like Aquinas's explanation, his defence of his position is unsatisfactory. The mere fact that a desire is internal to the agent in the same way as it is internal to a non-rational animal is not enough for the agent to be justly praised or blamed for it. But if agents are capable of affecting their desires or their influence on their actions, then Aristotle's claim is reasonable.

These arguments do not prove that Aquinas is right to rely on his conception of the will to explain voluntary actions that are not the direct product of rational deliberation; nor do they prove that Aquinas offers the best explanation of Aristotle's view, or the most Aristotelian account that might be offered to supplement Aristotle. Still, his account is worth mentioning, to forestall an obvious objection. It is easy to see that Aristotle does not mention *boulêsis* or *prohairesis* in all the places where Aquinas introduces the will; but Aquinas may still be right to believe that Aristotle needs to introduce the will in these places. If Aquinas is right on this point, he is right to claim that Aristotle explains voluntary action by appeal to the will.

While Aquinas at first seemed to be mistaken in intruding his own concept of the will into Aristotle's discussion of voluntary action, further examination shows that he actually explains Aristotle's intention more clearly than Aristotle explains it himself. For some of Aristotle's claims about voluntary actions are difficult to defend unless Aristotle relies on something like Aquinas's concept of the will. We would not be justified in attributing such a concept to Aristotle simply to defend his remarks about the voluntary, if we did not have some further reason for attributing it to him; but his views about *boulêsis* give us the further reason we need.

5. The Role of a Concept of the Will

If, as I have suggested, Aquinas can offer a reasonable defence of the genuinely Aristotelian character of his account of the will, he has also given us a good reason for supposing that Aristotle has a concept of the will. If we accept this conclusion, however, can we use the concept of the will that we have found in Aristotle to answer the questions that seem to require a reference to the will?

Aquinas believes that a conception of the will as essentially rational desire identifies the sort of thing that Augustine refers to; he believes that it is a third element in rational choice besides belief and mere desire. Aquinas believes that we are capable of rational choice between our different desires in so far as we are capable of deliberation about them in the light of our views of the overall good, and capable of choice in accordance with the result of this deliberation. Our belief that we are free agents, not passive spectators of our current desires, is explained, in his view, by our belief that we have wills, understood as capacities for rational desire. For this reason Aquinas believes that Aristotle has a concept of the will, because Aristotle's conception of *boulêsis* is a conception of the sort of rational desire that can properly be identified with the will.

We might agree with Aquinas's claim that Aristotle's conception of *boulêsis* matches his own conception of the will, but still deny that this is really an adequate conception of the will. For we may argue that the rational desire for the good is simply one of the desires between which the will has to choose, so that it cannot be identified with the will. According to this 'voluntarist' criticism of Aquinas, the will must be independent of beliefs about the good, and we must conclude that Aquinas stays too close to Greek intellectualism. A defender of Aquinas's position will reply that the voluntarist attempt to free the rational will from dependence on beliefs about the good really leaves no plausible conception of a rational will at all; for (it is argued) the voluntarist view leaves the will with no basis for a free and rational choice once it is severed from any appeal to the overall good.

This dispute between voluntarism and intellectualism is clearly relevant to discussion of Aquinas's attempt to find a concept of the will in Aristotle. Indeed, some critics who claim that Greek philosophers have no concept of the will may really mean that they do not hold a voluntarist conception of the will. It would be both a historical and a philosophical mistake, however, to claim that Greek philosophers lack a concept of the will, if we simply mean that they are not voluntarists. For the debate between voluntarism and intellectualism is a debate between two views of the will, among disputants who share a concept of the will.

If we allow ourselves, as we should, to be influenced by the history of discussion about the will, we see that we miss part of the point of this discussion if we refuse to recognize a concept of the will in Greek philosophers. One of the main issues in disputes about the will is about the plausibility of an intellectualist conception of the will, of the sort that Aquinas defends. We miss the significance of this issue if we refuse to attribute any concept of the will to Aquinas; but if we admit that Aquinas has a concept of the will, and if we attend to his account of Aristotle, we must also attribute a concept of the will to Aristotle.[43]

Notes

1. W.D. Ross, *Aristotle* (London: Methuen, 5th ed., 1949), p. 199. Ross does not entirely agree with this complaint, since he believes that Aristotle's doctrine

of *prohairesis* is an attempt to formulate a conception of the will (though he does not think it is completely successful).

2. R.A. Gauthier and J.Y. Jolif, *Aristote: L'Éthique à Nicomaque* (Louvain: Publications Universitaires, 2nd ed., 4 vols., 1970), Commentary, p. 218.

3. A.C. MacIntyre, *Three Rival Versions of Moral Enquiry* (Notre Dame: Notre Dame UP, 1990), p. 111.

4. See N.W. Gilbert, 'The concept of the will in early Latin philosophy', *Journal of the History of Philosophy* 1 (1963), pp. 17-35.

5. This is MacIntyre's view. It is defended at length by A. Dihle, *The Theory of the Will in Classical Antiquity* (Berkeley: U. of California Press, 1982). See also C.H. Kahn, 'Discovering the will', in *The Question of 'Eclecticism'*, ed. J.M. Dillon and A.A. Long (Berkeley: U. of California Press, 1985), ch. 9.

6. See Gauthier, Introduction, pp. 262-6.

7. Dihle's failure to identify the relevant issues is justly remarked in C.A. Kirwan's review, *Classical Review* 34 (1984), pp. 335-6. Among the other writers I have mentioned, Gauthier describes the issues most clearly.

8. This statement of the case is derived from Gauthier.

9. This is an inadequate account of Plato (in the *Republic*) and Aristotle; some of its inadequacies will be suggested by my later remarks about Aristotle. But it captures one apparent aspect of their view that provides a contrast with Socrates.

10. See *De Duab. Anim.* 14: Nobis autem voluntas nostra notissima est; neque enim scirem me velle, si quid sit voluntas ipsa nescirem. Definitur itaque isto modo: voluntas est animi motus cogente nullo ad aliquid vel non amittendum vel adipiscendum.

11. *De Lib. Arb.* iii 3: non enim quidquam tam firme atque intime sentio, quam me habere voluntatem, eaque me moveri ad aliquid fruendum; quid autem meum dicam prorsus non invenio, si voluntas qua volo et nolo non est mea; quapropter cui tribuendum est, si quid per illam male facio, nisi mihi? Cum enim bonus Deus me fecerit, nec bene aliquid faciam nisi per voluntatem, ad hoc potius datum esse a bono Deo, satis apparet. Motus autem quo huc aut illuc voluntas convertitur, nisi esset voluntarius, atque in nostra positus potestate, neque laudandus cum ad superiora, neque culpandus homo esset cum ad inferiora detorquet quasi quemdam cardinem voluntatis... .
    See also *Conf.* vii 5: ...liberum voluntatis arbitrium causam esse, ut male faceremus... . Sublevabat enim me in lucem tuam, quod tam sciebam me habere voluntatem quam me vivere. Itaque cum aliquid vellem aut nollem, non alium quam me velle ac nolle certissimus eram et ibi esse causam peccati mei iam iamque animadvertebam.

12. *Lib. Arb.* i 21: Nothing external can make a mind subject to sin: nulla res alia mentem cupiditatis comitem faciat, quam propria voluntas et liberum arbitrium. Cf. iii 2: [it is agreed that] nulla re fieri mentem servam libidinis, nisi propria voluntate.

13. See *CD* xiv 6: Interest autem qualis sit voluntas hominis; quia si perversa est, perversos habebit hoc motus; si autem recta est, non solum inculpabiles, verum etiam laudabiles erunt. Voluntas est quippe in omnibus; immo omnes nihil aliud quam voluntates sunt. Nam quid est cupiditas et laetitia nisi voluntas in eorum consensione quae volumus? Et quid est metus atque tristitia nisi voluntas in dissensione ab his quae nolumus? Cf. xiv 9: the citizens of the city of God still have affections; et qua rectus est amor eorum, istas omnes adfectiones rectas habent.

14. At *ST* 1-2 q55 a1 obj 2, Aquinas attributes Augustine's description of virtue as

'bonus usus liberi arbitrii' to *Lib. Arb*. ii. The words do not actually appear there, though they are a fair summary of ii 51. In fact they are Augustine's own summary in *Retrac*. i 9.6: ...in mediis quidem bonis invenitur liberum voluntatis arbitrium, quia et male illo uti possumus; sed tamen tale est, ut sine illo recte vivere nequeamus. Bonus enim usus eius virtus est, qui in magnis reperitur bonis, qua male uti nullus potest.

15. On the relation of love to will see *Trin*. xv 41, describing the Holy Spirit: De spiritu autem sancto nihil in hoc aenigmate quod ei simile videretur ostendi nisi voluntatem nostram, vel amorem seu dilectionem quae valentior est voluntas, quoniam voluntas nostra quae nobis naturaliter inest sicut ei res adiacuerint vel occurrerint quibus allicimur aut offendimur ita varias affectiones habet.

16. *CD* xv 22: Unde mihi videtur, quod definitio brevis et vera virtutis ordo est amoris. Cf. xiv 7: Recta itaque voluntas est bonus amor et voluntas perversa malus amor.

17. On the connexion of wills for means and ends see *Trin*. xi 10: Rectae enim sunt voluntates et omnes sibimet religatae si bona est illa quo cunctae referuntur; si autem prava est, pravae sunt omnes. Et ideo rectarum voluntatum conexio iter est quoddam ascendentium ad beatitudinem quod certis velut passibus agitur; pravarum autem atque distortarum voluntatum implicatio vinculum est quo alligabitur qui hoc agit ut proiiciatur in tenebras exteriores.

18. On the will as applying other mental capacities to a situation see *Trin*. xi 15: Voluntas porro sicut adiungit sensum corpori, sic memoriam sensui, sic cogitantis aciem memoriae. Quae autem conciliat ista atque coniungit, ipsa etiam disiungit et separat, id est voluntas.

19. For the translation see Cicero, *Tusculan Disputations*, iv 12, translating the Stoic term in (e.g.) Diogenes Laertius, vii 116. The mss. here read 'nos appellamus voluntatem', suggesting that Cicero is drawing attention to an established usage of 'voluntas' rather than coining or adapting (as he often does) a term in a special Stoic sense. R.M. Henry (in T.W. Dougan and R.M. Henry (edd.), *Tusculan Disputations*, vol. 2 [Cambridge: Cambridge University Press, 1934], ad loc.) prefers the emendation 'appellemus' on grounds that strike me as doubtful. The fact that Cicero regularly uses the subjunctive for coinages and adaptations does not imply that he should use the subjunctive in this passage; for it is open to dispute whether he is announcing a coinage or simply describing ordinary usage.

20. Hence 'wish' is perhaps the least unsatisfactory uniform translation of '*boulêsis*' in Aristotle. Normally, however, I will leave the term untranslated.

21. Voluntas nominat rationalem appetitum, *ST* 1-2 q6 a2 ad 1. Cf. 1a q81 a1; 87.4; 1-2, q6 introd.; q8 a1. I use 'desire' for 'appetitus', since Aquinas uses 'appetitus' to translate '*orexis*'. This can easily cause confusion, since one way of characterizing will distinguishes it from desire. But 'appetite' seems even less suitable, except on etymological grounds. I use 'appetite' to translate '*epithumia*' (for which Aquinas uses 'concupiscentia').

22. This might be the point of describing *boulêsis* as a 'desire without pain' (*Topics* 146a36-b6); Aristotle does not, however, accept this description as an adequate definition of *boulêsis*. The same conception of *boulêsis* may explain why Aristotle in one passage allows children to have *boulêsis*, as well as other forms of desire, before they acquire reason (*Politics* 1334b17-25).

23. As Gauthier puts it (Commentary, pp. 193-4), 'For the scholastics, the will is precisely a rational desire, in the sense that it is an activity of the rational soul, which possesses in itself a desiring faculty distinct from the irrational desiring faculty—an idea totally foreign to Aristotle.' In Gauthier's view, Aristotle consistently treats *boulêsis* as a movement of the desiring part of the soul, and

hence of a non-rational part, which becomes rational, 'in obeying the voice of reason, allowing itself to be moulded by the rule pronounced by reason'. Gauthier finds support in Alexander, *De Anima*, 74.6-13.

24. 434a11-14 is a notoriously difficult passage. I think Ross (in his Oxford Classical Text [Oxford: Clarendon Press, 1956]) goes too far, however, in accepting an emendation that omits *tên boulêsin* altogether. Though it is missing in three mss., it is not an obvious gloss, since *boulêsis* has not been mentioned in the immediate context. Moerbeke translates as though he had read *bouleusin* instead of *boulêsin*, and Aquinas assumes this in his commentary, §843. If he had found a reference to *boulêsis*, and hence to voluntas, he might have had some difficulty in explaining how an agent's voluntas could be overcome in incontinent action.

25. Hence some are inclined to identify the will with *prohairesis* rather than with *boulêsis*. See Ross, *Aristotle*, p. 200; J. Burnet, *The Ethics of Aristotle* (London: Methuen, 1900) p. 109; G. Rodier, *Aristote: Traité de l'âme* (Paris: Leroux, 1900), p. 532.

26. Or 'the most important part of *prohairesis*' (*to kuriôtaton tês prohaireseôs*).

27. *Commentaria in Aristotelem Graeca* vol. 19, ed. C.G. Heylbut (Berlin: Reimer, 1889), 68.27-32. Unfortunately the Greek has a lacuna in the last sentence. The translation of the sentence is based (see Heylbut's app. crit.) on Felicianus' Latin translation, which uses 'velle' and 'voluntas' where the Greek presumably has 'boulesthai' and 'boulêsis'.

28. See 1113a12. I incline, following Gauthier, to read *kata tên boulêsin*, as the lectio difficilior. *DA* 434a12 is another place where an original ms. reading *boulêsin* may have been corrupted into *bouleusin*. For the relation of *prohairesis* to *boulêsis* see also 1113b3-5, and on the deliberation of the incontinent person see 1142b17-20.

29. This view about the broad scope of *holôs orektikon* is accepted by J.A. Stewart, *Notes on Aristotle's Ethics* (Oxford: Clarendon Press, 1892), ad loc., and by Burnet, *Aristotle's Ethics*. Curiously, it is rejected by Gauthier, even though he accepts the anti-rationalist line that requires the broad scope; he takes Aristotle to be alluding only to *thumos* as well as *epithumia*, not to *boulêsis* as well (though he gives no reason for his view).

30. Some of the Greek commentators show that they take the non-rational part to consist only of *epithumia* and *thumos*. See Heliodorus, *Commentaria*, vol. 19, 24.20; Aspasius, 35.22, 36.2 (*to orektikon kai pathêtikon*); Eustratius, *Commentaria*, vol. 20, 118.33-5. They do not discuss the role of *boulêsis*. It is mentioned, however in Eustratius, 116.11-12: *houtô kai epi tês psuchês epi ta beltiô tou logou tas alogous dunameis kinein boulomenou...* .

31. An alternative translation is: 'the impulses of incontinent people go in directions contrary [to the instructions of the rational part].' This is the view of (apparently) Aquinas (§237), Burnet, and F. Dirlmeier, *Aristoteles: Nikomachische Ethik* (Berlin: Akademie-Verlag, 1969). Stewart's view is not clear. I follow the interpretation of Gauthier (who again fails to recognize the damage it apparently does to his anti-rationalist view). His view, taking 'contrary' to mean 'contrary to each other' rather than 'contrary to the instruction of the rational part', fits better with the immediately preceding illustration of the movements of partly paralysed bodies, and makes better sense of the plural in *hormai*.

32. Gauthier argues that the use of '*hormê*' belongs to a stage of Aristotle's thought at which he did not yet use '*orexis*' as a generic term for all desire, but confined it to non-rational desire. I doubt whether Gauthier is right to rely on a chronological hypothesis here; but if he is right to claim that '*hormê*' is the generic term for

desire, of which 'orektikon' indicates two of the three species, the passage actually seems to be good evidence for the rationalist view that Gauthier rejects. (Gauthier's reference to boulêsis at the top of p. 96 shows how the rationalist view might be defended.)

33. This seems to be the view of Aquinas, in EN §243.

34. I use 'voluntary' to translate 'hekousion', without meaning to beg any question in favour of Aquinas's view.

35. This claim about a lower degree of voluntariness also applies to children. But it needs to be modified, as Aquinas realizes, to account for the gradual acquisition of reason, and hence of free choice, in children. See 1a q99 a1; q101 a2; 3a q80 a9 ad 3.

36. In EN iii 1-5 Aristotle does not explicitly deny that non-rational animals are open to praise and blame. But none of his remarks about praise and blame suggest that he has animals in mind as appropriate candidates. All his remarks suggest that praise and blame mark the agent's degree of virtue or vice; indeed, the voluntary and involuntary are mentioned because they are relevant to praise and blame, which is relevant to virtue (1109b30-5). The virtues of character and intellect are introduced as praiseworthy states (1103a8-10), and Aristotle suggests that when we praise a person for good actions we are actually praising his virtue (1101b12-18, 31-4). In EN vii Aristotle insists that animals are incapable of virtue or vice (1149b30-1150a1) or incontinence (1147b3-5); and in his ethical works he never suggests that agents incapable of these conditions could be open to praise or blame. Similarly, his account of praise in Rhetoric i 9 is about praise of the virtues of rational agents. He mentions the possibility of some sort of praise of 'things without souls and any at all of the other animals' (Rhet. 1366a30), but he clearly distinguishes this from the sort of praise that is appropriate for virtue. (For examples of the other sorts of praise alluded to here see E.M. Cope, Aristotle's Rhetoric [Cambridge: Cambridge University Press, 1877], ad loc.) If we sought to describe a reduced sense of 'praise' in which it would be appropriate for animals, it would be reasonable to appeal to something like Aquinas's notion of a lower degree of voluntariness.

37. Since Moerbeke translates 'eph' hêmin' by 'in nobis', Aquinas does not notice that a move from 'the origin of x is en hêmin' to 'x is eph' hêmin' is as non-trivial as it seems to be in Aristotle. But if Aquinas had noticed this, he would have had another argument for the line of interpretation he favours. In fact his paraphrase brings out Aristotle's claim better than Moerbeke's translation does: Ea autem quae fiunt ex principio intrinseco sunt in potestate hominis ut ea operetur vel non operetur, quod pertinet ad rationem voluntarii (§391).

In saying that Aristotle takes x's having its origin in me to imply x's being up to me, I am speaking only of the EN. I think the claim is defensible for the EE too; but the question is more complicated.

38. See Nemesius, De Natura Hominis, ed. M. Morani (Leipzig: Teubner, 1987), 325-6 = p.117.23-118.1.

39. Aquinas quite reasonably takes Aristotle to be considering control exercised by the will (§508).

40. Aquinas takes Aristotle to mean that the activities of the virtues are voluntary because they are in accordance with decision. ('...sint secundum electionem, et per consequens sint voluntaria. Quia electio voluntarium est, ut supra dictum est', §496.)

41. In EN vii 5 Aristotle lists 'bestial' pleasures that appeal not only to people with diseased natures, but also to those who have suffered from 'morbid' conditions

that result from bad habits. He regards all these conditions as outside the area of virtue and vice (1148b15-1149a1). Though it is sometimes up to us to prevent ourselves from acting on these morbid impulses, Aristotle does not suggest that it is up to us to acquire them; but he could not reasonably deny that our desires play a crucial role in our acquiring the impulses.

42. See 1-2 q6 a7 ad 2-3; q6 a8; q77 a2; 2-2 q155 a3; q156 a1.

43. I have benefited from comments on a version of this paper read at the Institute for Classical Studies, London, and especially from remarks by Richard Sorabji, Myles Burnyeat, Norman Kretzmann, and Gail Fine.

GOD'S OBLIGATIONS

Eleonore Stump
University of Notre Dame

Introduction

The notion that God has no moral obligations is not new in the history of philosophical theology; it was apparently held by Duns Scotus, for example.[1] But in recent times it has been forcefully revived by William Alston. In "Some Suggestions for Divine Command Theorists,"[2] Alston holds that God has no moral obligations, that there is never anything God ought to do or ought to bring about, that it is never true to say of God that he ought not to act in a certain way. This is a view which has profound implications for philosophical theology, and the fact that it is defended by Alston only enhances its significance for current discussion in philosophy of religion. In this instance, however, my own intuitions are opposed to Alston's. I find it altogether natural to say that God has a moral obligation not to lie to his creatures, that God ought to keep his promises, that God ought not to betray those who trust in him.

In earlier discussions of this issue with Alston, I put forward as an objection to his position the claim that if God were to break his promise to one of his creatures, he would be doing what he ought not to do. In his article, Alston replies that my objection shows only that "'ought' would be applicable to God under certain counterfactual conditions (indeed counterpossible conditions if God is essentially perfectly good), not that 'ought' is applicable to Him as things are" (265). Alston does recognize the point, of course: if God makes promises or covenants, then he is subject to obligations, since, as Alston observes, "the very concept of a promise or of a covenant involves engendering obligations" (265). But he holds that we ought to take biblical talk of God's promises and covenants as analogical or metaphorical speech. The literal truth behind such speech is just that God expresses an intention to act in certain ways, and we can rely on God's intentions. I think, on the other hand, that the conviction that God does really make promises and does really enter into covenants with his creatures is strong and widely held among many reflective religious people; I myself would be reluctant to give it up. Making promises to a person produces a bond to that person which the sheer expression of intentions, however reliable, cannot produce.

So my intuitions and inclinations are strongly against the claim that God has no moral obligations, and they are not weakened by Alston's arguments to the contrary. In this paper, I will examine those arguments, and I will try to account for the differences between my intuitions and Alston's.

Arguments Alston Rejects

It is helpful to consider first a couple of arguments which support Alston's claim, but which he himself finds inadequate.

Here is the first one. (I) "The position [that God has no moral obligations] has been argued for from the premise that God lacks 'significant moral freedom'. It is assumed that terms of the 'morally ought' family apply to a being only if that being has a choice between doing or failing to do what it ought to do. But if God is *essentially* perfectly good, as I shall be assuming in this essay, it is, in the strongest way, impossible for God to fail to do what is right. Therefore it can't be correct to speak of God's duties or of what He ought to do. I am not happy with this line of argument" (p. 257). God might act from the necessity of his nature, Alston says, and yet be acting freely "in a way that is required for moral obligation". In other words, Alston assumes that the ability to act freely is required for being subject to moral obligation, but he rejects the claim that the ability to do otherwise is required for acting freely. This position seems to me entirely right. Freedom does seem a prerequisite for moral obligation, but the extensive discussion in recent literature of Frankfurt-type counterexamples to the principle of alternate possibilities seems to me abundantly persuasive that the ability to do otherwise is not a general or universal prerequisite for freedom.[3]

Here is the second argument Alston considers and rejects: (II) "we can point to the conditions under which it is appropriate to use these terms ['ought', 'obligation', and so on].To the extent that we think there is no possibility of S's failing to do A, we don't tell him that he ought to do A or speak of S's duty or obligation to do A...the possibility of deviation is a necessary condition of the applicability of terms in the 'ought' family" (258). Argument I depended on supposing that since God doesn't have the ability to do otherwise with respect to moral actions, he isn't free; on that basis, it claims that God doesn't have moral obligations. Argument II depends on supposing that since God doesn't have the ability to do otherwise with respect to moral actions, terms of moral obligation aren't appropriately applied to him; for that reason, it claims that God doesn't have moral obligations. Alston rejects Argument II also, on the grounds that we can't infer the absence of moral obligation from the inappropriateness of invoking moral terminology. He says, "it may be inappropriate to say something, or to say it with a certain illocutionary force, that is, nevertheless, perfectly true. ...Utter dependability [with respect to performing moral actions]...does not cancel obligations but merely ensures their fulfillment" (259).

Both these arguments have at their heart the claim that God cannot do otherwise than he does with respect to moral actions. The first argument invalidly infers from this claim that God is not free, and on that basis infers that God has no moral obligations. The second argument infers from this claim that it is pointless to use moral terminology of God and on that basis invalidly infers that God has no moral obligations. So Alston is right to reject both these arguments.

Alston's Argument

Alston explains that he himself doesn't have a "knockdown" argument for his claim that God has no moral obligations. He thinks that the "possibility of deviation" is one of the most fundamental and obvious features of moral obligation, and it is something which doesn't apply to God. I do not share his view about the connection between the possibility of deviation and moral obligation. It seems to me that *freedom* is one of the most fundamental and obvious requirements for moral obligation, but I am persuaded, as I have argued at length elsewhere,[4] that the ability to do otherwise is not required for freedom. So although freedom seems to me essential to moral responsibility, the possibility of deviation does not.

Although he doesn't think he has a conclusive argument for his claim that God has no moral obligations, Alston thinks he can support it with considerations of this sort.

In the first place, he makes a distinction between what is morally good and what is morally obligatory. This is a familiar distinction, which gives rise to the notion of the supererogatory. Giving all of one's goods to the poor is morally good but hardly obligatory; a person who does so has done something supererogatory.

Given this distinction, Alston asks what we have to add to the notion of morally good to get moral obligation, and he answers his question in this way: "One thing required for my having an obligation to do A...is that there are general principles, laws, or rules that lay down conditions under which that action is required. ...Call them 'practical rules (principles)'. Practical principles are in force, in a nondegenerate way, with respect to a given population of agents only if there is at least a possibility of their playing a governing or regulative function: and this is possible only where there is a possibility of agents in that population violating them" (262). He goes on to spell out what he means in some detail: "[where there is a possibility of agents' violating practical principles] behavior can be guided, monitored, controlled, corrected, criticized, praised, blamed, punished, or rewarded on the basis of the principles. There will be social mechanisms for inculcating and enforcing the rules, positive and negative sanctions that encourage compliance and discourage violation. Psychologically, the principles will be internalized in higher-level control mechanisms that monitor behavior and behavioral tendencies and bring motivational forces to bear in the direction of compliance and away from violation. ...I take it that terms like 'ought', 'duty', and 'obligation' acquire a use only against this kind of background, and that their application presupposes that practical principles are playing, or at least can play, a regulative role, socially and/or psychologically" (263).

Because God is essentially perfectly good, so that there is no metaphysical possibility of his doing what he ought not to do, such general moral principles have no regulative force for him. Therefore, moral terms do not apply to him. Alston says, "the closest we can get to a moral law requiring God to love others is the conjunction of the evaluative statement that it is a good thing for God to love others, plus the statement that God necessarily does so" (263).

Problems with Alston's Argument

What about this argument for the claim that God has no moral obligations? I have two different sorts of worries about it.

(i) God and Supererogation

Alston begins his argument with the familiar distinction between moral goodness and moral obligation; some morally good actions are not obligatory but supererogatory. It is, of course, possible that there might be some other way of driving a wedge between moral goodness and moral obligation besides the supererogatory, but Alston himself provides no clue about what that alternate way might be. If it is the case that the only way to pry moral goodness and moral obligation apart is by means of the supererogatory, then Alston's account runs into problems at the outset, because it isn't clear that the category of the supererogatory can be applied to a being who is omniscient, omnipotent, and supremely good.[5]

When an action is supererogatory for a person, it is so at least in part because although the action may be good, it makes a call upon her resources or her strength (including her spiritual strength or strength of character) which we feel no one has a right to demand of her, and which it isn't morally wrong of her to decline. It might be morally good of her to give all she has to the poor, but no one has a right to demand of her that she impoverish herself in that way; and if she fails to give all she has to the poor, she won't have acted in ways she ought not to act. God's resources, on the other hand, are infinite; he can never exhaust them, in the way that a human person can if she gives all she has to the poor. What counts as supererogatory for God then?

I certainly don't mean to deny that God sometimes does a great deal more good than anyone has any right to ask of him, but this claim by itself doesn't show that God does supererogatory acts, unless we suppose that rights and obligations are always correlative. If they are correlative, then when God gives a person some good the person has no right to, God is engaging in an act which is morally good but not morally obligatory to do, that is, a supererogatory act. But there are reasons for thinking that obligations and rights are not correlative in this way.

In the first place, there are some intuitive reasons for supposing that rights and obligations can be pried apart. Consider mercy, for example. Mercy is giving people more than they deserve or have a right to. But, as every parent knows, there are times in dealing with human persons when it seems as if it would be morally wrong not to act out of mercy. If justice would cement an adolescent in rebellion but mercy would soften his angry heart and restore him to civilized society, then (other things being equal) it seems morally wrong not to employ mercy in dealing with him. Forgiveness is a similar sort of case. Consider the man who tried to assassinate the Pope. It seems counter-intuitive to suppose that he has a right to be forgiven. But if he is sincerely repentant and pleads earnestly for forgiveness, then (other things being equal) it seems that the Pope *ought* to forgive him and would be worthy of moral blame if he did not forgive him. So in the case of both mercy and forgiveness, it appears that a person A can be obligated to treat a person B in a certain way, even though B has no correlative rights against A.[6]

There are also theoretical reasons for supposing that rights and obligations are not always correlative. For example, Onora O'Neill has recently argued that we sometimes have obligations to perform or omit an act for unspecified others but not all others, and that in such a case there are no corresponding rights.[7] Furthermore, allowing obligations without rights helps explain some oddities in contemporary ethical theory. For example, the peculiar categories of the "quasi-obligatory," the suberogatory, and acts of offence are easier to understand if we are willing to separate rights and obligations.[8]

The quasi-obligatory is supposed to be the category of actions which are not obligatory to do but nonetheless morally substandard to omit. Examples of the quasi-obligatory include small acts of kindness to which the recipients have no right, e.g., giving up one's seat to a pregnant woman on a crowded bus.[9] The line between acts which are quasi-obligatory and those which are supererogatory is not always easy to find. For example, is giving a certain small percentage of one's income to charitable causes supererogatory or quasi-obligatory? Suberogatory acts are described as those acts which it is morally praiseworthy not to do but not morally obligatory not to do. It is, for example, morally praiseworthy not to spread to one's neighbors the delicious story of a colleague's imbecility in a public meeting, but it is apparently not morally obligatory not to disseminate the story since the self-disgracing colleague has no right to confidentiality. Actions falling into categories of this sort can seem puzzling since they suggest that there can be actions which agents ought not to do but which they aren't obligated not to do.[10] Finally, acts of offence are acts which are morally blameworthy to do but not morally obligatory not to do. It is morally blameworthy to insist on the timely repayment of a loan when you have no need of the money and the debtor is in financial straits, but it is apparently not morally obligatory not to require repayment at the appointed time since the debtor has no right to an extension on his loan.[11] This category seems even more counter-intuitive than the category of the suberogatory since it is hard to understand how an act can be genuinely blameworthy but also permissible.

But if we are willing to separate rights and obligations, the problems with these peculiar categories of actions are alleviated. Obligation is not exhausted by meeting the demands of rights; there can be obligations even where there are no rights. On this view, we can take the quasi-obligatory as the category of actions which are morally obligatory to do but which are not required to be done by anyone's rights. They are then appropriately distinguished from supererogatory acts, which are morally praiseworthy to do but not morally obligatory. Furthermore, suberogatory acts and acts of offence can be collapsed into one group, the category of acts which are morally obligatory not to do but which are not required not to be done by anyone's rights. Understood in this way, these categories seem considerably less counter-intuitive. For example, we no longer have to ask in connection with the category of acts of offence how there can be acts for which an agent is morally blameworthy even though he is not morally obligated to omit them. The simplicity resulting from collapsing the categories of acts of offence and suberogatory acts also seems a gain since the difference between what is praiseworthy not to do and what is blameworthy to do is not so easy to see.[12]

So there are some theoretical as well as intuitive reasons for supposing that rights and obligations are separable. And if they are, then from the fact that God is merciful or gives people more than they have a right to, it won't follow that the supererogatory applies to him.

But perhaps there are other reasons for supposing that the supererogatory applies to God. Perhaps in creating a world as good as the world God creates, God engages in acts of supererogation. But I think that even with respect to creation there are reasons for doubting whether the supererogatory applies to God. It might be true, as Robert Adams has argued,[13] that in not doing some sorts of good actions, say, in not creating the best of all possible worlds, God wrongs no one or violates no one's rights. But if rights and obligations are separable, as I have been arguing, then it won't follow from this claim that God can do supererogatory actions. He might be obligated to do certain good actions even if no one has a right to have God perform such actions. And it certainly seems true that we can feel moral revulsion even at actions which violate no rights. Consider, for example, a case drawn from George Eliot's *Middlemarch*. Think about the moral revulsion we feel at Bulstrode's refusal to help Lydgate in his hour of need, even though Lydgate has no right to Bulstrode's help and in fact deserves to be in the financial straits that drive him to Bulstrode. At least part of what prompts our strong moral disapproval is not that Lydgate has a right to Bulstrode's help which Bulstrode ought to acknowledge, but rather just that Bulstrode's help would cost Bulstrode so little and do Lydgate so much good, so that it seems wrong of Bulstrode to refuse.

Someone might suppose that if there is no best of all possible worlds, then God might be obligated to create worlds only up to a certain threshold of goodness; creating any world containing good above that threshold would then be a supererogatory act for God.[14] Aquinas thought that the notion of the best of all possible worlds was ambiguous between (1) a world whose entities are ordered in the best possible way, and (2) a world which has the greatest number of good entities. Since good entities can be multiplied indefinitely, Aquinas thought that in sense (2) there was no best of all possible worlds and also no obligation to create the best of all possible worlds in that sense. Furthermore, on his view, an agent doesn't gain in moral goodness just in virtue of introducing more good entities into the world; an agent who produces a world with $n+1$ good entities is not thereby morally better than an agent who produces a world with just n good entities, other things being equal. On sense (2) God doesn't have an obligation to produce worlds up to a certain level of moral goodness, and he doesn't gain in moral goodness by producing worlds above that threshold. As for sense (1), Aquinas thinks that it is possible that a world be best in this sense, and he thinks that God does have an obligation to produce a best possible world of this sort. So on either understanding of best possible world, the supererogatory doesn't apply to God in creation. I think Aquinas's way of looking at this issue is basically correct.[15]

So it's hard for me to comprehend how the notion of the supererogatory, as distinct from the generous or the merciful, applies to God.[16] While we may have no rights to many of the good things which God is said to do for us, the failure of an omnipotent and omniscient being to do such things might well fill us with some moral revulsion or inspire us to attribute some moral blame. If the notion of supererogatory acts can't be applied to God, however, then in God's case we can't drive the wedge Alston wants between moral goodness and moral obligatoriness. Failing some other proposal for separating moral goodness from moral obligation, we can't suppose that moral goodness can be attributed to God while moral obligatoriness cannot.[17]

But this trouble with Alston's argument seems to me, in the end, not as significant as other problems it has. So, for the sake of argument, suppose that I am wrong on this score. Suppose that the category of the supererogatory does after all apply to God, or suppose that there is some other way besides the supererogatory to divide moral goodness from moral obligation and that this way can be applied to God. In that case Alston will be right to hold that moral goodness and moral obligation are different, in God's case as well as in ours. But now some other and more worrisome problems with the argument emerge.

(ii) The Soundness of Alston's Argument

Alston says that (A) one requirement of an agent's having a moral obligation to do an action is that there are "general principles, laws, or rules that lay down conditions under which that action is required" (262). (A) seems right. A person has a moral obligation not to break promises, for example, only if there is a general moral principle specifying that breaking promises is morally wrong and laying down the conditions under which keeping promises is required. Why is it that Alston thinks this requirement isn't met in God's case? The main reason is that, on his view, (B) general moral principles are in force only in case they play a governing or regulative function; and (C) they can play a governing or regulative function only in case it is possible that agents might violate them.

So I take Alston's argument here to have something of this form:

(A) An agent has a moral obligation to do an action only if there is a general moral principle laying down conditions under which that action is required.

(B) A general moral principle is in force only if it plays a governing or regulative role.

(C) A general moral principle plays a governing or regulative role for agents only if it is possible that they violate that principle.

(D) It isn't possible that God violate any general moral principle.

(E) Therefore, God doesn't have any moral obligations.

Clearly, this argument assumes that there *is* a general moral principle laying down conditions under which an action is required only if that general moral principle is *in force*. Is that assumption right? The answer depends on how we interpret Alston's (B).

We can think about the notion of a principle's playing a governing role or having a regulative function in two different ways. We might suppose that

(B1) a moral principle is in force only if it morally governs or morally regulates action; that is, we might suppose that a moral principle that is in force is one which is not overridden or abrogated by something in the circumstances. Aquinas, for example, thinks that the moral principle which says that adultery is wrong is always in force, but he doesn't feel the same way about the principle that taking someone else's property is wrong. In extreme cases, in which the human convention that some created things belong to a particular human person might result in the death of other people, the principle that taking someone else's property is wrong is abrogated;[18] in such circumstances, we might say, the principle is no longer in force.

This sense of a principle's being in force is not, however, the sense Alston has in mind. He seems to think a moral principle is in force only if it governs or regulates action in a practical way; that is, a moral principle is in force only if there are "social mechanisms for inculcating and enforcing the rules, positive and negative sanctions that encourage compliance and discourage violation. Psychologically, the principles will be internalized in higher-level control mechanisms that monitor behavior and behavioral tendencies and bring motivational forces to bear in the direction of compliance and away from violation" (262). In this sense, then, (B2) a moral principle is in force only if it plays a social and psychological role in controlling behavior.[19]

If we understand (B) as (B2), then we need to take (C) in the corresponding sense as (C2): (C2) moral principles play a social and psychological role in controlling behavior only if it is possible for agents to violate those principles. (C2) seems true. In this sense of a principle's being in force, it seems quite right to say that a principle can be in force with respect to certain agents only in case it is possible for those agents to violate the principles. If it is impossible for agents to violate moral principles, then those principles can hardly play any social or psychological role in controlling the behavior of those agents.

But with (B) and (C) understood in this sense, the argument that God has no moral obligations isn't valid. On (B2) a principle's being in force is a practical matter. It requires social or psychological machinery, to make the principles effective, to promulgate and enforce them; it needs socially instituted systems of punishments and rewards; it requires mechanisms for instilling these principles in the young, so that they come to function in a regulative way psychologically as well as socially.[20] There is a great distinction, then, between *a principle's being in force*, on the one hand, and *there being a principle at all*, on the other.

We can see this distinction in three ways. In the first place, to determine whether *there is a principle*, that breaking promises is morally wrong we need to think about promises. But to determine whether *that principle is in force* in a given society, we (or somebody from whom we could get the information) would have to learn about the people in that society. Secondly, we know of cultures where there are no psychological or social mechanisms for enforcing a moral principle—no social sanctions for violating it and no psychological "higher-level control mechanisms" which tend to produce compliance with it—and yet few of us would be willing to suppose that in consequence for that society there was no moral principle of the relevant sort.[21] For example, among the Yanomama Indians in the Venezuelan Amazon it is apparently customary for any woman without male protection to be repeatedly gang-raped. There are no social mechanisms penalizing or discouraging such rapes; none of the men who participate in such a rape shows any signs of guilt over his behavior, and the raped women themselves seem to accept their fate without question. In such a society, the moral principle prohibiting the rape of women is obviously not *in force*, in Alston's sense of a moral principle's being in force.[22] Nonetheless, it seems to me clear that the moral principle that women ought not to be raped applies to the Yanomama, too; even for the Yanomama, there *is* a moral principle prohibiting the rape of women.[23] Thirdly, even if we restrict our scope just to cases in which people or societies are invariably good, the distinction between there being a principle and a principle's being in force still seems to me to hold. In this case, the distinction bears a family resemblance to one which Alston uses in rejecting argument II. There he relied on the distinction between the obtaining of moral obligation, on the one hand, and the appropriateness of moral terminology, on the other hand. From the fact that moral exhortations or prohibitions are inappropriate, Alston says, it doesn't follow that there are no moral obligations, only that their fulfillment is ensured. A related point seems to me to hold with respect to Alston's own argument. There is a distinction between the obtaining of moral obligation and the appropriateness of the talk or promulgation of moral principles. And here a claim analogous to Alston's seems to me to hold and to count against his own argument: from the fact that (in the cases of restricted scope under consideration) talk or promulgation of moral principles seem inappropriate because they have no social or psychological role in governing behavior, it doesn't follow that there are no moral obligations—what follows is only that their fulfillment is ensured, so that pointing to or promulgating moral principles, setting up machinery to enforce them, instituting a system of rewards and punishments, and so on, is inappropriate and pointless.

So if we understand Alston's (B) as (B2), the assumption underlying the argument then becomes the claim that there are moral principles laying down conditions under which certain actions are required only if those principles play a social and psychological role in controlling behavior; but this claim isn't true, and therefore Alston's argument for the conclusion that God has no moral obligations isn't valid.

Suppose, then, that we understand (B) as (B1): (B1) a moral principle is in force only if it isn't abrogated or undermined in the circumstances. If there were no moral principles which were ever in force for God in this sense, it would seem right to conclude that he had no moral obligations; there would be no moral principles which laid out conditions under which God's actions were morally obligatory and which were not abrogated or overridden. On this understanding of (B), it is not implausible to suppose that there are general moral principles laying down conditions under which actions are required only if those moral principles are in force. So if we take (B) as (B1), we ought perhaps to grant the assumption underlying Alston's argument.

But in this case (C) becomes worrisome. We will now have to interpret (C) in a way corresponding to (B1), so that it becomes (C1): (C1) general moral principles are not abrogated or overridden only if it is possible for those principles to be violated. (C1) makes an agent's ability to do otherwise necessary for a moral principle's not being abrogated or undermined. Why should we think it is?

One reason for thinking it is the notion that the ability to do otherwise is essential to freedom. Agents who aren't able to do otherwise aren't free, we might suppose; and if they aren't free, then moral principles which might otherwise apply to them are abrogated or undermined. But the claim that agents who aren't able to do otherwise aren't free is a claim crucial to argument (I), which does depend on the claim that an agent is free with respect to an action only if he could have done otherwise. And Alston rejects argument (I) because he doesn't accept this connection between freedom and the ability to do otherwise.

We might just have an intuition that the ability to do otherwise is essential to moral obligation. Alston apparently has an intuition of this sort. But that is not a view I share. One reason for my not sharing it has to do with variations on Frankfurt-type counterexamples to the principle of alternate possibilities. In Dostoevsky's *The Possessed*, Peter Verkhovensky wants an escaped convict named Fedya to kill the Lebyatkin family, and he plans to offer him a large sum of money to do the murders. We can alter Dostoevsky's story and add that Verkhovensky also has an alternate plan. If Fedya shows the first signs of what might turn into hesitancy to do the murders, Verkhovensky will enlist the help of a mad neurosurgeon who will install a device in Fedya which will fire just those neurons necessary for Fedya's deciding to do the murders.[24] But in the event, Fedya, who is a hardened criminal and desperate for cash, accepts the money with enthusiasm. In this case, Fedya does not have the ability to do otherwise than to kill the Lebyatkins, but it seems to me clear that, even so, Fedya violates a moral obligation when he murders the Lebyatkins, that moral blame is appropriate in Fedya's case. This and other Frankfurt-type cases seem to me to suggest that the ability to do otherwise isn't essential for moral obligation.[25]

So for these reasons I am inclined to suppose that (C1) is false and that a version of Alston's argument which intends (B) and (C) as (B1) and (C1) is not sound. On either reading of (B) and (C), then, Alston's argument that God has no moral obligations seems unacceptable.

Another Version of Alston's Requirement on Moral Obligation

In comments on an earlier draft, Alston objected to the entire strategy of attacking his argument using Frankfurt-style counterexamples. He claimed that although in his article he does often put his point about moral obligation in terms of possibility, he meant it to refer only to tendencies: an agent has moral obligations in a certain case only if he has tendencies to do something other than the good in such cases. In fact, Alston says, he wants his requirement on moral obligation to refer only to tendencies in the *kind* to which the agent being evaluated belongs; his "requirement is not that the individual in question have some tendency to deviate from the morally good, but that it belong to a kind members of which have such a tendency." This revised requirement will indeed successfully ward off any attack on Alston's argument based on Frankfurt-style examples, but it raises difficulties of its own. The problem now will be to find a principled way to specify the kind with respect to which an agent is to be evaluated such that the requirement seems at all plausible and yet still has the result that God fails to meet it.

For example, it is apparently the case that among the Yanomama Indians there is no child abuse whatsoever nor any tendency on anyone's part towards that evil.[26] If the Yanomama Indians count as a kind, then on Alston's principle we would have to say that the Yanomama Indians have no moral obligations not to abuse their children, and that result would strike many of us as counter-intuitive. On the other hand, if a narrow construal of kinds makes Alston's principle seem implausible, we might try drawing the boundaries of the kinds more broadly. Unless there is some reason which prevents us from drawing the kind very broadly, we might, for example, specify the kind as that which includes all persons. In that case, God also would belong to a kind members of which have a tendency to do moral evil. Then God would after all meet Alston's requirement for moral obligation, contrary to what Alston himself supposes.

Even if we try for a principle which is both plausible and effective by stipulating that the kinds in question must be natural kinds, so that human beings must be evaluated with regard to the kind *human person*, and God must be evaluated with respect to the kind *divine person*, it isn't clear that Alston's requirement on moral obligation rules out attributing moral obligation to God in Christianity. On traditional views of the Trinity and the Incarnation, there are three divine persons, one of whom was incarnate as Jesus; and since traditional theology claims that Jesus was tempted just as we are, it seems reasonable to suppose that he had tendencies to sin, even if he didn't (even if he couldn't) act on them. Therefore, even if we stipulate that the kind with regard to which any divine agent must be considered is the kind *divine persons*, traditional views of the Trinity and Incarnation enable us conclude that any divine agent belongs to a kind at least one member of which has a tendency to deviate from the morally good, in which case God does meet Alston's requirement for moral obligation.

So although this version of Alston's requirement on moral obligation protects his argument from one sort of attack, based on Frankfurt-style counterexamples, it leaves the argument vulnerable in another way, since on this version of Alston's requirement plausible construals of the requirement do not rule out attributing moral obligation to God.

Conclusion

In this paper I have had only a negative thesis, that Alston's argument for the claim that God has no moral obligations is unsuccessful; and it is clear that the reasons I have mustered in support of my thesis don't themselves constitute an argument for the positive claim that God *does* have moral obligations. But Alston's argument strikes me as the best available for the claim that God has no moral obligations. And without a good argument for the somewhat surprising claim that God has no moral obligations, I see no reason for theists and atheists alike not to accept the common view that God, if he exists, does have moral obligations—that he can make promises and enter into covenants, which he is then obligated to keep, that he ought not to betray those who trust in him, that he ought to deal with his creation in some ways rather than others.[27]

Notes

1. See Marilyn Adams, "Duns Scotus on the Goodness of God," *Faith and Philosophy* 4 (1987) 486-505.
2. In *Christian Theism and the Problems of Philosophy*, ed. Michael Beaty (Notre Dame, IN: University of Notre Dame Press, 1989); reprinted in *Divine Nature and Human Language. Essays in Philosophical Theology* (Ithaca, NY: Cornell University Press, 1989), pp. 253-273. References to this paper will be given in parentheses in the text.
3. See, for example, Harry Frankfurt, "Alternate Possibilities and Moral Responsibility," *Journal of Philosophy* 66 (1969) 828-839. For a helpful introduction to the literature on this subject, see David Schatz, "Free Will and the Structure of Motivation" *Midwest Studies in Philosophy*, vol. x, Peter French, Theodore Uehling, Jr., and Howard Wettstein, eds. (Minneapolis: Minnesota University Press, 1986), pp. 451-482.
4. See "Intellect, Will, and the Principle of Alternate Possibility," in *Christian Theism and the Problems of Philosophy*, op. cit., pp. 254-285.
5. In helpful and generous comments on an earlier draft of this paper, which was presented at a symposium at the Pacific Division APA, 1991, Alston maintained

that he intended the supererogatory as sufficient but not necessary for dividing moral goodness from moral obligation. If the supererogatory can be applied to God also, then Alston has all he needs for his argument whatever other ways there might be to separate moral obligation and moral goodness. On the other hand, if the supererogatory does not apply to God, as I will argue here, then in order to evaluate Alston's argument on this score we will need to learn from him on what other basis he thinks moral goodness and moral obligation can be separated and then we will have to consider whether that other basis can itself be applied to God.

6. For an argument supporting this intuition, particularly with regard to forgiveness, see Neera Badhwar, "Friendship, Justice, and Supererogation," *American Philosophical Quarterly* 22 (1985) 123-132.

7. She has in mind particularly the obligation to be kind and considerate to children. She maintains that this obligation isn't owed to all children or to antecedently specified children, and consequently there are no right-holders. See Onora O'Neil, *Constructions of Reason* (Cambridge University Press, 1989), pp. 189ff.

8. For a discussion of this category, see, e.g., Aurel Kolnai, "Forgiveness," *Aristotelian Society Proceedings* 64 (1973) 91-106. I am indebted to Gregory Mellema for this reference. In a forthcoming paper, "Quasi-obligation, Supererogation, and Virtue Ethics" Mellema argues that quasi-obligations are best understood by supposing that aretaic judgments and deontic judgments give different results and that quasi-obligations are part of a virtue ethics.

9. Other examples include certain acts of friendship which friends are not morally obligated to do for one another but which are such that friends are morally substandard if they fail to do them. See, for example, Badhwar 1985.

10. See, for example, Gregory Trianosky, "Supererogation, Wrongdoing, and Vice: On the Autonomy of the Ethics of Virtue," *Journal of Philosophy* 83 (1986) 26-40. Trianosky formulates his puzzle in somewhat different terms from these. And he resolves it by arguing that there is only a loose fit between deontic and aretaic judgments.

11. For a discussion of acts of offence, see Gregory Mellema, "Offence and Virtue Ethics," *Canadian Journal of Philosophy* forthcoming.

12. But for those who think these categories need to be kept distinct, they can be reformulated this way: (a) a suberogatory act A is such that it is morally obligatory to do something other than A, although not doing A isn't required by anyone's right; (b) an act of offence A is such that it is morally obligatory to omit A, although not doing A isn't required by anyone's right.

13. "Must God Create the Best?," *The Philosophical Review* 81 (1972) 317-332.

14. Philip Quinn raised this objection in comments on an earlier draft.

15. For a discussion of Aquinas's position, which I have only sketched here, see Norman Kretzmann, "Goodness, Knowledge, and Indeterminacy in the Philosophy of Thomas Aquinas," *Journal of Philosophy* 80 (1983) 631-649.

16. Norman Kretzmann has suggested to me that examples illustrating the argument from evil are often presented as cases in which God would have done something supererogatory, rather than morally obligatory, if he had prevented the evil in question. "Couldn't God have prevented the suffering of just this one child?," someone might say, indicating not that any obligations to prevent the suffering attach to God but only that a God who prevented the suffering would be a more admirable person than a God who didn't. I am inclined to think, however, that if the circumstances of the case are as suggested—God could effortlessly spare the child the suffering; and if he did so, no greater evil would result or no greater

good would be lost—then God's failing to prevent the suffering is not a case of God's failing to do something supererogatory but rather a case of God's failing to do something he ought to do. And the tone of moral indignation with which people tend to raise questions such as "Couldn't God have prevented the suffering of just this one innocent child?" seem to me to indicate that the questioners share my view.

17. Philip Quinn has suggested that the suberogatory is another way of distinguishing between moral goodness and moral obligation and that this category might apply to God. But as I indicated above, it seems to me that the common understanding of the suberogatory is counterintuitive. If we pry apart moral obligations and rights, then this category can be understood as the category of acts it is morally obligatory not to do but not required not to be done by the rights of others. So understood, the category does not apply to God since God is essentially perfectly good.

18. See, e.g., ST II-II q.66 a.7.

19. In comments on an earlier draft of this paper, Alston indicated that his primary concern was with a principle's psychological role in controlling behavior and that, on his view, a principle need not have a social role in controlling behavior in order to count as being in force. In order to be faithful to the words in his article, I·have not taken account of this refinement in his position here; the points remain generally the same even if we bracket references to the social roles of principles in controlling behavior.

20. John Hare and Philip Quinn have both suggested to me that this view of morality is Kant's. In comments on an earlier draft, Quinn, supporting what he takes to be Kant's view, claimed that there is something imperatival about moral principles and that moral obligation has an imperatival character because agents subject to it have inclinations at variance with those obligations. Therefore, moral obligation does not apply to agents with no inclination to disobey the moral law. But even if Quinn's claim were true, the conclusion he draws from it doesn't seem to me to follow. At best, what follows is that for agents without inclinations contrary to moral law, moral obligation doesn't have an imperatival character. It might make no sense to address moral imperatives to such agents. But it isn't at all clear that moral obligations hold *only in case* they have an imperatival character, as I will argue below.

21. I am grateful to Norman Kretzmann for this point.

22. See Kenneth Good, *Into the Heart* (NY: Simon and Schuster, 1991).

23. In comments on an earlier draft, Alston wrote, "Moral obligation... is essentially a practical rather than a theoretical affair. It has to do with the governance of behavior...if it is impossible for a being with my nature to have any tendency at all to do A, I can't be obliged to do A. Moreover, and this may be a bit more controversial, if I am sincerely convinced, after as much investigation of the matter as could reasonably be expected of me, that I should do A, I can't be morally obligated to do not-A. No being that fails to satisfy such conditions as these can have the obligation in question. Where such conditions are not satisfied, the being *does not have* the obligation in question..." And Alston takes these considerations to constitute support for his general claim that moral obligation requires the possibility of doing otherwise than the good. But I think these considerations which Alston adduces as support for this general claim are not acceptable. I take it that the Yanomama have made " as much investigation of the matter" of rape "as could reasonably be expected" of them, and nonetheless they find the practice perfectly appropriate. We might even suppose that Yanomama men think they

should engage in gang rape whenever the opportunity presents itself. It seems to me clear, however, that even if we feel Yanomama men deserve no penalty— maybe even no blame—for raping their women, the moral prohibition against the rape of women still holds for them as well. Similarly, the nineteenth-century attitude opposing higher education for women seems to me a counterexample to Alston's claim. After as much reflection as was reasonable to demand of the men of that culture, they still felt that women should not receive higher education; but moral principles prohibiting oppression of women seem to me to hold nonetheless and to be applicable even to Victorian males. In general, any culture in which moral principles have no role in governing behavior because the society ("after as much investigation of the matter as could reasonably be expected") engages wholeheartedly in immoral behavior will constitute a counterexample to Alston's claim that in such cases agents don't have the moral obligation in question. So for these reasons, as well as others, I am inclined to dispute Alston's view that morality is "a practical rather than a theoretical affair," and that where moral obligations have no role in "the governance of behavior" of certain agents, there are no such moral obligations for those agents. Therefore, these considerations of Alston's don't seem to me to constitute support for his general claim that there is moral obligation only where there is a possibility of doing other than the good.

24. In comments on an earlier draft, Philip Quinn argued that this sort of example will be unacceptable to dualists, since they won't accept the equation of mind and brain which this example apparently presupposes. Since the issues in this paper lie in the intersection between religion and morality, and since many religious believers are dualists, it is worth pausing to consider Quinn's objection. The strategy for all Frankfurt-style examples is to contrast an actual sequence in which an agent appears to act freely with an alternate sequence in which the agent does the same thing but under coercion. One common way to formulate such an alternate sequence is in terms of a neurosurgical device. If dualism is correct, then such devices don't act on the mind. It doesn't follow, of course, that they don't *affect* the mind, as Quinn's objection seems to assume. Even Descartes thought that there was interaction between the brain and the mind, so that we might be able to affect even an dualistic mind by operating on the brain. But suppose that for the sake of argument we simply stipulate that neurosurgical devices can't affect the mind, because the mind is an incorporeal substance. Is it now impossible to construct Frankfurt-style counterexamples to the principle of alternative possibilities? I think the answer is clearly 'no'. Within the religious traditions which have espoused dualism in the past, it is also commonly accepted that God can act causally on human minds. Consider, for example, the story of God's hardening Pharaoh's heart (cf., e.g., Exodus 9:12) or the story of God's sending an evil spirit on Saul so that he seeks to kill David (I Sam.19: 9-10). We can then construct Frankfurt-style counter-examples tailored to dualists by telling some appropriate story about God's motivation and letting God serve the function of the neurosurgical device in the alternate sequence.

25. Alston maintained, in comments on an earlier draft, that his argument depends not on the general principle that moral obligation requires the ability to do otherwise, but only on the narrower principle that (NP) moral obligation requires the ability to do other than the good in a given case. His position thus is almost the mirror image of one held by Susan Wolf, who argues that moral responsibility requires the ability to do other than evil in a given case. See, for example, Susan Wolf, *Freedom Within Reason* (Oxford: Oxford University Press, 1990), esp. pp.

85-89. But it is not hard to construct Frankfurt-type counterexamples to the narrower principle Alston wants to espouse. To turn my Fedya example into a counterexample to (NP), let some third person offer Fedya the money to commit murder, substitute Fedya's saintly and long-suffering mother for Verkhovensky, let Fedya of his own accord refuse to do the murders, and let his mother's alternate plan involve a mad neurosurgeon who will install a device which will trigger just those neurons necessary for Fedya's *refusing* to do the murders if Fedya shows the first signs of what might turn into a willingness to murder the Lebyatkins. In this example, Fedya's mother is likely to feel that since Fedya rejects the money of his own accord, he has fulfilled his moral obligations (for once) and therefore merits moral praise even though he was unable to do anything other than the good, and my intuitions would be on her side.

26. See Kenneth Good, *Into The Heart*, op. cit.

27. This paper was read to the philosophy departments at Calvin College and at the University of Notre Dame and has benefitted from the discussions on both occasions. I am grateful to Norman Kretzmann and Philip Quinn, who gave me many helpful comments and suggestions, and I am particularly indebted to William Alston, for generous and detailed comments on and discussion of an earlier draft of this paper.

Philosophical Perspectives, 6, Ethics, 1992

THE PRIMACY OF GOD'S WILL
IN CHRISTIAN ETHICS

Philip L. Quinn
University of Notre Dame

In this paper I argue that some form of theological voluntarism ought to be the ethical theory of choice for Christian moral philosophers. The audience I hope my argument will convince consists of Christians of a fairly traditional cast of mind, and so my assumptions are things I take to be widely shared in conservative Christian communities. They will not be shared by all communities of moral inquiry. Those who do not share them may be persuaded that they cohere well with theological voluntarism; they are not likely to be convinced of its truth by my argument. It should therefore be read as a contribution to a debate within a distinctively Christian tradition of moral reflection and as an attempt to promote progress internal to that tradition. It does not aim to convince the adherents of rival traditions that are not Christian.

The argument has two parts. The first part is an attempt to build a cumulative case for a divine command conception of Christian morality. The case has three elements. None of them by itself is decisive; together they have considerable force. The first element in the case appeals to a conception of the divine nature that is not restricted to Christian theism. I argue that a particularly strong form of the doctrine of divine sovereignty can be used to furnish theists of all sorts with a positive theoretical reason for divine command ethics. The second element in the case appeals to narratives from the Hebrew Bible that have some authority for Jews, Christians and Muslims. I argue that the cases often described as the immoralities of the patriarchs have in Christian tradition been interpreted in a way that provides Christians with a positive historical reason for divine command ethics. And the third element in the case appeals to the Gospel accounts of the command to followers of Jesus to love their neighbors. I argue that these accounts should, for reasons that Kierkegaard made clear, be interpreted so as to provide a positive moral reason for divine command ethics. As I see it, then, divine command ethics rests securely on a tripod whose legs come from philosophical theology, scriptural interpretation and Gospel morality. But I make no claim that mine is a complete cumulative case for a divine command conception of Christian morality. There are, no doubt, other considerations Christians can mobilize that will also furnish positive reasons for divine command ethics. The three elements of my case do, however, illustrate the range of factors that converge in support of theological voluntarism.

Such considerations as these do, I think, suffice to show that a divine command conception of morality is a serious contender for the allegiance of Christian moral philosophers. But there are rivals also in contention within the arena of Christian ethical thought. So the second part of my argument is an effort to show that theological voluntarism is superior to the rival contender that currently enjoys the greatest popularity among Christian philosophers. It is a virtue theory of Aristotelian provenance. Of course it would be silly to maintain that there is no place in Christian ethics for virtues, but I shall argue that they should not have pride of place in Christian moral philosophy. They should instead be confined to a subordinate role. Making human virtue primary in ethics is an inversion of the Christian order in which God's will is primary and the human response to it is secondary. Seen from within a Christian perspective, virtue looks very different from what it appears to be when observed from the point of view of pagan Aristotelianism. So incorporating parts of Aristotle's ethical legacy into Christian moral philosophy will inevitably involve radical transformation in order to enforce the required theoretical subordination.

The first three sections of the paper will be devoted to the three elements of my cumulative case for divine command ethics. The final section will concentrate on showing that the rivalry with virtue theory is best brought to an end by assigning the virtues to a secondary and derivative place in the architecture of Christian moral theory. One disclaimer is needed before the argument begins. This paper does nothing by way of offering a defense of the divine command conception against various philosophical objections. It is not that I regard the task of constructing such a defense as unimportant. On the contrary, I think it is sufficiently important that I have made it a central project in my previous work on divine command morality.[1] And others who have made major contributions to the recent revival of divine command ethics in the philosophical world have also done much to show that it can be successfully defended against objections.[2] But I think the time has come in the campaign to refurbish divine command morality when a purely defensive strategy no longer promises to yield the greatest benefits. It seems to me that the time is now ripe for supporters of the divine command conception to make the positive case on its behalf to the community of Christian philosophers. It is the chief aim of this paper to do part of what needs to be done on this score if the case is to succeed in persuading that community.

Divine Sovereignty

There are a number of reasons for including a strong doctrine of divine sovereignty in one's philosophical theology. Two of the most important among them pertain to creation and providence. Theists customarily wish to insist on a sharp distinction between God and the world, between the creator and the created realm. According to traditional accounts of creation and conservation, each contingent thing depends on God's power for its existence whenever it exists. God, by contrast, depends on nothing external to himself for his existence. So God has complete sovereignty over contingent existence. Theists usually also wish to maintain that we may trust God's eschatological promises without reservation. Even if God does not control the finest details of history because he has chosen to create a world in which there is microphysical chance or libertarian freedom, he has the power to insure that the cosmos will serve his purposes for it and its inhabitants in the long run. So God also has extensive sovereignty over contingent events. Considerations of theoretical unity of a familiar sort then make it attractive to extend the scope of divine sovereignty from the contingent to the necessary and from the realm of fact into the realm of value.

How far can such extensions be pushed? In recent philosophical theology, there have been speculative attempts to push them very far indeed. Thomas Morris has advanced the metaphysical thesis "that God is absolute creator of necessary as well as contingent reality, and thus that literally all things do depend on him."[3] As Morris sees it, in order to be absolute creator "God must be responsible for the necessary truth of all propositions with this modality as well as for their mere existence as abstract objects."[4] If this view is tenable, Morris notes, "moral truths can be objective, unalterable, and necessary, and yet still dependent on God."[5] Thus, for example, even if it is necessarily true that such things as murder, theft and adultery are morally wrong, the absolute creationist holds that God is somehow responsible for the necessary truth of the proposition that murder, theft and adultery are wrong. But is this view tenable? In order to answer this question, we need to look at the details of the accounts the friends of absolute creation propose of the relation of dependence that is supposed to hold between God and such propositions.

As far as I can tell, it is Michael Loux who has provided the best worked out theory of how necessary truths might depend upon God. It is based on the idea that there is an asymmetrical relation of dependence between certain divine beliefs and facts being necessarily as they are. Taking notions of believing and entertaining as primitives, Loux defines a concept of strong belief as follows: a person S strongly believes that p if and only if S believes that p and does not entertain that not-p. Since God is omniscient, divine beliefs correlate perfectly with truth and divine strong beliefs correlate perfectly with necessary truth. But there is more than mere correlation here; there is also metaphysical dependency.

> God is not in the relevant strong belief states because the facts are necessarily as they are. On the contrary, the facts are necessarily as they are because God has the relevant strong beliefs. So it is the case that 2 + 2 = 4 because God believes that 2 + 2 = 4; and it is necessarily the case that 2 + 2 = 4 because God strongly believes that 2 + 2 = 4.[6]

And, of course, this idea can easily be extended to the moral realm. It is the case that murder, theft and adultery are wrong, on this view, because God believes that murder, theft and adultery are wrong; and if it is necessarily the case that murder, theft and adultery are wrong, this is so because God strongly believes that murder, theft and adultery are wrong.

Loux apparently means his account to be quite general, for he makes an explicit exception only for the case of free action. Thus he goes on to tell us that "if we turn to the realm of contingent facts (other than those consisting in rational agents freely performing actions), then, on the account I have given, it is most natural to suppose that the facts stand as they do because God has the beliefs God does."[7] It is an advantage of this way of thinking, he observes, that it furnishes a way to capture the dependence of the contingent on its divine creator and conserver. Similarly, it might be alleged by absolute creationists to be a merit of the claim that necessary facts are necessarily as they are because God has the relevant strong beliefs that it captures the dependence of the necessary on its divine absolute creator.

Unfortunately, however there are more exceptional cases than Loux acknowledges. Microphysical indeterminacy in the contingent realm is likely to be one sort of exception, but there are also theologically significant exceptions in the necessary realm. According to a leading theistic tradition, it is a necessary truth that God exists. Applied to this case, Loux's theory tells us that it is the case that God exists because God believes that God exists and that it is necessarily the case that God exists because God strongly believes that God exists. This is surely not correct and, indeed, seems to have the order of dependence backwards. God's beliefs neither produce nor explain his own existence. We cannot use Pirandello's slogan, 'Right you are if you think you are!', as a principle for bootstrapping God into existence from his own beliefs. Similarly, it is a necessary truth that God is omniscient. So according to the theory, it is the case that God is omniscient because God believes that God is omniscient, and it is necessarily the case that God is omniscient because God strongly believes that God is omniscient. Again, the actual order of dependence appears to be just the reverse of what the theory claims. I take it that these and similar theological examples suffice to refute Loux's version of the absolute creationist claim that God is responsible for the necessary truth of all propositions with this modality. A little less absolutism is, I think, called for here.

I am not sure exactly how to restrict the scope of the absolute creationist thesis in order to lend it maximal plausibility, though I have set forth one suggestion elsewhere.[8] However, in the present context it is not necessary to solve this problem. We can, I believe, avoid it by narrowing our focus of attention from global questions about truth in general to local questions about moral truth, and we can then ask how the kinds of considerations that motivate Morris and Loux should be applied within the moral realm. At the vert least, I suggest, they would lead one to hold that moral truth depends in some way on divine beliefs. A principle about wrongness proposed by Wierenga can be adapted to illustrate this idea.[9] The modified principle is this: For every agent x, state of affairs S, and time t, (i) it is wrong that x bring about S at t if and only if God believes that x ought not to bring about S at t, and (ii) if it is wrong that x bring about S at t, then by believing that x ought not to bring about S at t God brings it about that it is wrong that x bring about S at t. Less formally but more generally, the idea is that moral facts are as they are because God has the beliefs he does about what creaturely moral agents ought and ought not to do and necessary moral facts, if there are any, are necessarily as they are because God has the strong beliefs he does about what creaturely moral agents ought and ought not to do. This idea gets support from the doctrine of divine sovereignty because it extends God's sovereignty to cover the entire moral realm. I conclude from this that the doctrine of divine sovereignty provides a positive reason for a theoretical conception of this general kind.

So far I have been following the lead of Morris and Loux and discussing the dependence of morality on God in terms of divine doxastic states rather than divine volitional states. So it might be thought that the view I claim is supported by the doctrine of divine sovereignty is unconnected with theological voluntarism. My next task is therefore to elucidate the connections between them. There are several ways to do this; which of them is best will depend on other theological considerations.

If the doctrine of divine simplicity is true, intellect and will are not distinct in God, and so divine believings and divine willings are identical. If, for ease of exposition, we elide divine willings of a certain sort and divine commands, then to refer to a divine belief that an agent ought not to bring about a state of affairs at a time and to refer to a divine command that this agent not bring about that state of affairs at the time in question is to refer twice to just one thing. Divine strong beliefs will be identical with divine commands that are invariant across all possible worlds, which might be thought of as divine strong commands. Hence, to the extent that a strong doctrine of divine sovereignty is a positive reason for making moral truth dependent on divine beliefs across the board, it is also a positive reason for making such truth dependent on divine commands across the board. Wierenga's principle about wrongness, a modified version of which I set forth above, reads as follows: "For every agent x, state of affairs S, and time t (i) it is wrong that x bring about S at t if and only if God forbids that x bring about S at t, and (ii) if it is wrong that x bring about S at t, then by forbidding that x bring about S at t God brings it about that it is wrong that x bring about S at t." If the doctrine of divine simplicity is true, this principle and my modification of it are alternative formulations of what amounts to a single claim, and so whatever is a positive reason for one of them is also a positive reason for the other.[10]

If, as I tend to think, the doctrine of divine simplicity is not true, things are a bit more complicated. But intellect and will are nevertheless tightly integrated in God, and so divine normative believings and divine willings are perfectly correlated. Though I think it would smack of presumption to claim to know much about the internal mechanisms of the divine cognitive and conative apparatuses and their interactions, several simple models of the relations of divine beliefs and the divine commands I am assimilating to certain divine willings to moral truths can easily be constructed. One might suppose that moral truths are causally overdetermined and that perfectly correlated divine beliefs and divine commands operate independently to bring it about that moral propositions are true. Alternatively, one might assign causal priority either to the divine will or to the divine intellect. In the former case, divine volitions would bring about divine beliefs, which would, in turn, bring about the truth of moral propositions. By transitivity, divine volitions would bring about the truth of moral propositions, and so they would be remote causes of moral status. In the latter case, divine beliefs would bring about divine volitions and hence divine commands, which would in turn, bring about the truth of moral propositions. Thus divine commands would be proximate causes of moral status. I favor the third of these ways of thinking in the present context because it seems to me to have a slight edge over the other two in terms of intuitive naturalness or plausibility. On this view, to the extent that a strong doctrine of divine sovereignty is a positive reason for making moral truth dependent on divine beliefs, which are remote causes of moral truth, it is also a positive reason for making moral truth dependent on divine commands, which are effects of divine beliefs and proximate causes of moral truth. Moral truth, one might say, is the product of commands in perfect conformity with divine normative beliefs; it is thus the product of a "supremely rational will."[11]

Quite recently William P. Alston has argued that the most plausible form of divine command ethics will be one in which moral obligation, but not moral goodness, is dependent on God's will.[12] If that is right, then considerations of theoretical unity will allow us to extend the scope of divine sovereignty into the moral realm but may not permit us to extend it so far that it covers the entire moral realm. Whether the latter extension can be made will depend on further considerations such as the plausibility of Alston's suggestion that God himself is the supreme criterion of moral goodness and whether, if this is true, God is sovereign over moral goodness in a sense analogous to that in which he is sovereign over moral obligation because it depends on his will. The upshot, I think, is that there is a positive reason to suppose that divine sovereignty has, at the very least, a large territory to rule in the realm of value. But its claim to rule the entire realm may have to be scaled back or qualified just as Loux's extravagant claims have to be cut back in the theological realm.

The Immoralities of the Patriarchs

Speculative theistic metaphysics is not the only source of support for the divine command conception to be found within Christian traditions. Another is scripture itself. When we turn our attention to its narratives of God's dealings with his human creatures, we discover a picture of a deity who commands extensively. And in a prominent medieval tradition of interpreting scriptural stories about divine commands we find independent positive reasons for favoring an account of morality in which the primacy of God's will is acknowledged.

In medieval discussions it is sometimes disconcerting to see a philosophical question answered by appeal to the authority of scripture. For the most part, philosophers in our era would not make such appeals, but there is a good deal to be said for the practice, particularly in moral philosophy. The Hebrew Bible is authoritative for Judaism, Christianity and Islam. I think this authority operates in two ways. First, scriptural narratives propose paradigms of moral good and evil. They thereby help train the theist's faculty of moral discrimination and even contribute to the constitution of theistic moral concepts. Second, within theistic traditions canonical scriptures are cognitive authorities because they are supposed to contain divine revelation. Of course interpreting scripture has always been a delicate task, and hermeneutical controversies are both abundant and persistent. But plausible interpretations must within these traditions be granted evidential force just because scripture is at least a source and, on some views, is the only independent and ultimate source of sound doctrine about God. There can be no serious doubt that the Hebrew Bible portrays God as a commander. He is to be obeyed.

The Pentateuch records divine commands laying down the law about all sorts of things, including but not restricted to matters such as homicide that are clearly moral. Both Exodus 20:1-17 and Deuteronomy 5:6-21, which recount the revelation of the Decalogue, picture God as instructing his people about what they are to do and not to do by commanding them. He reveals his will and does not merely transmit information. So it is natural enough to assume that the authority of the Decalogue depends upon the fact that it is an expression of the divine will. Even if one doubts some of the details of these narratives because one thinks, for example, that God would not bother to regulate diet or ritual to quite the extent they say he does, it can hardly be denied that the conception of God the stories embody is that of a lawgiver. This conception surely invites development along just the lines proposed by divine command theories of morality. But, though such a development coheres very well with the narratives, they do not force the conclusion that God is the source of moral obligation. They can be interpreted so as to portray God as merely promulgating to his people moral laws that hold independent of his will if there are good reasons to suppose that such laws exist. After all, if there were such laws, a perfectly good God would will that his people obey them. And divine commands governing such things as ritual could be thought of as imposing religious rather than moral obligations.

There are, however, scriptural stories that can serve as a basis for a direct argument to the conclusion that God is the source of moral obligation. These are the incidents sometimes described as the immoralities of the patriarchs. They are cases in which God commands something that appears to be immoral and, indeed, to violate a prohibition he himself lays down in the Decalogue. Three such cases come up again and again in traditional Christian discussions. The first is the divine command to Abraham, recorded in Genesis 22:1-2, to sacrifice Isaac, his son. The second is the divine command reported in Exodus 11:2, which was interpreted as a command that the Israelites plunder the Egyptians. And the third is the divine command to the prophet Hosea, stated first in Hosea 1:2 and repeated in Hosea 3:1, to have sexual relations with an adulteress. According to these stories, God has apparently commanded homicide, theft and adultery (or at least fornication) in particular cases in a way that is contrary to the general prohibitions of the Decalogue. Such cases were bound to attract comments. How are we to interpret them?

The commentators I am going to discuss take scripture for literal truth; they assume that God actually did command as he is said to have done by the stories. They also suppose that these commands were binding on those to whom they were directed. In *The City of God*, Augustine uses the case of Abraham to make the point that the divine law prohibiting killing allows exceptions "when God authorizes killing by a general law or when He gives an explicit commission to an individual for a limited time." Abraham, he says, "was not only free from the guilt of criminal cruelty, but even commended for his piety, when he consented to sacrifice his son, not, indeed, with criminal intent but in obedience to God."[13] And in his *Questions on the Heptateuch*, Augustine disposes of the Exodus case with the remark that "the Israelites did not engage in theft, but, with God commanding this, they performed an office."[14] It is clear that Augustine thinks Abraham did what he should do in consenting to kill Isaac and the Israelites did what they should do in plundering the Egyptians because these things had been commanded by God. He also thinks that these things, which would have been wrong in the absence of those commands, were not wrong given their presence. So Augustine holds that divine commands addressed to particular individuals or groups determine the moral status of actions they perform out of obedience.

This general line on the immoralities of the patriarchs crops up over and over again in the works of Augustine's medieval successors. In his *On Precept and Dispensation*, Bernard says this:

> *You shall not kill, You shall not commit adultery, You shall not steal*, and the remaining precepts of that table, precepts which are such that, although they admit no human dispensation absolutely, and neither was it permitted nor will it be permitted to any human being to give release to something from those precepts in any way, yet God has given release from those which he wished, when he wished, whether when he ordered that the Egyptians be plundered by the Hebrews, or when he ordered the Prophet to have intercourse with a woman who was a fornicator. Certainly would nothing but a grievous act of theft be ascribed to the one, and nothing but the turpitude of a shameful act done in the heat of passion, to the other, if the authority of the commander should not have excused each act.[15]

So Bernard takes the Exodus case and the case of Hosea to show that God's authority is such that by his commands, he and only he dispenses people from the obligation to obey the precepts of the second table of the Decalogue. Plundering the Egyptians and having intercourse with a woman who was a fornicator, which would have been wrong in the absence of the divine commands to the Hebrews and Hosea, respectively, because they violate the precepts of the Decalogue, were in fact not wrong because God commanded them. Like Augustine, Bernard holds that divine commands make all the difference in the moral status of these actions.

The connection of these cases to a full-fledged divine command ethics is made quite explicit in the work of Andreas de Novo Castro, a fourteenth century philosopher who is judged by Janine M. Idziak to have conducted "the lengthiest and most sophisticated defense of the position."[16] He claims that there are actions which, "known per se by the law of nature and by the dictate of natural reason, are seen to be prohibited, as actions which are homicides, thefts, adulteries, etc.; but, with respect to the absolute power of God, it is possible that actions of this kind not be sins."[17] After citing the passage by Bernard I have quoted, which he thinks makes this evident, de Novo Castro appeals to the case of Abraham for additional confirmation. Abraham, he says, "wished to kill his son so that he would be obedient to God commanding this, and he would not have sinned in this if God should not have withdrawn the command."[18] For de Novo Castro, God's absolute power is such that acts such as homicides, thefts and adulteries, which are seen to be prohibited and so sins when known per se by means of natural law and natural reason, would not be sins if they were commanded by God as some in fact have been. He shares with Augustine and Bernard the view that divine commands can and do determine the moral status of actions.

What may be unexpected is that Aquinas too shares this view. He devote
an article of the *Summa Theologiae* to the question of whether the precept
of the Decalogue are dispensable, and in it he pronounces a verdict on ou
three cases. Not surprisingly, Aquinas maintains that those precepts "admi
of no dispensation whatever," and so he disagrees with Bernard on thi
point.[19] But when he treats our three cases in the course of responding t
an objection, he agrees with Bernard in exonerating the patriarchs. How doe
he manage to pull off this trick? The paragraph deserves to be quoted in full

> Consequently when the children of Israel, by God's command, took away
> the spoils of the Egyptians, this was not theft; since it was due to them by
> the sentence of God.—Likewise when Abraham consented to slay his son, he
> did not consent to murder, because his son was due to be slain by the
> command of God, Who is Lord of life and death: for He it is Who inflicts the
> punishment of death on all men, both godly and ungodly, on account of the
> sin of our first parent, and if a man be the executor of that sentence by
> Divine authority, he will be no murderer any more than God would be.—
> Again Osee, by taking unto himself a wife of fornications, or an adulterous
> woman, was not guilty either of adultery or of fornication: because he took
> unto himself one who was his by command of God, Who is the author of
> the institution of marriage.[20]

The main ideas in this passage are simple enough. Because God commande
the Israelites to plunder the Egyptians, what the Israelites took was due t
them and not to the Egyptians. Since theft involves taking what is not one'
due, the plunder of the Egyptians was no theft. Hence the Israelites neede
no dispensation from the prohibition on theft because their action did no
come within its scope. Similarly, because God, who is Lord of life and death
commanded Abraham to slay Isaac, Isaac was due to receive the punishmen
of death all humans deserve in consequence of original sin. Since murde
involves slaying someone who is not due to be slain, the slaying of Isaac woul
have been no murder, and so Abraham did not consent to murder and neede
no dispensation from the prohibition on murder. And because God, who i
the Author of marriage, commanded Hosea to take the adulteress as his wife
she was his wife and so he was guilty of neither adultery nor fornication i
having intercourse with her.

Aquinas and de Novo Castro differ in some respects about what the divin
commands do in our three cases. De Novo Castro seems to think that God'
command to Abraham brings it about that the slaying of Isaac would not b
wrong while remaining a murder. By contrast, Aquinas clearly supposes tha
God's command to Abraham brings it about that the slaying of Isaac woul
be neither wrong nor a murder. But this disagreement should not blind u
to the fact that they are of one mind in thinking that divine commands mak
a moral difference in all three cases. Both hold that the slaying of Isaac b
Abraham, which would be wrong in the absence of the divine command t
Abraham because of the Decalogue's prohibition, will not be wrong in th

presence of that command if Abraham carries it out. And they think similar things about the plundering of the Egyptians by the Israelites and Hosea having intercourse with the adulteress. We might sum up the agreement by saying that what the divine commands do in all three cases is to make obligatory patriarchal actions that would have been wrong in their absence. And because divine commands make this kind of moral difference in virtue of something necessarily restricted to God alone such as absolute power or lordship over life and death, human commands could not make a moral difference of this sort.

It is worth noting that agreement with Augustine, Bernard, Aquinas and de Novo Castro about these cases and others like them need not be restricted to those Christians who share their belief that there actually were such divine commands as the scriptural stories say there were. Some may choose to think of cases like these as merely possible but concur with the tradition of interpretation I have been describing in believing that divine commands would make a moral difference of the sort our medieval authorities thought they did in fact make. I think there would be enough agreement about some such cases among reflective Christians who considered them carefully to make it fair to claim that Christian moral intuitions about scriptural cases support the conclusion that God is a source of moral obligation. Moreover, it is only a contingent fact that there are at most a few such cases. The properties such as absolute power or lordship over life and death in virtue of which divine commands are authoritative would remain unchanged if such commands were more numerous or even universal. So it is hard to resist the conclusion that any act of homicide, plunder or intercourse with a person other than one's spouse would be obligatory if it were divinely commanded. Most, if not all, such acts are not obligatory because God refrains from commanding anyone to perform them. Hence the moral intuitions that lie behind the tradition of scriptural interpretation I have been discussing also support the stronger conclusion that whether any action is obligatory or not depends on whether God commands it or refrains from doing so. Reflection on scripture and how it has been interpreted in an impressive tradition of Christian thought furnishes another positive reason for thinking that divine commands are both necessary and sufficient to impose moral obligations.

Commanded Love

It is a striking feature of the ethics of love set forth in the Gospels that love is the subject of a command. In Matthew's Gospel, Jesus states it in response to a question from a lawyer about which commandment of the law is the greatest. He says:

> You shall love the Lord your God with your whole heart, with your whole soul, and with all your mind. This is the greatest and first commandment. The second is like it: You shall love your neighbor as yourself. On these two commandments the whole law is based, and the prophets as well.[21]

Mark 12:29-31 tells of Jesus giving essentially the same answer to a question by a scribe, and Luke 10:27-28 speaks of a lawyer giving this answer to a question from Jesus and being told by Jesus that he has answered correctly. And in his last discourse, recorded in John's Gospel, Jesus tells his followers that "the command I give you is this, that you love one another."[22] So the authors of those books concur in thinking that Jesus expressed, or approved others expressing, the ethical demand that we love one another in the form of a command.

It might be thought that this manner of expression is inessential to a Christian ethics of love of neighbor, arising merely from the fact that Jesus is portrayed as propounding the ethics of love in the course of discussion with lawyers or scribes who are concerned about his views on questions of law. Because the questions being discussed are legalistic in nature, it might be said, it is not surprising that Jesus uses or approves legalistic rhetoric involving talk of commands in the specific context of answering them. By itself, the fact that a Christian ethics of love can be put in terms of commands does not imply that it must be formulated or is best articulated in such terms. To be sure, Jesus commands love not only when addressing Pharisees who are hostile to him but also when addressing followers who are committed to him. But I suppose that even this consideration need not be regarded as decisive in the absence of a reason for thinking that the particular sort of love Jesus wants people to have must, at least in the first instance, be commanded. Is there such a reason?

I think there is. To a first approximation, it is that the love of neighbor of which Jesus speaks is unnatural for humans in their present condition. It does not spontaneously engage their affections, and so training, self-discipline and, perhaps, even divine assistance are required to make its achievement a real possibility. For most of us most of the time, love of neighbor is not an attractive goal, and, if it were optional, we would not pursue it. It must therefore be an obligatory love with the feel of something that represents a curb or check on our natural desires and predilections. Because the divine command conception holds that all obligations depend on God's will, such an obligatory love is properly represented as subject to being commanded by a divine lawgiver. It is, then, no accident that the love of neighbor the Gospels propose to us is a commanded love.

In my opinion, no Christian thinker has seen with greater clarity than Kierkegaard just how radical the demands of love of neighbor are. In *Works of Love*, he addresses the reader in his own name, presenting, as the subtitle indicates, some Christian reflections in the form of discourses. The discourse on Matthew 22:39, which was quoted above, draws a sharp contrast between erotic love and friendship, on the one hand, and Christian love of neighbor, on the other. Both erotic love and friendship play favorites; the practical love of neighbor Christians are commanded to display by performing works of love does not. Kierkegaard says:

> The object of both erotic love and friendship has therefore also the favorite's name, *the beloved, the friend*, who is loved in distinction from the rest of the world. On the other hand, the Christian teaching is to love one's neighbor, to love all mankind, all men, even enemies, and not to make exceptions, neither in favoritism nor in aversion.[23]

One's neighbor is, in short, everyone. Since the command tells us that the neighbor is to be loved as we love ourselves, everyone without exception ought to be regarded as just as near to us as we are to ourselves according to Kierkegaard. In terms of this spatial metaphor, what is wrong with selfish self-love is that one is nearer to oneself than to anyone else. Erotic love and friendship represent only a partial break with selfish self-love because they are exclusive. The beloved or the friend is nearer to oneself than those who are not bonded to one by such relationships of partiality. Kierkegaard endeavors to drive the point home by putting it in terms that smack of paradox. His claim is this:

> If there are only two people, the other person is the neighbor. If there are millions, everyone of these is one's neighbor, that is, again, one who is closer than *the friend* and *the beloved*, inasmuch as these, as objects of partiality, lie so close to one's self-love.[24]

The air of paradox is generated by the thought that the friend or the beloved is also one's neighbor, for this seems to have the consequence that one and the same person is nearer to us under one description than she or he is under another. But the point Kierkegaard is trying to make is not paradoxical at all, though it may seem shocking. I take it to be that the obligation to love imposed by the command places absolutely every human, including one's beloved, one's friend and one's very self, at the same distance from one as one's worst enemy or millions of people with whom one has had no contact. And so it is an obligation that extends to all alike, excludes no one and does not even permit distinctions among persons rooted in differential preferences. It is, perhaps, easy to imagine God loving all his human creatures in this undiscriminating way. It is much more difficult to see how it could be either desirable or feasible for humans to respond to one another in this fashion. But if Kierkegaard is right, this is exactly what the command to love the neighbor bids us to do.

The offense to common sense would be mitigated but not altogether removed if the scope of the obligation to love were narrowed. One might, for example, construe the command quoted above from the last discourse of Jesus as imposing an obligation to love that does not extend beyond those who are his followers. But even the first disciples of Jesus were a mixed bag; the members of the household of faith today are a very motley crew indeed. It would not square with the natural inclinations or predilections of the Christians of any era to love one another equally and without distinction. Not all Christians are alike in erotic attractiveness; nor are they all equal with respect to the charms of virtuous character. So a nondiscriminatory love of all alike is bound to go against the grain of our natural affections and their partialities.

Kierkegaard is acutely aware of this partiality. He insists that "in erotic love and friendship the two love one another in virtue of differences or in virtue of likenesses which are grounded in differences (as when two friends love one another on the basis of likeness in customs, character, occupation, education, *etc.*, consequently on the basis of the likeness by which they are different from other men or in which they are like each other as different from other men)."[25] He is also sensitive to the fact that the dependence of erotic love and friendship on the characteristics of the beloved and the friend make them vulnerable to changes in their objects. If the beloved loses the traits in virtue of which she or he was erotically attractive, then erotic love dies. If the friend who was prized for having a virtuous character turns vicious, then the friendship is not likely to survive unless one is corrupted and turns vicious too. But love of neighbor is invulnerable to alterations in its object. Kierkegaard puts the point this way:

> To be sure, you can also continue to love your beloved and your friend no matter how they treat you, but you cannot truthfully continue to call them beloved and friend when they, sorry to say, have really changed. No change, however, can take your neighbor from you, for it is not your neighbor who holds you fast—it is your love which holds your neighbor fast. If your love for your neighbor remains unchanged, then your neighbor also remains unchanged just by being.[26]

If there is to be such a love that alters not where it alteration finds, it cannot depend on mutable features of the neighbor or ways in which they engage our spontaneous and natural affections. According to Kierkegaard, it will have the requisite independence only if it is a duty, for only then can it be motivated by a sense of duty instead of by changeable affections or preferences. "In this way," he says "the 'You shall' makes love free in blessed independence; such a love stands and does not fall with variations in the object of love; it stands and falls with eternity's law, but therefore it never falls."[27] Only if love of the neighbor is required of us will our response to that unvarying demand remain stable in the face of changes in the neighbor and our natural reactions to them.

There are, then, two reasons for supposing that Christian love of neighbor has to be a matter of duty or obligation. The first is that only a dutiful love can be sufficiently extensive in scope to embrace everyone without distinction. Erotic love and friendship are always discriminating and so exclusive. The second reason is that only a dutiful love can be invulnerable to alterations in its objects. Erotic love and friendship are apt to change when the valued features of their objects alter. "In love and friendship preference is the middle term," Kierkegaard says; "in love to one's neighbor God is the middle term."[28] In Christian love of neighbor God is the middle term in two ways. First, love of neighbor arises from loving God above all else and then loving his human creatures, including oneself, in the steadfast and nondiscriminating way in which he loves them. And, second, it is God's will, made known to us by Jesus, that we humans love one another in this manner. As Christians see it, Jesus is at least the Son of God who reveals the will of his Father by commanding love of the neighbor. Christians who also accept the astonishing claim that Jesus Christ is God Incarnate seem to be committed to the view that the obligation to love the neighbor as oneself is a duty imposed by a direct divine command.

I think this commanded love is foundational for Christian ethics; it is what sets Christian ethics apart from all its rivals. There is nothing like it in the pagan ethics of antiquity or in the secular moralities of the modern era. The command is apt to give offense, and even Christians in their present condition find it difficult to acknowledge its full force. "Only acknowledge it," Kierkegaard exhorts his readers, "or if it is disturbing to you to have it put in this way, I will admit that many times it has thrust me back and that I am yet very far from the illusion that I fulfill this command, which to flesh and blood is offense, and to wisdom foolishness."[29] In our lucid moments all of us would have to agree with Kierkegaard on this point and admit that we fall far short of perfect obedience to the command that we love everyone as we love ourselves. But I concur with Kierkegaard in considering it important to highlight rather than downplay the stringency of the duty to love the neighbor even if in consequence some people are thrust back or offended. Loving everyone as we love ourselves is, I want to insist, obligatory in Christian ethics, and it has this status, as the Gospels show us, because God has commanded this all-inclusive love. So I find in what is most distinctive about the Christian ethics of the Gospels another reason for Christians to favor a divine command conception of moral obligation. It seems to me that Christians who take the Gospels seriously would be in no position to deny that they teach us that we have been commanded by God to love the neighbor and so are obliged to do our best to fulfill the command perfectly.

This completes my argument in three parts for the conclusion that a divine command conception of morality has in its own right a serious claim to be regarded as a good way to understand Christian ethics because it acknowledges the primacy of God's will in the moral realm. The strength of my case rests in part on the diversity of sources within Christian tradition to which it appeals. Considerations from speculative philosophical theology, Christian commentary on incidents portrayed in the Hebrew Bible, and the distinctively Christian ethical demands set forth by Jesus in the Gospels converge in supporting theological voluntarism. But it is a conception that has had rivals within the history of Christian moral thought, and so something must be said about how it stacks up against its competitors. I therefore conclude with a sketch of how the rivalry with currently fashionable virtue theories might be brought to an end by incorporating what is of lasting value from such theories into divine command morality.

Divine Commands and Aristotle's Virtues

Virtue ethics has undergone something of a renaissance in recent philosophical discussion. Virtue theorists agree in tracing their roots back to Aristotle, but he is a philosopher who can be used to serve many purposes. It is important to realize that not all philosophers who acknowledge having benefitted from studying him have learned the same lessons. On the contemporary scene, Aristotle is being appropriated by the adherents of at least two deeply divergent projects of moral inquiry.

One is wholly secular and is attracted by Aristotle's optimistic paganism. Martha Nussbaum represents this sort of interest in reviving Aristotle. She remarks that Aristotle "holds that human beings are naturally drawn toward virtue rather than vice, love more than repudiation—and that, given sufficient education, material support, and personal effort, most people will be able to make good and reasonable lives *for themselves*" (my emphasis).[30] On this view, the attractive prospect Aristotle's thought offers us is that, if fortune favors them, human beings can, operating on their own steam, so to speak, flourish and so be happy over the course of an earthly lifetime. And these achievements are independent of religion. Noting that Aristotle does not place piety on his list of virtues, Nussbaum conjectures that "this probably indicates his interest in separating practical reason from religious authority, and in keeping reason, rather than such authorities, in control of the most important matters."[31] Practical reason operating apart from religious influences offers humans their best shot at working out for themselves good lives.

All this is, needless to say, deeply alien to traditional Christian thought It would insist that humans in their present condition are fallen and, if left to themselves, incapable of flourishing in this life. Such human flourishing as is possible must take place against a background of ceaseless struggle to overcome interior evil. It can never be a wholly human achievement something people make for themselves if they are lucky. It must always be at least in part a divine gift. Nor is reason itself exempt from the infirmities of the present human condition; it too is fallen and enfeebled. A traditional

Christian is therefore likely to regard as naive any confidence in the ability of unaided human practical reason to rule well in the most important matters in our lives.

Aristotle's perspective allows him to see nothing beyond completed earthly lives, and so he must judge human flourishing and happiness in secular terms. From this point of view, it is quite reasonable to emphasize the way in which good fortune is essential for human flourishing, for the activities that, according to Aristotle, constitute a happy life are not possible in the absence of such conditions as good health and a modicum of wealth. Christianity's larger eschatological vision opens up other possibilities. Misfortune, far from ruling out ultimate happiness, may prove a blessing in disguise by furnishing to the one who suffers it an opportunity to become more intimately related to the suffering Jesus on the Cross. Providence may be giving to the wretched of the earth—those most sorely afflicted by disease and poverty—chances to imitate Christ that the comfortably situated ought to envy. Aristotle clearly would not have counted as blessed all the people Jesus did: the poor in spirit, the sorrowing, the lowly, those who hunger and thirst for holiness, the merciful, the simple-hearted, the peacemakers, and those who are persecuted for holiness's sake.[32] Not many such people would flourish in an ancient *polis* or, for that matter, in a modern secular polity. But Jesus promises them a great reward in heaven.

Moreover, Aristotelian friendships have just those characteristics in virtue of which a sharp contrast has to be drawn between even the best sort of friendship and genuine Christian love of the neighbor. Aristotle restricts the highest kind of friendship to good people who are equal in virtue and insists that we must rest content with only a few friends of this kind. "One cannot be a friend to many people in the sense of having friendship of the perfect type with them," Aristotle tells us, "just as one cannot be in love with many people at once (for love is a sort of excess of feeling, and it is the nature of such only to be felt towards one person); and it is not easy for many people at the same time to please the same person very greatly, or perhaps even to be good in his eyes."[33] But Christian love of neighbor, unlike both Aristotle's friendship of the perfect type and his love based on an excess of feeling, is something we are obliged to direct toward everyone. Aristotle also says this: "Now equality and likeness are friendship, and especially the likeness of those who are like in virtue; for being steadfast in themselves they hold fast to each other, and neither ask nor give base services, but (one may say) even prevent them; for it is characteristic of good men neither to go wrong themselves nor to let their friends do so."[34] But, again, Christian love of neighbor cannot be so exclusive; it must also be directed towards those who are not one's like in virtue. We are commanded to love not only our equals in virtue but also both those who are more virtuous and those who are less virtuous than we are. Aristotelian friendship between equals in virtue is, no doubt, an admirable thing, and secular moralists are right to praise it. It is, however, a far cry from Christian love of one's neighbor and the divine love for all humans that is its paradigm.

Another contemporary project of moral inquiry that treats Aristotle as a valuable resource is a tradition in Christian ethics whose distinguished ancestry can be traced back at least as far as Aquinas. Unlike the secular retrieval of Aristotle, this project must be very selective in appropriating Aristotelian materials, for Aristotle's optimistic paganism and the grim realities of the Christian drama of sin and salvation are worlds apart, as the contrasts I have mentioned above only begin to indicate. It can learn from Aristotle and other virtue theorists provided their insights are transformed by being situated in a theoretical context that focuses moral inquiry on discerning God's will.

Divine command moralists should, I think, be prepared to engage in such selective appropriation and transformation of Aristotelian conceptions of virtue. After all, divine command theorists will not wish to deny that there are such things as moral virtues; they will, however, want to dispute characteristic Aristotelian claims about their importance and centrality in moral thinking. For Aristotle, the virtues hold pride of place in ethical theory. They are not properly understood as dispositions to produce independently defined or recognizable good actions or states of affairs; rather good actions or states of affairs are defined as those a virtuous person would voluntarily produce in the appropriate circumstances. From the point of view of the divine command theorist, Aristotle has got things backwards. The will of God, the commands that express it, and the moral laws those commands establish are primary for ethics, and so obligations to obey God's moral legislation will be the fundamental facts of morality. The virtues will have a distinctly secondary role to play; they will be construed as habits of obedience to various standing divine commands or other expressions of God's will for humans. The virtue of obedience itself will be the master moral virtue and should occupy center stage in moral theory.

Aquinas recognizes the importance of obedience to God's will for Christian ethics. When engaged in moral thinking, he is a bit of a magpie, picking up bits and pieces of lore from a variety of sources. In portraying Aquinas as a moral *bricoleur*, Jeffrey Stout notes that "his real accomplishment was to bring together into a single whole a wide assortment of fragments—Platonic, Stoic, Pauline, Jewish, Islamic, Augustinian, and Aristotelian."[35] To be sure, he tries to assemble these fragments into a coherent pattern by subsuming them under a largely Aristotelian conceptual scheme. But scheme and content do not always fit well together, as the case of obedience shows. A single question is devoted to it slightly more than half way through the second part of the second part of the *Summa Theologiae*. It is classified as a part of a part of the virtue of justice. Yet Aquinas returns a positive answer to the question of whether obedience to God is the greatest of the moral virtues

He argues that moral virtues are to be ranked in accord with the principle that the greater the thing a person contemns in order to adhere to God, the greater the virtue. Human goods that may be contemned for God's sake are, in order of increasing greatness, external goods, goods of the body, and goods of the soul. Among goods of the soul, the will is the highest because it is by the will that humans make use of all other goods. It follows that "properly speaking, the virtue of obedience, whereby we contemn our own will for God's sake, is more praiseworthy than the other moral virtues, which contemn other goods for the sake of God."[36] What is more, other acts of virtue have no merit in God's eyes unless they are done out of obedience to God's will. "For were one to suffer even martyrdom, or to give all one's goods to the poor," Aquinas insists, "unless one directed these things to the fulfillment of the divine will, which pertains directly to obedience, they could not be meritorious."[37] Neither would such things be meritorious if they were done without charity, he continues, but that theological virtue "cannot exist apart from obedience."[38] So obedience to God's will is not only the most praiseworthy of the moral virtues but also a necessary condition of both merit before God and charity.

It is interesting to note that Aquinas returns to the immoralities of the patriarchs in the course of a discussion of the question of whether God is to be obeyed in all things. These cases now form the basis of an objection. No one, Aquinas assumes, is bound to do anything contrary to virtue. But it seems that the divine command to Abraham to slay his innocent son and the divine command to the Jews to plunder the Egyptians are contrary to justice and that the divine command to Hosea to take to himself a woman who was an adulteress is contrary to chastity. Hence it seems that God is not to be obeyed in all things. The reply to this objection puts the case for the primacy of God's will in Christian ethics in a striking and forceful way. "God can command nothing contrary to virtue," Aquinas assures us, "since virtue and rectitude of human will consist chiefly in conformity with God's will and obedience to His command, although it be contrary to the wonted mode of virtue."[39] And he proceeds to deal with the three cases in a manner that should by now seem quite familiar. God's command to Abraham to slay his innocent son is not contrary to justice because God is the author of life and death. God's command to the Jews to plunder the Egyptians is not contrary to justice because all things really belong to God and he gives them to whom he will. And God's command to Hosea to take unto himself an adulteress is not contrary to chastity because, God being the ordainer of human generation, the right manner of sexual intercourse is that which he appoints.

I am of the opinion that Christian moral philosophers ought to join Aquinas in holding that virtue consists chiefly in conformity with God's will and obedience to his commands. As I see it, this should be the ruling idea of any account of the virtues that claims it is part of a genuinely Christian ethics. Plausible claims about the virtues deriving from sources such as Aristotle should be incorporated into Christian ethics just to the extent that they can be made to cohere with and subordinated to this ruling idea. When this cannot be accomplished, Christian moral philosophers should reject such claims. So a Christian ethics of virtue would not be a rival of theological voluntarism but a proper part of a fully developed divine command morality. Such an account of the moral virtues may well, as the example of Aquinas suggests, overlap Aristotle's doctrine of the virtues at quite a few points. But those engaged in trying to construct such an account ought to keep clearly in mind the thought that complete coincidence with Aristotle's ethics is out of the question. There are bound to be radical disagreements with Aristotle and with his contemporary secular heirs in any moral theory that insists, as I have argued Christian ethics should, on the primacy of God's will as a norm for human conduct and character.[40]

Notes

1. Philip L. Quinn, *Divine Commands and Moral Requirements* (Oxford: Clarendon Press, 1978) and "Divine Command Ethics: A Causal Theory," *Divine Command Morality: Historical and Contemporary Readings*, ed. Janine M. Idziak (New York and Toronto: Edwin Mellen Press, 1979).
2. See, for example, Robert M. Adams, "A Modified Divine Command Theory of Ethical Wrongness," reprinted in his *The Virtue of Faith* (New York: Oxford University Press, 1987), Edward R. Wierenga, *The Nature of God* (Ithaca and London: Cornell University Press, 1989), Chapter 8, and Richard J. Mouw, *The God Who Commands* (Notre Dame: University of Notre Dame Press, 1990), Chapter 1.
3. Thomas V. Morris, *Anselmian Explorations* (Notre Dame: University of Notre Dame Press, 1987), p. 163.
4. *Ibid.*, p. 166.
5. *Ibid.*, p. 171.
6. Michael J. Loux, "Toward an Aristotelian Theory of Abstract Objects," *Midwest Studies in Philosophy* 11, ed. P. A. French, T. E. Uehling and H. K. Wettstein (Minneapolis: University of Minnesota Press, 1986), p. 510. It is important not to confuse Loux's notion of entertaining with other concepts of entertaining that are, perhaps, more familiar. He supposes that if S believes that p then S entertains that p. There seems to be a familiar sense of entertaining in which it is the case that if S entertains that p then S believes that it is possible that not-p. But if this principle were conjoined to Loux's suppositions, a consequence would be that God believes that it is possible that $2 + 2 \neq 4$, which is plainly false.
7. *Ibid.*
8. Philip L. Quinn, "An Argument for Divine Command Ethics," *Christian Theism and the Problems of Philosophy*, ed. M. Beaty (Notre Dame: University of Notre Dame Press, 1990).
9. Wierenga's original principle, which I quote a little later, is to be found on p. 217 of his *The Nature of God*.
10. For further discussion of the bearing of the doctrine of divine simplicity on the

foundations of Christian ethics, see Norman Kretzmann, "Abraham, Isaac, and Euthyphro: God and the Basis of Morality," *Hamartia: The Concept of Error in the Western Tradition*, ed. D. V. Stump *et. al.* (New York and Toronto: Edwin Mellen Press, 1983).

11. William E. Mann, "Modality, Morality, and God," *Noûs* 23 (1989): 99. Mann's argument, like mine, starts from divine sovereignty, but the two arguments proceed along different paths to similar conclusions.

12. William P. Alston, "Some Suggestions for Divine Command Theorists," included in his *Divine Nature and Human Language: Essays in Philosophical Theology* (Ithaca and London: Cornell University Press, 1989).

13. Augustine, *The City of God* I, 21.

14. Augustine, *Questions on the Heptateuch* II, 39.

15. Bernard, *On Precept and Dispensation* III, 6. I quote an unpublished translation by Janine M. Idziak.

16. Janine M. Idziak, "In Search of 'Good Positive Reasons' for an Ethics of Divine Commands: A Catalogue of Arguments," *Faith and Philosophy* 6 (1989): 63.

17. Andreas de Novo Castro, *Primum Scriptum Sententiarum*, d. 48, q. 2, a. 2, concl. 2. I quote from an unpublished edition and translation by Janine M. Idziak.

18. *Ibid.*

19. Thomas Aquinas, *Summa Theologiae* I-II, q. 100, a. 8.

20. *Summa Theologiae* I-II, q. 100, a. 8, ad 3. Aquinas also discusses these three cases in *Summa Theologiae* I-II, q. 94, a. 5; there the question is whether the natural law can be changed.

21. Matthew 22:37-40.

22. John 15:17.

23. Soren Kierkegaard, *Works of Love*, tr. Howard and Edna Hong (New York: Harper Torchbooks, 1964), p. 36.

24. *Ibid.*, p. 38.

25. *Ibid.*, p. 69.

26. *Ibid.*, p. 76.

27. *Ibid.*, p. 53.

28. *Ibid.*, p. 70.

29. *Ibid.*, p. 71.

30. Martha Nussbaum, "Recoiling from Reason," *The New York Review of Books* 36 (December 7, 1989): 40.

31. *Ibid.*

32. Matthew 5:3-10.

33. Aristotle, *Nicomachean Ethics* 1158a10-14.

34. *Nicomachean Ethics* 1159b2-7.

35. Jeffrey Stout, *Ethics After Babel: The Languages of Morals and their Discontents* (Boston: Beacon Press, 1988), p. 76.

36. *Summa Theologiae* II-II, q. 104, a. 3.

37. *Ibid.*

38. *Ibid.*

39. *Summa Theologiae* II-II, q. 104, a. 4, ad 2.

40. Much of what I say in the first two sections of this paper is a slightly revised version of material that was included in my "The Recent Revival of Divine Command Ethics," *Philosophy and Phenomenological Research* 51 (1990). Some of the material in the final section, also revised, comes from my "A Response to Hauerwas: Is Athens Revived Jerusalem Denied?," *The Asbury Theological Journal* 45 (1990).